SOCIAL PROBLEMS

THIRD CANADIAN EDITION

IN A DIVERSE SOCIETY

Diana Kendall
Baylor University

Vicki L. Nygaard
University of British Columbia

Edward G. Thompson
McMaster University

SOCIAL PROBLEMS

THIRD CANADIAN EDITION

PROBLEMS

IN A DIVERSE SOCIETY

Pearson Canada
Toronto

Library and Archives Canada Cataloguing in Publication

Kendall, Diana Elizabeth
  Social problems in a diverse society / Diana Kendall, Vicki L. Nygaard, Edward G. Thompson.—3rd Canadian ed.

Includes bibliographical references and indexes.
ISBN 978-0-205-66390-3

  1. Social problems—Textbooks. 2. Social problems—Canada—Textbooks. I. Nygaard, Vicki Leanne, 1964– II. Thompson, Edward G., 1945– III. Title.

HN17.5.K45 2011   361.1   C2009-905869-3

ISBN 978-0-205-66390-3

Vice-President, Editorial Director: Gary Bennett
Editor-in-Chief: Ky Pruesse
Editor, Humanities and Social Sciences: Joel Gladstone
Marketing Manager: Arthur Gee
Developmental Editor: Rema Celio
Production Editor: Melissa Hajek
Copy Editor: Marcia Gallego
Proofreader: Sally Glover
Production Coordinator: Avinash Chandra
Composition: Integra
Permissions and Photo Research: Christina Beamish
Art Director: Julia Hall
Cover and Interior Design: Anthony Leung
Cover Image: Veer.com

5   14

Printed and bound in Canada.

DEDICATION

This book is dedicated to the memory of Dr. Paul Morgan Baker (1949–2009), close friend and mentor, who, despite often having dramatically different views from mine, taught me how to be a sociologist.

Vicki L. Nygaard

This book is dedicated to my dear partner, Helen.

Edward G. Thompson

CONTENTS

PREFACE

Learning about social problems can be a highly rewarding experience. Although we live in challenging times, a course on social problems provides an excellent avenue for developing critical thinking skills and for learning how to use sociological concepts and perspectives to analyze specific social concerns ranging from war and terrorism, media concentration, drug addiction, and violence to the inequalities of racism, sexism, classism, ageism, homophobia, and ableism.

Our first and foremost goal in writing this book is to make the study of social problems interesting and relevant for students. To stimulate interest in reading the chapters and participation in class discussions, we have used lived experiences (personal narratives of real people) and statements from a wide variety of analysts to show how social problems impinge on people at the individual, group, and societal levels. Moreover, we have applied the sociological imagination and relevant sociological concepts and perspectives to all the topics in a systematic manner.

The third Canadian edition of *Social Problems in a Diverse Society* focuses on the significance of racialization and ethnicity, age, sexual orientation, class, ability, and gender in understanding social problems in Canada and around the globe. Throughout the text, people—especially those from marginalized groups—are shown not merely as "victims" of social problems, but also as individual actors with agency who resist discrimination and inequality and seek to bring about change in families, schools, workplaces, and the larger society. To facilitate the inclusion of previously excluded perspectives, Chapters 2 through 6 examine wealth and poverty, racialized/ethnic inequality, gender inequality, and inequalities based on age and sexual orientation. Thereafter, concepts and perspectives related to racialization and ethnicity, class, sexual orientation, age, and gender are intertwined in the discussion of specific social problems, such as education, health care, and the environment.

This third Canadian edition is balanced in its approach to examining social problems. However, it includes a more comprehensive view of feminist and postmodern perspectives on a vast array of subjects—such as the effect of new technologies and how the media depict social issues—than other social problems textbooks. As sociologists who integrate social theory into our lectures, we were disheartened by the minimal use of sociological theory in most social problems texts. Those that discuss theory typically do so in early chapters but then fail to use these theories as a systematic framework for examining specific social issues in subsequent chapters. Similarly, many texts give the impression that social problems can be solved if people reach a consensus on what should be done. But *Social Problems in a Diverse Society*, Third Canadian Edition, emphasizes that how people view a social problem is related to how they believe the problem should be reduced or solved. Consider poverty, for example: people who focus on individual causes of poverty typically believe that individual solutions (such as teaching people a work ethic and reforming welfare) are necessary to reduce the problem, whereas those who focus on structural causes of poverty (such as chronic unemployment and inadequate educational opportunities) typically believe that solutions must come from and through the larger society. Moreover, what some people see as a problem, others see as a solution for a problem (e.g., the sex trade as a source of income, or abortion to terminate a pregnancy). The epilogue allows students to explore the question, "How can social problems be solved?"

Finally, we wrote *Social Problems in a Diverse Society,* Third Canadian Edition, in hopes of providing students and instructors with a text that covers all the major social concerns we must deal with today, but does not leave students believing that the text—and perhaps the course—was a "depressing litany of social problems that nobody can do anything about anyway," as many students have stated about different texts. We have written this book in hopes of resolving those students' concerns, because we believe the sociological perspective has much to add to our individual, local, national, and global dialogues on a host of issues, such as environmental degradation; Canadian involvement in overseas military missions; discrimination based on racialization and ethnicity, class, gender, age, sexual orientation, or other attributes; and problems in media and education. Welcome to an innovative examination of social problems—one of the most stimulating and engrossing fields of study in sociology! We welcome your presence in the effort to make the world a better place.

ORGANIZATION OF THIS TEXT

Social Problems in a Diverse Society, Third Canadian Edition, has been organized with the specific plan of introducing disparities in wealth and poverty, racialization and ethnicity, gender, age, and sexual orientation early on so that the concepts and perspectives developed in these chapters may be applied throughout the text. All chapters offer theoretical analyses from structural functionalism, conflict or Marxist perspectives, symbolic interactionism, and feminist theories. In addition, other theories are introduced where most relevant.

- Chapter 1 explains the sociological perspective and provides an analysis of attempts at problem solving at the microlevel, mid-range, and macrolevel of society and highlights the issue of worldwide violence and the new Canadian *Youth Criminal Justice Act.*

- Chapter 2 looks at wealth and poverty in Canada and around the world. Students will gain new insights into disparities between the wealthy and the poor and into problems such as workfare,

homelessness, food insecurity, and poverty. The chapter concludes with a thematic question, "Can class-based inequality be reduced?" This question will be asked throughout the text as new topics are discussed.

- Chapter 3 integrates the previous discussion of class-based inequalities with an examination of racialized and ethnic inequality. The chapter looks at issues of democratic racism and White privilege in Canada, and at the ways that racism manifests throughout Canadian institutions and practices.

- Chapter 4 highlights factors such as mainstream gender socialization and social barriers that contribute to the unequal treatment of women in the workplace, in the family, at school, and at other social institutions. Transgender issues and global gender issues are also introduced for discussion.

- Ageism and inequality based on age are discussed in Chapter 5, and inequality based on sexual orientation is examined in Chapter 6, placing these important topics in a context similar to the studies of prejudice and discrimination rooted in racism and sexism in contemporary societies. In addition, Queer theory is highlighted as a way of analyzing sexual orientation issues.

- Chapter 7 links previous discussions of racialization and ethnicity, class, and gender to an analysis of the sex trade. The chapter provides up-to-date information on the globalization of prostitution and gives students insight into "johns" and how sex workers view themselves, why they engage in this line of work, and why some people view sex workers as a social problem.

- In Chapter 8, social problems caused by addictions—alcohol, tobacco, and other drugs and gambling—are discussed in depth, and students are provided with information about the drug commonly called the "date rape" drug; the abuse of prescription drugs, over-the-counter drugs, and caffeine; and the characteristics of problem gambling.

- Chapter 9 discusses crime and criminal justice and takes an incisive look at sociological explanations of crime.

- Beginning with Chapter 10, a look at health care and its problems, we examine some of the major social institutions in our society and note aspects of each that constitute a social problem for large numbers of people.

■ Chapter 11 explores the changing family, emphasizing diversity in intimate relationships and families, and child-related family issues. It also explores the dark side of family life.

■ Chapter 12 presents contemporary problems in education, tracing the problems to such issues as what schools are supposed to accomplish, how they are financed, and why higher education may become less widely accessible with increasing tuition fees.

■ Chapter 13 explores current issues in the global economy and politics such as the current global recession and soaring student and consumer debt loads.

■ Chapter 14 discusses ongoing concerns regarding the Canadian and global media such as media concentration, new media technology, and consequences of exposure to violent and/or racist and sexist media.

■ Chapter 15 provides a survey of problems associated with population and the environmental crisis, focusing particularly on the causes and consequences of high rates of global migration and particular types of pollution. It also includes a look at urban problems, detailing the powerful impact of urbanization on both high-income and low-income nations of the world.

■ Chapter 16 presents an overview of Canada's roles in the ongoing U.S. "war on terror," examining the consequences of war for people and the environment. The politics of war as well as global and domestic terrorism are highlighted.

■ The epilogue asks, "How can social problems be solved?" and includes a review of the four main sociological theories used to explain social problems, plus some thought-provoking questions about everyone's role in creating solutions to social problems.

DISTINCTIVE FEATURES

A number of special features have been designed to incorporate racialization and ethnicity, class, sexual orientation, and gender into our analysis of social problems and to provide students with new insights on the social problems that they learn about in the news. The following sections discuss the text's distinctive features.

Lived Experiences throughout Each Chapter

These authentic, first-person accounts are used as vignettes—"real words from real people"—to create interest and show how the problems being discussed affect people as they go about their daily lives. Lived experiences provide opportunities for students to examine social life beyond their own experiences ("to live vicariously," as one student noted) and for instructors to systematically incorporate into lectures and class discussions examples of relevant, contemporary issues that have recently been on the evening news and in newspaper headlines.

■ Cathy Crowe, a street nurse in Toronto, describes her experiences in working with homeless people for 20 years (Chapter 2, "Poverty in the Canadian Context").

■ Lawrence Hill, award-winning Canadian novelist and memoirist, talks about what it means to be both Black and White in Canada (Chapter 3, "Racism and Ethnic Inequality").

■ Anonymous Canadian youth speak about how they became involved in the sex trade (Chapter 7, "The Sex Trade in Canada").

■ Helen Stauffer, former vice-president of PRIDE (People to Reduce Impaired Driving Everywhere) and mother of a son who was killed by an impaired driver describes how that driver "took the sunshine from [her] life" (Chapter 8, "Addictions").

■ A 14-year-old woman who was forced to marry someone she hated reports her feelings in the discussion of the prosecution of polygamy in Bountiful, B.C. (Chapter 11, "The Changing Family").

■ Many Indigenous people report on their experiences at a residential school (Chapter 12, "Problems in Education").

■ Dr. Sunera Thobani, UBC women's studies professor, speaks about the hope people around the world share that new U.S. President Barack Obama will use his considerable influence to work toward peace (Chapter 16, "Global Social Problems").

Interesting and Highly Relevant Boxed Features

Four different boxes—Social Problems and Information Technology, Social Problems in the Media, Social Problems and Social Policy, and Social Problems in Global Perspective—highlight current hot topics involving various long-term social problems. Examples of each type of box are

- *Social Problems and Information Technolog:* Net Neutrality: Our Newest Endangered Species (Chapter 14, "Problems Related to Media");
- *Social Problems in the Media:* Media Ageism: Preferring Younger and Stereotyping Older Age Groups (Chapter 5, "Inequality Based on Age");
- *Social Problems and Social Policy:* The Battle over Harm Reduction: The Insite Program (Chapter 8, "Addictions"); and
- *Social Problems in Global Perspective:* 'Weapons of Mass Destruction': Political Spin and Media Framing of a War (Chapter 16, "Global Social Problems").

Built-in Study Features

These pedagogical aids promote students' mastery of sociological concepts and perspectives:

- Chapter Outlines: A concise outline at the beginning of each chapter gives students an overview of major topics.
- What Can You Do? Sections: This section gives students suggestions about how they can tackle social problems on their own, as individuals, or collectively in a group.
- Key Terms: Major concepts and key terms are defined and highlighted in bold print within the text. Definitions are also available in the glossary at the back of the text.
- Summaries in question-and-answer format: Each chapter concludes with a concise summary in a convenient question-and-answer format to help students master the key concepts and main ideas in each chapter.
- Questions for Critical Thinking: End-of-chapter questions provide opportunities for students to

develop important critical-thinking skills about the issues raised in each chapter.

Supplements

The following supplements specific to this text can be downloaded by instructors from a password-protected location of Pearson Education Canada's online catalogue (**vig.pearson.ca**). Contact your local sales representative for further information.

- Instructor's Manual. The Instructor's Manual is a comprehensive resource that provides you with tools for classroom discussion, assignments, and recommendations for related films and readings.
- PowerPoint Presentations. PowerPoint slides highlight the key concepts in each chapter of the text.
- MyTest/Test Item File. The MyTest/Test Item File contains multiple choice, true/false, and essay type questions. Each question is classified to difficulty level and includes the appropriate page reference.
- For the Student: A wealth of information and online resources can be found on MySocKit which accompanies this text.

CourseSmart for Instructors

CourseSmart goes beyond traditional expectations—providing instant, online access to the textbooks and course materials you need at a lower cost for students. And even as students save money, you can save time and hassle with a digital eTextbook that allows you to search for the most relevant content at the very moment you need it. Whether it's evaluating textbooks or creating lecture notes to help students with difficult concepts, CourseSmart can make life a little easier. See how when you visit **www.coursesmart.com/instructors**.

CourseSmart for Students

CourseSmart goes beyond traditional expectations–providing instant, online access to the textbooks and course materials you need at an average savings of 50%. With instant access from any computer and the ability to search your text, you'll find the content you need quickly, no matter where you are. And with online tools like highlighting and note-taking, you can save time and study efficiently. See all the benefits at **www.coursesmart.com/students**.

ACKNOWLEDGMENTS

We wish to personally thank the many people who have made this new edition a reality. First, we offer our profound thanks to the following reviewers who provided valuable comments and suggestions on how to make this text outstanding. Whenever possible, we have incorporated their suggestions into the text. The reviewers are Constance deRoche, Cape Breton University; Daniel Dorogi, Thompson Rivers University; Korbla P. Puplampu, Grant MacEwan College; and Robert Tucker, St. Lawrence College.

The third Canadian edition of *Social Problems in a Diverse Society* has benefited from the expertise and excellence of Rema Celio, Developmental Editor; Joel Gladstone, Acquisitions Editor; and Melissa Hajek, Production Editor. We sincerely appreciate all the support and encouragement they provided throughout this revision.

I could not have written this book without the assistance of my husband, Terrence Kendall, who has done so much outstanding advising, editing—and sometimes consoling—on this and other texts I have written that I have declared him to be not only a lawyer but also an "honorary sociologist."

—*Diana Kendall*

My heartfelt gratitude and appreciation go to my wonderful daughters, Freja Nygaard and Phoenix Nygaard, who teach me so much about life every day; to my brother, Adrian Nygaard; to my parents, Peter and Marilyn Hardy, for continuing to believe in me; to all my fabulous friends, for their encouragement, support, and the howls of laughter; to the Sangha, for the ongoing compassion, companionship, and generosity; and last but certainly not least, to Heather A. Robinson, Jillian A. Sweetnam, and Kelly-Ann S. Connor, for all of their hard work.

—*Vicki L. Nygaard*

I could not have written this book without the assistance of my partner, Helen Barron, who has not only provided continuing support, but also edited each of my original chapters.

—*Edward G. Thompson*

To each of you reading this preface, we wish you the best in teaching or studying social problems and hope that you will share with us any comments or suggestions you have about *Social Problems in a Diverse Society*, Third Canadian Edition. The text was written with you in mind, and your suggestions (with appropriate attribution) will be included whenever possible in future editions. Let's hope that our enthusiasm for "taking a new look at social problems" will spread to others so that together we may resolve some of the pressing social problems we encounter during our lifetime.

—*Diana Kendall*
—*Vicki L. Nygaard*
—*Edward G. Thompson*

TAKING A NEW LOOK AT SOCIAL PROBLEMS

1

We drive stolen cars to the States and sell them. And lots of partying. Drinking and chemicals. I started when I was nine. And I'm a skin. So we're into violence a lot. And we hang out at arcades and malls.

<hr>

"Brian," a young gang member from Ontario, speaking about typical activities he and his male friends engage in (quoted in Totten 2001:158)

Being a "tough guy," that's what I was called in school. I enjoyed that—getting that title at a young age. It gave me power, you know, over people.

<hr>

Derek Powder, speaking about his path to involvement with a gang in Alberta (quoted in Minaker and Hogeveen 2009:241)

What were his thoughts, were they only thoughts of survival or were they thoughts of never seeing his daughter again, never seeing his new baby, never seeing me. Did he struggle in vain to stay alive, knowing that to be left without him would break me into pieces? I walk through these images daily whether I want to or not and even put myself in the passenger seat of his van so he doesn't have to die alone . . . The completely selfish act of two people has not only left my husband dead, it has left me on the brink of insanity, struggling to survive to the next day . . . My daughter will never have that golf lesson with her dad. My son will never play that hockey game with his father. I will never be able to fill his shoes. I am learning to live without him, but it requires just settling with what life has dealt me rather than living every moment to the fullest. Nothing is the same . . . I am not the same. Bill would be destroyed to know the suffering everyone has had to endure, and that is hard to live with.

<hr>

Kim Hancox, wife of murdered Toronto police constable William Hancox, speaking through her victim impact statement to the two women convicted of murdering her 32-year-old husband as he sat in his vehicle (quoted in Schmalleger and Volk 2008:121)

At the time, [violence] was a high. A power high. It was a feeling of being king-shit—no one could touch you . . . We felt really important—because we were white—because we were guys. I mean skins don't exactly respect females either. A lot of them pounded on their girlfriends too. It wasn't just blacks. And gays as well. People think skins just hate blacks. It's not true. They hate gays, women—you name it.

<hr>

"Marty," a former racist skinhead, speaking about the feelings created by belonging to a violent gang (quoted in Totten 2001:141)

I wanted to take my anger and frustration out on a stranger, to be in control, to do what I wanted to do. I wanted to use and abuse someone as I felt used and abused. I was killing my girlfriend. During the rapes and murders, I would think about my [ex] girlfriend. I hated the victims because they probably messed men over. I hated women because they were deceitful and I was getting revenge for what happened to me.

<hr>

A young man convicted of raping and murdering five women as revenge against his ex-girlfriend for getting involved with another man when she went away to college (quoted in Scully and Marolla 2005:323)

An eye for an eye only ends up making the whole world blind.

<hr>

Mohandas Karamchand Gandhi, political and spiritual leader of the Indian Independence Movement, speaking on the path of non-violence (quoted in O'Grady 2007:199)

If you want to know who is going to change this country, take a look in the mirror.

<hr>

Maude Barlow, national chairperson of the Council of Canadians

Whether it takes place in a small-town schoolyard or on a busy city street, violence leaves shock and anguish behind. **Violence** is the use of physical force to cause pain, injury, or death, or damage to property. However, violence is relational: its destructiveness is aimed at some targeted "other." Alberta sociologists Minaker and Hogeveen argue that "in violence there is no reverence for life, no respect for another who is like us but unlike us. We do not esteem and honour those to whom we do violence. It is human—and world destroying" (2009:220). Around the world, violence is a major social problem. On a daily basis, the Internet and television news channels quickly spread word of the latest bombing, the latest massacre, the latest sexual assault, the latest murder. In Canada, a place not known for the level of violence reported daily in the United States, murders of youth by other youth have made sensational headlines. Along with several recent murders of youth in Toronto, a young South Asian woman, Reena Virk, was beaten by a group of mainly female peers in Victoria, B.C., in November 1997, and later killed by one of the young women and a young man. Other than Virk, the youth were White, adding a racialized dimension to the situation. In Vancouver in 2003, 17-year-old

Jomar Lanot was beaten to death on his way home from playing basketball at a nearby school by a group of teens led by 16-year-old Muzil Abdullah. Additionally, following the Columbine High School murders in Littleton, Colorado, on April 20, 1999, a 14-year-old boy in Taber, Alberta, brought a gun to school and shot 17-year-old Jason Lang to death and injured another boy; in April 2006, a 12-year-old girl and her boyfriend in Medicine Hat, Alberta, shot and killed her parents and her 8-year-old brother; and in September 2006, 25-year-old Kimveer Gill shot one person to death and injured 19 others at Montreal's Dawson College, marking the fourth similar tragedy in Quebec's recent history.

In 2006, Canadian Police Services reported that an average of more than three young people each day are accused of a gun-related violent offence and that Canada ranks fifth out of 26 countries for the rate of firearm deaths of children under age 14 (City of Toronto 2009a). In the wake of each new episode of gun violence, a renewed call for gun control goes out from advocates of restricted access to guns and other weaponry. Firearms are the third leading cause of death of Canadians aged 15 to 24, and the economic cost of gun deaths and injuries is estimated to be at least CN$6 billion annually (City of Toronto 2009a). Advocates of gun control point to Department of Justice information showing that the province with the highest percentage of homes with guns is Alberta, followed by New Brunswick and Saskatchewan; the provinces with the highest rate of youth aged 15 to 25 killed by firearms are, in order, New Brunswick, Saskatchewan, and Alberta (CBC 1999). A corresponding cry arises from gun enthusiasts across the country and such organizations as the National Firearms Association, who oppose further tightening of gun laws. In fact, in a 2002 news release, the National Firearms Association called the federal government's gun control program, which required Canadian citizens to register their firearms with a government gun registry, "a dog and pony show." Seemingly in accordance with this viewpoint, and after millions of dollars in overspending within the program, in June 2006, the Harper government introduced legislation to abolish the long-gun registry. This repeal was never brought to a vote in the House of Commons, however, and currently, rifle and shotgun owners who failed to register their guns have been granted amnesty from prosecution through a series of one-year extensions of these regulatory changes. The handgun registry and bans on automatic weapons will remain in place.

Many of us are ambivalent about violence. We condemn drive-by shootings and cold-blooded murders, yet enjoy watching action movies with lots of "blood and guts" or contact sports such as wrestling, hockey, football, and boxing. However we explain these contradictory attitudes, violence is a major social problem, in this country and around the world.

WHAT IS A SOCIAL PROBLEM?

Although not all sociologists agree about what constitutes a social problem, most would agree with this general definition: a **social problem** is a social condition (such as poverty) or a pattern of behaviour (such as violence against women) that people believe warrants public concern and collective action to bring about change. Social conditions or certain patterns of behaviour are defined as social problems when they systematically disadvantage or harm a significant number of people (or a number of "significant" people?) or when they are seen as harmful by many of the people who wield power, wealth, and influence in a group or society. To put it another way, social problems are social in their causes, consequences, and possible sources of resolution.

The study of social problems is one area of inquiry within **sociology**—the academic and scholarly discipline that engages in systematic study of human society and social interactions. A sociological examination of social problems focuses primarily on issues that affect an entire **society**—a large number of individuals who share the same geographical territory and are subject to the same political authority and dominant cultural expectations—and the groups and organizations that make up that society. Because social problems are social in their causes, public perception of what constitutes a social problem can change. Consider, for example, how public perception of what constitutes a social problem has changed over the past 50 years. In the 1950s, people worried about the problem of nuclear war. More recently, people have been worried about unemployment (early 1980s, early 1990s, and today); government debt (mid-1990s); cutbacks to health care, education, and social services (early 2000s); and, most recently, health care, the economy, poverty, and the environment (Angus Reid 2008; *Maclean's* 1999, 2002).

BOX 1.1 Violence around the World

In its first *World Report on Violence and Health,* released in October 2002, the World Health Organization (WHO) stated that violence kills 1.6 million people annually. About one-half of these deaths are due to suicide; one-third are due to homicide; and 20 percent are due to armed conflict. One person commits suicide every 40 or so seconds; one person is the victim of a homicide every minute; and one person is killed in armed conflict every two minutes. During the 20th century, about 191 million people were killed in armed conflict. Many more people were injured, physically and psychologically. Young people aged 15 to 44 are especially affected. Violence is a major cause of death for this group: 14 percent of young males and 7 percent of young females die violently.

Some patterns of victimization are experienced worldwide. For example, up to 70 percent (in Canada, close to 50 percent) of murdered women are killed by intimate or former intimate partners (see Chapters 4 and 9). Patterns also vary by region. For example, the rate of violent death is twice as high in low- and middle-income countries than in high-income countries, and whereas in Europe and Asia, suicides exceed homicides, in Latin America, homicides exceed suicides.

Following its mandate, the WHO promotes a public health approach to understanding the problem of violence. Thus, its *World Report on Violence and Health* could be considered part of the process of the medicalization of crime and deviance (see Chapter 9). To solve the problem of violence, the report recommends dealing with the social, cultural, economic, and psychological root causes of violence and taking advantage of opportunities to prevent violence. Developing community projects such as parent training and gun-safety training, strengthening responses of victims to violence, collecting better data on violence, and seeking practical international agreements to combat the drug and arms trades are among the recommendations put forward.

In November 2005, the World Health Organization released findings from another major study about violence called the *WHO Multi-Country Study on Women's Health and Domestic Violence Against Women.* This study reported data from 10 countries,

including Ethiopia, Bangladesh, Peru, and the United Republic of Tanzania, where few data were available; and one high-income country, Japan. A sample size of 24 000 women was obtained from cities and rural parts of these countries, and topics of physical and sexual violence were studied. The percentage of women who had experienced physical and sexual violence by an intimate partner in their lifetime ranged from 15 percent in Japan to 71 percent in Ethiopia. In Ethiopia, Bangladesh, Peru, and the United Republic of Tanzania, more than 50 percent of married women had experienced both physical and sexual violence. Other topics studied were abuse outside marriage, abuse before age 15, forced sex in marriage (a major problem because of the inability of women to protect themselves from HIV infection), and abuse during pregnancy. The report included several recommendations to create programs to help women, to enlist local leadership, and to make physical environments safer for women.

In 2009 the WHO released another report on worldwide violence, this one on traffic fatalities. Approximately 1.3 million people die each year on the world's roads, and between 20 and 50 million sustain non-fatal injuries. The results showed that road traffic injuries remain an important public health problem, particularly for low-income and middle-income countries. Pedestrians, cyclists, and motorcyclists make up almost half of those killed on the roads. Many of these fatalities could be prevented by laws regarding speeding, seat belt use, and blood-alcohol concentration limits. Canada has such laws, though not yet uniformly against cell phones and driving, and its fatalities have fallen from 25 per 100 000 people in 1971 to less than 10 in 2006. Unless more countries bring appropriate laws into effect, the WHO expects that traffic fatalities will rise to be the fourth leading cause of death in 2030.

Sources: World Health Organization (WHO), 2002, World Report on Violence and Health. *Retrieved July 23, 2006 (http://www.who.int/violence_injury_prevention/violence/world_report/en/);* WHO, 2005, WHO Multi-Country Study on Women's Health and Domestic Violence Against Women. *Retrieved July 23, 2006 (http://www.who.int/gender/en/);* WHO, 2009, Global Status Report on Road Safety. *Retrieved July 21, 2009 (http://www.who.int/violence_injury_prevention/raod_safety_status/2009/en/).*

Sociologists apply theoretical perspectives and use a variety of research methods to examine social problems. Some social problems—such as violence and crime—are commonly viewed as conditions that affect all members of a population (see Box 1.1). Other social problems—such as racialized discrimination and sexual harassment—may be viewed (correctly or incorrectly) as conditions that affect some members of a population more than others. However, all social problems may be harmful to all members in a society whether they realize it or not. Sociological research, for example, has documented the extent to which White racism wastes the energies and resources of people who engage in racist actions as well as those of the targets of the actions (see Feagin and Sikes 1994; Feagin and Vera 1995).

Social problems often involve significant discrepancies between the ideals of a society and their actual achievement. For example, in Canada, the rights of individuals are guaranteed by the *Charter of Rights and Freedoms,* which also provides the legal basis for remedying injustices. Significant discrepancies exist, however, between the democratic ideal and its achievement. One such discrepancy is **discrimination**—actions or practices of dominant group members (or their representatives) that have a harmful impact on members of subordinate groups. Sociologists define the **dominant group** as the group whose members are disproportionately at the top of the hierarchy, "with maximal access to the society's power resources, particularly political authority and control of the means of economic production" (Marger 1999:273). **Subordinate groups** are those whose members, in relation to the dominant group (or groups), do not occupy such positions of power. The term usually used for a subordinate group is *minority group* (see Chapter 3).

Discrimination may be directed along a number of lines—class, race, gender, and age. It also may be directed against subordinate group members whose sexual orientation, religion, nationality, disability, or other attributes or characteristics are devalued by those who discriminate against them. Sometimes, discrimination is acted out in the form of violence. This type of violent act is referred to as a **hate crime**—an act of violence motivated by prejudice against people on the basis of racialized identity, ethnicity, religion, gender, or sexual orientation. This can include the dissemination of materials intended to incite hatred. Although hate crimes were added to the *Criminal Code* only quite recently, the crimes themselves date back hundreds of years (see Chapters 3, 6, and 9 for further discussion of hate crimes).

WHY STUDY SOCIAL PROBLEMS?

Studying social problems helps us understand the social forces that shape our lives on both personal and societal levels. In our daily lives, we rely on common

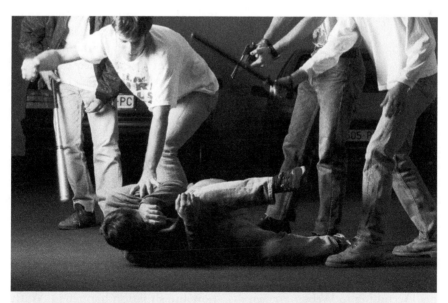

What does this photo show us about the discrepancies that exist between the democratic ideals and the social realities of our society? Does discrimination against subordinate group members take place in other societies as well?

sense—"what everybody knows"—to guide our conduct and make sense of human behaviour. But many common-sense notions about why people behave the way they do, who makes the rules, and why some people break rules and others follow them are *myths*—beliefs that persist even when the actual truth is different. Myths about social problems frequently garner widespread acceptance and sometimes extensive media coverage.

A sociological examination of social problems enables us to move beyond common-sense notions, to gain new insights into ourselves, and to develop an awareness of the connection between our own world and the worlds of other people. According to sociologist Peter Berger (1963:23), a sociological examination allows us to realize that "things are not what they seem." Indeed, most social problems are multifaceted. When we recognize this, we can approach pressing local, national, and global concerns in new ways and make more effective decisions about those concerns. In taking a global perspective on social problems, we soon realize that the lives of all people are closely intertwined, and that any one nation's problems are part of a larger global web of interrelated problems.

THE SOCIOLOGICAL IMAGINATION AND SOCIAL PROBLEMS

Just like other people, sociologists usually have strong opinions about what is "good" and "bad" in society and what might be done to improve conditions. However, sociologists know their opinions are subjective. Thus, they use systematic research techniques and report their findings to other social scientists for consideration. In other words, sociologists strive to view social problems *objectively*. Of course, complete objectivity may not be an attainable—or desirable—goal in studying human behaviour. Max Weber (1864–1920), an early German sociologist, acknowledged that complete objectivity might be impossible and pointed out that *verstehen* ("understanding," or "insight") was critical to any analysis of social problems. According to Weber, *verstehen* enables individuals to see the world as others see it and to empathize with them. *Verstehen*, in turn, enables us to develop what is called the sociological imagination.

According to sociologist C. Wright Mills (1959b), the **sociological imagination** is the ability to see the relationship between an individual's experiences and the larger society in which they are contextualized. The sociological imagination enables us to connect the private troubles of individuals to the public issues of a society. Public issues (or social problems) are matters beyond a person's control that originate at the regional or national level and can be resolved only by collective action. In *The Sociological Imagination*, Mills used unemployment as an example of how people may erroneously separate personal troubles from public issues in their thinking. The unemployed individual may view his or her unemployment as a personal trouble concerning only the individual, other family members, and friends. However, widespread unemployment resulting from economic changes, corporate decisions (downsizing or relocating a plant abroad), or technological innovations (computers and advanced telecommunications systems displacing workers) is a public issue. The sociological imagination helps us to shift our focus to the larger social context and see how personal troubles may be related to public issues.

Sociologists make connections between personal and public issues in society through microlevel and macrolevel analysis. **Microlevel analysis** focuses on small-group relations and social interaction among individuals. Using microlevel analysis, a sociologist might investigate how fear of unemployment affects workers and their immediate families. In contrast, **macrolevel analysis** focuses on social processes occurring at the societal level, especially in large-scale organizations and major social institutions such as politics, government, and the economy. Using macrolevel analysis, a sociologist might examine how globalization and the attendant labour market restructuring have impacted Canadian workers and their families.

As Mills suggested, a systematic study of a social problem such as unemployment gives us a clearer picture of the relationship between macrolevel structures such as the Canadian economy and microlevel social interactions among people in their homes, workplaces, and communities. It does not get the individual his or her job back, but it provides a better understanding of how the situation happened. With a clearer understanding of how we find ourselves in the situations we do, we may be able to develop more effective levels of prevention and intervention.

SOCIOLOGICAL PERSPECTIVES ON SOCIAL PROBLEMS

To determine how social life is organized, sociologists develop theories and conduct research. A **theory** is a set of logically related statements that attempt to describe, explain, and occasionally predict social events. Theories are useful for explaining relationships between social concepts or phenomena, such as "ethnicity and unemployment" or "gender and poverty." They also help us interpret social reality in a distinct way by providing a framework for organizing our observations. Sociologists refer to this theoretical framework as a **perspective**—an overall approach or viewpoint toward some subject. Four major theoretical perspectives have emerged in sociology: the functionalist perspective, which views society as a basically stable and orderly entity; the conflict perspective, which views society as an arena of competition and conflict; the interactionist perspective, which focuses on the everyday, routine interactions among individuals; and the feminist perspective, which focuses on the gendered (and racialized and classed) inequalities between groups and on strategies for positive social change. The functionalist and conflict perspectives are based on macrolevel analysis because they focus on social processes occurring at the societal level. The interactionist perspective is based on microlevel analysis because it focuses on small-group relations and social interaction. The feminist perspective involves both macro- and microlevel analysis by looking at the ways, for example, that the dominant gender ideology (macro) impacts the specific interactions (micro) between woman X and man Y within a capitalist and patriarchal White-dominant culture.

The Functionalist Perspective

The functionalist perspective grew from the works of early social thinkers such as Auguste Comte (1798–1857), who is thought to be the founder of sociology. Comte compared society to a living organism. Just as muscles, tissues, and organs of the human body perform specific functions that maintain the body as a whole, the various parts of society contribute to its maintenance and preservation. According to the **functionalist perspective**, society is a stable, orderly system composed of several interrelated parts, each of which performs a function that contributes to the overall stability of society (Parsons 1951). These interrelated parts are social institutions (such as families, the economy, education, and the government) that a society develops to organize its main concerns and activities so that it meets social needs. Each institution performs a unique function, contributing to the overall stability of society and the well-being of individuals (Merton 1968). For example, the functions of the economy are producing and distributing goods (such as food, clothing, and shelter) and services (such as tourism services and dry-cleaning), whereas the government is responsible for coordinating activities of other institutions directed to such ends as health care, education, maintaining law and order, dealing with unmet social needs, and handling international relations and peace.

Manifest and Latent Functions

Though the functions of the economy and the government seem fairly clear-cut, functionalists suggest that not all the functions of social institutions are intended and overtly recognized. In fact, according to the functionalist perspective, social institutions perform two different types of societal functions: manifest and latent. *Manifest functions* are intended and recognized consequences of an activity or social process. A manifest function of education, for example, is to provide students with knowledge, skills, and cultural values. In contrast, *latent functions* are the unintended consequences of an activity or social process that are hidden and remain unacknowledged by participants (Merton 1968). The latent functions of education include the babysitter function of keeping young people off the street and out of the full-time job market while their parents work, and the matchmaking function whereby schools provide opportunities for students to meet and socialize with potential marriage partners. These functions are latent because schools were not created for babysitting or matchmaking, and most organizational participants do not acknowledge that these activities take place.

Dysfunctions and Social Disorganization

From the functionalist perspective, social problems arise when social institutions do not fulfill their functions or when dysfunctions occur. *Dysfunctions* are the undesirable consequences of an activity or social process that inhibit a society's ability to adapt or adjust (Merton 1968). For example, a function of education is to prepare students for jobs, but if schools fail to do so, then students have problems finding jobs, employers or governments have to spend millions of dollars on employee training programs, and consumers have to pay higher prices for goods and services to offset worker-training costs. In other words, dysfunctions in education threaten other social institutions, especially families and the economy.

Dysfunctions can occur in society as a whole or in a part of society (a social institution). According to functionalists, dysfunctions in social institutions create social disorganization in the entire society. **Social disorganization** refers to the conditions in society that undermine the ability of traditional social institutions to govern human behaviour. Early in the 20th century, sociologists Robert E. Park (1864–1944) and Ernest W. Burgess (1886–1966) developed a social disorganization theory to explain why some urban areas had higher rates of *social deviance,* which they defined as a pattern of rule violation, than other areas. Social disorganization causes a breakdown in the traditional values and norms that serve as social control mechanisms, which, under normal circumstances, keep people from engaging in nonconforming behaviour. **Values** are collective ideas about what is right or wrong, good or bad, and desirable or undesirable in a specific society (Williams 1970). Although values provide ideas about behaviour, they do not state explicitly how we should behave. Norms, on the other hand, have specific behavioural expectations. **Norms** are established rules of behaviour or standards of conduct. French sociologist Emile Durkheim (1858–1917) suggested that social problems arise when people no longer agree on societal values and norms. According to Durkheim, periods of rapid social change produce *anomie*—a loss of shared values and sense of purpose in society. During these periods, social bonds grow weaker, social control is diminished, and people are more likely to engage in nonconforming patterns of behaviour, such as crime.

Early sociologists, examining the relationship between social problems and rapid industrialization and urbanization in Britain, Western Europe, and the United States in the late 19th and early 20th centuries, noted that rapid social change intensifies social disorganization. **Industrialization** is the process by which societies are transformed from a dependence on agriculture and handmade products to an emphasis on manufacturing and related industries. At the beginning of the Industrial Revolution, thousands of people migrated from rural communities to large urban centres to find employment in factories and offices. New social problems emerged as a result of industrialization and **urbanization,** the process by which an increasing proportion of a population lives in cities rather than in rural areas. During this period of rapid technological and social change, urban social problems such as poverty, crime, child labour, inadequate housing, unsanitary conditions, overcrowding, and environmental pollution increased sharply.

Applying the Functionalist Perspective to Problems of Violence

Some functionalists believe that violence arises from a condition of anomie, in which many individuals have a feeling of helplessness, normlessness, or alienation. Others believe that violence increases when social institutions such as the family, schools, and religious organizations weaken, and the main mechanisms of social control in people's everyday lives are external (i.e., law enforcement agencies and the criminal justice system).

Other functionalist explanations of violence focus on how changes in social institutions put some people at greater risk of being victims of violent crime than others. According to the **lifestyle–routine activity approach,** the patterns and timing of people's daily movements and activities as they go about obtaining such necessities of life as food, shelter, companionship, and entertainment are the keys to understanding violent personal crimes and other types of crime in our society (Cohen and Felson 1979). Several changes over the past 50 years may have put people at increased risk for violent crime victimization in Canada, such as more people living by themselves, shopping hours extended into the night, and more people eating outside the home (Parker 1995). Social structure may also put constraints on behaviour, thus making certain people more vulnerable to violent attack (e.g., people who are required to work at night). The lifestyle–routine activity approach suggests that people who willingly put themselves in situations that expose them to the potential for violent crime should modify their behaviour, or that society should provide greater protection for people whose lifestyle routine leaves them vulnerable to attackers. The lifestyle–routine activity approach offers some insight, but does not address the issue of violence in the home and other supposedly safe havens. Further, it does not explain the violence itself; it simply points out that people are at risk, which tells us nothing that would assist in eliminating violence.

How would a functionalist approach the problem of violence? Most emphasize shared moral values and social bonds. They believe that when rapid social change or other "disruptions" occur, moral values may erode, and problems such as school violence or hate crimes are likely to occur more frequently. Functionalists believe that to reduce violence, families, schools, religious organizations, and other social institutions should be strengthened so that they can regenerate shared values and morality. Most functionalists also believe that those who engage in violent criminal behaviour should be prosecuted to the full extent of the law.

The Conflict Perspective

The **conflict perspective** is based on the assumption that groups in society are engaged in a continuous power struggle for control of scarce resources. Unlike functionalist theorists, who emphasize the degree to which society is held together by a consensus on values, conflict theorists emphasize the degree to which society is characterized by conflict and discrimination. According to some conflict theorists, certain groups of people are privileged while others are disadvantaged through the inequitable use of political, economic, or social power. Not all conflict theorists hold the same views about what constitutes the most important form of conflict. We will examine two principal perspectives: the value conflict perspective and the critical-conflict perspective.

The Value Conflict Perspective

According to value conflict theorists, social problems are conditions that are incompatible with group values. From this perspective, value clashes are ordinary occurrences in families, communities, and the larger society, in which individuals commonly hold many divergent values. Although individuals may share certain core beliefs, they do not share all values or a common culture. *Culture* refers to the knowledge, language, values, customs, and material objects that are passed from person to person and from one generation to the next in a human group or society.

Discrepancies between ideal and real culture are a source of social problems in all societies. *Ideal culture* refers to the values and beliefs that people claim they hold; *real culture* refers to the values and beliefs they actually follow. In Canada, members of such diverse groups as B'nai Brith, the Heritage Front, the Aryan Nations, and the Urban Alliance on Race Relations all claim to adhere to ideal cultural values of equality, freedom, and liberty; however, these ideal cultural values come into direct conflict with real cultural values when issues of racialized/ethnic relations arise.

The value conflict perspective has been criticized by critical-conflict theorists, who argue that it overlooks the deeper social problems of inequality and oppression based on class, racialization, and gender.

Critical-Conflict Perspective

Unlike the value conflict approach, critical-conflict theorists suggest that social problems arise out of the major contradictions inherent in the way societies are organized. Some critical-conflict perspectives focus on class inequalities in the capitalist economic system; others focus on inequalities based on "race"/ethnicity or gender.

Most class perspectives on inequality have been strongly influenced by Karl Marx (1818–1883), a German economist and activist who recognized that the emergence of capitalism produced dramatic and irreversible changes in social life. **Capitalism** is an economic system characterized by private ownership of the means of production, from which personal profits can be derived through market competition and without government intervention. According to Marx, members of the *capitalist class* (the *bourgeoisie*), who own and control the means of production (e.g., the land, tools, factories, and money for investment), are at the top of a system of social stratification that affords them different lifestyles and life chances from those of the members of the *working class* (the *proletariat*), who must sell their labour power (their potential ability to work) to capitalists. In selling their labour power, members of the working class forfeit control over their work, and the capitalists derive profits from the workers' labour.

Marx believed that capitalism leads workers to experience increased levels of impoverishment and *alienation*—a feeling of powerlessness and estrangement from other people and from oneself (Marx and Engels 1847/1971:96). He predicted that the working class would eventually overthrow the capitalist economic system. Although Marx's prediction has not come about, Erik Olin Wright (1997) and other social scientists have modified and adapted his perspective to apply to contemporary capitalist nations. In today's capitalist nations, according to Wright (1997), ownership of the means of production is only one way in which people gain the ability to exploit others. Two other ways in which individuals gain control are through control of property and control over other people's labour. In this view, upper-level managers and others in positions of authority gain control over societal resources and other individuals' time, knowledge, and skills in such a manner that members of the upper classes are able to maintain their dominance.

Some critical-conflict perspectives focus on racialized and gender subordination instead of class-based inequalities. Critical-conflict theorists who emphasize discrimination and inequality based on "race" or ethnicity note that many social problems are rooted in the continuing exploitation and subordination of people of colour and Indigenous people by White people, or, more accurately, by institutions and systems set up by and for White people. For example, Frideres (1999:142–44) has shown how Indigenous people in Canada are greatly disadvantaged relative to any other ethnic group: they have considerably lower family incomes and substantially higher rates of unemployment than non-Indigenous people.

Throughout this text, where we discuss conflict theory, we will use critical-conflict theory (rather than the value conflict approach) to highlight the power relations that result in social problems.

Applying the Conflict Perspective to Problems of Violence

Conflict theorists who focus on class-based inequalities believe that the potential for violence is inherent in capitalist societies. In fact, say these theorists, the wealthy engage in one form of violence, and the poor engage in another. They note that the wealthy often use third parties to protect themselves and their families from bodily harm as well as to secure their property and investments in this country and elsewhere in the world. For example, the wealthy who live in Canada or other high-income nations and who own factories (or own stock in factories) in middle- and low-income nations use the governments and police of those nations—third parties—to control workers who threaten to strike. The wealthy also influence Canadian government policy, by supporting or not supporting peacekeeping or military intervention in nations where they may have investments or desire to have investments.

In contrast, these theorists say, when the poor engage in violence, the violence is typically committed by the individual and may be a reaction to the unjust social and economic conditions he or she experiences daily on the bottom rung of a capitalist society. The economic exploitation of the poor, these theorists note, dramatically affects all aspects of the individual's life, including how the person reacts to daily injustices, stress, and other threatening situations. In violent street crimes, the vast majority of offenders—as well as victims—are poor, unemployed, or working in low-level, low-paying jobs. In fact, most violent street crime is an intra-class phenomenon. Arrest and conviction data suggest that poor and working-class people typically victimize others who are like themselves. In part, this is due to the fact that violence committed by middle- and upper-class individuals is not investigated and/or prosecuted to the same degree. Moreover, middle- and upper-class individuals are likely to enlist the services of people from lower classes when they wish to commit violence. For example, in a televised interview, Brett Hayes, a past member of a neo-Nazi skinhead organization in Canada, stated that certain individuals are targeted for violence by the organization's elite (many allegedly in prominent positions in society), but the actual violence is carried out by the "foot soldiers," or "dogs," of the movement, the mainly working-class and youthful "skins" (CTV 1995).

The conflict perspective argues that the criminal justice system is biased in favour of the middle and upper classes. Because it is, its definition of violence depends on where a person's ethnicity, class, and gender locate him or her in the system of stratification. In this way, violent crimes are but one part of a larger system of inequality and oppression. Sexism and racism are reinforced by the overarching class structure that benefits the powerful at the expense of the powerless. The conflict perspective that focuses on racialized/ethnic inequalities points out that racism is an important factor in explaining such violent acts as hate crimes. Recently, a number of White supremacists spouting racist and anti-Semitic dogma have been convicted of violent crimes. This kind of brutality—for example, the 1998 murder of a Sikh man in Surrey, B.C., by a group of White supremacists—is fuelled by racist ideologies that suggest that problems with the economy and growing unemployment for young people are due to increased immigration. Leaders of White supremacist groups foster these discourses as a way of fuelling hate and inciting violence (see Chapter 3).

No matter what approach conflict theorists take, they all agree on one thing: violence is unlikely to diminish significantly unless inequalities based on class and ethnicity are reduced at the macrolevel in society.

SOCIAL PROBLEMS IN THE MEDIA

BOX 1.2   The New Canadian *Youth Criminal Justice Act:* Dealing Differently with Canada's Youth "Folk Devils"?

On February 4, 2002, the Canadian House of Commons passed Bill C-7, bringing into effect on April 1, 2003 Canada's *Youth Criminal Justice Act* (YCJA). The new act replaced the 1984 Canadian *Young Offenders Act* (YOA). There are several differences between the two acts, but most notable are changes that allow children to be tried as adults and penalized as adults, particularly for violent crimes such as murder and sexual assault. Under the old act, children aged 12 to 17 were viewed as having not reached full maturity and as such should be shown leniency. However, even under the old act, a youth aged 14 or over who was charged with murder, attempted murder, manslaughter, or aggravated sexual assault could be transferred to adult court and receive an adult sentence. Adult sentences were imposed if the court felt that a youth sentence would be insufficient in making the youth accountable for the crime (Department of Justice 2006).

The repeal of the 1984 YOA and subsequent creation of the 2002 YCJA were accomplished after much heated debate in Canada, the result, some say, of a multi-pronged public relations campaign begun in 1998 by the Government of Canada. On one side were the advocates of the "law and order" agenda, who painted youth as "out of control" "super-predators" who were "getting away with murder" (Martin 2002:96; Young and Gainsborough 2000:2). As Hartnagel states,

> The YOA was under frequent criticism almost from its inception in 1984. Many argued that the act was too soft on young offenders and that the available sentences were too light, particularly for repeat or more serious offences. The minimum age of legal culpability (12) was claimed to be too high; and the age of adulthood (18) was seen as "mollycoddling" young adult criminals. (2004:361)

On the other side of the debate were those who followed a "children's rights" discourse, believing the new YCJA would be too harsh, "too 'offence oriented' and/or too 'tough' on young people" (Doob and Sprott 2006:229).

The "law and order" approach to youth violence was aided by a concept advanced by Stanley Cohen and Jock Young, called a "moral panic" (1971/1980), where "the youth of today" are presented as "a threat to the established way of life" (Thompson 1998:1). A moral panic is defined as a campaign sustained over a period of time that appeals to people worried about the risks of a disintegrating social order, that lacks clear moral guidelines, that politicians and media are eager to act on in order to be seen as suppressing the threat, and that leaves the real causes of social breakdown (if a breakdown exists) unaddressed (Thompson 1998:3). Moral panics, as described by Kenneth Thompson, have five key stages or elements:

1. Something or someone is defined as a threat to values or interests.

2. This threat is depicted in an easily recognizable form by the media.

3. There is a rapid buildup of public concern.

4. There is a response from authorities and opinion makers.

5. The panic recedes or results in social changes (1998:8).

For at least 100 years, society has endured moral panics of one sort or another, disproportionately with youth as the perceived threat. That media and politicians created a moral panic in the 1980s and 1990s about the so-called rising tide of youth violence cannot be in doubt.

Several Canadian criminologists argue that public opinion in Canada about youth crime and youth justice has been carefully socially constructed through savvy government public relations strategies (including well-timed "leaks" to the media) and relentless media sensationalism that implies that statistically rare serious and violent crimes committed by youth have, in fact, become commonplace. The perceived goal of this PR campaign was the political ejection of a party that was viewed as being too soft on youth crime (Doob and Sprott 2006; Hartnagel 2004; Martin 2002; Pedicelli 1998). Various Canadian public opinion polls over these years indicated that Canadians believed violent youth crime was on the rise, and, as a result, became increasingly fearful of youth (Hartnagel 2004). Hartnagel, citing the work of Schissel (1997), states:

> The Canadian media constructed folk devils of youth, symbolically targeting them as scapegoats for various ills of society. [Schissel] illustrated his argument with newspaper articles claiming that youth crime had become endemic, characteristic of a certain kind of youth, and required stern intervention [and he] concluded that the media present an ideological portrait of youth crime and criminals by using selected extraordinary crimes as evidence of a general crime wave. (2004:366)

We can see clear evidence of Hartnagel's (and Schissel's) argument in the sensationalized media accounts of the trials of Kelly Ellard and Warren Glowatski, convicted April 2005 (Ellard) and June 1999 (Glowatski) of killing Reena Virk in Victoria, B.C.; of Muzil Abdullah, convicted July 2006 of killing Jomar Lanot in Vancouver, B.C.; and of Sonny Head, convicted June 2002 of killing Barbara Danelesko in Edmonton, Alberta.

What is significant about these well-publicized trials and Canadians' newfound comfort with the YCJA is that there are actually no demonstrable changes in our responses to youth who commit violent crimes. In fact, the level of punitiveness—demonstrated, for example, by increased rates of imprisonment, increased transfers to adult court, and harsher penalties—toward serious and violent youth offenders has not increased since the YCJA came into effect. Certainly the sensationalized cases mentioned earlier bear this out. Ellard and Glowatski were sentenced to life imprisonment and are eligible for parole after seven years. Head was sentenced to seven years in prison. Abdullah was sentenced to seven years in prison, with Judge Bernard stating that he would have sentenced Abdullah to 10 years in an adult jail *but for his age,* the fact that he pleaded guilty, and his failure to express remorse for the crime.

It remains the case that Canadian youth are still incarcerated at a high rate, higher than any other Western country, and that most Canadian youth, even violent offenders, are sentenced to alternatives to incarceration. Whether or not you view this as positive or negative, the evidence stemming from research on Canadian youth justice over the past 15 years appears to demonstrate that the new YCJA was a political tool used by politicians, via the media, to ensure political victory. In no appreciable way has it impacted either the rate or type of violent crimes committed by Canadian youth, nor the penalties for committing such crimes. Those who worried the YCJA would be too harsh should feel more at ease now, despite the media sensationalism.

The Interactionist Perspective

Unlike the conflict perspective, which focuses on macrolevel inequalities in society, the interactionist perspective focuses on microlevel analyses of how people act toward one another and how they make sense of their daily lives. The **interactionist perspective** views society as the sum of the interactions of individuals and groups. Most interactionists study social problems by analyzing how certain behaviour comes to be defined as a social problem and how individuals and groups come to engage in activities that a significant number of people view as a major social concern.

German sociologist Georg Simmel (1858–1918), a founder of the interactionist approach, investigated the impact of industrialization and urbanization on people's values and behaviour within small social units. Simmel (1902/1950) noted that rapid changes in technology and dramatic urban growth produced new social problems by breaking up the "geometry of social life," which he described as the web of patterned social interactions among the people who constitute a society. According to Simmel, alienation is brought about by a decline in personal and emotional contacts. How people *interpret* the subjective messages they receive from others and the situations they encounter in their daily life greatly influence their behaviour and perceptions of what constitutes a social problem.

Labelling Theory and the Social Construction of Reality

While Simmel focused on how people interpret their own situations, other interactionists have examined how people impose their shared meanings on others. According to sociologist Howard Becker (1963), *moral entrepreneurs* are people who use their own views of right and wrong to establish rules and label others as deviant (nonconforming). *Labelling theory,* as this perspective is called, suggests that behaviour that deviates from established norms is deviant *because* it has been labelled as such by others. According to this theory, deviants (nonconformists) are people who have been successfully labelled as such by others. Labelling theory raises questions about why certain individuals and certain types of behaviour are labelled as deviant but others are not. The answer is suggestive of an analysis of power, which this theory has no real view of.

According to some interaction theorists, many social problems can be linked to the *social construction of reality*—the process by which people's perception of reality is shaped largely by the subjective meaning that they give to an experience (Berger and Luckmann 1967). From this perspective, little shared reality exists beyond that which people socially create. It is, however, this social construction of reality that influences people's beliefs and actions. Other interactionists suggest that how we define a situation affects our reactions to it. According to sociologists William I. Thomas (1863–1947) and Dorothy S. Thomas (1899–1977), when people define situations as real, the situations become real in their consequences. Elaborating on the Thomas Theorem (1928), as it has come to be called, sociologist Robert Merton (1968) suggested that when people perceive a situation in a certain way and act according to their perceptions, the end result may be a **self-fulfilling prophecy**—a false definition of a situation that evokes a new behaviour that makes the original false conception become true. For example, a teenager who is labelled a "juvenile delinquent" may accept the label and adopt the full-blown image of a juvenile delinquent as portrayed in television programs and films: wearing "gang" colours, dropping out of school, and participating in violence or other behaviour that is labelled as deviant. If the teenager is subsequently arrested, the initial label becomes a self-fulfilling prophecy.

Applying Interactionist Perspectives to Problems of Violence

Interactionist explanations of violence begin by noting that human behaviour is learned through social interaction. Violence, interactionists state, is a learned response, not an inherent characteristic, in the individual. Some of the most interesting support for this point of view comes from studies done by social psychologist Albert Bandura (1973), who studied aggression in children. Showing children a film of a person beating, kicking, and hacking an inflatable doll produced a violent response in the children, who, when they were placed in a room with a similar doll, duplicated the behaviour shown in the film and engaged in additional aggressive behaviour. Others have noted that people tend to repeat their behaviour if they feel rewarded for it. Thus, when people learn that they can get their way by inflicting violence or the threat of violence on others, their aggressive behaviour is reinforced. It is important to point out that the "reward" may only be perceived as a reward in the eyes of that person.

Interactionists also look at the types of social interactions that commonly lead to violence. According to the **situational approach**, violence results from a specific interaction process, termed a "situational transaction." Criminologist David Luckenbill (1977) has identified six stages in the situational transaction between victim and offender. In the first stage, the future victim does something behavioural or verbal that is considered an affront by the other (e.g., a glare or an insult). In the second, the offended individual verifies that the action was directed at him or her personally. In the third, the offended individual decides how to respond to the affront and may issue a verbal or behavioural challenge (e.g., a verbal threat or a raised fist). If the problem escalates at this point, injury or death may occur in this stage; if not, the participants enter into the fourth stage. In this stage, the future victim further escalates the transaction, often prodded by onlookers siding with one party or the other. In the fifth stage, actual violence occurs when neither party is able to back down without losing face. At this point, one or both parties produce weapons (if they have not already appeared), which may range from guns and knives to bottles, pool cues, or other bludgeoning devices, and the offender kills the victim. The sixth and final stage involves the offender's actions after the crime: some flee the scene, others are detained by onlookers, and still others call the police themselves.

The situational approach is based first on the assumption that many victims are active participants in the violence perpetrated against them and second on the idea that confrontation does not inevitably lead to violence or death. As Robert Nash Parker (1995) has noted, in the first four stages of the transaction, either the victim or the offender can decide to pursue another course of action and most often does.

According to interactionists, reducing violence requires changing those societal values that encourage excessive competition and violence. These changes must occur at the microlevel, which means agents of socialization must transmit different attitudes and values toward violence. The next generation must learn that it is an individual's right—regardless of gender, racialized status, class, religion, or other attributes or characteristics—to live free from violence and the devastating impact it has on individuals, groups, and the social fabric of society.

Feminist Perspectives

Feminist theorists begin their analysis by pointing out that mainstream sociological thought and theory is both androcentric and Eurocentric (Alvi, DeKeseredy, and Ellis 2000:19). This means most sociological theory is based on the experiences, ideas, and issues of concern for males of European and Western extraction. European and male perspectives are valid, of course, and they are partial. All perspectives are partial, but in the past, these perspectives were treated as though they were representative of the experiences, ideas, and issues of all people. Today, we know this is impossible; hence feminist theories, anti-racist theories, post-colonial theories, Indigenous theories, and so on have been created and employed to account for more of social life, in addition to maintaining the mainstream theories previously discussed.

There are no "feminist issues" per se. Every issue is a feminist issue. Basically, when feminist theorists engage in analysis, they "gender" the issues under study. This means that theorists look at the differential impacts of social phenomena for men and women, and more recently for transgendered or non-gendered people as well. This does not mean that feminists study only gender, although in the past that may have been more true. Feminist theories typically examine dynamics of power in relationships between individuals, roles, structures, and so on. The focus on power differentials is shared with conflict and Marxist theories, but feminist theories add a focus on gendered power and patriarchy. A final defining feature of feminist theories is the idea

of beginning one's analysis from a particular "standpoint." This is to say that social life is examined from the situated vantage points of the individuals and/or groups involved.

Since there is no one feminist perspective, there is no one feminist perspective on social problems. Many authors put forth summaries of numerous variations of feminist theory (liberal, Marxist, radical, socialist, anti-racist, lesbian, cultural, and so on); however, it may be more useful to distinguish between the types of theories instead of the specific variants. Lengermann and Niebrugge-Brantley (1992:319) provide a classification system that categorizes various feminist theories as (a) theories of difference, (b) theories of inequality, or (c) theories of oppression. Theories are distinguished from one another by the approach taken to answering the question, Why are women's situations as they are? Theories of difference are premised on the idea that men and women experience different realities based on their differential locations in most situations. Theories of inequality assert that women's situations are not only different from men's but are also less privileged or are disadvantaged relative to men's. Theories of oppression suggest that not only are women's situations different from and unequal to men's but that women are actively subordinated and kept disadvantaged, both by patriarchal structures and by individuals reinforcing sexist socialization and ideologies.

Feminist theories and the people who advance them have been appropriately criticized for perpetuating the same kinds of injustice based on "difference" that mainstream sociological theories perpetuated because of their androcentrism and Eurocentricity. Most feminist theory in the past (and today) comes from a White, middle-class, heterosexual, educated women's bias. The issues assumed to be central by these theories, then, are the issues of interest and concern to these groups of people. Criticism arose, for example, because where White and educated feminists saw men and patriarchy as denying them reproductive freedom (e.g., access to birth control and abortion), Indigenous women and women of colour saw racism and acts of discrimination (e.g., in employment or housing) affecting both the men and the women of racialized groups as *the* issue of importance. Poor feminists saw academic elitism and poverty as *the* issue of importance for men and women. Lesbians and women with disabilities saw their perspectives silenced or marginalized. So, the locations or situations of the particular theorists deter-mine what issues are defined as the most important feminist issues to be taken up.

Modern-day feminist theories, if they are reflex-ive, turn the lenses back upon themselves. If one is supporting a particular theory, is it sexist? Is it racist? Is it homophobic? Is it classist? Is it ableist? Many con-temporary feminists spend a good deal of time deconstructing the theories they favour—the underly-ing assumptions, exclusions, inclusiveness, impacts of the analysis, and dissemination of the analysis. While this exercise may seem academic—and it is, in some senses—it is also important to know where the theory is weak, where it cannot be used to see an issue clearly, what the bias is, whose voice is missing, and so on. Several feminist theorists today call for simultaneous analyses of interlocking oppressions (see Chapter 3). These feminist theorists view the social world as a matrix of domination where sexism, racism, hetero-sexism, classism, and other marginalized statuses meet in myriad ways over issues. Theoretical analysis focuses on how these interlocking oppressions play out in different contexts. Other concepts important to contemporary feminist theorists are "public and private spheres, ideology [and] relations of ruling" (Swingewood 2000:240). Focusing on these concepts allows us to analyze macro and micro issues and the interplay between the two, an important feature if we are to have the ability to understand social life from a broader perspective. This leads to a final defining feature of feminist theory—a propensity to propel its adher-ents toward engaged social action.

Applying Feminist Perspectives to Problems of Violence

Feminist perspectives of violence highlight issues of dominance and power. Inequalities between groups can result in violence. People who enjoy power and privilege likely commit as many acts of violence as those who are disenfranchised. The main difference between groups is that those without power are disproportion-ately targeted as the perpetrators or viewed as bringing it on themselves. So, for example, in an analysis of Reena Virk's murder in Victoria, B.C., the media chose to focus on personal characteristics of the murdered young woman—her apparent "flaws"—while ignoring structures of domination and sexist and racist ideologies that create the context for this type of violence and that support and perpetuate gendered and racialized vio-lence. In an incisive anti-racist feminist analysis, Yasmin Jiwani (1997:2–3) concludes that

> [the murderers'] power and dominance, legitimized by and rooted in the sexism and racism of the dom-inant white culture and its attendant sense of superiority, was used to force [Virk] into submission—a submission that amounted to her death and erasure from society . . . The implicit mes-sage [in the media] was that had she been white and had she been thin, she would have fit in, and there would have been no reason for her to be killed . . . What happened to Reena could have happened to any number of us who are visibly different and dou-bly or triply marked in this society by virtue of race [sic], gender, sexual orientation and disability.

Feminists also add social class oppression as a loca-tion of domination. For example, in Chapter 4, the fact that the 1989 Montreal Massacre at École Polytechnique gained such notoriety is contrasted with the comparatively little stir created by the murders of many poor women from the downtown East Side of Vancouver.

Finally, one feminist perspective suggests that vio-lence against women is a means of reinforcing patriarchy. According to this analysis, in a patriarchal system, the sexual marketplace is characterized by unequal bargaining power, making transactions between men and women potentially coercive in nature. Gender strat-ification is reinforced by powerful physical, psychological, and social mechanisms of control, including force or the threat of force. Fear of violence forces women to adapt their ways of being in the world—living, acting, and dressing—to ensure they are not in a position to be victimized by men, and thus they are deprived of many basic freedoms (see Gardner 1995).

SOCIAL CHANGE AND REDUCING SOCIAL PROBLEMS

The concept of social change is important to any discussion of reducing social problems. **Social change** is the alteration, modification, or transformation of public policy, culture, or social institutions over time (Kendall

2000). Notice that this definition states that social change occurs "over time"; social change has a temporal dimension. Some efforts to deal with social problems are *short-term* strategies, whereas others are *middle-term* remedies, and still others constitute *long-term* efforts to alleviate the root causes of a social problem. In other words, efforts to alleviate individual unemployment or reduce unemployment rates in a community have a different temporal dimension than efforts to change the political economy in such a manner that high levels of employment and greater wage equity are brought about throughout a nation or nations. Clearly, efforts to alleviate individual unemployment are a short-term solution to the problem of unemployment, while efforts to reduce unemployment in a community or to change the entire political economy are middle-term and long-term solutions, respectively. Sometimes discussions of social change sound idealistic or utopian because they are middle-term or long-term strategies that attempt to target the root causes of a social problem. For most social problems, however, a combination of strategies is required to eliminate or reduce them.

Microlevel Attempts to Solve Social Problems

Earlier in this chapter, we described sociologist C. Wright Mills's (1959b) belief that we should apply the sociological imagination to gain a better understanding of social problems. According to Mills, the sociological imagination is the ability to see the relationship between an individual's experiences and the larger society. For Mills, social problems could not be *solved* at the individual level because they are more than personal troubles or private problems. However, sometimes social institutions cannot deal with a problem effectively, and political and business leaders are unwilling, or unable, to allocate the resources necessary to deal with the issue. In these situations, we typically begin to deal with the problem in an individualized way.

Seeking Individual Solutions to Personal Problems

Microlevel solutions to social problems focus on how individuals operate within small groups to try to remedy a problem that affects them, their family, or their

friends. Usually, when individuals have personal problems, they turn to their **primary groups**—small, less-specialized groups in which members engage in face-to-face, emotion-based interactions over an extended period of time (Kendall 2000). Primary groups include one's family, close friends, and other peers with whom one routinely shares the more personal experiences in life.

How can participation in primary groups help us reduce personal problems? According to sociologists, members of our primary groups usually support us even when others do not. For example, some analysts believe that there are many more people without a domicile (technically homeless) than current statistics suggest, but whenever possible, these people live with relatives or friends, many of whom already live in overcrowded and sometimes substandard housing. Many people who seek individualized solutions to personal troubles believe the situation will be temporary. However, if the problem is widespread or embedded in the larger society, it may stretch out for months or years without resolution. At best, individualized efforts to reduce a problem are short-term measures that some refer to as a "band-aid approach" to a problem because they do not eliminate the causes of the problem: they merely ameliorate the effects of it for a few, for a while.

Some microlevel approaches to reducing social problems focus on how individuals can do something about the problems they face. For example, a person who is unemployed or among the "working poor" because of low wages, seasonal employment, or other factors may be urged to get more education or training and work experience in order to find a "better" job and have the opportunity for upward mobility. Individuals who appear to have eliminated problems in their own lives through such efforts are applauded for their "determination," and are often held up (sometimes unwillingly or unknowingly) as examples that others are supposed to follow.

Mid-Range Attempts to Solve Social Problems

Mid-range solutions to social problems focus on how secondary groups and formal organizations can assist individuals in overcoming issues such as drug addiction or domestic violence. Some groups help people cope with their own problems, and some groups attempt to bring about community change.

Groups That Help People Cope with Their Problems

Most mid-range solutions to social problems are based on two assumptions: (1) some social problems can best be reduced by reaching one person at a time; and (2) prevention and intervention are most effective at the personal and community levels. Groups that attempt to reduce a social problem by helping individuals cope with it, or eliminate it from their own lives, are common in our society. Among the best known are Alcoholics Anonymous (AA) and Narcotics Anonymous (NA); however, a broad range of "self-help" organizations exists in most Canadian communities. Typically, self-help groups bring together individuals who have experienced the same problem and have the same goals. For example, a shared goal may be quitting a particular behaviour that has caused the problem, which can be anything from abuse of alcohol, tobacco, and other drugs to overeating, gambling, and chronic worrying. Volunteers who have had similar problems (and believe they are on the road to overcoming them) often act as role models for newer members. For example, AA and NA are operated by recovered alcoholics and/or other recovered substance abusers who try to provide new members with the support they need to overcome alcohol addiction or drug dependency. According to some analysts, AA is a subculture with distinct rules and values that alcoholics learn through their face-to-face encounters with other AA members (Maxwell 1981). Social interaction is viewed as central for individual success in the programs. Confessing one's behavioural problems to others in an organizational setting is believed to have therapeutic value to those who are seeking help.

Like other mid-range approaches, organizations such as AA and NA may bring changes in the individual's life; however, they usually do not systematically address the structural factors (such as unemployment, work-related stress, and aggressive advertising campaigns) that may contribute to the problems. For example, AA typically does not lobby for more stringent laws pertaining to drunk driving or the ready sale and consumption of alcoholic beverages. In British Columbia, for example, fairly recent legal changes have made the purchase of alcohol easier by expanding the hours it can be made available to consumers and expanding the kinds of outlets where it can be sold. As a result, larger societal intervention is necessary to reduce the problems that contribute to individual behaviours.

Grassroots Groups That Work for Community-Based Change

Some grassroots organizations focus on bringing about a change that may reduce or eliminate a social problem in a specific community or region. **Grassroots groups** are organizations started by ordinary people who work in concert to deal with a perceived problem in their neighbourhood, city, province or territory, or nation. Using this approach, people learn how to empower themselves against local, provincial, territorial, and national government officials, as well as corporate executives and media figures who determine what constitutes the news in their area:

By their nature, grassroots groups emerge to challenge individuals, corporations, government agencies, academia, or a combination of these when people discover they share a grievance. In their search for redress, they have encountered unresponsive, negative public agencies, self-serving private businesses, or recalcitrant individuals and groups. The answer for them is to select specific issues and find like-minded others. (Adams 1991:9)

A central concern of those who attempt to reduce a social problem through grassroots groups is the extent to which other people are apathetic about the problem. Some analysts suggest that even when people are aware of problems, they do not think that they can do anything to change them or they do not know how to work with other people to alleviate them:

The biggest problem . . . is not those issues that bombard us daily, from homelessness and failing schools to environmental devastation and the federal deficit. Underlying each is a deeper crisis. Some see that deeper problem in the form of obstacles that block problem solving: the tightening concentration of wealth, the influence of money in politics, discrimination, and bureaucratic rigidity, to name a few. These are powerful barriers. But for us the crisis is deeper still. The crisis is that *we as a people don't know how to come together to solve these problems.* We lack the capacities to address the issues or remove the obstacles that stand in the way of public deliberation. Too many [people] feel powerless. (Lappé and Du Bois 1994:9)

According to social analysts, more community dialogue is needed on social issues, and more people need to become involved in grassroots social movements. A **social movement** is an organized group that acts collectively to promote or resist change through collective action (Goldberg 1991). Because social movements are not institutionalized and are outside the political mainstream when they begin, they empower outsiders by offering them an opportunity to have their voices heard (Kendall 2000).

An example of a mid-range group is Pollution Probe, a Canadian environmental organization, whose purposes, according to its website (**http://www.pollution probe.org**), are

■ to define environmental problems through research;

■ to promote understanding through education; and

■ to press for practical solutions through advocacy.

The organization has four major programs:

1. An air program to promote tougher controls on urban smog;

2. A water program to ensure safe, clean drinking water and to help develop a global water ethic;

3. An energy conservation program; and

4. A climate change program.

Pollution Probe started in 1969, when a few University of Toronto students began working with faculty members such as Donald Chant, then chair of the Department of Zoology. Early concerns were dangers of pesticides for birds, high levels of phosphates in detergents for freshwater lakes, and smog in cities. To help deal with these concerns, Pollution Probe undertook a variety of programs. For example, in 1970, a community development project was devised to send people to different parts of southern Ontario's cottage country to encourage summer camp participants, cottage association members, and townspeople to look into problems of water pollution and

waste management in their area. Over its 40-year history, Pollution Probe has had a wide variety of accomplishments, including limiting the phosphate content of detergents, encouraging household recycling, helping to launch the Coalition on Acid Rain, contributing to an Ontario act that guarantees the right of residents to participate in environmental decisions, and being instrumental in the passage of an act for mandatory emissions testing of vehicles in Ontario. An example of a recent Pollution Probe action is the June 2009 "Nothing Is Possible: Clean Air Commute," an initiative designed to get people to commute to work for one week in the Toronto area in a way that contributes nothing to pollution. Pollution Probe has an enviable combination of accomplishments and trust that should ensure its continued effectiveness.

Many social movements, such as Mothers Against Drunk Driving (MADD), begin as community-based grassroots efforts (see Box 8.1). Over time, many mid-range organizations evolve into national groups; however, their organization and focus often change in the process (Adams 1991). Table 1.1 provides examples of activist organizations that seek to reduce specific social problems in communities.

Grassroots organizations and other local structures are crucial to national social movements because national social movements must recruit members and gain the economic resources that are necessary for nationwide or global social activism. Numerous sociological studies have shown that the local level constitutes a necessary microfoundation for larger-scale social movement activism. In fact, Bob Ratner (1997:275), a UBC sociologist, notes that the politics of new social movements have prompted a shift from national politics to local grassroots action and the formation of a vast and profound solidarity grounded in the validity of communal experience. Such movements, as they multiply and spread, represent a different sort of globalization, one tantamount to a "globalization from below."

To understand how grassroots organizations aid national social movements, consider the problem of environmental degradation. Leaders of national environmental organizations often participate in local or regional rallies, protests, and letter-writing or e-mail campaigns, particularly when politicians are making decisions that environmentalists believe will have a negative effect on the environment. By working with

TABLE 1.1   Selected Organizations That Seek to Reduce a Social Problem

Category	Organization	Website Address
Environment:	Earth First	http://www.earthfirst.org
	Greenpeace	http://www.greenpeace.ca
	Sierra Club	http://www.sierraclub.org
	Student Environmental Action Coalition	http://www.seac.org
	Western Canada Wilderness Committee	http://www.wildernesscommittee.org
Drunk driving:	Mothers Against Drunk Driving	http://www.madd.ca
Wages and working conditions:	Canadian Labour Congress	http://clc-ctc.ca
	Industrial Workers of the World	http://iww.org
Poverty, hunger, and homelessness:	Food Banks Canada	http://foodbankscanada.ca/main.cfm
	Canada Without Poverty	http://www.cwp-csp.ca/Blog/
	PovNet	http://www.povnet.org
	Raising the Roof (Homelessness)	http://www.raisingtheroof.org
Violence and war:	Food Not Bombs	http://www.foodnotbombs.net
	I Wage Peace.org	http://www.iwagepeace.org
	Canadian Peace Alliance	http://www.acp-cpa.ca/en/index.html

Note: Web addresses often change. Those given here were accurate at the time of publication.

local and regional activists and seeking to influence local and regional power structures—city councils, provincial and territorial planning commissions, and legislatures—national organizations assert the need for their existence and attempt to garner additional supporters and revenue for their efforts nationwide or around the globe. By intertwining local, regional, and national organizational structures, these groups create a powerful voice for social change. In this sense, then, many social movement groups participate in what well-known Canadian sociologist William Carroll (1997:29) has defined as counter-hegemonic practice—"a coherent practical and ethical alternative" to prevailing hegemony. The danger of creating counter-hegemonies is one that social movement groups need to be aware of: by defining a group's issues as "the" issues of the day, thereby relegating other groups' issues to the back burner, a group risks the possibility of creating new injustices (Carroll 1997). However, a paradigm shift that moves people away from notions and practices of competition is one way of ensuring this does not happen. If social movements are truly counter-hegemonic, then they leave us with a "hopeful prognosis for social and political transformation" (Carroll 1997:25).

Macrolevel Attempts to Solve Social Problems

Macrolevel solutions to social problems focus on how large-scale social institutions such as the government and the media may be persuaded to become involved in remedying social problems. Sometimes individuals who view themselves as individually powerless bind together in organizations to make demands on those who make decisions at the national or global level. As two social analysts explain,

Most individuals are largely powerless in the face of economic forces beyond their control. But because millions of other people are affected in the same way, they have a chance to influence their conditions through collective action. To do so, people must grasp that the common interest is also their own personal interest. This happens whenever individuals join a movement, a union, a party, or any organization pursuing a common goal. It happens when people push for a social objective—say universal health care or human rights—which benefits them by benefiting all those similarly situated. It underlies the development of an environmental movement which seeks to preserve the environment on which all depend. (Brecher and Costello 1998:107)

For example, when Canadian workers organize to support the rights of workers in low-income nations and are able to bring about changes that keep them from competing with these workers, they not only help workers abroad, they also help themselves (Brecher and Costello 1998).

Working through Special-Interest Groups for Political Change

At the national level, people seeking macrolevel solutions to social problems may become members of a *special-interest group*—a political coalition composed of individuals or groups sharing a specific interest they wish to protect or advance with the help of the political system (Greenberg and Page 1993; see Box 1.3). Examples of special-interest groups include the

---

SOCIAL PROBLEMS IN GLOBAL PERSPECTIVE

BOX 1.3 Sex Boycott as Political Action

I am positive. If we douse ourselves in perfume but ignore them when they pine—if we cook there'll be no resisting us. If we truly shut them out, it will drive them mad. They will miss us! Not just our husbands and boyfriends, but all of our fathers, brothers, sons and male friends! Our men will do whatever it takes to get back with us. The longer we neglect them on account of the war, the more desperate they'll be to end it.

Lysistrata, planning a sex strike to end the Peloponnesian War (Aristophanes)

Approximately 2400 years ago, Aristophanes wrote a play, *Lysistrata,* about a group of women led by Lysistrata, who, in protest against the 28-year-old Peloponnesian War, withheld sex from their husbands until the men laid down their swords. In early 2003, the Lysistrata Project—to have coordinated readings of the play—was conceived by Sharron Bower and Kathy Blume, who were frustrated that "we could do nothing but sit and watch in horror as the Bush Administration drove us toward a unilateral attack on Iraq" (Greene 2003). So they decided to e-mail "all [their] friends and put up a website. The response has been enormous." Blume added, "Many people have e-mailed us to say they now feel empowered to do something, and foster dialogue in their own communities about the dangers of this war."

The Lysistrata Project took off via the Internet. Over 900 play readings in over 50 countries were planned for March 3, 2003. Countries participating included Russia, China, Thailand, Greece, and Iceland. Many famous actors volunteered to participate, including F. Murray Abraham, Kevin Bacon, and Julie Christie in New York and Los Angeles, and David Hare and Vanessa Redgrave in London. In Canada, at least 37 readings took place, with some in almost every province. The Web has frequently been harnessed for peace demonstrations, but this was the

first worldwide theatre event for peace. The website (**http://www.lysistrataproject.org**) is still active in 2009.

Most recently in 2009, women in Kenya conducted a sex boycott to protest the chaos and devastation political parties created after a disputed election in 2007. According to the Center for Rights, Education and Awareness (CREAW) report *The Kenya Sex Boycott* (September 2009), in "the two months that followed the election results:

- More than 1500 people were killed;
- Hundreds of thousands were injured;
- Nearly half a million were displaced; and
- An estimated 3000 women and girls were raped.

Women bore the brunt of the violence." Women organized and drew up a set of demands to end political divisiveness and address security, hunger, and poverty issues. They then called on all Kenyan women to support a one-week sex boycott to achieve these ends. Organizers judged the boycott a success. Within two weeks, leaders of opposing parties met, a cabinet was convened, and a police task force on security was formed. Ann Njogu, CREAW chairperson, was pleased with the outcome and expressed, "For the first time in the tumultuous history of Kenya, we took the debate of national governance right into peoples' homes regardless of their social setting. And whether people agreed with the option we chose or not, the point remains that we succeeded in raising the country's awareness for the need to hold our leaders accountable. It also brought home the fact that 'the personal' is also 'the political.'"

Sources: The Lysistrata Project. 2006. Retrieved July 28, 2006 (http://www.lysistrataproject.org); Center for Rights, Education and Awareness, 2009, The Kenya Sex Boycott (http://creawkenya.org/).

Canadian Labour Congress, the Reform Party, and REAL Women.

Through special-interest groups, which are sometimes called *pressure groups* or *lobbies,* people seek to change social situations by exerting pressure on political leaders. These groups may be categorized on the basis of four factors:

1. *Issue focus:* Some groups focus on single issues, such as abortion, gun control, or teaching acceptance for family diversity in Canadian schools; others focus on multiple issues, such as equal access to education, employment, and health care (Ash 1972; Gamson 1990).

2. *View of the present system of wealth and power:* Some groups make radical demands that would involve the end of patriarchy, capitalism, governmental bureaucracy, or other existing power structures; others do not attack the legitimacy of the present system of wealth and power but insist on specific social reforms (Ash 1972; Gamson 1990).

3. *Beliefs about elites:* Some groups want to influence elites or incorporate movement leaders into the elite; others want to replace existing elites with persons whom they believe share their own interests and concerns (Ash 1972; Gamson 1990).

4. *Type of political action:* In recent decades, many special-interest groups have been single-issue groups that focus on electing and endorsing politicians who support their views. There may be more than one single-interest group working to reduce or eliminate a specific social problem. Usually, however, these groups do not agree on the nature and extent of the problem or on proposed solutions. For this reason, competing single-interest groups may aggressively place their demands in front of elected officials and bureaucratic policymakers.

Working through National Social Movements to Reduce Problems

Collective behaviour and national social movements are significant ways in which people seek to resolve social problems. **Collective behaviour** is voluntary, often spontaneous activity of a large number of people that typically violates dominant group norms and values (Kendall 2000). Public demonstrations and riots are examples of collective behaviour. Since it was first used in the 1919 Egyptian Revolution against British occupation, one popular form of public demonstration has been **civil disobedience**—non-violent action that seeks to change a policy or law by refusing to comply with it. People often use civil disobedience in the form of sit-ins, marches, boycotts, and strikes to bring about change. When people refuse to abide by a policy or law and challenge authorities to do something about it, they are demanding social change with some sense of urgency. Since Thoreau first wrote about it in 1849 in his essay "Civil Disobedience," it has been implemented by many mass movements seeking change through non-violent means. Protestors at the 1999 WTO meeting in Seattle used civil disobedience strategies by sitting on the street, linking arms together, and chanting over and over the words "non-violent protest" in response to the advancing lines of the National Guard in full riot gear. It has also been used to great effect in India, East Germany, South Africa, and Czechoslovakia since the early 1900s.

Groups that engage in activities that they hope will achieve specific political goals are sometimes referred to as *protest crowds.* For example, on February 23, 2002, in Victoria, B.C., thousands of demonstrators blocked traffic in the downtown core for an entire afternoon as they marched to the parliament buildings in an extensively organized and festive "Provincial Day of Action" against the budget-cutting measures of the then newly elected government of Gordon Campbell and the B.C. Liberals. The protest brought together an enormous range of groups: seniors, union activists, students, firefighters, hospital employees, teachers, children, Indigenous groups, environmentalists, religious leaders, peace activists, and others, who joined together in one of the largest and most multi-stakeholdered demonstrations ever to take place in Canada. It was reminiscent of the scope of the WTO protest that had preceded it.

There are several types of national and international social movements that may be used to reduce social problems. National social movements may be divided into five major categories: reform, revolutionary, religious, alternative, and resistance movements. *Reform movements* seek to improve society by changing some specific aspect of the social structure. Environmental groups and disability rights groups are examples of groups that seek to change (reform) some specific aspect of the social structure. Reform movements typically seek to bring about change by working within the existing organizational structures of society,

Collective behaviour is a powerful form of social protest against perceived injustices. Numerous protests have been staged in Canada against environmental degradation caused by logging, pollution, hunting, and other activities.

whereas *revolutionary movements* seek to bring about a total change in society. Examples of revolutionary movements include utopian groups and radical terrorist groups that use fear tactics to intimidate and gain—at least briefly—concessions from those with whom they disagree ideologically. Some radical terrorists may kill people in their pursuit of a society that more closely conforms to their worldview.

Religious movements (also referred to as *expressive movements*) seek to rejuvenate people through inner change. Because they emphasize inner change, religious movements are often linked to local and regional organizations that seek to bring about changes in the individual's life. National religious movements often attempt to persuade political officials to enact laws that will reduce or eliminate what they perceive to be a social problem. For example, some national religious movements view abortion as a social problem and thus lobby for a ban on abortions. In contrast, *alternative movements* seek limited change in some aspects of people's behaviour. Currently, alternative movements include a variety of so-called New Age movements that emphasize such things as the development of a collective spiritual consciousness.

Finally, *resistance movements* seek to prevent change or to undo change that has already occurred. In public debates over social policies, most social movements advocating change face resistance from reactive movements, which hold opposing viewpoints and want social policy to reflect their own beliefs and values. Examples of resistance movements include groups opposing same-sex marriage initiatives for gay or lesbian couples; anti-abortion groups, such as "Operation Rescue," which seek to close abortion clinics and make abortion illegal; and anti-immigrant groups seeking to close Canadian borders to outsiders or place harsher demands on immigrant workers.

Maude Barlow was instrumental in the formation of the not-for-profit group Council of Canadians.

Can national activism and social movements bring about the changes that are necessary to reduce social problems? Some analysts believe that certain social problems can be reduced through sustained efforts by organizations committed to change. An example of national social movements is the Council of Canadians. The not-for-profit council was formed in 1985 by a group of prominent Canadians and has become Canada's pre-eminent citizen watchdog organization. According to its website (http://www.canadians.org),

Strictly non-partisan, the Council lobbies Members of Parliament, conducts research, and runs national campaigns aimed at putting some of the country's most important issues into the spotlight: safeguarding our social programs, promoting economic justice, renewing our democracy, asserting Canadian sovereignty, advancing alternatives to corporate-style free trade, and preserving our environment.

The Council of Canadians is sustained by volunteers and financed by its members. The organization helps people take action through more than 70 chapters across the country. As a public interest organization, it does not take money from corporations or governments. Past campaigns include combatting bank mergers, control of newspapers by conglomerates, changes in public and unfair trade deals. Recently, the Council has focused its work to protect Canadian values by promoting progressive, independent national policies on fair trade, clean water, safe food, public health care, and other issues of social and economic concern to Canadians.

A major successful campaign was the fight against the Multilateral Agreement on Investments (MAI) in 1998. The Council of Canadians called it a charter of rights and freedoms for global corporations. As part of the campaign to free up the movement of capital and protect investors, the MAI was criticized for wanting standardized national policies that could potentially erode environmental legislation, culture, and sovereignty and bring in a two-tiered health system. The council sent a letter to then Prime Minister Chrétien, supported by prominent Canadians such as Carol Shields, David Suzuki, Judy Rebick, and Buzz Hargrove, emphasizing five principles that should govern all international trade and investment agreements. The principles were

1. Upholding the rights of citizens;
2. Protecting the common good;
3. Promoting the development of sustainable communities;
4. Guaranteeing the sovereignty of democratically elected governments over corporations; and
5. Ensuring effective citizen participation in the development of trade and investment policies. (Council of Canadians 1999)

The Council of Canadians called on Canada to pull out of MAI negotiations. The MAI was defeated because, in 1998, France, and later Australia, also concerned about the MAI's encroachment on their national sovereignty, pulled out of the negotiations.

What about global activism? Once again, we turn to the environmental movement for an example. According to Jared Diamond (2000), a physiology professor and director of the World Wildlife Fund, some transnational corporations are becoming aware that they have a responsibility for the environment. Diamond believes that a new attitude has taken hold of corporations such as Chevron and Home Depot, both of which now claim to realize that it is better to have a clean operation than to have costly industrial disasters. Of course, consumers have also demanded that corporations become more accountable for their actions: "Behind this trend lies consumers' growing awareness of the risks that environmental problems pose for the health, economies, and political stability of their own world and their children's world" (Diamond 2000:A31). For example, growing consumer awareness has led some companies that buy and retail forest products to no longer sell wood products from environmentally sensitive areas of the world and instead give preference to certified wood—that is, lumber that has been derived from forests where guidelines for environmentally sound logging practices have been met (Diamond 2000). Consumer power should not be underestimated when it comes to impacting corporations' profits. Indeed, consumer power is so great that many companies have rushed to assure the public that their products and services are environmentally friendly, even when they are not—a new practice called "greenwashing."

According to some analysts, what is needed is the "globalization from below" mentioned previously (Brecher and Costello 1998). In other words, people cannot rely on corporations to solve environmental problems. Indeed, it is necessary to develop a human agenda that will offset the corporate agenda that has produced many of the problems in the first place. Social activists Jeremy Brecher and Tim Costello (1998) suggest these criteria for any proposed human agenda:

- It should improve the lives of the great majority of the world's people over the long run.

- It should correspond to widely held common interests and should integrate the interests of people around the world.

- It should provide handles for action at a variety of levels.

- It should include elements that can be at least partially implemented independently but that are compatible or mutually reinforcing.

- It should make it easier, not harder, to solve social problems such as environmental degradation and war.

- It should grow organically out of social movements and coalitions that have developed in response to the needs of diverse peoples.

Based on these guidelines, the only way that a major global social problem such as environmental degradation or world poverty can be reduced is through a drastic redirection of our energies, as Brecher and Costello (1998:184) explain:

The energies now directed to the race to the bottom need to be redirected to the rebuilding of the global economy on a humanly and environmentally sound basis. Such an approach requires limits to growth—in some spheres, sharp reductions—in the material demands that human society places on the environment. It requires reduced energy and resource use; less toxic production and products; shorter individual work-time; and less production for war. But it requires vast growth in education, health care, human caring, recycling, rebuilding an ecologically sound production and consumption system, and time available for self-development, community life, and democratic participation.

Do you believe such human co-operation is possible? Will it be possible for a new generation of political leaders to separate *politics* from *policy* and focus on discovering

the best courses of action for Canada and the world? Where do ideas regarding possible social policies come from? Some of the ideas and policies of tomorrow are being developed today in public policy organizations and think tanks like the right-wing Fraser Institute or the left-leaning Canadian Centre for Policy Alternatives. If, as some analysts believe, these think tanks are increasingly setting the Canadian government's agenda, how much do we know about these groups, their spokespersons, and the causes they advocate?

Perhaps gaining more information about the current state of Canadian and global affairs is the first step toward individual efforts to be part of the solution rather than part of the problem in the future.

IN SUM

Sociologists view social problems from a variety of perspectives. Each perspective involves different assumptions. Functionalists, who emphasize social cohesion and order in society, commonly view social problems as the result of institutional and societal dysfunctions, social disorganization, or cultural lag, among other things. Conflict theorists, who focus on value conflict or on structural inequalities based on class, ethnicity, or other socially constructed attributes, suggest that social problems arise either from disputes over divergent values or from exploitative relations in society, such as those between capitalists and workers or between different ethnic groups. In contrast, interactionists focus on individuals' interactions and on the social construction of reality. For interactionists, social problems occur when social interaction is disrupted and people are dehumanized, when people are labelled deviant, or when the individual's definition of a situation causes him or her to act in a way that produces a detrimental outcome. Feminist theorists focus on gendering their analyses of inequalities that are maintained and perpetuated by structures and ideologies of domination. The ways that individuals play out oppressive relationships together can be traced to the unequal ways that structures and relations are organized in a capitalist, patriarchal society. This is the root of social problems, according to feminist theorists. We will use these theoretical perspectives, along with selected others, throughout the book.

It is important not only to have an analysis of social problems but also to see a means for solving them. The concept of social change is important to any discussion of reducing social problems. Strategies people use to deal with social problems are either short-term, middle-term, or long-term. An example of a short-term strategy is an attempt to help individuals find jobs through a "back-to-work" program or a resumé-writing service. An example of a middle-term strategy may be to reduce unemployment in a community by developing a new resort and golf course. An example of a long-term strategy could be to shift the whole political economy of a nation to a system that endorses 100 percent employment. For most social problems, a combination of strategies is required to eliminate or reduce them.

The remedies that people seek to social problems are microlevel, mid-range, or macrolevel remedies. Microlevel solutions to social problems focus on that ways that individuals work within small groups to try to solve a problem that affects them, their family, or their friends. Mid-range solutions focus on how secondary groups and formal organizations can deal with problems or assist individuals or groups in overcoming problems. Macrolevel solutions focus on getting large-scale social institutions such as the government or media to become involved in remedying social problems.

This chapter has examined violence from four sociological perspectives. As with many other social problems, people do not always agree on the causes of violence. They also do not always agree on what should be done about violence. However, this does not mean that we should simply give up and do nothing. The perspective taken by the authors of this text is that Canadians have a number of pressing social problems to address and that it is our responsibility to work toward a better world, however we conceive that world and however we decide to do that work. This book explores a range of social issues—and ways by which we may eliminate or reduce the harmful effects of those issues we collectively define as "problems." If an issue sparks something in you and you want to get involved, you will find some ideas for social action in the "What Can You Do?" section of each chapter. Of course, there are many more ideas and ways of being involved in the issue(s) of your choice than those we have indicated. Feel free to explore and do your part to make the world a better place. We would love to hear about it! As summarized by UNICEF in 1995 in *The Progress of Nations* (Ecumenical Coalition for Economic Justice 1996),

The day will come when the progress of nations will not be judged by their military or economic strength, nor by the splendour of their capital cities and public buildings, but by the well-being of their peoples: by their levels of health and education; by their opportunities to earn a fair reward for their labours; by their ability to participate in the decisions that affect their lives; by the respect that is shown for their political and civil liberties; by the provision that is made for those who are vulnerable and disadvantaged; and by the protection that is afforded to the growing minds and bodies of their children.

Please join us now in exploring many of the crucial issues of the 21st century with a view to changing the world for the better.

SUMMARY

How Do Sociologists Define a Social Problem?

According to sociologists, a social problem is a social condition (such as poverty) or a pattern of behaviour (such as substance abuse) that people believe warrants public concern and collective action to bring about change.

How Do Sociologists View Violence?

Sociologists view violence as a social problem that involves both subjective awareness and objective reality. We have a subjective awareness that violence can occur in such public settings as schools, daycare centres, businesses, and churches. Our subjective awareness becomes an objective reality when we can measure and experience the effects of violent criminal behaviour.

How Do Sociologists Examine Social Life?

Sociologists use both microlevel and macrolevel analyses to examine social life. Microlevel analysis focuses on small-group relations and social interaction among individuals; macrolevel analysis focuses on social processes occurring at the societal level, especially in large-scale organizations and major social institutions.

How Does the Functionalist Perspective View Society and Social Problems?

In the functionalist perspective, society is a stable, orderly system composed of interrelated parts, each of which performs a function that contributes to the overall stability of society. According to functionalists, social problems such as violence arise when social institutions do not fulfill the functions that they are supposed to perform or when dysfunctions occur.

How Does the Conflict Perspective View Society and Social Problems?

The conflict perspective asserts that groups in society are engaged in a continuous power struggle for control of scarce resources. This perspective views violence as a response to inequalities based on "race," class, gender, and other power differentials.

How Does the Value Conflict Perspective Differ from the Critical-Conflict Perspective?

According to value conflict theorists, social problems are conditions that are incompatible with group values. From this perspective, value clashes are ordinary occurrences in families, communities, and the larger society, where people commonly hold many divergent values. In contrast, critical-conflict theorists suggest that social problems arise out of major contradictions inherent in the way societies are organized.

Why Are There So Many Different Approaches in the Conflict Perspective?

Different conflict theorists focus on different aspects of power relations and inequality in society. Perspectives based on the works of Karl Marx emphasize class-based inequalities arising from the capitalist economic system.

How Does the Interactionist Perspective View Society and Social Problems?

Unlike the functionalist and conflict perspectives, which focus on society at the macrolevel, the interactionist perspective views society as the sum of the interactions of individuals and groups. For interactionists, social problems occur when social interaction is disrupted and people are dehumanized, when people are labelled deviant, or when the individual's definition of a situation causes him or her to act in a way that produces a detrimental outcome.

What Is the Feminist Perspective?

Feminist perspectives focus on patriarchy—a system of male dominance in which males are privileged and women are oppressed. Other perspectives emphasize that "race," class, and gender are interlocking systems of privilege and oppression that result in social problems. However, these perspectives are based on the assumption that inequality and exploitation, rather than social harmony and stability, characterize contemporary societies.

What Is Social Change? Why Is It Important in Reducing Social Problems?

Social change refers to the alteration, modification, or transformation of public policy, culture, or social institutions over time. Social change is important in reducing social problems because a combination of strategies, some previously untried, are usually required to reduce major social problems.

What Are Microlevel Solutions to Social Problems? What Are the Limitations of This Approach?

Microlevel solutions to social problems focus on how individuals operate within small groups to try to remedy a problem that affects them, their family, or their friends. Most people turn to their primary groups for help in dealing with a problem. However, solving social problems one person at a time does not take into account the fact that secondary groups and societal institutions play a significant part in creating, maintaining, and exacerbating many social problems.

What Are Mid-Range Attempts to Deal with Social Problems? What Are the Limitations of This Approach?

Mid-range attempts to deal with social problems focus on how secondary groups and formal organizations deal with problems or seek to assist individuals in overcoming problems, such as addiction to drugs or alcohol. Grassroots groups often work to change a perceived wrong in their neighbourhood, city, province or territory, or nation. Although local efforts to reduce problems affecting individuals and collectivities in a specific city or region have brought about many improvements in the social life of individuals and small groups, they usually lack the sustained capacity to produce the larger systemic changes needed at the national or international levels to reduce or eliminate the problems.

What Are Macrolevel Attempts to Deal with Social Problems? What Are the Limitations of This Approach?

Macrolevel solutions to social problems focus on how large-scale social institutions such as the government and the media may become involved in remedying social problems. Some people work through social movements, others through special-interest groups, and still others through various forms of collective behaviour. While macrolevel approaches are necessary for reducing or eliminating many social problems, some analysts believe that these approaches overemphasize structural barriers in society and give people the impression that these barriers constitute insurmountable walls that preclude social change. Macrolevel approaches may also de-emphasize the importance of individual responsibility.

What Are Four Key Factors That Differentiate Special-Interest Groups?

The four factors by which special-interest groups may be categorized are (1) issue focus (single-issue vs. multiple demands); (2) view of the present system of wealth and power (positive vs. negative); (3) beliefs about elites (whether to try to influence elites or seek to replace them); and (4) type of political action.

What Is Collective Behaviour? How Does Civil Disobedience Occur?

Collective behaviour is voluntary, often spontaneous activity of a large number of people that may violate dominant-group norms and values. As a form of collective behaviour, civil disobedience refers to non-violent action that seeks to change a policy or law by refusing to comply with it. In 1999, in Seattle, many WTO protestors engaged in this form of direct action by linking arms, sitting in the streets, and chanting.

What Are the Key Characteristics of the Five Major Categories of National Social Movements?

National social movements are divided into five major categories: reform, revolutionary, religious, alternative, and resistance movements. Reform movements seek to improve society by changing some specific aspect of the social structure. Revolutionary movements seek to bring about a total change in society. Religious movements seek to renovate or renew people through "inner change." Alternative movements seek limited change in some aspects of people's behaviour and currently include a variety of so-called New Age movements. Resistance movements seek to prevent change or undo change that has already occurred.

KEY TERMS

capitalism,   p. 9
civil disobedience,   p. 21
collective behaviour,   p. 21
conflict perspective,   p. 9
discrimination,   p. 5
dominant group,   p. 5
functionalist perspective,   p. 7
grassroots groups,   p. 17
hate crime,   p. 5
industrialization,   p. 8
interactionist perspective,   p. 12

lifestyle–routine activity
     approach,   p. 8
macrolevel analysis,   p. 6
microlevel analysis,   p. 6
norms,   p. 8
perspective,   p. 7
primary groups,   p. 16
self-fulfilling prophecy,   p. 13
situational approach,   p. 13
social change,   p. 15
social disorganization,   p. 8

social movement,   p. 18
social problem,   p. 3
society,   p. 3
sociological imagination,   p. 6
sociology,   p. 3
subordinate groups,   p. 5
theory,   p. 7
urbanization,   p. 8
values,   p. 8
violence,   p. 2

QUESTIONS FOR CRITICAL THINKING

1.   What are some of the impacts on a nation when high levels of violence exist within its borders?

2.   Value conflict theorists suggest that social problems are conditions that are incompatible with group values. How would value conflict theorists view debates over gun control laws?

3.   Some critical-conflict theorists believe that social problems arise from the major contradictions inherent in capitalist economies. What role does violence play in a capitalist economy?

4.   Using feminist and interactionist perspectives, what kind of arguments can you make to explain why males are more frequently involved in acts of physical violence than females? What do your own observations tell you about the relationship between social norms and violent behaviour?

5.   Do you believe that corporations can be trusted to "do the right thing" when it comes to reducing or eliminating existing social problems? Is good corporate citizenship a possibility in the global economy today? Why or why not?

6.   Suppose you were given the economic resources and political clout to reduce a major social problem. Which problem would you choose? What steps would you take to alleviate this problem? How would you measure your success or failure in reducing or eliminating the problem?

PEARSON

Explore the topics covered in this chapter at **www.mysockit.com** using the access provided with this text. Interactive resources for studying include video clips, practice tests, learning objectives, and Internet resources.

2

POVERTY IN THE CANADIAN CONTEXT

Quite suddenly, the global recession arrived and Canadians looked for a social safety net.

Canadian economist Lars Osberg (2009:5)

If there's one thing I've learned after seventeen years as a street nurse, it's that there's no such thing as a typical homeless person. The stereotype of a man lying prone on a sidewalk or heating grate, has never fit with the people I knew to be homeless. Over the years I've met artists, engineers, truckers, hydro workers, highly skilled steelworkers, professionals like police officers and nurses, war vets, and of course, families. Some ended up living on those grates, but mostly I saw people upright, struggling 24/7 to survive, caught in a labyrinth to find food, shelter, health care.

Cathy Crowe, Toronto street nurse (2007:139)

We can't depend on charity to do the work of inadequate social services.

Loren Freid, executive director of the North York Harvest Food Bank, Ontario (Canadian Association of Food Banks 2005)

Poverty is always praying that your husband must not lose his job. To me that's poverty.

A participant at an anti-poverty forum in Toronto (Galabuzi 2008:86)

It was hard for me to find a job . . . because whenever I applied they said that they need Canadian experience. . . . Where am I going to get the Canadian experience?

An immigrant participant from British Columbia in a study on welfare use among racialized individuals (Mirchandani and Chan 2007:60)

Growing inequality is a trend that usually unfolds during recessionary periods, when the bottom half of the labour market loses access to jobs or to hours of work. If inequality has grown so markedly over the past decade—a time of strong and sustained economic and job growth—what can we expect as we head into a recession?

Trish Hennessy and Armine Yalnizyan, senior economists with the Canadian Centre for Policy Alternatives (2008:9–10)

Last week I went two days without food (I had some for the kids) until I got my cheque. They want me to get a job but I can't afford to send out resumés or take the bus to deliver them, as well as there is the cost of photocopying.

A participant in the YWCA of Metropolitan Toronto's Teen Mother Program (Ricciutelli et al. 1998:57)

The process is, it is very difficult to, it is very impersonal first of all. It is a very impersonal process. You go in and you feel like utter crap first of all. It is very demoralizing. I don't care who says, it is very demoralizing to be on social assistance.

An immigrant participant from Ontario in a study on welfare use among racialized individuals (Mirchandani and Chan 2008: 171)

First off, the hostels don't take couples, okay, and Karen and I have a dog and so there is absolutely no place that would allow you to go with a dog. A lot of these places we had to go last year, they're called Out of the Cold—places that just open up in the wintertime, and they're scattered all over the city so you have to go to a different location every night, which means that everything you bring with you, you have to take with you during the day and bring it to the next place you go. So you can't really accumulate possessions because you have no place to put them. . . . It's impossible to find affordable housing in Toronto. It's a really, really desperate situation, which is why there are so many people living on the streets and in hostel situations.

Brian Boyd, a Toronto man who became homeless when he could no longer afford rent after pay rates in his electronics trade declined (Crowe 2007:106–107)

My main priority was getting as much work as I can to keep a roof over my head. Now they hire more temps. I know I've proven myself. I feel like I'm being used right now through my work. . . . I was willing to give up part of my pay, to be permanent and have medical. I don't care about vacation or sick leave. What have I got to fall back on? What have my kids got to fall back on?

Chris, a lone-parent mother who has children with recurrent health problems (Seccombe 2007:59)

Since the 1970s in Canada, social programs have increasingly ended up on the chopping block. A great deal of research has focused on looking at the impacts of social program cuts and the concomitant governmental focuses on "fraud." Despite the ongoing shredding of Canada's safety net, needs for services among Canada's population have increased, not decreased. Cuts in federal and provincial funding today make the experiences described in the quotes above a reality for too many people across Canada. Decreases in real wages, as well as unemployment and underemployment, mean that cuts to services not only impact those people who are on income assistance but also lead to increased poverty for those who work full- and part-time. This chapter examines these issues as well as some of the impacts of poverty and the ways we deal with poverty and income inequalities as a nation.

For decades, Canada has been described as a "land of opportunity"—or a place where the "American dream" can be realized. Simply stated, the *American dream* is the belief that the members of each generation can have a higher standard of living than that of their parents (Danziger and Gottschalk 1995). Implicit in the American dream is the belief that all people—regardless of ethnicity, colour, national origin, gender, ability, age, sexual orientation, or religion—should have an equal opportunity for success. This is the same as saying that Canadians view themselves as living in a **meritocracy**, a nation where the best person can rise to the top in any situation, despite his or her antecedents. Sociologists John Macionis and Linda Gerber (2002:257) define meritocracy as a "system of social stratification based on personal merit." But do all the people in this nation and other parts of the world really have an equal opportunity for success? How equally divided are national and global resources? What kinds of inequalities exist in Canada today?

POVERTY IN GLOBAL PERSPECTIVE

Today, more than 1.3 billion people live in **absolute poverty**, a condition that exists when people do not have the means to secure the most basic necessities of life (food, clothing, and shelter). Absolute poverty is life threatening. People living in absolute poverty may suffer from chronic malnutrition or die from hunger-related diseases. Current estimates suggest that more than 600 million people suffer from chronic malnutrition and more than 40 million people die each year from hunger-related diseases. To put this figure in perspective, the number of people worldwide dying from hunger-related diseases each year is the equivalent of more than 300 jumbo jet crashes *per day* with no survivors and half the passengers being children (Kidron and Segal 1995). In recent years, the number of people living in absolute poverty in high-income nations such as Canada has been increasing, drawing the criticism of many worldwide, including the United Nations.

ANALYZING INEQUALITY IN CANADA

Despite the notion that anyone can get ahead if she or he tries hard enough, one of this country's most persistent social problems is that it is a highly stratified society. **Social stratification** is the hierarchical arrangement of large social groups on the basis of their control over basic resources (Feagin and Feagin 1999). Today, the gap between the rich and the poor in Canada is wider than it has been for decades.

This widening gap, which is linked with global systems of stratification, has a dramatic impact on everyone's life chances and opportunities. Affluent people, the higher classes, typically have better life chances than the less affluent lower classes because the affluent have greater access to quality education, safe neighbourhoods, high-quality nutrition and health care, police and private security protection, and an extensive array of other goods and services. In contrast, people who have low and poverty-level incomes tend to have limited access to these resources.

How are social classes determined in Canada? Most contemporary research on class has been influenced by either Karl Marx's means of production model or Max Weber's multidimensional model. In Marx's model, class position is determined by people's relationship to the means of production. Chapter 1 described Marx's division of capitalist societies into two classes: the bourgeoisie or capitalist class, which owns the means of production; and the proletariat or working class, which sells its labour power to the capitalists to survive. According to Marx, inequality and poverty are inevitable by-products of the exploitation of workers by capitalists (Vanneman and Cannon 1987:39).

Like Karl Marx, German sociologist Max Weber (1864–1920) believed that economic factors were important in determining class location and studying social inequality, but he also believed that other factors were important. Weber was interested in people's **life chances**—the extent to which individuals have access to important societal resources such as food, clothing, shelter, education, and health care. He developed a multidimensional class model that focused on the interplay of wealth, power, and prestige as determinants of people's class position. **Wealth** is the value of all economic assets, including income and savings, personal property, and income-producing property, minus one's liabilities or debts. While some people have great wealth and are able to live off their investments, others must work for wages. Wealth should be differentiated from income. **Income** refers to the economic gain derived from wages, salaries, and income transfers (governmental aid such as income assistance [welfare] or ownership of property) (Beeghley 1989). Like wealth, income is extremely unevenly divided in Canada. According to a recent international study on income conducted by Statistics Canada, Canada has higher income inequality than Europe and lower inequality than the United States (Statistics Canada 2005h). **Power** is the ability of people to achieve their goals despite opposition from others. People who hold positions of power can achieve their goals because they can control other people; on the other hand, people who hold positions that lack power must carry out the wishes of others. **Prestige** is the respect, esteem, or regard accorded to an individual or group by others. Individuals who have high levels of prestige tend to receive deferential and respectful treatment from those with lower levels of prestige.

Recent theorists have modified Marx's and Weber's theories of economic inequality. According to sociologist Erik O. Wright (1997), neither Weber's multidimensional model of wealth, power, and prestige nor Marx's two-class system fully defines classes in modern capitalist societies or explains economic inequality. Wright sets forth four criteria for placement in the class structure: (1) ownership of the means of production; (2) purchase of the labour of others (employing others); (3) control of the labour of others (supervising others on the job); and (4) sale of one's own labour (being employed by someone else). Based on these criteria, Wright (1979, 1985) has identified four classes: the capitalist class, the managerial class, the small-business class, and the working class.

Although most people are aware of the wide disparity in lifestyles and life chances between the rich and the poor, far fewer of us stop to analyze the differences between middle-class and poverty-level living arrangements in Canada. Should social policies be implemented to equalize opportunities for people? Why or why not?

Wealth and Income Inequality

According to Forbes.com, a U.S. business e-publication, Bill Gates is the richest person in the world today. At age 53, he is worth US$40 billion. Down 23 ranks from Gates is the richest Canadian, David Thomson, whose total net worth in 2009 was US$13 billion, or approximately CN$15 billion. No other Canadian comes close to owning that kind of wealth, although Canada has a respectable number of billionaires (see Table 2.1), including the Westons, the Bronfmans, and the Irvings, and even British Columbia's own "rags to riches" story maker, Jimmy Pattison. The vast majority of Canadians will never amass even a fraction of the wealth these people possess. However, even billionaires have experienced dramatic declines in their fortunes. In 2009, the average net worth of the world's billionaires was US$3 billion, a figure that is down 23 percent from the year prior. In fact, in 2009, there were 793 billionaires, compared with 1125 in 2008 (Forbes.com 2009). Even though the net worth of all of Canada's millionaires and billionaires has declined, they are still a long way from experiencing the economic recession the way people with low incomes or those who are impoverished do. The face of poverty is increasingly diverse with regard to family type, as more Canadians experience layoffs, lack of real wage gains, and reduced work hours.

How is the unequal distribution of wealth associated with social problems? According to sociologists

TABLE 2.1   Canada's Billionaires, 2009

Rank[1]	Name	Worth (CN$ billion)
24	Thomson, David, and family	15.0
98	Weston, Galen, and family	5.8
146	Irving, James, Arthur, and John	4.5
246	Desmarais, Paul	3.0
261	Laliberte, Guy	2.9
261	Sherman, Bernard (Barry)	2.9
318	Azrieli, David, and family	2.4
318	Miller, Robert	2.4
318	Pattison, Jim	2.4
334	McCain, Wallace	2.3
397	Bronfman, Charles	2.1
397	Mike Lazaridis	2.1
397	Skoll, Jeffrey	2.1
397	Balsillie, James	2.0
468	Katz, Daryl	1.7
559	Saputo, Emanuele (Lino)	1.5
559	Schnaider, Alexander	1.5
601	Jarislowsky, Stephen	1.4
647	Cheriton, David	1.3
701	Lee-Chin, Michael	1.2

[1]Rank = rank in world

Source: Forbes.com, 2009, The World's Billionaires 2009 (Special Report, March 11). Retrieved June 25, 2009 (www.forbes.com/2009/03/11/worlds-richest-people-billionaires-2009-billionaires_land.html).

Melvin L. Oliver and Thomas M. Shapiro (1995:2), wealth is a particularly important indicator of individual and family access to life chances:

> Wealth signifies the command over financial resources that a family has accumulated over its lifetime along with those resources that have been inherited across generations. Such resources, when combined with income, can create the opportunity to secure the "good life" in whatever form is needed—education, business, training, justice, health, comfort, and so on. Wealth is a special form of money not used to purchase milk and shoes and other life necessities. More often it is used to create opportunities, secure a desired stature and standard of living, or pass class status along to one's children.

Income is clearly correlated with life chances, as well. Overall, when we talk about income, it is helpful to divide the population into fifths, or quintiles. If there was no inequality in income in Canada, each fifth of the population would receive 20 percent of the available income. Of course, we know that is far from the case. What is particularly interesting is that the distribution of market income and total income for each quintile of the Canadian population has remained amazingly stable since 1951, with minor fluctuations in predictable directions. The share of income in the highest quintile rose from 42.8 percent in 1951 to 46.5 percent in 2003. The share for the lowest quintile went from 4.4 percent in 1951 to 4.3 percent in 2003. The gap between the richest and the poorest in the nation continues to widen, despite income taxes and transfer payments designed to lessen inequality. The continuance of this pattern today is supported by Statistics Canada (2008r), which reported that "earnings of full-time full-year earners rose for those at the top of the earnings distribution, stagnated for those in the middle and declined for those at the bottom."

The Canadian Lower Classes

The lower class in Canada makes up approximately 20 percent of the population and comprises the working poor and the chronically poor. The working poor are those who work full-time in (often) unskilled positions, such as seasonal or migrant agricultural workers or the lowest-paid service sector workers, but still remain at the edge of poverty. Minimum wages in this country no longer keep people out of poverty, despite the fact that that was what they were designed to do.

When the minimum wage was introduced in Canada in 1974, an individual with full-time, full-year employment earning minimum wage could expect to live 10 percent above the poverty line. Today, an individual needs to earn considerably more than $10 per hour, full-time, full-year, to even reach the poverty line. It is easy, therefore, to see why so many Canadians fall into this class, despite the overall wealth of the nation. As of June 2009, the only province or territory in Canada to have raised the minimum wage to $10 was Nunavut; therefore, no minimum wages in any part of Canada reach the poverty line. When one considers that low-wage work is often not full-time and full-year, the risk of poverty is all the greater.

Although the poor constitute between 11 and 16 percent, depending on the measure used, of the Canadian population, they receive only about 5 percent of the overall Canadian income. Individuals who are chronically poor include people of working age who are unemployed or outside the labour force and children who live in poor families caught in long-term deprivation. Overrepresented among low-income and poverty-level individuals are those who are unable to work because of age or disability and lone-parent mothers who are heads of households, along with their children. The term *underclass* is sometimes used to refer to people who are chronically poor, but this term not only negatively labels poor people, it also puts them outside the mainstream of society.

POVERTY IN CANADA

The fact that Canada is a wealthy nation, but one in which such a high proportion of the population lives in low-income and poverty situations, has made it the target of international criticism, particularly from the United Nations. In Canada, the picture of poverty is multifaceted. Estimates of the homeless population range between 150 000 (officially) and 300 000 (unofficially), depending on whether one is counting only emergency shelter users or also those people who are sleeping in their cars, couch surfing, or sleeping on hot-air grates and in cardboard boxes, tents, or ATM entrances (Crowe 2007; Duffy and Mandell 2001; Laird 2007). People trying to survive on social assistance number in the hundreds of thousands. The shortage of affordable housing is one of the most critical issues facing people on a limited or poverty-level income and is the chief driver of increases in homelessness in Canada today (Crowe 2007; Food Banks Canada 2009c; Laird 2007). As eloquently pointed out by George Laird, Canadian homelessness researcher and Media Fellow at the Sheldon Chumir Foundation for Ethics in Leadership (2007:6), "Poverty has become a leading cause of homelessness, trumping substance abuse and mental illness, with some cities estimating as many as half of their street homeless have jobs." Laird raises an important issue in identifying the increasing and diverse

group of what has recently come to be called "the new homeless" or "the new poor": those Canadian "families, women, new Canadians, students and children—a broad demographic whose common trait is poverty" (Laird 2007:10) and who are not saved from homelessness or the need to access food banks because they are employed (Food Banks Canada 2009b). In fact, the most recent annual study conducted by Food Banks Canada (2009b), an organization whose member food banks feed 85 percent of the Canadians who use emergency food programs each year, found that 14.5 percent of food-bank users are employed (see Table 2.2 and Figure 2.1).

While the cost of living, as measured by Statistics Canada's Consumer Price Index, rose 9.2 percent between 2002 and 2006, average household incomes rose only 1.7 percent (Canadian Council on Social Development [CCSD], 2009a). Many sources point out that cost of living increases, coupled with wage stagnation, a decreasing number of full-time jobs, increasing unemployment, a frayed social safety net that makes income assistance and employment insurance next to impossible to get, and a dearth of affordable housing are pushing Canadians out onto the streets (CCPA 2009; CCSD 2009b; Crowe 2007; Food Banks Canada 2009c; Laird 2007; Osberg 2009). At the end

TABLE 2.2 Percentage of Food-Bank Clients Reporting Employment as Their Main Source of Income: March 2007 and March 2008

	2007	2008
British Columbia	11.5	14.4
Alberta	27.0	28.3
Saskatchewan	7.0	12.1
Manitoba	14.0	13.0
Ontario	14.2	17.1
Quebec	12.6	10.3
New Brunswick	10.7	11.2
Nova Scotia	9.4	9.7
Prince Edward Island	23.7	19.5
Newfoundland and Labrador	9.5	10.3
Canada	13.5	14.5

Source: Food Banks Canada, 2009, HungerCount 2008. *Retrieved June 30, 2009 (http://www.foodbankscanada.ca/documents/HungerCount_en_fin.pdf).*

FIGURE 2.1   Primary Income Source of Households Assisted by Food Banks, March 2008

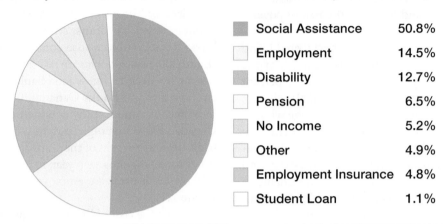

Social Assistance	50.8%
Employment	14.5%
Disability	12.7%
Pension	6.5%
No Income	5.2%
Other	4.9%
Employment Insurance	4.8%
Student Loan	1.1%

Source: Food Banks Canada, 2009, HungerCount 2008. *Retrieved June 30, 2009 (http://foodbankscanada.ca/documents/HungerCount_en_fin.pdf).*

of Canada's most recent economic boom and going into the global recession, increasing numbers of Canadians have been forced to choose between a roof over their heads or food in their bellies. As summarized by Food Banks Canada (2009c), Canadians turn to food banks because "they do not have enough money to pay for food on top of what is required for housing and other necessities." This situation is one that most Canadians find unnecessary and appalling, as indicated in the autumn 2008 Environics Focus Canada survey. The 2008 poll of over 2000 people found, among other things, that 90 percent of Canadians felt it was "time for strong [political] leadership to reduce the number of poor people in Canada," and 77 percent felt that in a recession, "it's more important than ever to make helping poor Canadians a priority" (Hennessy and Yalnizyan 2008:3).

The second critical issue facing low-income Canadians is food security. Food Banks Canada (2009c) reports that "insufficient income is the single most important variable influencing hunger in Canada." In an average month in 2008, Canadian food banks assisted over 700 000 people, almost 40 percent of whom were children. However, despite providing assistance to so many people, food banks are still unable to provide assistance to most of the 2.7 million Canadians who experience food insecurity during the year (Food Banks Canada 2009c:3).

Over the past decade, in a time of strong national economic growth, many governments continued their

severe cuts to social programs, disqualifying many people from eligibility for employment insurance and income assistance, changing criteria so fewer people qualify for benefits, decreasing benefit amounts, and decreasing the amount of time one can collect benefits. The result has been a reduction in the number of people receiving all types of social assistance benefits, but not a reduction in need. What happens to people who no longer qualify or do not qualify in the first place for any type of social assistance? What happens if the current economic recession drags on?

Sociologists make a distinction between absolute poverty and relative poverty. **Relative poverty** exists when people may be able to afford basic necessities, such as food, clothing, and shelter, but cannot maintain an average standard of living in comparison to that of other members of their society or group (Ropers 1991). Many Canadians do not suffer from absolute poverty, as the homeless do, but do experience relative poverty on the basis of what is available to other people in Canada.

Since 1997, Canada's gross domestic product (GDP) has grown by more than 73 percent, ranking Canada's economy as the ninth-largest in the world (Hennessy and Yalnizyan 2008). Despite this, Canada has a very high rate of poverty (over 11 percent, using conservative, after-tax measures in 2006) compared with other advanced industrial nations, and the "benefits of this last decade of expansion have passed the majority by" (Hennessy and Yalnizyan 2008:5). The **poverty rate** is the proportion of the population whose income falls below the government's official poverty line—the level of income below which a family of a given size is considered to be poor. In Canada, the government has never actually established a formal "poverty line" as such, but rather has created a low-income cut-off (LICO) line, which allows us to see how many people in Canada spend significantly more than the average on the necessities of life. The LICO also allows us to see how far below the cut-off some people live. As stated in a report by the National Council of Welfare (2001), "All measures of poverty are relative. The issue is not so much about measurement as it is about values. How poor and excluded are we willing to allow some people to be in our wealthy society?"

The number of families who live below the unofficial poverty (LICO) line in Canada increased throughout the two recessionary periods of the 1980s and 1990s, although around 1996, the numbers began to drop marginally each year, reflecting the better overall economic conditions coming out of the recession of the early 1990s (Statistics Canada 2002e). The National Council of Welfare (2001) cautions, though, that the drop in numbers living in poverty is not equivalent to the economic increases experienced by the nation overall, suggesting, for poor people, stagnation at best. Indeed, Canadian post-secondary students may soon find themselves among the poor—for longer than their in-school years—due to increasing debt loads and decreasing job opportunities for young people (see Box 2.1). As mentioned previously, in 2008 Statistics Canada reported that the trend of stagnation continued throughout the past decade (2008r). Facing the global economic recession now will result in a worsening situation for all, but particularly for people who are already poor.

As strongly stated by the National Council of Welfare (1999:4), "Statistics Canada has consistently maintained that it does not regard the LICOs as poverty lines, presumably because the federal government

SOCIAL PROBLEMS AND SOCIAL POLICY

BOX 2.1   Drowning in Student Debt

Canadian students who must rely on federal and/or provincial student loans may be unintentionally yoking themselves to years of debt. Despite the fact that government loans are made available to students with interest rates close to prime, many students are finding it difficult to pay their loans off as quickly as they had imagined they would after graduation. Human Resources and Skills Development Canada (HRSDC) reported that the proportion of students having trouble repaying student loans increased in the decade 1990–2000 (Dubois 2006), a theme that has continued in the decade since. In fact, according to a study released by Statistics Canada in April 2009, only just over one-quarter of students had paid off their outstanding loans two years after graduation. Those who were still paying down their student debt after two years were earning less than those who had already paid them off (Statistics Canada 2009h).

Structural shifts in the labour market are responsible for many people's inability to gain employment that pays more than minimum wage, even when they hold a baccalaureate degree. People with a master's degree fare a little better, but for how long? Further, as pointed out in a new

study of the impacts of Canada's Employment Insurance program, economist Lars Osberg contends that "since low wage individuals are especially likely to experience unemployment, the downloading of recessionary risk is having its biggest impacts on disadvantaged Canadians" (Canadian Centre for Policy Alternatives 2009). Exacerbating the repayment problem is the rising unemployment rate for students. While Canada saw another increase in the unemployment rate in May 2009 to 8.4 percent, workers aged 15 to 24 saw their unemployment rate rise to 15 percent in that same month. Compared to May 2008, 59 000 full-time jobs usually performed by students aged 20 to 24 disappeared by May 2009 (Canadian Labour Congress 2009a). The Canadian Labour Congress (CLC), representing 3.2 million Canadian workers, noted that the unemployment rate for that group of students was at an unprecedented high of 18.3 percent (CLC 2009a).

A 2006 HRSDC study also found that the average size of student debt had increased (Dubois 2006). Besides cost of living increases, Canadian students have encountered extremely high tuition increases, especially in some provinces,

TABLE 2.3 Canada Student Loan Repayment by Principal and Repayment Period

Principal	Repayment Period	Monthly Payment	Interest Paid	Total cost of education
$20 000	10 years	$218.62	$6 233.47	$26 233.47
$20 000	15 years	$165.12	$9 720.92	$29 720.92
$25 000	10 years	$273.27	$7 792.07	$32 792.07
$25 000	15 years	$206.39	12 152.06	$37 152.06
$32 000	10 years	$349.49	$9 973.68	$41 973.68
$32 000	15 years	$264.19	$15 553.42	$47 553.42

Source: Canadian Federation of Students, 2009, "Campaigns and Lobbying: Canada Student Loan Program." Retrieved July 1, 2009 (http://www. cfs-fcee.ca/html/english/campaigns/canstudentloan.php).

over the past decade, making the cost of post-secondary education higher than it has ever been (Canadian Federation of Students 2009c). While debt loads vary by province, with students in the Maritimes having the highest average debt loads and students in Quebec having the lowest, the average debt two years after graduation is $20 000 across Canada. Additionally, graduates from doctoral programs owe the most, with an average debt of $22 500, while those who graduated with a master's degree owe on average $19 500, with a baccalaureate degree $20 400, and with a college diploma $11 800 (Statistics Canada 2009h).

Canadians with student loans have been ineligible to claim bankruptcy involving their student loans since 1998. Those who had declared bankruptcy involving student loans before the 1998 prohibition came into effect were most likely to be female, to be low-waged (earning approximately $14 000 per year), to work in low-skill employment, and to have received income assistance at some point (Schwartz 1999). Difficulties replaying student loans still disproportionately affect Canadian women. Because women in Canada make lower average incomes than men (approximately $0.72 per male dollar), repayment is that much more costly. Statistics Canada reports that female graduates, because of the gendered wage gap, face 16 years of student debt compared to the 11 years male graduates face (2009h). And, because they take longer to repay their debt, women pay more for their education overall.

This pattern is echoed in the United Kingdom, where tuition fees for post-secondary education were recently introduced, as Kat Stark, the Women's Officer at the National Union of Students, notes:

Women are taking longer than men to pay off their student loans because they are paid less, not because they are taking time off to have children. Within three years of graduating, over 40% of men are earning over £25,000, compared to just over a quarter of women. The pay gap is not a new problem—the government knew it when it introduced the tuition fees system that female graduates would end up saddled with debt to a worse extent than their male counterparts. In the run-up to the 2009 review of higher education funding, the government should consider whether they wish to perpetuate this injustice. (Curtis 2008)

Student debt, unlike other forms of debt, is generally taken on to secure a more prosperous future. However, student debt today often significantly contributes to people's financial problems as high repayment schedules and stagnant wages force many students to rely later on high-interest and sub-prime loans (Uribe 2008). A recent study on Canadians and sub-prime lending found student loans to be a major source of concern for indebted Canadians. Additionally, "borrowing and more particularly heavy debt burden can have an adverse impact on future personal decisions such as the timing for buying a home, starting a family, saving for retirement, participation in adult education, etc." (Dubois 2006).

HRSDC found that, although the burden of student debt had increased, the proportion of students taking on student loans has remained stable (Dubois 2006). This may be because some students are "debt shy." Research by the Canadian Federation of Students (CFS), as well as by the private research firm Malatest and Associates, found that students who had never participated in post-secondary education cited financial issues as barriers, coupled with strong debt aversion (CFS 2009b; Malatest and Associates 2007). Not only does debt aversion keep people from enrolling, the fact of having debt impacts current students as well. Statistics Canada and other researchers found an inverse relationship between program completion and student debt: the higher the debt, the lower the rate of completion (McElroy 2005; Statistics Canada 2009h). Further, having student debt is related to increased tension, anxiety, and difficulty sleeping, and even low debt levels have been shown to impact achievement levels (Cooke et al. 2004). Interestingly, research conducted in the United Kingdom found additional components to this phenomenon: students who came from lower-class backgrounds, who were from racialized communities, or who were lone parents were more likely to have negative opinions about taking on student debt (Callender 2003; Callender and Jackson 2004). This viewpoint may be more beneficial than they realized as many, particularly those who have amassed a small fortune in student loan debt, wonder if they would have been better off financially without the post-secondary education.

In January 2009 the amount of money owed to the federal government for student loans surpassed $13 billion for the first time in Canadian history. The $13 billion does not include approximately $5 to $8 billion in provincial student debt or other personal debts students may have such as credit cards, lines of credit, and family and bank loans (CFS 2009c). Loans dispersed through the Canada Student Loans Program are increasing the total amount owed by $1.2 million a day, or by more than $430 million per year. The total amount of student loans, $13 billion, is more than the debt of some provinces and, to put it into another perspective, equals approximately the cost of the Afghanistan mission to date (CFS 2009b). The Canadian Federation of Students calls for an immediate reduc-tion in tuition fees as one way of managing the enormous debt students are accruing: "Reducing both tuition fees and stu-dent debt is well within the government of Canada's grasp. The $1.44 billion scheme of education tax credits could be converted to student grants, immediately reducing student debt by approximately 75%" (CFS 2009b).

Are you accruing debt for your post-secondary educa-tion? What kind of salary will you need to make in order to be debt-free in two years?

does not want to give official recognition to poverty." In Canada we need an official measure of poverty in order to begin to deal with the crisis afflicting the nation.

Consequences of Poverty

Poverty statistics are more than just a snapshot of who is poor and how the poor live: these statistics are also predictors. As such, they tend to predict a grim future for individuals who live below the poverty line and for the entire nation (Gleick 1996). As one social analyst (Ropers 1991:25) has noted, "Poverty narrows and closes life chances . . . . Being poor not only means eco-nomic insecurity, it also wreaks havoc on one's mental and physical health."

Health and Nutrition

According to the Canadian Association of Food Banks (2002:5), "[w]ithin a domestic context, hunger and food insecurity are best understood as consequences of extreme poverty."

Good nutrition, which is essential to good health, depends on the food consumed, and when people are poor, they are more likely to purchase cheap but filling foods such as beans, rice, and potatoes that may not meet all daily nutritional requirements or to go without food altogether. As a woman interviewed by the Peterborough Social Planning Council in Ontario (1998:126) reported, "I've been visiting my doctor regularly. He feels I'm not eating properly. My kids are fed three times per day, whereas I eat three times per week. I've lost 60 lbs. in the last year." Research about income assistance recipients in British Columbia demonstrated that this situation is an all-too-common reality for lone mothers. Using data from the 2005 Canadian Community Health Survey conducted by Statistics Canada, the Canadian Council on Social Development (CCSD) reported that 3.3 percent of Canadian households were food insecure without hunger, and another 1.8 percent were food insecure with moderate to severe levels of hunger (CCSD 2009b).

Poor children particularly are at risk for inadequate nutrition and hunger (Community Childhood Hunger Identification Project 1995). In 2005, for example, 2.8 percent of Canadian households with children reported that they could not afford enough food for their children, and a further 11.1 percent reported that this was "sometimes true" (CCSD 2009b). Emergency food assistance is especially pronounced in urban areas, but recently, there has been greater need in rural com-munities as well. Rural food banks make up almost half of the nation's food banks and serve more children and seniors than do urban food banks (Food Banks Canada 2009c). Since 2000, more than 51 new food banks have opened in rural areas (Canadian Association of Food Banks [CAFB] 2005).

Since the first food bank opened its doors in Edmonton, Alberta, in 1981, high numbers of peo-ple annually rely on it and other related food and meal programs to meet their nutritional needs. It is impor-tant to recognize that food hampers generally provide only enough food for five days and that most food banks are able to allow people access only once per month (Food Banks Canada 2009c). The nutritional value of most food bank hampers is dubious, consid-ering the kinds of foods that are typically donated. Imagine trying to provide adequate nutrition for a growing child from a food-bank hamper, which con-tains few fresh fruits and vegetables or high-quality foods.

Food Banks Canada (formerly the Canadian Association of Food Banks) outlines some of the impacts of poverty and deprivation:

> Food insecurity . . . elicits feelings of alienation, impoverishment and social exclusion. While parents deprive themselves in order to protect their children from the impacts of poverty and food insecurity, some simply do not have the resources to ensure an adequate diet for their children. Inadequately nourished children are more likely to experience compromised health, iron deficiency, frequent stomach aches and head aches, colds, ear infections, anemia, and asthma. Children with poor diets also have slower recovery periods from illness and reduced immune systems. Food insecurity is associated with major depression in adults, hyperactivity in children, and dysthymia, suicidal ideation and attempted suicide in adolescents. (CAFB 2002:4)

In evaluations of the contents of food-bank hampers, nutritionists unsurprisingly found that the donated groceries did not allow a person to meet basic daily nutritional requirements (CAFB 2002:15). When these hampers are used in emergency situations, as they were originally intended, this does not present many problems. However, when people rely on food-bank hampers over the long term, the consequences are detrimental and severe. Prolonged malnutrition can contribute to or result in such medical problems as rickets, scurvy, parasitic worms, and developmental disabilities. Since 2001, the Dieticians of Canada, B.C. Region, has found that welfare incomes are far below the amount of money required to meet basic food costs for a healthy and nutritious diet. About 40 percent of all children living in poverty consume significantly less than the federally recommended guidelines for caloric and nutritional intake (Brown 2002). The long-term health care costs of cuts to income assistance should be clear.

Problems associated with food and shelter are intricately linked. When parents are forced to decide between paying the rent and putting food on the table, many choose to pay the rent in hopes of keeping a roof over their children's heads. Sometimes, however, they cannot afford to do either.

Housing

The lack of affordable housing in many regions in Canada has become a crisis. Over the past three decades, low-cost housing units in many areas have been replaced by expensive condominiums or single-family residences for affluent residents in a process known as "gentrification." This shift to condominiums and single-family residences has made finding housing even more difficult for individuals and families living in poverty. When low-income housing is available, it may be located in high-density, often overcrowded areas. The housing often has inadequate heating and plumbing facilities, infestations of insects or rodents, and dangerous structural problems due to faulty construction or lack of adequate maintenance. Studies conducted by food banks in Canada show that most food-bank clients spend more than 30 percent of their income on housing (CAFB 2002:14). Further, the 2001 Census reported that 24 percent of Canadians spent 30 percent or more on housing, with even higher proportions spending 30 percent or more in British Columbia, Ontario, and Quebec, a situation that continues today (CCPA BC 2008; see Figure 2.2). The Canada Mortgage and Housing Corporation (CMHC) describes people in this situation as "in core housing need and at risk of becoming homeless" (CAFB 2002:14).

Evidence so far suggests that more people are joining the ranks of the homeless every day. Today at least one-third of all homeless people are entire families and one-third are youth aged 16 to 24 (Laird 2007). In fact, children are the fastest growing group of homeless people in Canada (Macionis and Gerber 2002:289), and one out of every seven emergency shelter users is a child (Laird 2007). The city of Vancouver announced in 2007 that its population of homeless seniors had tripled between 2002 and 2005 (Laird 2007). Even worse, the 2008 Metro Vancouver Homelessness Count demonstrated that homelessness there had increased by 22 percent since 2005 and 137 percent since 2002 (CCPA BC 2008). Vancouver's 2005 homeless count uncovered that 66 percent of those surveyed cited "lack of income" or "cost of housing" as the cause of their homelessness (Laird 2007:5). This is less surprising when one considers that 44 percent of B.C. renters spend more than 30 percent of their income on housing (CCPA BC 2008).

FIGURE 2.2   Housing Situations of Food-Bank Clients, March 2008

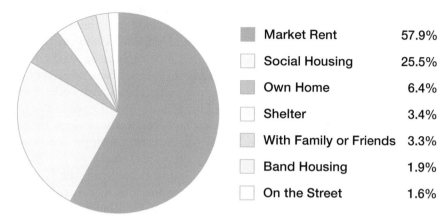

Market Rent	57.9%
Social Housing	25.5%
Own Home	6.4%
Shelter	3.4%
With Family or Friends	3.3%
Band Housing	1.9%
On the Street	1.6%

Source: Food Banks Canada, 2009, **HungerCount 2008.** *Retrieved June 30, 2009 (http://foodbankscanada.ca/documents/HungerCount_en_fin.pdf).*

In recent years, increased rates of homelessness reflect one of the most devastating effects of poverty. As described earlier, the composition of the homeless population has shifted to include many more families, young children, youth, and elderly (see studies by CCPA BC 2008; Liebow 1993; Lundy 1995; Rossi 1989). Regardless of age, gender, ethnicity, or marital status, homeless people are the poorest of the poor.

How Canada Deals with Poverty

In Canada, as part of an overall retrenchment of government programs and services, structural poverty is dealt with as though it is an individual problem. Rather than examining ways of eliminating poverty or dealing with poverty at a societal level, we offer temporary assistance. More often than not that temporary assistance is through charity—both individual charity, such as serving a meal at a soup kitchen or making a donation of money or goods, and charitable organizations, such as soup kitchens, sandwich trucks, and food banks, which almost always rely on volunteer labour and community donations and, rarely, receive some base year-to-year funding from the government. In 1980 there were no food banks in Canada. In 2005, 650 food banks, along with 2864 affiliated agencies, provided "emergency" food rations and meals to Canadian citizens. Food banks in

Canada have served more than 700 000 people every month since 1997, although Canada made a commitment in 1996, as a signatory to the Rome Declaration on World Food Security, to attain food security and end hunger (CAFB 2002). Today, food banks and affiliated agencies number in the thousands, and in a news release alerting Canadians to the June 2 "National Hunger Awareness Day," Food Banks Canada (2009a) estimated that since the March 2008 HungerCount was conducted, food-bank use has increased approximately 20 percent per month—a situation caused by the current economic climate.

Food-bank use in some regions has climbed even higher. For example, in the same news release, Food Banks Canada (2009a) reported an increase of 37 percent in Penticton, British Columbia, as a result of layoffs, and a similar situation occurred simultaneously in North Bay, Ontario, for the same reason. We can expect this situation to grow increasingly grim, as the Canadian Labour Congress (CLC) reported in June 2009 that Statistics Canada labour force figures for May 2009 showed net job losses of 41 800 that month (an increase of 83 800 unemployed people) and a still-rising national unemployment of 8.4 percent, the highest in several years (CLC 2009a). Further, the CLC reports that there are currently 1.55 million unemployed Canadians, 406 100 of whom lost their jobs since October 2008, an increase of 34.5 percent.

Despite the federal government's 1989 pledge to end child poverty, 37 percent of food-bank users in Canada are children (and over 40 percent in rural areas are children). The number of shelters has grown in recent years as well, and there are not nearly enough spaces for all who need them. Sociologists Ann Duffy and Nancy Mandell (2001:95) state that Toronto front-line workers estimate that two to four homeless people die each week in the city, and, as previously mentioned, the number of homeless people in Canada continues to grow.

Following a great deal of lobbying by Canadian activists and non-governmental organizations (NGOs) in the late 1990s and early 2000s, including the delivery of a "State of Emergency Declaration" to the United Nations, the federal government began taking baby steps toward looking at the problem of poverty. Over the past decade, several agreements have been signed between the federal government and the provincial, territorial, and municipal governments to cost-share expenses for some infrastructure spending (Crowe 2007). While it was thought that the agreements would mainly focus on funding new social housing, it became quickly evident that most of the money would be spent on sewers and water supply. While sewers and water are terribly important, and while the funding agreements are a welcome shift away from funding cuts, this does nothing to address poverty and homelessness in Canada.

So our national "non-strategy," so far, is to temporarily fund shelters and food banks in Canada as though poverty and it attendant problems are fleeting aberrations. Yet poverty did not significantly decrease, despite strong overall economic growth over the past decade, and state welfare programs, such as Employment Insurance (EI) and Income Assistance (IA), continue to be retrenched, resulting in heightened risks of poverty for income-insecure individuals. As Macionis and Gerber (2002:289) state, "Structural changes in the Canadian economy coupled with declining government support for lower-income people have all contributed to homelessness."

By way of example, revisions to the employee- and employer-funded Employment Insurance program have resulted in drastically narrowed eligibility criteria and shorter benefit periods, even though the program has always run at a surplus. Most recent data demonstrate that a mere 37 percent of the applicants meet new criteria, compared to more than 74 percent one decade ago (Canadian Labour Congress 2006). Additionally, waiting periods for benefit receipt have been lengthened, and individuals who need income assistance while waiting for a decision about their EI claim must agree to pay that money back when they receive EI benefits. In the past, unemployed workers were able to achieve EI benefits of up to 75 percent of their previous earnings; however, today workers are only able to receive *up to* 55 percent of their previous earnings, and often for only a few short weeks.

Since its inception, the Employment Insurance program has run at a surplus—perhaps the only government-handled program that has. Employers and employees both continue to pay into the EI fund, so why have there been so many cuts? Where has the EI money gone? As of 2005, the federal government had siphoned more than $45 billion to pay off the deficit, pay for tax cuts, and pay down government debt (CAFB 2005:32). Currently there is $57 billion in EI surplus (CAFB 2005:29). Ken Georgetti, Canadian Labour Congress president, stated in June 2009, "This is a scandal . . . . [Canadian] workers contributed to Employment Insurance in good faith and now they are being left to fend for themselves" (CLC 2009a). If you are laid off tomorrow, your chances of accessing any of the surplus you and your employer helped create are very low. Think about what you would do to survive for six weeks or more while your eligibility was being determined. *If* you were successful in getting EI, how well could you make ends meet on half your current monthly income? How long do you think it would take you to find another job at your current salary? What about your parents, if they are still in the labour force?

SOCIAL WELFARE IN CANADA

Canada, like many other advanced capitalist nations, is a **welfare state**—a nation in which the government intervenes in the welfare of its citizens through various social policies, programs, standards, and regulations (see Olsen 2002 and Teeple 2000 for a thorough discussion). Most Canadians are so accustomed to the benefits of the Canadian welfare state that we take them for granted. All of our social programs, such as universal health care, education, pension plans, worker's compensation, minimum wage, employment standards, environmental regulations, health and safety standards, social or income assistance, child tax benefits, and so

on, are subsumed under the mantle of the welfare state. From their inception, government programs have been viewed as "good" if recipients are thought to be deserving of assistance and "bad" if recipients are considered undeserving (see Box 2.2).

SOCIAL PROBLEMS AND SOCIAL POLICY

BOX 2.2   Workfare in Canada: Betraying a National Trust

In 1966, the federal government brought into effect the Canada Assistance Plan (CAP). The purpose of the plan was to outline the ways the federal government would cost-share income assistance with the provinces and to establish national social assistance standards. The criterion upon which people could access CAP was need, based on the idea that all Canadian citizens had certain basic human rights. These rights, enshrined in CAP, were (a) the right to income assistance when in need; (b) the right to an amount of income assistance that meets basic requirements; (c) the right to appeal decisions if the person disagrees; (d) the right not to have to work or train in order to collect income assistance; and (e) the right to collect income assistance, regardless of the province of origin (Swanson 2001:108). Historically derived from a charity model, income assistance based upon need became a right for all citizens in Canada.

Following a Keynesian economic model, the government had great incentive to stabilize the domestic market. Unemployment had to be kept low. Business cycles needed to be stabilized. All of this protected corporations and citizens from the worst of the cyclical nature of capitalism (Shragge 1997). CAP was just one of many social programs that were part of the welfare state, along with universal health care and education, pension plans, and unemployment insurance.

In July 1995, the Liberal government passed Bill C-76, which signalled the end of the Canada Assistance Plan, and on April 1, 1996, replaced it with the *Canada Health and Social Transfer Act* (CHST). Replacing CAP with CHST was part of a broader strategy of retrenchment by the government, decreasing its responsibilities in general for the welfare of citizens through the reduction of various social services (Morel 2002). Sociologist Gregg M. Olsen (2002), in a comparative analysis between Canada, the United States, and Sweden, states that while all three are advanced capitalist nations, Canada has always existed somewhere between the other two with regard to policies and programs and their effects. With globalization stepping up, Canada has been becoming increasingly

similar to the United States in terms of social policies, cost-cutting measures, and cutbacks in social services and programs (Olsen 2002:3). Welfare state retrenchment in Canada has had farther-reaching and more "acute, punitive, and brutal" changes, because we are becoming more like the United States than like Sweden (Olsen 2002:3). Political scientist Sylvie Morel (2002:19) notes that one of the distinctive features of Canadian welfare-policy reform is the classification of social assistance recipients according to a criterion of fitness for work. One of the major effects of replacing CAP with the CHST was that it ended our participation in the United Nations Covenant of Social, Economic, and Cultural Rights, which we signed in 1976. Among other things, the covenant declared that all citizens have the right to "freely chosen" employment and to "an adequate standard of living . . . including adequate food, clothing and housing and . . . the continuous improvement of living conditions" (UN 1992, in Swanson 1997:158). Every five years, each nation that has signed the covenant must report to the UN how it is complying. In the past, Canada used the CAP to demonstrate its commitment to the covenant. No more.

Another and related effect of the CHST was to make workfare legal in Canada. The term *workfare* is generally used to describe a particular direction taken by governments as they reform social assistance, with a particular focus on the shift from income assistance based on need to some type of mandatory employment activity in exchange for benefits (Morel 2002; Shragge 1997). Workfare programs are based on the assumption that there are two groups of poor: the deserving and the undeserving. The deserving poor are those who, for reasons completely beyond their control (for example, extreme old age or extreme disability) are unable to work. The undeserving poor, rated as the vast majority of people on income assistance, are those who suffer from the "damaging consequences of dependence on the welfare system" (Shragge 1997:17). According to proponents of workfare schemes, the undeserving poor need the "tough love of workfare" to give them "a hand up and not merely a hand out" (Shragge 1997:19). Ideally, this tough love would improve the moral conduct of the undeserving poor, who, it is supposed, must be taught "appropriate sexual conduct" and a "life of thrift and humility," rather than squandering their meagre incomes on alcohol, tobacco, bingo, and other luxuries (Hardina 1997; Shragge 1997; Swanson 2001).

The official rationale for retrenchment and for workfare is to save money and reduce welfare dependency. It is believed by many that "the poor" are unmotivated, or do not value work, or have no work ethic, or have, through a "culture of poverty," "cultural values and attitudes which preclude a commitment to work" (Hardina 1997:132). In fact, social scientist Donna Hardina (1997:132), following a comprehensive analysis of U.S. workfare programs, noted that conservatives throughout the 1990s blamed "single mothers [on income assistance] for both the federal deficit and moral decay." Anti-poverty activist Jean Swanson (1997) calls this "Newspeak," based on the language made up by government officials in George Orwell's famous novel *1984*. In Orwell's novel, new terms are created in order to shape and direct citizens' understandings of social and political life in particular ways. Swanson (1997:151) argues that "social policy 'experts,' corporate lobby groups, and right-wing politicians" have devised a new language of blame that serves to obscure the truth about welfare and workfare programs and to create a climate where cuts can be justified. Newspeak about workfare is based on two myths: (1) that people on welfare need to be forced to take employment because they are lazy; and (2) that enough employment, paying living wages, exists. A coalition of social justice groups concerned with poverty, End Legislated Poverty (ELP), catalogued at least 15 Newspeak terms currently in use and their meanings (Swanson 1997). The following reflects a sampling of these terms. Have you heard these expressions before?

Breaking the Cycle of Poverty: This phrase implies that children are taught to be poor by poor adults who pass their preference for poverty onto their children. ELP notes that "no one is exhorted to 'break the cycle of wealth' where rich people pass their wealth on to children who pass it on to their children, perpetuating inequality of income distribution" (Swanson 1997:152–153).

Bring Social Programs into the 21st Century: This phrase typically means to "cut and slash social programs so that people will have to work at low-wage jobs [if they can find them] so they can compete with people in Mexico making $5 a day" (Swanson 1997:153).

Self-Esteem: This phrase is most often used in conjunction with the idea that people need employment to build and maintain their self-esteem. "It implies that a single parent must build her self-esteem at a low-wage, exploitative paid job, rather than by staying home to raise her children to be good citizens" (Swanson 1997:154).

Training for the Jobs of the Future: Quoting Swanson (1997:154–155), this "phrase is used to imply that if only we got ourselves trained in computer programming or air traffic controlling, we could get off welfare or [EI] and be set for the future. In fact, we don't need 1.5 million (the number of unemployed in Canada) people in new high-tech jobs. Training does not create jobs. Available jobs are mostly low wage. Tens of thousands of people get trained and then can't find work. They are pushed out into the labour force to compete with those who do have jobs and pull wages down."

Newspeak therefore suggests that workfare programs are good for people on welfare, as a way of curbing their substance-abuse–like dependence on the system, on "taxpayers." Nowhere does Newspeak suggest that people's generally short-term and temporary sojourns on income assistance are caused by the lack of decent-paying jobs, or by downsizing and restructuring and other structural shifts in the paid labour market. This reflects an individualizing of poverty, where the cause of poverty is viewed as resting with the individual instead of being found in social and structural factors. Critics of workfare point to these structural factors as the reason workfare schemes and the retrenchment of other social programs and services will not work to eradicate poverty.

In fact, long-term research in Canada and the United States has shown that workfare programs are not successful in moving people off income assistance in the long term (Hardina 1997; Shragge 1997; Swanson 1997), likely because the only people who are now eligible for it are those who are most severely disadvantaged. As Hardina (1997:131) states,

> There is no sound empirical research that confirms that mandatory work and job training programs are effective in helping people leave the welfare system. On the contrary, most evaluations of welfare state reform projects have not produced statistically significant differences in job acquisition, earnings or decreases in welfare benefits.

Canadian economist Lars Osberg (2009:15), in his research on cuts to EI and other social programs, points out that the only thing that has ever worked to move people off income assistance is employment, and this fact, along with changes to the CHST, will spell trouble ahead for the provinces and territories in the years to come:

> The most significant influence of social assistance rates appears to be the availability of jobs . . . . Since the 1990s . . . a minority of the unemployed are eligible for EI and any increase in social assistance costs produced by a downturn in labour demand will be entirely borne by provincial treasuries. The shift to block funding of

transfers to the provinces, embodied in the CHST, means that the federal government's participation in increased social assistance payments in a recession is now zero.

Demands on the social assistance system are likely to be more sensitive to future business cycle downturns because the dramatic decline in eligibility for unemployment insurance payments under EI means that provincial social assistance programs will be called on to carry the burden earlier, and to a far greater degree, than in past recessions.

Speaking about so-called welfare dependency, Swanson (1997:150), citing 40 years of research in British Columbia, makes the further point that "welfare benefits are so low, the welfare system so controlling and demeaning, that the vast majority of people engineer their own escapes from it as soon as they can." Her comments are based on provincial governmental research showing that only 10 percent of assistance recipients stay on it for more than two years. Hardina (1997:137) further points out that conservative politicians assert that income assistance is the "cause" of deficits, but in Canada, *all* social program spending (including health care and education spending) accounts for a mere 2 percent of the budget, and in the United States, AFDC (Aid to Families with Dependent Children) spending accounts for less than 1 percent. Income assistance programs in Canada cost taxpayers as much money as tax breaks to RRSP holders do, and yet the latter group of citizens is not held to blame for Canadian deficit problems (Swanson 1997, 2001). Further, tax breaks to corporations far outweigh the amount of money spent on social programs and yet few people lobby for an end to the corporate dole. If it is true that most people only use income assistance as a safety net in times of real need, as was intended, and if forced work programs have not been shown to be effective for their stated purpose (to save money and reduce the numbers on income assistance), and if these social programs do not cost Canadian taxpayers much money, why do governments persist in moving ahead with workfare programs and the like?

Several writers have developed incisive critiques of workfare, putting forth alternative reasons for governmental promotion of workfare programs while cutting benefits and eligibility for income assistance and EI. Tying people's income assistance benefits to training and/or to low-waged, temporary employment undermines existing jobs and wages and depresses labour standards throughout society (A Commitment for Training and Employment for Women [ACTEW] 1998; Hardina 1997; Morel 2002; Osberg 2009; Shragge 1997; Swanson 1997, 2001). Basically, these programs create a pool of cheap, subsidized, and "flexible"

(disposable) labour that governments, the private sector, and community organizations can access. In effect, workfare creates the perfect reserve army of labour, a pool of workers who have few rights and who can be moved into and out of the labour market as needed, without regard to the creation of permanent jobs, living wages, or benefits. This pool of labour is not only flexible (available to serve the cyclical expansion and contraction of a capitalist market), but is also used to destabilize so-called good jobs (those with decent wages, labour practices, stability, and benefits) and help bust unions. Social scientist Eric Shragge (1997:30–31) summarizes, "Workfare becomes a means of mobilizing a surplus population to undermine the conditions of public sector and community employment."

What are the social policy implications following from these analyses? Long-term forecasts for employment predict that, with globalization, generally, unemployment in Canada will get worse. Indeed, the current global recession is ushering this in at a rapid pace. Shragge (1997) suggests that in shaping future social policy we need to look at the polarizations that are taking place in the labour market and in society in general between those with wealth and employment and those without. Many people find themselves forced to work longer hours and take more jobs, while others are being "downsized" right out of the labour market. In order to create a more equitable distribution of income and employment, then, some policies may need to address restrictions on overtime and shorter average work weeks (Shragge 1997). Further, the National Council of Welfare conducted a study that found that if minimum wage was set at a rate people could live on (now at least $11 per hour), there would be no disincentive (Swanson 1997).

Canadian social welfare policy has been based, in the past, on two distinct traditions. The first of these is the British Poor Laws of the 1600s, which established notions of deserving and undeserving poor (Graham et al. 2000:64). Social scientist Francis J. Turner (1995:6), in an overview of social welfare in this country, described the nature of this historical dichotomy:

The *deserving* were those persons and groups who, through no fault of their own, but by birth, accident, or disaster, were not able to care for themselves, either temporarily or permanently. Since they were deemed not to be responsible for their state of need, it was considered fitting that society, through one of its subsystems, provide assistance to them. What has never been clear in this matter is who decided, and on what grounds, what criteria could be applied in determining who was deserving or undeserving.

The *undeserving* were those people who, in the opinion of persons of influence, were in need through their own fault or failings. Such persons were considered to be lazy, irresponsible, improvident—and indeed, evil—members of society and thus were not considered to have a claim on assistance. To help such persons was considered as an unfair drain on the resources of society and as a way of contributing to further indolence. Any help that was made available was provided only grudgingly, was made as unattractive as possible, and was kept to an absolute minimum.

The second tradition informing Canadian social welfare policies has been the racist Social Darwinism of the 19th century, which helped to establish ideas about hierarchies and majority–minority relations (Graham et al. 2000:64). Poverty in Canada kills more people than cancer, despite the fact that we have a cure for poverty through changes to social policies (see Table 2.4), should we choose to exercise it (Swanson 2001:185). So far, however, we have chosen not to. What do you think will happen in the future if we refuse to intervene in the problem of poverty in Canada?

TABLE 2.4   Differences in Canadian and Western European Family Policies

	Canada	Western Europe
Value assigned to children and the role of parents	<ul><li>children considered "life style choices" or "private commodities" to be pursued with private means</li><li>family presumed to be essentially private and self-sufficient</li><li>government role/community support only when children are "at risk" or families "in need"</li><li>parenting role is undervalued because children are undervalued</li></ul>	<ul><li>children considered collective responsibility or "public goods" who contribute to the well-being of the whole society</li><li>important contribution parents make to the larger society is recognized</li><li>state commitment to contribute to the cost of raising children</li></ul>
Ideas about who should benefit from social programs	<ul><li>"public charity" model results in growing unwillingness to contribute to "undeserving" welfare poor</li><li>pits modest-income families against poor families; threatens social cohesion</li><li>privatization of child rearing and targeting basic benefits primarily to the poor</li><li>median-income families excluded from significant benefits</li></ul>	<ul><li>willingness of people to contribute public revenues for the common good of all families</li><li>not only those with the lowest incomes benefit from social programs</li><li>policies provide significant benefits to all or most families, reflecting sense of collective responsibility.</li><li>universality and higher family allowances</li></ul>
Ways of supporting families/women	<ul><li>reducing/preventing poverty are explicit goals of public policy, yet unsuccessful at preventing poverty</li><li>women not supported adequately as mothers or workers</li><li>mothers of young children expected to be in the labour market yet very little support is provided (income support, child care, parental leave programs)</li><li>gender-neutral individual responsibility model</li></ul>	<ul><li>reduction/prevention of poverty among families with children are by-products of family support policies and programs</li><li>two different approaches: family-oriented or employment-oriented</li><li>both approaches extremely successful at preventing poverty, even among lone parents</li><li>social responsibility model to support family ethic and/or care ethic for women</li></ul>
Different outcomes	<ul><li>social assistance primary form of income support for many families with children</li><li>high poverty rates for children, particularly in female lone-parent families</li><li>large income gaps and inequalities</li></ul>	<ul><li>social assistance truly residual</li><li>low poverty rates even for female lone-parent families</li><li>smaller income disparities generally</li></ul>

Source: Christa Freiler and Judy Cerny, 1998, Benefiting Canada's Children: Perspectives on Gender and Social Responsibility, *Ottawa, ON: Research Directorate, Status of Women Canada. March. Reproduced with the permission of the Minister of Public Works and Government Services Canada, 2003.*

The modern welfare state, or Keynesian welfare state, came into existence in Canada following World War II. Economist John Maynard Keynes proposed that nation-states intervene between their citizens and capitalism in order to create

a political compromise with the working classes. This compromise included the goals of moderating the business cycle (to prevent a repeat of the unrest of the 1930s), helping rebuild the war-destroyed economies of Europe (to ensure the re-establishment of capitalism), and containing or diminishing the growing interest in socialism stemming from the experience of the 1930s and the devastation of war. (quoted in Teeple 2000:440)

One of the unintended, but useful, consequences of the welfare state has been to ameliorate the worst contradictions created by capitalism's normal "ebb and flow" cycle; therefore, as Teeple (2000:442) points out, the welfare state soothes "the worst effects of economic inequality and . . . placate[s] resistance to all political and social implications of such inequality." A harsher view of this is proposed by sociologists Shahid Alvi, Walter DeKeseredy, and Desmond Ellis (2000:60), who observe that capitalists and conservatives view the poor as

"social junk" because they are not formally attached to the capitalist economy, . . . [and] are seen by the ruling class as requiring discipline. Thus, the "invisible hand" of the capitalist market is replaced by the "visible fist" of the government. For example, the government intervenes to ensure that the process of capital accumulation is not hindered by these potential troublemakers.

In the early 1970s, capitalism shifted from a national to an international economic system—in short, capitalism became global. Capitalist enterprises were no longer reliant on the purchasing power of any particular nation-state when a whole world was now the market. Additionally, workers in any particular nation no longer had to be placated when capitalist enterprises could easily move production from nation to nation: one reason why cuts to social programs like EI have been so devastating. Under various trade agreements, capitalists sought to level ("harmonize") social and economic policies between nations so as to facilitate easier and more profitable trade (see Chapter 13).

A newly internationalized capitalism put increased pressure on governments to enact new neo-liberal policies that would have the effect of reducing government interventions such as income assistance, EI, universal health care, publicly funded education, and so on, called "barriers to trade" by neo-liberals. These "interventions," in the form of social programs and public protections, are being retrenched or cut back more each year, using a variety of justifications, from the "deficit-mania" hysteria in the 1990s to the superficially convincing arguments that Canadian health care is "just too expensive," when the facts underlying these sophisticated advertising campaigns demonstrate much different realities. Can a welfare state provide a solution to poverty? The answer to this question may depend on how poverty itself is explained.

PERSPECTIVES ON POVERTY AND CLASS INEQUALITY

Social-class inequality and poverty can be understood from various perspectives. The framework that is applied influences people's beliefs about how poverty might be reduced.

The Symbolic Interactionist Perspective

Symbolic interactionists examine poverty from the perspective of meanings, definitions, and labels. How is poverty defined? How are people who are poor viewed by non-poor society members? How do people who are poor define themselves and their situations? What stigma is attached to poverty, or homelessness, and how do people live with, or manage, that stigma? What are the consequences of being labelled as "poor" or "low income" or "homeless"?

Canada is a meritocracy, and much of contemporary rhetoric suggests, then, that if people wish to succeed, they can. Definitions of *success* are rarely explicitly discussed; instead, a common understanding of the term is assumed and taken for granted. If someone fails to succeed, it follows that the fault lies with the individual, who is "irresponsible," "lazy," "immoral," "lacking in motivation," and so on. This is the "land of opportunity," and people who do not succeed have no one but themselves to blame for their lacks and flaws (Feagin 1975). Workfare programs for social assistance recipients are based on individualistic explanations for poverty (see Box 2.2). To many sociologists, however, individual explanations of poverty amount to **blaming the victim**—a practice suggesting that the cause of a social problem emanates from within the individual or group who exhibits the problem, by virtue of some inherent lack or flaw on the part of the individual or group. Conversely, symbolic interactionists also examine what it means to be wealthy. How are those with wealth viewed by others? While impoverished people tend to be negatively stigmatized, wealthy individuals tend to be seen as hard working and deserving of their wealth. Where do we get information about the relative merits of whole groups of people? As author and journalist Jeremy Seabrook (2002:129) points out, "while it is easy to find a table of the 20 richest people in the world, it would be impossible to do the same with the 20 poorest." Further, since wealthy people have the means to avoid being observed and investigated in ways that poor people do not, sociologists know relatively little about them. In the absence of evidence about the hard-working (or other) practices of wealthy people, we must rely simply on ideology.

Symbolic interactionists are also interested in what it means to people to be poor and what impact stigma has on people's self-concepts. Some researchers have focused on how cultural background affects people's values and behaviour. Among the earliest of these explanations is the "culture of poverty" thesis by anthropologist Oscar Lewis (1966). According to Lewis, poor people have different values and beliefs than people from the middle and upper classes and so develop a separate and self-perpetuating system of attitudes and behaviours that keeps them trapped in poverty. Among these attitudes and behaviours are the inability to defer gratification or plan for the future; feelings of apathy, hostility, and suspicion toward others; deficient speech and communication patterns; female-headed households; and a decided lack of participation in major societal institutions. People trapped in the "culture of poverty" socialize their children into this cycle of poverty, and hence the culture supposedly perpetuates. The "culture of

poverty" thesis has provided political leaders, social analysts, and many other Canadian citizens with a reasonable-sounding rationale for blaming the situations endured by poor people on the poor themselves. The "culture of poverty" thesis, while popular, has been soundly criticized. Critics point out that people who are poor, just like people who are not poor, develop attitudes and behaviours as *responses* and ways of coping with stigma and other limitations and barriers placed on their participation. The "culture of poverty" thesis has also been critiqued for suggesting that poor people both enjoy their impoverished situations and do not know any better. Besides being incorrect, these notions are paternalistic and based on stereotypes.

More recent cultural explanations of poverty have focused on the lack of **cultural capital**—social assets, such as values, beliefs, attitudes, and competencies in language and culture, that are learned at home and required for success and social advancement (Bourdieu and Passeron 1990). From this perspective, low-income people do not have adequate cultural capital to function in a competitive global economy. According to most sociologists, cultural explanations again deflect attention from the true structural sources of poverty (unemployment, racism, sexism, and so on) and shift blame from the affluent and powerful to the poor and powerless (Sidel 1996:xvii–xviii).

The Structural Functionalist Perspective

Unlike individual and cultural explanations of poverty, which operate at the microlevel, structural explanations of poverty focus on the macrolevel, the level of social organization that is beyond an individual's ability to change. One structural explanation of poverty (Wilson 1996) points to changes in the economy that have dramatically altered employment opportunities for people, particularly those who have the least wealth, power, and prestige. According to the functionalists who espouse this explanation, social inequality serves an important function in society because it motivates people to work hard to acquire scarce resources. In 1945, sociologists Kingsley Davis and Wilbert Moore published a paper explaining that social stratification exists in every society in some form and must, therefore, be functional. Davis and Moore asserted that some occupations require more training and investment than others, or are difficult or unpleasant to do, so should be compensated more, through prestige and pay. This explains, they felt, why doctors and judges have high prestige and pay, while restaurant servers and truck drivers do not. This thesis has been criticized for several reasons, among them the idea that inequities in pay and prestige are functional for society. Why are women paid less than men? For whom is this functional? Is the work of a child-care provider really worth millions of dollars less per year than the work of an NHL star? Why are occupations that are overly dirty or dangerous not rewarded with high salaries? Functionalists also assert that it is functional to maintain a pool of more desperate workers in order to fill the occupations that no one wants to do. This is deemed "functional" but is likely problematic for those "desperate few" who are forced to work in unfavourable conditions, often for low wages. This is a main criticism of functionalist perspectives generally—we must always ask the question, Functional for whom? Lastly, poverty may be seen as functional for those who work in the "poverty industry" (for example, financial assistance workers) and for those who need a market for second-rate or inferior-quality items.

The Conflict Perspective

Another structural explanation for poverty is based on a conflict perspective that suggests poverty is a side effect of the capitalist system. Using this explanation, analysts note that workers are increasingly impoverished by the wage squeeze and high rates of unemployment and underemployment. The *wage squeeze* is the steady downward pressure on the real take-home pay of workers that has occurred over the past three decades. During these decades, shareholders in major corporations have had substantial increases in dividends, and chief executive officers have received extremely lucrative salaries and compensation packages (Gordon 1996). In a February 2006 interview with Vancouver's *The Georgia Straight,* Barry Cook, an executive compensation expert at Western Management Consultants, stated that executive pay has risen at a faster rate than pay for other occupations every year since the early 1990s (Smith 2006). As an example, the average increase in CEO pay at "Standard and Poor 500" firms from 1993 to 2003 was 146 percent! In contrast, average workers' wages increased very little

and in some cases declined (CLC 2006:2). Corporate downsizing and new technologies that replace workers have further enhanced capitalists' profits and contributed to the impoverishment of middle- and low-income workers by creating a reserve army of unemployed people whom the capitalists use for casual labour and as a means to keep other workers' wages low. Corporations' intense quest for profit results in low wages for workers, a wide disparity in the life chances of affluent people and poor people, and the unemployment and impoverishment of many. Sociologist Harley D. Dickinson (2000) notes that unemployment is a normal consequence of capitalism and, in fact, is necessary. Conflict between the capitalists (Marx's bourgeoisie) and the workers (Marx's proletariat) has in part been ameliorated in past decades by welfare state programs like EI or income assistance (Dickinson 2000). What effect will continued retrenchment have on class conflict in Canada? Although some analysts suggest that high rates of poverty will always exist in advanced capitalist societies, others believe that inequality and poverty can be reduced, even eliminated, if the political will exists.

Feminist Perspectives

Many feminist perspectives on poverty or class inequality focus on the gendered character of stratification and poverty. Most of the people living in poverty are women and their children. This trend of women being disproportionately represented among individuals living in poverty has been called the **feminization of poverty.** Feminist theorists look at the differential valuing of occupations and roles within Canadian society, noting who has power and prestige, which occupations are deemed more or less valuable, and so on. Feminist theorists examine what factors propel women into poverty and keep them there, looking, for instance, at women's economic positions following divorce or marital dissolution. The fact that women are more likely than men to have children living with them after marital breakup disproportionately burdens them, particularly if fathers are not contributing to the new household financially. This can be especially problematic as women make lower wages in nearly every occupation in Canada. Further, women are more likely to be widowed than men, and, currently, older women's pensions, because many were not in the paid labour force for long, are negligible. Lastly, work that is considered to be "women's work" (i.e., any paid work that mimics that done in the home—cleaning, caregiving, and so on) is compensated poorly as it is deemed more a "labour of love" than real "work" requiring proper compensation.

In work that later became the foundation of a socialist–feminist analysis of the intersection of gender and class, or patriarchy and capitalism, Engels theorized that the fact of private property was at the heart of patriarchy. With capitalism came private property. With private property came the desire to pass it on along with the wealth it generated to the children of the bourgeoisie. This then made knowing one's genetic offspring very important to the bourgeoisie, which then made the establishment of a system for ensuring paternity very important. In order to ensure a man's children were indeed his own, monogamy and the subjugation of women became necessary. Engels (1884/1972:120) referred to this, in a famous phrase, as "the world-historical defeat of women." One of the criticisms of a socialist–feminist perspective is that it is deterministic; it lacks an explanation of why capitalism must unfold this way (Muszynski 2000). More recently, instead of seeing women and men as oppositional classes, scholars have analyzed the variety of ways that gender, racialization, and class intersect within a capitalist economic system, recognizing the complexities in an analysis of who is poor and who is wealthy, who is an oppressor and who is oppressed. In addition to the fact that poverty is gendered, Abolmohammad Kazemipur and Shiva Halli (2000:112) point out in their book on poverty in Canada that

poverty is too diverse and complicated a phenomenon to be adequately explained by a uni-dimensional theory. It varies, for example, from one city to another; from one ethnic group to another; from one segment of population (e.g., immigrants) to another; and even within each segment, it varies from one generation to another.

If we are going to understand poverty, if indeed this is a necessary precursor to ending it, our explanations will need to become more comprehensive. Is it possible to reduce or eliminate class inequality and poverty without a theoretical understanding?

HOW CAN POVERTY BE REDUCED?

Chapter 1 made the point that how people view a social problem is related to how they believe the problem should be reduced or solved. Poverty and social inequality are no exception. Analysts who focus on individualistic explanations of poverty typically suggest individual solutions: "Low-income and poverty-level people should change their attitudes, beliefs, and work habits." For example, economist George Gilder (1981:69) stated that "the only dependable route from poverty is always work. . . . The poor must not only work, they must work harder than the classes above them."

Similarly, people who use cultural explanations seek cultural solutions; they suggest that poverty can be reduced by the enhancement of people's cultural capital. They urge the development of more job training and school enrichment programs to enhance people's cultural capital and counteract negative familial and neighbourhood influences. Seeking cultural solutions, the federal government developed job training and young entrepreneur programs to provide children and adolescents from low-income families with the cultural capital (White, middle-class values, really) they need to succeed in the White, middle-class world.

Although some analysts seeking structural solutions suggest that poverty can be eliminated only if capitalism is abolished and a new means of distributing valued goods and services is established, others state that poverty can be reduced by the creation of "a truly open society—a society where the life chances of those at the bottom are not radically different from those at the top and where wealth is distributed more equitably" (MacLeod 1995:260). The latter analysts feel that federal, territorial, and provincial governments can and should play a vital role in reducing poverty and lessening people's need for social assistance. Policy analysts point to polls conducted throughout this early part of the 21st century that demonstrate that Canadians are becoming increasingly alarmed by their elected governments' lack of action on poverty. For example, an autumn 2008 poll of 2023 Canadians by Environics Canada (stratified random sample and accurate to plus or minus 2.2 percent) reports the following highlights:

- 90 percent say it's time for strong leadership to reduce the number of poor people;

- 92 percent say if countries like Great Britain and Sweden can do it, so can Canada;

- 86 percent believe if government took concrete action, poverty could be greatly reduced;

- 89 percent say the prime minister and premiers need to set concrete targets and timelines to reduce poverty and measure their progress;

- 81 percent support reducing poverty by at least 25 percent over the next five years;

- 90 percent of Canadians say they would be proud if their premier took the lead in reducing poverty in their province;

- 88 percent want Canada to be a leader in poverty reduction;

- 77 percent say a recession is all the more reason to act now; and

- there is resounding majority support to raise the minimum wage, improve income support programs to help poor families raising children, create low-cost child-care spaces, create more affordable housing, make sure welfare rates rise with the cost of living, and invest in jobs and skills training for those in between jobs (CCPA 2008).

Canadians of every political persuasion (poll results were remarkably similar for all political affiliations) are ready for action on poverty, and they want all levels of government to take leadership. What is particularly interesting about this poll is that the majority of people indicated that that they would be more likely to support a political party that pledged to make poverty reduction a priority (CCPA 2008).

Dr. David Hay, a research and information management consultant, also believes that Canadians "feel that their current social reality is disconnected from long standing, essential and shared Canadian values" (2009:9). So how might we get back on track and become more aligned with our social values?

Taking concrete and immediate action on poverty reduction is one way. According to Hay (2009), who reviewed performance on poverty reduction in Canada and other nations, the development of effective programs and benefits can work to reduce poverty. However, what might a poverty reduction strategy look like? The Canadian Centre for Policy Alternatives (CCPA) published a poverty reduction strategy in

December 2008. Based on research of other jurisdictions that have successfully reduced poverty, the report (CCPA BC 2008) described the following common characteristics of the most effective poverty reduction plans:

- *Targets and timelines:* The plan must have clear targets and timelines, using multiple and widely accepted measures of progress. The benchmarks for the timelines must be concrete enough, and frequent enough, that a government can be held accountable for progress within its mandate. The targets and timelines should be legislated.

- *Accountability:* Accountability mechanisms are key to an effective and credible plan. The plan should lay out overarching goals for the whole of government and include the development of implementation plans within key ministries. The lead minister responsible should be required by legislation to submit an annual progress report to the legislature.

- *Comprehensiveness:* The plan must deal comprehensively with the multiple dimensions and causes of poverty and homelessness. Policy measures put in place must aid those in the low-wage workforce and those who cannot work in paid labour (either temporarily or long term), as well as enhance the social programs/public goods that are relied upon by everyone, but in particular, low- and middle-income households (such as housing, child care, and accessible post-secondary education).

- *Focus on marginalized groups:* The plan must include measures that focus specifically on populations where poverty and marginalization are most acute—namely, Indigenous people, recent immigrants, lone mothers, single senior women, people with disabilities, and people with severe mental illness, addictions, and other health problems.

- *Community involvement:* An official government strategy should be the product of a meaningful province-wide consultation process—one that hears in particular from those most affected by poverty. That said, there are policy actions that require immediate implementation and should not wait for further consultation.

Hay (2009:18) cites the National Council of Welfare following a national consultation on "solving poverty" in 2007, stating that "the Council concluded that 'if there is no long term vision, no plan, no one accountable for carrying out the plan, no resources assigned, and no accepted measure of result, we will continue to be mired in poverty for generations.'" According to the Canadian Centre for Policy Alternatives, B.C. Office 2008b:8–9), an effective poverty reduction plan should include the following, each with targeted priority actions and timelines, and with clear channels of accountability specific to the province or territory in question:

1. Provide adequate and accessible income support for the unemployed;
2. Improve earnings and working conditions for low-wage workers;
3. Address the needs of those most likely to be living in poverty;
4. Address homelessness and the lack of affordable housing;
5. Provide universal, publicly funded child care;
6. Provide support for training and education; and
7. Promote the health of all citizens.

Although poverty reduction plans like the one presented here will not "solve" the problem of poverty overnight, they will temper and reduce the price poor people pay for living in the "land of opportunity."

WHAT CAN YOU DO?

- Lobby politicians to support real job-creation strategies, higher minimum wages, universal child care, and affordable housing.
- Volunteer at a local food bank, shelter, or soup kitchen.
- Donate money, food, or time to an organization such as a food bank or an anti-poverty organization.
- Write a letter to the local newspaper or your university or college paper outlining some little-known facts about poverty, welfare, "wealthfare," workfare, or hunger in your region. Send a copy of your letter to Food Banks Canada at **info@food bankscanada.ca**.

- Participate in alternative economies such as food-share programs and car-share programs.
- Grow a garden and donate some of your efforts to a local food program.
- Bookmark on a computer you use some of the websites for organizations that keep up-to-date statistics on hunger and homelessness in Canada.
- Engage a homeless person in conversation and find out about his or her life.
- Bake cookies and hand them out to homeless people.
- Make a phone call to your city hall and ask what programs and services the municipality has in place for homeless people. Use your voice as a housed person!
- Become a member of Food Banks Canada or a local anti-poverty organization.
- Attend demonstrations and protests on poverty issues in order to gain information about what the issues are locally. For example, recently in Victoria, B.C., a group of temporary shelters made of cardboard, erected in an out-of-the-way place, was torn down by police at the directive of the municipality. Taking away people's belongings and a semi-dry place to sleep did not stop the problem of homelessness in that city. Use your privilege as a literate person with more media access than most homeless people to get these issues heard.
- Organize a food drive for your local food bank. For example, at Christmas time in some urban centres, municipal garbage collection workers, organized through the Canadian Union of Public Employees (CUPE), ask citizens to leave wrapped, non-perishable food donations outside on garbage collection days and will ensure they get to the local food bank. Some university campuses organize an annual "Trick or Eat" campaign and go door to door on Halloween collecting food for the local food bank. Remember, good advance publicity is the key to a successful campaign.
- Visit a local grocery store, deli, or bakery and ask if they donate leftover food to the local food bank or soup kitchens. Call places that do and thank the managers of those stores. This encourages people to

- continue to operate with their civic responsibilities in mind.

- Send a donation to Food Banks Canada (an organization whose member food banks and agencies feed over 85 percent of Canada's hungry). For every dollar you donate, Food Banks Canada can move $75 worth of food.

- Attend all-candidates forums and ask political hopefuls what they and their party are doing to reduce homelessness, hunger, and poverty in Canada. Ask to see their poverty reduction strategies.

- Intervene when you hear someone poor-bashing or negatively stereotyping poor people. Educate friends, family members, and classmates or professors who are not as knowledgeable about the issues. Keep up to date about the facts so you are comfortable educating others.

- In the words of Toronto street nurse Cathy Crowe (2007:170), "be angry that our governments are not working together to fund the right to safe and truly affordable housing. Your anger is vital to the momentum needed to create the wind for social change." Get angry about the injustice of poverty in Canada.

SUMMARY

Why Is Social Stratification a Social Problem?

Social stratification refers to the hierarchical arrangement of large social groups based on their control over basic resources. In highly stratified societies, low-income and poor people have limited access to food, clothing, shelter, education, health care, and other necessities of life.

Who Makes Up the Lower Classes In Canada?

The Canadian population is divided into several classes. Members of the lower class include the working class and the poor. The working class holds occupations such as semi-skilled machine operator or counter help in a fast-food restaurant. The poor include the working poor and the chronically poor. The working poor are those who are attached to the labour market but whose wages are not sufficient to provide them with the necessities. The chronically poor include individuals of working age who are outside the labour force and children who live in poor families.

What Are Individual and Cultural Explanations of Poverty?

Individual explanations of poverty focus on the attitudinal and motivational problems of individuals or the amount of human capital a person possesses. Cultural explanations of poverty focus on how cultural background affects people's values and behaviour. These explanations focus on the microlevel, and most sociologists view them as attempts to blame the victim for the problem.

What Are Structural Explanations of Poverty?

Structural explanations of poverty focus on the macrolevel, the level of social organization that is beyond an individual's ability to change. These explanations consider how changes in the economy have altered employment opportunities or how inequality and exploitation are inherent in the structure of class and gender relations in a capitalist economy.

What Solutions Have Been Suggested for Poverty?

Most individual and cultural solutions focus on the importance of work. Individual perspectives suggest that people should work harder. Cultural perspectives suggest enhancing people's cultural capital to make them better prepared for employment. Structural perspectives are based on the assumption that society can reduce poverty by creating real jobs and by investing in people through provision of child care, health care, and affordable housing.

KEY TERMS

absolute poverty,   p. 32
blaming the victim,   p. 48
cultural capital,   p. 48
feminization of poverty,   p. 49
income,   p. 33

life chances,   p. 33
meritocracy,   p. 32
poverty rate,   p. 37
power,   p. 33
prestige,   p. 33

relative poverty,   p. 36
social stratification,   p. 32
wealth,   p. 33
welfare state,   p. 42

QUESTIONS FOR CRITICAL THINKING

1.   What would happen if all the wealth in Canada were redistributed so that all adults had the same amount? Some analysts suggest that within five years most of the wealth would be back in the possession of the people who hold it today. What arguments can you give to support this idea? What arguments can you give to refute it?

2.   Forcese (1997:215) states that "employers can, if obliged, produce jobs as well as products. Educational institutions, if obliged, can generate mobility. Political parties, if obliged, can legislate benefits." Assess the implications of "obliging" employers, educational institutions, and political parties to do these things.

3.   Assess the implications of Canada's immediate adoption of a poverty reduction strategy like the one introduced in this chapter.

PEARSON

Explore the topics covered in this chapter at **www.mysockit.com** using the access provided with this text. Interactive resources for studying include video clips, practice tests, learning objectives, and Internet resources.

RACISM AND ETHNIC INEQUALITY

3

[About 30 years ago] it was hijacked by the UN as the International Day for the Abolition of Apartheid. With the fall of South Africa in 1994, it was renamed "the International Day for the Elimination of Racism," which I interpret really means the International Day for the Elimination of the White Race—as black or Oriental racism is never condemned.

Paul Fromm, director of the Canadian Association for Free Expression, explaining to some of the participants of the March 21, 2009, White Pride Parade in Calgary that the White nationalist movement was reclaiming March 21—the spring equinox, a day long sacred in the cycle of the seasons to the European people. (Stormfront 2009)

I expect that being an interracial couple in Toronto would be a very different experience. Our smaller community seems at times to exoticize my Indianness and at other times to ostracize us as a couple. I remember when we decided to tell my parents about our relationship and felt as though the burden of the world had been lifted from our shoulders. Walking down the street for the first time, hand-in-hand, without fear that we would be seen was like walking on cloud nine. Do you remember? What popped my balloon was that guy on the park bench who yelled out to us, "You fucking White bastard, what are you doing with that Paki woman?" It jarred me into a reality that our differences were not just cultural but also racial, and that we would not only have to deal with the problem of my family's acceptance of you as my husband, but also that of society's acceptance of us. This is the difference that has been the most difficult with which to cope. The cultural stuff like food, language and clothing can be negotiated. But racism is something not so easily negotiated.

Bina Mehta in a dialogue with her husband, Kevin Spooner (2000:155)

Racism is like a fleet-footed bed bug that runs for cover under a sweet-smelling duvet stuffed with politeness and tolerance for multiculturalism. . . . [As a result] Canadians are quick to point out what we of mixed race are not—we are not white and we are not black—but they don't tell us what we are. . . . This is the quintessential Canada: the True North, Proud and Vague.

Lawrence Hill, award-winning Canadian novelist and memoirist, in 2001, on what it means to be Black and White in Canada

We looked around at the other women at the table. Nobody said hello. They looked and I looked back. . . . We sat and we waited. The other women talked amongst themselves in what resembled a huddle. They glanced furtively in our direction. We sat and waited—I watched. Whispers. Whispers coming from the huddle. Whispers that called out, too loud, clanging around in my ears, "Smells like Indians!" Instinctively I breathed in deeply. Did they mean us? I could see them staring at us. My mother's head was down. Tears? I looked back at them. I knew it was us. We moved to another table. We do not speak about what was said about us. We do not recognize them. We cannot give them more power. My anger grows. My mother's spirit staggers. . . . How can they make a judgment about Native people without knowing or caring to know about us?—judgments made in ignorance. I decided that someday I would tell them about things they did not want to hear, about things they were afraid to ask. I decided to talk back. There was nothing to lose. People hated us anyway.

Valerie Bedassigae Pheasant recollecting "growing up different" in Canada (2001:39–40)

"We're all the same. Just because you're Black doesn't matter." I realized there was a lot more work to do than just explaining my feelings. I was shocked to realize that many of my classmates—professional people living in Canada, one of the most multicultural countries in the world—simply didn't get it. For them, the Canadian Mosaic was not much of a reality. . . . I asked my classmates, "How can I, an African, be the same as you, an Irish immigrant?" . . . "Our experiences are not the same, our lives are not the same, and by God I am thankful that we are not the same." My reaction surprised them.

Gifty Serbeh-Dunn speaking about when she realized that many Canadians had no desire to discuss culture and "race" (Serbeh-Dunn and Dunn 2001:270)

It astonishes and saddens me as a Canadian. . . . I don't think the findings reflect well on Canada at all.

Andrew Grenville, chief research officer for pollster Angus Reid on Canadians' negative biases toward religions other than Christianity (Geddes 2009:21)

As the preceding quotations illustrate, racism in Canada continues unabated in both subtle and overt forms. While many in Canada know that racism is unacceptable, their privileged positions blind them to ways they participate in and perpetuate it. Non-White Canadians, regardless of class position, gender, sexual orientation, ability, age, size, educational level, or occupation, may experience prejudice and discrimination on any given day in what is supposed to be a multicultural society. We know from experience that right now many of you suspect that we are non-White people writing this, because our socialization in Canada teaches us that issues of racialized prejudice and discrimination (racism) are not White issues, that they are issues for Indigenous people or so-called visible minorities only. We are White people, and therefore are every bit as implicated in the racism we are speaking about in this chapter as most of the readers. This chapter will not only discuss many of the manifestations of racist discrimination in Canada but will also raise issues of privilege and dominance and examine possibilities for change.

As described in Chapter 1, *discrimination* is the actions or practices of dominant group members that have a harmful impact on members of subordinate groups (Feagin and Feagin 1999). Like many other social problems, racialized and ethnic discrimination signals a discrepancy between the ideals and realities of Canadian society today. While equality and freedom for all—regardless of country of origin, skin colour, creed, or language—are stated ideals of this country, many subordinate group members experience oppression based on racializing factors, regardless of their other statuses.

RACISM AND ETHNIC INEQUALITY AS A SOCIAL PROBLEM

A decade into the 21st century, racism is still among the most divisive social problems facing Canada. At the same time, sociologists such as William J. Wilson (1996) suggest that we all—regardless of racialized or ethnic background—share certain common interests and concerns that cross "race" and class boundaries. Some of the problems are unemployment and job insecurity, declining real wages, escalating medical and housing costs, a scarcity of good-quality child-care programs, worries about the quality of public education, and violence in many neighbourhoods. From this perspective, racialized and ethnic inequality is a problem for everyone, not only for people "of colour." Additionally, all people can be allies in working toward the elimination of racism. While the anti-racism torch has been

lit and carried by non-White people for many years in Canada, it is time for White people to exercise some of their considerable privilege to join this campaign. Who better to speak out against racism than those who benefit most from it? Who better than those who are viewed as credible sources (as opposed to those viewed as "whining special-interest groups") to take up this discussion publicly and to press for the necessary changes? Changes for the better have already been made, and there is no doubt, despite backlash, that they will continue. The process of change can, however, move more quickly when alliances across difference are forged.

What Are Ethnicity, "Race," and Racialization?

In Canada, the terms *ethnicity* and *"race"* are often used interchangeably, while *racialization* is a term many people have never heard of. It is useful, therefore, to define these concepts at the outset. In this country, we talk mainly of "ethnicity," and Statistics Canada censuses have historically collected data based primarily on ethnic group. An **ethnic group** is a category of people who are distinguished, by others or by themselves, on the basis of cultural or nationality characteristics (Feagin and Feagin 1999). These can include language, country of origin, and adherence to a culture. Briefly stated, members of an ethnic group share five main characteristics: (1) unique cultural traits; (2) a sense of community; (3) a feeling that one's own group is distinct; (4) membership from birth; and (5) a tendency, at least initially, to occupy a distinct geographic area (such as a Chinatown, Little Italy, or Greektown). "White ethnics," such as Norwegian Canadians, Ukrainian Canadians, and Jewish Canadians, are also examples of ethnic groups. Ethnicity can be, and often is, used as a basis to judge an individual or group as inferior or superior. Ethnicity is a contested issue. Some, like sociologist J. Milton Yinger (1994), support a more narrow definition of ethnicity based on three criteria: (1) members of a group must view themselves as distinct; (2) others must view the group as distinct; and (3) group members must participate in collective "activities that have the intent or the effect of affirming their distinctiveness" (Fleras and Elliott 1999:104). Sociologists Augie Fleras and Jean Leonard Elliott (1999) point out, however, that these criteria render invisible the most dominant group in Canada—White Canadians—a conclusion they find problematic. It is problematic to assert that most members of the dominant group have no ethnicity. It presents White existence as a neutral standard and masks the ethnicized nature of our institutions, practices, and beliefs (see Box 3.2 on page 67). Moreover, it suggests that ethnicity is really a euphemism for "minority group," which again puts White experience at the centre, a standard against which "others" (e.g., non-White ethnics) are measured. Fleras and Elliott (1999:104) caution, "To ignore white ethnicity is to redouble its hegemony by naturalizing whiteness."

Where ethnic groups are defined on the basis of cultural or nationality characteristics, sociologists note that racialized groups are usually defined on the basis of alleged physical characteristics. As with ethnicity and gender, sociologists view "race" as a **social construct**—the classification of people based on social and political values—rather than as a biological given (see Omi and Winant 1994). However, because physical features such as skin colour, hair texture, or eye shape are often used to determine "race," many people believe that "race" stems from real and immutable genetic differences, as opposed to subjective and arbitrary perceptions of differences—an important distinction. As the Thomas Theorum so aptly reminds us, "if a situation is perceived as real, it *is* real in its consequences." In humans, genetic differences by population do not exist—we share a generalized gene pool. The only "race" that exists with regard to humans is the "human race," or human species. Socio-culturally, however, the concept of race has been and continues to be salient. European, Chinese, and Arab people were active in attempting to classify humans into racialized groups as early as the 15th century, although Europeans became the first to use "science" to legitimate and popularize race as a classification system (Fleras and Elliott 1999). Several authors suggest that popular use of the concept of race stems from the need to justify slavery and/or capitalist exploitation (Fields 1990; Johnson 2006). Canadian political scientist Grace-Edward Galabuzi notes that while arguments like these are compelling, and while the definitions of "races" have been fluid (for example, the Irish, along with several other European ethnic groups, were often described as "Black" or "Negro" by writers like John Beddoe and Robert Knox in the middle and late 1800s), the use of "race" as a means to differentiate some "other" dates back to ancient times, pre-dating both capitalism anywhere and the slave trade in the United States (2006).

In contrast to an attempted biological definition of "race," sociologists define a **racialized group** as a category of people who have been singled out, by others or themselves, as inferior or superior on the basis of subjectively selected physical characteristics such as skin colour, hair texture, and eye shape. Blacks, Whites, Asians, and Aboriginals are all examples of categories of people who have been racialized. Racialization is therefore a process that occurs to or with a group in that it becomes "racialized," or comes to be seen as having certain distinct traits that are supposed to mean something. In addition to persistent efforts to classify people along "racial" lines despite the continued lack of biological substantiation, it is in the definition and ranking of traits where racism can be seen, because definitions applied to certain features or characteristics are completely arbitrary: they vary across cultures and change over time. This is not the same as saying "race" doesn't matter. Race does matter, not because of innate differences between people, but because racialized individuals and groups have been treated as though certain characteristics matter in certain ways (discussed in Box 3.2). As Grace-Edward Galabuzi explains, "The process of racialization therefore involves the construction of racial categories as real, but also unequal, for purposes that impact the economic, social and political composition of a society . . . and has led to differential treatment and outcomes in Canada [for racialized groups]" (2006:34).

Historical and Political Roots of "Race"

Fleras and Elliott (1999:47) define "race" as the classification of people into categories on the basis of preconceived attributes; each group is defined as different by virtue of predetermined properties that are seen as fixed and permanent because of real or alleged characteristics.

Several classification schemes were developed from the 1700s onward, beginning with Swedish naturalist Carl von Linne's (Linnaeus') four-category scheme from 1735. Others since have come up, with anywhere from 30 to 150 categories (Fleras and Elliott 1999). The best known of these typologies is the one still often employed today: Mongoloid (for Yellow people), Caucasoid (for White people), and Negroid (for Black people). It is curious that this three-category typology has remained so stubbornly in our lexicon when there are such serious flaws with its use, not the least of which is, under which category do we classify Red people or Brown people? Several other arguments against the use of "racial" typologies deserve mention. Discrete boundaries between "races" are indefinable and, hence, arbitrary. "Racial" purity is a myth. The selection of traits defined as meaningful in some way is completely arbitrary. Why skin colour, for example, and not eye colour or length of big toe or shape of ear? It is important to understand that there is more variation on any criterion within a supposed race than between "races"; for example, there are more variations in skin tone within any racialized grouping than between two racialized groupings.

The politics of race are hotly debated and highly divisive because people who are attached to racial classifications often attempt to "rank diversity along an ascending/descending order," with implicit and explicit messages about concomitant superiority or inferiority (Fleras and Elliott 1999:49). Others acknowledge that racialization is what is significant and not the socially constructed notion of race. In any case, no one disputes the significance of the concept in justifying or legitimating ways of treating people. The concept of "race" has historically been used to justify inequitable treatment—sometimes economic and social disadvantage, sometimes death—in all cases, not contributing anything satisfactory to our understanding of human behaviour. As summarized by Fleras and Elliott (1999:36), "Race matters because people perceive others to be different and rely on these perceptions to justify unequal treatment and condone indifference."

The Meaning of Majority and Minority Groups

When sociologists use the terms *majority group* and *minority group,* they are referring to power differentials among groups, not to the numerical sense in which the words *majority* and *minority* are generally used. A **majority (or dominant) group** is one that is advantaged and has superior access to resources and rights in a society (Feagin and Feagin 1999). Majority groups often are determined on the basis of racialized factors or

ethnicity, but they can also be determined on the basis of gender, sexual orientation, class, age, or physical ability. A **minority (or subordinate) group** is one whose members, because of supposed physical or cultural characteristics, are disadvantaged and subjected to negative discriminatory treatment by the majority group and regard themselves as objects of collective discrimination (Wirth 1945). In Canada, people "of colour," all women, people with disabilities, gay men, lesbians, and trans people tend to be considered minority group members, regardless of their proportion in the overall population. The term "minority" is formally applied to non-White people in Canada, as in the official government category "visible minority." This label, Grace-Edward Galabuzi (2006:31) contends,

> implies the imposition of an inferior status. They are often set apart by the majority group as incompetent, abnormal or dangerous because of differences pertaining to race, gender, culture and religion. Majority or dominant groups use these differences to distance themselves from minorities for the purposes of acquiring or maintaining privilege and power.

White Privilege and Internalized Dominance

In Canada, the racialized and ethnic majority group is associated with *White privilege*—privilege that accrues to the people who have "white" skin, trace their ancestry to Northern and Western Europe, and think of themselves as European Canadians or WASPs (White Anglo-Saxon Protestants). Women's studies scholar Peggy McIntosh (1995:76–77) describes White privilege as

> an invisible package of unearned assets that I can count on cashing in each day, but about which I was "meant" to remain oblivious. White privilege is like an invisible weightless knapsack of special provisions, assurances, maps, guides, codebooks, passports, visas, clothes, compass, emergency gear, and blank cheques.

In a paper called "Deconstructing Whiteness," Gabriel Bedard (2000:45) makes the point that "in Canada, Whiteness holds political, economic and moral power." In addition, Whiteness is a condition that White people every day can count on to ease their lives *because* they are White. In general, having "white" skin in Canada confers two overarching benefits: the invisibility and normalization of privilege and the choice of whether or not to support the struggle against racialized oppression (Wildman and Davis 2002). The normalization of privilege means that characteristics and attributes associated with Whiteness or White people's cultures are viewed as the standard, as the "normal" way of doing things. Normalization of privilege is manifested when all members of a society are judged against the characteristics or attributes of those who are privileged, and typically this is seen as a neutral process—the standard is typically invisible to those who do the judging. Objectivity is the dominant group's subjectivity. In this system, when people—usually those who are most like the privileged norm—succeed, it is seen as the result of individual effort or merit, not due to any invisible or unearned privilege (Wildman and Davis 2002:93). Janet Sawyer (1989) called this **"internalized dominance"**—all the ways that White people learn they are normal, feel included, and do not think of themselves as "other" or "different." White people carry this privilege around with them at all times, everywhere they go, and they are generally unaware of it. Sawyer (1989:23) concludes a discussion of internalized dominance by saying,

> In any way we are in a dominant group, we have been taught to internalize our own dominance. That is not our fault. It does not mean we are bad people. It does mean that our learned values, assumptions and behaviours are actively hurting other people. It does mean that it is our responsibility to change.

The second benefit conferred on people with "white" skin is having the choice about whether to work against oppression. If White people choose, they do not have to engage in working against racist oppression. This privilege is commonly exercised as silence when witnessing racist behaviour or hearing racist comments. As legal scholars Stephanie Wildman and Adrienne D. Davis (2002:94) conclude, "Privilege is not visible to its holder; it is merely there, a part of the world, a way of life, simply the way things are. Others have a *lack,* an absence, a deficiency." Most White Canadians are unaware of the benefits that they derive from White privilege (see Bishop 2002; Johnson 2006; McIntosh 1995; Rothenberg 2008; Wellman 1993).

What is also true is that many White people in Canada suffer from a clear lack of privilege, associated with class, gender, ability, age, and/or sexual orientation or preference. What White privilege does for people who experience oppression on other measures is reflect one place where they are not discriminated against in a White-dominant society. Non-White people may experience gendered oppression or be impoverished and *also* have to contend with racism, the kind of multiple jeopardy or intersectionality discussed elsewhere in this chapter and text. Nevertheless, the advantage/disadvantage and power/exploitation relationships of majority and minority groups in this country are deeply rooted in patterns of prejudice and discrimination.

RACISM, PREJUDICE, AND DISCRIMINATION

Racism is a set of attitudes, beliefs, and practices used to justify the superior treatment of one racialized or ethnic group and the inferior treatment of another racialized or ethnic group. In sociology, racism is sometimes referred to as White racism. *White racism* refers to socially organized attitudes, ideas, and practices that deny Indigenous people and people "of colour" the dignity, opportunities, freedoms, and rewards that are typically available to White Canadians (Feagin and Vera 1995:7). From this perspective, Indigenous people and people "of colour" pay a direct, heavy, and immediately painful price for racism, while White discriminators pay an indirect and seldom-recognized price.

Prejudice is a negative attitude about people based on such characteristics as racialization, gender, age, religion, or sexual orientation (Allport 1958). If we think of prejudice as a set of negative attitudes toward members of another group simply because they belong to that group, we quickly realize that all people have prejudices, whether or not they acknowledge them. Prejudice is rooted in **ethnocentrism**—the assumption that one's own group and way of life are superior to all others. For example, most school children are taught that their own school and country are the best. Singing the national anthem is a form of *positive ethnocentrism.* However, *negative ethnocentrism* can result if individuals come to believe, because of constant emphasis on the superiority or "normalcy" of their own group or nation, that other groups or nations are inferior and should be treated accordingly (Feagin and Feagin 1999). Negative ethnocentrism is manifested in stereotypes that adversely affect many people.

Stereotypes are fixed and distorted generalizations about the appearance, behaviour, or other characteristics of all members of a particular group. Stereotypes are rigid perceptions that are believed to be true for all members of a group, even in the face of contradictory evidence. They ignore individual differences and specific situations (Speier 1991). Stereotypes should be distinguished from generalizations. **Generalizations** are ideas held about a group of people that are open to revision or change and that can be rejected entirely at any time. Everyone generalizes——it is an efficient way to organize our experiences and a useful method of applying information from situation to situation without having to relearn it every time (Speier 1991). Stereotyping often leads to discrimination, while generalizing does not.

Discrimination may be carried out by individuals acting on their own or by individuals operating within the context of large-scale organizations or institutions, such as schools, corporations, and government agencies. **Individual discrimination** consists of one-on-one acts by members of the dominant group that harm members of the subordinate group or their property (Carmichael and Hamilton 1967). Individual discrimination results from the prejudices and discriminatory actions of bigoted people who target one or more subordinate group members. The taxi driver who refuses to pick up passengers who are members of Indigenous groups in Canada is practising individual discrimination. The neo-Nazi member of an organized racist group who paints a swastika on a synagogue is practising individual discrimination. Another common example in Canada involves the treatment of non-White-looking Canadians, who, regardless of how many generations their families have been in Canada, and who may even be of mixed ethnic origins, are assumed to be from somewhere other than Canada, in ways White-looking Canadians are not. Greg Taylor (2000:61), a man with a White mother and Black father, recollects a fairly typical experience he had growing up in eastern Ontario:

I was playing at a soccer game at a local high school in Grade 10 or 11 and developed what I thought was a friendly competitive rivalry between myself and the guy on their team I was always

paired up against. This happens a lot and generally isn't much of a big deal. Anyway, this other guy decides to increase the competition by elbowing me. I (because I hate conflict) started walking away. To my back he says to me: "Why don't you go back to your own fucking country, you fucking nigger?" . . . I always thought it was interesting that he told me to go back to my own country. Where would that be exactly, if not Canada? This is my country and I belong here as much as he does.

Additionally, people who embody mixed racialized or ethnic backgrounds and who look visibly non-White are often asked by strangers, "Where are you from?" The desired response that is being sought is one that differs from "from Canada" or "from Winnipeg." The desired response is one that emphasizes the person's "exoticness" (e.g., she or he should be from a culturally "different" and non-White nation) and, in the bargain, revokes her or his claims to Canadianness (Taylor 2008). Canadian educator Leanne Taylor (2008:86) notes that "the more that mixed-race identities challenge the norms of what is understood as 'Canadian,' the more mixed-race people will be positioned as doubly different, doubly strange, and doubly foreign."

In contrast to individual discrimination, **institutional discrimination** consists of the day-to-day practices of organizations and institutions that have a harmful impact on members of subordinate groups. For example, many mortgage companies are more likely to make loans to White people than to people "of colour" or to members of Indigenous groups (see Squires 1994). Institutional discrimination is carried out by the individuals who implement policies and procedures that result in negative and differential treatment of subordinate group members. Jewish immigrants in the late 1800s experienced institutional discrimination in accommodations and employment. Signs in hotel windows often read "No Jews Allowed," and many "help wanted" advertisements stated "Christians Only" (Levine 1992:55). Such practices are referred to as **anti-Semitism**—prejudice and discriminatory behaviour directed at Jews. Anti-Semitism is not the same as racism, although both have to do with prejudice and discrimination against a group of people presumed to have certain characteristics.

Anti-Semitism is one of the longest-standing recorded forms of discrimination in history. Today, in Canada and throughout the world, discrimination against Jews is often carried out in the destruction and defacing of property, as this photo illustrates, and in the distribution of hate propaganda.

Anti-Semitism is one of the longest-standing forms of discrimination recorded in history (Fleras and Elliott 1999). A little-known fact about Canada is that in 1939, authorities refused to admit to Canada, as refugees, 900 German Jews who were fleeing the Holocaust. They were forced to return to Nazi Germany, where many were imprisoned and killed in concentration camps. In Toronto, Jews (and dogs) were disallowed public beach access at Lake Ontario. Public signage warning Jews (and Catholics) not to apply for police work was posted by the Metropolitan Toronto Police Force, and many other types of employment and education in Canada were closed to Jews (see Abella 1989; Abella and Troper 1991). Today, discrimination against Jews is often carried out through the destruction and defacing of property and the distribution of hate propaganda, increasingly over the Internet. Based on the pernicious history of intolerance and overt discrimination against Jews in

Canada, there is a long-standing debate about whether or not anti-Semitism should be taken up under the anti-racism banner. In defence of keeping the issues separate, but co-operating as allies with common interests, activist Joshua Goldberg (1998), a White Jew, wrote in correspondence to a friend, "Solidarity is not built on pretending we all experience the same struggles. As a white Jew, I get all the race-based privileges afforded Gentile white people." While this is no doubt true, Jewish people today still experience being on the receiving end of negative stereotyping, prejudice, and discrimination. In fact, with the upsurge of organized racist activity around the world, Jews are active targets of virulent hatred. In addition, they are often disbelieved when they try to raise issues of anti-Semitism. Short (1991:37), for example, states that even "anti-racists appear to have eschewed any interest in anti-Semitism." Reasons for the neglect of anti-Semitism in anti-racist work may be remnants of anti-Semitism among those who are active anti-racists or a belief in the stereotype of Jews as powerful people in society who are therefore not subject to economic and educational disadvantage in the same ways that people "of colour" (Jewish or not) or Indigenous people are. Racism and anti-Semitism come from different histories of oppression: colonization and slavery on the one hand and expulsion and persecution on the other.

In all anti-oppression work, it is important to acknowledge people's distinct histories and distinct struggles and not become complicit in furthering people's oppression through competition. Isobel Yrigoyei, a student of professor bell hooks, wrote,

> We are not equally oppressed. There is no joy in this. We must speak from within us, our own experiences, our own oppressions—taking someone else's oppression is nothing to feel proud of. We should never speak for that which we have not felt. (in hooks 1984:57)

This last point speaks also to the issue of analogizing as a way of unintentionally furthering the oppression of people as we try to understand their situations. Legal scholars Tina Grillo and Stephanie Wildman (1996:86) talk about the contradictory use of analogies as both "the key to greater comprehension and the danger of false understanding." Trying to understand another's experience by comparing it with an experience one has had is common. This can ease the process of comprehension and pave the way for greater understanding. It can also, however, perpetuate existing relations of domination and, thus, cause more pain by centring on and shifting the focus back to the analogizer's issues or by taking over or denying the existence of pain through the analogizer's belief that she or he understands the pain the other is experiencing. As Grillo and Wildman (1996:98) conclude,

> The use of analogy exacerbates this natural desire to have our own struggles receive recognition. For if we can convince ourselves that another's experience is "just like" ours, we are then exempt from having fully to comprehend that experience.

A final type of institutional discrimination that deserves mention occurs in what American anti-racism trainer and diversity consultant Byron Kunisawa (1996) refers to as an "institutional design of omission." Kunisawa points out that the design of the whole range of systems, from education to health care and not-for-profit organizations, government, and judicial systems, reflects the needs, values, practices, and priorities of those who created them. Members of every group in society were not consulted. Their needs and priorities were not considered. It may have nothing to do with intentional exclusion but rather may reflect the (racist) protocols and values consistent with the era in which the systems were developed. Kunisawa contributes to understanding and overcoming racism by pointing out that we have never actually dealt with the exclusionary nature of the system design. Rather, we attempt to remedy situations by "adding on" another piece. For example, in his model Institutional Designs of Omission (see Figure 3.1), Kunisawa shows, in phase one, how a system or an organization gets designed by people who represent 70 percent of the population but who *think* they represent 100 percent. In phase two, those left out of the original design want inclusion. The way of balancing people's demands for inclusion is to create separate systems, or add-ons, with the belief that these add-ons will sufficiently meet the needs of those previously excluded. The add-ons do not, however, because people are still not included in the original or "mainstream" systems. People are still set apart and, given how pervasive racism is, not treated equally. What we need to do, according to Kunisawa, is work toward changing the fundamental design criteria of the organizations and systems we take part in by including historically marginalized people in their redesign. This

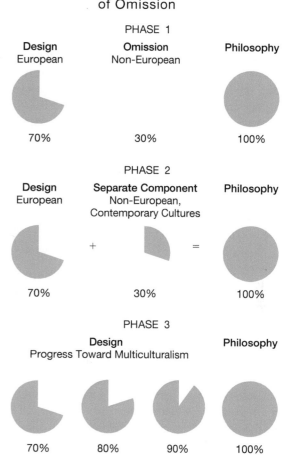

FIGURE 3.1   Institutional Designs of Omission

Source: Byron Kunisawa, www.byronkunisawa.com. Reproduced by permission of the author.

Historically, Canada and the United States have maintained a philosophy of equality and opportunity. However, our systems and institutions have never had the design to match this philosophy. The three phases illustrated here reflect the past and present system designs and future design for systemic change. If we are going to become truly multicultural nations in the 21st century, we will need to work toward the model reflected in phase three.

process will take time but will yield an inclusive and truly multicultural society; however, we still have a long way to go when one considers how little progress has been made historically.

Historical Roots of Racism

As Europeans participated in campaigns to expand their empires, they increasingly came into contact with "exotic others." Their responses to these others ranged from benign curiosity to outright hostility. As a way of making sense of the diversity they encountered, they employed the pseudoscientific "race" theories that were gaining a foothold in society. It was the time known as the Enlightenment, and people searched for rational and scientific ways to classify and explain their worlds. Using the legitimacy of the scientific enterprise (but arbitrary criteria), these theories explained that some people were superior to others. That these systems of classification also aided Europeans in colonization, by justifying the exploitation and domination of people all over the world, is not accidental:

> Europeans not only racialized the "other" as unassimilable or as a threat; they also racialized themselves by defining Europeans as a group held together by the inevitable superiority of white to non-white. (Fleras and Elliott 1999:53)

The most common doctrine of "racial" supremacy, widely accepted in the first part of the 19th century, was what later became known as social Darwinism (Fleras and Elliott 1999). Notions of "survival of the fittest," the "struggle for survival," and unilinear evolution legitimized colonial expansion with the rationale that those who were better adapted would thrive; those less adapted would become extinct. As with all who have the power to define, the Europeans defined themselves at the top of the evolutionary hierarchy, with all others ranked according to how closely they emulated European civilization and Christianity. Therefore, colonialism was viewed as a "natural" and inevitable process, just like capitalism and imperialism. Colonialists saw themselves as assisting those whom they were exploiting in their evolutionary progression from savagery through barbarism to civilization. Civilization meant European and Christian civilization, of course. This doctrine added legitimacy to many practices, such as slavery and forced labour, the appropriation of land and resources, and the destruction of whole cultures and ways of life.

The Many Forms of Racism in Canadian Society

Racism is not a uniform process. It has many permutations and varieties, demonstrating its complexity and multidimensionality. Several authors have created a typology of the forms of racism in Canada as a way of pointing to the necessity for a range of diverse solutions to the problem (Fleras 2001; Fleras and Elliott 1999; Henry et al. 2000). Fleras and Elliott (1999) outline three broad categories of racism, each with specific subcategories: interpersonal, which includes redneck racism and polite racism; institutional, which includes systematic racism and systemic racism; and societal, which includes everyday racism and cultural racism.

Interpersonal Racism

Interpersonal racism occurs between individuals and is directed at an individual because of who or what he or she stands for. The typical depiction of a racist is the redneck racist whose racism is explicit and who generally is not intimidated by the label "racist." This is the "Bubba" stereotype of our collective view. "Bubba" participates in highly personalized attacks on others, such as name calling or racial slurs, based on the notion that his or her culture is superior. An example of redneck racism is be the type of racism exhibited by members of White supremacist groups in Canada, such as the Heritage Front or the White nationalist Aryan Guard, which parades in Calgary each year on March 21 to protest the International Day for the Elimination of Racism (see Box 3.1 for more discussion).

The use of the "Bubba" stereotype in our cultural view can be dangerous for two reasons. First, it is a stereotype, and as such can be misleading and inaccurate and can be applied to people erroneously. Second, and more subtle, is the fact that if we define racism as only the type of behaviour exhibited by "Bubba," we miss the majority of racism that goes on in Canada; the stereotype provides a cover for other harmful attitudes and practices. Human rights legislation and the *Charter of Rights and Freedoms* have done a great deal to erode redneck racism in public discourse. In its place, due to increasing risks of legal and social consequences, polite racism has evolved. *Polite racism* refers to the ways that people may couch criticisms of racialized others in bland tones or use language that appears non-prejudicial on the surface. Polite racists are often good at phrasing a sentence so as to deliver a racist message to anyone looking for it but make it obscure enough to enable the deliverer to deny that there was any racist intent. Unsurprisingly perhaps, polite racists tend to be those with higher education. Polite racism can be difficult to prove and therefore difficult to combat. An example is when a member of a

BOX 3.1   Organized Racism—Canada's Links to a World of Hatred

Organized racist groups have been increasing in membership around the world since the fall of apartheid in South Africa and the decline of communism in Europe and the former U.S.S.R. Racist groups worldwide have fairly easily traceable links to a number of networks and groups in Canada. While it may be surprising to many Canadians, the history of organized hate groups in Canada is, unfortunately, a long one. The Ku Klux Klan (KKK), which began as a U.S. group, became a thriving organization in Canada in the 1920s and 1930s and has recently resurfaced here. Along with the KKK, however, we have seen the growth and proliferation of more of these groups, both in Canada and abroad. British Columbia and Ontario experience the highest rates of organized racist activity.

Organized racism is often referred to as neo-fascism, neo-Nazism, White supremacism, or organized hate. It differs from other forms of Canadian racism in both its virulence and its intent. Organized racists differ from regular racists in that their hatred of non-White people, and of Jews in particular, coupled with their active membership in a hate group, gives them a predisposition to *act* on their racism by committing violence, publishing messages of hate, recruiting others to their cause, and participating in a host of other activities.

The intent of the many hate groups ranges, but they have one basic activity in common—to rid the province/state/nation/world of "undesirables"; to fight against what they view as the "racial takeover" of "their" geographic space. As anthropologists Frances Henry and Carol Tator, lawyer Winston Mattis, and race relations and diversity specialist Tim Rees (2000:99) state, "All these groups share an ideology that supports the view that the Aryan, or White, 'race' is superior to all others, morally, intellectually, and culturally, and that it is Whites' manifest destiny to dominate society." Also, as the term implies, organized racism is an organized activity. Typically, the group has a designated leadership and a well-established hierarchy of followers. Most Canadians are completely unaware of this kind of organized activity. Those who are aware of the existence of such groups tend to dismiss their adherents as "nutters" or people on the fringe. Contrary to what many people believe or want to believe about these groups, they do exist, they have resources, and they are dangerous. While many of us do not wish to believe it when a 65-year-old Sikh janitor is beaten to death at a Surrey, B.C., temple, or an elderly Calgary journalist is beaten savagely in a surprise attack at his home, or Jewish synagogues are defaced across Canada, or burning crosses are placed on the lawns of people believed to be non-White or Jewish, it is difficult to discount White supremacists as harmless.

Augie Fleras and J.L. Elliott reported that in Canada there may only be "1500 hard-core supremacists" (1999:80) who are

members of a proliferation of groups, including known racist organizations such as the KKK, the Western Guard, the Aryan Nations, White Aryan Resistance, the Heritage Front, the Nationalist Party, Posse Comitatus, and the Church of the Creator, and alleged groups such as the Canadian Free Speech League, the Council on Public Affairs, and the Coalition for Humanistic British Canada. Information about organized hate groups in Canada is now easy to access through the Internet and telephone call-in lines, such as Canadian Liberty Net, although organized hate groups still carry out physical recruitment drives as well.

The question is, What do these people want? Different groups have different aims. Some of the more radical right-wing groups desire the downfall of the Canadian state (viewed as traitorous because it has allowed non-White and Jewish immigration) and political control over a bounded territory (a sovereign "Aryan Nation") completely free of non-White and Jewish people and of "race traitors" (those who associate with non-Whites or Jews). For many, violence is an acceptable means for achieving these ends, and in preparation for the coming "race war," paramilitary training is carried out in several areas of Canada (for example, northern British Columbia, Alberta, and Ontario) and at some "Whites only" compounds in the United States (Hayden Lake, Idaho, and other areas in the southern States, for example).

Organized hate groups adhere to an extreme right-wing and very often Christian ideology. Sociologist Stanley Barrett (1991:90–91) reports that the main tenets of the White supremacist's ideology are "anticommunism, antiliberalism, racism and anti-Semitism" and a belief that the "survival of the whites is precarious." Barrett (1991:90) also points out that, in contrast to their views of Jewish people, who are supposedly responsible for all of society's ills, "White supremacists see themselves as the saviours of the white race [sic] and Western Christian civilization." In this way, many right-wing racists interpret their racism as a positive force rather than a negative one, "a 'natural' preference of people for their own race and repugnance for other races" (Barrett 1991:95). Many believe that it will take an extreme incident, like the near-extinction of Whites, before White people will wake up and realize they need to join supremacist groups and "take back" their nation. While some are content to wait for the majority of Whites to "wake up," many others take matters into their own hands by actively recruiting members.

Recruitment into hate groups takes many forms. It may be a simple pamphlet left in a mall washroom or on a city bus seat. It may be a racist comic book given out to elementary school children. It can be a book table at a public lecture. It can be a personal visit to a person's home. It can be through political platforms in legitimate democratic elections. (Wolfgang Droege, a now deceased Heritage Front leader, ran in a municipal election in Scarborough, Ontario, in 1993 and won an alarming 14 percent of the vote. It is worth noting that Droege, a very public racist figure, was murdered outside his apartment in April 2005.) Recruitment can be through music. For example, the alternative hate rock band RaHoWa (which stands for Racial Holy War) was managed by George Burdi, who was also the band's lyricist and vocalist. Burdi was a self-proclaimed leader of the violent Church of the Creator and a Heritage Front member. Bands like RaHoWa and others, such as Odin's Law from Surrey, B.C., market and distribute their hate-filled lyrics worldwide. George Burdi, whose real name is George Eric Hawthorne, recently left the White Power movement after a stint in prison for assault. He is now married to a non-White woman, is a Buddhist, and is involved in a multiethnic music group called Novacosm. His comments in a recent interview are indicative of his shift:

George Burdi

My advice for today's [White Power] musicians is to remember that every lyric you ever write will be read by your children someday, that once it's out there you can't take it back, and that you have to speak out to the kids who listen to your records, keep them out of jail, and make the concerts more family oriented and culturally uplifting. Focus more on what you love, not what you hate. Also do not concentrate only on your racial identity, for can "what is impermanent, changeable, and non-substantial be considered thus: this is mine, this am I, this is my self?" (http://www.vanguardnewsnetwork.com/2004b/42704burdiinterview.htm, retrieved June 1, 2006)

While membership in organized hate groups tends to increase during economic recessions, it is by no means restricted to the working class. On the contrary, although much of the membership may be from economically disenfranchised classes, leadership and financial support are often from middle- and upper-middle classes (CTV 1995). As Barrett (1991:87) concludes, "It is improbable that such organizations could exist unless there was some degree of compatibility with the institutional fabric of the larger society." This comment may explain how it is that organized hate groups are able to access tolerance from many liberal thinkers who otherwise claim to be non-racist. The racists play on people's deep emotions about personal freedoms and democracy. Making a heartfelt case for an issue such as freedom of speech, organized racists say that even if most Canadians do not like exactly what they are saying, as Canadians they should have the right not to be censored. Fleras and Elliott (1999:80) point out that because of a deeply rooted history of racism and the ability of organized racists to hide behind this liberal facade, extremists may always have the ability to undermine societal values and practices. Leo Adler, the director of national affairs for a Toronto Jewish human rights organization, notes that there are approximately 6000 Internet sites operating today that promote hatred. Fleras argued recently that even though "there is no way of gauging the number of hardcore supremacists in Canada . . . even a small number of racist ideologues have the potential to destabilize a society where prejudice is pervasive and the economy is sputtering" (2010:74).

What do you think? Do you think people in Canada should have the freedom to publicly express views and messages of hatred against groups?

dominant group makes a comment to another member of a dominant group about a subordinate group that he or she would not make, knowingly, to a member of the subordinate group in question. The comment is often carefully benign on the surface, to allow room for the denial of racism, but the receptor of the comment *knows* what the thrust of the comment is.

Institutional Racism

Institutional racism refers to various organizational practices, policies, and procedures that discriminate, either purposely or inadvertently. If there is the intent to deny privilege or to exclude, it is referred to as systematic. If not, it is referred to as systemic. *Systemic racism* is embedded in the design of the organization, is formalized, and is legally sanctioned by the state. Discriminatory practices reflect the values of the dominant culture and act to deliberately prevent certain groups from participating in the culture. Examples are the exclusion of Indigenous people and Black Canadians from movie theatres and restaurants until the 1950s, the restricting of the enrolment of Jewish Canadians in Canadian universities in the 1940s, and the disallowing of Japanese Canadians from voting in British Columbia until 1949 (Fleras and Elliott 1999). Indigenous people were only allowed the vote provincially starting between 1949 and 1969 and were disenfranchised federally until 1960.

Systemic racism is also embedded in the organization, procedures, and norms of an organization. It tends to be impersonal and unconscious in that discrimination is unintended but has the effect of discriminating anyway. It occurs because seemingly neutral rules are applied evenly to all, even when this may be inappropriate. The impact is the favouring of certain groups whose members most closely resemble the rule makers while disadvantaging those who are different. An example is the height and weight requirements once used for police recruits in Canada, which inadvertently disallowed most Asians, Indigenous people, and women from participation. A well-publicized example was the headgear policy for the RCMP that stated that members had to wear RCMP-issue headgear. This policy, which was fought and defeated, effectively disenfranchised Sikhs who, for religious reasons, wear a turban.

Societal Racism

Societal racism refers to the generalized, and typically unconscious, patterns of interaction between people that perpetuate a racialized social order. It is part of the general functioning of society and is said to precede other forms of racism (Henry et al. 2000).

Everyday racism refers to general, and seemingly benign, ideas about the relative superiority and inferiority of certain groups. These ideas are widely accepted as normal by dominant group members. The main way that ideas are perpetuated is through language that is held to be neutral. Language, of course, is far from neutral, as through it we socially construct our reality. Words convey images and associations, both positive and negative, that we draw upon to order and imagine our worlds. As Fleras and Elliott (1999:84) point out, "[Language] provides a cultural frame of reference for defining what is desirable and important."

Some examples of everyday racism can be found in the use of colour symbolism (e.g., associating white with good, black with evil) or the use of emotionally loaded terms like "Indian massacres" (Fleras and Elliott 1999:85) or "Islamic terrorist." Everyday racism can be further distinguished into active and passive racism (Henry et al. 2000:55). *Active racism*, according to social psychologist Philomena Essed (1990), includes any act (including the use of language) that is motivated by the intention of excluding or making a person or group feel inferior *because* of his/her/their minority group status. *Passive racism* includes being complicit in another's racism, for example laughing at a racist joke or "not hearing" racist comments (Essed 1990). *Cultural racism* refers to cultural values that reinforce the interest of the dominant group while undermining the interests of subordinate groups. Cultural racism is manifested in the notion that minority groups are acceptable in Canada, as long as they know and understand their place in society and act in ways the dominant majority wants them to. Cultural values support equality, but measures toward ensuring that it happens are resisted. An example can be cultural support for the notion of equal opportunity in employment in all sectors but hostility toward employment equity programs or the *Canadian Employment Equity Act*. This type of racism is discussed in depth in Box 3.2.

SOCIAL PROBLEMS AND SOCIAL POLICY

BOX 3.2   Undermining Democratic Racism in Canada

Most non-White Canadians know that prejudice and discrimination based upon racializing factors are very much alive and well in Canada. While there are many White Canadians who are aware of this fact, there are more who are perplexed when they hear allegations of racism. Pointing to our official multiculturalism policies, our recent hate crimes legislation, our federal employment equity policy, and our *Charter of Rights and Freedoms*, people question how racism can coexist with policies and laws that enshrine people's rights to be culturally and linguistically different from the mainstream. The fact of these liberal democratic policies and laws may be precisely what makes racism in Canada so elusive. Frances Henry and Carol Tator (1999:107) have published a number of articles and books addressing this paradox. In fact, they assert that "social inequality continues to operate and is reproduced and legitimated through the state." Racism in Canada, although often cloaked, is thus made possible by way of a process called "democratic racism."

Democratic racism refers to the tension between two contradictory sets of values and the process enabling them to simultaneously exist (Henry and Tator 1999, 2000; Henry et al. 2000). This is played out in Canada through, on the one hand, ideologies consistent with liberal democracies, with ideals like "justice," "fairness," "equality," "tolerance," "acceptance," and "individual rights"; and, on the other hand, pervasive and widespread racist practices, beliefs, and attitudes. This racism is inherent in, and promoted by, not only individuals but also institutions and the Canadian state itself, through its policies and practices. As Henry and Tator (1999:89–90) state,

> State responses have largely failed to achieve the goal of eliminating or even controlling racial bias and discrimination because racism and notions of racial superiority are deeply embedded in the collective belief system and in the norms and practices of Canadian society.

We typically think of racism as the attitudes and actions of individuals. More dangerous, perhaps, because it is more easily hidden, is racism rooted in our collective belief system that holds up one culture's beliefs, values, norms, and practices as superior and others as inferior. Individuals' attitudes and practices are connected, however, to institutions and the whole system: "Racist attitudes are derivative in nature and grow out of and are sustained by the structures of social relations of which they are a mere reflection" (Henry and Tator 2000:286).

We have developed a set of arguments in Canada that justify and rationalize racism. Philosopher Michel Foucault used the term *discourse* to describe these sets of arguments as a form of communication that is used as a "vehicle for social processes" (1980, quoted in Henry and Tator 2000:291). In deconstructing an overall discourse of domination, Henry and Tator (2000:292–298) outline 12 myths or discourses that support and perpetuate democratic racism. A sample of these is briefly featured below.

The Discourse of Denial: The main assumption underpinning this discourse is that racism simply does not exist here. The systemic nature and embeddedness of racism is ignored. Examples of this discourse include, "Canada is not a racist nation"; "I am not a racist"; "The justice system is not racist."

The Discourse of Equal Opportunity: The point of this discourse is to convey the message that if we treat everyone equally, fairness will follow. The unexplored, ahistorical, and incorrect assumption is that everyone is coming from an 'equivalent place and has an equal opportunity to succeed or fail. This discourse ignores the power and privilege assigned to people based on gender, language, skin colour, sexual orientation, and so on.

The Discourse of Reverse Racism: The main point of this discourse is the assertion that White people are now on the receiving end of oppression and exclusion. Policies and programs that are designed to redress inequities in Canadian society are viewed as anti-democratic and symptomatic of a "creeping totalitarianism" that discriminates against Whites.

After identifying 12 discourses that underlie democratic racism in Canada, Henry and Tator (2000:298) conclude that:

> Many Canadians see themselves as egalitarian and have little difficulty in rejecting the more overt expressions of racism. They may make symbolic gestures of inclusivity. However, beyond these tokenistic efforts, the struggles of people of colour [and Indigenous people] are met with arbitrary use of political, economic, and cultural institutional power in the interest of "maintaining democracy."

Democratic racism plays out at all levels in Canadian society and carries with it many consequences for all citizens. One consequence is a general lack of support for anti-racist or equity initiatives. As an example, employment equity strategies, or affirmative action strategies by employers, are painted in mainstream society as "unfair" and "undemocratic." The argument is based on the idea that these hires are not based on "merit" but rather on some ascribed characteristic such as skin colour, ancestry, or gender. What is conveniently overlooked in this argument is that we have always had precisely this kind of affirmative action—*for members of dominant groups*. When people from dominant groups are no longer automatically preferred or privileged, they cry "unfair," "*reverse* racism," "discrimination," and so on. While, strictly speaking, affirmative action is discriminating and selectively preferring, as an interim strategy it is necessary if we are to build a truly fair and just society based on something other than ascription. This is not to suggest that people hired through employment equity strategies are in any way unqualified. Unfortunately, often a member of a minority group must be many times more qualified than a member of the dominant group in order to be hired. A message of "lack of qualifications" is often the implicit message in these complaints, however, and it needs to be exposed for its underlying racism. We must make an effort, even if temporarily, to redress past exclusion and discrimination. When we have true equity, we will no longer need specific policies and legislation.

Many Canadians seem to resist equity and anti-racist initiatives because it is easier to believe the rhetoric of democratic racism. It is easier to believe that things are running smoothly for us all and to blame the victim when we hear stories that contradict our beliefs. It is easier to do this than to critically question our own deeply held beliefs and value systems because, ultimately, upon examination, if our real practices do not support our stated values, we are placed in an untenable position. If we know about this contradiction and choose to do nothing, it makes us hypocrites; and if we choose to do something, where and how do we begin? Additionally, we may be in the uncomfortable predicament of having to give up some of our invisible and often uncontested privilege. As philosopher Elizabeth Kamarck Minnich (1995:424) noted more than a decade ago, "Most seem to want to give up the harm without giving up the privilege."

Given the pervasive and sometimes subtle nature of democratic racism, it is difficult to know how to approach meaningful change. Henry and colleagues (2000:390–400) offer five strategies as starting points that offer hope that we can work toward

the elimination of racism in Canada. These strategies are the development of reflective skills and practices, changing our responses to allegations of racism, empowering communities to push for peaceful change, monitoring anti-racism initiatives, and emphasizing the roles of major institutions in dealing with racism.

Despite measures that have already been taken in Canada to reduce inequalities based on ethnicity and racialization, they persist at alarming levels. The concept of democratic racism, with its confounding discourses, allows us to understand how it is possible to hold two sets of conflicting values simultaneously. The impact of these contradictions is not merely intellectual but, rather, has serious and derogatory impacts on the real material conditions of people's lives—their abilities to participate equally and be treated equally as citizens in a rich and prosperous land. We must all take action to eliminate racism. Besides being morally and ethically wrong, it is a shocking waste of human potential.

Racism manifests in a diversity of ways. This being so, it is imperative that strategies and measures to combat it be equally diverse and multidimensional.

PERSPECTIVES ON RACIALIZED AND ETHNIC INEQUALITY

Over the course of more than 100 years, sociologists have developed different perspectives to explain why racialized and ethnic inequality occurs and why it persists. Some perspectives focus on sociological factors such as migration, assimilation, conflict, and exploitation, while others focus on more social-psychological factors.

The Symbolic Interactionist Perspective

Related to social-psychological explanations of prejudice and discrimination are theories based on the interactionist perspective. One interactionist approach emphasizes how racialized socialization contributes to feelings of solidarity with one's own racialized or ethnic group and hostility toward all others. *Racialized socialization* is a process of social interaction that contains specific messages and practices concerning the nature of one's racialized or ethnic status as it relates to (1) personal and group identity; (2) inter-group and inter-individual relationships;

and (3) one's position in the social stratification system. Although racialized socialization may occur through direct statements about "race" made by parents, peers, teachers, and others, it may also include indirect modelling behaviours, which occur when children imitate the words and actions of parents and other caregivers (Thornton et al. 1990). Racialized socialization affects how people view themselves, other people, and the world. Here, for example, racialization and ethnic relations scholar and historian Manning Marable (1995:1) describes how racialized socialization makes "race" a prism through which Canadians who are Black or members of other visible minorities view their daily lives:

Black and white. As long as I can remember, the fundamentally defining feature of my life, and the lives of my family, was the stark reality of race. . . . It was the social gravity which set into motion our expectations and emotions, our language and dreams. . . . Race seemed granite-like, fixed and permanent, as the centre of the social universe. The reality of racial discrimination constantly fed the pessimism and doubts that we as Black people felt about the apparent natural order of the world, the inherent unfairness of it all, as well as limiting our hopes for a better life somewhere in the distant future.

Though all groups practise racialized socialization, White racialized socialization emphasizes White "racial" bonding. According to multicultural education scholar Christine E. Sleeter (1996), White racial bonding occurs when White people act in ways that reaffirm the common stance on ethnic or cultural issues and draw "us–them" boundaries, thus perpetuating racism and discrimination. Such people choose to live near other Whites, to socialize with other Whites, and to vote for other Whites, thus maintaining racialized solidarity. Although many Whites do not support racist beliefs, actions, or policies, they fear breaking bonds with other Whites and may simply remain silent in the face of prejudice and discrimination (Sleeter 1996).

The Structural Functionalist Perspective

To functionalists, social order and stability are extremely important for the smooth functioning of society. Consequently, "racial" and ethnic discord, urban unrest, and riots are dysfunctional and must be eliminated or contained. One functionalist perspective focuses on **assimilation**—the process by which members of subordinate racialized and ethnic groups become absorbed into the dominant culture. Functionalists view assimilation as a stabilizing force that minimizes differences that otherwise might result in hostility and violence (Gordon 1964). In its most complete form, assimilation becomes **amalgamation**, a process in which the cultural attributes of diverse racialized or ethnic groups are blended together to form a new society incorporating the unique contributions of each group. Amalgamation occurs when members of dominant and subordinate racialized or ethnic groups intermarry and procreate to produce "mixed-ethnicity" children.

Early assimilation in Canada focused primarily on the Anglo-conformity model, rather than amalgamation. The **Anglo-conformity model** refers to a pattern of assimilation in which members of subordinate racialized/ethnic groups are expected to conform to the culture of the dominant (White) Anglo-Saxon population. Assimilation does not always lead to full social acceptance. For example, many successful members of designated minority groups have been excluded from membership in elite private clubs and parties in the homes of co-workers.

Another functionalist perspective emphasizes **ethnic pluralism**—the coexistence of diverse racialized/ethnic groups with separate identities and cultures within a

society. In a pluralistic society, political and economic systems link diverse groups, but members of some racialized/ethnic groups maintain enough separation from the dominant group to guarantee that their group and ethnic cultural traditions continue (Gordon 1964). Ethnic pluralism is the formal model of ethnic relations in Canadian society; however, Anglo-conformity is such a strong force that pluralism may be more of a myth than a reality for ethnic groups. In Canada, pluralism can take the form of *segregation* because subordinate racialized/ethnic groups have less power and privilege than do members of the dominant group (Marger 1994). **Segregation** is the spatial and social separation of categories of people by racialization, ethnicity, class, gender, religion, or other social characteristics. Some recent sociological studies have found that when high levels of segregation based on racialization are followed by inter-ethnic contact, competition may ensue, which creates the potential for conflict between groups (Olzak et al. 1996).

The Conflict Perspective

Conflict theorists explain racialized and ethnic inequality in terms of economic stratification and access to power. As discussed in Chapter 1, there is more than one conflict perspective. This chapter focuses on the critical-conflict approach, which explains racialized and ethnic inequality in terms of economic stratification and unequal access to power. We will briefly examine class perspectives, split-labour market theory, internal colonialism, and the theory of "racial" formation.

Class perspectives on racialized and ethnic inequality highlight the role of the capitalist class in racialized exploitation. For example, according to sociologist Oliver C. Cox (1948), the primary cause of slavery was the capitalist desire for profit, not racialized prejudice. People were enslaved because, through force, they could be made to do heavy labour and other duties for basically the costs of feeding and housing them. A contemporary class perspective suggests that members of the capitalist class benefit from a split-labour market that promotes racialized divisions among workers and suppresses wages. According to the *split-labour market theory*, the economy is divided into two employment sectors: a primary sector composed of higher-paid workers in more secure jobs and a secondary sector composed of lower-paid workers in jobs that often involve hazardous working conditions and little job security (Bonacich 1972, 1976). Dominant group members are usually employed in primary sector positions; subordinate group members are concentrated in the secondary sector. Workers in the two job sectors tend to have divergent interests and goals because of their different relations to the labour market; therefore, worker solidarity can be difficult to achieve (Bonacich 1972, 1976). Members of the capitalist class benefit from these divisions because workers are less likely to band together and demand pay increases or other beneficial changes in the workplace. Historically, White workers in the primary sector who accepted racist arguments attempted to exclude subordinate group members from higher-paying jobs by barring them from labour unions, lobbying against employment equity, and opposing immigration. Some of these tactics still occur today.

A second critical-conflict perspective examines **internal colonialism**—a process that occurs when members of a racialized/ethnic group are conquered or colonized and forcibly placed under the economic and political control of the dominant group. According to sociologist Robert Blauner (1972), people in groups that have been subjected to internal colonialism remain in subordinate positions in society much longer than do people in groups that voluntarily migrated to this country. For example, Indigenous peoples were forced into subordination when they were colonized by Europeans. Hundreds of culturally and linguistically diverse Indigenous groups lost property, political rights, components of their culture, and often their lives; some Indigenous groups were virtually extinguished as victims of **genocide**—the deliberate, systematic killing of an entire people or nation. Meanwhile, the capitalist class acquired cheap labour and land, frequently through government-sanctioned racialized exploitation (Blauner 1972). The legacy of internal colonialism remains visible today in the number of Indigenous people who live in poverty, particularly those who live on federal reserves, often lacking essential services such as water, electricity, and sewage disposal.

Psychologists Michael Chandler and Christopher Lalonde have been studying Indigenous youth suicide on reserves in Canada, primarily in British Columbia, for over a decade. Studying the wide discrepancy in youth suicide rates—some Indigenous communities have zero youth suicides, while others have rates as high as 800 times the national average—they convincingly

demonstrate that the more protective factors a band has in place, the fewer suicides their community experiences (see Figures 3.2 and 3.3). Chandler and Lalonde note that in British Columbia, more than 90 percent of the suicides by youth occur in only 10 percent of the communities (2004). The protective factors they identify have to do with overcoming the legacy of internal colonialism described above. In terms of factors, they articulate the following:

> We have also demonstrated that bands that are well on their way to preserving or rehabilitating their threatened cultures, and that have met with measurable success in recovering community control over their civic lives (i.e., that, in addition to having taken concrete steps to preserve their cultural past, have achieved a measure of self-government, have effectively militated for title to traditional lands, and have gained a measure of control over their own health, education, child protection and jural systems) suffer no suicides, while those who fail to meet all or most of these standards of self-determination have [significantly higher] youth suicide rates. (2004:111)

The last critical-conflict perspective we will look at is the **theory of racial formation**, which states that the government substantially defines racialized and ethnic relations. From this perspective, racialized bias and discrimination tend to be rooted in government actions, ranging from the passage of "race"-related legislation to imprisonment of members of groups that are believed to be a threat to society. According to sociologists Michael Omi and Howard Winant (1994), governments are responsible for shaping the politics of racialized inequality through actions and policies that have resulted in the unequal treatment of Indigenous people and visible minorities. Immigration legislation, for example, reveals specific racialized biases. Fleras (2010:250), for example, notes that "initial practices regarding whom to let in and whom to keep out could be described as essentially racist in orientation, assimilationist in objective, nativist in content, and exclusionary in outcome." As an example, until the 1960s, Western Europeans were the preferred immigrants, and when immigration was extended to Eastern Europeans, Jewish and Mediterranean people required special permits. Further, Asians of Chinese and Indian origin were only reluctantly admitted during times of capitalist expansion, when the state required large pools

FIGURE 3.2   Suicide Rate by Community Factors

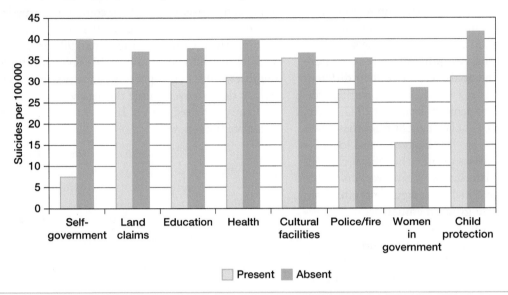

Source: M. Chandler and C. Lalonde, 2004, "Transferring Whose Knowledge? Exchanging Whose Best Practices?: On Knowing about Indigenous Knowledge and Aboriginal Suicide," In J. White, P. Maxim, and D. Beavon (Eds.), Aboriginal Policy Research: Setting the Agenda for Change, *Vol. II (pp. 111–123), Toronto: Thompson Educational Publishing.*

of cheap labour, and even then, only males were permitted to immigrate. Family members were not allowed. Overtly racially selective immigration policies, closely following Canada's nation-building requirements, were in force until the first major revision in 1962. As Canadian sociologist Victor Satzewich (1989:132) notes,

Racism is an ideology imposed from above by those who own the means of production on those who do not: racism acts to mystify social reality, justifies the exploitation of certain groups of people's labour power, and contributes to the maintenance of the status quo.

FIGURE 3.3   Suicide Rate by Number of Factors Present (B.C., 1993 to 2000)

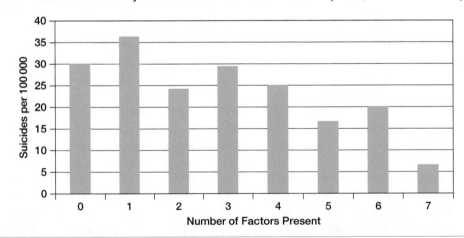

Source: M. Chandler and C. Lalonde, 2004, "Transferring Whose Knowledge? Exchanging Whose Best Practices?: On Knowing about Indigenous Knowledge and Aboriginal Suicide," In J. White, P. Maxim, and D. Beavon (Eds.), Aboriginal Policy Research: Setting the Agenda for Change, *Vol. II (pp. 111–123), Toronto: Thompson Educational Publishing.*

Feminist and Anti-Racist Perspectives

One feminist perspective is based on a critical-conflict perspective and links racialized inequality and gender oppression. **Gendered racism** may be defined as the interactive effect of racism and sexism in exploiting Indigenous women and women "of colour." According to Essed (1991), not all workers are exploited equally by capitalists. For many years, the majority of jobs in the primary sector of the labour market were held by White men, while most people of colour and many White women were employed in secondary sector jobs. Below the secondary sector, in the underground sector of the economy, many Indigenous women and women "of colour" worked as domestic servants and nannies, in sweat shops, or in the sex trade to survive. Work in this underground sector is unregulated, and people who earn their income in it are vulnerable to exploitation by many, including unscrupulous employers, greedy pimps, and corrupt police officers (Amott and Matthaei 1991).

In Canada, anti-racist feminist theorizing—deconstructing the interconnectedness of racism and sexism, colonialism and imperialism—has been engaged in since the 19th century (Dua 1999). Anti-racist feminist theorizing differs from mainstream feminist theorizing: it challenges the notion of a common experience that all women share under capitalism; it focuses on the specific ways that class, gender, *and* ethnicity play out as interconnections. Anti-racist feminist scholar and critical theorist Himani Bannerji (1995:77) points out that "the erasure of the factors 'race,' racism, and continual immigration prevents an adequate understanding of the Canadian economy." Building on this, women's studies scholar Enakshi Dua (1999:21) concludes that "the discourse of race is as 'foundational' to the creation and maintenance of the Canadian political economy as are capitalist relations and patriarchy." Dua (1999:16) outlines three priorities within much of Canadian anti-racist feminist thought: (1) to interrogate feminist theory and practice to assess its complicity in perpetuating racism; (2) to raise questions about ways of theorizing about the connections between gender and racialization; and (3) to continue to document the ways that racialized differences are created and maintained among women.

Many proponents of anti-racist feminism also investigate the impacts of racism on women of colour, examining the ways that gender, racialization, and class intersect, for example, when well-to-do White women employ racialized and poor women from non-industrialized nations to do domestic labour for them on temporary work visas. Other impacts that have been examined are the wages of women of colour and Indigenous women compared to White women's wages and the ways that equity measures for women disproportionately privilege White women relative to non-White women. Some anti-racist feminist theorists have suggested a *standpoint analysis*; that is, beginning theorizing and analysis from the situated standpoint of the person and her experiences—employing a kind of "outsider-within" perspective (Dua 1999:19). However, women's experiences with racialization vary along class lines according to sexual orientation and personal history. Therefore, it is important to account for the whole of a person's identity or locations.

Taking anti-racist feminism a step further, sociologist Daiva Stasiulis (1999) makes a convincing case for feminist intersectional theorizing. Feminist intersectional theorizing, or intersectionality, is a trend away from what Stasiulis (1999:350–351) calls the "race-gender-class trinity" or the "iron triangle of race-gender-class" and a move toward an understanding of the myriad ways that oppressions are linked and the impacts on individuals and groups of those intersections. In addition to a focus on the triad of issues mentioned, nationality, language, religion, sexuality, citizenship, ability, and so on are interrogated, with the emphasis on seeing the ways the "simultaneity of racism, sexism and class exploitation" plays out (Satzewich and Liodakis 2007:24). Sociologist Von Bakanic describes how intersectionality works:

> The ordering of groups in the hierarchy is complex because one's place in the hierarchy is not determined by a single characteristic. Race, class and gender are but three important dimensions of inequality, but they are not the only components contributing to social inequality. Age, disabilities, sexual orientation, religion and even physical attractiveness are but a few of the influences affecting placement in the stratification system. Unfortunately, we can't just add up subordinate and dominant group memberships to figure out a person's placement. Race, class and gender intersect, so that the effect of each is mitigated by the

other two traits. Being White, being male, or belonging to an affluent class opens the door of opportunity. All of these three exposes one to an interlocking, invisible system of advantage. Unfortunately, the reverse is also true. Being a racial or ethnic minority, being female and belonging to the working or poor class results in multiple disadvantages that are often difficult to sort out. (2009:145–146)

With the increase in economic globalization, interest in this mode of analysis has been heightened and developed. However, in developing an analysis of intersectionality, the challenge is to steer clear of the trap of essentializing all women this way and all people "of colour" that way, and so on, as well as to avoid using terms euphemistically, such that "gender" means "women" and "racialized" means "brown," and so on.

HOW CAN RACIALIZED AND ETHNIC INEQUALITIES BE REDUCED?

According to symbolic interactionists, prejudice and discrimination are learned, and what is learned can be unlearned. As sociologist Gale E. Thomas (1995:339) notes,

In the areas of race, ethnic, and human relations, we must learn compassion and also to accept and truly embrace, rather than merely tolerate, differences . . . through honest and open dialogue and through the formation of genuine friendships and personal experiential . . . exchanges and interactions with different individuals and groups across cultures.

In other words, only individuals and groups at the grass-roots level, not government and political leaders or academic elites, can bring about greater ethnic equality. Many authors point to anti-racist education as an important means of promoting change and building alliances (Bakanic 2009; Bishop 2002; Fleras 2001; Fleras and Elliott 1999; Henry et al. 2000; Kivel 1996, 2002; Robertson 1999).

How do functionalists suggest reducing racialized/ethnic inequality? Because they believe a stable society requires smoothly functioning social institutions and people who have common cultural values and attitudes, functionalists suggest restructuring social institutions to reduce discrimination and diffuse racialized/ethnic conflict. According to sociologist Arnold Rose (1951), discrimination robs society of the talents and leadership abilities of many individuals, especially people of colour. Rose suggests that societies invest time and money fostering racialized/ethnic inclusion and eliminating institutionalized discrimination in education, housing, employment, and the criminal justice system. Employing a global perspective, functionalists argue that Canadian racialized discrimination should be reduced because it negatively affects diplomatic and economic relations with other nations made up of diverse racialized/ethnic groups (Feagin and Vera 1995).

From a conflict perspective, racialized and ethnic inequality can be reduced only through struggle and political action. Conflict theorists believe that inequality is based on the exploitation of subordinate groups by the dominant group, and that political intervention is necessary to bring about economic and social change. They agree that people should mobilize to put pressure on public officials. According to social activist Paul Kivel (1996, 2002), racialized inequality will not be reduced until this country has significant national public support and leadership for addressing social problems directly and forcefully.

Feminists and anti-racist feminists advocate critical analysis that begins from the myriad standpoints and situated experiences of people. In addition to building on insights developed from various standpoints, they advocate rendering the connections between locations or standpoints visible so that silences can be heard, hypocrisies can be exposed, and myths can be evaporated. When White people become more clearly aware of their complicity in perpetuating racism and systems of domination, the foundation for solid alliances can be built. We must work toward those ends tirelessly if we intend to create a better place for all.

Whether or not the people of Canada will work for greater equality for all racialized/ethnic groups, one thing is certain: the Canadian population is rapidly becoming increasingly diverse. Statistics Canada (2009b) released its latest analysis of 2006 Census data on ethnic diversity in January 2009, and stated that 20 percent of the population in Canada today is foreign-born. This is the highest rate of foreign-born Canadians since 1931, when 22.2 percent of the population was foreign-born. Foreign-born citizens are increasingly diverse, both culturally and linguistically, adding credence to the notion of a "Canadian mosaic," a concept that in recent decades has been little more than a catchphrase. For example, in 2006, 5.1 million people, or 16.2 percent of the population, claimed "visible minority" status. The population of Indigenous people in Canada has also been increasing, accounting for a total of 3.8 percent of the population (1.2 million people). In addition to responding to the challenges and richness accompanying increased diversity, we also need to deal with longstanding tensions, based on a legacy of colonization, between Indigenous peoples and those of European ancestry. A vision of the future in Canada must be inclusive and be based on a collective endeavour to bring about the thorough eradication of racism at all levels of society—the individual, the institutional, and the societal. The time to begin is immediately.

WHAT CAN YOU DO?

- Join (or start) a local anti-racism group and develop or take part in a "social action" mandate.

- Learn how to address racist comments and jokes when you hear them. This can sometimes be accomplished by asking people for clarification about their comments and providing information counter to their stereotypes. This can also sometimes mean just clearly telling the perpetrator that you find these remarks upsetting or unsettling and do not wish to hear them.

- Join and/or monitor anti-racist discussion groups online such as **http://icare.to.**

- Make an effort to get to know people from cultural groups different from your own. Take stock of your friendship circle right now. Do you regularly hang out with people who are different from you? If not, why do you think that is?

- Report suspected or known hate crimes or White supremacist activity to **http://www.stopracism.ca.**

- Attend cultural activities that are open to the public in order to get to know people different from you and find out about cultures different from your own. What things do you have in common? What things are different? What differences can you celebrate?

- Do not assume that eating sushi or falafel or listening to "world music" gives you enough cross-cultural experience! It's often a beginning. Challenge yourself and others to broaden that knowledge.

- To begin to learn how to unlearn racism, enroll in an anti-racism or diversity course or workshop.

- Get educated about contemporary Indigenous issues such as land claims, treaty rights, and self-determination. Recognize that what you may read or hear in the media is usually only one perspective and that careful attention to information from legitimate sources on both (or more) sides of an issue may be something you need to research to find out.

- Attend public forums on issues concerning immigration, refugees, and Indigenous people. Check into Canada's immigration and refugee policies and investigate recent immigration and refugee statistics to get a better understanding of what is fact and what is fiction.

- Look at the cultural makeup of the boards, staff and volunteers at organizations you belong to or at places you frequent. Where there is diversity, what positions do people fill in your organization? Are there any non-White people in positions of authority or working on the front lines (e.g., visible to the public as soon as they walk in?).

- Carefully read the policies of organizations you are part of. Are they inclusive? Are they welcoming of diversity? If you are unsure, contact a local anti-racism organization and have them come in to do a policy workshop, or consult with them, using your policies as examples.

- Address stereotypical comments that may be made by your family and friends. Do not let any such remarks go by. Ask them for more information about a stereotype they hold, or why they believe the stereotype to be true; or, if they really believe the stereotype to be true, ask them what evidence they have that it is. Ask yourself what investment they may have, if any, in continuing to hold a certain view.

- March in solidarity with people of all backgrounds when the opportunity to publicly declare your stance against racism arises. If you are a White person, demonstrate your position as an ally.

■ Write letters or editorials for your local or post-secondary newspaper debunking stereotypes. Interview people of diverse groups.

■ If you are White, do not make your unlearning of racism the work of people of colour or Indigenous people. Make this your own project. Read. Talk to other White people who are grappling with these

issues. Be reflective about the biases and stereotypes you hold and analyze them critically. Do not wallow in guilt. This serves no one. Become a force for positive change. "No one is free, until all are free."

■ Think about your social locations and determine which of your statuses confer privilege on you and which ones confer disadvantage. Think carefully about what you are willing to give up or to do to ensure equality for all people in Canada. This is a hard one!

SUMMARY

How Do Racialized and Ethnic Groups Differ?

According to sociologists, racialized groups are defined on the basis of arbitrarily selected characteristics, and ethnic groups are defined on the basis of cultural or nationality characteristics. "Race" does not exist biologically but does exist as a socio-cultural phenomenon.

What Are Majority and Minority Groups?

When sociologists use the terms *majority group* and *minority group,* they are referring to power differentials. A majority (or dominant) group is one that is advantaged and has superior resources and rights in a society. A minority (or subordinate) group is one whose members are disadvantaged and subjected to unequal treatment by the dominant group and regard themselves as objects of collective discrimination.

How Are Prejudice and Discrimination Related?

Prejudice is a negative attitude that may or may not lead to discrimination, which is an action or practice of dominant group members that has a harmful impact on subordinate group members.

How Do Individual Discrimination and Institutional Discrimination Differ?

Although individual discrimination and institutional discrimination are carried out by individuals, individual discrimination consists of one-on-one acts by members of the dominant group; institutional discrimination refers to actions and practices that are built into the day-to-day operations of large-scale organizations and social institutions.

How Do the Interactionist and Functionalist Perspectives View Racialized and Ethnic Relations?

Interactionists focus on microlevel issues, such as how people develop a racialized/ethnic identity and how individuals from diverse racialized/ethnic groups interact with each other. Functionalists focus on macrolevel issues, such as how entire groups of people assimilate or do not assimilate into the mainstream of society.

What Are the Major Conflict Explanations for Racialized/Ethnic Inequality?

Conflict perspectives include class perspectives, split-labour market theory, internal colonialism, and racial formation theory.

How Do Feminist and Anti-Racist Feminist Theories Explain Racialized/Ethnic Inequality?

Feminists and anti-racist feminists advocate using critical analysis, beginning from the lived experiences of people. Additionally, they advocate an analysis that examines the intersections of locations, such as gender, ethnicity, sexual orientation, and class.

What Types of Discrimination Have Been Experienced by Minority Group Members in Canada?

Minority group members have experienced every type of discrimination in Canada, from exclusion and expulsion to cultural genocide, slavery, and internment; from discrimination in hiring and retention and in housing to physical violence on a personal level. The legacy of racism for Indigenous people is particularly acute.

What Commonalities Can Be Seen in the Experiences of All Subordinate Racialized/Ethnic Groups?

Members of most subordinate racialized/ethnic groups have these commonalities in their experiences in Canada: (1) each has been the object of negative stereotypes and discrimination; (2) each has resisted oppression and continued to strive for a better life for their members and their children; and (3) each has been the object of some government policy that has shaped its place (or lack thereof) in Canadian ethnic relations over the past four centuries.

KEY TERMS

amalgamation,   p. 70
Anglo-conformity model,   p. 70
anti-Semitism,   p. 61
assimilation,   p. 70
ethnic group,   p. 57
ethnic pluralism,   p. 70
ethnocentrism,   p. 60
gendered racism,   p. 73
generalization,   p. 61

genocide,   p. 71
individual discrimination,   p. 61
institutional discrimination,   p. 61
internal colonialism,   p. 71
internalized dominance,   p. 60
majority (or dominant)
   group,   p. 59
minority (or subordinate)
   group,   p. 59

prejudice,   p. 60
racialized group,   p. 58
racism,   p. 60
segregation,   p. 70
social construct,   p. 58
stereotypes,   p. 61
theory of racial
   formation,   p. 71

QUESTIONS FOR CRITICAL THINKING

1. Do you consider yourself part of the dominant racialized/ethnic group or part of a subordinate racialized/ethnic group in Canada? Consider what specific ways your life might be different if you were in another group.

2. Sociologists suggest that we acquire beliefs about our self and others through socialization. What specific messages have you received about your racialized/ethnic identity? What specific messages have you received about dealing with people from other racialized/ethnic groups? What hidden, subtle, or covert messages do you think you have received about your cultural group and about others?

3. Have all White Canadians, regardless of class, gender, or other characteristics, benefited from racialized prejudice and discrimination in Canada? Why or why not? In what ways have White people benefited from racism against non-Whites? In what ways have they been harmed by racism against non-Whites?

4. Compare recent depictions of Indigenous people, Black Canadians, Asian Canadians, and other racialized/ethnic groups in Canada in films, television shows, and advertisements. To what extent have we moved beyond the traditional stereotypes of those groups? To what extent have the stereotypes remained strong?

PEARSON
mysockit™

Explore the topics covered in this chapter at **www.mysockit.com** using the access provided with this text. Interactive resources for studying include video clips, practice tests, learning objectives, and Internet resources.

4

GENDER INEQUALITY

Would you note that if I commit suicide today 89-12-06 it is not for economic reasons (for I have waited until I have exhausted all my financial means, even refusing jobs) but for political reasons. Because I have decided to send the feminists, who have always ruined my life, to their Maker. For seven years life has brought me no joy and being totally blasé, I have decided to put an end to those viragos. . . . Even if the Mad Killer epithet will be attributed to me by the media, I consider myself a rational erudite that only the arrival of the Grim Reaper has forced to take extreme acts. . . . The feminists have always enraged me. They want to keep the advantages of women . . . while seizing for themselves those of men.

Partial text of the suicide letter left by the shooter who killed 14 women on December 6, 1989, at Montreal's École Polytechnique. The letter was followed by a list of names of 19 women and the following appended note : "The lack of time (because I started too late) has allowed these radical feminists to survive." (Quoted in Malette and Chalouh 1991:180–181)

The killing of 14 women in Montreal, Quebec, on December 6, 1989, shocked the nation. Most news reports in the days and weeks following cited the act as that of a madman—an isolated, bizarre event carried out by a deranged individual. While there can be no doubt that the act was extreme, feminists and other analysts continue to question this individualistic analysis, pointing instead to the pervasiveness of sexism in a patriarchal society, a pervasiveness they say creates a climate for actions such as this, and other forms of violence against women, to play out. **Sexism** is the subordination of one sex, female, based on the assumed superiority of the other sex, male, while **patriarchy** refers to a hierarchical system of social organization in which cultural, political, and economic structures are controlled by men. According to some social analysts, problems of sexism are overblown: sexism was a problem in the past when women were underrepresented in organizations and the paid labour force generally; now, however, women have made significant inroads in education and employment. By 2004, for example, 58 percent of Canadian women aged 15 and over were employed for pay, up from 30 percent in 1961, and by 2004, women made up nearly one-half of the total labour force population at 47 percent (Statistics Canada 2006g). By contrast, in 2004, only 68 percent of males were in the paid labour force, a figure significantly lower than in the late 1970s. Many more women

today have gained post-secondary degrees (15 percent of women in Canada, versus 16 percent of men) and are employed in an increasing variety of professional fields; women are also increasingly represented among the self-employed (11 percent of all employed women are self-employed). With obvious changes such as these, some people believe that women should just be happy and stop complaining about the "past." Many feel that, while the events of December 6, 1989, were tragic, conditions that may have caused such an event (assuming a social *versus* an individualized analysis) to occur are over now—they are historical conditions that we have overcome in the years since. These people believe that today women and men in Canada are equal.

However, despite women's advances in the labour market, education, and so on, gender equality appears to be rhetoric. Nowhere is gender inequality more clearly illustrated than in the persistence of violence against women. As Charlotte Bunch, past president of MATCH, a Canadian NGO, stated in a public speech in the early 1990s, "Violence against women is the most pervasive human rights abuse in the world today. If any other group in society were as systematically battered and killed in order to be controlled, it would be a civil emergency . . . the war on women must end." The United Nations and Amnesty International have recently issued similar statements about the persistence of violence against women and its clear links to gender inequality.

The B.C. Ministry of Community Services reports that every minute of every day, a woman or girl is sexually assaulted somewhere in Canada—as of 1999, 60 percent of those assaulted were under the age of 18 (B.C. Ministry of Community Services 2006). The 1993 National Violence Against Women Survey (VAWS) conducted by Statistics Canada represents the only comprehensive report on women's experience of violence, although Statistics Canada added questions to the quintennial General Social Survey (GSS) about family violence and gendered violence that allow some ongoing statistical comparisons. The 1993 VAW survey, which asked a sample of 12 300 women to report their lifetime experiences of assault, sexual assault, and sexual harassment, found that most assaults go unreported to police. Only 14 percent of all assaults had been reported; wife assaults were reported at a rate of 26 percent. Fifty-one percent of Canadian women had experienced at least one incident of physical or sexual assault since the age of 16. Forty-five percent of these women were assaulted by men known to them, and an additional 23 percent were assaulted by a stranger. Thirty-nine percent of women experienced sexual assault; 34 percent of women experienced non-sexual assault. Some of the sexual assaults and most of the non-sexual assaults were perpetrated by the women's spouses (Johnson 1996:49). The two most recent GSS surveys, which asked questions about victimization, found similar results. Additionally, the GSS supported earlier findings that three-quarters of the victims of spousal assault and over 90 percent of victims of sexual assault still do not report the crimes to official agencies (Sauve and Burns 2009).

In October 2006, Statistics Canada released a comprehensive summary of information from various official sources, including the GSS and the VAWS, as well as police data, transition house surveys, and so on, that enabled a snapshot of the prevalence and severity of violence against women, one that would allow ongoing comparisons. Overall, the report found that women continue to be more likely than men to be victims of spousal homicide, sexual assault, criminal harassment (stalking), and the most severe forms of spousal assault. On a positive note, the 2006 report found that the rates of spousal homicide had decreased somewhat for both sexes, and that the severity of non-lethal assaults of women had also declined marginally. The rate of reported sexual assaults also declined slightly but, because the rates reported in GSS victimization surveys have remained constant, Statistics Canada cautions that we cannot know if the actual occurrences have decreased or people's reporting behaviours have changed, with fewer crimes coming to police attention in recent years (Brennan and Taylor-Butts 2008; Statistics Canada 2006e).

Every week in Canada, at least one woman is murdered by her boyfriend or spouse (B.C. Ministry of Community Services 2006; Statistics Canada 2006f). In a study of 569 women's shelters and transition houses in Canada, in the one-year period ending March 31, 2008, 61 690 women, along with 37 902 dependent children, were admitted (Sauve and Burns 2009). In a previous study in 2000, 57 182 women and 39 177 children were admitted to 448 shelters: 41 percent of the children were under age 5, and 32 percent were between the ages of 5 and 9 (Dauvergne and Johnson, 2001).

One study of women who experience violence found that over 1 million Canadian children have witnessed violence by their fathers against their mothers (Fitzgerald 1999). The 2006 Statistics Canada *Measuring Violence Against Women* report found that the number of women accessing shelters in Canada has remained stable. It also noted, however, that on any given day (in this case, April 14, 2004), 221 women and 112 children were turned away from 93 shelters surveyed, indicating that the need for services exceeds availability (Statistics Canada 2006e).

In 2006, Statistics Canada published the fifth edition of *Women in Canada: A Gender-Based Statistical Report*, which reported the results of a national study of police departments. Researchers found that of all violent crimes reported to police in 2004, women represented 51 percent of victims, and 78 percent of them had been victimized by someone they knew, whereas men had been victimized by someone they knew just over half of the time. Women were over six times more likely than males to be victims of sexual assault and were over three times more likely to be victims of criminal harassment than males (Statistics Canada 2006h). Additionally, women made up 84 percent of all spousal homicide victims. Clearly, violence against women by men is a tremendous social problem in Canada linked to sexism.

Just as women are not viewed as equal to men, not all women are viewed as equal to one another. For example, the murders of the 14 women in Montreal sparked annual December 6th memorials to raise awareness of the violence against women that continues today. The White Ribbon campaign, begun in 1991 and carried out by Canadian men to raise awareness and educate men and boys about violence against women, continues to gain support each year. In fact, this campaign is the largest worldwide effort by men to end violence against women and is currently operating in over 55 countries (see **http://www.whiteribbon.ca/about_us/#1**).

A national monument in Vancouver's Thornton Park commemorates women's deaths at the hands of male violence. Women's groups from Vancouver's downtown East Side question why the disappearances of at least 68 Vancouver women since 1983 have not created the same kind of public concern. No one criticizes the increased attention to issues of violence against women, but many point out the difference in public interest and attention the two groups of women

Eat your vegetables.

Don't play with matches.

Finish your homework.

Respect women.

AWAITING INSTRUCTIONS.

Violence against women is a tragic reality. We must teach our sons early and often what it means to be a real man – that women deserve honor and respect, and that violence never equals strength. A safer world is in their hands. Help them grasp it.

Family Violence Prevention Fund
www.endabuse.org

It is important that children are brought up to respect women.

have received. Analysts highlight the class, ethnic, and lifestyle differences between the groups; for instance, the Montreal Massacre, as it quickly came to be called, involved 14 young, White, middle-class women, most of whom were enrolled as students in engineering at the "Poly." The disappearances in Vancouver have mainly involved women believed to be drug users and/or sex-trade workers, many of whom are also Indigenous. These women are commonly viewed as "disposable" people, societal "throwaways." In a critique of the way the 68 disappearances have been handled by the RCMP to date, John Lowman of Simon Fraser University's Department of Criminology stated in a February 2002 newspaper interview, "If [68] women in any other category, whether housewives or women of a certain age or anyone else, went missing, believe me, the police reaction would have been entirely different" (Matas 2002:A4). Similar critiques have emerged about the lack of attention, from media and ordinary citizens alike, in the serial murders of three Indigenous women in Saskatoon in the late 1990s (Hanon 2005) and about the disappearances or murders of at least seven young women, six of whom are Indigenous, along a lonely stretch of northern British Columbia's Highway 16, now known as the Highway of Tears (Hall 2005).

Violence against women in its many forms is one particularly devastating result of sexism and gender inequality. Other manifestations of sexism discussed on the following pages include inequalities in the paid labour force and in domestic labour. The ways that gender socialization perpetuates these inequalities are highlighted, as are various theories for analyzing gender inequality.

GENDER INEQUALITY AS A SOCIAL PROBLEM

Similar to the ways that racialized ethnic group members experience discrimination based on supposed innate characteristics, women experience discrimination based on their sex. Since 51 percent of the people in Canada are female, women constitute a numerical majority. However, they are often referred to as the country's largest minority group because as a group, they do not possess as much wealth, power, or prestige as men. As a telling example involving income alone, for all full-time workers in Canada in 1967—the first year the data were gathered on male to female earnings—women earned 58.4 percent of what men earned. In 1995, this had increased to 73.0 percent. But by 2000, the earnings differential had decreased again, to 72.0 percent, and by 2003 it was 71.0 percent (Nelson 2010:236; Statistics Canada 2002a; Statistics Canada 2006g).

The differences between women's and men's earnings are more striking when we examine all earners' wages, since women are more often employed only part-time. Sometimes this is by choice, though often it is instead the result of persistent gender stereotypes that women's incomes are "pin money" or otherwise merely "supplemental" to men's. In 1991, for all Canadian earners, full- and part-time, women earned 61.3 percent of men's earnings. In 1995, a banner year, they earned 64.8 percent, and in 2000, women earned 64.0 percent of what men earned (Statistics Canada 2002a). More recent data state that women today earn approximately 62 percent of what men earn (Statistics Canada 2006h; see Figure 4.1). If the pattern from past decades continues to hold, we cannot expect much change.

Defining Sex and Gender

What is the difference between sex and gender? Although many people use these terms interchangeably, sociologists believe that there are significant differences in their meanings. **Sex** refers to the biological, physiological, hormonal, and chromosomal attributes of females, males, and intersex people. Our sex is the first label we receive in life and is an ascribed status. Before birth or at the time of birth, we are typically identified as either male or female on the basis of our sex organs and genes. Despite the fact that many children do not exhibit the genitalia or chromosomes consistent with either a male or female designation, most people act as though there are only two dichotomous and "opposite" sexes. For example, when a child is born **intersexed**—that is, with either unrecognizably male or female genitalia or with both male and female genitalia—we surgically alter the child to fit our current two-sex model of reality. Within the two-sex model, males are seen as the central or standard sex against which females, the

FIGURE 4.1   Average Income of Women and Men, 1993, 1997, and 2003*

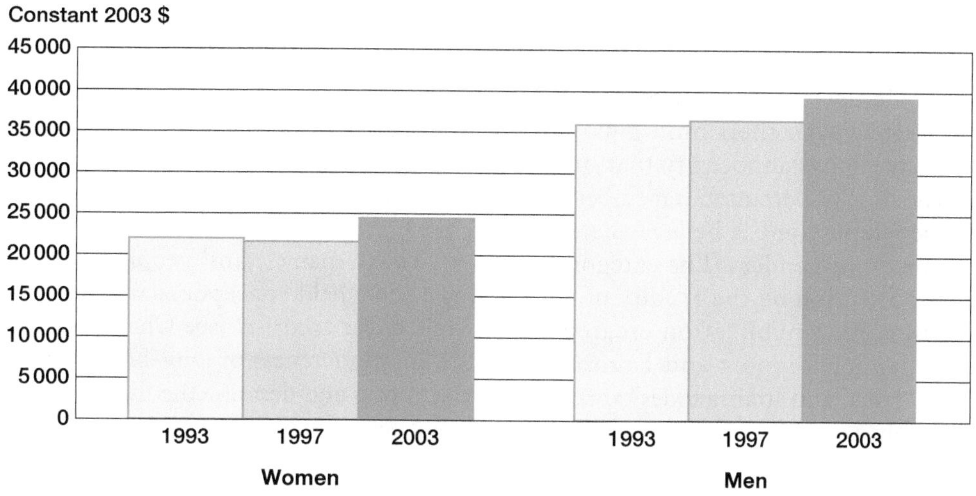

Data for 1993 and 1997 include 15-year-olds.
Source: Statistics Canada, 2006, Women in Canada: A Gender-based Statistical Report (5th ed.). *Ottawa: Minister of Industry. Retrieved July 16, 2009 (http://www.statcan.gc.ca/pub/89-503-x/89-5-3-x2005001-eng.pdf).*

"opposite" sex, are measured. This practice of putting males at the centre is known as **androcentricity.** As an illustration of the fluidity of our notions, even in something as seemingly fixed or static as biology, in the past, Westerners had a one-sex model of humanity, with the one sex being male. Females and their bodies were viewed as imperfect or flawed versions of the male. Historian Thomas Laqueur (1992:4), in a book called *Making Sex,* states that several early "scientists," such as Galen and Herophilus,

> demonstrated at length that women were essentially men in whom a lack of vital heat—of perfection—had resulted in the retention, inside, of structures that in the male are visible without. . . . In this world the vagina is imagined as an interior penis, the labia as foreskin, the uterus as scrotum, and the ovaries as testicles . . . for two centuries, the ovary . . . had not even a name of its own.

Scholars and lay people alike were "caught up in the female-as-male model" until approximately 1800, when many began to insist that there "were fundamental differences between the male and female sexes" (Laqueur 1992:5).

Following, then, from a two-sex model, **gender** refers to the socially constructed sets of attitudes that dictate whatbehaviours, thoughts, and emotions are appropriate for each sex—these are culturally specific, change over time, and are associated with notions of femininity and masculinity. For many people, being *masculine* means being aggressive, independent, and unemotional, while being *feminine* means the opposite—being passive, dependent, and emotional. Understanding the difference between sex and gender is important, according to sociologists, because what many people think of as *sex differences*—for example, being aggressive or independent—are actually socially constructed *gender differences* based on widely held assumptions about men and women (Gailey 1987). In other words, males are supposed to be aggressive and independent not because they have male sex organs but because that is how people in this society think males should act. Psychologist S.L. Bem (1974) talked about masculinity and femininity being represented on two continuums. Where individuals are located on each continuum gives an indication as to their personal combination of masculine and feminine traits. Again, though, masculinity and femininity are presented as the central elements in a dichotomy instead of as simply two out of a multiplicity of possibilities for genders.

Because gender is socially constructed, people can choose a gender identity that is in keeping with the way they view themselves. Some people choose a more feminine gender identity, while others choose a more masculine identity. Most people choose a gender identity that is consistent with their biological sex. However, some may choose an identity that others feel is inappropriate. It is important to remember that currently, most people in Canada believe there are two sexes and hence two genders. The category of "trans" focuses our attention on the fluidity of gender. According to a 2001 publication created by Transcend Transgender Support and Education Society, the terms "trans" and "transgender" are used, often interchangeably,

to refer to anyone who has a gender identity that is not as simple as "man" or "woman," who expresses their gender in a way that contravenes societal expectations of the range of possibilities for men and women, or who experiences transphobia as a result of having physical characteristics outside the norms of male and female. (2001:9)

Today, many "trans" people are publicly challenging widely held conceptions of gender (see Box 4.1), while queer theorists (see Chapter 6) are challenging the appropriateness of long-held binary categories to encompass and describe the fluidity of sex and gender many people experience.

SOCIAL PROBLEMS AND SOCIAL POLICY

BOX 4.1   *Trans*-gressing Gender Norms

On October 15, 2002, directors and chairs at the University of Victoria received a memo from the Office of the President. The University of Victoria president, along with the vice-president academic and the new dean of graduate studies, was advising the university community that the dean of graduate studies, also a tenured professor in the Department of Sociology, wished henceforth to be known as a man. The memo communicated the upper administration's "unequivocal personal support for this decision and . . . a great appreciation for his valued contributions to the university" and called for people's understanding and consideration of the wishes of the dean to now "live as a man." Aaron (formerly Holly) Devor is the well-known Canadian author of many publications on gender and transgender issues, including the books *Gender Blending: Confronting the Limits of Duality* (1989) and *FTM: Female to Male Transsexuals in Society* (1997).

Aaron Devor's experience of "unequivocal" institutional support, economic well-being, and a high-status, high-profile position is precisely what we wish to see achieved for all trans people. The unfortunate reality, however, is that this experience is not at all typical among transgendered people. A recent study by trans activist Emilia L. Lombardi and her colleagues (2001) documents that violence and economic discrimination are more common responses to gender nonconformity. Several other studies confirm that trans people experience high rates of prejudice, marginalization, discrimination, harassment, stalking, and other violence (Appelbe 2001; Donavon 2001;

MacDonald 1998/2000; Nangeroni 2001; Towle and Morgan 2002). In addition to external threats, pervasive victimization has been shown to lead to a higher incidence of depression, substance abuse, and suicide in trans people (Donavon 2001; Lombardi et al. 2001; Nangeroni 2001). As with homophobia and biphobia (see Chapter 6), it is important to remember that it is not the fact of being a transsexual or transgendered person that causes ill health and heightened risks; rather, it is transphobia, or the hatred and fear of trans people, that does. Sadly, transphobia may come as much from gays and lesbians as it does from heterosexuals.

Trans people have begun to speak out about their experiences and the issues they face living in a transphobic culture. As Nick Matte, a history professor in the Sexual Diversity Studies Program at the University of Toronto, points out,

When we're thinking about the barriers faced by "trans" people, what's really sad is that people often have to spend so much time educating themselves and breaking down the barriers they help to create, that it's easy to forget to make time to celebrate the fact that "trans" people have already been breaking those barriers down for them/ourselves. (2003, author's files)

Recently, Tina Donavon (2001:20), a member of Senior Action in a Gay Environment (SAGE)/Queens, described a little of her experience coming out as a transgendered woman in the mid-1970s:

I am a woman, 61 years old and transgender. I have lived the last 27 years as a woman, much to the chagrin of my parents and some friends. They did not understand the nature of my struggles since early childhood. I knew all along that I was female, not a male. When I revealed this information to my parents, my father said I was "nuts" and my mother cried. They both thought that my gender identification was a result of their failing to raise me in the correct way.

Trans issues have increasingly come into public focus over the past decade. Ethnographic research, largely by anthropologists, has been used to provide supposed cross-cultural "proofs" that the "Western binary gender system is neither universal nor innate" (Towle and Morgan 2002:469). In many publications, examples of people who belong to a "third gender" are presented: the Hijras in India, the so-called Berdache[1] of North America, the female husbands of West Africa, the Xanith of the Arabian Peninsula, and the Sambia of Papua New Guinea. While these people around the world provide interesting examples of a variety of socially constructed roles and statuses, they cannot just be slotted unproblematically into the North American context; one must carefully examine the cultural and historical contexts from which these groups spring. As anthropologists Evan B. Towle and Lynn M. Morgan (2002:490) point out,

> Invoking "third gender" examples in an oversimplified way or citing them out of context to underwrite Western social agendas is an unwitting kind of neocolonial (or at least ethnocentric) appropriation that distorts the complexity and reality of other people's lives.

The term *transgender* was originally coined by Virginia Prince in a 1970s conference presentation titled "The Transsexual and His Wife" (MacDonald 1998/2000). We use and have used in the past a great many terms to refer to trans people: transgendered, transsexual, transvestite, butch, femme, drag king, drag queen, female to male (F to M), male to female (M to F), intersex, third gender, non-op, pre-op, post-op, androgyne, epicene, and two-spirited—to name only a few. Providing definitions of a range of trans experiences is beyond the scope of this feature. Moreover, it is not necessarily appropriate, given that an often common thread of trans experiences is precisely the challenge to identity-based categories and to the way we think about identity. Political scientist Eleanor MacDonald (1998/2000:284), for example, provides this provocative notion:

> What transgender identity specifically problematizes is identity itself. Transgender identity is about identity experienced as problematic; the experience of being transgender problematizes the relationship of the self to the body, and the self to others. In doing so, it also

problematizes issues of identity boundaries, stability and coherence. . . . What is radical, then, to the definition of "transgender" is its origin in problem, a disjunction between one's feelings of who one is or is not, and how one is (or has once been) perceived, recognized, and understood by others.

The existence of trans people, trans bodies, and trans identities may be useful in understanding all gender relations, the normative and the transgressive. Towle and Morgan (2002) suggest that through an interrogation of trans we may be able to get at what the differences between men and women really are: Through what acts is gender identity communicated? What consequences are there for social interactions if one fails to communicate a gender identity? And what is the meaning of inhabiting a gendered body? David Valentine and Riki Anne Wilchins subvert the typical lines of questioning with their point that "[bodies that] are suspect . . . are not what have to be explained. Rather, the requirement that they explain themselves should itself be investigated" (in Towle and Morgan 2002:491–492). Konnor Brett, researcher and educator with the British Columbia NGO "Transcend," adds, "I'm not sure that my transitioning broke down many aspects of the binary gender system in our society as a whole. I do know that I see my future with happiness" (2003, author's files).

The Canadian general public has responded to trans issues in a range of ways, from support and confusion to intolerance and hostility. Mainstream movies such as *Transamerica* and *Kinky Boots* have provided more balanced insights into some of the issues faced by trans people. While many people are supportive and may even constitute a silent majority in some sectors of the population, MacDonald (1998/2000) outlines three general responses to trans people that she has observed and that can present problems. One response has been hostility and/or exclusion in the form of denouncing trans individuals as dangerous to progressive enterprises, such as women's centres, for example. Trans people, particularly F to M, have been viewed by some as traitors or turncoats, while M to F have been treated as deceptive, as "Trojan horses," and as violators of women-only spaces. It is interesting to note both the essentialism and the sexism inherent in this response: essentialist because trans people are stereotyped a certain way, using the sex they were born into; and sexist because women are often portrayed, through sexist stereotypes, as "sneaky deceivers." Further, females who transition may be seen as "switching sides," suddenly developing all the characteristics supposedly attributed to males, including a complete inability to understand women's concerns, issues, or experiences.

A second response has been to medicalize trans people's experiences, seemingly rendering them apolitical. Finally, a third response has been to "celebrate trans identity as emblematic of

This young F to M couple is celebrating graduation from university. They have to contend not only with transphobia in their daily lives, but also with homophobia.

the subversiveness of post modern theory"—where "gender doesn't [or shouldn't] matter" (MacDonald 1998/2000:282, 285). This can create a lot of inappropriate pressure for trans individuals to think and feel and act in certain ways.

While this third response is more supportive, it does not adequately capture the complexity of lived experiences of trans identities. Trans people may "playfully or seriously" choose identities that are grounded firmly in gender-stereotypical notions of masculinity or femininity. What is sometimes overlooked is that a sense of relief and pleasure can accompany the ability to identify with a recognizable and easily understood gender, especially for those for whom a gender identity has been denied or has felt uncertain. Additionally, becoming firmly situated within a recognizable gender may be necessary from a strategic perspective, as many physicians and psychiatrists view this as the "proof" necessary to endorse a sex change or to dispense hormones.

Political scientist and activist Paisley Currah (2001:192) takes a different stance, stating that it is imperative that trans (and non-trans) people push beyond the gender stereotypes that "reinforce heteronormative notions":

We need to give sustenance to gender-variant traditions, to preserve them, to make sure they get reproduced, not play into the larger ideological erasure of them. We need to contest, rather than support ideologies that

assert that queer, gay, lesbian, bisexual, questioning, and transgender kids are pathological.

In a study about the extent to which trans people are at risk for violence and discrimination, Lombardi and colleagues (2001:99) report that trans youth are exposed to heightened risks of "attempted suicide, substance abuse, unsafe sexual practices, of being exposed to STDs (including HIV), of being homeless, dropping out of school, and of experiencing high levels of distress, as well as experiencing many forms of discrimination, harassment and violence." Widespread transphobia and its devastating consequences indicate that a series of policies is required to create ways to protect trans Canadians' fundamental human rights, such as the following:

- Tracking all incidents of violence against members of trans communities in order to better understand the nature of these hate crimes.

- Designing and implementing education for law enforcement personnel, social service workers, and other professionals who come into contact with members of trans communities so that they can recognize issues and lend assistance.

- As with other hate crimes in Canada, ensuring that penalties for hate-motivated crimes against members of trans communities are enhanced (e.g., made more severe). This will require the addition of gender identity and/or presentation to hate crimes legislation.

- ■ Ensuring that unless it is absolutely necessary to know, sex should not have to be reported to bureaucracies, employers, and other officials. As with other personal information, such as age, sexual orientation, or ability, knowing someone's sex is usually unnecessary, and requiring this information could violate human rights. To require it complicates the lives of trans people unnecessarily and may even set them up for negative or harmful experiences.

- ■ Where possible, providing gender-neutral washroom spaces, either in addition to male and female washrooms or in place of them. We often provide gender-neutral washroom space in public places already, so there is no logical reason why trans people should not also be afforded this measure of privacy. As the public becomes more relaxed about co-ed worlds, many public spaces, such as restaurants, are already doing away with gendered designations. (Appelbe 2001; Devor 2003; Lombardi et al. 2001).

While trans issues are often misunderstood and marginalized (even writing this feature as a boxed item instead of as part of the regular text may illustrate this fact), trans issues are finally coming into the mainstream in positive and empowering ways. As you read at the beginning of this box, some trans people are experiencing support in their workplaces. Many find support for their transitions through their relationships with family, friends, and peers. One trans individual, in a relationship with another trans person, related that "the most common question we get asked is about family support and I have to say that both our families love and support us in all aspects" (2003, author's files). Many trans people also report feelings of joy in having the ability to finally feel as though they are living authentically, in ways they have chosen. As one undergraduate student recently stated,

> Before I knew about transitioning, I basically had accepted my life would be lived in a depressed state. Since my transition, I have been constantly amazed about what I was missing. I feel truly happy and balanced for the first time in my life. (2003, author's files)

These positive reports do not in any way diminish the ongoing need to be vigilant about ridding Canadian society of prejudice and discrimination against trans people, but they do help us to see that life as a trans person is not all negative and, in fact, can be cause for celebration. As one trans individual concluded, "What you see in the media is only going to give you the miserable story" (2003, author's files). Clearly, there is much more to trans life than that.

Note: [1]Use of the term "Berdache" reflects the mistaken assumptions about same-sex relations among Indigenous peoples made by Europeans at contact. The word "Berdache" originated as a Persian term meaning "slave youth." It later came to mean a "kept boy" in a gay relationship. Neither meaning depicts any North American Indigenous traditions or practices, nor was either term accepted as appropriate by Indigenous people. The continued widespread use of the term demonstrates, if nothing else, the pervasiveness of colonialism (Roscoe 1995, in Goldie 2001:10).

BIOLOGICAL AND SOCIAL BASES OF GENDER ROLES

Is there something in the biological and genetic makeup of boys or girls that makes them physically aggressive or passive? As sociologist Judith Lorber (1994:39) notes, "When little boys run around noisily, we say 'Boys will be boys,' meaning that physical assertiveness has to be in the Y chromosome because it is manifest so early and so commonly in boys." Similarly, when we say "She throws like a girl," according to Lorber, people mean that "she throws like a female child, a carrier of XX chromosomes." However, Lorber questions these widely held assumptions: "But are boys universally, the world over, in every social group, a vociferous, active presence? Or just where they are encouraged to use their bodies freely, to cover space, take risks, and play outdoors at all kinds of games and sports?"

According to Lorber, boys and girls who are given tennis racquets at the age of 3 and encouraged to become champions tend to use their bodies similarly. Even though boys gradually gain more shoulder and arm strength and are able to sustain more concentrated bursts of energy, after puberty girls acquire more stamina, flexibility, and lower-body strength. Coupled with training and physical exercise, these traits enhance, compensate for, or override different physical capabilities (Lorber 1994). Thus, the girl who throws "like a girl" is probably a product of her culture and time: she has had more limited experience than many boys at throwing the ball and engaging in competitive games at an early age. The implication that social roles "are an unproblematic reflection of biology (sex)" is analytically flawed (Marshall 2000:24).

The social basis for gender roles is known as the gender belief system or **gender ideology**—ideas of masculinity and femininity that are held to be valid in a given society at a specific historical time (Lorber 1994). Gender ideology is reflected in what sociologists refer to as the **gendered division of labour**—the process whereby productive tasks are separated on the basis of gender. How do people determine what constitutes "women's work" or "men's work"? Evidence from cross-cultural studies shows that social factors, more than biological factors, influence the gendered division of labour in societies. In agricultural societies, for example, women work in the fields and tend to their families' daily needs; men typically produce and market cash crops but spend no time on household work. In industrialized nations, an increasing proportion of women are in paid employment but still have heavy household and family responsibilities. For example, in Canada in 2005, men spent 2.4 hours per day on housework and other unpaid work while women spent 4.3 hours per day (Statistics Canada 2006b). Across cultures, women's domain is viewed as the private and domestic, and men's domain is viewed as the public, economic, and political. This difference in how labour is divided, how workers are rewarded, and what cultural value is accorded to paid versus unpaid labour affects access to scarce resources such as wealth, power, and prestige. Given their domain, men have greater access to these resources, a situation that leads to gender inequality in other areas.

To explain gender inequality, some sociologists use a *gender-role approach*, focusing on how the socialization process contributes to male domination and female subordination. Other sociologists use a *structural approach*, focusing on how large-scale social structures determine the boundaries of individual behaviour. Let's look first at how socialization can perpetuate gender stereotyping and inequality.

GENDER INEQUALITY AND SOCIALIZATION

Numerous sociological studies have found that gender-role stereotyping is one of the enduring consequences of childhood gender socialization.

Socialization into appropriate "feminine" behaviour makes women less likely than men to pursue male-dominated activities, and socialization into appropriate "masculine" behaviour makes men more likely than women to pursue leadership roles in education, religion, business, politics, and other spheres of public life (Peterson and Runyan 1993). We learn our earliest and often most long-lasting beliefs about gender roles from a variety of *agents of socialization*—those people, groups, or institutions that teach us what we need to know to participate in society.

This young man challenges gender conformity through his choice of clothes.

Among the most significant agents of socialization are parents, peers, the education system, and the media. Although all four agents of socialization are important, this chapter will focus on gender socialization in media, given its preeminence in contemporary culture.

The Media and Gender Socialization

Females' acceptance or praise for being "good" and/or "compliant" is consistently reinforced throughout all types of media. From television to the Internet, from magazines to billboards, we are inundated by media on a daily basis. Because media are socially constructed, they reflect the realities and/or fantasies of their creators. Communications scholar Julia T. Wood (2001) identifies three themes in contemporary media that reflect gender. The first theme is the underrepresentation of women and other minority groups. The overrepresentation of able-bodied, youngish, White men in media conveys the message that they make up the majority of the population (which they do not) and, as such, that they are the cultural standard. When women and other minority groups are depicted in media, they are typically shown in ways that reinforce and perpetuate, subtly or overtly, negative stereotypes about the group. The second theme is the stereotypical fashion in which males and females are presented. Males continue to be presented as competent, powerful, serious, confident, and independent, while females continue to be presented as incompetent, unintelligent, young, thin, beautiful, dependent, and passive sex objects (Nelson 2010; Wood 2001:283–284). To redress past voids, contemporary media have made attempts to show women involved in activities outside the domestic sphere; however, they have not made a corresponding attempt to show men involved in the domestic sphere. Where men are shown involved in domestic labour or child care, they are typically portrayed as helpless ("hopeless"?) buffoons (Wood 2001:284), reinforcing men's lack of "suitability" for child care and domestic activities. Family sociologists historically have referred to this phenomenon as "learned incompetence." The third theme is the portrayal of male–female relations along traditional lines and in ways that perpetuate and normalize violence against women (Wood 2001:281). Wood (2001:287–294) suggests there are four themes that reflect and promote gender-stereotypical, and perhaps even dangerous, relations between the sexes: (1) women's dependence and men's independence; (2) women's incompetence and men's authority; (3) women as primary caregivers and men as primary breadwinners; and (4) women as victims and sex objects and men as aggressors.

While some critics argue that the media simply reflect existing gender roles in society, others point out that the media also have a unique ability to shape ideas. Sociologist Linda Lindsey (2005:69) notes that "heavy television viewing is strongly associated with traditional and stereotyped gender views, a pattern that is demonstrated for all [ethnic groups] and age groups." From children's cartoons to adult shows, television programs offer many more male than female characters. Furthermore, the male characters often act in a manner strikingly different than female ones. Male characters in both children's programs and adult programs are typically aggressive, constructive, and direct, while female characters defer to others or manipulate them by acting helpless, seductive, or deceitful (Basow 1992). Nurturant males, along with females generally, are most often found in comedies with females who inhabit highly stereotypical roles, suggesting that they need not be taken seriously (Nelson 2010). Furthermore, in cartoons, where male characters outnumber female characters five to one, females are typically cast in minor supportive roles (e.g., the wife or the younger sister) and display only a small repertoire of stereotypical behaviours and emotions such as fear, support, romance, or good manners (Nelson 2010:198). Males, particularly in the many police and detective dramas available today, tend to be stereotyped as hypermasculinized: they are either aggressive, criminal, thrill-seeking, and callous toward women ("bad guys"), or aggressive, thrill-seeking, and tough ("good guys") (Nelson 2010:200). Some have argued that even educational programs such as *Sesame Street* perpetuate gender stereotyping and male dominance because most of the characters have male names and masculine voices and participate in "boys' activities" (Wood 2001).

Recent studies of televised music videos have found that they often show stereotyped gender roles and condone harassment of and discrimination against women. In the words of Linda Lindsey, "The misogyny in most rock videos is blatant" (2005:358). A 1992 study found most female characters were dressed in revealing clothing, made sexual advances toward men, and usually were presented as sex objects. Further studies from 1999 and 2002 demonstrate that women do not appear at all or appear only in the background in over half of music videos, but where they do appear, sexual images are increasingly combined with violence. Male characters routinely pursue fantasy adventures or engage in aggression and violence (Seidman 1992). Further, women are shown either satisfying male sexual fantasies or being ostracized or punished for not engaging in this way. Sociologist Sut Jhally, in his *Dreamworlds* documentaries, links music videos and sexual assault, describing the fantasy world of music videos as the male videographer's and consumer's dreamworld. This "dreamworld" objectifies and dehumanizes women and denies them subjectivity, all of which puts women at risk for violence by reinforcing a **rape culture**—the pervasive system of cultural values, attitudes, and practices that support and perpetuate sexualized violence against women. It includes rigid gender scripts for males and females and equally rigid notions of gender-appropriate behaviours. Many music videos overtly depict male violence against women, and increasingly, over the years, rape scenes have been enacted in music videos (Lindsey 2005). Jhally, in the most recent edition of *Dreamworlds* (III, 2007) makes the case that many music video producers and directors today are also producers and directors of pornography and that the line between music video and pornography is now indistinct. Psychologists Harmony Sullivan and Maureen McHugh (2009:746) note that Jhally's film "elucidates how the dominant cultural narrative expressed in music videos and other media confers to men a sense of entitlement to comment on and even touch women's bodies in public" and that through indoctrination by various media, such as music videos, "women may be seen, by men but also by women ourselves, as decorative, dehumanized and perhaps deserving of abuse." Further, research by Dieter (1989) demonstrated that women who watched sexualized violence on MTV were more accepting of violence in their own intimate relationships with men than women who did not view the images (cited in Wood 2001).

While changes have occurred in the roles men and women play in movies, most still embrace stereotypes. Even though there are many movie stars who are female, with a few exceptions, there are few notable roles for women, and even fewer films that examine women's lives and issues from their perspectives. Movies featuring boys and men focus on saving the nation, the world, or the universe, while films featuring girls and women focus on saving money on shoes by finding *the most fabulous discount ever!* Females are usually depicted as "bimbos," as shopaholics, and as sexually available. Things may be changing somewhat: in some recent films, women are not portrayed as helpless, even if they are conventionally attractive, and even the token "smart females" are sometimes portrayed as also attractive. However, even when females are portrayed positively as smart *and* attractive, as characters in the *Harry Potter* and *Star Wars* series are, they are still only supporting characters to the males who save the day. Recently, there has been a spate of movies featuring "kick-ass" females (*Underworld, Mr. and Mrs. Smith, The Matrix*); however, these women are depicted as cold-blooded killers, very masculine in their approach to the world and dressed in highly sexualized attire. According to social psychologist Hilary Lips (1993:19), "We are surrounded with the message that masculine males can be powerful, but feminine females cannot, or that women's only effective source of feminine influence is beauty and sex appeal." Moreover, the dominant message conveyed still remains that females must use their influence, however paltry, in an attempt to garner that pinnacle of feminine achievement and self-definition—an intimate relationship with a man.

Why is awareness of gender socialization important for understanding gender discrimination and gender inequality? Social analysts who use a gender-role approach say that because parents, peers, teachers, and the media influence our perceptions of who we are and what our aspirations should be, gender-role socialization contributes to a gendered division of labour, creates a *wage gap* between women and men workers, limits occupational and other choices for women and men, and perpetuates gendered violence and shapes our (lack of) responses to it. It is important, therefore, to keep in mind that gender is a social construction and, in the words of sociologist Judith Lorber (1986:576), "what is socially constructed can be reconstructed, and social relations can be rearranged." In this way, social change is always possible.

However, some social analysts say that the decisions that people make (such as the degrees they choose to achieve and the occupations they choose to pursue) are linked not only to how they were socialized but also to how society is structured. We now examine structural features that contribute to gender inequality.

CONTEMPORARY GENDER INEQUALITY

How do tasks in a society get defined as either "men's work" or "women's work," and why are they differentially rewarded? Many sociologists believe that through various social institutions and structures, people assign different roles and responsibilities to women and men based on notions of gender appropriateness and, in the process, restrict women's opportunities. According to feminist scholars, gender inequality is maintained and reinforced through individual and institutionalized sexism. The term *individual sexism* refers to individuals' beliefs and actions that are rooted in anti-female prejudice and stereotypical beliefs. The term *institutionalized sexism* refers to the power that men have to engage in sex discrimination at the organizational and institutional levels of society. This pattern of male domination and female subordination is known as *patriarchy*, defined earlier as a hierarchical system of social organization in which cultural, political, and economic structures are controlled by men. According to some analysts, the location of women in the workforce and on the economic pyramid is evidence of patriarchy (Epstein 1988). In this section, we focus on five structural forms that contribute to contemporary gender inequality: the gendered division of labour, the wage gap, sexual harassment, the glass ceiling and the glass escalator, and the double shift.

The Gendered Division of Paid Work and the Wage Gap

Whether by choice or economic necessity, women have entered the paid labour force in unprecedented numbers in recent years. Today, Canadian women have among the highest labour force participation rates in the world (Wilson 2001). In 1946, fewer than 20 percent of women over the age of 25 were employed in the Canadian paid labour force. This number had risen to 30 percent as of 1961. Today, women represent nearly 50 percent of the total Canadian workforce (47.1 percent in 2006). Until the 1950s, employed women were typically single, young, and childless. Today, however, many women with preschool children are in the paid labour force. As of 2003, 80 percent of all married Canadian women are in the paid labour force, with the largest increases in participation coming from those aged 25 to 44—those most likely to have dependent children at home (Mitchell 2009; Nelson 2010; Wilson 2001).

There are several reasons for these dramatic increases in participation. First, economic growth after World War II saw an increase in available jobs, particularly jobs that were deemed suitable for women such as "supportive" clerical jobs, nursing, and teaching (Mitchell 2009:96). Additionally, structural pressures such as inflation necessitated higher incomes generally, and the shift from a goods-producing or manufacturing economy to a service economy—with the attendant lower wages—and cost-of-living increases in the 1960s drove the increase in dual-earner families. As well, service jobs are ones in which we disproportionately find women. Along with this, cultural values about women's roles, paid employment, marriage, and parenting shifted to the point where today, women working for pay, regardless of their marital or parental status, are no longer so negatively stigmatized as they once were (Mitchell 2009; Nelson 2010; Wilson 2001). Even as women's labour force participation has been increasing, male participation has been gradually declining due to young men staying in school longer, layoffs in the industrial sector, downsizing of business and government, and the long-term trend toward early retirement, either voluntary or involuntary, by men in their 50s and older (i.e., "buyouts"; Nelson 2010).

While many people who know these statistics are optimistic about the gains Canadian women have made in paid employment, this should be a cautious optimism given that women's position in the labour force is still lower than men's in terms of status, opportunities, and salaries. Today, most women and men remain concentrated in occupations that are segregated by gender (see Table 4.1). The term *gender-segregated work* refers to the extent to which men and women are concentrated in different occupations and places of work (Reskin and Padavic 1994). For example, women are predominant in word-processing pools and child-care centres, whereas men are predominant in the construction trades.

Women continue to be concentrated in jobs where they receive lower wages, less prestige, and fewer benefits, on average, than men. However, this inequity is even more compounded by racialization and (dis)ability, a

situation known as *multiple jeopardy* or **intersectionality.** For those who experience multiple barriers to employment, it is nearly impossible to determine which particular barrier was most salient in a given instance of discrimination.

The **wage gap**—the disparity between women's and men's earnings—is the best-documented consequence of gender-segregated work (Reskin and Padavic 1994). No matter what group men belong to in terms of age, racialization, or ability, they earn more than women of that same group. A wage gap persists in Canada across full- and part-time employment and in both annual income and hourly wages (Nelson 2010; Wilson 2001). The fact that women have historically been a cheaper source of labour has been one of the factors in their attractiveness to employers. In 1967, women made 58 percent of men's wages for full-time, full-year work (i.e., 58 cents for each male dollar earned). However, by 2003, women

TABLE 4.1   Women as a Percentage of Total Employed in Occupation, 1987, 1994, 2003, 2006

	1987	1994	1999	2003	2006
Managerial					
Senior management	16.9	19.8	26.8	24.2	26.3
Other management	30.6	36.9	35.7	36.1	36.9
Total management	28.9	35.1	35.1	35.4	36.3
Professional					
Business and finance	40.7	44.6	49.4	48.4	51.6
Natural sciences/engineering/mathematics	16.7	17.0	19.6	22.0	22.0
Social sciences/religion	47.8	56.5	58.2	63.8	71.3
Teaching	57.3	59.4	62.1	62.9	63.9
Doctors/dentists/other health-related	44.1	48.7	47.1	52.1	55.3
Nursing/therapy/other health-related	87.3	87.1	86.5	87.7	87.4
Artistic/literary/recreational	50.4	53.6	54.6	53.4	54.1
Total professional	49.8	52.2	51.8	53.4	55.9
Clerical and administration	74.4	74.9	75.3	75.1	75.0
Sales and service	55.7	56.4	58.7	58.7	56.8
Primary	20.0	21.3	21.6	19.7	20.5
Trades, transport, and construction	5.3	5.4	6.2	6.6	6.5
Processing, manufacturing, and utilities	30.2	29.2	29.8	28.9	31.1
Total*	43.0	45.3	45.9	46.6	47.1

*Includes occupations that are not classified.

Source: Adapted from Statistics Canada, Women in Canada: Work Chapter Updates, 2003, Cat. No. 89F0133X (March 25, 2004). Adapted in Gender in Canada, Fourth Edition *by Adie Nelson, 2010, p. 227, Pearson Canada. Reprinted with permission of Pearson Canada Inc.*

still earned only 71.3 percent of what men earned (Nelson 2010:236). Statistics Canada (1999a) notes that one-half the differential in the data can be explained by "male–female differences in labour market experience, education, and major field of study, occupation, job responsibilities, and industry" (see Figure 4.2). This leaves one-half of the wage differential unexplained. Wilson (2001:224) notes "the unexplained portion is presumed to be due to discrimination." The Canadian Labour Congress's latest pay-equity awareness campaign includes the following tongue-in-cheek headline: "Hurry! 30 percent off women's labour—when they're equal, the savings will be gone! Valid for most workplaces without a union" (Canadian Labour Congress 2009b). Interestingly, the main force driving the overall narrowing of the gendered wage gap has been the stagnation and long-term decline of men's wages generally (Nelson 2010; Roos and Reskin 1992; Wilson 2001).

I SAID...
"YOU'VE COME A LONG WAY BABY!"...

Women   Men

EARNING POWER

Source: Gable, Regina Leader Post 84. *Reprinted by permission of Brian Gable and the* Regina Leader Post.

Sexual Harassment

Millions of men never harass women in the workplace or elsewhere, but so many men do, that, sadly, it is almost impossible for women to avoid the experience (Langelan 1993). In fact, the 1993 Violence Against Women Survey conducted by Statistics Canada found that 87 percent of Canadian women had experienced some form of sexual harassment; just over one-half had been harassed by men they knew (Johnson 1996). **Sexual harassment** is a form of intentional, institutionalized gender discrimination that includes all unwelcome sexual attention affecting an employee's job conditions or creating a hostile work environment. Sociologists Walter S. DeKeseredy and Ronald Hinch (1991:103) define it as "unsolicited, unreciprocated male behaviour that values a woman's sex role over her function as a worker." Sexual harassment includes, but is not limited to, verbal abuse or threats, touching, staring or leering, making jokes, demanding sexual interactions, making repeated propositions, offering comments or questions about a person's sex life, displaying sexually offensive materials, and sexual assault on the job (Benokraitis and Feagin 1995; Nelson 2010). A recent study of female and male undergraduates found that both sexes experienced sexual harassment but that males were generally likely to identify sexual attention from a woman (including instructors and professors) as "non-threatening," even "entertaining," ego-satisfying, and "validating of their masculinity" (Nelson 2010:185). This was especially likely to be the interpretation, regardless of how blatant or forceful the harassing behaviour was, if the female harasser was identified as "attractive." In contrast, a national survey

FIGURE 4.2   Wages of Full-Time Employees,* by Occupation and Sex, 2006

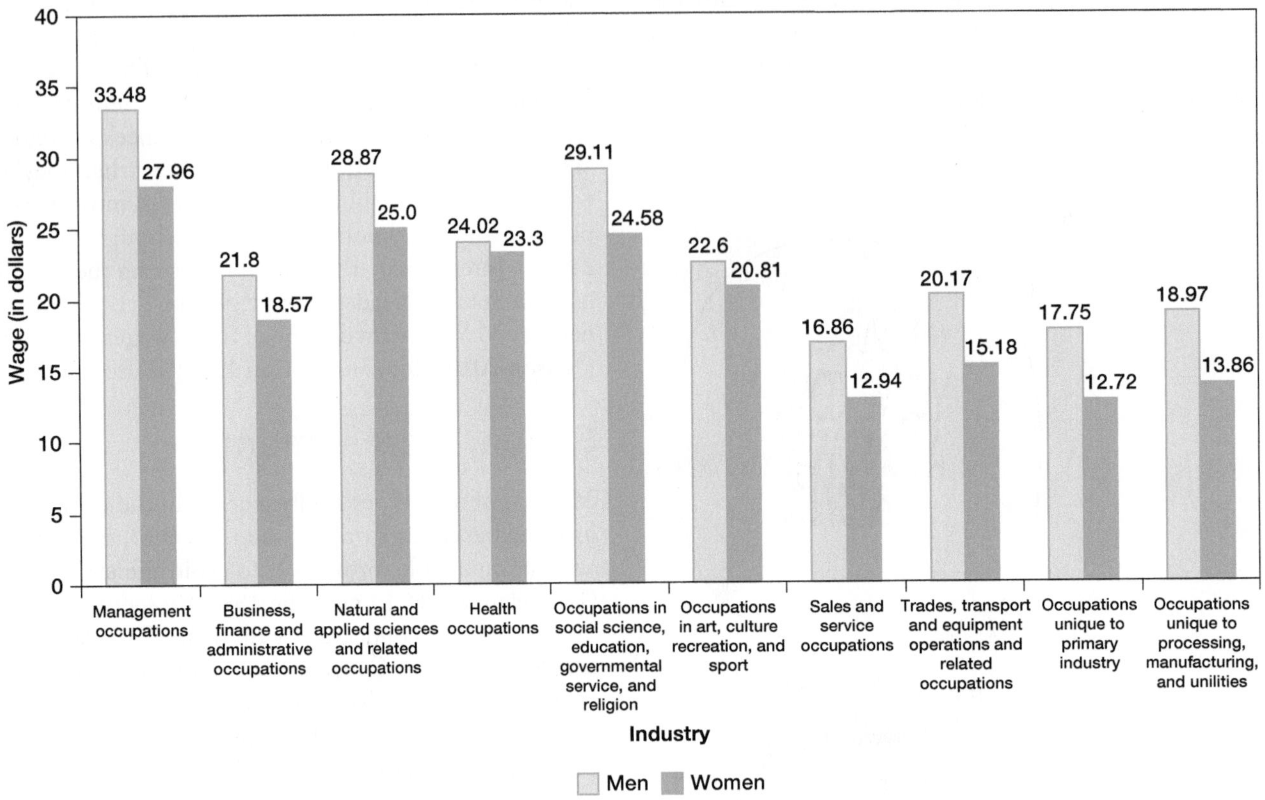

Source: Used with permission of the House of Commons, Government of Canada.

of sexual harassment against employed women found that 90 percent reported at least one incident of unwanted male sexual attention in a public place that resulted in them feeling emotionally shaken and with "the nagging, gnawing sense that something horrible *could* happen" (Smith 1993:70).

People who are accused of sexual harassment frequently claim that their actions were merely harmless expressions of (supposedly) mutual sexual attraction. Sociologist Adie Nelson reports that "research has indicated that behaviour that women defined as unacceptable or offensive, especially in the workplace, was viewed by men as normal and appropriate" (2006:179). Sexual harassment is not about attraction; it is about abuse of power. Sexual harassment constitutes a form of intimidation and aggression: the recipient has no choice in the encounter or has reason to fear repercussions if she or he declines.

The Glass Ceiling and the Glass Escalator

More recently, feminist researchers have used the advancement (or lack of advancement) of women into top-tier management jobs as a litmus test for how well women are faring in the labour force as a whole. They have found that women hold only a handful of top positions. Although they are inching their way up the corporate ladder, women almost always encounter barriers when they try to enter the lucrative and prestigious top positions of their occupations. This is because of what is known as the **glass ceiling**—the invisible institutional barrier constructed by male management that prevents women from reaching top positions in major corporations and other large-scale organizations. Among the reasons cited for this barrier are male executives who believe that male workers will not work for female supervisors, that female workers are supposed to be in support roles only, that the prestige of the profession will decrease if females are admitted, and/or that "the ideal worker is normatively masculine" (Benokraitis and Feagin 1995; Martin 1992:220; Nelson 2010).

The glass ceiling is particularly evident in the nation's 500 largest companies. Catalyst, a not-for-profit global research organization that focuses on women in business, found in their 2008 census that Canadian women continue to be disproportionately underrepresented within *Financial Post* 500 companies (Catalyst 2009). In dramatic contrast to women's overall labour force representation at almost half of the Canadian labour force, Catalyst states that, at current rates of growth, "the number of women reaching the top ranks in Corporate Canada will not reach a critical mass of 25 percent until the year 2025" (Tallarico and Black 2005:1).

Overall, women are most likely to reach top positions in the service sector (for example, banking and diversified finance, publishing, retailing, food services, and entertainment), a sector in which they have traditionally been employed in great numbers.

Even with nearly equivalent numbers of women and men in a workplace, a chilly climate may exist. The *chilly climate* is a concept used to draw attention to the fact that equality of access does not necessarily guarantee equality of treatment within any given institution. The chilly climate can be manifested as an inhospitable workplace for a person of "the wrong sex" through exclusionary, isolating, dismissive, or generally "cool" behaviours, based on cultural notions of gender-appropriate labour (The Chilly Collective 1995; Nelson 2010:240).

Unlike women who enter male-dominated occupations, men who enter female-dominated occupations are apt to find little difficulty rising to the top. In research on men working as registered nurses, elementary teachers, librarians, and social workers, sociologist Christine L. Williams (1995) found that they tended to rise in disproportionate numbers to administrative positions at the top of these occupations. Further, they very often "receive preferential treatment in hiring and promotion" and gain "accelerated access to desirable work assignments and higher salaries" (Nelson 2010:230). Williams (1995:12) calls the upward movement of men in "women's professions" the *glass escalator*

effect because, as she notes, "like being on an invisible 'up' escalator, men must struggle to remain in the lower (i.e., 'feminine') levels of their professions."

The Double Shift

Although there have been dramatic changes in the participation of women in the labour force, the household division of labour by sex has remained unchanged in many families. While more married women now share responsibility for earning part— or all—of the family income, many married men still do not participate in routine domestic chores (Reskin and Padavic 1994). Consequently, many employed women must deal with a double workload. In the words of sociologist Arlie Hochschild (1989), women with dual responsibilities as wage earners and unpaid household workers work "the second shift." However, the most recent data on housework and other unpaid labour demonstrates that men's participation in this type of work has increased from 72 percent in 1986 to 79 percent in 2005. Women's participation has remained steady at approximately 90 percent (Marshall 2006). Interestingly, there have been some changes recently in the daily participation rate of what has been identified as "core housework"—tasks such as meal preparation, cleaning, and laundry. Men's participation went from 40 percent in 1986 to 59 percent in 2005, while women's participation actually decreased from 88 percent to 85 percent (Marshall 2006). There has also been an increase in women's hours per day at paid labour, from 4.5 hours to 5.4, and a corresponding decrease in hours spent doing housework (see Figure 4.3). Basically, "more people today are doing some daily housework than in the past but they are spending less time at it" (Marshall 2006:9). As Statistics Canada reports in *The Daily* (2006b), "while women have made dramatic breakthroughs in the job market, men have only gradually been getting into housework."

While things are becoming slightly more equitable, albeit slowly, on the domestic labour front, the kinds of chores men and women do vary significantly. Women do most of the *daily* chores, such as making beds, cooking, cleaning up after meals, chauffeuring, and taking care of children ("core" household work). As sociologist Adie Nelson states, "women's tasks tend to be routine, repetitive, monotonous and invisible

FIGURE 4.3   Hours per Day Spent on Paid and Unpaid Work: Males and Females, 1986 and 2005

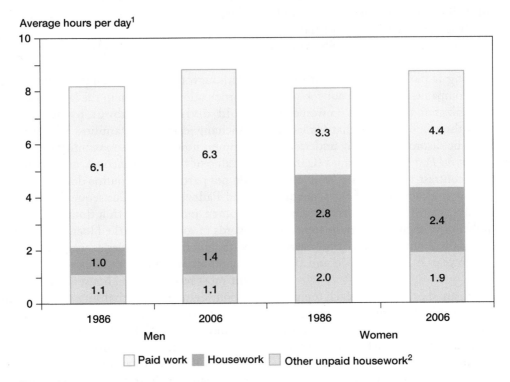

Average hours per day[1]

Men		Women	
1986	2006	1986	2006

Men bars:
- 1986: Paid work 6.1, Housework 1.0, Other unpaid housework 1.1
- 2006: Paid work 6.3, Housework 1.4, Other unpaid housework 1.1

Women bars:
- 1986: Paid work 3.3, Housework 2.8, Other unpaid housework 2.0
- 2006: Paid work 4.4, Housework 2.4, Other unpaid housework 1.9

☐ Paid work ■ Housework ☐ Other unpaid housework[2]

[1]Numbers may not add due to rounding.
[2]Primary child care and shopping for goods and services.

Source: Reprinted with permission from the House of Commons, Parliament of Canada.

(i.e., not noticed unless undone)" (2006:253). Men are more likely to do chores that do not have to be done every day ("non-core" work) and hence allow considerable scheduling autonomy. For example, men typically mow the lawn, repair cars or other equipment, clean out the eavestroughs, and do home improvements (Marshall 2006; Nelson 2006; Shelton 1992).

Since 1996, the Census has included questions on unpaid labour. Data from the 2006 Census demonstrate that the current value of unpaid work in Canada, at least two-thirds of which is performed by women, is approximately 41 percent of Canada's GDP (Mitchell 2009:98), conceding, as sociologist Augie Fleras points out, "the collapse of Canada's market economy" without the invisible labour of women's

unpaid work (Fleras 2005:114). Globally, unpaid work is worth US$11 billion (Mitchell 2009:98).

PERSPECTIVES ON GENDER INEQUALITY

Unlike functionalist and conflict perspectives, which focus on macrolevel sources of gender inequality, feminist perspectives focus on both macro structural levels and micro interactional levels. Interactionist perspectives typically focus on social constructs such as language. It is language, interactionists say, that structures our thinking and discourses about domination and subordination.

The Interactionist Perspective

Symbolic interactionists focus on the differential socialization processes that create masculinity and femininity in people. When a child is assigned a gender at birth, typically corresponding to sex, culturally appropriate gender socialization begins wholeheartedly. Children learn which attitudes, skills, behaviours, likes and dislikes, and so on are appropriate for each gender. Many people believe that socialization today has changed, with fewer restrictions on the ways children are taught to act, think, and feel. It is important to recognize that some differences may exist that are class-based, with people from working classes typically enforcing greater conformity to stereotypical roles, as this may mirror the expectations many of them face in their work lives. People from the middle classes often allow children more autonomy, in keeping with their occupations. In all cases, however, despite our ideas that things have changed, gender roles based on stereotypes are so entrenched and pervasive in the dominant culture that pressure to conform is enormous for most children.

Interactionists, who view society as the sum of people's interactions, consider language extremely significant in defining social realities because it provides people with shared meanings and social realities. Historically, what men have thought, written, and concluded has been the givens of our discourse (Peterson and Runyan 1993). Today, however, English and other languages are being criticized for *linguistic sexism*—that is, for words and patterns of communication that ignore, devalue, or sexually objectify women.

Linguistic sexism, some analysts believe, perpetuates traditional gender-role stereotypes and reinforces male dominance. These analysts note that the idea that women are secondary to men in importance is embedded in the English language: the masculine form (*he*) has traditionally been used to refer to human beings generally, and words such as *chairman* and *mankind* are considered to include both men and women (Miller and Swift 1991). When a woman enters a profession such as medicine or law, she is frequently referred to as a "female doctor" or "woman lawyer"; such terms linguistically protect these male-dominated professions from invasion by females (Lindsey 1994).

Language can also be used to devalue women by referring to them in terms that reinforce the notion that they are sex objects. Terms such as *fox, bitch, babe, kitten,* or *doll* further devalue women by ascribing pet-like, childlike, or toylike attributes to them (Adams and Ware 1995). According to one analyst, at least 220 terms exist for women considered sexually promiscuous, but only 22 terms exist for men considered sexually promiscuous (Stanley 1972). Further, the terms for women are more likely to be derogatory, while those reserved for men are complimentary.

Research by scholars in a variety of disciplines has demonstrated not only the importance of language in patterning our thoughts but also how gender—and the hierarchy it constructs—is built into the English language (Peterson and Runyan 1993). According to sociologists Claire M. Renzetti and Daniel J. Curran (1995:151), "Given that women are denigrated, unequally defined, and often ignored by the English language, it serves not only to reflect their secondary status relative to men in our society, but also to reinforce it."

Linguist Deborah Tannen (1990) has examined how power differentials between women and men at home and in the workplace are reflected in their communication styles. According to Tannen (1990), men and women speak different *genderlects:* women are socialized to speak and hear a language of intimacy and connection, while men are socialized to speak and hear a language of status and independence. For example, women's conversations tend to focus more on relationships with others and include "rapport talk." Men's conversations are more likely to convey messages about their position in the workplace or social hierarchies and include "report talk." In explanation, Tannen (1990:77) states,

For most women, the language of conversation is primarily a language of rapport: a way of establishing connections and negotiating relationships. Emphasis is placed on displaying similarities and matching experiences. . . . For most men, talk is primarily a means to preserve independence and negotiate and maintain status in a hierarchical social order. This is done by exhibiting knowledge and skill and by holding center stage through verbal performance such as story telling, joking, or imparting information.

Men's and women's communication styles also differ. Men are taught to have a more direct style of communication and are more likely to dominate conversations than women are. Men are taught to seek immediate solutions for problems, while women are taught to consider a variety of alternatives before reaching a decision. From this perspective, communication not only reflects women's and men's relative power in society but also perpetuates gender inequalities.

At the microlevel of interactions, we can see some of the ways that male dominance is perpetuated through non-verbal forms of communication, such as bodily movement, posture, eye contact, use of personal space, and touching. Men typically control more space than women do, whether they are sitting or standing. Men tend to invade women's personal space by standing close to them, touching them, or staring at them. Such actions are not necessarily sexual in connotation; however, when a man pats and fondles a flight attendant or a co-worker in the office, these actions do have sexual overtones that cannot be dismissed. Recent sexual harassment cases show that women do not appreciate such acts and feel threatened by them, especially when the toucher is the employer (Lindsey 1994:79).

Although the interactionist perspective has been criticized for ignoring the larger, structural factors that perpetuate gender inequality, it is important to note that language and communication patterns are embedded in the structure of society and pass from generation to generation through the socialization process.

The Functionalist Perspective

In focusing on macrolevel issues affecting gender inequality, functionalists frequently examine employment opportunities and the wage gap between men and women.

According to such early functionalists as Talcott Parsons (1955), gender inequality is inevitable because of the biological division of labour: men generally are physically stronger than women and have certain abilities and interests, whereas women, as the only sex able to bear and nurse children, have their own abilities and interests. Given these biological attributes, Parsons said, men find themselves more suited to *instrumental* (goal-oriented) *tasks* and women to *expressive* (emotionally oriented) *tasks*. In the home, therefore, husbands perform such instrumental tasks as providing economic

support and making the most important decisions for the family, while wives perform such expressive tasks as nurturing children and providing emotional support for all family members. The division of labour by gender ensures that important societal tasks—such as procreation and the socialization of children—are fulfilled and that the family is socially and economically stable.

According to Parsons, this division of labour continues in the workplace, where women again do expressive work and men again do instrumental work. Thus, women cluster in occupations that require expressive work, such as elementary school teaching, nursing, and secretarial work, because of their interests and abilities. Women also are concentrated in specific specialties within professions such as law and medicine because of their aptitude for expressive work and their desire to spend more time with their families than men, who are in the more lucrative specialties. For example, many women in law specialize in family law, and many women in medicine specialize in pediatrics (infants and children), obstetrics and gynecology (women), or family practice. In corporations, women are thought to be more adept at public relations and human resources; men are viewed as more adept at financial management.

In recent years, however, critics have rejected the dichotomy between men's instrumental work and women's expressive work set forth by functionalists (see Scott 1996). These critics have noted that the functionalist explanation of gender inequality does not take into account sex discrimination and other structural barriers that make some educational and occupational opportunities more available to men than to women. It also fails to examine the underlying power relations between women and men and does not consider the fact that society places unequal value on tasks assigned to men and women (Kemp 1994). Functionalist theories tend simply to justify and perpetuate gender inequities rather than provide any real explanations. Furthermore, they implicitly perpetuate heterosexual unions and two-parent families.

Other functionalist explanations of gender inequality focus on the human capital that men and women bring to the workplace. According to human capital explanations, what individuals earn is based on choices they have made, including choices about the kinds of training and experience they accumulate. For example, human capital analysts argue that women diminish their human capital when they leave the labour force to engage in child-bearing and child-care activities, which, of course, are not valued and therefore do not increase human capital. While women are out of the labour force, their human capital deteriorates from non-use. When they return to paid employment, they earn lower wages than men do because they have fewer years of work experience and "atrophied human capital" because their education and training may have become obsolete (Kemp 1994:70).

Critics of the human capital model note that it is based on the false assumption that all people, regardless of gender, racialization, or other attributes, are evaluated and paid fairly on the basis of their education, training, and other job-enhancing characteristics. It fails to acknowledge that White women, Indigenous people, people of colour, and people with disabilities tend to be paid less when they are employed in occupations dominated by White males and even when they take no time off for family duties (Lorber 1994).

Conflict Perspectives

Conflict perspectives on gender inequality are based on the assumption that social life is a continuous struggle in which members of powerful groups (males, in this case) seek to maintain control of scarce resources such as social, economic, and political superiority. By dominating individual women and commanding social institutions, men maintain positions of privilege and power. However, as conflict theorists note, not all men are equally privileged: men in the upper classes have greater economic power because they control elite positions in corporations, universities, the mass media, and government (Richardson 1993).

Conflict theorists using a Marxist approach believe that gender inequality primarily results from capitalism and private ownership of the means of production. The gendered division of labour is seen to be inherent in capitalism and, therefore, will disappear with its demise (Mackie 1987). With the development of private property and inheritance based upon primogeniture, women were transformed from equal, productive members of society in hunting-and-gathering and feudal economies into subordinate wives (and also into property or "chattel"). Further, with the institution of bourgeois marriage, women found it necessary to exchange their sexual and reproductive services for economic support (Mackie 1987).

As industrialization progressed and production moved further from the home, women's skills and education became increasingly separate from those required in the paid labour force. Therefore, according to conflict theorists, the subordinate position of women is the result not of biology, as functionalists believe, but of structural and historical relations.

Conflict theories have been criticized for their view that gender inequality is an inherent and inevitable feature of capitalist relations and for the simplistic and androcentric view that the liberation of women is dependent solely on the liberation of the working class. As sociologist Rosalind Sydie (1983:216) points out, "history would take care of the 'woman question'; therefore the issue [could] be ignored and the 'proper' focus of attention—class relations—be attended to."

Feminist Perspectives

Feminist perspectives in general challenge the status quo with regard to the unequal position of females in society. Feminism, however, is far from being a unified voice. Instead, it is multifaceted, critical, and activist, seeing both the scope of the problem of gender inequality and its solutions differently. Basing their work on a Marxist approach, *socialist feminists* state that under capitalism, men gain control over property and over women. Thus, *capitalism* exploits women in the workplace, and *patriarchy* exploits women at home (Kemp 1994). According to this perspective, capitalists benefit from the gendered division of labour in the workplace because they can pay women lower wages and derive higher profits. Cultural ideas about the appropriateness of women in the home ensure that women return to the home after any stints in the paid labour force (for example, as a worker in the reserve army of labour required by a capitalist economy—see Chapter 2). At the same time, individual men benefit from the unpaid work women do at home by simply not having to do it and by having more leisure time to recuperate from labouring in the capitalist marketplace. The capitalist economic system is maintained because women literally reproduce the next generation of workers while also providing current employees (often including themselves) with food, clean clothes, and other goods and services that are necessary for those who must show up at the workplace each day (Hartmann 1976). Sociologist Marlene Mackie (1987:40) notes that "to pay women for their efforts would mean a massive redistribution of wealth." In addition, men who labour under capitalism can feel a sense of power by having a superior social position to women and may be less apt to agitate. Marxist feminist perspectives have been criticized for their emphasis on male dominance without a corresponding analysis of how men may also be oppressed by capitalism and/or patriarchy.

Unlike socialist feminists, *radical feminists* focus exclusively on *patriarchy* as the primary source of gender inequality. From this perspective, men's oppression of women is deliberate, with ideological justification provided by other institutions such as the media and religion. The subordination of women is naturalized through gendered assumptions inherent in patriarchy. Radical feminism challenges patriarchy and male hegemony, seeing many traditional institutions—the nuclear family in particular—as sites of female enslavement and "domestic servitude" (Fleras 2001:133). Radical feminists are criticized for their focus on patriarchy to the exclusion of other structures of domination (such as class oppression and racism).

Liberal feminists believe that gender inequality is rooted in *gender-role socialization,* which perpetuates women's lack of equal rights and educational opportunities. This type of feminism arises out of classical liberal notions of individual freedoms or liberty. Women are seen to be unequal because they are not given access to the opportunities to make comparable wages and so on. The aim of this type of feminism, therefore, is to ensure that women are equally distributed in education and the paid labour force, alongside men. The system is seen as inherently sound and would be transformed with the removal of discriminatory barriers. Liberal feminism is criticized for its lack of focus on the structural roots of inequalities.

Black feminists, Indigenous feminists, and other feminists "of colour" believe that Indigenous women and women of colour face heightened inequalities based on the multiplicative effect of racialization, class, and gender as simultaneous forces of oppression (Andersen and Collins 1997). Oppressions are seen as intersecting patterns of subordination that cannot be viewed or treated as separate issues, but rather must be seen as a complex whole (see Chapter 3). Solutions to gender inequality, therefore, are inextricably linked with solutions to oppression generally. Lesbians and women with disabilities also experience the effects of this matrix of domination in our hierarchically organized society. Feminists from the so-called margins, those who experience multilayered oppressions, have led the much-needed critique of other feminist perspectives, advancing the incisiveness of feminist perspectives overall and strengthening activism across difference.

HOW CAN GENDER INEQUALITY BE REDUCED?

Although the rights and working conditions of women have improved during the past 50 years, much remains to be done before gender inequality is eradicated or even significantly reduced. As for how, specifically, to go about reducing gender inequality, a point that was made in previous chapters bears repeating: how people view social problems directly affects how they think the problem should be solved. Interactionists, for example, think that one way gender inequality can be reduced is to redefine social realities such as linguistic sexism. In their view, language should be modified so that it no longer conveys notions of male superiority and female inferiority, which are then transmitted intergenerationally through the socialization process.

Some functionalists believe that traditional gender roles should be redefined for the well-being of individuals and society, but other functionalists suggest that women should become more aware of how their human capital is diminished by decisions they make. From this perspective, to be competitive in the workplace, women must have the same educational background and qualifications for positions that men have. Some functionalists also suggest that overt sex discrimination can be reduced by enforcing existing legislation such as the *Canadian Charter of Human Rights and Freedoms* or various provincial human rights codes, which forbid discrimination on the basis of sex or gender. However, this approach would not affect covert or institutionalized discrimination, which has a negative and differential impact on White, non-White, and Indigenous women.

While some conflict theorists view elimination of sex discrimination as the primary solution for gender inequality, those using a Marxist approach believe that gender equality will occur simultaneously when capitalism is abolished. Socialist feminists agree that it should be discarded and a new economy that eliminates the gendered division of labour and the wage gap between women and men should be developed. Liberal feminists say that we could reduce gender inequality by dramatically changing gender socialization and what children learn from their families, teachers, and the media about appropriate masculine and feminine attitudes and behaviour. Radical feminists suggest that gender inequality can be reduced only when patriarchy is abolished. To achieve this goal, they say that the legal system must continue to provide relief for sex discrimination, especially sexual harassment in schools and the workplace, and that alternative institutions must be developed to replace existing gendered social institutions. For example, women's health care centres should replace male-dominated medical practices, and childcare and elder-care centres should assume some of women's caregiving burdens. Finally, Black feminists and other feminists "from the margins" believe that equality will occur only when all women—regardless of racialization, class, gender, age, religion, sexual orientation, and ability or disability—are treated equitably (Andersen and Collins 1997).

Clearly, many gender issues remain unresolved. As a result of technological changes and the proliferation of service jobs, such as information clerk, nurses' aide, and fast-food restaurant worker, which often are equated with "women's work," gender-segregated jobs may increase rather than decrease. Moreover, if the number and quality of "men's jobs" shrink, some men at all class levels may become more resistant to women entering traditionally male-dominated occupations and professions (Reskin and Padavic 1994). Many analysts suggest that for a significant reduction in gender inequality to occur, women have to become more involved in the political arena and take action themselves (see Chapter 13). Again, however, this view implies that the system itself is essentially sound and that reform is possible using the tools that have been traditionally available. What do you think?

WHAT CAN YOU DO?

Gender inequality is a complex social problem that is rooted in structural sexism and manifests itself every day in actions in interpersonal interactions. In terms of proactive things that you can do, then, much depends

on the situations you most often find yourself in, as well as what your interests are. Below are a few suggestions for social action that is either preventative or interventionist. What others can you think of?

- Get involved in political actions in your province or territory by joining in protests and teach-ins and by writing letters to MPs/MLAs and the newspapers (e.g., about pay equity).

- Lobby government to restore and increase core funding for women-serving organizations such as women's shelters, women's centres, and sexual assault centres by writing letters to government officials linking your thoughts with your vote.

- Fundraise alone (smaller-scale effort) or with others (larger-scale effort) to support women-serving organizations in your municipality.

- Create coalitions, along with other justice-seeking groups, to raise awareness of the gender inequality issue of interest to you.

- Start or join a group aimed at effecting change on an issue of interest to you. (For example, many small groups of men at university and college campuses across Canada have started groups and campaigns to end violence against women. As a specific example, in 2001, a group of men at the University of Victoria started the Men Against Sexualized Violence Group. They undertook the White Ribbon campaign, which involved linking up with the National White Ribbon campaign, and came to many classrooms to talk to their peers about the relationship of men to sexualized violence against women.)

- Sign on to Internet listservs and websites of groups and organizations whose interests you share as a means of keeping up to date on the issue and informing others.

- Break the cultural taboo about wage secrecy and share information about wages as widely as possible with co-workers. Many businesses explicitly instruct employees not to discuss their wages. It is very possible that these places are paying people inequitably. You may be surprised to find where you are on the wage scale, despite what company representatives imply. If there are inequities, expose them and lobby the company to redress the situations of underpaid workers.

- When you are being told a sexist joke (or a joke that is typically inherently sexist, like the "blonde joke"), explain to the person that the joke perpetuates harmful and derogatory stereotypes about women and that you do not find demeaning others amusing.

- Be alert and open to hearing about (other) women's experiences with sexism or violence. Ask women you know what their experiences have been. Educate yourself about people's differing experiences—talk to males and females, White women and non-White women, lesbians, trans people, and so on. Try to hear the experience without judgment.

- Report violence whenever you see or hear it by calling 911. Do not get involved in a situation that is unsafe physically: call law enforcement.

- Go to court and watch the trials of men charged with sexual assault, assaulting a woman, or femicide. Critically analyze the approach of the justice system to the case. How did police handle it? How did lawyers handle it? How did the judge handle it? Write a letter to the local newspaper and/or your college/university newspaper with your analysis.

- Think about all the words you use that are gender exclusive and/or sexist. Think of words you can use to replace them and begin practising (don't worry about not being perfect! It takes a long time to unlearn this).

- Educate yourself and others about trans issues. You may even know a trans person and be unaware of it. Try not to assume. Support trans people when and wherever they are.

- Support people's inalienable right to feel comfortable in their own skin.

- Include trans issues whenever you talk or write about gender. In the words of renowned feminist scholar Adrienne Rich (1984:13), "When someone with the authority of a teacher describes the world and you are not in it, there is a moment of psychic disequilibrium, as if you looked into a mirror and saw nothing."

- Next time you, a friend, or a relative has a child, look for gender-neutral clothing, accessories, and toys and books that promote gender equality.

- Think of any gender-stereotypical assumptions you own and challenge them.

- Consumerism is power. Begin a boycott campaign against companies that use women in narrow, stereotypical, and objectified ways in advertising.

Write to the company and tell it what you are doing and why and in what ways you are planning to get your boycott message out (examples can be found on the Canadian White Ribbon Campaign site (**http://www.whiteribbon.ca**).

- Write a letter to the newspaper or advertise in some other way about companies that have gender-equitable policies, wages, and so on. This demonstrates to all companies that the public is watching and does care.

- Report offences and breaches to the appropriate person or office (e.g., to police, ombuds offices, or anti-harassment offices on campuses). Be persistent. Get support. Be an advocate for people whose voices are marginalized in these systems. Help them to report and follow up, if appropriate.

- Volunteer for crisis lines, sexual assault centres, and women's shelters (men can volunteer in many of these places by going out and doing community education and/or fundraising, for example). It is important to demonstrate to the community that violence against women is not a women's issue—it is a community issue.

- If you witness sexual harassment in a public place, lend support to the person suffering and/or make it uncomfortable for the perpetrator to harass (again, do not take risks to your own safety, but intervene where and when possible).

- Think about ways in which your actions and words maintain current beauty standards. Think of ways to celebrate and support all women.

- Read books by pro-feminist men that analyze and help unravel male privilege and that suggest alternatives to "going with the flow" and perpetuating sexism. Some great examples are *The Macho Paradox* by Jackson Katz, *Unraveling the Gender Knot* by Allan Johnson, *New Black Man* by Mark Anthony Neal, and *Guyland* by Michael Kimmel.

- Begin discussions with your family and friends about an issue of sexism that interests you. Inform people about some of the facts you have learned and explain why you feel the situation is unjust.

- Make music, make art, make word collages, make zines—whatever—that promote the message that gender inequality is unjust and has got to go. Get your message out there!

SUMMARY

How Does Sex Differ from Gender?

Sex refers to the biological and physiological aspects of being male or female or intersex; gender is the socially constructed sets of attitudes that dictate what is deemed appropriate, in term of masculinity and/or feminity, for the sexes. In short, sex is what we (generally) are born with; gender is what we acquire through socialization. We currently operate under a two-sex, two-gender system that views male–female and masculine–feminine as not only different, but also binary opposites.

What Are the Primary Socializing Agents?

The key socializing agents are parents, peers, teachers and schools, and the media, all of which may reinforce gender stereotypes and gender-based inequalities as they attempt to teach culturally based gender-appropriate behaviour.

How Are Sexism and Patriarchy Related?

Individual and institutional sexism are maintained and reinforced by patriarchy, a hierarchical system in which cultural, political, and economic structures are dominated by males.

What Are Some of the Primary Causes of Gender Inequality?

Gender inequality results from economic, political, and educational discrimination against women as evidenced in gender-segregated work, which in turn results in a disparity—or wage gap—between women's and men's earnings. Even when women are employed in the same job as men, on average they do not receive the same (or even comparable) pay.

What Is the Second Shift? Why Is It a Problem for Women?

The second shift is the unpaid household work and child care performed by employed women. Many women have a second shift because of their dual responsibilities in the workplace and at home. The typical woman in Canada who combines paid work in the labour force with parenting and housework does not have enough hours in the average day to fulfill all her responsibilities, and many men have been unwilling or unable to pick up some of the slack at home. Women, thus, employ a variety of creative strategies for coping with this problem such as sacrificing leisure time and sleep.

How Does Symbolic Interactionism Explain Gender Inequality?

Symbolic interactionists view gender inequality as the result of faulty gender-role socialization, in which language use, including body language, plays a significant role. Inequality between the sexes is seen to exist and be perpetuated through the use of gender-exclusive and/or sexist language and through non-verbal actions, such as male invasion of female space or males touching females in mixed-gender interactions.

How Do Functionalist and Conflict Analysts Explain the Gendered Division of Labour?

According to functionalist analysts, women's caregiver roles in contemporary industrialized societies are crucial in ensuring that key societal tasks are fulfilled. While the husband performs the instrumental tasks of economic support and decision making, the wife assumes the expressive tasks of providing affection and emotional support for the family. According to conflict analysts, the gendered division of labour within families and the workplace results from male control and dominance over women and resources.

What Are the Major Feminist Perspectives? How Do They Explain Gender Inequality?

In liberal feminism, gender equality is connected to equality of opportunity. In radical feminism, male dominance is seen as the cause of oppression. According to socialist feminists, women's oppression results from capitalism and patriarchy and women's dual roles as paid and unpaid workers. Anti-racist feminism and other feminisms focus on matrices of oppression, linking gender inequality with other forms of oppression, such as class oppression, racialization, sexual orientation or preference, ability, and age.

KEY TERMS

androcentricity, p. 83
gender, p. 83
gendered division
    of labour, p. 88
gender ideology, p. 88

glass ceiling, p. 94
intersectionality, p. 92
intersexed, p. 82
patriarchy, p. 79
rape culture, p. 90

sex, p. 82
sexism, p. 79
sexual harassment, p. 93
wage gap, p. 92

QUESTIONS FOR CRITICAL THINKING

1.   Examine the various administrative offices and academic departments at your college or university. What is the gender breakdown of administrators, faculty, and staff in selected departments? Can you identify a gender-related pattern associated with women's and men's work at your school? What conclusions can you draw about the relationship between gender and employment, based on your observations? Are there any policies in place to counteract gendered inequities in that workplace? Do they work? Why or why not?

2.   Will the increasing numbers of women in higher education, the workplace, and the military, particularly in non-traditional positions or majors, tip the balance of power between men and women and result in greater gender equality in the future? Explain why or why not.

3.   What is the role of violence against women in our culture? In what ways do music videos perpetuate a "rape culture" and violence against women in Canada? What could be done to change this?

4.   In what ways does traditional gender socialization support capitalism?

Explore the topics covered in this chapter at **www.mysockit.com** using the access provided with this text. Interactive resources for studying include video clips, practice tests, learning objectives, and Internet resources.

INEQUALITY BASED ON AGE 5

In spite of several debilitating chronic conditions, Ann Elizabeth Carson, aged 79, is an active writer, sculptor, painter, and poet. Since her retirement as counsellor, supervisor, and instructor at York University in Toronto, she has written *Shadows Light*, a collection of poetry accompanied by colour photographs of her sculptures, and *My Grandmother's Hair*, a social memoir in prose, poetry, and visual images about how we are shaped by family and social contexts. Her latest book, *We All Become Stories: Creating Memory*, is 12 profiles of older people recounting the changing experience of memory over their lifetimes. Ann maintains a part-time private psychotherapy practice; leads workshops that explore how art, movement, and writing broaden our perspective; and reads from her books at various venues. She participates in a study group on international affairs, two book clubs, and the work of the Older Women's Network (OWN), and keeps fit with circuit training, rebounding, and walks on the Beaches boardwalk.

Author's personal communication, November 2008

It has been frequently noted that our society is aging. Figure 5.1 shows the growth of the proportion of seniors in our population from less than 5 percent in 1982 to about 13 percent today, and to a projected 25 percent by the middle of this century. But this aging might not be very negative when so many seniors like Ann Carson are contributing to our society.

Ann Carson's example indicates that it is still possible to make a substantial contribution to society years after the traditional retirement age. Two terms can help us distinguish between people's actual age and their performance. Although Ann's *chronological age*—age based on date of birth—is quite high, her *functional age*—individual attributes such as physical appearance, mobility, strength, coordination, and mental capacity that are used to assign people to age categories (McPherson 1990:31)—is considerably lower. A wide range of physical, psychological, and intellectual factors can influence our functional age (Chudacoff 1989). Although we may appear to be younger or older than our chronological age, there are some things that we do in life, such as driving a car or voting, that are determined by our chronological age rather than our functional age. For the younger person, then, changes in chronological and

FIGURE 5.1   Growth of Senior Population, Canada, 1982 to Mid-21st Century

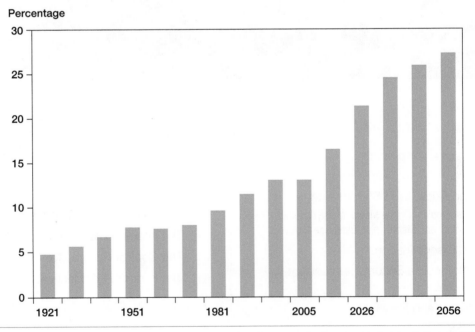

Source: Martin Turcotte and Grant Schellenberg, 2007, A Portrait of Seniors in Canada, *Ottawa: Statistics Canada, Social and Aboriginal Statistics Division.*

functional age are positive. However, as some people age, they begin to lose some of the functional abilities, such as vision or hearing, that are necessary for driving. Thus, the older person may view changes in chronological and functional age negatively. The field of *gerontology* examines the biological, physical, and social aspects of the aging process. In this chapter, we focus primarily on **social gerontology**—the study of the social (nonphysical) aspects of aging—as we examine age classifications in Canada and such problems as ageism, workplace discrimination, retirement, income security, leisure, health, illness and health care, victimization, family relationships, housing and long-term care, and death and dying. To provide a comparative portrait of the situation and experiences of seniors, we also make several comparisons to younger people.

Finally, the sociological perspectives are used to help explain aging problems. The chapter concludes with a discussion of ways to reduce inequality based on age and what you can do about it.

CHARACTERISTICS OF LATER MATURITY AND OLD AGE

Later maturity is usually considered to begin in the 60s. The major changes associated with this stage are social. Although many people in their 60s retain sufficient physical strength to be able to carry on an active social life, their peer groups can shrink noticeably as friends and relatives die. Many people in later maturity find themselves caring for people of their own age and older.

Old age is usually considered to begin in the late 60s or in the 70s. Although some people continue to work past age 70, most have left paid employment by their 70th birthday. Problems are not just social but also increasingly biological. Some physical changes, such as arteriosclerosis (the loss of elasticity in the walls of the arteries) are potentially life threatening (Belsky 1990). As bones become more porous, they become more brittle; a simple fall may result in broken bones that take longer to heal than those of a younger person. Strength, mobility, and height may decline, and the abilities to see, hear, taste, touch, and smell

may diminish. Because taste and smell work together to allow us to enjoy food, eating may become less pleasurable, contributing to poor nutrition in some older adults (Belsky 1990). Although it is not true of all elderly people, the average person over age 65 does not react as rapidly (physically or mentally) as the average person who is younger than 65 (Lefrançois 1999).

The chances of heart attacks, strokes, and cancer increase along with the likelihood of some diseases that primarily affect the elderly. Alzheimer's disease, a degenerative disease that attacks the brain and severely impairs memory, thinking, and behaviour, may be the best-known example. People with this disease have an impaired ability to function in everyday social roles; over time, they cease to be able to recognize people they have always known, and they lose all sense of their own identity. Finally, they may revert to a speechless childishness, at which point others must feed them, dress them, sit them on the toilet, and lead them around by the hand. Alzheimer's and other dementias strike 8 percent of those over age 64, according to the 1991 Canadian Study of Health and Aging. Today in Canada there are likely over 350 000 people suffering from dementia, according to Mary Anne Burke and her colleagues (1997:25). Most of the people with dementia (78 percent) live in institutions (Statistics Canada 1999b:63). In spite of promises for cures in the future, the disease can last 8 to 20 years, ending only with death (Lefrançois 1999).

Gerontologists have come to realize that there are significant differences among people who are now called the "young-old" (ages 65 to 74), the "middle-old" (ages 75 to 84), and the "old-old" (ages 85 and older). Although more than half of all people aged 65 and older are in the young-old category, the old-old category has grown more rapidly over the past two decades than has any other age group in Canada. Between 1981 and 2005, the number of seniors aged 85 and older increased from 196 000 to 492 000 (Turcotte and Schellenberg 2007). As with other age categories, it is difficult to make generalizations about older people. But it is not true that all old people feel lonely and lost in retirement, live in institutions, and are uniform in their health, activities, and financial situation (Novak and Campbell 2006:291).

PROBLEMS LINKED TO BEING ELDERLY

Ageism and Age-Based Stereotypes

Ageism—prejudice and discrimination against people on the basis of age—is a social problem that particularly stigmatizes and marginalizes older people. Gerontologist Robert Butler (1969) introduced the term *ageism* to describe how myths and misconceptions about older people produce age-based discrimination. According to Butler, just as racism and sexism perpetuate stereotyping and discrimination against people of colour and all women, ageism perpetuates stereotyping of older people and age-based discrimination. Most research has therefore focused on the negative and differential impact ageism has on older people. There are more stereotypes about the physical and mental abilities of older people than there are about the abilities of people in any other age category.

Older people are stereotyped in numerous ways. Some stereotypes depict them as slow in their thinking and movement; as living in the past and being unable to change; and as cranky, sickly, and lacking in social value (Novak and Campbell 2006:7). Examples of this kind of stereotyping are common in the workplace, but are also appearing in universities where "mature students" are looking to improve their skills. According to an article by Nadja Sayej in the *Globe and Mail*, "Dozens of groups [are] taking aim at mature students with members from Melbourne to Glasgow, Toronto to Halifax, popping up on Facebook." Expressions such as "down with mature students," "go back to your life and stop trying to reinvent yourself," and "old, boring and balding" are used to describe mature students (Sayej 2008:L4). Other stereotypes suggest that older people are "greedy geezers," living an affluent lifestyle and ignoring the needs of future generations (Toner 1995). When many people accept age-based stereotypes, they can affect how people vote and what types of social policies legislators enact. Negative stereotypes of older people reinforce ageism and influence how younger people interact with older people.

Although most of us do not believe that we engage in stereotypical thinking about older people, researcher William C. Levin (1988) found that college students in his study evaluated people differently on the basis of their assumed age. Levin showed students three photographs of the same man, who had been made up to appear 25 in the first photo, 52 in the second, and 73 in the third. He then asked them to evaluate these (apparently different) men for employment purposes. Many students described the "73-year-old" as less competent, less intelligent, and less reliable than the "25-year-old" and the "52-year-old." Older people also give low ratings of the elderly. In a survey of older people, Ian D. Graham and Paul M. Baker (1989) found an inverted U-shaped curve of status ratings on a six-point scale: older and younger people were rated lower than middle-aged people. Clearly, our place in the social structure changes during our life course, and if we live long enough, any of us may become the target of stereotyping and discrimination directed at older people (Hooyman and Kiyak 2008).

SOCIAL PROBLEMS IN THE MEDIA

BOX 5.1   Media Ageism: Preferring Younger and Stereotyping Older Age Groups

Although media coverage of teenagers can be negative, as soon as teenagers turn 18 years of age, the media want to attract them. Advertisers want the 18- to 34-year-olds because the advertisers believe that if this segment is attracted to products, they will maintain "brand loyalty." Older segments of the population, according to the advertisers, have already made up their minds.

One of the other consequences of advertisers' beliefs is that television and radio networks change or drop programs well established with the 50+ age group to appeal to younger viewers and listeners. Whereas many programs with older actors, such as Angela Lansbury (*Murder She Wrote*), Andy Griffith (*Matlock*), and Betty White and the rest (*The Golden Girls*), were on prime time until the mid-1990s, and *The West Wing* until mid-2006, few shows now have older actors (MacDonald 2004). Perhaps surprisingly, a continuing demand exists for *The Golden Girls*. In June 2009, Betty White said, "When the DVD came out, I thought who's going to watch it? We're on four times a day.

They know the lines better than we ever did. But sure enough, the DVD keeps selling all over the world. I hear from Finland, Bangladesh, Sri Lanka" (Ehrbar 2009:49). More people want to watch older women than advertisers think.

In addition, media portrayal of seniors is often degrading. At the World Congress of Gerontology held in Vancouver in July 2001, journalist and now senator Laurier LaPierre said, "Older people are essentially represented with ridicule" and "Older people have no life of their own beyond these media-imposed titles (bewildered grandfather or meddling mother-in-law)" (Muggeridge 2001:5). In the same article, Dolores Ewan reported on an ad from a major department store chain, which pictured the surveying of seniors. If the seniors disliked a style, that was taken as an indicator of the style being fashionable. But society does not complain about this kind of stereotyping. Ewan went on to say that if the ad had shown Blacks or Indigenous people in this light, "there would have been a hue and cry about bigotry and racism" (Muggeridge 2001:5). In mid-2009, TD Canada Trust (a bank) ran several commercials featuring older men who seemed very much behind the times. They did not believe that a bank would give them ideas about saving money, although they were ultimately convinced. But most of the commercial was devoted to their stereotypical old-fashioned ways.

What should media do about the nature of their coverage of elderly people? To what extent should the media, particularly public media like the CBC, organize their programming to appeal to different age groups?

Workplace Discrimination

Despite the *Canadian Charter of Rights and Freedoms,* which protects all Canadians against discrimination based on many characteristics including age, many subtle forms of age discrimination in the workplace remain. This does not include mandatory retirement, which has now been eliminated in all the provinces and territories (CBC News 2008c). Still, some employers prefer younger workers to older workers, whom they believe have health problems, poor motivation, and low ability. Employers may hire younger workers because they believe that they can pay them less than older workers and make more demands on their time and energy. Older employees sometimes find that their employers have downgraded their job descriptions, failed to promote them or grant them raises, or are trying to push them out of their jobs so that cheaper workers can be hired. In a study of Statistics Canada's employment numbers from 2000 to 2004, Chhinzer and Ababneh reported that younger workers aged 25 to 34 were a third less likely to experience a layoff than an older worker (Grant 2008:B10).

Despite the negative stereotypes, some employers have found it profitable to keep or hire older employees, and some older employees are able to continue working. In 2004, 1.7 percent of the Canadian labour force (about 300 000 people) over 64 years of age had a job, mostly in agricultural and religious occupations (Turcotte and Schellenberg 2007). To support employers who are attempting to overcome these stereotypes, the Canadian Association for Retired People (CARP) created an award for best employers for 50-plus Canadians to recognize and reward those companies that value older workers. The 2004 recipients of this award were RBC Royal Bank, Global Banking Service Centre, Merck Frosst, The Home Depot Canada, and Avis Rent A Car (CARP 2005a). Unfortunately, this award has not been continued, but it is to be hoped that those companies who treated older workers well would continue to do so.

With the end of mandatory retirement, some of these problems will vanish. However, new ones will emerge, likely around removing people who are thought to be unable to do the job.

Retirement: Income Security and Leisure Activities

The *retirement principle* is the "idea that at a fixed age, regardless of mental or physical ability, a person leaves work" (Novak and Campbell 2006:212). In the past, people in many occupations and professions (including tenured faculty members at universities, police officers, and fire fighters) faced mandatory retirement at age 65, regardless of their health or desire to continue working. It was simply assumed that everyone experienced a decline in physical and mental ability at a specific age. Although the median age of retirement decreased from 65 to about 60 years of age in the 1990s, it has since increased slightly, at least for males (see Figure 5.2).

The severe decline in the value of pensions and investments that occurred the fall of 2008 may cause many more people to continue to work after age 65. An October 2008 study by Desjardins Financial found

FIGURE 5.2   Median Age at Retirement, by Sex, Canada, 1976 to 2005

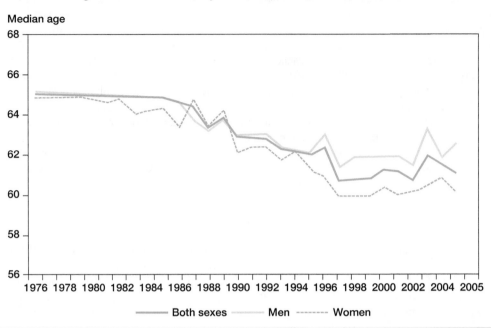

Source: *Martin Turcotte and Grant Schellenberg, 2007,* A Portrait of Seniors in Canada, *Ottawa: Statistics Canada, Social and Aboriginal Statistics Division.*

that 42 percent of Canadians over the age of 40 plan to delay retirement because of the global recession (Grant 2008:B10).

The next problem to deal with is the orientation of the retiree. Many are well prepared with good health, friends, and financial resources. Others are not so well prepared. There remains a small percentage of people who are enjoying life less after retirement, and these are the people whose health is fair or poor, who do not have much financial support, and who did not plan for retirement (Turcotte and Schellenberg 2007).

While some retirees are enjoying life less than others, fewer Canadians are suffering now from income insecurity in their retirement than in the past, and most retirees are far from being dependent. Some actually provide financial support to children and grandchildren. The results of a global study conducted by Oxford University's Institute of Ageing showed that "16 percent of those in their 60s and nearly one third of those in their 70s provide financial support to grandchildren" (Galt 2007:B5). To be more precise about how well off seniors are, we turn to figures from Statistics Canada. Using data collected from 1983 to 2004, on average, Canadian workers had family disposable incomes at

age 75, when most are retired, that were 80 percent of their incomes at age 55, when they were working. Naturally, the extent to which Canadians maintained their income in retirement varied with their level of income and availability of pensions, but those with the lowest incomes did not experience a worse financial situation, whereas wealthier Canadian workers experienced a substantial financial decline after they retired. The richest workers, those in the top 20 percent of the income distribution at 55, received on average about 70 percent of their working income during their 70s. The people in the lowest 20 percent of income earners saw no decline in their income because they received various transfer payments, such as Old Age Security (OAS) and Guaranteed Income Supplement (GIS), an income supplement for those with a low income or no income other than OAS, and, if they were working, the Canada or Quebec Pension Plan (CPP/QPP). Over this period, as illustrated in Figure 5.3, the percentage of senior low-income earners declined substantially. The percentage of low-income earners aged 65 and older declined from more than 20 percent to just over 5 percent. Interestingly, the percentage of low-income earners of other ages remained the same.

FIGURE 5.3   Incidence of Low-Income, by Age Group, Canada, 1980 to 2003

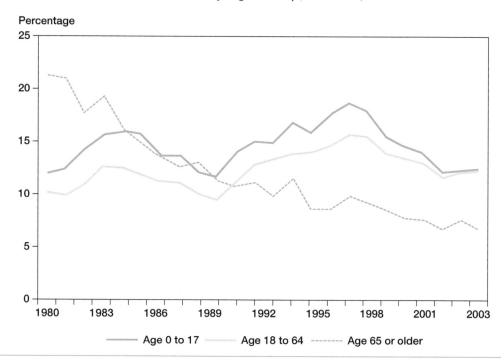

Source: Martin Turcotte and Grant Schellenberg, 2007, A Portrait of Seniors in Canada, *Ottawa: Statistics Canada, Social and Aboriginal Statistics Division.*

However, the above studies took place before the stock market meltdown in the fall of 2008. In late 2008, Mercer, the benefits consulting firm, reported that assets available in Canadian pension plans fell to their lowest level in a decade. Whereas the ratio of assets to liabilities was 1.20 in 2000, the ratio had fallen to .72 in the third quarter of 2008 (Daw 2008:B2). Thus, in the future, retirees with a pension or investments could experience a greater drop in their standard of living.

Although most seniors are doing well now, not all subgroups of seniors are as comfortable. Figure 5.4 shows that in 2000, people living alone, especially women and recent immigrants, did not fare so well. Whereas 30 percent of males and 40 percent of females living alone had low income, among very recent immigrants these percentages rose to 60 and 70 percent respectively. These people have less opportunity to save for retirement or to have a substantial return from CPP/QPP.

Another problem that is often mentioned with retirement is people being at a loss regarding their use of leisure time. But here again, Canadians generally participate in many hours of active and passive leisure on a daily basis. Statistics Canada has surveyed elderly Canadians about four types of leisure activity: passive leisure, cognitive leisure, social leisure, and physical leisure:

- Passive leisure consists of such activities as watching television, listening to the radio, and taking pleasure drives.

- Cognitive leisure is made up of reading books or newspapers, taking part in educational activities, attending entertainment events, participating in hobbies, playing cards, and using the computer or the Internet.

- Social leisure includes socializing with friends and relatives and talking on the phone.

- Physical leisure includes all physical recreation.

Cognitive leisure, social leisure, and physical leisure can be combined to form active leisure in comparison to the passive leisure activities.

FIGURE 5.4   Percentage of Low-Income among Seniors Living Alone, by Sex and Period of Immigration to Canada, 2000

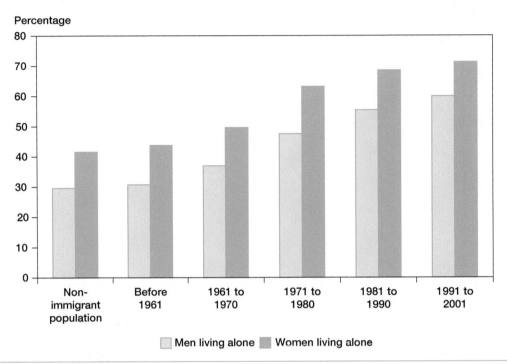

Percentage

Men living alone   Women living alone

Source: Martin Turcotte and Grant Schellenberg, 2007, A Portrait of Seniors in Canada, *Ottawa: Statistics Canada, Social and Aboriginal Statistics Division.*

Passive and active leisure both increase after 65 years for men and women. Men participate in about four hours of active and passive active leisure, and women participate in four hours of active leisure and slightly more than three hours of passive leisure (Turcotte and Schellenberg 2007).

Health, Illness, and Health Care

At age 93, Malcolm Clarke plays doubles tennis four times a week and sails his boat; he also shops and cooks for himself (Brody 1996). Although Clarke attributes his longevity and good health to "luck," studies show that many older people are not developing the disabling diseases that were common in the past, and the vast majority function quite well. Improvement in the health status of older people has been attributed, at least in part, to better education (knowing what to do and not to do to stay healthy), nutrition, and public health care. Figure 5.5 shows that a high percentage of people 65 years of age and older with university education report having excellent or very good health. Since the number of people with university education is increasing, it is likely that in the future a higher percentage of people will report excellent or very good health.

However, this positive outlook is not true for Indigenous people in Canada. Figure 5.6 shows that for both Indigenous males and females, the percentage of seniors who report excellent or very good health is much below that of the total Canadian population. The percentage of Indigenous seniors who report a high level of health is just lower than those with less than high-school education in the total population (see Figure 5.5). This finding might also be predicted from the fact that 79 percent of Indigenous seniors have less than high-school education.

While the data about Indigenous seniors may be discouraging, the percentage of Indigenous people with a university education increased from 9 percent in 1996 to 13 percent in 2001 (Turcotte and Schellenberg 2007). So, we might expect that the outlook for reported health

FIGURE 5.5   Percentage of Canadians Reporting Excellent or Very Good Health, by Age Group and Level of Education, 2003

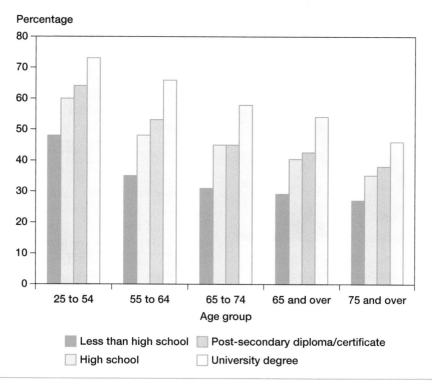

Source: *Martin Turcotte and Grant Schellenberg, 2007,* A Portrait of Seniors in Canada, *Ottawa: Statistics Canada, Social and Aboriginal Statistics Division.*

for Indigenous seniors, like that for the total population of seniors, will improve in the future.

Despite feeling healthy, people aged 65 and older account for about one-third of all dollars spent on health care, and this figure is expected to rise dramatically with the aging of the Canadian population. Many believe the cost problems associated with health care will be further intensified by the feminization of aging—the formerly increasing proportion of older people who are female—because women, on average, have a greater likelihood of being poor and having no spouse to care for them (Weitz 1996). Some researchers state that dire predictions of skyrocketing costs are greatly overstated. Robert Evans and his colleagues (2001:160) report that numerous studies show that the effects of aging on health care costs are relatively small, as a result of the "compression of morbidity" and falling needs among the elderly. Studies in British Columbia, for example, show minimal effects of population aging on health costs. Everybody—not just the elderly—is

using more complex and costly services. The claims that the aging of the population will bankrupt the system, while having intuitive appeal, serve the interests of those who provide care and who wish to privatize parts of health care (Evans et al. 2001:187).

Victimization

Although older people are in fact less likely than younger people to be victims of violent crime, they fear this type of crime more than people in other age categories do. According to police-reported statistics, in 2007, seniors were victimized at a rate of 160 incidents per 100 000 population, and they were more likely to be victimized by someone they knew than by a stranger. Senior victims of violence were more likely to be victimized by an adult child or a current or former spouse. While overall rates of violence were greater for senior men than women, women were more likely to be victims of family violence than men (Statistics Canada 2008g:7).

Retirement is a time for leisure and reflection if it comes by choice and the individual is healthy and financially prepared. But for others, adapting to less income, increased dependency, and the loss of roles can be difficult.

pre-existing health problems or inhibit an older person's ability to function independently. Many analysts believe that family violence is under-reported because people who know of the abuse are unwilling to report it, and older people who are the victims are either too ashamed or afraid to notify authorities. Although some analysts initially believed that younger people were likely to exploit older people who were psychologically and economically dependent on them, just the opposite has often proven true: younger people are more likely to exploit elders on whom they themselves are dependent (Novak and Campbell 2006:311).

Now safe havens have been created for abused seniors. The first one was created in Calgary. Edmonton has one that has expanded to seven apartment units. There are now apartments in Surrey, B.C., Winnipeg, and Toronto, the last one called Pat's Place (addresses are not given to protect the seniors). Pat's Place is not a traditional shelter, but rather an apartment where a person can receive counselling and will be helped to create a long-term plan (Javed 2008: A17).

Family Problems and Social Isolation

Older people can easily become socially isolated from their families. Younger family members who once asked for advice stop asking, perhaps because they think that their older relatives are out of touch or perhaps because of some miscommunication. Sometimes, younger family members feel unduly burdened by the concerns of their elders, which don't seem truly important to them. For one reason or another, older people can come to believe (rightly or wrongly) that they are isolated from the rest of the family.

In 1996, 29 percent of people aged 65 and above lived alone versus 9 percent of people aged 15 to 64 (Statistics Canada 1999b:31). Many older people live alone voluntarily, but others live by themselves because they are divorced, widowed, or single. The 1996 General Social Survey showed that 75 percent of Canada's widows aged 65 and older live alone (Bess 1999:2). But, living alone is not always the equivalent of social isolation. Many older people have networks of family and friends with whom they engage in activities. Contrary to

However, older people are often the targets of other types of crime. Con artists frequently contact them by mail or telephone to perpetrate scams that often promise prizes or involve a "stockbroker" selling a "hot" stock or other commodity (Hays 1995). In 1998, CARP, an advocacy group for those 45-plus years of age and/or retired, created a National Forum on Scams and Frauds, which produced recommendations such as providing more information to seniors, instituting cooling-off periods for contracts, and freezing assets of scam artists. A new brochure has been prepared with more scams to watch for, such as the Nigerian e-mail or letter asking for money with the promise of larger sums later, and pyramid schemes (CARP 2005b). The appendix of the 1998 edition of the CARP brochure highlighted the Illinois law that makes defrauding a person of $5000 or more a more serious felony if the victim is over 60 years of age (CARP 1998). Is this a positive kind of discrimination that Canadian lawmakers should consider?

Victims of violence may be more vulnerable to complications resulting from physical violence than younger victims, since physical injuries may worsen

FIGURE 5.6   Percentage of Total Canadian and Indigenous Off-Reserve Population 25 Years and Older Reporting Excellent or Very Good Health, 2000 and 2001

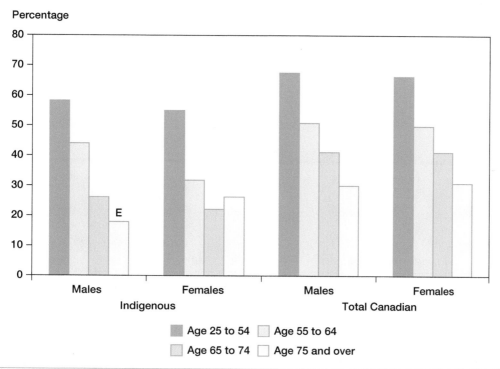

Source: Martin Turcotte and Grant Schellenberg, 2007, A Portrait of Seniors in Canada, *Ottawa: Statistics Canada, Social and Aboriginal Statistics Division.*

the myth that older people are abandoned by their families, Canadian research has shown that most seniors live in a situation called "intimacy at a distance"—families usually provide much support for their older members (C. Rosenthal 1987). For those without children, many form other ties (McMullin and Marshall 1996). Many seniors also engage in a variety of work, as shown by Ann Elizabeth Carson in the vignette at the beginning of this chapter and by Turcotte and Schellenberg in their report *A Portrait of Seniors in Canada* (2007). To a large degree, the extent to which they associate with others has to do with social class: people with more money are able to pursue a wider array of activities and take more trips than are those with more limited resources.

Perhaps one of the saddest developments in contemporary society is the growing number of older people who are homeless. While some older homeless people have lived on the streets for many years, others have become homeless because they have been displaced from low-income housing, such as single-room occupancy (SRO) hotels. In recent years, many SROs in cities such as Vancouver and Toronto have been replaced by high-rise office buildings, retail space, and luxury condominiums. Older people who are homeless typically lack nutritious food, appropriate clothing, adequate medical care, and a social support network. They tend to die prematurely of disease, crime victimization, accidents, and weather-related crises, such as winter blizzards, when an individual without shelter can freeze to death on a park bench. Fortunately, the picture is not this bleak for many older people who remain in residences they have occupied for many years.

Housing Patterns and Long-Term Care Facilities

Many people mistakenly assume that most older people live in long-term care facilities such as nursing homes. As Figure 5.7 shows, even for those 85 years and over,

FIGURE 5.7   Percentage of Seniors Living in Institutions, by Age Group and Sex, 2001

Percentage

[Bar chart showing percentage of seniors living in institutions by age group and sex. Y-axis ranges from 0 to 40 in increments of 5. X-axis shows three age groups: "65 to 74", "75 to 84", and "85 and over". Men shown in light bars, Women in darker bars. For 65 to 74: Men approximately 2, Women approximately 2.5. For 75 to 84: Men approximately 6, Women approximately 10. For 85 and over: Men approximately 23, Women approximately 36.]

Age group

Men   Women

Source: Martin Turcotte and Grant Schellenberg, 2007, A Portrait of Seniors in Canada, *Ottawa: Statistics Canada, Social and Aboriginal Statistics Division.*

only about a quarter of the men and a third of the women live in institutions.

More than people of any other age category, older people are likely to reside in the housing in which they have lived for a number of years and own free and clear of debt. Because of the high cost of utilities, insurance, taxes, and repairs and maintenance, older women, who are more likely to live alone than are older men, are at a distinct disadvantage if they attempt to maintain their own homes. And, as shown in Figure 5.4, a high percentage of women living alone have a low income.

Some low-income older people live in planned housing projects that are funded by federal and local government agencies or private organizations, such as religious groups. Older people with middle and upper incomes are more likely to live in retirement communities or in seniors' residences that provide amenities such as housekeeping, dining facilities, and transportation services. In recent years, religious organizations and for-profit corporations have developed *multilevel* facilities, which provide services ranging from independent living to skilled nursing care all at the same site.

Although only about 7 percent of older people live in nursing homes or other long-term care facilities in Canada, living in an institutional setting remains the only option for some older individuals. What alternative living arrangements can you suggest for older people in the future?

When we refer to housing the elderly, it is important to distinguish between residences for the elderly and long-term care facilities. Long-term care is defined as a

> range of services needed for persons who are dependent on help with basic activities of daily living (ADL) such as bathing, dressing, eating using the toilet, and moving around. This central personal care component is frequently provided in combination with help with basic medical services such as help with wound dressing, pain management, medication, health monitoring, prevention, rehabilitation or services of palliative care. (Huber 2005:17)

Long-term care is expensive. How much does Canada spend for this essential service? The Organization for Economic Cooperation and Development (OECD), an organization of the major Western industrialized nations and Japan, has provided some data about provision of long-term care among most of its members. Canada spends 1.23 percent of its GDP on long-term care (.99 percent is public, .24 percent is private funding, 1.06 percent is for institutions, and .17 percent is for home care). The OECD average for 19 countries is 1.25 percent of GDP in total, with a similar public/private distribution, slightly higher support for home care, and slightly lower support for institutions. Thus, Canada is an average contributor to long-term care among industrialized nations. As might be predicted, Sweden, with a higher percentage of elderly and a collective orientation, contributes a higher percentage of GDP to long-term care, and the United States, with a lower percentage of elderly and an individualist orientation, contributes a lower percentage of GDP to long-term care (Huber 2005:26).

While some long-term care facilities may be excellent, others have undergone extensive media scrutiny and public criticism for violations of regulations and harmful practices such as elder abuse. These facilities are also very expensive. In Ontario, for example, the annual cost of a long-term care placement is $43 000 (Steed 2008). As a result, many people select home care, adult day care, or assisted living for older relatives rather than institutional settings, which tend to depersonalize individuals and "reify the image of age as inevitable decline and deterioration" (Friedan 1993:516). Home care is being seen now as a way to reduce costs in the health care system. The annual price of home care in Ontario is about $3000 (Steed 2008). Although home care has received increased resources in the past decade, problems of getting home care still exist (Segall and Chappell 2000; see Chapter 10). In Ontario, the Aging at Home Strategy, a government initiative, has been expanded from $700 million over three years to $1.1 billion over four years (Steed 2008).

Death and Dying

In previous generations, death was a common occurrence in all stages in the life course, but today most deaths occur among older people. About 52 percent of deaths among Canadians are due to heart disease and cancer, with cancer being the leading cause of death (Statistics Canada 2008l). Stroke, chronic lower respiratory diseases, diabetes, influenza and pneumonia, Alzheimer's disease, and kidney disease follow these causes of death for older people. Between 2000 and 2004 the death rates declined for most of these diseases (Statistics Canada 2008l), but it is still true that most deaths occur among older people. According to social gerontologists, the increased association of *death* with the process of *aging* has caused many people to deny the aging process and engage in ageism as a means of denying the reality of death, particularly their own (Atchley 2000). Euphemisms such as "pass away" or "sleep" are often used to refer to death by those who are trying to avoid its reality. Researchers have found, however, that many people do not actually fear death itself as much as they fear the possibility of pain and suffering, loss of control, and the consequences of their death for survivors (Marshall and Levy 1990). Given a chance to choose, most people would choose a painless death over prolonged physical and mental deterioration and the prospect of being a burden on their families. Quoting Ann Elizabeth Carson again:

> At age 79 death will come sooner rather than later. Like so many others I've talked to, it's not death I fear, but the process of dying. As the result of an adverse drug reaction 13 years ago most of the commonly used drugs are toxic for me, or cause an allergic reaction. In dealing with chronic pain over the years I have researched alternative methods of pain control like acupuncture, coditron (a little gizmo that delivers electrical stimulation

to the meridian points identified by Chinese acupuncture), and meditation and am now looking into these and other ways to alleviate pain during palliative care. However, it is very difficult to find allopathic (traditional) medical practitioners willing to discuss the toxic or allergic consequences of anaesthetics and painkillers. I can only hope that there will soon be significant advances in this respect, or that I will not need surgery in my last years. (personal communication, November 2008)

Some researchers have also found that older people have less fear of death than younger people do (Gesser, Wong, and Reker 1986, quoted in Novak and Campbell 2006:323); others have found that education and religious beliefs are important factors in how people view death and dying (Kalish 1985).

There are three widely known frameworks for explaining how people cope with the process of dying: the stage-based approach, the dying trajectory, and the task-based approach. The *stage-based approach* was popularized by Elisabeth Kübler-Ross (1969), who proposed five stages in the dying process: (1) denial ("Not me"); (2) anger ("Why me?"); (3) bargaining and asking for divine intervention to postpone death ("Yes me, but . . . "); (4) depression and sense of loss; and (5) acceptance. According to some social scientists (Kalish 1985; Marshall 1980), Kübler-Ross's study is limited because she focused primarily on the attitudes of younger people who had terminal illnesses. These scientists argue that the same stages may not apply to older people who believe that they have already lived a full life.

In contrast to Kübler-Ross's five stages, the concept of the *dying trajectory* focuses on the perceived course of dying and the expected time of death. From this perspective, not all people move toward death at the same speed and in the same way. A dying trajectory may be sudden (e.g., a heart attack) or slow (e.g., lung cancer) and is usually shaped by the condition causing death. A dying trajectory involves three phases: the *acute* phase, in which maximum anxiety or fear is expressed; the *chronic* phase, in which anxiety declines as the person confronts reality; and the *terminal* phase, in which the dying person withdraws from others (Glaser and Strauss 1968).

The *task-based approach* suggests that daily activities can still be enjoyed during the dying process and

that fulfilling certain tasks makes the process of death easier, not just on the dying person, but on everyone involved. *Physical tasks* are performed to satisfy bodily needs and to minimize physical distress. *Psychological tasks* help to maximize psychological security, autonomy, and richness of experience. *Social tasks* sustain and enhance interpersonal attachments and address the social implications of dying. *Spiritual tasks* are performed to identify, develop, or reaffirm sources of spiritual energy and to foster hope (Corr et al. 1994). Most important in any approach are the rights of the dying person and the way in which care is provided.

Technological advances in medicine have helped to focus attention on the physical process of dying and, in recent years, the needs of dying patients and their families. Many people are choosing to sign a *living will*—a document stating a person's wishes about the medical circumstances under which his or her life should be allowed to end. Rejecting the idea of being kept alive by elaborate life-support systems and other forms of high-tech medicine, some people choose to die at home rather than in a hospital or nursing home. The hospice movement has provided additional options for caring for the terminally ill. **Hospices** are organizations that provide a homelike facility or home-based care (or both) for persons who are terminally ill. Some hospices have facilities where care is provided, but hospice is primarily a philosophy that affirms life, not death, and offers holistic and continuing care to the patient and family through a team of visiting nurses, on-call physicians, and counsellors. Home care enables many people to remain in familiar surroundings and maintain dignity and control over the dying process (Corr et al. 1994). Sophia Mumford summarizes the feeling of many older people about death:

I'm afraid of one thing. I want my death to be dignified. My fear is that something will cause me to live past the point where my life has value. I don't want to live on. . . . From now on, if life says it's leaving, I'm not doing anything about it. If I get a bad pain and it's diagnosed as cancer, then I won't wait, I'll go. I'm ready, because I feel I've had a good life. (quoted in Terkel 1996:429)

Because many people want a dignified death, the topic of euthanasia will likely become very prominent in the future (see Box 5.2).

SOCIAL PROBLEMS AND SOCIAL POLICY

BOX 5.2   Euthanasia

According to Greek etymology, *euthanasia* means, literally, a "good death," and it comes in several types. *Passive euthanasia* means withholding or ceasing treatment of someone not likely to recover from a disease or injury. *Active euthanasia* means intervening to hasten someone's terminal illness, with, for example, a lethal dose of sedatives. *Assisted suicide* means helping someone end his or her life with, for example, drugs. Since advances in medical technology have made it possible to keep people alive longer than in the past, questions are arising about the best time and method of dying.

A number of high-profile cases, such as those of Sue Rodriguez and Robert Latimer, have highlighted the problems in this area. Sue Rodriguez was a 42-year-old woman suffering from ALS (Lou Gehrig's disease) who appealed all the way to the Supreme Court of Canada to have the legal right to have someone help her commit suicide when she wanted to die. In 1993, the Supreme Court decided against her, supporting the law prohibiting assisted suicide. Sue Rodriguez actually did die with the assistance of an unidentified doctor and Svend Robinson, an NDP MP from British Columbia. Robert Latimer is a Saskatchewan farmer who administered a lethal dose of carbon monoxide gas to his daughter, Tracy, who suffered from severe cerebral palsy. He was accused of second-degree homicide. After his first trial, at which he was found guilty, the judge imposed a two-year sentence. This sentence was appealed to the Saskatchewan Court of Appeal, which sentenced Latimer to the mandatory penalty for second-degree homicide, life imprisonment with no chance of parole for 10 years. Later, in 2001, the Supreme Court of Canada refused to review that sentence. In 2008 Latimer was granted day parole (Hunter 2008).

An Angus Reid poll inquired about Canadians' attitude to the Latimer case and to mercy killing. This poll indicated that Canadians were very supportive of Latimer: almost three-quarters of them said that he had acted out of compassion and should have received a more lenient sentence (Sallot 1999:A5). It also found that Canadians are quite supportive of legalizing euthanasia: approximately 41 percent said mercy killing should not be against the law under appropriate circumstances; 38 percent said it should be illegal, but perpetrators should be treated with leniency; and 18 percent said it should be treated like any other murder (2 percent had no opinion). Notably, the young (18 to 34 years of age) were slightly less lenient than older Canadians.

Some countries are making euthanasia legal. In April 2001, the Netherlands became the first country in the world to legalize euthanasia, and later that year, Belgium did the same. In 2005, the number of reported legal euthanasia cases in the Netherlands was 1933. In Canada, much emphasis is put on individual rights, and the *Charter of Rights and Freedoms* supports this emphasis. In late November 2009, Quebec's College of Physicians cautiously endorsed limited euthanasia. Polls in Quebec showed 75 percent of the people support euthanasia. However, the spokesperson for federal Justice Minister Rob Nicholson said the government has "no intention to come forward with legislation on this" (Perreax 2009:A8).

Should we have a right to die when and how we want to? With the increasing cost of health care, should we ever consider rationing health care so that younger people have more access to care than older people? Do you believe that Canada should legalize euthanasia? Do you think that young people might want to euthanize older relatives to make their own lives easier? If we do legalize euthanasia, what safeguards do you think should be imposed?

PERSPECTIVES ON AGING AND SOCIAL INEQUALITY

Although each of the major sociological perspectives focuses on different aspects of aging and social inequality, they all provide insights into how people view the aging process and how ageism toward the young and the old contributes to social inequality in society.

The Functionalist Perspective

According to functionalists, dramatic changes in such social institutions as the family and the economy have influenced how people look at the process of growing old. Because of these influences, both the complexity and the stability of society require that people spend much time preparing for occupational roles and then leaving them at an arbitrary time, such as age 65, when it is likely that they are no longer able to keep up with the role demands and jobs must be available to younger people. Encouraging older people to leave is referred to as *disengagement theory*; this theory suggests that older people want to be released from societal expectations of productivity and competitiveness. At the same time, disengagement facilitates a gradual and orderly transfer of statuses and roles from one generation to the next instead of an abrupt change, which might result in chaos. Retirement policies, then, are a means of ensuring that younger people with more up-to-date training (for example, newer computer skills) move into occupational roles while ensuring that older workers are recognized for years of service (Williamson et al. 1992).

Critics of this perspective object to the assumption that disengagement is functional for society and say that it is dysfunctional. Older people may not want to disengage when they are still productive and gain satisfaction from their work. Some have suggested that CPP/QPP and other pension systems will be strained by the proportionately fewer workers who are paying into the plans, which must support an increasing number of retired workers (see *elderly dependency ratio* on page 121). As mentioned above, mandatory retirement has been eliminated in Canada, so pension plans will be less strained if people continue to work after age 65.

The Interactionist Perspective

Interactionist perspectives on aging focus on the relationship between life satisfaction and levels of activity. The *interactionist activity theory* is based on the assumption that people who are active are happier and better adjusted than are less-active persons. According to this theory, older people shift gears in late middle age and find meaningful substitutes for previous statuses, roles, and activities (Havighurst et al. 1968). Those who remain active have a higher level of life satisfaction than do those who are inactive or in ill health (Havighurst et al. 1968). In contrast to disengagement theory, activity theory suggests that older people must deny the existence of old age by maintaining middle-age lifestyles for as long as possible. But some older people are themselves critiquing this idea. According to an interview study conducted by Stephen Katz, some older people object to the idea that those preferring their inner world to being active are thought to be problem people. Katz (2000) suggests that this emphasis on activity could be transformed into a means of controlling older people.

The Conflict Perspective

In analyzing the problems of older people in contemporary capitalistic societies, conflict theorists focus on the political economy of aging. From this perspective, class constitutes a structural barrier to older people's access to valued resources, and dominant groups attempt to maintain their own interests by perpetuating class inequalities. According to conflict theorists, aging itself is not a social problem. The problem is rooted in societal conditions that older people often face without adequate resources, such as income and housing. People who were poor and disadvantaged in their younger years become even more so in old age. Today, in Canada, a much smaller percentage of seniors live in low-income situations now than as recently as two decades ago (see Figure 5.3). Whereas in 1980, 22 percent of seniors had a low income (the low-income cut-off [LICO] is discussed in Chapter 2), in 2003 that percentage had declined to 7 percent. However, health care costs could be a greater problem in the future as programs are delisted from health care support and new, expensive drugs are not included in support plans.

In the capitalist system, many older people are set apart as a group that depends on special policies and programs. Fortunately, in Canada, seniors do not have to depend on special government programs; Canada's health program is universal. But it is under siege by those who would like to see greater privatization of services and who claim among other things that seniors will bankrupt the system (Evans et al. 2001).

Conflict analysts draw attention to the ways that class, gender, and racialization divide older people, just as they do everyone else. The conflict perspective adds to our understanding of aging by focusing on how capitalism devalues older people, especially women. Critics assert, however, that this approach ignores the fact that industrialization and capitalism have been positive forces in society, greatly enhancing the longevity and quality of life for many older people.

The Feminist Perspective

Feminist theorists emphasize inequalities between men and women. It is well known that although women live longer than men, they are subject to higher rates of disability (see Chapter 10) and their incomes are lower. In 2003, whereas unattached men had median after-tax incomes of $20 200, unattached women had median after-tax incomes of $18 200 (Turcotte and Schellenberg 2007:Table 2.2.1). And we have seen that women living alone are more likely to have low income than men (Figure 5.4).

In addition, feminists argue that more attention should be paid to the health problems of women, as in the study done by the Ontario Women's Health Council to determine whether this difference in disability is alterable.

HOW CAN AGE-BASED INEQUALITY BE REDUCED?

The inequality experienced by older people needs to be addressed. People who have had no opportunity to engage in leisure activities earlier in their life are unlikely to suddenly become leisure-oriented. Employment, family responsibilities, and leisure must become less compartmentalized, and changes in technology and employment may make this possible. At present, however, it is difficult for most people to have *free time* and *money* at the same time.

For older people many dimensions must be addressed. As we have seen, technological innovations and advances in medicine have contributed to the steady increase in life expectancy in Canada. Advances in the diagnosis, prevention, and treatment of diseases associated with old age, such as Alzheimer's, may revolutionize people's feelings about growing older. Technology may bring about greater equality and freedom for older people (Novak and Campbell 2006:90–94). Home-based computer services, such as online banking and shopping, make it possible for older people to conduct their daily lives without having to leave home to obtain services. Computerized controls on appliances, lighting, and air conditioning make it possible for people with limited mobility to control their environment. Soon, sensing devices may be developed that could monitor a person's daily behaviour, such as the use of a kettle or motion, and report any deviation over the Internet to a concerned relative or central office. Technology also brings recreation and education into the home. For example, Senior Net is a computer network that encourages discussion of diverse topics and provides hands-on classes in computer use. Robotics and computer systems may eventually be used by frail older people who otherwise would have to rely on either family or paid caregivers to meet their needs or move to a nursing home. However, class is again a factor: while much of home care is covered by the health care system in Canada, many of the home accessibility features are paid for by users or their families.

Economic concerns loom large in the future as baby boomers (those born between 1946 and 1964) will be retiring soon if they have not already done so, bringing about a dramatic shift in the **elderly dependency ratio**—the number of workers necessary to support those over age 64 or the ratio of seniors to 100 workers aged 20 to 64. Obviously, as the percentage of seniors in the population rises, there would be a smaller percentage of workers to support them, and ultimately, according to some speculation, seniors would bankrupt the system. In Canada, this ratio was 14.7 in 1960 and 20.3 in 2000, and it is projected to rise to 43.7 in 2040 (Huber 2005:104). If this projection were the only important consideration, transfer payments to seniors would be overwhelming. However, other factors make this unlikely: unlike in the American system, changes in the pension systems in Canada have brought about a decline in the number of low-income seniors without creating many high-income seniors (Myles 2000:312–313) and, thus, fewer candidates for the epithet "greedy geezer." Moreover, the federal government has increased the pension contributions of current workers so that the plans will not go bankrupt. However, the wealth inequality could change in the future with the increased value of employment and personal (RRSP) pension plans going to the higher-income retirees. Advocates of *productive aging* suggest that instead of pitting young and old against each other, we should change our national policies and attitudes. We should encourage older people to continue to create their own roles in society, not to disengage from it. To some extent, as mentioned, this will happen with the end of mandatory retirement. In addition, real value should be placed on unpaid volunteer and caregiving activism, and settings should be provided in which older people can use their talents more productively (Hooyman and Kiyak 2008).

Functionalists suggest that changes must occur in families and other social institutions if we are to resolve problems brought about by family diversification and increased workplace demands. Some adult children have to provide economic and emotional support for aging parents and grandparents at the same time as they are caring for their own children. These people are called the *sandwich generation.* According to the 2002 GSS, almost 3 in 10 people aged 45 to 64 years with unmarried children under 25 in the home were also caring for a senior (Statistics Canada 2004i). This is some 712 000 people in Canada. Various sacrifices made by these people included changing hours, losing income, missing promotional opportunities, and incurring medical expenses. Women tend to devote more hours than men to caring for seniors, and they tend to provide more personal care while men provide economic and transportation care. Although some tax incentives are available for those taking care of seniors, given that the sandwich generation reports generally feeling stressed, more support would certainly be welcomed by them.

Other social analysts suggest that people need to rely more on themselves for their retirement and old age. Younger workers should be encouraged to save money for retirement in RRSPs. As conflict theorists have pointed out, however, many young people have loans to repay or do not have jobs or adequate income to meet their current economic needs, much less their future needs.

From the conflict perspective, age-based inequality is rooted in power differentials, and short of dramatic changes in the structure of political and economic power in society, the only way for older people to hold on to previous gains is through continued activism. Advocacy groups like CARP make presentations to government and hold forums (e.g., on scams and frauds) about policies that would benefit many older people. According to interactionists, however, individuals like Ann Elizabeth Carson who maintain strong relationships with others and remain actively involved throughout their lifetime have reason to be optimistic about life when they reach old age.

WHAT CAN YOU DO?

- Study the amount of caregiving that your elderly relatives and those of your friends require.

- Volunteer for an agency that helps seniors in your neighbourhood. Helping a senior person may be as simple as listening to one on a regular basis.

- Set up a system of habits, such as exercise, recreational reading, and saving for retirement in an RRSP, to establish an activity pattern that will prepare you for later years.

- Help some seniors lobby for some improvements, such as educational and fitness programs in communities.

- Challenge some of the ageist stereotypes held by some young people. When one of the authors was showing a news clip about people over 80 years of age and their romantic interests, he heard sounds of disgust from the back of the classroom. You might start a discussion of ageism with questions about romantic expectations after 80. The vast majority of your age group will be there someday.

- Study the differences in problems currently faced by senior men and women. To what extent will these problems change as more women become more self-supporting?

SUMMARY

What Do We Experience in Later Maturity and Old Age?

The life course is generally divided into infancy and childhood, adolescence and young adulthood, middle age, later maturity, and old age. In later maturity, we increasingly find ourselves involved in caring for people of our own age and older people. Problems of older adults vary widely because of the diverse needs of the "young-old" (ages 65 to 74), the "middle-old" (ages 75 to 84), and the "old-old" (ages 85 and older).

Problems Linked to Being Elderly

Ageism is prejudice and discrimination against people on the basis of age. Ageism is a social problem because it perpetuates negative stereotypes and age-based discrimination, particularly against older people.

Despite laws to the contrary, older workers may experience overt or covert discrimination in the workplace. Retirement brings about changing roles and a loss of status for those older people whose identity has been based primarily on their occupation, but Canadians have until now maintained income security and been active in leisure activities. For some older people, low incomes, disease, and lack of health care or home care are problems. Older people may become the victims of scams by con artists and elder abuse by family members or nursing-home personnel, but they experience the lowest rates of violent crime for any age group. For some older people, moving into a nursing home represents a loss of autonomy.

How Do People Cope with the Process of Dying?

Three explanations have been given for how people cope with dying. Kübler-Ross identified five stages that people go through: (1) denial; (2) anger; (3) bargaining; (4) depression; and (5) acceptance. However, the dying trajectory suggests that individuals do not move toward death at the same speed and in the same way. The task-based approach suggests that daily activities can still be enjoyed during the dying process and that fulfilling certain tasks makes the process of death easier not just on the dying person but on everyone involved.

How Do Functionalist and Interactionist Explanations of Age-Based Inequality Differ?

According to functionalists, disengagement of older people from their jobs and other social positions may be functional for society because it allows the smooth transfer of roles from one generation to the next. However, interactionists suggest that activity is important for older people because it provides new sources of identity and satisfaction later in life.

How Do Conflict and Feminist Theorists Explain Inequality Based on Age?

According to conflict theorists, aging itself is not a social problem. The problem is rooted in societal conditions that older people often face when they have inadequate resources in a capitalist society. In the capitalist system, older people are set apart as a group that depends on special policies and programs. Feminists argue that older men tend to be in a more advantageous social and economic position than older women. Since this disadvantage for women begins much earlier, institutions such as schools and businesses should work to eliminate the inequality they generate.

KEY TERMS

ageism,   p. 108
elderly dependency ratio,   p. 121

hospice,   p. 118
social gerontology,   p. 107

QUESTIONS FOR CRITICAL THINKING

1.   If you were responsible for reducing ageism, what measures would you suggest to bring about greater equality? What resources would be required to fulfill your plan?

2.   Since we have eliminated laws regarding retirement for older people, are there limits we should consider?

3.   Does disengagement theory or activity theory more closely reflect how you plan to spend your later years? What other approaches to aging can you suggest?

4.   Think of synonyms, both formal and informal, for *senior,* and look up the word *senior* in a thesaurus. How ageist are these synonyms? Make up new synonyms that are not ageist.

PEARSON

Explore the topics covered in this chapter at **www.mysockit.com** using the access provided with this text. Interactive resources for studying include video clips, practice tests, learning objectives, and Internet resources.

INEQUALITY BASED ON SEXUAL ORIENTATION

6

The State has no business in the bedrooms of the nation.

Pierre Elliott Trudeau, past prime minister of Canada, and justice minister in 1969

Ironically, where bisexuals are presumed to have access to heterosexual privilege, we are in fact contending with both externalized and internalized homophobia and heterophobia, all at the same time.

Ruby Rowan, in "Sleeping With the Enemy and Liking It: Confessions of a Bisexual Feminist," 2001

I have a lesbian daughter and only a handful of people know about it. I have not told any close family member aside from one brother. I have not told my best friend. I have only told one colleague at work, and that was someone I trust completely not to blab. So if I don't tell people about my gay daughter, if I keep her gayness a big dark secret—which is easy to do because she lives in Toronto with her partner who can easily be referred to as her roommate—how am I any better than the people who avoid gay people or who tell gay jokes or even those who physically harm people just for being gay? If I am willing to be silent about my own daughter's gayness—and it's more than that—I am afraid to tell people about it—because I am not sure how they will react—how am I any better than the worst homophobe?

Marilyn Totten, in A Mother's Story: Critical Consciousness, Conscience, and Homophobia, *2004*

Schools are meant to develop civic virtue and responsible citizenship, to educate in an environment free of bias, prejudice and intolerance.

Supreme Court of Canada decision in Trinity Western University v. British Columbia College of Teachers, *May 17, 2001, para 13*

There was only one person who figured out that I was gay and I find that pretty shocking; but in school I was afraid to be out. Now I have to be careful because my sister might suffer if the kids at school know.

"Svend" in Queer Youth in the Province of the "Severely Normal" *(Filax 2006)*

When I was in high school I can't remember any deep and challenging discussions with my friends about homosexuality. The only time it came up, really, was when we'd yell "fag" down the hall after a boy we didn't like or found effeminate. On reflection, the cruelty and homophobia are clear, but thirty years ago these comments were just considered to be part of high school life. I can't imagine what it must have been like for youth who were questioning their orientation and scared by our bullying.

Hazelle Palmer, executive director of Planned Parenthood of Toronto, in Hear Me Out: True Stories of Teens Educating and Confronting Homophobia, *2005*

To be fully accepted for who I am as a queer person ... well that would be perfect.

"Chastity" in Queer Youth in the Province of the "Severely Normal" *(Felax 2006)*

I found myself having sex with boys to prove I wasn't gay.

"Lisa" in "Everyday Acts of Survival and Unorganized Resistance: Gay, Lesbian and Bisexual Youth Respond to Oppression" (Dobinson 2004)

As the opening quotations illustrate, there are a number of diverse issues that need to be considered when looking at sexual orientation and discrimination. This chapter will examine many issues surrounding sexual orientation, beginning with a look at definitions of various orientations and the extent of homosexuality, bisexuality, homophobia, and biphobia in Canada.

We will try to understand how and why prejudice and discrimination against people based on sexual orientation still happen in Canadian society, a society that prides itself on its high levels of "tolerance" and even "acceptance." We will review some of the laws that deal with sexual orientation and look specifically at hate crimes and ways they are being dealt with. Finally, we will review several theories that pertain to sexual orientation and discrimination and consider ways we can advocate for social change.

Simplistically, **sexual orientation** refers to a preference for emotional–sexual relationships with individuals of the "same" sex (homosexuality), the "opposite" sex (heterosexuality), or both (bisexuality) (Lips 1993). This type of definition, however, encourages us to think of sexual orientation as an "either–or" proposition—you are *either* heterosexual *or* you are homosexual *or* you are bisexual—when, in fact, not only do many people exhibit a shifting sexual orientation over their lifetimes, they may identify differently depending upon whether we are talking about behaviour, attraction, fantasy, desire, or self-identity. This will be discussed further shortly.

The terms *homosexual* and *gay* are most often used in association with males who prefer "same"-sex relationships; the term *lesbian* is used in association with females who prefer "same"-sex relationships. Heterosexual individuals, or those who prefer "opposite"-sex relationships, are sometimes referred to as *straight* (e.g., "Is everyone else in your family straight?"). It is important to note, however, that heterosexual people are much less likely to be labelled by their sexual orientation than are people who are gay, lesbian, or bisexual, because their heterosexuality is presumed normal and is taken for granted. We will discuss this presumption of normalcy later in the chapter when we examine heterosexual privilege. It is also important to note that although in lay terms, we talk about the "opposite" sex, there are biologically, physiologically, cognitively, and emotionally very few differences between males and females. In effect, there is no such thing as an "opposite" sex. The myth of the opposite sex is one of the most persistent and foundational binaries we adhere to in our culture.

What criteria do social scientists use to classify individuals as gay, lesbian, or bisexual? In a ground-breaking study of sexual orientations published in the mid-1990s, researchers at the University of Chicago established three criteria for identifying people as homosexual or bisexual: (1) *sexual attraction* to persons of one's own sex, (2) *sexual involvement* with one or more persons of one's own sex, and (3) *self-identification* as gay, lesbian, or bisexual (Michael et al. 1994). According to these criteria, then, engaging in a homosexual act does not necessarily qualify a person as homosexual. Many participants in the Chicago study indicated that although they had had *at least* one homosexual encounter when they were younger, they were no longer involved in homosexual conduct and never identified themselves as lesbians, bisexuals, or gay. In fact, self-definition plays a critical role in confounding attempts to classify people definitively. For example, many people who engage in same-sex behaviours on an occasional or even regular basis may not perceive themselves as homosexual or bisexual at all. In fact, among many (mostly young) people, bisexual behaviour at parties or raves has achieved a sort of cachet, sometimes called "bisexual chic" in academic literature.

NATURE AND EXTENT OF INEQUALITY BASED ON SEXUAL ORIENTATION

How many homosexuals and bisexuals are there in Canada? That question is likely impossible to answer definitively for all the reasons discussed above. The 2001 Canadian Census was the first to ask questions specifically about same-sex couples, a full four years before same-sex marriage was legalized. In that year, 34 200 Canadian couples, or one-half of 1 percent of all couples, claimed same-sex common-law status (Statistics Canada 2002j). In 2006, the number reporting same-sex couple status (common law and married) increased 11 percent to 37 885 couples (0.6 percent of all couples in Canada) (Statistics Canada 2008s). Of these, 7500 couples were legally married, representing 0.1 percent of all married couples—a percentage comparable to other nations who sanction same-sex marriage (Statistics Canada 2008s). Independent and Statistics Canada researchers caution, however, that the reported numbers of same-sex couples may be quite low in relation to the actual number of same-sex couples in Canada, as reporting same-sex couple status to the government is very new and many people are understandably wary. Indeed, in their report of recent research of Canadian lesbians, researchers for Status of Women Canada Irene Demczuk, Michele Caron, Ruth Rose, and Lyne Bouchard (2002:viii) state that "to this day, most lesbian couples still hide their sexual orientation and their conjugal situation, especially in the workplace, in order to protect themselves against the negative reactions of those around them." Jerome Ryckborst, a Vancouver writer, described the conflict that many gay and lesbian Canadians had to grapple with when faced with reporting, in essence, their sexual orientation to the Canadian government: "It does feel risky . . . but the need for our community to grow up, stand up and be counted outweighs the personal concerns" (Anderssen 2002:A9). Approximately 53 percent of reported same-sex couples were male, and only about 3 percent of these couples have children living with them. In contrast, and in keeping with gender socialization norms and typical post-divorce custody arrangements in Canada, approximately 16 percent of the female couples had children living with them; female couples were slightly more than five times more likely than male couples to have children living with them (Statistics Canada 2007c).

While we now have a count, however inaccurate, of same-sex common-law and married couples in Canada, the general population census has yet to count people according to their sexual orientation. Most estimates of the homosexual population have historically placed percentages between 1 and 10 percent. While there are many reasons, discussed later in this chapter, why people in Canada may wish to keep information about their sexual orientation from being scrutinized by government agencies, legalization of same-sex marriage has opened the door for the collection of official statistics. For example, the 2003 Canadian Community Health Survey (CCHS) was the first Statistics Canada survey to include a question on sexual orientation (Statistics Canada 2008i). The CCHS is an annual survey of Canadians aged 12 and up regarding health-related matters, such as health status and health care usage. The CCHS found that of Canadians aged 18 to 59, 1.0 percent identified themselves as gay or lesbian, and a further 0.7 percent identified themselves as bisexual (see Table 6.1).

Further, in the 2004 GSS (released February 2008), a survey of criminal victimization conducted every five years found that 1.5 percent of Canadians identified as homosexual, 94 percent identified as heterosexual, and 5 percent did not identify their sexual orientation (Statistics Canada 2008i). Regardless of the numbers of people who identify as other than heterosexual, the central issue is the need to eliminate prejudice and discrimination against people based on sexual orientation.

Homosexuality has existed in most, if not all, societies throughout human history. Acceptance (and tolerance) of homosexuality and bisexuality exist along a continuum. Most tribal societies regard some homosexual acts as socially acceptable at least some of the time. For example, the Siwans, the Azande, the Dahomy, and the !Kung of Africa, and the Sambians of New Guinea regard same-sex relations as a "normal" part of maturing (Blackwood 1986). In contrast, for most of the past 2000 years, there have been groups—sometimes entire societies—that considered homosexuality "a crime against nature," "an abomination," or "a sin" (Doyle 1995:224). In any case, most societies have norms pertaining to **sexuality**—attitudes, beliefs, and practices related to sexual attraction and intimate relationships with others. Cultural sexuality norms are based on the assumption that some forms of attraction and relationships are *normal* and *appropriate* while others are *abnormal* and *inappropriate*. Up until very recently, in many societies, including modern North American and European societies, homosexuality had been classified as a form of deviance. This classification has made people the targets of prejudice and discrimination so severe that some have even been killed for being gay. Prejudice toward gay men and lesbians is known as **homophobia**—the irrational and excessive fear or intolerance of homosexuals and homosexuality. Additionally, **biphobia** refers to fear and intolerance of bisexuality. According to sociologists, homophobia and biphobia are actually *socially determined prejudices*, not medically recognized *phobias* (Lehne 1995; Wilton 2000).

Elisabeth Young-Bruehl, a psychotherapist on faculty at Columbia University in the United States, classifies what she calls "primary prejudices," such as racism, sexism, homophobia, and anti-Semitism, into three categories: obsessive, hysterical, and narcissistic

TABLE 6.1   Sexual Orientation, 2003

| | Homosexual or Bisexual | |
	Number	Percentage of Total Population
Total	316 800	1.7
Newfoundland and Labrador	4100*	1.3*
Prince Edward Island	**	**
Nova Scotia	5900*	1.1*
New Brunswick	7200*	1.6*
Quebec	103 400	2.3
Ontario	107 200	1.5
Manitoba	9600*	1.5*
Saskatchewan	6600*	1.2*
Alberta	23 400*	1.2*
British Columbia	47 700	1.9
Male	172 600	1.8
Female	144 300	1.5
18–34	139 200	2.0
35–44	101 900	1.9
45–59	75 700	1.2

* Use with caution.

** Suppressed due to high sampling variability.

Source: Statistics Canada, 2004, "Canadian Community Health Survey," **The Daily** *(June 15). Retrieved February 24, 2009 (http://www.statcan.gc.ca/daily-quotidien/040615/dq040615b-eng.htm).*

(1996, in Baird 2007). People who embody *obsessive* prejudices feel the objects of their prejudice are "omnipresent conspirators or enemies set on one's destruction" and as such, they "must be eliminated" (Baird 2007:80). Anti-Semitism is an example of obsessive prejudice. People who embody *hysterical* prejudices are those who view the objects of their prejudice as "'other,' as inferior, and as sexually threatening" (Baird 2007:80). Racism is an example of hysterical prejudice. Finally, people who embody *narcissistic* prejudices "cannot tolerate the idea that there exist people who are not like them" (Young-Bruehl 1996, quoted in Baird 2007:80). Young-Bruehl notes that homophobia alone represents all three categories, a factor that may help to explain its pervasiveness (1996, in Baird 2007:80).

Homophobia and biphobia are intensified by the ideology of **compulsory heterosexism,** a belief system that offers no options other than heterosexual behaviour and feelings and denies, denigrates, and stigmatizes gay, lesbian, or bisexual behaviour, identity, relationships, and community. Somewhat like institutional racism and sexism, compulsory heterosexism is embedded in a society's social structure and maintained by ideologies that are rooted in religion and law (Herek 1995). **Heterosexism** is the belief that heterosexuality is the only normal, natural, and moral mode of relating, and hence is superior to homosexuality or bisexuality (Wilton 2000). What makes the Heterosexual Questionnaire in Table 6.2 humorous is that it turns the assumptions of heterosexism upside down.

TABLE 6.2   The Heterosexual Questionnaire

1. What do you think caused your heterosexuality?
2. When and how did you decide you were a heterosexual?
3. Is it possible that your heterosexuality is just a phase you may grow out of?
4. Is it possible that your heterosexuality stems from a neurotic fear of others of the same sex?
5. If you have never slept with a person of the same sex, is it possible that all you need is a good gay lover?
6. Do your parents know that you are straight? Do your friends and/or roommate(s) know? How did they react?
7. Why do you insist on flaunting your heterosexuality? Can't you just be who you are and keep it quiet?
8. Why do heterosexuals place so much emphasis on sex?
9. Why do heterosexuals feel compelled to seduce others into their lifestyle?
10. A disproportionate majority of child molesters are heterosexual. Do you consider it safe to expose children to heterosexual teachers?
11. Just what do men and women do in bed together? How can they truly know how to please each other, being so anatomically different?
12. With all the societal support marriage receives, the divorce rate is spiraling. Why are there so few stable relationships among heterosexuals?
13. Statistics show that lesbians have the lowest incidence of sexually transmitted diseases. Is it really safe for a woman to maintain a heterosexual lifestyle and run the risk of disease and pregnancy?
14. How can you become a whole person if you limit yourself to compulsive, exclusive heterosexuality?
15. Considering the menace of overpopulation, how could humanity survive if everyone were heterosexual?
16. Could you trust a heterosexual therapist to be objective? Don't you feel s/he might be inclined to influence you in the direction of his/her own leanings?
17. There seem to be very few happy heterosexuals. Techniques have been developed that might enable you to change if you really want to. Have you considered trying aversion therapy?
18. Would you want your child to be heterosexual, knowing the problems that s/he would face?

Source: From "The Language of Sex: The Heterosexual Questionnaire," **Changing Men** *(Spring 1982). Martin Rochlin, West Hollywood, CA.*

IDEOLOGICAL BASES OF INEQUALITY BASED ON SEXUAL ORIENTATION

Support for Elisabeth Young-Bruehl's idea that homophobia constitutes a special case of prejudice is echoed in the work of cultural critics such as Bruce Bawer (1994:81). Bawer also believes that homophobia differs significantly from other forms of bigotry:

In a world of prejudice, there is no other prejudice quite like [homophobia]. Mainstream writers, politicians, and cultural leaders who hate Jews or Blacks or Asians but who have long since accepted the unwritten rules that forbid public expression of those prejudices still denounce gays with impunity. For such people, gays are the Other in a way that Jews or Blacks or Asians are not. After all, they can look at Jewish or Black or Asian family life and see something that, in its chief components—husband, wife, children, workplace, school, house of worship—is essentially a variation of their own lives; yet when they look at gays—or, rather, at the image of gays that has been fostered both by the mainstream culture and by the gay subculture—they see creatures whose lives seem to be different from theirs in every possible way.

According to Bawer, heterosexuals cannot identify with the daily lives of lesbians and gay men, who—unlike them—exist as identifiable categories primarily because there is such strong anti-gay prejudice in Canada. In fact, the stereotypical beliefs that dominant (heterosexual) group members hold about gay men and lesbians are a major impediment to reducing inequalities based on sexual orientation (Nava and Dawidoff 1994).

Stereotypical beliefs about lesbians and gay men often equate people's sexual *orientation* with sexual *practice*. For example, all gay men and lesbians—regardless of the nature and extent of their sexual activity—are still stereotyped as "sex obsessed, sexually

compulsive, and sexually predatory" (Nava and Dawidoff 1994:32). Despite increases in the profile of homosexuals in mainstream media, media depictions still tend to reinforce stereotypes of gay men as sexual predators or effeminate sissies while lesbians are still depicted as butch, man-hating "dykes" (Nava and Dawidoff 1994; Wilton 2000). Recently, movies such as *The Family Stone, Imagine Me and You,* and *A Touch of Pink* have attempted to demonstrate the normalcy of same-sex partnerships, while others, including *Brokeback Mountain* and *I Now Pronounce You Chuck and Larry,* have attempted to demonstrate some of the harms to bisexual and other non-heterosexual people caused by living in a homophobic culture. Television shows such as *Will and Grace, The L Word,* and *Ellen* have sought to bring gay and lesbian issues into prime-time programming, while hit series such as *House* and *Grey's Anatomy* profile bisexual characters. Although some shows perpetuate negative stereotypes about lesbians and gay men, others have attempted, with varying levels of success, to change public perceptions about issues related to sexual orientation (see Box 6.1).

SOCIAL PROBLEMS IN THE MEDIA

BOX 6.1   Getting Better All the Time? Representations of LGBT Life on TV

Alice: We don't have to split the rent exactly down the middle.

Tasha: Yes, we fucking do. Alice, can we just keep looking? Because our relationship will be unbalanced if you pay a bigger portion of the rent.

Alice: I will be out of balance if you make me live in a shithole.

—"Alice" and "Tasha" (a lesbian couple played by Leisha Hailey and Rose Rollins) discuss renting a place together on Showcase's six-season series *The L Word.*

Are issues such as same-sex marriage or same-sex adoptions becoming less controversial to media audiences, particularly as they have been legal in Canada for some years? There is a lack of consensus about the answer to this question. Unlike controversies generated by earlier shows such as *Dawson's Creek* and *Roseanne,* which showed gay or lesbian kisses that led to network boycotts by viewers, hate campaigns, and withdrawal of support by major advertisers, the "Prior Commitments" episode showing the gay commitment ceremony on ABC barely created a buzz among media critics and viewers.

Do shows such as this constitute a significant change in how gay men and lesbians are depicted in prime-time television programming? Although the writers of some television series now include one or more lesbian, gay, bisexual, and trans (LGBT) characters in the permanent casts of their shows, the actual number of these characters overall on the networks has been declining. Some of this is due to series ending—for example, the long-running program *ER* finally aired its last episode in April 2009, bringing a close to the role of Chaz Pratt, a paramedic who was gay. *The L Word,* a cable series, also finished its last season in March 2009, accounting for a large decrease in cable network representations of LGBT individuals as well. According to *Where We Are on TV,* an annual report conducted by the Gay and Lesbian Alliance Against Defamation (GLAAD), in the 2008–2009 season, lesbian, gay, bisexual, and trans scripted representations (as opposed to reality shows) on prime-time broadcast television improved in quality and, after a three-year decline, finally slightly in quantity as well: LGBT representations accounted for 2.6 percent of all regular cast members of scripted series, up from 1.1 percent in 2007, 1.3 percent in 2006, and 1.4 percent in 2005. Among the findings of the 2008–2009 study were the following:

- LGBT representations account for 2.6 percent of all series-regular characters on prime-time broadcast networks, but LGBT series regulars on mainstream cable networks have decreased from 40 to 32.

- There were four LBGT people of colour series regulars during the 2008–2009 prime-time television season, up from one the previous season.

- Of the 616 series-regular cast members on ABC, CBS, the CW, FOX, and NBC, 16 were LGBT.

- Fox, with 5 out of 97 LGBT characters, has the highest percentage of LGBT representation at 5 percent, while ABC, with the highest number of LGBT characters of any network at 7 out of 166, weighs in at 4 percent.

- There are more bisexual women and lesbian characters portrayed than previously (5 bisexual and 4 lesbian), but this has not come close to the number of gay male and bisexual male characters portrayed (23 gay and 1 bisexual).

- There are 2 trans characters portrayed on broadcast networks, up from zero in 2005–2006. (GLAAD 2009)

As this study suggests, clearly positive changes have occurred in regard to LGBT representations on network and cable television channels, including the introduction of two LGBT-focused cable networks, Logo and here! These two networks provide an additional 39 series-regular LGBT characters.

Despite these positive changes, a number of media analysts believe that much remains to be done in regard to the manner in which gay, lesbian, bisexual, and trans characters are portrayed in media and popular culture. For example, some television shows and films with a gay or lesbian character present a uni-dimensional portrayal of the individual that focuses only on the person's sexual orientation or on some quirk or mannerism supposedly associated with the "gay lifestyle," such as gay men being heavily into fashion or standing in a certain way. According to one analyst, the best way to portray LGBT characters is so "their sexuality [or gender identity] is not a punch line to laugh at or make the other characters—or the audience—feel uncomfortable" (Jensen 2007). In this regard, we have a long way to go both in media representations of gays and lesbians and in their treatment in everyday life: these individuals are viewed as one-dimensional people rather than as whole persons who possess many different—and praiseworthy—attributes and talents.

How do you think the portrayal of people, specifically in relation to their sexual orientation, might be improved on television, in films, and in other forms of popular entertainment? hat positive and negative examples can you give of media portrayals of people based on their sexual orientation?

Religion and Sexual Orientation

The major difference between homophobia and biphobia and other forms of discrimination such as sexism or racism is that many people believe that homosexuality or bisexuality is morally wrong. These beliefs are often, although not always, linked to religious affiliation. For example, health researcher Tamsin Wilton (2000:9) cites a strong association found by many researchers between homophobic and biphobic attitudes and strong religious beliefs. Some people use their religious affiliation as a way of reinforcing their existing prejudices against gays and lesbians, while others interpret their religious doctrines as genuinely forbidding same-sex relations (Wilton 2000:9). In Canada, while civil marriages are now legalized between same-sex couples, the law has stated that no religion or faith is compelled to endorse or marry same-sex couples in faith-based ceremonies.

Most of the major religions of the world—Judaism, Christianity, Islam, and Hinduism, as well as Confucianism—have historically regarded homosexuality as a sin. Indeed, the only major world religion that does not condemn homosexuality is Buddhism (Dynes 1990), although historically, even within Buddhism, acceptance of sexual diversity varied culturally (Baird 2007). This is not to suggest that all or even most practising religious people are homophobic, only that most of the major religions provide justifications for homophobia, should people want them. Religious fundamentalists in particular denounce homosexual conduct as a sign of great moral decay and societal chaos.

Some Canadian churches, such as the United Church of Canada, have declared that all people, regardless of sexual orientation, are entitled to become full members of the church, including the right to become ordained ministers. In this spirit, the Unitarian Universalist Church welcomes LGBT individuals and families to join their congregations through their website:

Unitarian Universalist congregations extend a warm welcome to Bisexual, Gay, Lesbian, and Transgender (BGLT) people and their families. We encourage you to seek your own spiritual path and visit our congregations, places where people gather to nurture their spirits and put their faith into action by helping to make our communities—and the world—a better place. (Unitarian Universalist Association of Congregations 2009)

Still, increasing numbers of lesbians and gay men are carving out their own niches in religious organizations. Some gay men and lesbians have sought to bring about changes in established religious denominations; others have formed religious bodies, such as the Metropolitan Community Church, that specifically focus on the spiritual needs of the gay community. Like anyone, gay men and lesbians believe that they should not have to choose between full participation in their church and a committed relationship (Dunlap 1996).

Law and Sexual Orientation

However divided Canadians are in their opinions about how many and what kinds of rights gays and lesbians should be afforded in society, both tolerance and acceptance of homosexuality and bisexuality have increased in Canada in past decades. Canadian citizens are much more tolerant of homosexual and bisexual relations than are U.S. citizens, although the vast majority of people in both countries believe that, with regard to employment, there should be no discrimination on the basis of sexual orientation. In a 1996 Gallup poll, 60 percent of Canadians said they believed that homosexuality was acceptable, compared with 44 percent of people in the United States. Similarly, 64 percent of Canadians believed that consensual homosexual acts between adults should be legal, while 48 percent of people in the United States agreed. The most recent poll on the issue, conducted by Leger Marketing in April 2006, offered respondents a list of 11 behaviours, with homosexuality third from the bottom (see Figure 6.1). When pollsters asked Canadians if they considered homosexuality immoral, the total percentage who responded yes was 31 percent—37 percent of men polled and 26 percent of women polled (Angus Reid 2006a). Clearly, Canadians are becoming increasingly accepting, or at least "tolerant," of same-sex relationships.

Over the past four decades, Canadians have witnessed first the decriminalization of sexual practices

associated with same-sex relations; second, the inclusion of sexual orientation as a prohibited ground in human rights legislation; and third, the enactment of federal and provincial legislation aimed at conferring rights on same-sex couples (Demczuk et al. 2002:viii). Therefore, in Canada, discrimination on the basis of sexual orientation is prohibited everywhere. In Alberta, the provincial legislation deliberately omitted sexual orientation as a prohibited ground for discrimination; however, the Supreme Court of Canada stated in a groundbreaking April 1998 case (*Vriend v. Alberta*) that Alberta's human rights legislation would be *interpreted* as including sexual orientation as a prohibited ground for discrimination, whether the legislation specifically stated this or not, in order to bring Alberta's legislation in line with that of the rest of the provinces and territories.

These advances have been diligently pushed for and won by gay, lesbian, bisexual, and queer advocates, mainly through successful legal challenges and not, as Demczuk and colleagues (2002:viii) point out, through "the expression of any political will on the part of the federal [territorial] and provincial governments to systematically eliminate discrimination."

In the late 1960s, the Canadian government debated many much-needed reforms to the *Criminal Code* in order to make it more reflective of current and changing Canadian values and practices. In a 1969 omnibus bill, sexual acts that were committed between consenting adults fell within the parameters of individual freedoms, and so many sexual practices, some believed to be associated with homosexuality—for example, anal sex or "sodomy"—were decriminalized. It still took until 1977 for the federal government to do away with the immigration regulation prohibiting homosexuals from immigrating to Canada.

The 1969 Act . . . did not represent "a legalization of homosexuality," but rather a partial decriminalization of certain sexual practices that were not limited to homosexuals but were often associated with them. Beyond these changes to the Criminal Code, violence, discrimination in employment, police harassment and distinctions in terms of conjugality continued to exist with impunity. (Demczuk et al. 2002:6)

FIGURE 6.1   Canadians Examine What Is Immoral

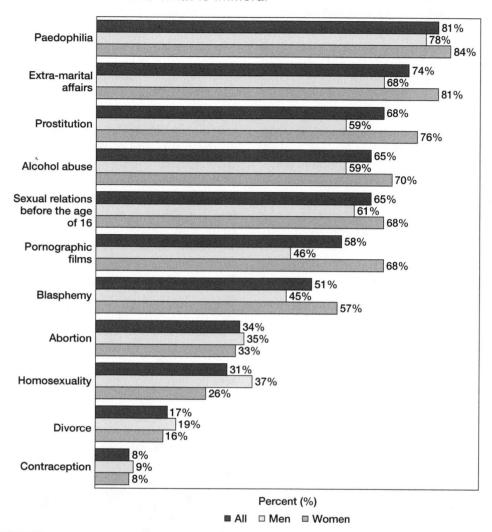

Source: Leger Marketing, 2006, "81% of the population consider pedophilia tops the list of immoral behaviours," Morality Barometer. Reproduced with the permission of Leger Marketing (http://www.legermarketing.com).

In the 1960s, the United Nations adopted the *Universal Declaration of Human Rights*. As a liberal democracy, Canada was obligated to both respect this and similar declarations and make illegal any government acts that infringe on people's individual rights. Along with the federal government, most provinces also enacted their own human rights legislation in the late 1960s and early 1970s. When Canada repatriated its Constitution in 1982, the *Canadian Charter of Rights and Freedoms* gained ascendancy, and its section 15 provided a vehicle for disenfranchised groups to seek remedy through court challenges. Section 15(1) of the *Charter* reads,

Every individual is equal before and under the law and has the right to the equal protection and equal benefit of the law without discrimination and, in particular, without discrimination based on race, national or ethnic origin, colour, religion, sex, age, or mental or physical disability.

In 1977, Quebec became the first province to include sexual orientation as a prohibited ground of discrimination in its provincial human rights legislation. Ontario followed 9 years later, but it still took 21 years and the *Vriend* decision for sexual orientation to be extended as a prohibited ground in all Canadian provinces and territories.

Throughout the 1980s and 1990s, through legal challenges about pensions, bereavement leaves, alimony, and various other family-law issues, individuals pushed, with varying levels of success, for recognition of same-sex couples as analogous to heterosexual couples. Governments continued to make case-by-case decisions, in several cases insisting that the decisions be non–precedent setting and that they be given more time to integrate the rights of minority groups into existing law. Finally, in the *Vriend v. Alberta* case, the Supreme Court of Canada stated:

> The need for government incrementalism was an inappropriate justification for *Charter* violations. . . . In my opinion, groups that have historically been the target of discrimination cannot be expected to wait patiently for the protection of their human dignity and equal rights while governments move toward reform one step at a time. If the infringement of the rights and freedoms of these groups is permitted to persist while governments fail to pursue equality diligently, then the guarantees of the *Charter* will be reduced to little more than empty words. (*Vriend v. Alberta* 1998. S.C.R. 493, paragraph 122, cited in Demczuk et al. 2002:17)

One year later, following a Supreme Court ruling that made distinctions between heterosexual couples and homosexual couples unconstitutional, several provincial governments amended their *Family Law* acts to include provision for same-sex couples by changing the definition of "spouse." The first to make these changes were British Columbia, Quebec, and Ontario in 1999 and Nova Scotia in 2000 (see Figure 6.2). For example, in Quebec, the first Canadian province to allow same-sex partners the same benefits and responsibilities as heterosexual partners, Bill 32 committed the government to making changes to 39 provincial laws, including the Quebec Pension Plan, automobile and prescription-drug insurance, legal aid, low-cost housing, child and child-care

benefits, financial assistance, student assistance programs, taxation, tax credits, RSPs, employee retirement plans, and health insurance (Demczuk et al. 2002; Mooney et al. 2001). In British Columbia, through the *Definition of Spouse Amendment,* same-sex partners who have "lived and cohabitated with another person, for a period of at least two years . . . in a marriage-like relationship, including a marriage-like relationship between persons of the same gender" have all the rights and responsibilities of heterosexual couples, including the right to inherit if a partner dies without a will, the right to inherit property and pensions, and the right to apply to adopt a child together (Mooney et al. 2001:292). Today, same-sex couples are usually able to adopt an unrelated child with both potential parents formally applying and being listed as parent applicants. This follows the 1999 Supreme Court of Canada ruling in *M v. H* that opposite-sex definitions being read into the word "spouse" and were "unconstitutional." This ruling came into effect as of March 1, 2000, and had implications for adoption acts that stated that "spouses" could adopt children. Each province and territory in Canada oversees its own adoptions. Many same-sex couples have successfully adopted children in Canada.

In a June 2006 Angus Reid poll of attitudes toward same-sex marriage, 59 percent of Canadians agreed that in principle, "same-sex couples should have the same right to civil marriage as opposite-sex couples," while 33 percent disagreed (Angus Reid 2006b).

FIGURE 6.2   Provinces and Territories Permitting Same-Sex Marriage Before Nationwide Legalization in 2005

Permitted

Did not permit

Source: Map Courtesy of Ink Blot Visual Communications.

Same-sex couples in British Columbia, Ontario, and Quebec challenged Canada's marriage laws in 2000. Many advocates believed that until same-sex couples were granted the right to legally marry across Canada, they would not be viewed by society as legitimate and would continue to be disenfranchised from some of the financial and many of the social benefits—such as holding hands in public, bringing one's spouse to the company picnic, having one's partnership recognized by one's parents as more than a "phase" one is going through—enjoyed by heterosexual spouses. In July 2002, two men who married in a church ceremony but were denied a marriage licence by the Ontario provincial government took their case to court. Three Ontario Superior Court judges ruled that the law prohibiting

same-sex marriages was unconstitutional. The Government of Canada was appealing the ruling, but on June 17, 2003, on the recommendation of federal Justice Minister Martin Cauchon, Prime Minister Chrétien announced that the federal government would no longer engage in the legal battle and would support marriage for gays and lesbians across Canada. The prime minister said that his government would

■ Draft legislation aligned with the common-law definition of marriage that came into effect on June 10, 2003;

■ Protect faith communities from having to perform any marriage that does not conform to religious values;

■ Seek approval from the Supreme Court of Canada to ensure that the marriage law complies with the *Charter*, and that it is applicable to all provinces and territories; and

■ Introduce the new law in Parliament's next session (September 2003) for a "free vote."

In June 1999, members of the Canadian House of Commons voted overwhelmingly to oppose same-sex marriage. However, following Chrétien's statement and, much earlier, the inclusion of sexual orientation as a protected ground in the *Canadian Charter of Rights and Freedoms*, advocates continued to challenge all provinces to expedite marriage for gay and lesbian Canadians.

As Canadians debated the issue of same-sex marriage, the courts were doing their work. On December 9, 2004, the Supreme Court of Canada ruled that Ottawa *did* have the exclusive right to determine who had the right to marry in Canada. The government's same-sex marriage bill, Bill C-38, came up for the vote in Cabinet on June 28, 2005. It passed by a 158–133 margin, with the support coming from most Liberals, the NDP, and the Bloc Québécois. Bill C-38 became law on July 20, 2005, after being passed by Senate and receiving Royal Assent. Canada is now the fourth country, after the Netherlands, Belgium, and Spain, to legalize same-sex marriage. South Africa and Norway have also recently legalized it, and at least 21 additional countries offer some type of legal recognition of same-sex unions (Angus Reid 2009). As of June 2006, more than 10 000 marriage licences had been issued to gay and lesbian couples in Canada, and Statistics Canada counted 45 300 same-sex couples in Canada in the 2006 Census (Angus Reid 2006b; Statistics Canada 2008j).

Not everyone was excited about Bill C-38 becoming law. Conservative leader Stephen Harper stated at the time that if his party formed the next government, he would revisit the law. He argued that "most Canadians aren't buying the final decision as most Federalist MPs are opposed to same-sex marriage" ("Harper Questions 'Legitimacy'" 2005). While Harper's Conservatives did manage to form the next two governments, they have had no success in drumming up support for reopening the same-sex marriage debate.

In a June 2006 Angus Reid poll, 62 percent of Canadians stated clearly that the matter of giving same-sex couples the same right to civil marriage as opposite-sex couples was "settled," and 27 percent felt the government should reopen the issue (Angus Reid 2006b). The issue has not been raised in Canadian polls since.

Further to these positions, some Canadians suggest that the inclusion of homosexual couples in definitions of "family" and "marriage" and the like will act to destabilize those definitions and categories, perhaps fundamentally and radically altering them for the betterment of all persons (Blasius 2001b; Currah 2001; Gamson 1996; Goldie 2001). This debate mirrors the debate waged between those who use the term "queer" politically—as an essentialist category, to describe themselves, to be recognized and valued for who they are, and to be included as equals with the rest of society—and those who use the term "queer" more theoretically—as a destabilizing entity, a descriptor only in that it implies non-mainstream but refuses to define, in any essential way, what "queer" is or is not. This debate will be discussed in more detail later in the chapter.

DISCRIMINATION BASED ON SEXUAL ORIENTATION

As the campaigns for equal rights and an end to anti-gay discrimination have progressed, more people have come forward to declare that they are gay, lesbian, or bisexual and to indicate their support for LGBT organizations. Lesbian, gay, and bisexual people continue to seek all the same rights and privileges that heterosexual people enjoy. Many people, however, continue to find themselves the victims of hate (see Box 6.2).

Victimization and Hate Crimes

On November 17, 2001, Aaron Webster, a 41-year-old Vancouver resident and photographer, was viciously beaten to death near Second Beach in Stanley Park by a group of three or four men. While gay bashing in Vancouver, Toronto, and other large Canadian cities is well documented (see Janoff 2005), Webster's death marked the first time a person could have been charged with a hate crime in British Columbia regarding sexual orientation. In December of 2004, 22-year-old Ryan Cran was convicted of manslaughter and sentenced to six years in prison. His accomplices, young offenders at the time of the murder,

SOCIAL PROBLEMS AND SOCIAL POLICY

BOX 6.2   Politics and the Risks of Coming Out

In line with most social psychological models of identity formation, psychologist Jean Baker (2001:45) states that coming out is a "complex discovery process that children or adolescents go through as they gradually recognize their homosexual identity and acknowledge it to themselves and then to others." Unlike homosexuals or bisexuals, heterosexuals have no such process to undergo. As a member of the group that is the norm, or cultural standard, they learn from a very early age what social work researcher Janet Sawyer (1989) calls "internalized dominance." Internalized dominance refers to all the messages, overt and otherwise, that signify to White people or straight people or people with no disabilities or men that they are normal; they are the standard; they are acceptable just being who they are. They are in no way "other," as people of colour or Indigenous people are; as women are; as sexual minorities are; as people with disabilities are. One of the privileges of being part of the dominant group is the privilege of never having to consider how a fundamental aspect of your self—your sexual orientation, for example—impacts on your life. Contrast this with people who belong to a marginalized group, and it is easy to see that people in marginalized groups must, at least potentially, deal with or consider their status every day. They must consider how being openly gay or lesbian will impact their job search or apartment search or family holiday or grade in a class. Will it get them verbally or physically harassed or assaulted today?

Baker (2001:46) notes that "coming to terms with one's homosexual identity is a developmental task required of the gay, [lesbian or bisexual individual] but one for which he or she receives little guidance and for which successful role models are seldom available." Taking a slightly different approach from Baker, political theorist and LGBT activist Mark Blasius (2001a:155), in a discussion of an "ethos" of gay and lesbian existence, states that coming out is a multifaceted and lifelong process. Blasius believes that coming out, the goal of which is to live one's life as a lesbian or gay man, is not just about disclosure of one's gay or lesbian identity to one's self and others: "Rather than being an end-state in which one exists as an 'out' person, coming out is a process of becoming, a lifelong learning of how to become and of inventing the meaning of being a lesbian or a gay man in this historical moment." Coming out thus refers both to "an ontological recognition of the self by the self" and a "fundamental political act" (Blasius 2001a:155).

Defining oneself as gay or lesbian or bisexual can have serious, and often negative, consequences for youth due to the prevalence of homophobia and biphobia in society.

According to Parents and Friends of Lesbians and Gays (PFLAG) Canada, LGBT youth hear anti-gay slurs an average of 26 times every day (2009). Unsurprisingly, one-quarter of youth who identify as homosexual drop out of school due to harassment, and 40 percent report that their performance at school has been negatively affected by conflicts around sexual orientation (Dobinson 2004; Mooney et al. 2003). In a Canadian study conducted by sociologist Cheryl Dobinson (2004:55), homopohobia in schools is overt and includes "violence, threats of violence, intimidation, verbal abuse, and homophobic slurs." As one young woman states, "I wanted to just forget about the teasing. I thought, it'll just go away, but it didn't. It definitely affected my actions. I started ditching school" ("Amy," quoted in Dobinson 2004:66). Further, queer-friendly counselling and support services are often nonexistent in schools, as are positive role models and library and other resource materials (Dobinson 2004). Often, LGBT youth feel they cannot come out at home or at school, leading to violence against oneself and suicide attempts, the ultimate example of internalized oppression. One survey of gay youth found that 30 percent of those identifying themselves as homosexual had attempted suicide in the past year, compared with 7 percent of those identifying themselves as heterosexual (PFLAG 2009; Platt 2001, in Mooney et al. 2003). A Calgary study found that gay and bisexual males were nearly 14 times more likely to have seriously attempted suicide than heterosexual males were (Mooney et al. 2003). This study also demonstrated that non-heterosexual youth of colour (lesbians, gay males, and bisexuals) were "dramatically overrepresented in the attempted-suicide statistics" ("Pierre Tremblay" in Fisher 1999, in Mooney et al. 2004:299). As this young man relays, "I realize that I made some choices, but when I first started cutting [classes] I felt I was making the only choice. It was for simple survival. I wasn't choosing to fuck up, I was choosing to not kill myself . . . I decided I didn't feel pride in graduating from a school that had treated me in this way" ("Brent," in Dobinson 2004:66). When LGBT youth feel they have no choice but to quit school because the bullying is unbearable, not only are their lives impacted in that moment, but that "choice" affects their whole future, socially and with regard to employment and further education. Twenty-six percent of LGBT youth are told to leave home when their parents find out they are gay or lesbian, and LGBT youth are much more likely to become homeless at an early age (PFLAG 2009). There is also evidence that gay, lesbian, and bisexual youth are coming out at earlier ages today than in the past (Baker 2001; Dobinson 2004). This speaks to the need for more and earlier supports. Internet chat rooms and dedicated LGBT phone lines are two supports that youth can access from almost anywhere in Canada. Dobinson, who volunteered at an LGBT youth phone line, notes that "I have no doubt that being able to reach out over the phone and talk to another gay, lesbian or bisexual young person contributes directly to saving lives" (2004:69).

What do you think should be done to decrease the numbers of suicides and attempted suicides among non-heterosexual youth?

were both convicted of manslaughter and sentenced to three years, two-thirds of which had to be served in closed custody ("B.C. Man Guilty in Beating Death of Gay Man" 2004). Due to a lack of conclusive evidence, however, none of the three ended up being charged with a hate crime, which would have resulted in harsher sentencing.

This incident echoed the brutal October 1998 murder of 21-year-old Matthew Shepard, a University of Wyoming student who was lured to the outskirts of town by two young men who then tied him to a fence, savagely beat him, and left him to die. He was killed because of his sexual orientation (Shepard 1999). In Canada, under the *Criminal Code,* there is no "hate crime legislation" per se. Rather, under "Purposes and Principles for Sentencing," section 718.2 states that

> a court that imposes a sentence shall also take into consideration the following principles:
> (*a*) a sentence should be increased or reduced to account for any relevant aggravating or mitigating circumstances relating to the offence or the offender, and, without limiting the generality of the foregoing, . . .
> (i) evidence that the offence was motivated by bias, prejudice or hate based on race, national or ethnic origin, language, colour, religion, sex, age, mental or physical disability, sexual orientation, or any other similar factor. . . .
> (Department of Justice Canada 2006b)

Before the early 1990s, few acts of violence against gays and lesbians were ever reported in the media. Indeed, hate crimes against gay men and lesbians were not even acknowledged as such. Although research is finally taking place, the scope and extent of hate crimes based on sexual orientation is not known (MacMillan and Claridge 1998), but hate crimes appear to be most prevalent where homophobic attitudes and behaviours are tolerated or at least overlooked. The Webster murder was not an isolated hate crime—many other incidents are reported across the country every week. Alarmingly, though, the B.C. Hate Crimes Team estimates that only between 5 and 10 percent of all hate crimes are actually reported to police (MacMillan and Claridge 1998:2) and that "based on the number of hate/bias crimes 'reported' to the police in the late 1990s, gay males were the most victimized group in Vancouver" (MacMillan and Claridge 1998:5).

In June 2008, Statistics Canada (2008p) released a study of hate-motivated crime (see Table 6.3). While 6 out of 10 hate crimes are motivated by racism, 1 in 10 are motivated by homophobia. What is of particular note, corroborating the findings of the B.C. Hate Crimes Team a decade earlier, is that 56 percent of hate crimes based on sexual orientation are violent crimes, generally assault. This is in striking contrast to crimes motivated by racism (38 percent are violent crimes) or religious intolerance (26 percent are violent).

Statistics Canada's recent Hate-Motivated Crime study also found that youth aged 12 to 17 were the group most likely to be accused of a hate crime, at 38 percent of all accusations (Statistics Canada 2008p). Further, data from Ontario show that most hate crimes (95 percent) are committed by individuals who are not connected to an organized hate group, despite most people's beliefs that organized hate groups such as racist groups are most often responsible for hate crimes (MacMillan and Claridge 1998:6). Clearly, stronger and more pervasive measures must be taken to eliminate homophobia, biphobia, and the associated hate crimes.

PERSPECTIVES ON SEXUAL ORIENTATION AND SOCIAL INEQUALITY

Sexual orientation inequality can be understood from various perspectives. Sociological explanations focus primarily on how various aspects of sexual identity and homophobia are associated with social learning and/or social structural factors in society. We'll look at each perspective separately.

TABLE 6.3   Police-Reported Hate Crime by Type of Motivation and Crime Category, 2006

Type of motivation	Violent crime		Property crime		Other crime		Total	
	number	%	number	%	number	%	number	%
Race/ethnicity								
Black	90	37.8	122	51.3	26	10.9	238	100.0
South Asian	25	37.9	36	54.5	5	7.6	66	100.0
Arab/West Asian	30	49.2	24	39.3	7	11.5	61	100.0
East/Southeast Asian	12	48.0	9	36.0	4	16.0	25	100.0
Caucasian	11	45.8	11	45.8	2	8.3	24	100.0
Aboriginal	8	50.0	6	37.5	2	12.5	16	100.0
Multiple races/ethnicities	6	16.2	29	78.4	2	5.4	37	100.0
Other	10	34.5	14	48.3	5	17.2	29	100.0
Unknown	1	16.7	5	83.3	0	0.0	6	100.0
Total	**193**	**38.4**	**256**	**51.0**	**53**	**10.6**	**502**	**100.0**
Religion								
Jewish	32	23.4	96	70.1	9	6.6	137	100.0
Muslim (Islam)	19	41.3	19	41.3	8	17.4	46	100.0
Catholic	1	7.7	7	53.8	5	38.5	13	100.0
Other	6	30.0	11	55.0	3	15.0	20	100.0
Unknown	0	0.0	4	100.0	0	0.0	4	100.0
Total	**58**	**26.4**	**137**	**62.3**	**25**	**11.4**	**220**	**100.0**
Sexual orientation	45	56.3	29	36.3	6	7.5	80	100.0
Other[1]	5	56.3	11	36.3	6	7.5	22	100.0
Unknown	26	38.2	27	39.7	15	22.1	68	100.0
Total	**327**	**36.7**	**460**	**51.6**	**105**	**11.8**	**892**	**100.0**

1. "Other" includes motivations not otherwise stated above, such as language, disability, gender, profession, or political beliefs.
Note: Includes data from municipal and provincial police services as well as the Royal Canadian Mounted Police in British Columbia, covering 87% of the Canadian population.

Source: Statistics Canada, 2008, "Study: Hate Motivated Crime," The Daily (June 9). Retrieved April 5, 2009 (http://www.statcan.gc.ca/daily-quotidien/080609/dq080609a-eng.htm).

Interactionist Perspectives

Similar to some social psychological perspectives, interactionist perspectives view all sexual conduct—heterosexual and homosexual—as learned behaviour; therefore, they tend to focus on the process by which individuals come to identify themselves as gay, lesbian, bisexual, or straight. According to interactionists, most people acquire the status of *heterosexual* without being consciously aware of it, because heterosexuality is the established norm and they do not have to struggle over their identity. They have the privilege of not ever thinking about sexual orientation. But the same is not true of people who come to identify themselves as *homosexual* or *bisexual*. In fact, some sociologists suggest that sexual orientation may be a master status for many gay men, lesbians, and bisexuals (Schur 1965). A **master status** is the most significant status a person possesses, the one that most determines how the individual views him- or herself and how he or she is treated by others. Master status based on sexual orientation is particularly significant when it is linked to other subordinate racialized/ethnic group statuses. For example, working-class gay Latinos are more hesitant than White, middle-class gay men to come out to their families because of cultural norms pertaining to *machismo* (masculinity) and the fear that relatives will withdraw the support that is essential for surviving at the subordinate end of racialized and class hierarchies (see Almaguer 1995).

Interactionists have identified several common themes that people experience in the process of accepting a lesbian, gay, or bisexual identity (Weinberg et al. 1994). First, people can experience identity confusion—a situation in which they feel different from other people and struggle with admitting that they are attracted to individuals of the same sex. For example, "Brandon," a 17-year-old in Bass and Kaufman's 1996 study, stated,

> If my "naturalness" wasn't going to come by itself, then I was ready to force it on myself. . . . I did some really drastic things—all of which I hoped would make me do a complete turnaround and become a heterosexual. (quoted in Dobinson 2004:63)

Another youth in the same study, "Matt," explains his attempts to come to terms with the possibility that he might be gay, saying,

> I'll do anything for this not to be me. I decided I just won't have sex with men. I'll just have sex with women and get married and live a normal life. That was my attitude for a long time. I didn't know anyone gay, not anyone. So, I tried all this different stuff to make myself be straight, like going to dances with girls. (quoted in Dobinson 2004:63)

In the past, many gay and lesbian people had nowhere to turn in their quest for answers and support from others; today, many use the Internet and other forms of global communication to connect with others who share their concerns (Gabriel 1995). It is important to keep in mind, however, that in a more accepting and less homophobic society, young people would not need to feel their lives were "over" when experiencing feelings of attraction for those of the same sex.

A second part of the process of establishing a lesbian or gay identity can be seeking out others who are openly lesbian or gay and perhaps engaging in sexual experimentation or making other forays into the homosexual subculture. A typical third theme that many people report as part of their coming-out process is an attempt to integrate one's self-concept and acceptance of a label such as "homosexual," "gay," or "lesbian" by pursuing a way of life that conforms to their definition of what those labels mean (Cass 1984; Coleman 1981/2; Ponse 1978). This may take a variety of forms. As with most of the "stage" theories that deal with identity construction, it is important to note that not all people experience the same things in coming to terms with their sexual orientation, whatever it is.

Studies on how people come to accept their sexual identity as gay, bisexual, or lesbian show the significance of labelling in identity construction. Labelling, while potentially helpful in some instances, can also create barriers to full participation in Canadian society. However, studies on labelling to date have been typically based on a relatively narrow selection of people, which makes it difficult to generalize the findings to larger populations. That is, research participants who openly identify themselves as gay or bisexual may not be characteristic of the larger homosexual or bisexual population (Weinberg et al. 1994).

Functionalist and Conflict Perspectives

Unlike the interactionist approach, which focuses primarily on how individuals come to identify themselves as homosexual, bisexual, or heterosexual, functionalist perspectives focus on the relationship between social structure and sexual orientation. To functionalists, social norms and laws are established to preserve social institutions and maintain stability in society. From this perspective, then, many societies punish homosexual conduct because it violates the social norms established by those societies and thus undermines their stability. Sociologist David P. Aday, Jr., provides an overview of this perspective:

> Marriage and family are structural arrangements that contribute to the continuity of our contemporary society. . . . [Homosexuality undermines] arrangements that currently operate to replace societal members in an orderly way—that is, the arrangement has survival value. . . . If homosexual conduct were allowed to exist unchallenged and unpunished, then it might in time undermine norms and laws that underpin monogamous marital sex, at least some of which results in the production of offspring to repopulate the society. . . . The punishment of homosexual conduct, from ridicule and discrimination to imprisonment, reinforces expectations about heterosexual and marital sex and defines the boundaries of society. (Aday 1990:25)

The functionalist perspective supports the ideas of those people who do not believe homosexual conduct or marriages between lesbian or gay couples should be protected legally. It also explains why some religious and political leaders call for a renewal of heterosexual "family values" in this country. But, as pointed out by political scientist and gay rights activist Andrew Sullivan (1997:147), homosexual people are part of heterosexual families too:

> [They] are sons and daughters, brothers and sisters, even mothers and fathers, of heterosexuals. The distinction between "families" and "homosexuals" is, to begin with, empirically false; and the stability of existing families is closely linked to how homosexuals are treated within them.

Importantly, as a popular slogan states, "Hate is *NOT* a family value."

Critics suggest that the functionalist approach supports the status quo and ignores a need for more current definitions of marriage and family. If marriage is understood to be the decision of two people to live together in a partnership—to be a family—then the intention or the capacity to have children should not be a condition. Furthermore, when heterosexual couples do not have children, they can still be defined as a family, so reproductive capacity should not play a role. Critics of the theory say that nothing but custom mandates that marital partners must be of different genders (Nava and Dawidoff 1994).

Whereas the functionalist approach focuses on how existing social arrangements create a balance in society, the conflict approach focuses on *tensions* in society and *differences* in interests and power among opposing groups. From this perspective, people who hold the greatest power are able to have their own attitudes,

Many individuals seem to go through a process of accepting their identities as lesbian, gay, or bisexual over time. Seeking out others who are open about their sexual orientation and experimenting sexually can eventually lead to self-acceptance.

beliefs, and values—about sexual orientation, in this case—represented and enforced, while others are not (Aday 1990). Therefore, norms pertaining to *compulsory heterosexuality* reflect the beliefs of dominant group members who hold high-level positions in the federal, territorial, and provincial governments and other social institutions. However, critics assert that the conflict approach fails to recognize that some people who have wealth and power are gay or lesbian yet take no action to reduce discrimination based on sexual orientation.

According to Karl Marx, conflicts over values are an essential element of social life, and less-powerful people often challenge the laws imposed on them by those in positions of power. For example, adverse decisions by provincial courts and the Supreme Court of Canada have often resulted in increased political activism by gay and lesbian rights groups. In recent years, more openly lesbian and gay people can be found in public office, as elected or appointed officials; in the medical and legal professions; as educators and business leaders; and in all walks of life. However, regardless of their location in the power structure, most gay men, lesbians, and bisexuals remain acutely aware that many social barriers have not been lifted and that major shifts in people's attitudes toward homosexuality and bisexuality are still not realized.

With rapid Internet communications, lesbians and gay men around the world keep informed about political decisions that may adversely affect them. Many coalitions have been formed to organize gay pride marches and protests around the world. For example, the International Lesbian and Gay Association (ILGA) reports that more than 670 lesbian and gay groups exist, on every continent and in more than 110 nations (Hendriks et al. 1993; ILGA 2009).

Feminist and Queer Perspectives

Feminist perspectives on sexuality have shifted considerably over the past four decades. In the late 1960s and through the 1970s, sexual orientation was mainly discussed by radical feminists who, by embracing binary and essentialist notions of males and females, claimed that women everywhere were bonded together in a sisterhood founded on their common oppression by men everywhere. As feminist writer Robin Morgan wrote in 1969, "Women have been subjugated longer than any other people on earth" (1993:42). Feminist scholars

Robyn Rowland and Renate Klein echoed this in 1996: "The first and fundamental theme is that women as a social group are oppressed by men as a social group and that this is the primary oppression for women" (1996:11). Along with the radical feminist theories of patriarchy came, necessarily, the analyses of compulsory heterosexuality as the cornerstone of male privilege and sexism. Feminist writer Adrienne Rich (1984), in her now famous essay "Compulsory Heterosexuality and Lesbian Existence," pointed out that heterosexuality, far from being a "natural" inclination, was, in fact, systematically imposed upon women through various means, including violence, as well as through hegemonic notions that heterosexuality was natural, inevitable, and universal. The radical feminist response to compulsory heterosexuality was varying degrees of separatism, at least for the short term. As theorist Chris Weedon (1999:36) points out,

> a heterosexual lifestyle was often regarded as incompatible with feminism. To relate sexually to men was to consort with the enemy. This radical version of separatism implied having nothing to do with men, the first step in the process of freeing oneself from patriarchal power structures. This process involved a decolonization of patriarchally defined female consciousness, body image and ways of living. The result, it was thought, would be the discovery of a truly woman-defined womanhood.

This is not to suggest that men, and gay men in particular, are not oppressed by heterosexism or compulsory heterosexuality, but sociologist Mariana Valverde (1987/2000:257) points out, "it weighs particularly heavily on women [as] men do not need female validation for their identity."

The weight of this radical feminist perspective resulted for many heterosexual feminists in feelings of guilt and confusion, estranging some from feminism altogether and reducing many to silence on the question of sexuality (Overall 2000; Valverde 1987/2000; Weedon 1999). Recently, feminists, including radical feminists, discontented with past analyses, have again taken up the issue of sexuality, focusing on what it means to be both heterosexual and feminist. So, by the late 1980s, Valverde (1987/2000:260) argued that

> feminism asserts the right of all women to make their erotic choices, and this includes choosing men exclusively. Feminism also rejects the hierarchy of sexual practices, and so does not seek to substitute a lesbian priority for heterosexism. The goal of feminism in the area of sexuality is to establish true sexual pluralism, where no one choice is presented as "the norm."

Following on the notion of sexual pluralism, some feminist analyses focused on the possibility of being heterosexual and feminist but "conscious" of both the privileges and constraints of one's choice of heterosexuality (Overall 2000). What this question brings up is the thorny issue of privilege. Women as a group may be disenfranchised. Gay men, lesbians, and bisexuals may be disenfranchised. Men have privilege. Heterosexuals have privilege. Therefore, as sociologist Zoe Newman (2001:134) points out, "We need to map our complicity in structures of domination in order to 'move out of the subject position we claim on the margins and into the shifting and multiple subject positions of oppressed and oppressor.'" In effect, theorizing and identifying oneself as both heterosexual and feminist carries with it the discomfort of "disrupt[ing] identity posited on marginality, and reveal[ing] the coexistence of innocence and complicity" (Newman 2001:131). Despite some heterosexual feminists' claims that their relationships with men are completely egalitarian and non-oppressive,

> it nonetheless remains *possible* for the man to take advantage of his potential power. All that stands in the way of his using that power is his own good will, while he is not similarly dependent on the woman's good will. And he still benefits, however indirectly, from male hegemony, and "even the advantages that he is in a position to refuse are waiting for him if he changes his mind." (Overall 2000:267)

Newman draws upon the work of theorist Michel Foucault (2001:134), stating that "even the act of shedding power is born of power; power circulates throughout our relations, it enables and it restricts." Contemporary feminists, then, with regard to the question of sexual orientation, have been focusing on the politics of difference. This is to say that because of the "hierarchization of difference in heterosexist societies," homosexuality and bisexuality continue to be hotly debated political issues within feminism, as much as they are personal ones (Weedon 1999:46).

Common ground between gay men and lesbians is discussed much more in contemporary liberal feminist perspectives, due, as Weedon (1999) points out, to the achievements of the lesbigay rights movements. For example, feminist psychologist Celia Kitzinger (1987:44) states that "the lesbian and gay man are no longer a species apart, but human beings of equal worth and dignity to heterosexuals, contributing to the rich diversity of humankind." The shift from feminist critiques of patriarchy and male power to a more inclusive politics of difference perspective accompanied the rise of postmodern thought, in particular in the form of *Queer theory.*

The quintessential feature of Queer theory is its staunch theoretical repudiation of any defining features, of any "normality" or "fixedness." Accepting the basic tenets of postmodern thought generally, those who subscribe to Queer theory, or to notions of "queer" in general, allow that nothing is "normal," nothing is "natural"; everything is socially constructed and hence arbitrary. Queer theorists view gender and sexuality as performance and refuse to hierarchize any sex above another, any gender above another, any mode of sexual expression above another (Weedon 1999:73). Feminist psychologists Sue Wilkinson and Celia Kitzinger (1996:377) summarize one of the main thrusts of Queer theory, which is,

> most popularly . . . [the] "genderfuck" . . . or "fucking with gender." The genderfuck is supposed to "deprive the naturalizing narratives of compulsory heterosexuality of their central protagonists: 'man' and 'woman'" . . . and to illustrate the social constructedness of "sex" in all its multiple meanings.

While Queer theory seeks to subvert notions of "natural" and "normal," making any and every form of sexuality acceptable, many feminists and others find it problematic from a political or social change perspective, for a number of reasons. Queer theorists often view feminism as a "grand narrative," the assumptions and foundational propositions of which must be open to question and critique. Therefore, sexualized violence, pornography, and other heterosexually eroticized models of sexuality that are based in profoundly oppressive patriarchal relations may, within a Queer theory perspective, all be endorsed as "unimportant," "transitory," and "provisional" (Wilkinson and Kitzinger 1996:381):

"Power relations within and between heterosexuality and homosexuality become invisible, allowing for a liberalism which hides oppression" (Weedon 1999:76).

Equally problematic is the widespread practice of gays and lesbians reclaiming the term "queer" as a means of self-identification, shifting the term from the pejorative to the celebratory. In doing this, they subvert the radical potential of the term "queer" by using it as an almost essentialist, but certainly bounded or fixed, category that has political value on the one hand but subverts the "mind fuck" potential on the other. From this perspective, then, a more radical use of the term may be for "straights" to begin to identify as "queer," thereby highlighting the multiplicity and arbitrariness of "queer." Indeed, many heterosexual people whose sexuality does not fit the norm for a variety of reasons do identify as queer. In this case, the value of queer as a destabilizing element is highlighted, rather than the term being used as simply a new category; as Newman (2001:129) describes it, defining one's "identity as always founded on a sense of marginality." She further points out that, used in this way, "the potential of queer seems to be that we do not come together around an assumption of sameness, but around a critique of 'the normal'" (Newman 2001:132). Sociologist Joshua Gamson (1996:396) cites queer activists Allan Bérubé and Jeffrey Escoffier in saying that queer is often employed "to affirm sameness by defining a common identity on the fringes." Other critics of Queer theory note that while it may appear radical to reinterpret oneself as "queer," in terms of political activism, it is problematic. Anthropologist Max H. Kirsch (2000:97) cautions: "It is misguided as political action: it cannot generate the collective energy and organization necessary to challenge existing structures of power."

Defining oneself as queer—as "other" from a norm of heterosexuality—has concrete consequences. Some of these consequences include internalized and external oppression played out in depression, apathy, and violence. Kirsch (2000:97) notes, "We cannot simply refuse to acknowledge these facts of social life in our present society and hope that our circumstances will change." Queer theory therefore contains both the ability to be radical and destabilizing in challenging all things deemed natural or normal and, conversely, the potential to render one completely apolitical and paralyzed by apathy in the abyss of "anything goes." This is neatly summarized by political scientist Paisley Currah

(2001:193–194), who also quotes feminist legal scholar Kimberlé Crenshaw (1991):

> "At this point in history, a strong case can be made that the most critical resistance strategy for disempowered groups is to occupy and defend a politics of social location rather than to vacate and destroy it." The appropriation of queer theory's useful theoretical insights by advocates of gay rights and the rights of sexual minorities requires maintaining a delicate balance between the politics of location and the politics of deconstruction.

HOW CAN INEQUALITIES BASED ON SEXUAL ORIENTATION BE REDUCED?

As we have emphasized in previous chapters, how people view a social problem is related to how they believe the problem should be reduced or solved. Inequality based on sexual orientation is no exception. From an interactionist perspective, homosexual conduct is learned behaviour, and people go through a process in establishing a lesbian, gay, or bisexual identity. Society should, therefore, be more accepting of people as they come to accept their sexual identity. Legal and social barriers that prevent homosexuals and bisexuals from fully participating in society should be removed, thereby making the complex psychological and social process of coming out to friends, family, and co-workers easier for those who choose to do so.

According to the functionalist perspective, social norms and laws exist to protect the family and maintain stability in society. Given this, sexual orientation becomes a social issue: gay activists' demands for equal rights, including legal recognition of same-sex marriages, become major threats to the stability of society. With the legalization of marriage for gays and lesbians in Canada, some groups say there will be no stopping others who wish to strike down what remains of "foundational truths once thought to be self-evident" (Thomas 1996:A15).

Some advocates of this position believe that lesbians and gay men can change their sexual orientation:

> Homosexuals can and do change. My files bulge with stories of those who once engaged in sex with people of the same gender, but no longer do. They testify to the possibility of change for those who want to. The struggle to maintain what remains of the social fabric will ultimately determine whether we will continue to follow ancient Rome on the road to destruction, or come to our senses, turn around and re-enter a harbour of safety ordained by God for our own protection. (Thomas 1996:A15)

Whether gay, lesbian, and bisexual individuals can or should change their sexual orientation is the subject of some disagreement. However, most functionalists agree that homosexuality may be dysfunctional for society if it does not contribute to society's need for new members or if it undermines social norms and laws that preserve the family unit and maintain stability in society.

Conflict theorists believe that prejudice and discrimination against lesbians, gay men, and bisexuals are embedded in the social structure of society and are reinforced by those who hold the greatest power and thus are able to perpetuate their own attitudes, beliefs, and values about what constitutes "normal" sexual conduct. From this perspective, homophobia is similar to (but not the same as) racism, sexism, ableism, and ageism, and the overt and covert discrimination that gay men and lesbians experience is similar to (but not the same as) the discrimination experienced by people of colour, Indigenous peoples, all women, people with disabilities, older people, and children and youth. According to the conflict approach, the best way to reduce inequality based on sexual orientation is to continue to pass laws that ban all forms of discrimination against gay men, lesbians, and bisexuals as well as remove barriers to their equality with heterosexuals. However, to gain equal rights, activism is necessary: people must continue to demand social change.

In the past, feminist theorists, using a radical critique of patriarchy, advocated separation of men and women. Lesbianism was promoted as the only rational and non-oppressive mode of relationship. This perspective led to deep divisiveness in the movement as heterosexual feminists had difficulties reconciling their sexual orientation with the political demands of the radical feminist separatists. More recently, feminists have approached questions of sexual orientation from the perspective of sexual pluralism, with the idea that all people, regardless of sexual orientation or gender, need to support one another to combat oppression. Therefore, according to contemporary feminists, to reduce inequality based on sexual orientation, people need to understand their commonalities in the face of oppression and also need to be clear about their varying positions of privilege in order to form alliances across location. In this way, everyone can fight against inequality based on sexual orientation as well as other inequalities.

Queer theorists believe that gender is a social construction, and thus sexual orientation is also fluid. People use a queer perspective in one of two ways. Either they use the term "queer" as a descriptive category, or they use it as a stand-in for the terms "gay," "lesbian," or "bisexual." This use is political in that it represents a reclaiming of a term that, in most uses, has been regarded as disparaging. However, the radical potential of "queerness" as something fluid is thus subverted. From this perspective, the category or term is a means of overcoming people's homophobia by being "out," "loud," and "proud"—by demonstrating the normalcy of being outside the "norm" and raising challenging questions such as, "Who defines what or who is normal?" Using "queer" as a political category gives people something to rally around; it helps make collective action possible. Additionally, many people identify themselves as "queer" for a variety of reasons, and so it is an identity marker to use to provide common ground for all those who see themselves in opposition to "normal" sexuality, however that gets defined. Others use a queer perspective to refuse to define self or others, in this way enabling people to grapple with identity, subjectivity, and location. People may define themselves as queer but refuse to explain what makes them so, forcing people to engage with the questions about the importance of categorizing. From this perspective, by transgressing gender or sexuality norms (through cross-dressing, for example), people can flout the norms and demonstrate their arbitrariness and fluidity and thereby have an impact on changing or broadening norms and definitions. This is typically done on an individual basis, making collective actions difficult to organize. However, as pointed out by political scientist James Scott, "most of the political life of subordinate groups is to be found neither in overt collective defiance of powerholders nor in complete hegemonic compliance, but in the vast territory between these two polar opposites" (1990:136).

In the 21st century, gay advocacy is perhaps the most effective means of reducing homophobia and bringing about greater equality for gay men and lesbians. In fact, it took a small riot at the Stonewall Inn in 1969 in New York to make the general public really aware of inequality based on sexual orientation and the need for social change (Weinberg and Williams 1975). As recently as the 1970s in Canada, the RCMP conducted raids on bars known for or suspected of patronage by gays and lesbians, and police raids on "gay bath houses" continue today. Hundreds of organizations seek equal rights and protections for gay men, lesbians, and bisexuals; these groups represent a wide cross-section of the Canadian population.

Despite some changes in the attitudes and laws pertaining to homosexuality, discrimination and anti-LGBT prejudice remain strong. According to a recent study, gay, lesbian, and bisexual sociologists who advocate gay rights are more likely than their heterosexual colleagues to encounter difficulty in obtaining academic positions, to experience bias in the tenure and promotion process, and to be excluded from social and professional networks (Taylor and Raeburn 1995). However, not all of the study's findings were negative: for some sociologists, being involved in gay rights issues brings professional visibility, recognition, and opportunities for advancement (Taylor and Raeburn 1995):

> Gay rights advocates argue that gay men, lesbians, and bisexuals should not be the only ones responsible for reducing or eliminating inequality based on sexual orientation: It all comes down to this: Are people equal in this society by virtue of their citizenship, or not? If the answer is no, then we will be saying that equality does not exist ... anymore but has been replaced by tiers of citizenship, and that what tier you occupy depends on whether people like you or not. And if we accept this, then we will have repudiated the constitutional principles of liberty and equality.... We believe that you will join in this cause because it is your cause, too, the cause of individual liberty and human equality. (Nava and Dawidoff 1994:167)

Some analysts suggest that people in the future will ask, "What was all the fuss over gay men and lesbians (or sexual orientation) about?" Valverde (1998) takes the position that 20 years in the future, it will have become as socially unacceptable to discriminate against people based on sexual orientation as today it has become to discriminate against people based on skin colour. What do you think?

WHAT CAN YOU DO?

- Reflect on the assumptions you hold about homosexuals, heterosexuals, and bisexuals, and about sexual orientation in general.

- Attend a Pride Day or parade in your community, regardless of your sexual orientation.

- Consider voting in favour of same-sex marriages and other issues that support queer folk, in newspapers, on the Internet, and in opinion polls.

- Do not claim heterosexual privilege. Refer to your girlfriend or boyfriend or husband or wife as your "partner" or your "spouse." Don't let people assume heterosexual privilege. Keep people guessing.

- Incorporate sexual orientation issues into your relevant research papers.

- Do not refer to gay, lesbian, or bisexual friends or colleagues as "my gay friend Kim" unless you typically refer to your straight friends as "my straight friend Lee."

- Do not assume you know someone's sexual orientation. Instead, allow people to define their gender or sexuality for you if they wish.

- Write a letter to your MP asking that he or she speak against repeals of the legislation favouring equal marriage for same-sex couples if the issue comes up in the House of Commons again, and explain why he or she should do this.

- Do not treat bisexuality as an "identity of confusion" but accept it as a real and valid (and queer) identity of its own.

- Get educated about hate crime so you know what to do if you are targeted by one or if you witness or hear about one.

- Object to harassment, discrimination, and prejudice whenever you see or hear it. Don't ignore, condone, or accept this in others.

- Intervene when you hear homophobic or biphobic jokes or slurs. Your silence can be all the encouragement a person needs to continue this hurtful behaviour.

- Encourage diversity, inclusion, and respect in your school, your classrooms, your workplace, and your friendship circles.

- Work on being nonjudgmental about others' preferences and life choices.

- Use gender-inclusive and non-heterosexist language.

- Don't "out" anyone to others if you know she or he is gay, lesbian, or bisexual. Respect people's rights to disclose their sexual orientation if and when they choose. This is especially important as many people may be "out" only in certain spaces or with certain people they deem safe. Outing someone could put her or him at risk for many serious consequences such as losing friends, family members, employment, or housing.

- Don't assume that being LGBT is a negative thing or that LGBT people are always suffering. There is much to celebrate and much humour to be found and shared.

- Recognize people's complexity. Sexual orientation is just one part of identity that people carry around with them. This means that sexual orientation is only part of the picture, and it intersects with multiple other parts of our identities to both enfranchise and disenfranchise us, sometimes simultaneously.

- Never force anyone to "come out" or remain "out."

- Accept public displays of affection (PDAs) between people of the same sex as natural and normal. Participate in them, to show solidarity with same-sex couples, to whatever degree you are comfortable (e.g., linking arms with a same-sex friend while walking down the street; hugging a same-sex friend when you meet him or her).

- If you are heterosexual and involved in an intimate partnership with a person of the other sex, try to keep this relationship "in the closet" for one week. This could involve (a) having no physical contact with the person if anyone else (friends, family, general public) is around; (b) being careful where or even if you are seen together; (c) not mentioning this person or the relationship to anyone; and (d) not being seen or heard talking on the phone to this person.

SUMMARY

What Criteria Do Sociologists Use to Study Sexual Orientation?

Sociologists define sexual orientation as a preference for emotional–sexual relationships with persons of the "same" sex (homosexuality), the "opposite" sex (heterosexuality), or both (bisexuality). Recent studies have used three criteria for classifying people as homosexual or bisexual: (1) sexual attraction to persons of one's own gender; (2) sexual involvement with one or more persons of one's own gender; and (3) self-identification as a gay man, lesbian, or bisexual.

How Do Religion and Law Influence People's Beliefs About Homosexuality?

Most major religions, with the exception of Buddhism, regard homosexuality as a sin. Contemporary religious fundamentalists denounce homosexual conduct as a sign of great moral decay and societal chaos. Throughout Canadian history, moral and religious teachings have been intertwined with laws that criminalize homosexual conduct. While many religions do not condone homosexuality, many adherents to them do.

What Types of Discrimination Do Gay and Lesbian People Experience?

Although lesbians and gay men experience discrimination in many aspects of daily life such as housing, medical care, and employment, a major concern, because of the seriousness of its consequences, is hate crime.

How Have Changes in the Definition of Hate Crimes Affected Gay Men and Lesbians?

Despite sexual orientation being a "protected ground" in the Charter and in most provincial and territorial human rights legislation, Canada's *Criminal Code* still does not include specific hate crime legislation, except under section 718.2 on sentencing. Provincial hate crimes units,

however, such as British Columbia's, are going a long way to collect those data, perhaps influencing further and broader legislative changes in the future. Hate crimes against gays and lesbians appear to be most prevalent where homophobic attitudes are tolerated or overlooked.

How Do Interactionists Explain Problems Associated With Sexual Orientation?

According to interactionists, most people acquire the status of heterosexual without being consciously aware of it. For lesbians, gay men, and bisexuals, sexual orientation may be a master status because it largely determines how individuals view themselves and how they are treated by others. Interactionists identify a process of accepting the identity of lesbian, gay, or bisexual that some people may experience: (1) experiencing identity confusion; (2) seeking out others who are openly lesbian or gay and sometimes engaging in sexual experimentation; and (3) attempting to integrate self-concept and acceptance of a label such as "homosexual," "gay," or "lesbian."

How Do Functionalists Explain Problems Associated With Sexual Orientation?

Functionalists focus on how social norms and laws are established to preserve social institutions such as the family and to maintain stability in society. They also analyze reasons why societies find it necessary to punish sexual conduct that violates social norms prohibiting non-marital sex and same-sex sexual relations. According to functionalists, homosexual conduct is punished because it undermines social institutions and jeopardizes the society.

How Do Conflict Theorists Explain Problems Associated With Sexual Orientation?

Conflict theorists believe that the group in power imposes its own attitudes, beliefs, and values about sexual orientation on everyone else. Thus, norms enforcing compulsory heterosexuality reflect the beliefs of dominant group members in the federal and provincial governments, the military, and other social institutions. According to conflict theorists, social change can occur only if people demand that laws be changed to bring about greater equality for gay men and lesbians.

How Do Feminist Theorists Explain Problems Associated With Sexual Orientation?

Like conflict theorists, feminist theorists believe that the group in power can impose its own agenda. The group in power in this case is seen to be males, however, and notions of compulsory heterosexuality work to serve the interests of men in an unequal and gendered social system. Feminist theorists from a radical perspective first suggested that lesbianism was a rational, political choice, based on a critique of patriarchy. Today, many feminists reject the separatist stance of earlier writers on these issues and instead opt for a model that values all diversity and encourages acceptance of all people, regardless of gender, sexual orientation, and so on. Therefore, homosexuals and bisexuals need to be made equal within all institutions and facets of society.

How Do Queer Theorists Explain Problems Associated With Sexual Orientation?

Many Queer theorists believe that problems associated with sexual orientation are the result of a homophobic and biphobic culture. They advocate playing with the categories, labels, definitions, and understandings of the various genders, sexes, and sexual orientations as a way of subverting consciousness. Queer theorists believe that when people's taken-for-granted realities are disrupted, people will be enabled to see sex, gender, and sexual orientation as the social constructions they are, and thus, ease off of rigid and harmful stereotyping and actions.

How Have Gay Rights Advocates Sought to Reduce Inequality Based on Sexual Orientation?

Beginning with the Gay Liberation movement in the 1960s, advocates have argued that lesbians and gay men are citizens and entitled to the same rights and protections that all other citizens enjoy, including the right to equal employment and housing, legally sanctioned marriage, adoption of children, and protection from harassment and hate crimes. Some analysts suggest that future social change depends on the continued vigilance of gay, lesbian, and bisexual advocacy organizations.

KEY TERMS

biphobia,   p. 128
compulsory heterosexism,   p. 129
heterosexism,   p. 129

homophobia,   p. 128
master status,   p. 139

sexuality,   p. 128
sexual orientation,   p. 126

QUESTIONS FOR CRITICAL THINKING

1. Think of any assumptions you hold about homosexuals, bisexuals, and heterosexuals. What actions flow from your assumptions? What impact may your actions have on people whose sexual orientation or preference differs from your own?

2. Following a Queer theory approach, critically analyze the discomfort generated by allowing or asking people to define their gender, sex, and sexual orientation

for you. What assumptions are disrupted when you do this?

3. What things can heterosexual individuals and couples take for granted that homosexual individuals or couples cannot?

4. The B.C. Hate Crimes Team, created by the provincial government and including members of the RCMP, reports that gays, lesbians, and bisexuals

are often reluctant to report violence that is perpetrated against them. Explain why this might be so.

5.   How has the social institution of heterosexuality constrained and limited all Canadians—straight, gay, and bisexual?

Explore the topics covered in this chapter at **www.mysockit.com** using the access provided with this text. Interactive resources for studying include video clips, practice tests, learning objectives, and Internet resources.

7

THE SEX TRADE IN CANADA

I'd find a job and I would never be in the sex trade if I could live my life over again.

Female street worker, Victoria, B.C. (Hallgrimsdottir et al. 2006:276)

I won't even work for anything under $10 an hour, I won't. 'Cause what's the sense of busting my balls for that? and listen to somebody yelling at you, telling you what to do. 'Cause I can't take authority from nobody, I can't let nobody tell me what to do. This job [sex work], that's how it turned me. I'm kinda my own boss, and I get so much money off it. No, it [a "straight" job] just won't work

Male, Moncton, New Brunswick (Jeffrey and MacDonald 2006:322)

It's just a job, that's it. I don't come home and break down. There have been times when I'm not too happy with what I do but if I stay in that head space I get depressed. It's not about having sex, it's about the money, it's about providing a good living for myself.

Female, Victoria, B.C. (Hallgrimsdottir et al. 2006: 276)

I'm not addicted [to substances]. I'm used to the money and you know . . . the lifestyle. You know, you're used to having so much money for the day to use or whatever, and now you don't have it no more and you're drawn back out to go. . . . It's hard to pass up the money sometimes when someone is offering you a hundred dollars and you're really broke.

Female, Halifax, Nova Scotia (Jeffrey and MacDonald 2006:318)

Know those porn star shirts that say "XXX" or "Touch This" or whatever they say . . . all I can say is that you see 15-year-olds walking around in them and I'm sorry, but the first word that comes to my mind is sex. What is this? It has a lot to do with society.

Female youth, Mission, B.C. (Kingsley and Mark 2000:26)

This community around here, they think we're parasites as far as I'm concerned, that we're not real people. But everybody has to make a living and they have to realize that.

Female, Toronto, Ontario (Erickson et al. 2000:782)

You can buy a woman for $10,000 and you can make your money back in a week if she is pretty and she is young. Then everything else is profit.

Sex trafficker quoted in The Natashas: The New Global Sex Trade *(Malarek 2003:45)*

A lot of our issues are the same, all the way across the country, whether we want to see it or not, and it all comes back to the same thing, that abuse in our families and our communities.

Female youth, Halifax, Nova Scotia (Kingsley and Mark 2000:23)

There are a multitude of reasons why people enter the sex trade, and the voices of some Canadians involved in the sex trade quoted here speak to a few of those reasons. Some men and women involved in the sex trade view what they do and the causes of their involvement in it as exploitive, while other sex-trade workers view it simply as a career choice—with willing buyers and sellers, a purely economic exchange—that is no more or less degrading than any other profession (Aalbers 2005; Alexander 1987; Chapkis 1997; Doezema 1998; Kempadoo 1998, 2005; McWilliams 1996). Certainly, in this country, it is a thriving multimillion-dollar industry that includes prostitution, the film and video trade, printed pornography, escort services, massage parlours, and strip and table- and lap-dancing clubs. However, prostitution and other types of sex work have always been controversial; not all social analysts even agree on whether or not the sex industry is a social problem. To better understand the controversy over prostitution and other sex work, we will look at each of these issues and examine varying views on what the work means to those involved. Looking at the way elements of the sex trade are currently organized, as well as looking into the future, nationally and globally, may help you to decide if any of the explanations provided by various sociological and feminist perspectives clarify your opinions.

PROSTITUTION IN HISTORICAL AND GLOBAL PERSPECTIVE

Narrowly defined, **prostitution** is the sale of sexual services (of oneself or another) for money or goods and without emotional attachment. More broadly defined, systems of prostitution refer to any industry in which women's, men's, and children's bodies are bought, sold, or traded for sexual use (Giobbe 1994). According to this broader definition, systems of prostitution may include pornography, live sex shows, peep shows, international sexual slavery, and prostitution as more narrowly defined above. The vast majority of sex-trade workers around the globe are women and female children (80 to 90 percent), although men and male children also work in the sex trade. In all cases, regardless of the age or sex of the sex-trade worker, the clients or buyers are nearly always adult males (see Browne and Minichiello 1995; Lauer et al. 2006; Leuchtag 2003; McNamara 1994; Snell 1995; Wolff and Geissel 2000). What factors in our global society may help explain this fact?

The World's Oldest Profession?

Prostitution has been referred to as the "world's oldest profession" because references to it can be found throughout recorded history. Still, over the past 4000 years, prostitution has been neither totally accepted nor completely condemned. For example, while female prostitution was widely accepted in ancient Greece, where upper-class prostitutes were admired and frequently became the companions of powerful Greek men, the prostitutes themselves were refused the status of wife—the ultimate affirmation of legitimacy for women in Greek society—and were negatively compared with so-called virtuous women in a "bad woman–good woman" ("Madonna–Whore") dichotomy (see Bullough and Bullough 1987; Jolin 1994; Roberts 1992).

In other eras, attitudes and beliefs about prostitution have ranged from generally tolerant to strongly averse. Such early Christian leaders as St. Augustine and St. Thomas Aquinas argued that prostitution was evil but encouraged tolerance toward it. According to Aquinas, prostitution served a basic need that, if unmet, would result in greater harm than prostitution itself. Later Christian leaders such as Martin Luther in 16th-century Europe believed that prostitution should be completely abolished on moral grounds (Jolin 1994; Otis 1985).

In the 19th-century feminist movement, for the first time women voiced their opinions about prostitution. Some believed that prostitution led to promiscuity and moral degeneracy in men and should therefore be eradicated. Others believed that it should be legitimized as a valid expression of female sexuality outside of marriage. Recently, some advocates have suggested that prostitution should be viewed as a legitimate career choice (prostitute as sex worker), but others have argued that it is rooted in global gender inequality (prostitute as victim of oppression, as most prostitutes are women). This argument will be discussed further when we examine feminist perspectives on the issue.

In terms of prostitution being Canada's oldest profession, it is not. Sociologist Dan Allman (1999) notes that though there were some interpretations that describe "prostitution-like" relations among Indigenous people, sex work was not actually introduced in Canada until Europeans began to settle here. Early writings about the Canadian sex trade (late 1800s to early 1900s) are limited to females who were in the public eye.

The Global Sex Industry

The past three decades have seen the industrialization, normalization, and globalization of prostitution. Although *industrialization* typically refers to the mass production of manufactured goods and services for exchange in the market, sociologist Kathleen Barry (1995:122) suggests that this term should also apply to commercialized sex manufactured within the human self. Prostitution becomes *normalized* when sex work is treated as merely a form of entertainment and there are no legal impediments to promoting it as a commodity. Certainly the plethora of television advertisements encouraging viewers to call or text "hot singles" in their area help speed the process of normalization. The *globalization* of prostitution refers to the process by which the sex industry has become increasingly global in scope (e.g., international conglomerates of hotel chains, airlines, bars, sex clubs, massage parlours, brothels, and credit card companies that have an economic interest in the global sex industry), which has occurred as people's political, economic, and cultural lives have become increasingly linked globally (Barry 1995; Davidson 1996; Maticka-Tyndale et al. 2005). Political scientist and international relations specialist Cynthia Enloe (1990:36–37) critically comments that

sex tourism requires Third World [*sic*] women to be economically desperate enough to enter prostitution; having done so, it is made difficult to leave. The other side of the equation requires men from affluent societies to imagine certain women, usually women of colour, to be more available and submissive than the women in their own countries. Finally, the industry depends on an alliance between local governments in search of foreign currency and local and foreign business-men willing to invest in sexualized travel.

For evidence of exactly this sort of globalization, one has only to look at the recent increase in Canada of migrant—often trafficked—sex workers from the former Soviet Union and Eastern and Central Europe (see Box 7.1).

BOX 7.1 The Global Sex Trade Comes to Canada: The "Natashas" Case

Many women are trafficked as domestic workers or mail-order brides. Others are trafficked for the sex trade. How many women are trafficked into Canada for involvement in the sex trade is unknown, but the demand for "exotic" and foreign-born women is well documented. An estimated 1 million people, mainly women, are trafficked for the sex trade world-wide, and, historically, much of this traffic has involved women from various parts of Asia. Recent reports suggest that of the women who are trafficked annually globally, approximately 225 000 are from South East Asia, 200 000 from former Soviet republics, 150 000 from South Asia, 100 000 from Latin America and the Caribbean, 75 000 from Eastern Europe, and 50 000 from Africa (Farr 2005:4). According to Victor Malarek, a Canadian investigative journalist, the third largest money-making enterprise in the world, after drugs and weapons, is the traffic in human flesh (2003:4). A 2006 estimate puts the global dollar amount of trafficking at US$42.5 billion, and according to the 2005 U.S. State Department *Trafficking in Persons Report*, more than one person per minute is traf-ficked across international borders—approximately 600 000 to 900 000 people per year (Channel 4 2009; Malarek 2003:5). Indications are that today, Slavic women from Eastern and Central Europe and Russia, known colloquially as "the Natashas," are the main focus of traffickers and represent more than 25 percent of the global trade (Malarek 2003:6; McDonald et al. 2000:1).

The reasons for the increase in the traffic of Slavic women revolve mainly around the breakup of the Soviet Union in 1991 and the resultant economic upheaval. As Eastern Europe and the former Soviet Union struggled to make the transition from a communist economy to free-market capitalism, massive job loss and poverty ensued. Inevitably, around the world, women (and their children) have been the hardest hit by these struc-tural economic shifts. Many women view migration to richer nations as the key to their survival or view it as a means to bet-ter their and their families' situations. Additionally, there appears to be a growing demand for women racialized as White in Europe, the Middle East, China, Thailand, Korea, and Japan (Farr 2005; Sutdhibhasilp 2002; Yea 2005).

Through formal means (advertisements in local newspa-pers, on billboards, and on TV) or informal means (word of mouth by friends, relatives, and co-workers), women are recruited by sex-trade traffickers to work in Canada, the United States, Asia, and Western European countries. Worldwide, Kamala Kempadoo has argued that "most 'trafficked persons' express some personal desire to migrate, and about half of women in the global sex trade appear to be conscious of the fact that they will be involved in some form of sex work prior to migration" (2005:38). While some women may be aware of the working conditions and the goals of those who recruit them for the Canadian sex trade, many appear to be ill-informed, misled, or completely deceived. Sentences for traffickers are light as well as rare, making this a "highly profitable and enduring business" (Farr 2005:3).

In research for Status of Women Canada, Lynn McDonald, Brooke Moore, and Natalya Timoshkina (2000) conducted, for the first time, an exploratory study of women migrant sex workers in Toronto who had come to Canada from Eastern Europe and the former Soviet Union. Eighteen migrant sex workers, as well as service providers and other key informants such as police officers, immigration officials, and massage parlour owners, were inter-viewed in order to create a comprehensive picture of these women's experiences. The researchers found that trafficking networks varied in their degree of formalization, depending on size. Large-scale networks were ones with political and eco-nomic footholds in the countries of origin and destination and were "sophisticated" in terms of producing fraudulent docu-ments and having a "substantial infrastructure" for transit routes and destination nations (McDonald et al. 2000:5). Medium-scale networks were those that did not sell women to others but rather recruited women from one specific country to work in their own businesses in the destination country (McDonald et al. 2000:5). The small-scale networks operated typically by fulfilling orders for one, two, or more women, perhaps from a specific region, placed by a business owner. In these operations, the traffickers recruited and then accompanied the women, ultimately deliver-ing them to the contracting business owner (McDonald et al. 2000:5). Many women are also recruited informally, through word of mouth, by people they know who are either already here in Canada or are in the country of origin but know of contacts here.

While it would be incorrect to paint all trafficked women as innocent victims, some degree of deception is nearly always employed in recruiting them. Some women are promised legitimate employment and then forced into the sex trade, while others know they will be involved in the sex trade but are deceived about its legality in Canada, the specifics of what they are to do, the extent of their involvement, and the length of time they must be involved, as the interview comments of these Hungarian sex-trade workers in a Toronto strip-club illustrate:

> I call them and I meet with them, and they said it's a babysitting job and stuff . . . and then when I come to Canada I find out here that it's not a babysitting job. And then I just find out this group in Hungary it's really organized crime. (McDonald et al. 2000:44)

> The first, second, third, fourth night I didn't work at all. I said: "There is no way I'm going to dance. You can do anything with me. I'm not going to dance." On Sunday night he [owner/agent] said, "You've been here one week . . . you didn't make any money, and we are going to teach you how to make the money" . . . he sent four guys in the room so he could teach me how I have to make the money. They raped me for four days and four nights. (McDonald et al. 2000:54)

> I heard that they keep the rules very strictly so I shouldn't worry about the dance. They knew I'd never danced before and that's why they said it. That nobody can ever touch me . . . always security everywhere. And so I won't have any problems with any customers, nobody can come close to me. . . . The difference was that of course people tried to touch me, of course they were closer to me than I expected. There was no security where we danced. So the customers could do whatever they wanted. (McDonald et al. 2000:44–45)

McDonald, Moore, and Timoshkina (2000) found that none of the women in their study had worked in the sex-trade industry prior to being trafficked to Canada. Many believed they were coming to Canada to become legitimate chorus line–style dancers or entertainers. Most said they were aged 18 to 26, although some may have been younger than that. All had finished high school, with half the women having post-secondary certificates, degrees, and careers in their countries of origin. Most of the women were single, and one-quarter of them had children. All the women came to Canada with the idea of improving their economic situations, some having other reasons in addition, such as the actuality or threat of war in their homeland.

What many women found was that instead of making a great deal of money and living autonomous lives, their activities were often completely controlled; they found themselves living at places designated by the business owner or agent, being driven to and from work, working long hours, being videotaped or watched constantly, and earning just enough (if any) money to keep them perpetually engaged in the business, since against any earnings were charged creative fees for housing, food, the DJ's services, room rentals for sex with customers, fines for being late, and so on. Other women had more autonomy, earned decent money, and felt they could not make this kind of money elsewhere, so they remained tied to the industry due to lack of viable options (McDonald et al. 2000). Many of the women were brought into the country on visitor visas; when these expired, the owners or agents had that much more control over the women.

Many women are told they cannot leave the trade or the establishment because they will be arrested and deported, especially those women who are here on expired visas. Others have stayed in the work due to a (perceived) lack of options. Some women were expected to send money home to relatives or were trying to support families here and believed that they would not get comparably paid jobs due to language barriers and a lack of Canadian training or education:

> In one day you can make $200. It's a big difference when you used to make $50 a day. It means you can work for two days, just close your eyes on everything and you can survive already. I signed up my girl for dancing classes, signed her up for music classes, and she paints too. And I became happier. I can help out my mother. (Russian massage parlour worker, quoted in McDonald et al. 2000:61)

> You know, I've been working in this business for several years, and I can tell you that all the girls have goals. But, for some reason, even older women who keep saying: "Oh, I'll just save some money and go to school" . . . You see, it is so hard to get out of it, out of this business. Mainly because of the money. It's very difficult. I tried to get out three or four times. (Moldovian massage parlour worker, quoted in McDonald et al. 2000:61)

The traffic of women into Canada has serious implications for the women themselves and for all Canadians. Whether or not these women choose to remain in the sex industry, they should live in conditions free from coercion, abuse, danger, and economic insecurity. How to create the conditions for women to make free choices is a matter for policymakers and others to take up. McDonald, Moore, and Timoshkina (2000:66–68) make a number of recommendations that could have implications for the Canadian *Criminal Code* and for Canada's immigration laws. Some of the recommendations include

- distributing information in countries of origin and at immigration ports, in many languages, about the realities of trafficking, the legalities of the sex trade in Canada, exotic dancing, and so on;

- re-evaluating visitor's visas with a view to finding ways for women whose visas expire to avoid illegal status;

- finding ways to integrate migrant women and their partners into the core Canadian economy by offering more language classes (English/French) and by expediting the process for accreditation of immigrant professionals;

- intervening in establishments where women are working in unfavourable working conditions by having health inspectors do inspections on whole workplaces, not just kitchens;

- developing a system of regulating sex-trade businesses to ensure basic Canadian work-safety rules are followed;

- having written information posted in these businesses, in many languages, about free health and social services that are available;

- funding agencies and organizations that work with people in the sex trade and mandating their access to these businesses; and

- developing and funding joint initiatives for addressing organized sex-trade trafficking.

Kempadoo, using a Third World or transnational feminist perspective, notes that the sex industry is only one of several sites of global trafficking in a world increasingly dominated by globalized capitalism: "The continued demand for cheap labour by corporations, state military apparatuses, and leisure and professional classes, which are wholly complicit in sustaining conditions of economic inequality, exploitive conditions, and the criminalization of poor people, goes unfettered and unchallenged in this new crusade" (2005:51–52). Noulmook Sutdhibhasilp, an expert on migrant female workers' rights, concludes her look at migrant sex workers in Toronto by stating that "the government of Canada would be most helpful to these workers if they would abandon regressive and repressive immigration and prostitution laws" and policies that "serve to push the international sex trade further underground . . . [thereby increasing] women's reliance on potentially abusive individuals and organizations." Instead, "strategies [need to] be developed to assist migrants to travel, work and live legitimately. These measures should be based on the stated needs of migrants and avoid developing policies that work against their interests" (2002:187). In May 2007, Immigration Minister Diane Finley attempted to introduce Bill C-57, intended to prevent sexual exploitation and trafficking of foreign workers under the guise of exotic dancer visas. To date, nothing further has happened with the bill.

What do you think should be done about the global sex trade? In what ways is the global sex industry linked to the international division of labour and other forms of globalization?

Furthermore, Internet sites, such as Sly Guide, World Sex Archives, Craigslist, alt.sex.prostitution, and World Sex Guide, post listings for hundreds of cities all over the world. Would-be travellers can simply log on, click on their destination city, and find out about specific women and agencies in the area, rates, services offered (e.g., if she allows "oral" on herself, if she will perform "oral" on you, how "good" the experience is, etc.), photos, laws of the particular jurisdiction, and so on. Many Canadian cities are listed, along with detailed advice and reports from businessmen, tourists, long-haul truckers, and others who travel domestically. One has only to spend two minutes looking through the photo galleries of any of these sites to see the evidence of globalization.

World Bank consultant Saltanat Sulaimanova (2006:61) states that trafficking is one of the fastest-growing organized crime activities precisely because risks are relatively low while profits are extremely high, at US$7 billion to US$12 billion per year. The United Nations Economic Commission for Europe has slightly lower estimates, stating that worldwide trafficking is a US$5 billion to US$9 billion-per-year enterprise. The United Nations estimates that 4 million people are trafficked every year, with 50 000 brought into the United States and up to 16 000 people, mainly women, coming into Canada. The United Nations International Children's Emergency Fund (UNICEF) estimates that almost one-third of the women who are trafficked globally are actually minors, many under the age of 13 (Leuchtag 2003). Further, UNICEF estimates that the 1.2 million children who are trafficked each year are sexually exploited or used as cheap labour (UNICEF 2009). Over 1 million of the people who are trafficked are believed to be trafficked into the sex industry (Farr 2005). It is difficult to gain reliable statistics for any aspect of trafficking, however, because of the illicitness of the acts and because definitions and perceptions of "trafficking" vary. This dilemma has led many people to adopt the UN definition of trafficking proposed in its Protocol to Prevent, Suppress and Punish Trafficking in Persons in 2000:

"Trafficking in persons" shall mean the recruitment, transportation, transfer, harbouring or receipt of persons, by means of the threat or use of force or other forms of coercion, of abduction, of fraud, of deception, of the abuse of power or of a position of vulnerability or of the giving or receiving of payments or benefits to achieve the consent of a person having control over another person, for the purpose of exploitation. Exploitation shall include, at a minimum, the exploitation of the prostitution of others or other forms of sexual exploitation, forced labour or services, slavery or practices similar to slavery, servitude or the removal of organs. (UN 2000)

The Solicitor General for Canada estimated that in 1998, the money involved annually in the traffic into Canada was anywhere from $120 million to $400 million. Today, it is estimated to be at least $400 million.

Traditionally, the demand for prostitution was greatest when large numbers of men were congregated for extended periods of time in the military or on business far from home. Natural disasters or wars saw many displaced or marginalized women drawn to these areas to make a livelihood. As noted by anthropologists Martha Ward and Monica Edelstein, "Serving men sexually is one of the leading forms of employment and survival for women on the planet" (2009:220). Further, a connection between wartime rape and increased prostitution has been documented for the Vietnam War and, more recently, for the wars in El Salvador and Bosnia. Large populations of refugees and victims of rape and sexual violence tend to be exploited by networks of pimps and organized crime gangs such as the Yakuza in Japan, the Russian Mafia, and other international cartels (Leuchtag 2003; Seager 1997; Women's International Network 1995). Jyoti Sangera (1997) refers to this as the first or traditional tier of sex work. Linked to the first tier, but different from it, is a second tier, one tied to global tourism and business. In many countries, sex tourism began with the establishment of brothels that served foreign military bases (Seager 1997). The second tier has grown up around major tourist destinations and business centres. The size of the first tier has remained relatively stable, while the size of the second tier is ever expanding, providing "R and R for the corporate world workforce" (Sangera 1997:11).

In a recent case study of Windsor, Ontario, as a destination for sex tourism, Eleanor Maticka-Tyndale, Jacqueline Lewis, and Megan Street (2005:46) discuss the notion of liminal space (transitional or marginal space) as it relates to sex tourism. They suggest that people who travel to other locations are able to engage in exotic or forbidden practices because they "move into liminal space . . . [and are] 'betwixt and between,' in a socially condoned marginality, where they are bound neither by the mores of home, nor by those of the host community."

For residents of these tourist destinations, however, this is their home. Residents inhabit a space "where visitors come for the explicit purpose of violating the dominant norms and mores of Western sexuality" (Maticka-Tyndale et al. 2005:47). How people in sex-tourism destinations deal with this varies. In Thailand, for example, sex tourism and prostitution is big business, promoted by government. Leuchtag reports that 5 million sex tourists visited Thailand in 1996 from the United States, Canada, Western Europe, Japan, and Australia and brought in US$26.2 billion, "thirteen times more than Thailand earned by building and exporting computers" (2003:96). The money earned through sex tourism assists the Thai government to pay the interest on its foreign debt, which encourages government officials to view "women as a cash crop" (Leuchtag 2003:96). Unfortunately, with its focus on revenue generated by sex tourism, the government feels it must deny the enormous HIV/AIDS epidemic sweeping Thailand.

Although recent research has indicated that the global sex industry, especially prostitution, contributes to the transmission of HIV, the virus that causes AIDS (Gil et al. 1996; Purvis 1996), many agencies and governments have not come to grips with the problem. Moreover, the threat of HIV/AIDS may be fuelling the increased demand for children and younger, inexperienced sex workers as a "safe sex" strategy in the booming sex tourism business (Seager 1997). This strategy, along with myths in many cultures that sex with virgins cures HIV, leads to increasing sexual exploitation of children. The Japanese Foundation for AIDS Prevention, an organization affiliated with the Japanese government, launched a poster campaign featuring a grinning, middle-aged man wearing a business suit and displaying his passport, with a caption reading, "Have a nice trip! But be careful of AIDS." The Japanese government is clearly aware that many businessmen participate in sex tourism abroad (Sachs 1994), and the poster seems to endorse this while warning them about unsafe practices. What strategies do you think these businessmen might employ to try to avoid the risks of sexually transmitted diseases?

The picture of the global sex industry reflects the economic disparity between the poorest regions of the world—where women and children (mainly) may be bought, sold, or traded like any other commodity— and the richest regions, such as Europe and North America, where many of the global sex industry's consumers reside (see Bauerlein 1995; Davidson 1996; Seager 2003). For example, in terms of sex tourism, the countries that most sex tourists lived in and left from were Canada, the United States, Japan, Australia, Great Britain, France, Sweden, Germany, Norway, Saudi Arabia, China, Singapore, and Kuwait. Major destinations for these tourists were Hungary, Brazil, Indonesia, Thailand, Vietnam, Kenya, Cambodia, Bangladesh, Philippines, Costa Rica, Morocco, India, and the Dominican Republic (Seager 1997; 2003; Ward and Edelstein 2009). Additionally, as seen in Box 7.1, rich nations increasingly import the sexual services of people from poorer nations. As geographer and women's studies scholar Joni Seager (2003:56) notes, "As poverty deepens in Eastern Europe, it becomes a major source region for prostitutes; as wealth expands in China and Malaysia, men in those countries fuel an increased demand for the traffic in women and girls."

PROSTITUTION IN CANADA

Prostitution among consenting adults has never been illegal in Canada. However, sections 210–214 of the Canadian *Criminal Code* do prohibit many transactions that are quite necessary to prostitution. The activities that are illegal in Canada relating to the sex trade are communicating in a public place for the purposes of buying or selling sexual services (section 213); procuring or soliciting a person to exchange sexual services for money and living off the avails (section 212); being involved in a common bawdy house (section 210); providing direction to or transporting someone to a bawdy house (section 211); and purchasing sexual services from someone under the age of 18 (section 214[4]; Maticka-Tyndale et al. 2005:47; Millar 2002:38; Wolff and Geissel 2000:254). These activities are considered a threat either to public decency or to public order. Those convicted of prostitution-related offences are often fined, although jail terms are possible. For example, communicating for the purposes of prostitution carries the maximum penalty of a $2000 fine or six months in jail

or both. Given the economic situation of many street prostitutes, hefty fines may ensure continued sex-trade work and do not in any way act as a deterrent. As one female Saskatoon youth explains:

> [When I was arrested for prostitution] all my friends were there and it hurt so much, it made me feel much lower . . . they [the judicial system] treat you like such a bad person or that you're a slut, tramp, or whore. You're forced to go there [the streets], you were forced into that spot and if you said no, you were beat up or something worse, you could be killed. And they make it out like you're nothing, they don't try to help you, they just charge you and send you on your merry way . . . they know where you're going off to, you have to pay off your fine. (Kingsley and Mark 2000:27)

Federal laws on prostitution-related activities ensure that it is almost impossible to engage in the trade without breaking the law. Criminologist John Lowman (2000) reports that this fact adds to the already existing moral–political marginalization that sex-trade workers endure, increasing the risks of the work. Lowman (2000:1006) says our "system of quasi-criminalization"

1. contributes to legal structures that tend to make the prostitute responsible for her [or his] own victimization, and thus reinforces the line of argument that says that, if people choose to prostitute themselves, they deserve what they get—they are "offenders" not "victims";

2. makes prostitution part of an illicit market. As such, it is left to primitive market forces and creates an environment in which brutal forms of manager-exploitation can take root;

3. encourages the convergence of prostitution with other illicit markets, particularly the drug trade. Once the price of a habit-forming, mind-altering substance is driven up by criminal prohibition, a drug like heroin can be as demanding a "pimp" as any man; and

4. alienates persons who engage in prostitution from the protective-service potential of the police. Why would prostitutes turn to police for help when police are responsible for enforcing the laws against prostitutes? . . . Criminal law sanctions institutionalize an adversarial relationship between prostitutes and police.

This may be why, instead of going to the police when they are beaten, raped, or robbed, sex-trade workers report "bad tricks" or "bad dates" to various organizations that keep, post, and monitor Bad Date Sheets. One of the first organizations in Canada to publish a Bad Date Sheet was the Alliance for Safety of Prostitutes (ASP) in 1983. Bad Date Sheets typically report the type of offence, where the offender picked the worker up, the date and time of the offence, description of and characteristics of the offender (age, racialization/ethnicity, gender, other identifying features such as tattoos, etc.) and vehicle, the type of person victimized (e.g., woman, man, transsexual, youth), and whether the person is known to be a repeat offender or not. The sheets are then circulated monthly by street and other social service workers and posted in various agencies and places prostitutes are known to go for services (Lowman and Fraser 1996). John Lowman and Laura Fraser's study (1996) *Bad Trick Reports in Vancouver, B.C. 1985–1994* shows that most "bad tricks" are Caucasian males, perceived to be in their 20s and 30s, and most victims are adult females. The most common types of bad dates were physical and sexual assaults, followed by robbery, and, in a quarter of the cases, a weapon was used. Lowman and Fraser (1996) encourage us to see this violence as part of a continuum of male violence against women, not as acceptable risks associated with the job. In fact, in a recent study of 80 men who purchase sex in Vancouver, it was reported that only 6.5 percent of the men surveyed had ever committed a violent act against a commercial or non-commercial sexual partner: "Our findings are consistent with many contemporary accounts suggesting that the problem of violence against sex workers is perpetrated by a relatively small proportion of very violent men who prey on the marginalized social and situational position of street sex workers" (Lowman and Atchison 2006:293).

Many Canadian youth, women, and men are involved in the Canadian sex trade as sex workers, as "managers," or as customers, both overseas and at home. Prostitution has always been a feature of Western societies and, although some characteristics of it are changing with increasing globalization and economic disparity between more and less industrialized nations, it certainly appears to be here to stay. As this young ex-sex-trade worker in B.C. reports,

A sex worker friend of mine and I sat down one night and figured out how many tricks we'd had in our illustrious careers as street sex trade workers. We came up with about 10 000 each, so anyone who says there aren't very many men out there buying sex are just wrong. (Megan, in Rabinovich and Lewis 2001:7)

How we approach the myriad issues raised by the sex trade (e.g., some of the associated dangers, like violence, particularly against street sex-trade workers) will depend upon how we view it. In any case, it is interesting to note that while in 1985, 20 percent of Canadians identified prostitution as a pressing social problem, a decade later, fewer than 1 percent of Canadians felt it was a "very serious" social problem (Bibby 1995). However, a 2006 Angus Reid poll of 1508 Canadians found that 68 percent still believed prostitution was "immoral," with more women than men having this view (Angus Reid 2006a).

Some Characteristics of Prostitution in Canada

Clearly, not all sex-trade workers are alike: life experiences, family backgrounds, years of formal education, locales of operation, types of customers, and methods of doing business vary widely. Even with these differences, however, sociologists have identified five levels, or tiers, of prostitution, ranging from escort workers to street prostitutes to women exchanging sex for drugs in crack houses.

Top-tier prostitutes are typically referred to as *escorts* or *call girls* and *call boys*. They are considered the upper echelon in prostitution because they tend to earn considerably higher fees and typically have more years of formal education than other prostitutes do. Many of them do not even think of themselves as prostitutes. They usually dress nicely—and often conservatively—so that they do not call undue attention to themselves at the luxury hotels, clubs, and apartment buildings they may be called to work in. Maybe most importantly, escort sex workers have more selectivity in their working conditions and customers than do other prostitutes (Chapkis 1997; Macy 1996; Maticka-Tyndale et al. 2005). An escort worker named Terry clearly differentiates between herself and other, less fortunate workers:

One of the reasons I think I can enjoy my work, is because I carefully screen my clients. I have no tolerance for any assholes. I'm providing a service to these men, and as far as I'm concerned, they're privileged to have it. So they have to show me the proper respect. I deserve that respect. If they don't think so then they should keep their cock in their pants and their money in their pocket. It means that I may make less money than I might otherwise, but my safety is worth it. People in more desperate circumstances have to put up with a lot more. (Chapkis 1997:100)

Escort prostitutes work "on call," going out to see customers who are referred to them by their escort service, pimp, or other procurers such as hotel concierges and taxi drivers who may receive a percentage of the prostitute's fees. (See Table 7.1 for other terminology of the sex trade.) Other escorts may "freelance," brokering their own calls and deals, advertising in local newspapers, and so on. One home-based male escort in Victoria, B.C., speaks to his experience of the relative autonomy offered by freelancing, stating, "When it comes right down to it, I have full control over what I'm doing. I know that I can make my own decisions, my own rates, and I can make my own hours" ("Peter," cited in Hallgrimsdottir et al. 2006:277). Although their work is not as visible as that of many other sex workers, escorts generally may face some of the same hazards, including abusive customers and sexually transmitted diseases. A recent exploratory study in Vancouver by Simon Fraser University criminologist Tamara O'Doherty of off-street sex workers' experiences of violence reported that two-thirds have never experienced violent behaviour while working (Meadahl 2007). O'Doherty's findings support earlier research in Vancouver (see Lowman and Fraser 1996) and suggest that potentially violent men may actually target street workers: "No surprise . . . street sex workers, forced to work in isolation with little or no protection from police are ideal prey for violent men" (O'Doherty, quoted in Meadahl 2007). A global review of recent research on the sex trade by sociologist Ronald Weitzer (2005) supports the idea that "street workers are significantly more at risk for violence and more serious violence than indoor workers" (Lever and Dolnick, quoted in Weitzer 2005:216) because indoor workers "are in a better position to screen out dangerous customers and also have a greater proportion of low-risk, regular clients" (Weitzer 2005:216).

A 1995 task force on the use of city bylaws to regulate sex work was created by the municipal council in Windsor, Ontario. The task was to create a bylaw that would not violate the *Criminal Code* statutes on prostitution, nor be seen as licensing sex work, but at the same time provide sex workers with safety and autonomy and the police with the ability to monitor the industry. As one police representative stated at the time, "Escort work is particularly difficult to police. You can't find it. . . . When it's licensed we know who they are and where they are. We can keep tabs on it. . . . We can prevent the worst elements from moving in" (Maticka-Tyndale et al., 2005:49). Three factors were seen as important in the creation of a bylaw:

(a) escorts should remain integrated in their local communities and not be isolated in a red-light district; (b) escorts should be able to determine their own working conditions within the limits set by law; and (c) escorts should be provided with information that could help them conduct their work safely and contribute to their over-all well-being. (Maticka-Tyndale et al. 2005:49)

Windsor escorts and agency receptionists are able to work from their own homes or through an agency. Escorts are licensed after meeting certain criteria such as a minimum age of 18 and a clean police record. Work must be out-calls only, and workers are required to carry and produce their licences when asked by police. Agency personnel are required to keep records of who went where and when and to turn these records over to police if requested. By the end of 2002, there were a dozen agencies and 113 escorts licensed in Windsor. Many escorts like to maintain that their work does "not necessarily involve sexual services" (Maticka-Tyndale et al. 2005:50), and many see themselves as very different from other sex-trade workers, particularly from street prostitutes: "I'm not like them. They're disgusting, all dirty and smelly. Several of them look like they got AIDS. I'm not anything like them, no way, I'd never be a whore" (quoted in Maticka-Tyndale et al. 2005:50).

The second tier of prostitutes is composed of hustlers, strippers, and table dancers who engage in prostitution on the side. People in this tier work primarily out of nightclubs, bars, and strip joints. The hustlers are sometimes referred to as *bar girls* or *bar boys* because they are supposed to pressure (hustle) customers to buy drinks. Most hustlers are not paid by

TABLE 7.1   The Jargon of the Profession: Some Words and Phrases Commonly Used and Understood in the Canadian Sex Trade

Term	Definition
A Man	Pimp. For example, "Do you have a man?" or "You can't work here without a man."
Bad Date	Violent or abusive trick.
Bogus Call	About one in ten calls, the address can't be confirmed or it's a joke by a neighbour who is watching.
Booking On	Phoning into to an escort agency to report being available for calls.
Booking On Fee	This is a fee in order to be able to book on, which can be up to $300/month or a per shift fee of $10–$20.
Boystown	The stroll that the men and boys work.
Break	Get a customer.
Call	Trick or date sent by an escort agency.
Cancellation Fee	The $30–$100 fee charged if the date cancels because the woman is late, the driver can't find the address, or he doesn't like the look of a particular woman.
Coffee Fund	Escort agencies charge of $50–$75/month for beverages available to clients.
Date	Customer, trick, or john.
Deposit	First $100–$500 earned kept by the agency. Non-refundable.
Driver	Someone who drives women to their calls and waits. Mostly men.
Escort Service or Agency	Business where people buy time for money. They say what the two consenting adults do with their time is their business.
Exiting	Leaving, quitting the sex trade.
Experiential	People with direct, personal experience in the sex trade.
Fines	$50–$100 charged to woman by escort agency for any number of transgressions from not wearing the kind of lingerie the client wants to being late for work.
Forced Indebtedness	Period of partying which precedes entry into trade. No indication that repayment will be required and no mention of future payment. Girl is then told that she has spent thousands of dollars on drugs and someone else paid for them and repayment is demanded.
High Track	Sex trade workers who ask some of the highest prices and tend to be the "best kept" looking sex workers on the street. High track is almost always pimped.
John	Customer, date, or trick.
Keep Six	Take down the license number of cars as girls get in. Usually done by street kids for $5–$10 a car. Is also an expression for watching for the cops.
Kiddie Track	Generally 17 years old and under. Often pimped or working in partnership with other exploited youth.
Late Fine	$25 for every half hour booked on late.
Leaving Fee	Money paid to pimps or an escort agency to leave the trade. Generally a substantial amount, like $2000–$5000 in 1999.
Low Track	Usually in industrial areas. More of the women are older or more noticeably drug addicted and/or with mental health issues. They charge less but often make up for that in volume.
Mid Track or Renegade Stroll	Higher-end women who work without pimps or without formal pimping. Sometimes boyfriends or husbands act as pimps.
Regular	A customer that a sex trade worker sees regularly. Often have a slightly more personal relationship with one another.
Renegade	Sex worker without a pimp.
Sexually Exploited Youth	Youth in the sex trade; the term is used to differentiate them from adult sex workers or prostitutes. Sexually exploited youth are under 18 years old.
Sex Trade Worker	Adult who works in the sex trade. The term is used interchangeably with prostitute.
Spotter	Person who takes down license numbers of cars. Could be arranged by an escort agency or individual.
Square	Not in the sex trade and have never been in the trade.
Squared Up	Exited from the sex trade.

Stroll	Area where street prostitution takes place. Also called the track.
Trannie Stroll	Where male-to-female transsexuals and cross-dressers work.
Trick	Customer, client. Also: John or Date.
Trick Charge	Fee some hotels charge for taking a guest to the room.
Working	Engaging in the sex trade. "I've got to go to work" as compared with mainstream employment "I have to go to my job."
Working Clothes	Clothes worn for the sex trade

Source: Jannit Rabinovich and Megan Lewis, 2001, Impossible, Eh? The Story of PEERS: Prostitutes Empowerment, Education and Resource Society, Vancouver: Save the Children Canada.

the bar but earn their livelihood by negotiating sexual favours with bar customers, who often are lonely and want someone to talk to as well as to have sex with (Devereaux 1987).

The third tier is made up of *house girls* who work in brothels (houses of prostitution) run by a madam or a pimp, who collects approximately half of the fees earned by the women. Customers choose a "date" from women lined up in a parlour or receiving room. House prostitutes are not allowed to engage in "dirty hustling" (winking, running one's tongue over one's lips, or shaking a leg) or to turn down a customer (Devereaux 1987). Operating a bawdy house or living off the avails of prostitution is illegal in Canada, and thus houses of prostitution typically operate as body-painting studios, massage parlours, or other legal businesses. In Vancouver, although the city does not admit to licensing prostitution, criminologist John Lowman advises people to consider the fees that the city charges for different categories of business. In 1997, there were approximately 150 distinct business categories that require annual licensing. For 115 business categories, the fee was under $200. For another 24 categories, the fee was between $201 and $500. Only a very few had annual licensing fees above $500. Lowman reports these as "pubs and cabarets . . . $556.00; a public market is $886.00; concert halls vary between $1839.00 to $2644.00 depending on seating capacity; an amusement park is $3156.00; the horse race track is $7473.00; and the Pacific National Exhibition is $10,463.00" (1997:Appendix). As for personal service businesses, dating service agencies were charged $104 per year; health enhancement centres, $162; massage parlours, $172; escort services, $802; and body rub parlours, $6527 per year—the third most expensive licence to procure after the PNE and the race track!

A controversial proposition to open a co-operative brothel near Vancouver in time for the 2010 Olympics has raised many issues, from health and safety to complete decriminalization. Some of the arguments that may support the "pro" side include that hundreds of brothels already exist in the city but are merely quasi-hidden behind massage parlour and other "fronts"; that recent Canadian research has demonstrated that sex-trade workers' safety is nowhere near as at-risk in indoor work; that the brothel would provide other legitimate work opportunities and assist workers who wanted to exit the trade; that workers' health could be better monitored; that it would help reduce the stigma against sex workers; and that it would get the sex trade off the streets, out of the public view. To be considered alongside these arguments is journalist Victor Malarek's assertion that more than 40 000 women and girls were trafficked into Greece to service the 2004 Summer Olympics, and more than 20 000 women were imported for the 2006 FIFA Cup in Germany, both countries where prostitution is legal (2003). Those who are against the opening of a legal brothel in Canada, even as "an experiment," state that a co-operatively owned and operated brothel still won't solve any problems for those engaged in the sex trade for survival (e.g., those who are drug addicted, the abused); that it is still akin to slavery; that if prostitution is legitimized, it means legitimizing pimps and sex traffickers; and that prostitution in any form is violence against women (Joyce 2008; Lee 2007; Woolley 2008).

Near the bottom tier of prostitution are *streetwalkers,* who publicly solicit customers and charge by the "trick." This type of prostitution is believed to account for between 10 and 20 percent of the sex trade in most large urban centres in Canada (Lowman and Atchison 2006:285). Most street prostitutes work a specific location and many are "protected" by a pimp. Many streetwalkers derive status and some degree of protection from violent "johns" from their pimps, although in most cases, pimps are not out on the streets monitoring the workers enough to really provide protection (Weitzer 2005). Further, researchers have also documented the exploitative and too often violent nature of the pimp–prostitute relationship (B.C. Ministry of Attorney General 1996; Kingsley and Mark 2000; Lauer et al. 2006; Sexually Exploited Youth Committee of the Capital Regional District [SEYC-CRD] 1997). There is little available research on pimps or managers, and most information comes from the women who work for pimps and not the pimps themselves. However, one British study found pimps "exercised almost total control over their workers" (May et al. 2000, in Weitzer 2005:227). Whether at risk for violence from pimps or johns, street prostitutes are significantly more at risk than sex workers in indoor (and often screened and controlled) environments.

The very bottom tier of prostitution is occupied by women who are addicted to crack cocaine, heroin, or other drugs and who engage in drugs-for-sex exchanges (Fullilove et al. 1992; Kingsley and Mark 2000). Researchers have found that many crack-addicted women perform unprotected oral sex on men or have sexual intercourse with them in crack houses in exchange for hits of crack, a practice known as "freaking" (Erickson et al. 2000). According to one study,

> Some men will enter a crack house, purchase enough rocks for two people for several hours, and then make it clear to every woman in the house what he has in mind. . . . [There] seems to be an expectation [in the crack house] that if a man wants to have sex with a woman, she will not oppose the offer. The expectations are implicit. Everyone involved—the house owner, the male user/customer, and the female user/prostitute are all aware of what is expected. (Inciardi et al. 1993:74–75)

In the words of one young Winnipeg woman, "I met a bunch of guys I knew, they were always giving me rock [crack] for free, I never had to do anything, except for this one guy. Then we met these guys, [and] you had to go around the whole room to get a piece [of crack from each guy]" (Kingsley and Mark 2000:21).

Although less research has been done on prostitution tiers with males, the tiers appear to be similar to those of females except that with males, most customers are of the same gender as the sex worker. For example, in her report on escort services, journalist Marianne Macy (1996:249) found that some male escorts exist and "men normally go see men." Most of Canada's larger cities, for example Vancouver, Toronto, and Montreal, have some form of "Boystown," where male sex workers line the stroll, on display for the primarily male customers. Some male prostitutes work as hustlers in bars and nightclubs, where they typically wear blue jeans, leather jackets, and boots, seeking to project a strong heterosexual image. Julian Marlowe, a graduate student who is putting himself through school by working as an escort, reports that "the sugar daddy of a former acquaintance of [his] once admitted he used to get a rush from picking up hustlers on his lunch break due to the sheer element of danger: the person he picked up could conceivably beat him to a pulp" (1997:141).

Sexual orientation is frequently an issue with male prostitutes, some of whom do not define themselves as gay and limit the types of sexual acts they are willing to perform. Others view sex strictly as an economic exchange and define work-related sex as "not real sex" (Browne and Minichiello 1995). Other research suggests that for hustlers who are part of gay culture, "knowing that one is attractive enough to command payment raises, rather than lowers, one's self esteem. Why would a man have low self esteem if he's being sought out and given money for his body" (Marlowe 1997:143). Most research shows that although many males are involved in the sex trade as sex workers, there are not as many boys and men as girls and women. Status of Women Quebec estimated in 2002 that between 70 and 90 percent of sex-trade workers are women (Conseil du statut de la femme 2002:7). The Department of Justice in 1993 estimated that between 10 and 33 percent of street prostitutes in Canada are male, but that at least 80 percent of situations where sex is traded for money involve women as the worker (Allman 1999). This is reinforced by the B.C. provincial study: "Sexually procured youth and adults (those who receive money for sexual services) are predominantly female. Males are less visible and tend to work primarily on a party circuit or in private residences" (B.C. Ministry of Attorney General 1996:3).

Much research in Canada has been focused on identifying the factors that bring people into the sex trade, particularly into the relatively dangerous street prostitution tier. Recent studies of youth in the sex trade in British Columbia as well as Canada-wide studies reveal that several factors are nearly always implicated in engaging youth in the sex trade. The use of the term "youth" is not accidental here, as research shows that most people (96 percent) became prostitutes before age 18 (Hallgrimsdottir et al. 2006; Rabinovich and Lewis 2001;

Wolff and Geissel 2000). One cross-provincial study, a community consultation on prostitution in B.C., found that the average age of entry to prostitution in that province is 14, with some beginning as early as age 8 or 9 (B.C. Ministry of Attorney General 1996). Another study, conducted in Victoria, B.C., found the average age of entry to be 15.5 years, although some started as early as 11 (SEYCCRD 1997). Allman (1999) reported that approximately 10 to 12 percent of sex-trade workers were under 18 years of age, and most males in the trade admit to starting by age 16. There is evidence across Canada that males remain in the trade for much shorter durations than females, the average length of time being just over five years for men. Allman suggests that by the time males in the trade reach the age of 20 to 22, the youthful looks that attracted the customers are beginning to fade, so they move on to other things.

There is some evidence as well that males and females may enter the sex trade for slightly different reasons (Allman 1999). Most people involved, females and males alike, report that the money is an enticement (Allman 1999; Hallgrimsdottir et al. 2006; Jeffrey and MacDonald 2006a). A 1993 Montreal study found that prostitutes were earning anywhere from $600 to $2000 per week, with females earning considerably more than males per week (maybe due to demand; Allman 1999). Criminologist Tamara O'Doherty found, in her Vancouver study of off-street workers, that on average, the women worked four days per week and earned $60 000 per year (Meadahl 2007). Key factors leading to the sex trade for youth are generally reported to be homelessness and a lack of basic necessities for survival for themselves or their children (e.g., shelter, food, clothing); emotional abuse, sexual abuse, and other physical assaults at home; alcohol or drug addiction; a lack of satisfactory assistance with a health or mental health issue (e.g., depression, eating disorder, bipolar disorder); a lack of life skills and employment; dropping out of school; and low self-esteem (B.C. Ministry of Attorney General 1996; Kingsley and Mark 2000; Lauer et al. 2006; SEYCCRD 1997; Wolff and Geissel 2000). As stated by a female former street worker from Thunder Bay, Ontario, "[I wouldn't have worked in the trade if] I could have had better self-esteem, I didn't have any boundaries, and I didn't care. I didn't know my worth at that time" (Kingsley and Mark 2000:31). One Ottawa-area study of youth sex-trade workers found that the "sex for survival" motif was more common for females

than for males. Many homeless males were able to "couch surf," while females were expected to trade sex for food, shelter, or money (reported in Allman 1999).

The presence of several or even all of these factors obviously does not guarantee entry into the sex trade. It does, however, heighten the risk of a young person having fewer choices. As stated in one recent report, "They do not move directly from a 'normal' teenage life of home, school and extra-curricular activities to being a prostitute. Long before that, most have a long history of school problems or family problems or emotional problems or all three" (SEYCCRD 1997:4). Criminologist John Lowman, with Laura Fraser, reports that most female sex workers are from lower socio-economic backgrounds and are extremely dissatisfied with their home lives (1996). As clearly stated by Wolff and Geissel (2000:257), "Adolescent prostitution can be viewed as a survival behaviour." However, as B.C. sociologists Helga Hallgrimsdottir, Rachel Phillips, and Cecilia Benoit (2006:275) caution,

a more accurate interpretation [for why people enter the sex trade] of the empirical data is that persons involved in the sex industry represent populations that face barriers to mainstream employment, are more likely to belong to discriminated identities, and come from current and historical backgrounds of economic and social hardship. Such an interpretation positions sex industry workers as structurally disadvantaged, not morally corrupt or helpless victims.

The Extent of Prostitution in Canada

There are no reliable estimates of the extent of prostitution in Canada, for several reasons. First, the activity is quasi-legal, and hence most of it is clandestine or otherwise hidden behind massage parlours and escort services. Second, criminal charges, which are basically our only official source for quantitative data on prostitution, deal almost entirely with street prostitution. Although this is only one component of the sex trade, accounting for less than one-fifth of prostitution overall in Canada, it is the most visible, with 95 percent of all charges in recent years being for "communicating." Throw into all this confusion the fact that people don't always agree on how to define certain types of sex work (i.e., is it "prostitution" or not?) and the fact that people move around, change their names and addresses, and so on. Many people drift into and out of prostitution, considering it temporary work between full-time jobs or as part-time work while attending school (Allman 1999; Lowman 2000; Reynolds 1986; Potterat et al. 1990).

Prostitution and Age, Class, Education, Racialization, and Ethnicity

Although some Canadian prostitutes are as young as 8 or 9, the vast majority are between the ages of 17 and 24. The peak earning age appears to be about 22, although this may apply mainly to street workers; for example, O'Doherty's recent study of off-street sex workers in Vancouver found that the women involved were aged 22 to 45, and a recent Victoria study found the mean age of 201 sex workers they interviewed to be 32, with ages ranging from 18 to 63 (Clinard and Meier 1989; DePasquale 1999; Hallgrimsdottir et al. 2006; Meadahl 2007). Male customers are often considerably older than the sex workers they hire and are usually White and married, although some teenage and university-age males also hire prostitutes (Lowman and Atchison 2006; National Victims Resource Center 1991; Weitzer 2005). Often, the age difference between young prostitutes and older customers is striking, as a woman forced into prostitution at age 13 by a pimp explains:

> The men who bought me—the tricks—knew I was an adolescent. Most of them were in their 50s and 60s. They had daughters and granddaughters my age. They knew a child's face when they looked into it. . . . It was even clearer that I was sexually inexperienced. So they showed me pornography to teach me and ignored my tears as they positioned my body like the women in the pictures, and used me. (Giobbe 1993:38)

Although a small percentage of teenagers enter prostitution through coercion, most are runaways who have left home because of sexual abuse or other family problems. Some teen prostitutes are "throwaways"—thrown out of their homes by parents or other family members (Snell 1995; Vissing 1996). Regardless of their prior history, many teens become prostitutes because prostitution is the best—or only—job they can get. As "Dawn" explains,

> I have often heard men say that I had a choice, and I did, work as a prostitute or starve to death because it is illegal in Canada to work at 12, not to mention that no one will hire you if you have no address and are only 13 or 14. (quoted in Parrot and Cummings 2008:4)

Social class is directly linked to prostitution: lower-income and poverty-level women and men are far more likely to become prostitutes than are more affluent people (Hallgrimsdottir et al. 2006; Lowman and Fraser 1996; Miller 1986). Some people with little formal education and few job skills view prostitution as an economic necessity. As one woman stated, "I make good money [as a prostitute]. That's why I do it; if I worked at McDonald's for minimum wage, then I'd feel degraded" (quoted in McWilliams 1996:340). However, women working for exclusive escort services are more likely to have attended college and come from the middle or upper-middle class. O'Doherty's research supports this, as 90 percent of her sample of off-street sex workers had some postsecondary education, and more than one-third had a university degree (in Meadahl 2007).

Racialization is also an important factor in prostitution. Sociologist Patricia Hill Collins (1991) suggests that African-American women are affected by the widespread image of Black women as sexually promiscuous. Collins traces the roots of this stereotype to the era of slavery, when Black women—and Black men and children—were at the mercy of White male slave-owners and their sexual desires. Indigenous women are affected by similar stereotyping. Historically, First Nations women have been viewed as "exotic sexual commodities" (Farley and Lynne 2004:111) and as sexually freer than White women (Allen 1986), a view that has, over the years, translated into the stereotype of sexual promiscuity. This stereotype has had the effect of devaluing and even dehumanizing Indigenous women and has been used as a justification for sexualized violence against them. As psychologist Melissa Farley and social worker Jacqueline Lynne (2004:111) note, "Hierarchies within prostitution locate Indigenous women at the bottom of a brutal 'race' and class hierarchy." For example, sociologists Augie Fleras and Jean Leonard Elliott (1996:148) report on the prairie practice of "squaw hopping," the "acknowledged practice for White men to harass and sexually assault native women." Collins (1991:175) supports Farley and Lynne, stating that prostitution exists within a "complex web of political and economic relationships whereby sexuality is conceptualized along intersecting axes of 'race' and gender." Sexually-exploited-youth advocates Cherry Kingsley and Melanie Mark (2000:28–29), in a national consultation of sexually exploited Indigenous youth, found Indigenous women and girls overrepresented in the visible sex trade, with Indigenous youth accounting for as much as 90 percent of the visible trade in some communities. These findings are echoed in a recent Victoria study as well, where Indigenous people accounted for 15 percent of the workers but only 2.8 percent of the Census area population (Hallgrimsdottir et al. 2006). Farley and Lynne's research in Vancouver's downtown East Side found 52 percent of their sample identifying as "Native" and a further 5 percent identifying as "African Canadian" (2004:115). High rates of Indigenous participation in prostitution can be attributed, in part, to poverty and to many young people's experiences in foster care: "Consultations with [Indigenous] youth identified their care experiences as paving the way for their commercial sexual exploitation" (Kingsley and Mark 2000:26). Today, prostitution remains linked to the ongoing economic, political, and social exploitation of people of colour and Indigenous people, particularly women. As sociologist Ronald Weitzer notes from his recent research on

prostitution, "Street prostitution is stratified by 'race,' gender, age, appearance, income and locale—all of which shape worker's daily experience" (2005:215).

A Closer Look at "Johns"

Until very recently, there have been few comprehensive studies conducted in Canada about the sex-trade customer, or "john." This may be a reflection of the relative power of the john's social location in relation to the sex-trade worker's. Since both are, theoretically, equally liable for prosecution under Canada's communicating laws, we should have access to similar information about both groups. This power differential is well understood by one youthful sex-trade worker in Saskatoon:

> They are always looking down on us and blaming us, but it's not only us. It's their husbands that are picking us up. Everybody is in denial: everybody pinpoints us, and blames us because we're the ones out on the street. But they're the ones that are picking us up and giving us money. They're always calling us little sluts and whores, but they never say anything about the johns . . . like they're picture perfect guys. (Kingsley and Mark 2000:25)

This self-inking money stamp was made available by the Sex Workers Alliance of Vancouver, in 1999, to sex workers in the community. Its aim is to raise public awareness that money earned in the sex trade is an important part of the Canadian economy.

Source: Will Pritchard, Illustrator/Designer. Distributed by the Sex Workers Alliance of Vancouver © 1996, http://www.walnet.org/swav/. Reproduced with permission.

Available information indicates that most johns are men in their mid-20s to mid-40s (although older is common also), White, married, and gainfully employed (Brannigan et al. 1989; Lowman and Atchison 2006; Lowman et al. 1997; National Victims Resource Center 1991). A report by the Canadian Advisory Council on the Status of Women (1984:49) notes that most observers of prostitution report that johns are "ordinary men who go to prostitutes for simple reasons," such as experiencing sexual acts they cannot have in their other relationships, experiencing sexual relationships without lasting obligations or long-term complications, engaging in "therapy" for problems like impotence, or having a good time (see also Weitzer 2005).

A B.C. consultation with johns that was arranged through Sexual Addicts Anonymous provided some insights into some johns' behaviour that offer a contrast to the picture of them as ordinary, well-adjusted men. Given the nature of the group consulted, however, these men cannot be seen to be representative of all johns (B.C. Ministry of Attorney General 1996). This consultation found that many johns reported childhood sexual abuse and believed themselves to be "addicted" to sex. The use of prostitutes resulted in the men feeling a great deal of shame, which related to their childhood experiences and caused them to act in ways that perpetuated those feelings (engaging the services of a prostitute, for example). These johns also reported that part of the attraction to cruising for prostitutes and the use of their services was the risk of getting caught, therefore indicating that "shame the johns" campaigns may in fact work counter to the stated purpose of the campaigns. The view of the men interviewed was that stopping prostitution could be achieved only by ensuring there was a treatment component inherent in the sentencing—that punishments alone would not be successful.

Other strategies aimed at customers are being tried, such as charging a john but offering the removal of the charge from the man's record if he agrees to pay a fine and attend "John School." Typically the one-day workshop will provide a legal overview, show slides of various venereal diseases, and showcase former sex workers who talk about how much they despised their clients. The program seems to have been moderately successful in reducing people's return to buying sex, but only a small proportion of johns limit their sex buying to one time (Lauer et al. 2006). Most johns are repeat customers; for example, only 5 percent of the participants

in Lowman and Atchison's recent Vancouver study had purchased sex only once—the highest proportion, one-third of the study participants, had purchased sex between 11 and 50 times, with 10 percent reporting 51 to 100 times (2006:288). Lowman and colleagues further report that in a survey of 120 johns in the United States, a quarter of the people said they had seen a sex worker 51 or more times, and 16 percent reported seeing a sex worker more than 100 times. Another study of 101 johns found they used the services of sex workers over several years, with two-thirds of the men reporting weekly contact with a sex worker (reported in Lauer et al. 2006:36).

In an attempt to obtain a broader picture of people who buy sexual services, the B.C. Ministry of Attorney General funded an Internet survey in 1996–1997, conducted by John Lowman, Chris Atchison, and Laura Fraser (1997). The attitudes and behaviours of 130 men worldwide who buy sex are represented in this report. As in other Canadian studies (Brannigan et al. 1989; Lowman and Atchison 2006; Van Brunschot 2003), the mean age of johns was 37, with a range from 18 to 67. Most men were married or common-law; had children; were heterosexual, White, high-school graduates; and were employed full-time. Most of the men who responded online reported that their first sexual experience was with a friend or an acquaintance, not with a relative or a stranger. Twenty percent reported childhood sexual abuse. We do not have comparable figures for childhood sexual abuse for men generally.

When asked about attitudes, the men who participated in this survey believed that loneliness, sexual problems at home, the desire for specific sexual acts that partners would not perform, the desire for uncomplicated sex, and a strong male sex drive were important reasons for seeking out a prostitute. Just over one-half of the participants believed that travel to a city other than one's normal residence is important for the sex-trade transaction to occur. Most men believed female sex-trade workers are "normal," hard-working women who are "just doing another job" and "provid[ing] a valuable service"; most of the participants disagreed that prostitutes are the "victims of a sexist society" (Lowman et al. 1997). When asked whether prostitution should be criminalized, unsurprisingly then, most of these men believed it should not be. The exception here was that most of these men believed that sex with children under age 13, and snuff films—films where the actor, usually the female in the film, is actually killed in front of the camera—are morally reprehensible and should be prohibited. In terms of deterrents to buying sex, nearly all the men who responded stated they would buy sex even if it was completely illegal. However, when asked which strategies would be useful in preventing men from buying sex on the street, having viable off-street options was listed, as well as the fact of their spouses finding out, public exposure or public recognition by someone they know, and fear of HIV/AIDS (Lowman et al. 1997). A recent study of research on prostitution (Weitzer 2005:225) depicted some interesting attitudes toward prostitution held by 140 male customers who had been arrested (see Table 7.2).

The way that prostitution is dealt with under the *Criminal Code of Canada* makes the prostitution-related offence of "communicating" (s. 213) a "nuisance" offence. It is the most frequently prosecuted prostitution offence, but sentencing is minimal. Generally, when sentencing

TABLE 7.2 Customers' Attitudes toward Prostitution

	Agree (%)	Disagree (%)
Currently in a sexual relationship	59	41
Usually enjoys sex with prostitutes	36	64
Tried to stop using prostitutes	50	50
Patronizing prostitutes has caused problems for me	40	60
Prostitutes are victims of pimps	61	39
Prostitutes make a lot of money	44	56
Women are prostitutes because they want to be	42	58
Prostitutes enjoy their work	27	73
Prostitutes genuinely like men	43	57
There is nothing wrong with prostitution	46	54
Prostitution should be legalized	61	39
I would marry a prostitute	24	76
It would be okay if my son went to prostitutes	24	76
It would be okay if my daughter became a prostitute	8	92

N=140 men arrested for soliciting a prostitute in a Midwestern city and West Coast city in the United States.

Source: Ronald Weitzer, 2005, "New Directions in Research on Prostitution," Crime, Law and Social Change, 43:211–235.

occurs, it is female sex-trade workers who receive sentences of a few days in jail and the male customers who receive "discharges or negligible fines" (Department of Justice Canada 2006). Procuring (s. 212), an indictable offence, is viewed as much more serious, particularly when youth are involved, and currently carries a maximum sentence of 5, 10, or 14 years' imprisonment, depending on the sub-section of the code. Keeping a bawdy house (s. 210) is also an indictable offence and can result in a sentence of up to 2 years' imprisonment, while transporting (s. 211), not an indictable offence, can result in a summary conviction, as in s. 213. The Vancouver brothel pursued by The West Coast Co-operative of Sex Industry Professionals (WCCSIP), discussed earlier, would see an experimental exemption to *Criminal Code* sections 210, 211, and 213 similar to the kind of exemption awarded to the Vancouver safe-injection site during its pilot phase.

PERSPECTIVES ON THE SEX TRADE

Sociologists use a variety of perspectives to examine the sex trade as a social problem. Functionalists focus on the notion of deviance and on how deviance—sex work as deviant behaviour—serves important functions in society. Interactionists investigate microlevel concerns, such as how and why people become sex workers, how people come to buy sexual services, or how negative stigmatization affects sex workers' self-concepts and experiences. Conflict perspectives seek to explain how the powerful enact their moral beliefs into law and how prostitution is related to capitalism and patriarchy, and feminist theorists focus on sex-trade work as gendered (and generally inequitable) labour.

The Functionalist Perspective

Functionalists believe that the presence of a certain amount of deviance in society contributes to its overall stability. According to early sociologist Emile Durkheim, deviance clarifies social norms and helps societies to maintain **social control**—the systematic practices developed by social groups to encourage conformity and discourage deviance—over people's behaviour. By punishing those who engage in deviant behaviour such as prostitution, the society reaffirms its commitment to its sexual norms and creates loyalty to the society, particularly as people come together to oppose the behaviour.

Prostitution "is one of the few areas of consensual sexual activity that is still subject to legal control and punitive measures" in Canada (Sutdhibhasilp 2002:173). According to sociologist Kingsley Davis (1937), in societies such as Canada that have certain restrictive norms governing sexual conduct, prostitution will always exist because it serves important functions. First, it provides impersonal sexual gratification that does not require emotional attachment or a continuing relationship with another person (Freund et al. 1991). Second, prostitution provides a sexual outlet for those who do have difficulty finding a partner in a conventional relationship (Weitzer 2005). Third, prostitution provides people with the opportunity to engage in a variety of sexual practices and experiences—multiple sex partners, same-sex partners, "inter-racial" partners, fellatio (oral stimulation of the male genitalia), cunnilingus (oral stimulation of the female genitalia), anal intercourse, or any of a range of behaviours associated with BDSM (bondage, discipline, sadism, and/or masochism), including the use of devices such as restraints, gags, riding crops, and dildos. Fourth, prostitution protects the family as a social institution by making a distinction between "bad girls" or "bad boys"—with whom one engages in "promiscuous" sexual behaviour—and "good girls" and "good boys"—with whom one establishes a family. Finally, prostitution can benefit the economy by providing jobs for people who have limited formal education and job skills.

The Interactionist Perspective

Why do people enter the sex trade? Why do they stay? Why do some enjoy their work while others loathe it? What makes some people choose to pay for sex? How do sex trade workers experience their work? Interactionists investigate such questions by examining people's lived experiences and first-hand accounts. An excerpt from an interview with "Dolores" is instructive:

I set my own schedule. I set my own limits and made my own rules, and I didn't have to answer to anyone. I learned a lot about myself: what I would and would not do for money, and what I was willing to do for the right amount of money. . . . I didn't have to see anyone I didn't want to see. If a man was too boring or too rough or too crude or took too much time, I didn't have to see him again. I loved it. (French 1988:180)

"Dolores's" remarks suggest that some people become prostitutes because it provides them with greater autonomy and more career options than they otherwise would have. These reasons fit with sociologist Howard Becker's (1963) suggestion that entering a stigmatized or deviant career is similar in many ways to entering any other occupation. The primary difference is the labelling that goes along with a deviant career. Public labelling of people as deviant and their acceptance or rejection of that label can be crucial factors in determining whether or not a person stays in a deviant career or, at the very least, can determine their experience of it and of themselves. Some people are more willing than others to accept the label "deviant" or may believe they have no other option. Others successfully redefine their work and their roles within it:

See and the worst thing too, in the paper they try to fabricate . . . "prostitute," "prostitute." The way they talk about it: how dare you! I am more than a prostitute. I'm somebody's mother. I'm somebody's friend. I'm somebody's sister. I'm not just a prostitute, you now, I have, I have a story. I have lived, you know? I'm not just that. Get off it. . . . And what people are like nowadays, it's just the stigma of the whole thing. But it's . . . hey, walk in my shoes for a week, see if you survive. ("Alyssa" in Saint John, New Brunswick, quoted in Jeffrey and MacDonald 2006b:172)

There are now many qualitative Canadian studies that seek to understand the experiences of those involved in the sex trade at all levels. People's experiences vary widely, with conclusions showing that sex workers in Canada "overwhelmingly view sex work as a job" (Jeffrey and MacDonald 2006a:313). It has to be remembered that the vast majority of sex work is not street work. Many of those who work on the streets may define their experiences somewhat more negatively, and certainly do if they have been trafficked or victimized. As Weitzer states, "In general, the type of prostitution is the best predictor of worker experiences" (2005:219).

Why do some men prefer to pay for sex? Research by interactionists suggests that some young men seek out prostitutes to fulfill what they believe is a rite of passage from boyhood to manhood. Further, social analysts suggest that the desire of men of all ages to validate their sexual prowess or reaffirm their masculinity can be a factor in their seeking out prostitutes (Raphael 1988). Other research demonstrates that men who feel shy or awkward around women generally may enjoy the straightforward transactions with a prostitute (Weitzer 2005). Additionally, some clients may define the risk of "illicit or risky conduct thrilling" (Weitzer 2005:223). Interactionist perspectives such as these highlight the different ways that people define social realities—such as the importance of sexual prowess or the thrill of illicit behaviour—in light of competing and often contradictory values they have learned through socialization.

Conflict and Feminist Perspectives

Conflict perspectives on prostitution highlight the relationship between power in society and sex work: the laws that make certain activities associated with prostitution illegal are created by powerful dominant group members who seek to maintain cultural dominance by criminalizing sexual conduct that they consider immoral or in bad taste (Barry 1995).

Some conflict analysts using a liberal feminist framework believe that prostitution should be *decriminalized*—meaning that laws making activities around prostitution a crime should be eliminated. These analysts argue that prostitution is a **victimless crime**—a crime that many people believe has no real victim because it involves willing participants in an economic exchange. Therefore, neither sex workers nor johns should be harassed by police and the courts. According to Margo St. James, a former prostitute and founder of an activist group called COYOTE (Call Off Your Old Tired Ethics), "The profession itself is not abusive; it's the illegality; it's the humiliation and degradation that is dealt to them at the hands of the police" (quoted in McWilliams 1996:340). In other words, prostitution is sex work in the sex industry and should be treated and regulated as any other labour issue. In a September 2004 St. John's, Newfoundland, radio broadcast, Wayne Lucas, then provincial president of Canada's largest union—the Canadian Union of Public Employees—stated that sex workers should be unionized. Lucas said that

work is work. The people who work in that trade, they certainly deserve some of the benefits that other workers have traditionally received in their work fields. [They] should have access to benefits such as health care and pensions. They're people, just like your next-door neighbour. They could be a sister of ours, a mother, a cousin. They're out and they're in a dangerous field. ("Unionize Prostitutes" 2004)

Some conflict perspectives that use Marxist feminist and radical feminist frameworks suggest that women become prostitutes because of structural factors such as economic inequality and patriarchy (Jolin 1994). Capitalism and patriarchy foster economic inequality between women and men and force women, especially, to view their bodies as simply commodities: "When a man has bought a woman's body for his use as if it were like any other commodity . . . the sex act itself provides acknowledgment of patriarchal right. When women's bodies are on sale as commodities in the capitalist market . . . men gain public acknowledgment as women's sexual masters" (Pateman 1994:132). Taylor Lee, a young woman who entered the sex trade as a dancer, first acknowledges the roles of economics and power in a capitalist market: "Many believe that women profit from prostitution, when in fact the largest portion goes to pimps, club owners, and other businessmen. . . . The managers, owners, and investors are the ones in power" (2004:57). Summarizing a historical feminist position, the Canadian Advisory Council on the Status of Women (1984:3), in its report on prostitution in Canada, pointed out that

prostitution is not an exchange among equals. Men, who as a group, still hold most of the powerful positions of social, economic and political power in our society, buy services from the less powerful: women (often poor, young and under-educated women) and male and female adolescents and children. The sellers have little or no defense against the risks of physical or sexual abuse of economic exploitation. . . . The buyer . . . has the money: as a group, buyers do not depend on sellers for their income, while sellers generally do depend on buyers. This economic dependence reinforces the social vulnerability that prostitutes experience.

Feminists who hold this view believe that the exploitation involved in prostitution is an extension of the kind of exploitation women experience generally, not only with regard to economic disadvantages but

170   Social Problems in a Diverse Society

also with regard to cultural standards of female attractiveness, which are bound up in youthfulness, slimness, and so on. Male customers, on the other hand, like men in general in society, are not constricted by these cultural standards, as they make up the rules and have the economic means to reinforce their desires. Many feminists believe that women who are prostitutes do not understand their exploitation and need to be saved from the "false consciousness" that traps them in these degrading occupations. Taylor Lee explains,

> The first time I had sex, I was raped by someone close enough to my family to call my mother "mom." Now I was sure what I was for. I knew that my greatest asset was my sexuality and knew how badly it was desired. I also realized that I had little control over my sexuality, that it could be taken at will. It was easy to give it for profit; at least then I was in control. (2004:58)

The prostitute-as-victim stance continues to be challenged by many people who are advocates for and/or are engaged in the sex trade, including many prostitutes and other sex-trade workers who identify as feminists. As Jeffrey and MacDonald state, "Attempts to portray the sex worker as 'victim' infantilizes her [and] denies her agency" (2006a:314). Hallgrimsdottir and colleagues further note that in "victim" narratives, "sex workers appear to be legally and morally incapacitated, incapable of making safe and reasonable choices for themselves" (2006:272). These sociologists all have a view of prostitution as a service for which workers charge a fee, much like any other service in society. The difference, about which the workers are fully conscious, is that they are hiring out their bodies in ways most people would find too distasteful to engage in. They do not necessarily view themselves as exploited and often encourage those who view them as "victims" to instead respect them as self-directed, independent, hard-working women who have made the conscious choice to be involved in the sex trade, to do what they wish with their own bodies. This debate between feminists has been going on for decades and likely will continue. As Carol Queen, a well-known sociologist, filmmaker, and sex-trade worker, stated,

> Unfortunately, the exciting politics that promised me sexual freedom twenty-five years ago have veered toward dogma.... Please ... don't assume that you know what someone else's experience has been just because you can't imagine liking to do it yourself. Please don't require that all people be one certain "politically correct" way. Please don't assume I can't make my own decisions, that my exhibitionism somehow makes me a victim.... Don't tell me I don't have a soul. (Queen 1997:138–141)

According to some Marxist feminists, the only way to eliminate prostitution is to reduce disparities in income levels between women and men and eliminate poverty. However, most radical feminists believe that prostitution will not be eliminated until patriarchy is ended.

In examining social problems, conflict theorists and feminists focus on the interrelationship of racialization, class, and gender, and suggest that the criminalization of prostitution uniquely affects poor women, especially poor women of colour and Indigenous women, who are overrepresented among street prostitutes and the most vulnerable to violence, arrest, fines, and so on. According to these theorists, White male supremacy—which traditionally preserves the best-paying jobs for men—makes women of colour and Indigenous women particularly vulnerable to recruitment or coercion into prostitution. Kingsley and Mark (2000:14) found, in a national consultation of commercially sexually exploited Indigenous children and youth in Canada, that "for the Aboriginal youth who participated in these consultations, economic need dictated their actions ... [their] engagement in the sex trade."

Analysts using this framework also note that discrimination in law enforcement uniquely affects women of colour and Indigenous women, as these groups are overrepresented among prostitutes in Canada. For example, law enforcement officials typically target street prostitutes and other sex workers, particularly when political elites decide to crack down on "deviant" behaviour such as prostitution and pornography (Barry 1995). Lowman notes that there is a lack of political will to create safer conditions for prostitutes to ply their trade, as this would be seen as condoning prostitution, a stance Lowman calls "odd" as well as "hypocritical" given that prostitution in Canada is legal and hence already condoned (Lowman and Fraser 1996). Instead, Lowman contends that crackdowns, which disproportionately affect street prostitution, occur when property-holders get up in arms about their neighbourhoods, demonstrating that public propriety and property values heavily outweigh all other considerations. Most recently in many Canadian communities, police "sting" operations have targeted johns, arresting them for "communicating offences" and then publicizing their names, levying fines, and demanding community service hours and other conditions of probation.

In opposition to those analysts who view all sex work as violence against women, many Third World or transnational feminist analyses view sex work as a practice that emerges from the intersections of racism, patriarchy, imperialism, and capitalism. Women in this perspective are seen not simply as victims of patriarchal oppression but equally as

> agentic, self-determining, differentially positioned subjects who are capable of negotiation, complying with, as well as consciously opposing and transforming relations of power, whether these are embedded in institutions of slavery, prostitution, marriage, the household, or the labour market. (Kempadoo 2005:37)

Kempadoo concludes, therefore, that sex work or the sex trade itself is not necessarily problematic: much depends upon the will of the person involved in the sex trade (2005). She notes that many prostitutes' rights and anti-trafficking organizations, including feminist ones, now make a distinction between "free and forced prostitution," with "traffic in persons and forced prostitution [as] 'manifestations of violence against women'" being viewed entirely differently from that of "respect for the self-determination of adult persons who are voluntarily engaged in prostitution" (2005:37). As noted in anthropologist Denise Brennan's ethnographic account of sex workers' lives in the Dominican Republic, "sex work is never just about money and sex; it is about hopes, possibilities, and the realities of transnational capitalism and the local structures of class" (2004:ix–x). Brennan's research "unscrambles the transnational economies of desire and intimacy and shows how sex workers, with few opportunities and fewer resources, strategize to make a way for themselves in a global economy of enduring inequalities" (Brennan 2004:x).

THE FUTURE OF THE SEX INDUSTRY

Public opinion polls have consistently shown that people in Canada are mainly ambivalent about the sex industry. While they acknowledge that the industry may produce goods and services that serve as a "safety valve" for some, many believe that these goods and services can be a "trigger" for others.

In this chapter, we have focused on the sex trade. However, it is important to note that mainstream media—including magazines, movies, videos, television programming, and especially music videos—can also contribute to negative images of women and men and to the exploitation of children. Furthermore, the mainstream media can desensitize people to sexual assault, rape, violence, and murder through repeated exposure to depictions of women as victims and sex objects and men as aggressors, rapists, and killers. What do you think—Is the sex trade or the media in general more likely to encourage violence aimed at women and children?

WHAT CAN YOU DO?

- Find out what is happening regarding youth prostitution in your area and sit on an existing committee. For example, there may be a committee to establish a "safe house" for youth desiring to leave the trade.
- If your community has a safe house, volunteer at it or help educate others about the issues faced by people attempting to leave the sex trade.
- As many youth in prostitution come from abusive homes, get involved in child-abuse prevention programs in your area.
- Put together an education/information package, with others if you wish, to send to schools so that they may include the issue of sexual exploitation in career and personal-planning curricula.
- Lobby the school district to have such information available in public schools.
- Get involved in local organizations that support making the working conditions for people in the sex industry safer (e.g., Prostitutes Empowerment and Education Resource Society [PEERS]).
- Get involved in international organizations to work toward ending sexual exploitation of women and children (e.g., Global Alliance Against Trafficking in Women [GAATW]).
- Volunteer to teach English or French with immigrant and refugee settlement organizations.

Because cuts to funding for these programs often mean men have the first priority for language training (within certain racialized/ethnic communities and families), offer to teach women or youth.

- Lobby federal MPs and provincial MPPs/MLAs to have health inspectors tour entire establishments (not only kitchens) as parts of their job descriptions to ensure safer working conditions for people employed in clubs.
- Work with health care organizations to ensure that information on physical, mental, and emotional health-related issues is accurately translated into many languages and distributed in places where sex-trade workers convene.
- Write a letter to the newspaper discussing some of the issues for people in the sex trade from your point of view (e.g., Do you think prostitution should be decriminalized? Why or why not?).

- Lobby federal MPs and provincial MLAs to shift the focus in prosecution from those most vulnerable—sex-trade workers—onto pimps, traffickers, and so on—whomever you think should be prosecuted, if anyone.
- Work on a media awareness campaign with the goal of "deglamourizing" work in the sex trade.
- Get involved or create, with others, a public education campaign about why young people get involved in prostitution.
- Lobby in your community for higher minimum wages so that there may be less incentive to enter the sex trade rather than pursue other occupations.
- Work in your community to get better addiction services and housing for those who need it.
- If you have been (or are) involved in the sex trade, use your knowledge to mentor others who are involved about health and safety and options.

SUMMARY

What Is Prostitution? How Has It Changed in Recent Years?

Prostitution is the sale of sexual services (one's own or another's) for money or goods and without emotional attachment. According to some social analysts, prostitution has recently become industrialized, normalized, and globalized. The industrialization of prostitution refers to commercialized sex as a product manufactured within the human self. Normalization is the process whereby sex work comes to be treated as a form of entertainment with no legal impediments to promoting it as a commodity. The globalization of prostitution refers to the process by which the sex industry has increasingly become global in scope, spanning borders with relative ease.

What Levels, or Tiers, of Prostitution Have Sociologists Identified?

Sociologists have identified several categories: Escort prostitutes earn higher fees and can be more selective in their working conditions and customers than other prostitutes. Hustlers work out of nightclubs, bars, and strip joints, where they solicit their customers. House prostitutes work in brothels, and a substantial portion of their earnings goes to the house manager or pimp. Street prostitutes publicly solicit customers and charge by the "trick." The last tier includes those who exchange sex for drugs.

How Do Functionalists View Prostitution?

Functionalists point out that prostitution—like other forms of deviance—is functional for society. Prostitution continues because it provides people with (1) quick, impersonal sexual gratification without emotional attachment; (2) a sexual outlet for those who have no ongoing sexual relationships; (3) the opportunity to engage in non-traditional sexual practices; (4) protection for the family as a social institution; and (5) jobs for people with few traditional job skills.

How Do Interactionists View Prostitution?

Interactionists believe that prostitution—like other forms of deviance—is socially constructed. Entering a career such as prostitution is like entering any other occupation, but public labelling of the occupation as deviant—and the individual's acceptance or rejection of that label—determines whether a person stays in that career.

How Do Conflict Theorists and Feminists View Prostitution?

There are several conflict perspectives on prostitution. Liberal feminists consider prostitution a victimless crime—involving a willing buyer and a willing seller—that should be decriminalized. Marxist feminists see prostitution as linked to the capitalist economy. Radical feminists trace the roots of prostitution to patriarchy in society. Feminist theorists who focus on the intersection of racialization/ethnicity, class, and gender believe that the criminalization of prostitution is a form of discrimination against poor women, particularly poor women of colour and Indigenous women. Third World or transnational feminists view sex work and trafficking as one possibility emerging from the intersections of many relations of dominance that condition women's lives.

KEY TERMS

prostitution,   p. 151   social control,   p. 167   victimless crime,   p. 169

QUESTIONS FOR CRITICAL THINKING

1.   There have been ongoing suggestions by citizens to create "Red Light" districts in major urban centres in Canada. What arguments would you present in favour of this suggestion? What arguments would you present against it?

2.   In what ways is prostitution linked to sexism, racism, homophobia, and class-based inequality?

3.   In what ways does our Canadian culture generally sustain and perpetuate an environment where commercial sexual exploitation of children and youth in prostitution flourishes?

PEARSON

Explore the topics covered in this chapter at **www.mysockit.com** using the access provided with this text. Interactive resources for studying include video clips, practice tests, learning objectives, and Internet resources.

8

ADDICTIONS

You don't know what you are talking about.

A response that Kevin, 32, a former street person, received and reported (to the author) when he tried to talk with street youth who were using drugs. Kevin, who himself had contracted both HIV and hepatitis C from a syringe used to inject drugs, added, "The city will chew you up and spit you out."

It wasn't until I lost everything—savings in the bank, using tuition money and maxing out all my credit cards—that I realized my addiction needed to stop.

A former student's realization that her gambling was a severe problem (see fuller statement below)

A wide variety of people are affected by drugs and gambling. In the latest analysis, it was estimated that since the early 1990s, approximately 47 000 people have died annually because of tobacco (37 000 people), alcohol, and other drugs (Health Canada 2009b; Single, Robson et al. 1999), and the health, economic, and social cost to Canadian society in 1992 was $18.4 billion, 2.7 percent of GDP in that year (Single et al. 1996). These costs are a combination of workforce productivity losses, transfer payments, and the costs of prevention, research, law enforcement, and health care. While similar analyses have not been done for those affected by gambling, Tepperman (2009:8) estimated from the survey of Wiebe et al. (2006) that in a population of 32 million of whom 75 percent are over age 25, "roughly 1.2 million Canadians have a gambling problem or are at serious risk of a gambling problem."

In this chapter, we will examine legal drug use and abuse (e.g., alcohol, tobacco, and prescription drugs); illegal drug use and abuse (e.g., marijuana, narcotics, and stimulants); and gambling and severe problem gambling. To reduce unnecessary complexity of expressions, we will label all psychological and physiological need for these problems as addictions, and we will examine explanations of addictions, addiction prevention and treatment programs, and what you can do about addictions.

DRUG USE AND ABUSE

What is a drug? There are many answers to this question, so the definition is not always consistent or clear. For our purposes, a **drug** is any substance—other than food or water—that, when taken into the body, alters its functioning in some way. Drugs are used for either therapeutic or recreational purposes. *Therapeutic* use occurs when a person takes a drug for a specific purpose, such as reducing a fever or controlling an epileptic seizure. Sometimes, individuals who take prescription drugs for therapeutic purposes cross the line to drug abuse. *Recreational* drug use occurs when a person takes a drug for no other purpose than achieving some pleasurable feeling or psychological state. Alcohol and tobacco (nicotine) are *licit* (legal) drugs that are used for recreational purposes; heroin and cocaine are *illicit* (illegal) recreational drugs (Levinthal 2007). Licit drugs, which include such substances as vitamins, aspirin, alcohol, tobacco, and prescription drugs, are legal to manufacture, sell, possess, and use. Illicit drugs, such as marijuana, cocaine, heroin, and LSD (lysergic acid diethylamide), are socially defined as deviant, and using them is criminal behaviour and hence a social problem.

Defining Drug Abuse

What is drug abuse? *Drug abuse* is the excessive or inappropriate use of a drug that results in some form of physical, mental, or social impairment. A more difficult question to answer is, "What constitutes drug abuse?" When looked at from this perspective, drug abuse has both objective and subjective components. The *objective component* is physical, psychological, or social evidence that harm has been done to individuals, families, communities, or the entire society by the use of a drug. The *subjective component* refers to people's perceptions about the consequences of using a drug and the social action they believe should be taken to remedy the problem.

Sometimes when people talk about drug abuse, the subjective component—the perception of consequences—overrides the objective component. Consider, for example, the subjective and objective components underlying our society's view of the use of marijuana. The subjective component of marijuana use is the general belief that marijuana is harmful and therefore should not be legal, even though there is little evidence that marijuana use is detrimental to health. The subjective component of alcohol use is the general belief that it is harmless and acceptable, even though there is considerable evidence that it impairs more people and produces greater costs to individuals and society than marijuana use. Thus, the use of alcohol is legal.

Drug Addiction

The term **drug addiction (or drug dependency)** refers to a psychological and/or physiological need for a drug to maintain a sense of well-being and avoid withdrawal symptoms. Drug dependency has two essential characteristics: tolerance and withdrawal. **Tolerance** occurs when larger doses of a drug are required over time to produce the same physical or psychological effect that was originally achieved by a smaller dose. Tolerance is a matter of degree: some drugs produce immediate and profound levels of tolerance, whereas others produce only mild tolerance. For example, when a person first drinks a five-ounce cup of coffee, containing about 100 milligrams of caffeine, the stimulant effect is usually quite pronounced. After that person drinks the same amount of coffee over a period of several days or weeks, the effect is greatly diminished, and a second or third cup of coffee (for a total of 200 to 300 milligrams of caffeine) becomes necessary to duplicate the earlier feeling (Levinthal 2007). **Withdrawal** refers to a variety of physical and/or psychological symptoms that habitual drug users experience when they discontinue drug use. For example, people who suddenly terminate their alcohol intake after long-term, heavy drinking experience various physical symptoms ranging from insomnia to DTs (*delirium tremens,* or mental confusion often accompanied by sweating and tremor) and psychological symptoms such as a reduced sense of self-worth.

ALCOHOL USE AND ABUSE

Much of the data in this section comes from the Canadian Addiction Survey (CAS), the most recent national study of Canadians' use of alcohol and other drugs published in November 2004. The content is multidimensional, including physical, mental, and social components, and the method is in-depth telephone interviewing of over 13 000 Canadians aged 15 and older. In addition, results of a couple of the waves of the National Population Health Study (NPHS) are also reported. This study was conducted by Health Canada and Statistics Canada and consisted of in-depth interviewing of over 17 000 Canadians. It is an ongoing study to measure changes in the health status of Canadians.

The use of alcohol—ranging from communion wine in religious ceremonies to beer, wine, and liquor at business and social gatherings—is considered an accepted part of the dominant culture in Canada. *Alcohol* and *alcoholic beverages* are terms that refer to the three major forms in which ethyl alcohol (ethanol) is consumed: *wine,* which is made from fermentation of fruits and contains between 12 and 14 percent ethyl alcohol; *beer,* which is brewed from grains and hops and usually contains 3 to 6 percent alcohol; and *liquor,* which includes whiskey, gin, vodka, and other distilled spirits and usually contains 40 percent (80 proof) to 50 percent (100 proof) alcohol.

According to sales data in the year ending March 2006, Canadians (aged 15 years and older) purchased per capita 7 litres of spirits, 13.9 litres of wine, and 77.0 litres of beer for a total of 98 litres. Though high, this number is down from 104 litres purchased in 2002 and 134 litres purchased per capita in 1976 (Statistics Canada 2007a and 2002b). Since some people do not drink at all, if Canada follows the American pattern this rate means that 10 percent of the population could account for roughly half the total alcohol consumption (Levinthal 2007).

Many people do not think of alcohol as a drug because it can be purchased legally—and without a prescription—by adults. It is, however, a psychoactive drug that is classified as a *depressant* because it lowers the activity level of the central nervous system. The impairment of judgment and thinking associated with being drunk is the result of alcohol depressing brain functions. Alcohol also affects mood and behaviour. One to two drinks often bring a release from tensions and inhibitions. Three to four drinks affect self-control—including reaction time and coordination of hands, arms, and legs—and judgment, muddling the person's reasoning ability. Five to six drinks (binge or heavy drinking) affect sensory perception, and the person may show signs of intoxication, such as staggering, belligerence, or depression. At seven to eight drinks, the drinker is obviously intoxicated and may go into a stupor. Nine or more drinks affect vital centres, and the drinker may become comatose or even die. Of course, factors such as sex (women are more affected than men by the same amount of alcohol because they have a lower percentage of water in their bodies), body weight, physical build, and recent food and fluid consumption must be taken into account in estimating the rate of alcohol absorption in the body.

Although negative short-term effects of drinking are usually overcome, chronic heavy drinking or alcoholism can cause permanent damage to the brain or other parts of the body. Social scientists divide long-term drinking patterns into four general categories. *Social drinkers* consume alcoholic beverages primarily on social occasions; they drink occasionally or even relatively frequently. *Heavy drinkers* are more frequent drinkers who typically consume greater quantities of alcohol when they drink and are more likely to become intoxicated. *Acute alcoholics* have trouble controlling their use of alcohol and plan their schedule around drinking. *Chronic alcoholics* have lost control over their drinking and tend to engage in compulsive behaviour such as hiding liquor bottles and sneaking drinks when they are not being observed.

Heavy Alcohol Consumption and Gender, Age, Marital Status, and Class

Since alcohol is consumed by almost 80 percent of the population, and heavy or binge drinking is considered to be a problem, the discussion of demographic factors related to alcohol consumption will focus on heavy or binge drinking (five drinks or more when alcohol is used). Table 8.1 shows that 6.2 and 25.5 percent of Canadians are heavy drinkers on a weekly or monthly basis, respectively. A much higher percentage of men are heavy drinkers than women (9.2 versus 3.3 percent on a weekly basis). A higher percentage of young people than older people are heavy drinkers (approximately 15 percent versus less than half that for older ages). Single and never-married people are much more likely to be heavy drinkers than married, partnered, divorced, separated, and widowed people (10 versus less than 5 percent, respectively). People with university degrees are much less likely to drink heavily than those with lower educational attainment (2.4 versus 7.3 to 8.0 percent, respectively). But little difference is found among those with lowest, middle, and highest income adequacy.

Alcohol-Related Social Problems

Alcohol consumption is linked to many kinds of harm, both to oneself and to others. Harms to oneself refer to harm to physical health, family and work functioning, friendships, legal problems, and so on. Harms to others

TABLE 8.1   Prevalence of Weekly and Monthly Heavy Drinking among Past-Year Drinkers by Demographic Characteristics, Canada, Aged 15+, 2004

	Weekly Heavy Drinking (%)	Monthly Heavy Drinking (%)
Total (drinkers)	6.2	25.5
Sex		
Female (comparison group)	3.3	17.0
Male	9.2	33.9
Age Group (comparison group is previous age group)		
15–17	7.6	35.7
18–19	16.1	51.8
20–24	14.9	47.0
25–34	6.5	30.4
35–44	5.3	24.2
45–54	6.0	22.0
55–64	4.0	17.5
65–74	0.5	9.7
75+	1.5	9.1
Marital Status		
Married/partnered (comparison group)	4.6	20.2
Divorced/separated/ widowed	4.9	20.9
Single/never married	10.2	38.8
Education		
Less than secondary (comparison group)	7.7	26.1
Secondary	7.3	29.6
Some post-secondary	8.0	26.6
University degree	2.4	19.8
Income Adequacy		
Lowest (comparison group)	8.7	26.6
Middle	6.0	26.4
Highest	6.7	25.5
Not stated	5.2	23.7

Source: Canadian Addiction Survey (CAS), 2005, A National Survey of Canadians' Use of Alcohol and Other Drugs: Prevalence of Use and Related Harms: Detailed Report. *Ottawa: Canadian Centre on Substance Abuse.*

refer to their being insulted or humiliated, receiving verbal abuse, being in serious quarrels, family or marriage problems, or being assaulted.

According to the Canadian Addiction Survey (CAS), nearly 1 in 10 adult Canadians reported experiencing harm in the past 12 months due to their drinking. The most common harm was to physical health (5.4 percent). Smaller percentages reported harms to friendships and social life (2.7 percent) and financial position (4.7 percent). Table 8.2 shows the harm experienced because of drinking by others: 32.7 percent of Canadians 18 years or older experienced one or more harms. Equal percentages of males and females experienced harm. Younger people tended to experience more harm than older people. Single and never-married people experienced more harm than married, partnered, divorced, separated, and widowed people. A higher percentage of those with some post-secondary education experienced harm than those with other levels of attainment. Experienced harm was not related to income adequacy or rural/urban status, but it was related to being a heavy drinker. Those who were heavy drinkers were much more likely to report experiencing harm than non-heavy drinkers.

Health Problems

Although not all heavy drinkers and chronic alcohol abusers exhibit the major health problems that are typically associated with alcoholism, their risk of them is greatly increased. For alcoholics, the long-term health effects include *nutritional deficiencies* as a result of poor eating habits. Chronic heavy drinking contributes to high caloric consumption but low nutritional intake. Alcoholism is also associated with fluctuations in blood sugar levels that can cause adult-onset diabetes. Structural loss of brain tissue may produce *alcoholic dementia,* which is characterized by difficulties in problem solving, remembering information, and organizing facts about one's identity and surroundings (Levinthal 2007).

Chronic alcohol abuse is also linked to *cardiovascular problems* such as inflammation and enlargement of the heart muscle, poor blood circulation, reduced heart contractions, fatty accumulations in the heart and arteries, high blood pressure, and cerebrovascular disorders such as stroke (Levinthal 2007). However, studies show that moderate alcohol consumption—such as a glass of wine a day—may improve body circulation, lower cholesterol levels, and reduce the risk of certain forms of heart disease.

Over time, chronic alcohol abuse also contributes to irreversible changes in the liver that are associated

TABLE 8.2 Percentage Reporting at Least One Harm During the Past Year Because of Others' Drinking, by Demographic Characteristics

	%
Total (drinkers)	32.7
Sex	
Female (comparison group)	32.6
Male	32.9
Age Group (comparison group is previous age group)	
18–19	62.6
20–24	58.3
25–34	41.9
35–44	32.7
45–54	30.4
55–64	24.8
65–74	14.9
75+	5.4
Marital Status	
Married/partnered (comparison group)	28.2
Divorced/separated/widowed	27.9
Single/never married	46.8
Education	
Less than secondary (comparison group)	25.6
Secondary	31.9
Some post-secondary	38.6
University degree	30.8
Income Adequacy	
Lowest (comparison group)	37.9
Middle	33.4
Highest	34.1
Not stated	28.1

Source: Canadian Addiction Survey (CAS), 2005, A National Survey of Canadians' Use of Alcohol and Other Drugs: Prevalence of Use and Related Harms: Detailed Report. Ottawa: Canadian Centre on Substance Abuse.

with *alcoholic cirrhosis*—a progressive development of scar tissue in the liver that chokes off blood vessels and destroys liver cells by interfering with their use of oxygen. Given all the possible health problems, perhaps it is not surprising that alcoholics typically have a shorter life expectancy—often by as much as 10 to 12 years—than non-drinkers or occasional drinkers who consume moderate amounts of alcohol.

Abuse of alcohol and other drugs by a pregnant woman can damage the fetus. **Fetal alcohol spectrum disorder (FASD)** is an umbrella term used to describe the range of disabilities and diagnoses that result from drinking alcohol during pregnancy. This expression replaces *fetal alcohol syndrome* and *fetal alcohol effects*. Specific birth defects and the degree of the disability can depend on how much alcohol was drunk, and how often and when during the pregnancy; they can also depend on the state of health of the pregnant woman. No amount or type of alcohol during pregnancy is considered safe.

It is estimated that in Canada, more than 3000 babies a year are born with FASD, and about 300 000 people are currently living with the disorder (Health Canada 2009c).

Alcohol in the Workplace

Productivity losses due to absenteeism, tardiness, and workplace accidents from alcohol use amounted to $4.1 billion in 1992, according to Single and his colleagues (1996:247). Excessive alcohol consumption impairs the sensorimotor skills necessary to operate machinery, heavy equipment, and motor vehicles. Numerous studies have shown a relationship between alcohol—and other drugs—and many workplace injuries or fatalities (Macdonald 1995).

Driving and Drinking

Drivers who have been drinking often do not realize how much alcohol they have consumed or what effect it has on their driving ability. As a result, many people drive dangerously even when they are not legally drunk—that is, driving with a blood alcohol level over 0.08 percent, which is referred to as impaired driving. Alcohol-related driving accidents occur, for example, when drivers lose control of their vehicles, fail to see a red traffic light, a car, or a pedestrian in the street, or miss a sharp curve in the road (Gross 1983). The latest information from the Health Canada website states that alcohol-related motor vehicle crashes account for 13 percent of all alcohol-related hospitalizations and 12 percent of all alcohol-related days in hospital (Single et al. 1996). They also account for 22 percent of all alcohol-related deaths and 33 percent of all alcohol-related years of life lost (Single et al. 1996). Single et al. (1996) estimated that in 1992, alcohol-related collisions in Canada resulted in direct costs for damage of $482.8 million.

Much less is known about the prevalence of driving while impaired by drugs other than alcohol, and the risks associated with this behaviour. Groups such as Mothers Against Drunk Driving (MADD) continually develop new recommendations to ensure that public interest in the issue is maintained (see Box 8.1).

Family Problems

Chronic alcohol abuse or alcoholism makes it difficult for a person to maintain social relationships and have a stable family life. According to social scientist Charles F. Levinthal (2007), for every person who has a problem with alcohol, an average of at least four other people are directly affected on a daily basis. Domestic abuse and violence in families are frequently associated with heavy drinking and alcohol abuse by one or more family members. Women whose partners consume five or more drinks at one time, compared to those whose partners never drink, are at six times the risk of violence, and abused women frequently use drugs to deal with the pain (Health Canada 1993). Growing up in a family that is affected by alcohol can have a profound impact on children. The extent to which alcohol abuse affects other family members depends on the degree of alcoholism and the type of alcoholic. Some alcoholic parents are violent and abusive; others are quiet and sullen or withdrawn. To outsiders, the family of an alcoholic may appear to be normal, but family members may feel as though they have an "elephant in the living room," as journalist Joyce Maynard (1994:80–81) explains:

I grew up in an alcoholic household. But as difficult as it was dealing with my father's drinking, the greater pain for me was the secret keeping. Adult children of alcoholics refer to the phenomenon as "the elephant in the living room": You have a huge, inescapable fact about your life that affects everything in your home, but nobody mentions it, although everybody's behaviour is altered to accommodate or deal with it. . . . Our family squeezed past the elephant in the living room, felt his breath on our faces, and rearranged furniture to make room for him. I hid liquor bottles if a friend was coming over. To prevent my father from driving, I even stashed away the keys to his car. But I never uttered a word, and neither did the rest of my family, about what was behind those

BOX 8.1   Maintaining a Drumbeat against Drunken Driving

A selfishly drunk (BAC Blood Alcohol Concentration 240, three times the legal limit) driver took the sunshine from my life in July 1981—or was it just yesterday? That sunshine was our 19-year-old son, about to embark on his adult life: university, career, marriage. Instead, we are left with chronic emptiness: no hugs at the door on his weekends home; no daughter-in-law to love and admire; no grandchildren to be "just like so-and-so."

Like many other members of Mothers Against Drunk Driving (MADD), including Candace Lightner, who founded the organization in the United States in the early 1980s when her daughter was killed, Helen Stauffer has a personal reason for confronting the problem of drunk driving. Over the past two decades, MADD has campaigned for stricter laws against drunk driving, mounting media campaigns against drinking and driving, and promoting the idea of having a designated driver. According to studies commissioned by MADD, since 1999 the number of impaired crash fatalities has been averaging 1212 per year from 1999 to 2006 (Applied Research and Evaluation Services 2009).

One of MADD's campaigns was to reduce the *Criminal Code* BAC level from 0.08 percent to 0.05 percent. Police are reluctant to charge people with a BAC lower than 0.10 percent

because of measurement variation. The campaign to reduce the BAC led to much criticism and claims that MADD was trying to criminalize social drinking. MADD's national executive director, Andrew Murie, replied in the same press release, "A 0.05 percent BAC limit would not criminalize social drinking. What we want to stop are people who go out to drink four or five and then drive." Another campaign is to advocate passing a drug-impaired driving law (MADD Canada 2005).

MADD is also concerned about the influence of beer and wine advertising (distillers have informally agreed not to advertise hard spirits). Despite the fact that the annual number of alcohol-related auto accidents in this country remains high, images and fantasies associated with drinking make it seem far more exciting, romantic, and adventurous to drink than to abstain. What further policy steps do you think MADD should take to promote its message? Do you think that alcoholic beverage manufacturers have a responsibility to inform the public about the potential consequences of their products, through health facts and graphic photos on bottles like those found on cigarette packages? Why or why not?

Source: Helen Stauffer, former vice-president of PRIDE (People to Reduce Impaired Driving Everywhere) and its successor, MADD (Mothers Against Drunk Driving) Canada (e-mail to the author)

actions. . . . It wasn't until I became an adult myself that I recognized the unhealthiness of our family's conspiracy of silence.

As Maynard suggests, family members of alcoholics frequently become *enablers*—people who adjust their behaviour to accommodate an alcoholic. Enabling often takes the form of lying to cover up the alcoholic's drinking, absenteeism from work, and/or discourteous treatment of others. Enabling leads many families to develop a pattern of **codependency**—a reciprocal relationship between the alcoholic and one or more non-alcoholics who unwittingly aid and abet the alcoholic's excessive drinking and resultingbehaviour (Jung 1994). When codependency occurs, the spouse or another family member takes on many of the alcoholic's responsibilities and keeps the alcoholic person from experiencing the full impact of his or her actions. Children who grow up in alcoholic families tend to have

higher than normal rates of hyperactivity, antisocial behaviour, low academic achievement, and cognitive impairment (Leventhal 2007). However, although the statistical risk of becoming an alcoholic increases if one's parent has been an alcoholic, most children of alcoholics (as many as 59 percent) do not become alcoholics themselves (Sher 1991).

TOBACCO (NICOTINE) USE AS A SOCIAL PROBLEM

The nicotine in tobacco is a toxic, dependency-producing psychoactive drug that is more addictive than heroin. It is categorized as a *stimulant* because it stimulates central nervous system receptors, activating the release of adrenaline, which raises blood pressure, speeds up the heartbeat, and gives the user a sense of alertness. Some people claim that nicotine reduces their appetite, helps them to lose weight, and produces a sense of calmness and relaxation (Akers 1992). Perhaps these physical and psychological effects of nicotine dependency help to explain why though smoking rates have declined substantially (see Figure 8.1), just less than one in every four Canadian adults over the age of 15 (25 percent of men and 20 percent of women) smoked in 2007 (Statistics Canada 2008d).

Figure 8.1 also shows that a declining and a lower percentage (12 percent) of young people aged 12 to 19 are smoking.

Although the overall proportion of smokers in the general population has declined somewhat since the pioneering 1964 U.S. Surgeon General's warning that smoking is linked to cancer and other serious diseases, tobacco is still responsible for more than 37 000 deaths per year in Canada, or five times the number of deaths from car accidents, murder, suicides, and alcohol abuse combined, according to Health Canada (2009d). People who smoke cigarettes, cigars, or pipes have a greater

likelihood of developing lung cancer and cancer of the larynx, mouth, and esophagus than non-smokers because nicotine is ingested into the bloodstream through the lungs and soft tissues of the mouth (Akers 1992). Furthermore, many cases of bronchitis, emphysema, ulcers, and heart and circulatory disorders can be traced to nicotine consumption. When tobacco burns, it forms carbon monoxide, which disrupts the transport of oxygen from the lungs to the rest of the body and hence contributes to cardiovascular disease (Levinthal 2007).

Smoking typically shortens life expectancy. It is estimated that about half a pack (10 cigarettes) a day on average reduces a person's life expectancy by four years, and smoking more than two packs a day (40 cigarettes) reduces life expectancy by eight years. When a person uses both tobacco and alcohol, the cancer-causing effects of tobacco are exacerbated (Levinthal 2007).

Even people who never light up a cigarette are harmed by **environmental tobacco smoke**—the smoke in the air as a result of other people's tobacco smoking

FIGURE 8.1   Trends in Proportion of Current Smokers (Daily or Occasional), by Age and Sex, Canada (Excluding the Territories), 2000/2001 to 2007

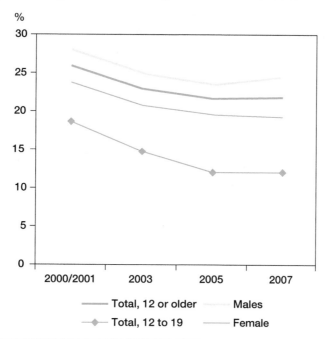

Source: Statistics Canada, 2008, "Canadian Tobacco Monitoring Use Survey," The Daily (June 18). Retrieved October 25, 2008 (http://www.statcan.gc.ca/daily-quotidien/080618/dq080618a-eng.htm).

(Levinthal 2007). When someone smokes a cigarette, about 75 percent of the nicotine ends up in the air. Researchers have found that non-smokers who carpool or work with heavy smokers are more affected by environmental smoke than non-smokers who are only occasionally exposed to it. Therefore, smoking has been banned in many public and private facilities throughout the country.

Not surprisingly, cigarette smoking adversely affects infants and children. Infants born to women who smoke typically have lower than average birth weights and sometimes slower rates of physical and mental growth. When a pregnant woman smokes, blood vessels constrict, which reduces the amount of oxygen reaching the fetus. Carbon monoxide transmitted from the mother's blood to the fetus interferes with the distribution of oxygen that does reach the fetus (DiFranza and Lew 1995). Children who grow up in households where one or both parents smoke are more apt to suffer from frequent ear infections, upper respiratory infections such as bronchitis and sinusitis, allergies, asthma, and other health problems than children whose parents do not smoke.

Why do so many people use nicotine if it is so dangerous? Several reasons have been suggested. First, nicotine creates a high level of dependency, so once a person has begun to use tobacco regularly, the withdrawal symptoms may be strong enough to make the person light up another cigarette. Some researchers have found that the majority of people who smoke recognize that smoking is bad for them and would like to quit but cannot (Levinthal 2007). Second, in the past, sophisticated marketing campaigns associated smoking with desirable cultural attributes such as achieving maturity, gaining wealth and happiness, or being thin and sexy. In Canada, the *Tobacco Act* of 1997 (amended in 1998 and 2000) prohibits cigarette manufacturers from advertising their products on radio or television or in magazines or newspapers; they are also prohibited from sponsoring sports and arts events. In addition, the manufacturers must print large health warnings and graphic anti-smoking pictures on cigarette packages and report marketing campaigns to the federal government. Finally, smoking has been used by youth as a form of rebellion and a method of showing solidarity with peers. Thus, many forces combine to promote the continuation of Canada's number one public health problem.

PRESCRIPTION DRUGS, OVER-THE-COUNTER DRUGS, AND CAFFEINE

When most people think of drug abuse, they picture unscrupulous drug dealers in dark alleys selling illegal drugs. But legal drugs may also be abused. Legal drugs fall into two categories: *prescription drugs*, which are dispensed only by a registered pharmacist on the authority of a licensed physician or dentist, and *over-the-counter (OTC) drugs*, which are available off the shelf and are restricted only by the customer's ability to pay.

Prescription Drugs

According to the NPHS, in 1998, opioid analgesics (morphine-type pain relievers) were used by 4.7 percent of Canadians aged 15 or older, antidepressants by 3.6 percent, sleeping pills by 3.5 percent, tranquilizers by 2.7 percent, steroids by 0.8 percent, and diet pills by 0.5 percent (Single, Minh et al. 1999:113). Pain medication is probably the prescription drug that is most frequently abused. Though millions of people benefit from *narcotics*—natural or synthetic opiates such as morphine (brand names Duramorph and Roxanol), propoxyphene (Darvon), and codeine—that relieve pain, suppress coughing, control chronic diarrhea, and reduce heroin withdrawal symptoms, there are risks of short-term abuse and long-term psychological and physical dependence. Over time, users develop tolerance for the drug they are taking and must continue to increase dosages to obtain the same effect that was derived from the lower dose. Drug dependency that results from physician-supervised treatment for a recognized medical disorder is called *iatrogenic addiction*. Iatrogenic addiction is most likely to occur with long-term use and/or high dosages of a prescription drug; it most often affects people from the middle or upper class who have no previous history of drug abuse or addiction (Levinthal 2007).

Two widely prescribed drugs that have been the subject of controversy regarding their use and abuse are methylphenidate (Ritalin) and fluoxetine (Prozac). Ritalin is a stimulant that is prescribed for children who are diagnosed with *attention-deficit hyperactivity disorder* (ADHD). According to the American Psychiatric Association, ADHD is characterized by emotionality, behavioural hyperactivity, short attention span, distractibility, impulsiveness, and perceptual and learning disabilities. Although some children are probably correctly diagnosed with this disorder, some commentators worry that Ritalin is overprescribed in Canada. According to the continuing survey of drug use among Ontario students conducted by drug-use researchers Edward Adlaf and Angela Paglia-Boak (2007), 1.0 percent of students used drugs for ADHD in 2007 (see Table 8.4 on page 185). Boys are slightly more likely than girls to be diagnosed with ADHD and to be prescribed drugs. Advocates believe that children with normal to above-average intelligence who are performing poorly in school can benefit from Ritalin, which has proven to be safe for more than 40 years. But critics argue that many parents, doctors, and teachers see Ritalin as a quick fix for dealing with troublesome children.

One of the most abused prescription drugs for adults is Prozac, an antidepressant. Introduced in 1987 as a breakthrough medication for clinical depression, Prozac has become a cure-all for the blues, a far milder form of depression. Advocates believe that Prozac enhances the quality of life for many people, freeing them from depression and suicidal thoughts. But the long-term side effects of the drug are unknown, and there is some evidence that Prozac is associated with intense, violent suicidal thoughts in some patients. Both Prozac and Ritalin are approved by Health Canada and are considered safe and effective if taken as directed.

Over-the-Counter Drugs

A fine line exists between prescription and over-the-counter (OTC) drugs. Today, both types of drugs are advertised in electronic and print media directly to the consumer, with suggestions to "ask your doctor or pharmacist about [our product] on your next visit." Some drugs are available both by prescription and over the counter, depending on their strength and dosage. For example, medication for stomach ulcers (e.g., Zantac and Tagamet) is sold over the counter in lower doses and by prescription in higher doses. Some drugs that are now sold over the counter were previously available only by prescription.

Widely used OTC drugs include analgesics, sleep aids, and cough and cold remedies. According to the NPHS, 65 percent of Canadians 12 years old and older took pain relievers, 20 percent took cold and cough

remedies, and 11 percent took stomach remedies. In each case, a higher percentage of women than men took the drugs (Statistics Canada 2001b:36). Abuse of aspirin and other analgesics can cause gastric bleeding, problems with blood clotting, complications during surgery and during labour and delivery, and Reye's syndrome (a potentially life-threatening condition that can arise when children with flu, chicken pox, or other viral infections are given aspirin). Overdoses of analgesics such as acetaminophen (e.g., Tylenol and Anacin-3), aspirin, and ibuprofen (e.g., Motrin, Advil, and Midol) have been linked to cases of attempted suicide, especially by White females between the ages of 6 and 17 years. Few of these suicide attempts have resulted in death except when the analgesics were combined with alcohol or other drugs (Levinthal 2007). Like analgesics, sleep aids are dangerous when combined with alcohol or some cough and cold remedies because they are depressants that slow down the central nervous system. Even cough and cold medications alone have side effects, such as drowsiness, that can be hazardous—if, for example, users attempt to drive a car or operate heavy machinery. To counteract drowsiness, some drug companies add caffeine to their products.

Caffeine

Although it is a relatively safe drug, caffeine is a dependency-producing psychoactive stimulant (Gilbert 1986). Caffeine is an ingredient in coffee, tea, chocolate, soft drinks, and stimulants such as NoDoz and Vivarin. Coffee lovers drank 86 litres in 2006, up 6.5 litres from 1997. The enjoyment of traditional and specialty coffees available from a number of coffee shops has likely fuelled coffee use (Statistics Canada 2007a). Most people ingest caffeine because they like the feeling of mental alertness and reduced fatigue that it produces. The extent to which caffeine actually improves human performance, however, is widely debated. Caffeine may improve concentration when a person is performing boring or repetitive tasks, but it has little effect on the performance of complex tasks such as critical thinking and decision making (Curatolo and Robertson 1983; Dews 1984). The short-term effects of caffeine include dilated peripheral blood vessels, constricted blood vessels in the head, and a slightly elevated heart rate (Levinthal 2007). Long-term effects of heavy caffeine use (more than three cups of coffee or five cups of tea per day) include increased risk of heart attack and osteoporosis—the loss of bone density and increased brittleness associated with fractures and broken bones (Kiel et al. 1990).

Overall, however, the social problems associated with the abuse of caffeine and prescription and OTC drugs are relatively minor when compared with the social problems associated with illegal drugs.

ILLEGAL DRUG USE AND ABUSE

Are some drugs inherently bad and hence classified as illegal? What constitutes an illegal drug is a matter of social and legal definitions that are subject to change over time. During the 19th and early 20th centuries, people in Canada had fairly easy access to drugs that are currently illegal for general use. In the early 1800s, neither doctors nor pharmacists had to be licensed. *Patent medicines*, which sometimes contained such ingredients as opium, morphine, heroin, cocaine, and alcohol, could be purchased in stores, through mail-order advertisements, and from medicine wagons run by people who called themselves doctors and provided free entertainment to attract crowds (Young 1961). Over time, because of the rapidly growing number of narcotics addicts, prescriptions became required for some drugs. Some forms of drug use were criminalized because of their association with specific minority groups. For example, in Canada, opium could be consumed legally in cough syrup, but smoking the same amount of opium was banned by the *Opium Act* of 1908 after an investigation by Mackenzie King on the use of opium. The reason for the ban was that opium smoking was a favourite pastime of the Chinese workers building railroads in Western Canada (Small 1978). In Canada, the Division of Narcotic Control was part of the Department of Health. Its head was Col. C.H.L. Sharman, who undertook the moral entrepreneurial role against drugs in Canada that Harry Anslinger played in the United States.

The most recent legislation dealing with drugs in Canada is the *Controlled Drugs and Substances Act*, which came into effect in 1997. This legislation, according to *Canada's Drug Strategy* (Health Canada 1998), has enforcement measures "for the interdiction and suppression of unlawful import, export, production, distribution, and possession of controlled substances and for the forfeiture of any property used or intended to be used in the commission of such offences and profits derived from such offences." Nevertheless, drugs are still widely available. The Canadian Addiction Survey (CAS) provides an aggregate portrait of illicit drug use in Canada.

Table 8.3 shows the lifetime use by Canadians of any of the following drugs: cannabis, cocaine, speed,

TABLE 8.3 Percentage Reporting Lifetime Use of Any of Six Illicit Drugs, by Demographic Characteristics

	%
Total	45.1
Sex	***
Female (comparison group)	39.9
Male	50.6
Age Group (comparison group is previous age group)	***
15–17	39.5
18–19	70.9
20–24	69.3
25–34	57.7
35–44	55.6
45–54	51.3
55–64	28.5
65–74	13.4
75+	3.3
Marital Status	***
Married/partnered (comparison group)	41.4
Divorced/separated/widowed	36.0
Single/never married	58.3
Education	***
Less than secondary (comparison group)	35.7
Secondary	42.9
Some post-secondary	53.0
University degree	44.7
Income Adequacy	***
Lowest (comparison group)	43.7
Middle	45.6
Highest	55.1
Not stated	35.2

Source: Canadian Addiction Survey (CAS), 2005, A National Survey of Canadians' Use of Alcohol and Other Drugs: Prevalence of Use and Related Harms: Detailed Report. *Ottawa: Canadian Centre on Substance Abuse.*

hallucinogens, ecstasy, and heroin, according to the CAS. Of Canadians aged 15 and over, 45.1 percent reported lifetime use of any of these six illicit drugs. A higher percentage of males than females have used them (50.6 versus 39.9 percent, respectively). A higher percentage of younger than older people has used them, but with the exception of the 15 to 17 group, the percentage using them remains above 50 until the age group 55 to 64 is reached. A higher percentage of people in the west than the east of Canada have used them. A higher percentage of those with some post-secondary education have used them than those with other levels of education. Finally, since illicit drugs are costly, it might be expected that income level would be related to their use. A higher percentage of people with the highest income have used them than those with lower levels. If drug incidents reported in the Uniform Crime Reporting Surveys are a measure of use, then the use of illegal drugs, particularly marijuana, is increasing. In 2004 almost 100 000 reported incidents occurred, an increase of 46 percent from 1994 (see Table 9.2 on page 204). The biggest increase in incidents, 120 percent, is for the cultivation of marijuana or grow-ops.

To show the use of these drugs by teenagers, we turn to the continuing (since 1977) study by Edward Adlaf and Angela Paglia-Boak (2007) of drug use among Ontario students. This study includes students from grades 7 to 12 inclusive (aged approximately 12 to 17 years). Table 8.4 shows the drug use during 2007 reported by male and female students.

Marijuana

Marijuana is the most extensively used illicit drug in Canada. According to the CAS, 7.4 percent of Canadians 15 years and older used marijuana in 1993, and a higher percentage of men than women reported using it (10 percent versus 4.9 percent) (Single, Minh, et al. 1999:144). According to the 2007 Ontario Student Drug Use Survey report, 25.6 percent of students used marijuana, with little difference between the sexes. Students often laugh to hear that marijuana use is still considered deviant behaviour. While the federal government was considering the decriminalization of marijuana possession during Liberal administrations, the present (2009) Conservative government has no plans to decriminalize it.

TABLE 8.4   Percentage of Ontario Secondary Students Reporting Past-Year Drug Use, by Total and Sex, 2007

	Total	Males	Females
Alcohol	61.2	61.7	60.7
Binge drinking	26.3	27.1	25.4
Cannabis	25.6	26.9	24.3
Opioid pain relievers (NM)	20.6	18.0	23.5 *
Cigarettes	11.9	11.7	12.1
Solvents	5.8	4.9	6.8
Stimulants (NM)	5.7	4.0	7.5 *
Other hallucinogens	5.5	6.6	4.3 *
OTC sleeping medication (NM)	4.0	3.2	4.9 *
Ecstasy (MDMA)	3.5	3.4	3.5
Cocaine	3.4	3.6	3.1
Jimson weed	2.6	2.7	2.4
Glue	2.5	2.1	3.0
Tranquilizers/sedatives (NM)	1.8	1.7	1.9
OxyContin (NM)	1.8	1.7	1.9
LSD	1.6	2.1	1.1 *
Methamphetamine	1.4	1.5	1.4
Ketamine	1.1	1.3	1.0
Crack	1.0	0.9	1.1
ADHD drugs (NM)	1.0	1.1	1.0
Heroin	0.9	1.3	0.6 *
ICE (Crystal Methamphetamine)	0.8	0.8	0.8
PCP	0.7	0.9	0.5
Rohypnol	0.6	s	0.8
GHB	0.5	s	0.7
Any illicit drug, including cannabis	28.7	29.3	28.1
Any illicit drug, excluding cannabis	11.7	11.7	11.6
Steroids (lifetime use)	1.3	2.0	0.5 *

Notes: Binge drinking (5+ drinks on one occasion) refers to the past four-week time period; NM = non-medical use; OTC = over-the-counter; s = estimate suppressed (less than 0.5 percent); * indicates a significant sex difference, not controlling for other factors

Source: Edward Adlaf & Angela Paglia-Boak, 2007, Drug Use Among Ontario High School Students. Toronto: Centre for Addiction and Mental Health.

Many teenage users report that marijuana is as easy to acquire as alcohol, and easier than cigarettes. According to one teenager, "It is so popular, so well known, it is around everywhere. Nobody is afraid of the consequences of selling it or buying it. . . . It is really easy to get" (quoted in Friend 1996:2A). Many young people buy the drug from friends who grow their own plants.

Marijuana is ingested by smoking it, either in a hand-rolled cigarette known as a *reefer* or *joint,* or through a pipe or other smoking implement. Potent marijuana—marijuana with high levels of the plant's primary psychoactive chemical, delta-9 tetrahydro-cannabinol (THC)—has existed for many years, but potency has increased in recent years because of indoor gardens. Indoor crops have levels of THC up to four times as high as plants grown outdoors and in other nations (Navarro 1996).

Marijuana is both a central nervous system depressant and a stimulant. In low to moderate doses, the drug produces mild sedation; in high doses, it produces a sense of well-being, euphoria, and sometimes hallucinations. Marijuana slightly increases blood pressure and heart rate and greatly lowers blood glucose levels, causing extreme hunger. The human body manufactures a chemical that closely resembles THC, and specific receptors in the brain are designed to receive it. Marijuana use disrupts these receptors, impairing motor activity, concentration, and short-term memory (Cowley 1997). As a result, complex motor tasks such as driving a car or operating heavy machinery are dangerous for a person who is under the influence of marijuana. Some studies show that heavy marijuana use can impair concentration and recall in high-school and college students (Wren 1996). Users become apathetic and lose their motivation to perform competently or achieve long-range goals, such as completing their education. Overall, the short-term effects of marijuana are typically milder than the short-term effects of drugs such as cocaine.

High doses of marijuana smoked during pregnancy can disrupt the development of a fetus and result in lower-than-average birth weight, congenital abnormalities, premature delivery, and neurological disturbances (Levinthal 2007). Furthermore, some studies have found an increased risk of cancer and other lung problems associated with inhaling, because marijuana smokers are believed to inhale more deeply than tobacco users.

Over the past decade, medical uses of marijuana have been widely debated. In 2001, Health Canada authorized the use of marijuana for medicinal purposes. As noted in the last edition of this book, the Canadian AIDS Society criticized this program in 2006. At the time, fewer than 200 people with HIV/AIDS took advantage of the program because most did not know of its existence or could not find a doctor to support their application (Kendall et al. 2008:216). Now this situation is very different. As of July 4, 2008,

- 2812 people are authorized to possess dried marijuana;
- 2017 people are allowed to cultivate it;
- 1476 doctors (in most provinces and territories) participate in the program; and
- hundreds of applications have been made since mid-2006 for authorization to possess. (Health Canada 2009e)

Thus, it would seem that the problems of the medical use of marijuana that did exist have been mostly overcome.

Stimulants

Cocaine and amphetamines are among the major stimulants that are abused in Canada. Cocaine is an extremely potent and dependency-producing drug derived from the small leaves of the coca plant, which grows in several Latin American countries. In the 19th century, cocaine was introduced as a local anesthetic in medical practice and a mood-enhancer in patent medicines (Akers 1992). It was an ingredient in Coca-Cola from the 1880s to the early 1900s (Miller 1994). Today, cocaine is the third most widely used psychoactive drug after alcohol and marijuana. Users typically sniff, or "snort," the drug into their nostrils, inject it intravenously, or smoke it in the form of crack—a potent form of cocaine that is specially processed for smoking.

According to the CAS and reported in the *Canadian Profile,* 0.7 percent of Canadians aged 15 and older had used cocaine in 1994—slightly more males than females reported use (0.8 percent versus 0.5 percent)—and this figure has remained relatively stationary over time (Single, Minh, et al. 1999:144). Table 8.4 shows that 3.4 percent of students reported using cocaine in 2007, and more males than females (3.6 versus 3.1 percent) used it. For some central-city residents living in poverty, with no hope of gainful employment, dealing cocaine is a major source of revenue and an entry point for other drug-related crime.

The effects of cocaine on the human body depend on how pure the dose is and what effect the user expects. Most cocaine users experience a powerful high, or "rush," in which blood pressure rises and heart rate and respiration increase dramatically. Reactions vary in length and intensity, depending on whether the drug is injected, smoked, or snorted. When the drug wears off, users become increasingly agitated and depressed. Some users become extremely depressed and suicidal; others develop such a powerful craving that they easily become addicted to the drug (Gawin and Ellinwood 1988). Occasionally, cocaine use results in sudden death by triggering an irregular heart rhythm.

People who use cocaine over extended periods of time have higher rates of infection, heart disturbance, internal bleeding, hypertension, cardiac arrest, stroke, hemorrhaging, and other neurological and cardiovascular disorders than non-users. Although these problems may develop gradually as cocaine use continues, some users experience the problems after a single dose. Intravenous cocaine users who share contaminated needles and syringes are also at risk for HIV/AIDS. The risk of contracting HIV is especially high in crack houses, where women addicts often engage in prostitution (see Chapter 7) to acquire drugs.

Cocaine use is extremely hazardous during pregnancy. Children born to crack-addicted mothers usually suffer painful withdrawal symptoms at birth and later show deficits in cognitive skills, judgment, and behaviour controls. "Crack babies" must often be cared for at public expense in hospitals and other facilities because their mothers cannot meet their basic needs or provide nurturance. But social scientist Philippe Bourgeois suggests that blame for the problem cannot be placed on the women alone. Instead, Bourgeois blames patriarchal definitions of "family" and the dysfunctional public sector that relegates the responsibility for nurturing and supporting children almost exclusively to women. For change to occur, fathers and the larger society must share women's burden (Bourgeois 1995).

Like cocaine, amphetamines ("uppers") stimulate the central nervous system. Amphetamines in the form of diet pills and pep formulas are legal substances when they are prescribed by a physician, but many people, believing that they cannot lose weight or have enough energy without the pills, become physically and/or psychologically dependent on them. Speed freaks—heavy users who inject massive doses of amphetamines several times a day—often do "runs," staying awake for extended periods of time, eating very little, and engaging in bizarre behaviour such as counting cornflakes in a cereal box or pasting postage stamps on the wall before "crashing" and sleeping for several days (Goode 1989). Recent concern about amphetamine abuse has focused on a smokable form called ICE that contains a high percentage of the pure drug and produces effects that last from 4 to 24 hours (Lauderback and Waldorf 1993). Table 8.4 shows that 0.8 percent of Ontario students used ICE in 2007. Chronic amphetamine abuse can result in *amphetamine psychosis,* which is characterized by paranoia, hallucinations, and violent tendencies that may persist for weeks after use of the drug has been discontinued. Overdosing on amphetamines can produce coma, brain damage, and even death.

Depressants

Many people who abuse stimulants also abuse depressants—drugs, including alcohol, that depress the central nervous system and may have some pain-killing properties. The most commonly used depressants are barbiturates (e.g., Nembutal and Seconal) and anti-anxiety drugs or tranquilizers (e.g., Librium, Valium, and Miltown). Table 8.4 shows that 1.8 percent of Ontario students used tranquilizers in 2007. Relatively low oral doses of depressants produce a relaxing and mildly disinhibiting effect; higher doses result in sedation. Users may develop both physical addiction to and psychological dependence on these depressants. Users sometimes use depressants for *potentiation*—the interaction that takes place when two drugs are mixed together to produce a far greater effect than the effect of either drug administered separately. Heroin users, for example, will sometimes combine heroin and barbiturates in hopes of prolonging their high and extending their heroin supply (Levinthal 2007).

Recently, Rohypnol and GHB (gamma-hydroxybutyrate), also known as "Grievous Bodily

Harm" or "Liquid X," have been topics of discussion on university and college campuses. Rohypnol is used as an anesthetic and sleep aid in other countries, but it is not approved for use in Canada. Rohypnol and GHB are popular among young people because they are inexpensive ("lunch money") drugs, and they produce a "floaty" state, a mild euphoria, increased sociability, and lowered inhibitions. Table 8.4 shows that 0.6 and 0.5 percent of students have used Rohypnol and GHB, respectively. For some people, Rohypnol works like a powerful sleeping pill.

Jenny Altick was a university student when she tried the drug:

> I'd just pass out.... It seemed like a very safe thing to take. It wasn't like acid or something that was totally chemical and bad. If you're thinking about trying coke [cocaine], you've heard how bad it is. There's that little thing in your head. But this one, no one had heard about it. It was one of those new things everyone was doing. (quoted in Bonnin 1997:E1)

For other users, however, the consequences are more dire. Rohypnol, a benzodiazepine, known colloquially as "roofies," is known as the "date rape drug" because a number of women have reported that they were raped after an acquaintance secretly slipped the drug into their drink. Victims, including men, become drowsy and pass out, not remembering what happened. The combination of alcohol and Rohypnol or GHB has also been linked to automobile accidents and deaths from overdoses, which occur because it is difficult to judge how much intoxication will result when depressants are mixed with alcohol (Bonnin 1997).

Narcotics

Narcotics, or opiates, are available in several forms: natural substances (e.g., opium, morphine, and codeine); opiate derivatives, which are created by making slight changes in the chemical composition of morphine (e.g., heroin and Percodan); and synthetic drugs, which produce opiate-like effects but are not chemically related to morphine (e.g., Darvon and Demerol). Because heroin is the most widely abused narcotic, we will focus primarily on its effects.

Who uses heroin? The percentage of Canadians using it is very small. The CAS combined several drugs together to report their use. The data, reported in the *Canadian Profile*, show that 1.1 percent of Canadians aged 15 and older used heroin, speed, and/or LSD in 1994, and that a higher percentage of men than women used these drugs (1.5 percent versus 0.7 percent) (Single, Minh, et al. 1999:144). Table 8.4 shows that 1.4 percent of Ontario students used methamphetamine and 0.9 used heroin in 2007. Some people who try the drug have adverse side effects, such as nausea and vomiting, and never use it again; others become addicted.

What effect does heroin have on the body? Most heroin users inject the drug intravenously—a practice known as *mainlining* or *shooting*—which produces a tingling sensation and feeling of euphoria that is typically followed by a state of drowsiness or lethargy. Heroin users quickly develop a tolerance for the drug and must increase the dosage continually to achieve the same effect. Heroin and other opiates are highly addictive; users experience intense cravings and have physical symptoms such as diarrhea and dehydration if the drug is withdrawn.

What are the long-term effects of heroin? Although some users experience no long-term physical problems, there are serious risks involved in use. In high doses, heroin produces extreme respiratory depression, coma, and even death. Because the potency of street heroin is unknown, overdosing is always a possibility. Street heroin also tends to be diluted with other ingredients that produce adverse reactions in some users. Shooting up with contaminated needles can lead to hepatitis or HIV/AIDS. As well, heroin use has been linked more directly to crime than have some other types of drug use. Because hard-core users have difficulty holding a job and yet need a continual supply of the drug, they often turn to robbery, burglary, shoplifting, pimping, prostitution, or working for the underground drug industry (Johnson et al. 1985).

Hallucinogens

Hallucinogens, or psychedelics, are drugs that produce illusions and hallucinations. Mescaline (peyote), lysergic acid diethylamide (LSD), phencyclidine (PCP), and MDMA (ecstasy) produce mild to profound psychological effects, depending on the dosage.

Mescaline or peyote—the earliest hallucinogen used in North America—was consumed during ancient Native American religious celebrations.

In the 1960s, LSD became a well-known hallucinogen because of Timothy Leary's widely publicized advice, "Turn on, tune in, drop out." LSD is one of the most powerful of the psychoactive drugs; a tiny dose (10 micrograms) of the odourless, tasteless, and colourless drug can produce dramatic, highly unpredictable psychological effects for up to 12 hours. These effects are often referred to as a *psychedelic trip,* and users report experiences ranging from the beautiful (a good trip) to the frightening and extremely depressing (a bad trip). Consequently, some LSD users take the drug only with the companionship of others who are familiar with the drug's effects. However, some studies have found that there is a possibility of *flashbacks* in which the user re-experiences the effects of the drug as much as a year after it was taken. Most long-term psychiatric problems associated with the drug involve people who were unaware that they had been given LSD, who showed unstable personality characteristics before taking the drug, or who experienced it under hostile or threatening circumstances (Levinthal 2007).

Among the most recent hallucinogens are PCP ("angel dust") and MDMA (ecstasy). PCP can be taken orally, intravenously, or by inhalation, but it is most often smoked. Initially, PCP was used as an anesthetic in surgical procedures, but it was removed from production when patients who received it showed signs of agitation, intense anxiety, hallucinations, and disorientation. Production then went underground, and PCP became a relatively inexpensive street drug that some dealers pass off as a more expensive drug, such as LSD, to unknowing customers.

In the mid-1980s, MDMA (ecstasy) hit the street market. Manufactured in clandestine labs by inexperienced chemists, ecstasy, or "E," is a "designer drug" that is derived from amphetamines and has hallucinogenic effects. Users claim that it produces a state of relaxation, insight, euphoria, and heightened awareness without the side effects of LSD. Ecstasy has a high abuse potential and no recognized medical use (Milkman and Sunderwirth 1987). Table 8.4 shows that 1.6, 0.7, and 3.5 percent of students reported using LSD, PCP, and ecstasy, respectively, in 2007.

Inhalants

Inhalants are products that people inhale to get high. Commonly available products that are used as inhalants include gasoline, glue, paints, cleaning fluids, and toiletries. Inhalants are often called solvents because so many of them are used as inhalants. Abuse is common because inhalants are inexpensive, easy to obtain, and fast acting. They contain poisonous chemicals that can make abusers sick, damage their nerve and brain cells, and even kill them. As with many kinds of substance abuse, precise figures about use are either unavailable or questionable. However, Table 8.4 shows that 5.8 percent of students used solvents in 2007.

While inhalant abuse is found in all ethnic groups in Canada, news stories suggest it is very prevalent among Indigenous children and adolescents. A study that shows a higher prevalence of inhalant use by Indigenous than White adolescents was conducted by psychologists Barbara Gfellner and John Hundleby (1995). In a survey of students (grades 7 to 12; N = 2353 White and 237 Indigenous adolescents) in a non-metropolitan centre in midwestern Canada, they found that a higher percentage of Indigenous than White adolescents sniffed glue (4.3 percent versus 3.5 percent) and solvents (6.4 percent versus 3.5 percent) in 1993 (Gfellner and Hundleby 1995). The usual explanation for this difference is a perception of a lack of opportunities for Indigenous adolescents.

Overall Harm from Drug Use

Table 8.5 shows the percentage of Canadians reporting harm to themselves because of illicit drug use, according to the CAS. Overall, 17.5 percent of Canadians reported harm in the past year from their drug use. Little difference was found between men and women for the past year, but a higher percentage of men reported a lifetime harm. A higher percentage of younger than older Canadians reported harm, and a higher percentage of lesser-educated and lowest income adequacy reported harm.

One might think that reducing harm due to drug use would be considered a good thing, but a new controversy has emerged about the topic of safe injection sites. Should governments pay for safe injection sites (see Box 8.2 on page 191)?

TABLE 8.5   Percentage Reporting One or More Harms from One's Own Drug Use: Past Year and Lifetime

	Past-Year Harm (%)	Lifetime Harm (%)
Total	17.5	23.8
Sex	NS	***
Female (comparison group)	16.0	19.8
Male	18.4	27.2
Age Group (comparison group is previous age group)	***	***
15–17	29.9	37.6
18–19	30.6	43.6
20–24	18.2	29.9
25–34	13.1	25.4
35–44	15.8	22.5
45–54	10.6	18.8
55–64	3.1	16.7
65+	S	52
Marital Status	***	***
Married/partnered (comparison group)	11.0	18.8
Divorced/separated/widowed	16.2	22.9
Single/never married	21.7	31.5
Education	***	888
Less than secondary (comparison group)	28.5	35.5
Secondary	24.3	26.8
Some post-secondary	11.2	22.3
University degree	9.4	17.1
Income Adequacy	NS	***
Lowest (comparison group)	18.9	36.3
Middle	17.7	25.0
Highest	13.1	17.8
Not stated	22.0	24.9
Location of Household	NS	NS
Rural (comparison group)	21.3	22.1
Non-rural	17.0	24.2

Notes: For lifetime harm, percentages are of current and former drug users; for past-year harm, percentages are of current drug users; drug used include any of the following: cannabis, cocaine, speed, hallucinogens, ecstasy, inhalants, heroin, and steroids.

NS—estimate suppressed due to high sampling variability

Source: Canadian Addiction Survey (CAS), 2005, A National Survey of Canadians' Use of Alcohol and Other Drugs: Prevalence of Use and Related Harms: Detailed Report. *Ottawa: Canadian Centre on Substance Abuse.*

GAMBLING AND PROBLEM GAMBLING

Although Canadians, like people everywhere, have always gambled, only recently has gambling become a billion-dollar business in Canada and have we learned about the characteristics of gamblers and the consequences of problem gambling. Since the early 1990s, great growth has occurred in the gambling industry. Net revenue from government-run lotteries, video lottery terminals (VLTs), casinos, and slot machines not in casinos rose from $2.7 billion in 1992 to $13.6 billion in 2007, and employment in the gambling industry rose from 11 000 in 1992 to 46 000 in 2007. As a share of total governments' revenue, proceeds from gambling have risen from 1.9 percent in 1992 to 4.8 percent in 2005 (Statistics Canada 2008h).

Types of Gamblers

A study conducted in Ontario in 2005 by psychologist Jamie Wiebe and colleagues provides a comprehensive and detailed picture of the types of gambling and consequences for participants. The researchers employed the Canadian Problem Gambling Index (CPGI), included in one cycle of the Canadian Community Health Survey, and within it the Problem Gambling Severity Index (PGSI). This study found that about 36 percent of the population were non-gamblers, 54 percent were non-problem gamblers, about 6 percent were at risk, 2.6 percent had moderate gambling problems (level 3–7), and 0.8 percent had severe gambling problems (level 8+) (Wiebe et al. 2006:41). The PGSI is a nine-dimension instrument that assesses several domains of gambling problems and is divided into four categories (0, 1–2, 3–7, and 8+) to indicate increasing levels of problems. The 3–7 level denotes a significant risk. It is associated with heavy gambling and related gambling problems, such as making increased wagers, returning to win back losses, and borrowing money or selling something to gamble, and it may or may not yet be accompanied by adverse consequences from gambling, including feeling guilty about gambling, experiencing financial problems, and developing health problems such as stress and anxiety. The 8+ level represents severe problem gamblers—those who have experienced adverse consequences from gambling and might have lost control of their behaviour. The severe problem gamblers participated more in every kind of

SOCIAL PROBLEMS AND SOCIAL POLICY

BOX 8.2   The Battle over Harm Reduction: The Insite Program

Insite is a safe injection (of drugs) site that opened in 2003 in Vancouver's downtown East Side. The video *FIX: The Story of an Addicted City* in the Video Library that accompanies this textbook shows the beginning efforts to set up this program. Vancouver's downtown East Side is a neighbourhood with high rates of drug addiction, mental illness, and prostitution. One of a number of programs developed for the neighbourhood, Insite is called a "harm reduction site" because drug users are given clean needles (not drugs) and a safe place to shoot up to prevent needle sharing and the subsequent spread of disease; given nursing help to prevent fatalities due to overdoses; and offered routes to rehabilitation.

The World Health Organization (WHO) has endorsed the site, and it is one of 49 safe injection sites, primarily in Europe and Australia. It also has the support of British Columbia premier Gordon Campbell. But it does not have the support of Prime Minister Stephen Harper. His opposition was expressed by then Health Minister Tony Clement, who asked, "Is it ethical for health-care professionals to support the administration of drugs that are of unknown substance, or purity or potency—drugs that cannot otherwise legally be prescribed?" (Editorial, *Globe and Mail*, August 20, 2008:A16).

Other criticisms have included the following:

■ Most drug users do not use the site.
■ Overdose deaths prevented amount to one per year.

■ The number of HIV and hepatitis C cases it has reduced is uncertain.
■ Insufficient data exist to draw conclusions about the overall cost/benefit effectiveness. (Wente 2008:A17)

The program is quite costly: expenses were $1.5 million for set-up; $2 million for annual operating costs, provided locally; and $1.5 million over three years for research, provided by the federal government (Bailey 2008:A3). However, a computer modelling analysis of the effectiveness of the site by Ahmed Bayoumi and his colleagues suggests that Insite will save the health care system at least $14 million and prevent more than 1000 HIV infections and 54 cases of hepatitis C over a 10-year period (Weeks 2008:L1). Dr Bayoumi, whose research is supported by the Ontario HIV Treatment Network, went on to say that compared to other health care interventions, investing in a supervised injection facility represents very good value for money.

Besides the support from this research, Insite also gained support from the B.C. Court's 2008 decision that allowed the site to remain because to deny access to its health care services would violate drug users' *Charter* rights. The federal government plans to appeal this ruling. Do you believe that Insite is providing a worthwhile program? If you were in charge of funding, would you place any restraints on the program?

---

gambling (tickets, electronic, games with friends, casinos, horse racing, bingo, sports betting, and speculative investments) than other gamblers (Wiebe et al. 2006:30). Individuals with severe gambling problems spent about 20 times as much money as an average gambler in any month. Whereas an average gambler spent 2.2 percent of his or her income on gambling, those with severe gambling problems spent about 21 percent of their income (Wiebe et al. 2006:34).

Gambling and Gender, Age, Income, and Marital Status

National gambling data show no difference in the percentage of men and women who gamble. While there is little difference in gambling by age, men's participation increases with age, and women 65 and over are least likely to gamble. People at all income levels participate,

and participation and expenditure rates increase with household income. For example, 54 percent of households with incomes of less than $20 000 gambled in 2006 and spent an average of $469 per year, while equivalent figures for those with incomes of $80 000 or more were 82 percent and $566, respectively. People living alone are likely to gamble more. One in seven women and men living alone reported spending money on casinos, slot machines, or VLTs; however, the men spent more than three times as much as the women ($1396 versus $434.3) (Statistics Canada 2008h).

Problem Gambling and Province, Gender, Age, Marital Status, Education, and Income

To determine the prevalence of problem gambling in Canada, psychologist Brian Cox and colleagues (2005) also used the CPGI and within it, the PGSI. Cox et al. found that while the vast majority of Canadians had not experienced gambling problems, about 2 percent of Canadians were problem gamblers (levels 3–7 and 8+) and that some variation occurred among the provinces, ranging from 1.5 percent of people in New Brunswick to 2.9 percent of people in Manitoba (Cox at al. 2005).

Since the Ontario study by Wiebe et al. contains more detailed data of severe problem gamblers, it will be used to create a more complete portrait of this type of person. A higher percentage of men than women were severe problem gamblers (1.2 versus 0.5 percent). A higher percentage of young people (18 to 24 years) were severe problem gamblers compared with older people (1.4 versus 0.4 to 0.8 percent). A higher percentage of severe problem gamblers were found among those who were single and never married than those married or living with a partner (1.2 versus 0.7 percent). Those who had completed post-secondary education were less likely to be severe problem gamblers. A higher percentage of those who had the highest level of income ($100 000+) were likely to be severe problem gamblers (2.4 versus 0 to 1.7 percent), but otherwise employment status was unrelated to severe problem gambling. Region of residence in Ontario was also unrelated to severe problem gambling (Wiebe et al. 2006:41–42).

Gambling-Related Social Problems

Wiebe et al. also identified difficulties experienced by gamblers. While few gamblers overall reported difficulties, almost half of severe problem gamblers reported one or more problems, including

- difficulty making a paycheque last (64.5 percent of severe problem gamblers);
- gambling with money budgeted for something else (51.6 percent);
- negatively affected personal relationships (45.2 percent);
- negatively affected work (13.3 percent); and
- thoughts of suicide. (9.7 percent; Wiebe et al. 2006:37)

The following three quotations from sociologist Lorne Tepperman's interview study *Betting Their Lives*:

The Close Relations of Problem Gamblers (2009) illustrate particular difficulties gamblers or their relations experience:

> I hope I can repay my debts as soon as possible and then rebuild my family. I had properties before. Now I have nothing. (2008:145)

> My father is very preoccupied with money, and everything revolves around gaining or losing money. It has affected our relationship because I find him very self-centred, very consumed with money-making and [he] doesn't really care about other people's well-being. (2008:147)

> My sister was worried about him. Like, she would buy a case of formula for the new baby, and [her husband] would take it back and get the money for gambling. (2008:147)

As mentioned, the highest percentage of severe problem gamblers were people aged 18 to 24. A former student of one of the authors reported the difficulties she experienced over gambling:

> I started off with on-line gambling. I was glued to my laptop; in the kitchen—place the bet, stir the food, place the bet, eat a mouthful, place the bet—and it kept going. I started to get bored with the on-line casino and started to hit the real thing. In school, instead of studying, I'd be at the casino between exams 12 to 13 hours a day. My average bet was $85 per spin. It wasn't until I lost everything—savings in the bank, using tuition money, and maxing out all my credit cards—that I realized my addiction needed to stop. (author's files)

EXPLANATIONS OF ADDICTIONS

As mentioned at the outset of this chapter, we will use the term *addictions* to describe dependence on alcohol, drugs, and tobacco and severe problem gambling. Since less research is available for severe problem gambling than the other addictions, the research reported here will refer to specific kinds of addictions. Why do people become addicted? Various explanations have been given. Some focus on biological factors; others emphasize environmental influences. Sociologists stress environmental factors. We will emphasize these factors, but it is important to remember that other factors contribute. For example, studies have found convincing evidence that drugs such as alcohol, heroin, and cocaine act directly on the brain mechanisms responsible for reward and punishment. As the drugs stimulate the areas of the brain that create the sensation of pleasure and suppress the perception of pain, the user receives reinforcement to engage in further drug-taking behaviour.

Drugs that provide an immediate rush or intense euphoria (e.g., cocaine and heroin) are more likely to be abused than drugs that do not. Similarly, drugs that produce pleasant but rapidly dissipating effects (e.g., alcohol) tend to encourage users to take additional doses to maintain the pleasurable effects. Prescription drugs, like dopamine agonists for Parkinson's disease, can also produce feelings of bliss after a gambling win. Patients can be so overcome that they continue in a compulsive fashion and can lose everything gambling (Lehrer 2009).

The Interactionist Perspective

Like social psychologists, sociologists who use an interactionist framework believe that an addiction is learned behaviour that is strongly influenced by families, peers, and other people. In other words, individuals are more likely to use or abuse drugs if they have frequent, intense, and long-lasting interactions with people who use or abuse drugs. For example, some children learn to be addicts by watching their parents' addictive behaviour. Other young people learn from their peer group. In his classic study of marijuana users, sociologist Howard S. Becker (1963) concluded that drug users learn not only how to "do" drugs from other users but also what pleasurable reactions they should expect to have.

People are also more prone to accept attitudes and behaviours favourable to drug use if they spend time with members of a **drug subculture**—a group of people whose attitudes, beliefs, and behaviours pertaining to drug use differ significantly from those of most people in the larger society. Over time, people in addictive subcultures tend to become closer to others within their subculture and more distant from people outside the subculture. Given this, participants in hard-core

subcultures quit them only when something brings about a dramatic change in their attitudes, beliefs, and values regarding drugs. Although it is widely believed that most addicts could change their behaviour if they chose to do so, *labelling theory* suggests that it is particularly difficult for individuals to discontinue once they have been labelled "alcoholics" or "drug addicts." Because of the prevailing ideology that alcoholism and drug addiction are personal problems rather than social problems, individuals tend to be held solely responsible for their behaviour.

The Functionalist Perspective

Why does the level of addiction remain high in Canada? Functionalists point out that there is virtually no society in which people do not use drugs of some kind (Schlaadt 1992) or do not gamble. Drugs contribute to many rituals, including weddings and other celebrations, and some drugs, such as alcohol, are often a part of daily mealtimes. Other functionalists would suggest that social institutions such as the family, education, and religion, which previously kept deviant behaviour such as addictions in check, have become fragmented and somewhat disorganized. Because they have, it is now necessary to use formal mechanisms of social control to prohibit people from taking illegal drugs or driving under the influence of alcohol or other drugs. External controls in the form of law enforcement are also required to discourage people from growing, manufacturing, or importing illegal substances. But these controls are not available for problem gambling. Because gambling is legal and provides employment and a substantial portion of government budgets—4.8 percent to the provinces in 2005 (Statistics Canada 2008h)—governments are doing little to prevent problem gambling.

Functionalists believe that activities in society continue because they serve important societal functions. Prescription and over-the-counter drugs, for example, are functional for patients because they ease pain, cure illness, and sometimes enhance or extend life. They are functional for doctors because they provide a means for treating illness and help to justify the doctor's fee. They are functional for pharmacists because they provide a source of employment; without pills to dispense, there would be no need for pharmacists. Gambling is also very profitable. The growth in the gambling industry in Canada has been noted. But dysfunctions also occur with addictions: patients may experience adverse side effects or develop a psychological dependence on the drug; doctors, pharmacists, and drug companies may be sued because they manufactured, prescribed, or sold a drug that is alleged to cause bodily harm to users. The dysfunctions of severe problem gamblers are losses of wealth and relationships.

Illicit drugs also have functions and dysfunctions. On the one hand, the illicit drug trade creates and perpetuates jobs at all levels of the criminal justice system, in the federal government, in social service agencies that deal with problems of alcoholism and drug addiction, and in criminology departments. What, for example, would employees in various police services do if Canada did not have an array of illicit drugs that are defined as the "drug problem"? On the other hand, the dysfunctions of illicit drug use extend throughout society. At the individual level, addictive drugs such as heroin, cocaine, and barbiturates create severe physical and mental health problems as well as economic crises for addicts, their families, and acquaintances. At the societal level, drug abuse contributes to loss of productivity, human potential and life expectancy, and money. Hundreds of millions of dollars in taxpayers' money that might be used for education or preventive health care are spent making and enforcing drug laws and dealing with drug-related crime and the spread of HIV/AIDS by addicts who shoot up with contaminated needles. Addiction to illegal drugs, the abuse of legal drugs, the abuse of alcohol and tobacco, and severe problem gambling exacerbate the loss of human potential and undermine the stability of society.

The Conflict Perspective

According to conflict theorists, people in positions of economic and political power make the sale, use, and possession of drugs abused by the poor and the powerless illegal. We mentioned earlier that opium smoking was outlawed because it was associated with the Chinese. Restricting the drugs that members of a subordinate racialized/ethnic group use is one method of suppressing the group and limiting its ability to threaten dominant group members or gain upward mobility in society. Those who control the nation's

political and legal apparatus decide whether a drug is legal or illegal.

Conflict theorists also point out that powerful corporate—and, in the case of gambling, corporate and government—interests perpetuate addictions. Corporations that manufacture, market, and sell alcohol, tobacco, and pharmaceuticals and the gaming industries reap huge profits from products that exact a heavy toll on the personal health and well-being of addicts, their families and communities, and the larger society. Using their wealth and political clout, elites in Canadian tobacco companies have spent years vigorously fighting measures to discourage smoking. Since sales of tobacco products are approximately $4 billion per year, tobacco companies are not likely to give up the fight.

The Feminist Perspective

Feminist theorists point out that a significant part of the explanation of drug abuse by women has to do with women's vulnerability and disadvantaged position in society. Chapter 4, "Gender Inequality," discussed many forms of inequality, such as vulnerability to sexual and spousal abuse, the wage gap and fewer promotional opportunities, and the second shift. To deal with the feelings these forms of inequality bring about, women sometimes turn to drug abuse. "Women use drugs to cope, to deal with stress, to nurture themselves, to escape from the pain of past events or of their current status, or to continue their social roles" (Harrison 1997:230).

A feminist approach to the problem emphasizes the different types of drug abuse by males and females. Data presented earlier in the chapter showed that males are much more likely to use alcohol and illicit drugs than females, and females are more likely to use licit, psychotherapeutic drugs than males. Several hypotheses have been suggested to account for gender differences in health behaviour. Two hypotheses that help to explain the differences in drug taking are the risk-taking behaviour of men and the willingness of women to adopt the "sick role" (see Chapter 10 for a discussion of the sick role). Men are socialized to take risks, and women are socialized to be more cautious and take care of their health (Waldron 1997). Thus, men would engage in risky behaviour such as drinking or illicit drug use to solve problems (see Table 10.2

on page 233: men show a higher rate of substance dependence than women), and women would seek out medical help and use prescription drugs for problems rather than engage in risky behaviour. On the other hand, the social acceptability hypothesis suggests that women are more willing than men to admit being sick, adopt a sick role, and accept medical help such as using drugs to deal with their problems (Gee and Kimball 1987).

Since a much smaller percentage of severe problem gamblers are women, it is less of an issue for feminists. The focus for feminists is the fact that many women and children suffer from the consequences of men's severe gambling problems.

THE FUTURE OF ADDICTIONS

How to prevent abuse of alcohol and other drugs and how to treat drug-related problems after they arise are controversial issues in contemporary society. What kinds of addiction prevention programs are available? Will future treatment programs for addicts differ from the ones that are available today? Regarding drugs, in Canada, the federal government has developed a comprehensive strategy—Canada's Drug Strategy. This is a national, concerted effort to address alcohol and other drugs in Canada. The long-term goal of Canada's Drug Strategy is to reduce the harm associated with the use of alcohol and other drugs to individuals, families, and communities. This is accomplished through pursuing the following five goals (Health Canada 2009a):

1. Reducing the demand for drugs
2. Reducing drug-related mortality and morbidity
3. Improving the effectiveness of and accessibility to substance abuse information and interventions
4. Restricting the supply of illicit drugs and reducing the profitability of illicit drug trafficking
5. Reducing the costs of substance abuse to Canadian society

Prevention Programs

Addiction prevention programs can be divided into three major categories: primary, secondary, and tertiary.

Primary prevention refers to programs that seek to prevent drug problems before they begin. Most primary prevention programs focus on people who have had little or no previous experience with drugs. In contrast, *secondary prevention* programs seek to limit the extent of drug abuse, prevent the spread of drug abuse to substances beyond those already experienced, and teach strategies for the responsible use of licit drugs such as alcohol (Levinthal 2007). For example, a program directed at college students who already consume alcohol might focus on how to drink responsibly by emphasizing the dangers of drinking and driving. Finally, *tertiary prevention* programs seek to limit relapses by individuals recovering from alcoholism or drug addiction. The purpose of tertiary prevention is to ensure that people who have entered treatment for some form of drug abuse become free of drugs and remain that way.

Prevention, according to Canada's Drug Strategy, is best done through a combination of public awareness campaigns, educational resources, training of service providers, and community action. The programs should be part of every year's school curriculum, should involve students in planning and conducting presentations, and should present honest factual material about why people use drugs and give alternatives to their use.

Scare tactics and negative-education programs do not work; they turn students off and do not achieve their desired goal. In fact, scare tactics appear to pique some students' curiosity about drugs rather than deter their use. Objective information programs often begin in kindergarten and progress through grade 12. Using texts, curriculum guides, videos, and other materials, teachers impart factual information about drugs to students, but as with scare tactics, students sometimes become more—instead of less—interested in drug experimentation. An 18-year-old student who smoked his first marijuana joint at age 13 explains why he thinks these programs are ineffective: "When someone tells you not to do it, that makes you want to do it even more" (Kolata 1996a:A12).

Future prevention programs will be family-, school-, and community-based. They will offer alternative activities and outlets to drug use. These programs—like other drug abuse prevention efforts—will take into account issues that affect people differently depending on their racialization/ethnicity, religion, or other factors. Reaching across lines of racialization, class, and gender, the next generation of drug abuse prevention programs will use cable television channels to make people aware of the effects of drugs on the human body and how to get help in dealing with alcoholism and drug addiction. The Internet will become a vital source of information. Current websites provide an array of information on drugs and offer unique features such as an online dictionary of street drug slang.

Treatment Programs

Tertiary prevention programs are programs that aim to ensure that people who have sought help for some form of drug abuse remain drug-free. It follows from the biological and social learning explanations for substance abuse and alcohol addiction that treatment must deal with the body's physiological and psychological responses. Therefore, *alcohol and drug treatment* involves the use of activities designed to eliminate physical and psychological addiction and to prevent relapse—returning to abuse and/or addiction. Most treatment programs are based on a medical model or therapeutic community.

The Medical Treatment Model

The *medical treatment model* considers drug abuse and alcoholism to be medical problems that must be resolved through medical treatment by medical officials. Treatment may take the form of *aversion therapy* or *behavioural conditioning*. For example, drugs such as Cyclazocine and Nalozone are given to heroin and opiate addicts to prevent the euphoric feeling that they associate with taking the drugs. Supposedly, when the pleasure is gone, the person will no longer abuse the drug. Some heroin addicts also receive methadone detoxification to alleviate withdrawal symptoms associated with stopping heroin use. Over a one- to three-week period, the patient receives decreasing doses of methadone, a synthetic opium derivative that blocks the desire for heroin but does not have its negative side effects.

Antabuse is used in the treatment of alcoholism. After the person has been detoxified and no alcohol remains in the bloodstream, Antabuse is administered along with small quantities of alcohol for several consecutive days. Because this combination produces negative effects such as nausea and vomiting, the individual eventually develops an aversion to drinking, which becomes associated with uncomfortable physical symptoms. Although the medical treatment model works for some people, it is criticized for focusing on the physiological effects of alcohol and drug dependency and not dealing with the psychological and sociological aspects of dependency.

Short- and Long-Term Services and the Therapeutic Community

According to a booklet entitled *Alcohol and Drug Treatment in Ontario: A Guide for Helping Professionals* published by the Centre for Addiction and Mental Health, many short- and long-term services (both live at-home and live-in) are available (at no charge, except for some specialized services) for people seeking help with addictions. (The authors acknowledge that some services may not be locally available.) Short-term services include withdrawal management (detox) services, which give people a place to stay while their bodies get rid of alcohol or drugs and adapt to a drug-free state, and services that provide a place to stay for a month and insight into leading a healthy life.

When substance abusers are perceived to have an underlying psychological problem, treatment generally involves long-term services like counselling, rehabilitation, and/or the therapeutic community. Counselling often employs rehabilitated alcoholics or addicts who encourage participants to take more responsibility for their lives so that they can function better in the community. Some counselling and rehabilitation programs take place on an outpatient basis or as day treatment; others involve residential treatment. *Outpatient programs* allow drug abusers to remain at home and continue working while attending regular group and individual meetings. *Day treatment* takes place in a hospital setting where the abuser participates in day-long treatment groups and individual counselling sessions and returns home in the evening. The *therapeutic community approach* is based on the idea that drug abuse is best treated by intensive individual and group counselling in a residential setting. Residential treatment takes place in a special house or dormitory where alcoholics or drug addicts remain for periods of time, ranging from several months to more than a year while they learn to rebuild their lives without alcohol or drugs.

Perhaps the best-known non-residential therapeutic communities are Alcoholics Anonymous (AA), founded in 1935, and its offshoots, Narcotics Anonymous (NA) and Gambling Anonymous (GA). AA, NA, and GA provide members with support in their efforts to overcome drug dependence and addiction. AA was established in 1935 in the United States by two alcoholics who were seeking a way of returning to sober life. Today, the organization has more than 4800 chapters with more than 95 000 members in Canada (Alcoholics Anonymous 1998). Members use only their first names to ensure anonymity, and recovering addicts serve as sponsors and counsellors for others. AA, NA, and GA are based on a 12-step program that requires members to acknowledge that they are addicts who must have the help of God and other people to remain sober or drug-free. Group support is central to success in these programs, as journalist Caroline Knapp (1996:253–254) explains:

A few months after my one-year anniversary [of sobriety] I went to the meeting . . . on the ground floor of a church. . . . One person tells his or her story for the first half-hour, and then the meeting opens up, first to those in their first month of sobriety, then to those with three months or less, then six months or less, and so on. . . . At the end of the meeting there was a presentation for a young guy named John, who was celebrating one year without a drink. . . . He was so happy that evening, so grateful to get that one-year medallion, and so moved by the amount of support he'd gotten over the year, that his eyes welled up and his voice kept cracking. "I can't thank you all enough," he said, and his face was the picture of hope. . . . Then I had an image of every person in that room . . . getting into our beds clean and sober, another day without a drink behind us. It was a simple image but it filled me with a range of complicated feelings: appreciation for the simple presence of all those people; admiration for their courage and strength; a tinge of melancholy for the amount of pain it must have taken each and every one of them to put down the drink; affection for their humanity. I didn't realize until hours later that there was a name for that feeling. It's called love.

Sociologists believe Anonymous programs are successful because they give former addicts the opportunity to be delabelled as stigmatized deviants and relabelled as former and repentant deviants. It should be kept in mind, however, that social class and personality factors affect people's ability to enter into the repentant role, which requires the participant to publicly admit guilt and repentance and to interact successfully with others in the program (Trice and Roman 1970).

WHAT CAN YOU DO?

- Volunteer at an agency such as Mothers Against Drunk Driving (MADD) or, if a local chapter exists, Students Against Drunk Driving (SADD). If a local chapter does not exist, contact MADD at **http://www.madd.ca** about founding a chapter.

- Participate in or organize a committee for challenging the various kinds of drug companies and their influence on universities. Since the influence of pharmaceutical companies on research practices is likely to be a continuing problem, much scope exists for future educational programs.

- Develop an educational program to help students stop binge drinking. Generally, the peer-initiated programs have better results. Several years ago, students at colleges in Ontario undertook a promotional campaign based on the slogan, "If you drink, don't bowl," based on the double meaning of *bowl* as a game and a place to vomit (toilet bowl). Try to devise a new catchy and effective slogan for your program. You might include some first-aid suggestions for dealing with consequences of binge drinking.

- Study the way students use prescription medicines, not only antidepressants, but also diet pills and stimulants, and study the relationship between alcohol consumption and acquaintance or date rape.

- Design a program to alert students, particularly women, to the problems of excessive body-consciousness (see also Chapter 10) as well as the need to use drugs with particular care when on dates.

SUMMARY

What Are the Major Patterns of Drinking?

Social scientists divide long-term drinking patterns into four categories: (1) *social drinkers* consume alcoholic beverages primarily on social occasions and may drink either occasionally or relatively frequently; (2) *heavy drinkers* are more frequent drinkers who typically consume greater quantities of alcohol when they drink and are more likely to become intoxicated; (3) *acute alcoholics* have trouble controlling their use of alcohol and plan their schedule around drinking; and (4) *chronic alcoholics* have lost control over their drinking and tend to engage in compulsive behaviour.

What Are the Major Hazards Associated with Tobacco Use?

Nicotine is a toxic, dependency-producing drug that is responsible for about 37 000 deaths per year in Canada. People who smoke have a greater likelihood of developing cardiovascular disease, lung cancer, and/or cancer of the larynx, mouth, and esophagus. Even those who do not smoke may be subjected to the hazard of environmental tobacco smoke—the smoke in the air as a result of other people's tobacco smoking. Infants born to women who smoke typically have lower-than-average birth weights and sometimes have slower rates of physical and mental growth.

What Problems Are Associated with Use of Prescription and Over-the-Counter Drugs?

Some prescription drugs have the potential for short-term abuse and long-term psychological and physical dependence. This form of dependency is known as *iatrogenic addiction*—drug dependency that results from physician-supervised treatment for a recognized medical disorder. Over-the-counter drugs, which are widely advertised and readily available, may be dangerous when combined with alcohol or other drugs.

In Canada, What Are the Major Stimulant Drugs?

Cocaine and amphetamines are the major stimulant drugs abused in Canada. Cocaine is an extremely potent and dependency-producing stimulant drug. Amphetamines can be obtained legally in the form of diet pills and pep formulas when they are prescribed by a physician.

What Are Depressants and What Health-Related Risk Do They Pose?

As the name indicates, depressants depress the central nervous system; they also may have some pain-killing properties. The most common depressants are barbiturates and anti-anxiety drugs or tranquilizers. Users may develop both physical addiction and psychological dependency on these drugs. There is also the risk of *potentiation*—the drug interaction that takes place when two drugs are mixed together and the combination produces a far greater effect than that of either drug administered separately.

What Is Severe Problem Gambling, and What Difficulties Do Such Gamblers Experience?

Severe problem gambling is associated with heavy gambling and related gambling problems such as increased wagers, returning to win back losses, and borrowing money or selling something to gamble. It may or may not yet be accompanied by adverse consequences from gambling, including feeling guilty about gambling, having financial problems, and experiencing health problems such as stress and thoughts of suicide.

How Do Sociological Perspectives View Alcohol, Drug, and Gambling Addiction?

Interactionists believe that these are learned behaviours that are strongly influenced by families, peers, and others who serve as role models. People are more prone to accept attitudes and behaviours that are favourable to drug use or gambling if they spend time with members of a subculture. Functionalists believe that drug and gambling-related problems have increased as social institutions such as the family, schools, and religious institutions have become fragmented and somewhat disorganized. However, use of alcohol and other drugs serves an important function, even though some aspects of drug use are dysfunctional for society. All of these addictions provide jobs for people, and most provide income for governments. According to conflict theorists, people in positions of economic and political power are responsible for making the sale, use, and possession of some drugs illegal. Conflict theorists also point out that powerful corporate interests perpetuate the use and abuse of alcohol, tobacco, other legal drugs, and gambling. Feminist theorists emphasize the vulnerability and disadvantaged position of women who abuse drugs.

What Is the Purpose of Prevention and Treatment Programs?

Primary prevention programs seek to prevent problems before they begin. Secondary prevention programs seek to limit the extent of abuse, prevent the spread of abuse to other substances beyond the problems already experienced, and teach strategies for responsible use. Tertiary prevention programs seek to limit relapses by individuals recovering from addiction. They may be based either on a medical model or the therapeutic community. The best-known therapeutic community is Alcoholics Anonymous (AA) and other Anonymous programs.

What Other Factors Must be Taken into Account in Efforts to Reduce Drug and Gambling Problems?

Addictions are intertwined with other social problems, such as dramatic changes in the economic and technological bases of society, the growing gap between the rich and poor, and inequalities based on racialization/ethnicity and gender.

KEY TERMS

codependency,   p. 180
drug,   p. 175
drug addiction (drug dependency),
   p. 176
drug subculture,   p. 193

environmental tobacco
   smoke,   p. 181
fetal alcohol spectrum disorder
   (FASD)   p. 179
primary prevention   p. 195

tolerance,   p. 176
withdrawal,   p. 176

QUESTIONS FOR CRITICAL THINKING

1.   Does public tolerance of alcohol and tobacco lead to increased use of these drugs? Why do many people view the use of alcohol and tobacco differently from the use of illicit drugs?

2.   If stimulants, depressants, hallucinogens, and inhalants have such potentially hazardous side effects, why do so many people use these drugs? If drug enforcement policies were more stringently enforced, would there be less drug abuse in this country?

3.   As a sociologist, how would you propose to deal with the problem of addictions in Canada? If you were called upon to revamp existing drug laws and policies, what, if any, changes would you make in them?

4.   How have changes in technology affected the problem of alcohol, drug, and gambling addictions over the past century? How have changes in the global economy affected drug-related problems in this country and others? (See Box 9.1 on page 210 about international organized crime.)

PEARSON
mysockit™

Explore the topics covered in this chapter at **www.mysockit.com** using the access provided with this text. Interactive resources for studying include video clips, practice tests, learning objectives, and Internet resources.

9

CRIME AND CRIMINAL JUSTICE

The video surveillance of public streets that the RCMP is carrying out in Kelowna is not necessary. There is no evidence that it is effective or is likely to be effective.

Privacy Commissioner George Radwanski, who launched a lawsuit in the Supreme Court of British Columbia, believed the cameras violated the Charter's *guarantee of the right to privacy (quoted in Lunman 2002:A1)*

The RCMP continually seeks to find appropriate means to ensure and increase public safety and security, be that through police or community-based initiatives.

RCMP Sergeant Paul Marsh, in reply to Privacy Commissioner George Radwanski (quoted in Lunman 2002:A8)

After the discovery of the images of four alleged suicide bombers before and on the day of bombings in London, July 7, 2005, the city's police chief Sir Ian Blair said that the results of Britain's 4 million closed-circuit TVs speak for themselves (Byrne 2005:A9).

The placing of cameras in what criminologists call "hot spots" (Sherman et al. 1989) is a way of deterring **routine activities crime**, crime that occurs when a motivated offender finds a suitable target in the absence of suitable guardianship. Some researchers suggest that crime that would be deterred by the cameras would, like street prostitution, just move to another location. In early August 2005, Canadians were asked in a Globe CTV poll conducted by the Strategic Counsel if they would support having video cameras in public places: 72 percent supported or strongly supported it, and 25 percent opposed or strongly opposed it ("Do Canadians Feel Secure?" 2004). What do you think? Would you feel safer with surveillance cameras in public places?

In this chapter you will learn about the problem of defining crime and measuring crime with official statistics or victimization surveys; the level of various kinds of crime (e.g., violent, property, and youth crime); and how the levels of some of these crimes in Canada compare to those in the United States. You will also learn about the nature of occupational and organized crime; why people commit crimes (the biological, psychological, and sociological explanations of crime); and the nature of the criminal justice system. The chapter concludes with some suggestions for ways you might help deal with the problem of crime.

CRIME AS A SOCIAL PROBLEM

Many people in Canada fear crime and are somewhat obsessed with it even though they have no direct daily exposure to criminal behaviour. Their information about crime comes from the media (Chermak 1995) and sometimes from watching real-crime dramas such as *America's Most Wanted* (sightings by Canadians have led to the arrest of a few of the suspects). They are also influenced by fictionalized crime stories on television, such as *The Border*. Media coverage of crime is extensive, but it is not because crime is increasing.

Crime rates have fallen now for almost two decades. Figure 9.1 shows an almost steady decline since 1991. That is not to say that crime isn't a problem. Crime statistics tell only part of the story. Crime *is* a significant social problem because it endangers people's lives, property, and sense of well-being. In 2007, over 2.3 million crimes (down from 2.6 million reported in the last edition of this textbook) were reported to police, a rate of 6984 per 100 000 population (Statistics Canada 2008e). Given that many victims do not report all crimes to the police (Statistics Canada 2005d), a substantial portion of Canadians have been victimized. Since much is spent on the police, courts, and prison system, even individuals who are not directly victimized by crime are affected because they have to pay taxes to fight it, high insurance rates for theft, high interest rates for credit card fraud, and so on.

Problems with Official Statistics

Over the past two decades, sophisticated computer-based information systems have not only improved rates of detection, apprehension, and conviction of offenders but also have provided immediate access to millions of bits of information about crime, suspects, and offenders. The leading source of information on crimes reported in Canada is the *Uniform Crime Report* (UCR). The UCR was developed by Statistics Canada with the co-operation and assistance of the Canadian Association of Chiefs of Police. The survey became operational in 1962 and collects crime and traffic statistics reported by all police agencies in Canada. UCR data are based on reported crime substantiated by police investigation (Logan

2001:13) and are made available by the Canadian Centre for Justice Statistics (CCJS) in its now online periodical, *Juristat*, for use in presentations such as this chapter. Since 1988, the UCR has been using an incident-based reporting system (collecting data on each criminal event, offender, and victim) instead of an aggregate system. It is thus providing a more complex portrait of crime in Canada. The crime rate reported here includes offences such as homicide, assault, sexual assault, break and enter, robbery, theft, motor vehicle theft, and fraud. It does not include other violations, such as traffic and drug offences.

How accurate are these crime statistics? Any answer to this question must take into account the fact that the statistics reflect only crimes that are reported to law enforcement agencies or that police officers see occur.

The downward trend in crime probably reflects several factors, including increasing job opportunities (at least until the recent recession) and an age shift in population (see Chapter 5). The percentage of the Canadian population under age 26—the age group most likely to commit crimes—began to decline in 1992.

FIGURE 9.1   Crime Rate, 1962 to 2007

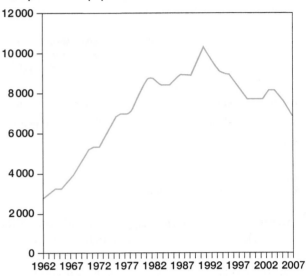

Source: Statistics Canada, 2008, "Crime Statistics 2007," The Daily *(July 17).* Retrieved October 29, 2008 (http://www.statcan.ca/Daily/English/080717/ d080717b.htm).

TABLE 9.1   Self-Reported Victimization Incidents Reported to the Police, 2004[1,2]

	Total No. of Incidents	Incidents Reported to the Police[3]		Incidents Not Reported to the Police		Don't Know/Not Stated	
	x 1000	x 1000	percent	x 1000	percent	x 1000	percent
Total	7723	2613	34	4962	64	148	2
Total violent	2109	687	33	1381	66	41[E]	1[E]
Sexual assault	512	42[E]	8[E]	448	88	F	F
Robbery	274	127	46	144	53	F	F
Physical assault	1323	519	39	789	60	16[E]	1[E]
Total household	3206	1188	37	1958	61	59	2
Break and enter	505	275	54	223	44	7	1
Motor vehicle/parts theft	571	281	49	285	50	5	1
Theft household property	1136	330	29	786	69	20	2
Vandalism	993	303	31	664	67	26	3
Theft personal property	2408	738	31	1623	67	47[E]	2[E]

[E]Use with caution.

[F] Too unreliable to be published.

[1] Figures may not add to total due to rounding.

[2] Spousal violence incidents are excluded.

[3] Includes incidents reported by the victim or by someone else.

Source: Statistics Canada, 2005, "General Social Survey: Criminal victimization," The Daily *(November 24). Retrieved March 30, 2009* (http://www.statcan.gc.ca/daily-quotidien/051124/dq051124b-eng.htm).

Because the number of crimes *reported* is not necessarily the number of crimes *committed*, Statistics Canada conducts victimization surveys, the most recent example being the General Social Survey (GSS) of 2004, which surveyed 24 000 randomly selected households to identify victims of personal crimes (e.g., theft of personal property, break and enter, assault, sexual assault, robbery, motor vehicle theft, and hate), and to determine whether the crime was reported or not (Statistics Canada 2005f). These surveys indicate that the number of crimes committed is substantially higher than the number reported. Table 9.1 shows that the percentage of crimes reported to police ranged from less than 10 percent for sexual assault to over 50 percent for break and enter. The main reason given for not reporting crimes to police was that the incident was not considered significant enough. Victims of sexual assault reported seeking help from social services and support centres.

However, the GSS has limitations, too:

1. Responses are based on recall, and some people don't remember specifically when a crime occurred. (They are supposed to report on the previous 12 months.)

2. For various reasons, respondents may not be truthful.

3. The surveys focus on theft and assault and do not measure workplace crimes, such as embezzlement or bribery, and organized crime.

Defining Crime and Delinquency

Crime is behaviour that violates the criminal law and is punishable by fine, jail term, or other negative sanctions. There are two components to every crime: the act itself, and *criminal intent*—expressed in the concept of *mens rea,* meaning "guilty mind." An individual's intent in committing a crime may range from willful conduct (hiring someone to kill one's spouse) to an unintentional act of negligence that is defined as a crime (leaving a small child unattended in a locked automobile in extremely hot weather, resulting in the child's death).

Criminal law is divided into two major categories: summary and indictable offences. **Summary conviction offences** are relatively minor crimes that are punishable

by a fine or less than a year in jail. Examples include public unlawful assembly, theft ($5000 and under), and traffic violations. **Indictable offences** are more serious crimes, such as murder or aggravated assault, that are punishable by more than a year's imprisonment. Adolescents (12 to 17 years of age) who commit illegal or antisocial acts usually are adjudicated as *delinquent* or *youth crime* by a youth court judge.

TYPES OF CRIMES

To make the study of crime—a large and complex subject—manageable, sociologists and criminologists categorize types of crime. In this section, we will look at seven categories of crime: violent crime, hate crime, property crime, occupational crime, corporate crime, organized crime, and youth crime. Table 9.2 shows the rate of particular crimes in 2007 and the percentage change since 1998.

Violent Crime

While it is well known to occur frequently in the United States, violent crime occurs much less frequently in Canada. **Violent crime** consists of actions involving force or the threat of force against others and includes homicide, attempted homicide, the three levels of assault and sexual assault, robbery, and other violent offences like criminal negligence causing death. Violent crimes are committed against people; non-violent crimes are usually committed against property. People tend to fear violent crime more than other kinds of crime because victims are often physically injured or even killed and because violent crime receives the most sustained attention from law enforcement officials and media (see Parker 1995).

Homicide

The UCR defines **homicide** as the unlawful, intentional killing of one person by another. (Killing by accident, in self-defence, or during wartime is not homicide.) By this definition, murder involves not only an unlawful act but also *malice aforethought*—the *intention* of doing a wrongful act. A person who buys a gun, makes a plan to kill someone, and carries out the plan has probably committed homicide. In contrast,

TABLE 9.2   Crime Rates for Selected Offences

| Type of offence | 2007 | | 2006 to 2007 | 1998 to 2007 |
	number	rate	% rate change	
Total *Criminal Code* (excluding traffic), crime rate	**2,302,900**	**6,984**	**-7.4**	**-14.4**
Violent crime	**306,559**	**930**	**-2.5**	**-5.3**
Homicide	594	2	-3.0	-2.6
Attempted murder	802	2	-5.1	-1.6
Robbery	29,600	90	-4.7	-6.5
Sexual assault (levels 1,2,3)	21,449	65	-4.5	-23.2
Other sexual offences	2,784	8	-0.1	-26.1
Assault level 1	179,586	545	-3.3	-10.7
Assault level 2, weapon/causing bodily harm	53,945	164	0.1	32.3
Assault level 3, aggravated	3,403	10	0.5	18.6
Other assaults	13,917	42	5.4	4.8
Abduction	479	1	-8.3	-47.2
Property crime	**1,094,703**	**3,320**	**-7.7**	**-27.3**
Breaking and entering	230,920	700	-9.0	-39.8
Motor vehicle theft	146,142	443	-8.8	-19.4
Theft over $5,000	17,369	53	0.6	-32.7
Theft $5,000 and under	579,211	1,756	-7.2	-25.8
Possession of stolen goods	32,775	99	-9.8	2.8
Fraud	88,286	268	-6.2	-14.8
Other *Criminal Code* incidents	**901,638**	**2,734**	**-8.6**	**4.8**
Mischief	375,816	1,140	-1.8	5.1
Counterfeiting currency	55,517	168	-54.0	27.5
Bail violations	110,115	334	0.2	37.9
Disturbing the peace	116,978	355	-1.1	63.3
Offensive weapons	18,709	57	-4.2	2.0
Prostitution	4,724	14	-17.6	-27.6
Arson	13,202	40	-3.8	-6.7
Forcible confinement/kidnapping	4,595	14	0.9	121.5
Other *Criminal Code* (not listed above)	201,982	613	-4.6	-24.4

Note: Rates are calculated per 100,000 population.

Source: Statistics Canada, 2008, "Crime Statistics 2007," The Daily (July 17). Retrieved October 29, 2008 (http://www.statcan.ca/daily/english/080717/d080717.htm)

manslaughter is the unlawful, *unintentional* killing of one person by another. An intoxicated person who shoots a gun into the air probably holds no malice toward the bystander who is killed by a stray bullet. Sometimes a person's intentions are clear, but many times they are not, and the lines between intentional, unintentional, and accidental homicides are blurred. As Table 9.2 shows, the homicide rate in 2007—two victims per 100 000 population—shows a slight decline over the previous 10 years.

Mass murder is the killing of four or more people at one time and in one place by the same person. Fortunately, the examples of mass murder in Canada are few. Marc Lepine's killing of 14 women in 1989 in the École Polytechnique in Montreal is an example of

mass murder. A more recent example is the killing of four Mounties by James Roszko in 2005.

According to criminologists, mass murderers tend to kill in the areas where they live. They are likely to be male, problem drinkers, and collectors of firearms and other weapons, which they often hide (Dietz 1986). Some mass murderers have been disgruntled employees or former employees who seek out supervisors and co-workers in the workplace. An example of this kind of mass murder was the 1992 killing of four faculty members by Valery Fabrikant, a professor of engineering, at Concordia University in Montreal. In the United States, a number of these violent eruptions have occurred in post offices, hence the term "going postal."

Serial murder is the killing of three or more people over more than a month by the same person. Serial murders account for few homicides, but receive extensive media coverage. In Canada, Clifford Olson, who killed 11 boys and girls and was sentenced to life imprisonment in 1982, and Michael Wayne McGray, who pleaded guilty to six murders in 1998, are examples of serial killers. The finding of many bodies at the pig farm owned by Robert Pickton in Port Coquitlam, a suburb of Vancouver, is another example of serial murder. In 2007 he was convicted of killing six people, and it was decided not to pursue convictions for the other crimes.

It is difficult to characterize serial killers, outside of the fact that the best-known ones are White males. Some travel extensively to locate their victims; others kill near where they live. One study identified four basic types of serial killers: (1) *visionaries,* who kill because they hear a voice or have a vision that commands them to commit the murderous acts; (2) *missionaries,*who take it on themselves to rid the community or the world of what they believe is an undesirable type of person; (3) *hedonists,* who obtain personal or sexual gratification from violence; and (4) *power/control seekers,* who achieve gratification from the complete possession of the victim (Holmes 1988).

Characteristics of Victims and Accused

Statistics on homicide are among the most accurate official crime statistics available. Homicides rarely go unreported, and suspects are usually apprehended and charged. Although annual rates vary slightly, murder follows certain patterns in terms of gender, age, racialization, and region of the country, as analyses from earlier years show. Men make up the vast majority of murder victims and offenders. In 2007, three-quarters of the victims were male and 90 percent of the accused were male. The median age of accused males was 24, and the median age of male victims was 29 and female victims 35.5 (Statistics Canada 2008a). In Canada, unlike the United States, homicide is not an urban phenomenon, and it is more likely to occur in western than eastern provinces (Statistics Canada 2008e).

In 2007, in 80 percent of solved homicides the victim knew the killer (Statistics Canada 2008e). Among spousal victims, the declining homicide rate was seven times greater for females than for males (38 versus 5 percent) (Statistics Canada 2008e).

Across the nation, in 2007, 126 homicides were committed with handguns, a doubling of the rate in the past 20 years (Statistics Canada 2008e). This is a fact that leads to ongoing political debate over gun control, especially of handguns.

Sexual Assault

Many people think of **sexual assault** (the term "rape" is no longer used in criminal law) as a sexually motivated crime, but it is actually an act of violence in which sex is used as a weapon against a powerless victim (Vito and Holmes 1994). Both men and women can be victimized by sexual assault. In Canada, it is classified into three levels:

- Level 1 includes touching, grabbing, kissing—the category of least physical harm to the victim.
- Level 2 includes assault with a weapon, threats to use a weapon, or causing bodily harm.
- Level 3, or aggravated assault, includes wounding, maiming, or endangering the life of the victim.

Date rape is forcible sexual activity that meets the legal definition of sexual assault and involves people who first meet in a social setting (Sanday 1996). This definition is preferred by some scholars because it encompasses dates and casual acquaintances but excludes spouses (marital rape) and relatives (incest). The phrase was coined to distinguish forced, non-consensual sex between people who know one another from forced, non-consensual sex between strangers—but both are against the law. Date rape is often associated with alcohol or other drug consumption (see "roofies" on page 188 in Chapter 8), especially among college students. We probably know much less about the actual number of date rapes than we do about the number of stranger assaults, because victims are less likely to report sexual attacks by people they know.

On university or college campuses, date or acquaintance rape sometimes takes the form of gang or party rape. Unlike individual acquaintance rape, gang rape is used as a reinforcing mechanism for membership in a group of men (Warshaw 1994). In fact, men who rape in groups might never commit individual rape. As they participate in gang rape, they experience a special bonding with each other and use rape to prove their sexual ability to other group members and thereby enhance their status among members.

Characteristics of Victims and Accused

Statistics on sexual assault are misleading at best because it is often not reported. According to the 1993 Violence Against Women Survey, which interviewed 12 300 women about their experiences of sexual and physical assault, 39 percent reported at least one incident of sexual assault since the age of 16 (CCJS 1999:278). According to UCR data for 2007 (see Table 9.2), sexual assaults constituted less than 7 percent of violent crime and have declined by about a quarter since 1998. Some women may not report that they have been assaulted because they believe that nothing will be done about it or that the attacker may try to get even.

Like homicide, sexual assault follows certain patterns in terms of gender, age, racialization, and education. With the proviso that inmates of correctional institutions may not fully represent the population that commits these crimes, we can gain much information from the last major inmate survey by consultant David Robinson and his colleagues (1999:275). According to the census of inmates conducted on October 5, 1996, incarcerated sexual offenders were male (99 percent), older than other violent offenders (35 versus 31 years of age), slightly more likely to be of Indigenous status than other violent offenders (23 versus 19 percent), and less educated (having grade 9 or less) than the rest of the population (41 versus 19 percent).

In most sexual assaults, according to the Violence Against Women Survey of 1993, the victim is young (18 percent for women aged 18 to 24 versus 1 percent for women aged 45 and over). Single and separated/divorced women were six times more likely to report sexual assault than women married or living common-law (CCJS 1999:278).

Gang Violence

Gang violence includes homicide, sexual assault, robbery, and aggravated assault. But actually defining a "gang" is difficult. Police define gangs so broadly—"two or more persons engaged in antisocial behaviour who form an allegiance for a common criminal purpose and who individually or collectively are creating an atmosphere of fear and intimidation within a community" (quoted in Abbate 1998:A10)—that to identify violence as gang violence using this definition is too inclusive. Criminologist Robert M. Gordon (2000:48) has identified six types of gangs in Vancouver:

1. *youth movements*, like skinheads and punks who perpetrate hate crimes;

2. *youth groups*, youth who hang out together in public places, like malls;

3. *criminal groups*, small groups who band together for a short time for illegal financial gain;

4. *"wanna-be" groups*, loosely structured groups, frequently substitute families, that indulge in impulsive criminal behaviour;

5. *street gangs*, young adults who plan criminal behaviour; and

6. *criminal business organizations*, older, well-established groups, sometimes with ethnic membership, like the Lotus, Flying Dragons, Hells Angels, and Bandidos.

Typically, gangs are composed primarily of young males of the same ethnicity. Some gangs are basically peer groups that hang out together, seeking a sense of belonging, like a family, but others are well organized and violent. In recent years, gang activity and gang-related violence have increased significantly not only in large metropolitan areas but also in smaller cities and suburbs. In Canada, gang-related killings tripled between 1995 and 2000, rising from 21 in 1995 to 71 in 2000 (Fedorowycz 2001:6). In 2007, this number grew considerably. There were 117 homicides reported as gang-related by police, 16 more than in 2006. This accounted for about one in every five homicides reported (Statistics Canada 2008e).

Some analysts have suggested that gang violence may be exacerbated by socialization of males for male dominance and by patriarchal social structures. Sociologist Martín Sánchez Jankowski (1991) suggests that violence attributed to gangs is often committed by gang members acting as *individuals* rather than as agents of the organization. According to Jankowski, most gang members do not like violence and fear that they may be injured or killed in violent encounters. As a result, gang members engage in collective violence only to accomplish specific objectives, such as asserting authority or punishing violations by their own members who are incompetent or who break the gang's code. Violence against other gangs occurs primarily when a gang feels threatened or needs to maintain or expand its operations in a certain area. In general, according to Jankowski, collective violence is used to achieve the goals of gang membership (proving masculinity and toughness, providing excitement, and maintaining reputation), mainly when gang members are provoked by others or are fearful.

Sociologists Jack Levin and Jack McDevitt (1993) suggest that some gangs look for opportunities to violently attack "outgroup" members because they are seeking a thrill and view their victims as vulnerable. When violent attacks are made because of a person's racialization, religion, skin colour, disability, sexual orientation, national origin, or ancestry, they are considered to be hate crimes (see Chapter 1) and are likely performed by the "youth movements" in Robert Gordon's typology.

Intervention by law enforcement officials and the criminal justice system has had only limited success In spring 2002, "Mom" Boucher, the closest thing to a godfather in the Hells Angels in Quebec, was convicted on several counts of homicide; and police arrested 36 members of the Bandidos, the second largest biker gang.

Hate Crime

Hate crimes are crimes that are motivated by the offender's hatred of certain characteristics of the victim, e.g., national or ethnic origin, language, colour, religion, gender, age, mental or physical disability, or other similar factors. In the GSS victimization survey, people were asked if the crime they reported could be a hate crime. Four percent of 273 000 incidents were reported as hate crimes, and the most frequently cited characteristics were the victim's ethnicity, cited by 43 percent of the victims; the culture, by 18 percent; and the gender, by 18 percent (Besserer and Trainor 2000:180). In 2007, 785 crimes were classified as hate crimes, down from 892 in 2006, and of these, 62 percent were motivated by race/ethnicity; 24 percent were motivated by religion; and 10 percent were motivated by sexual orientation. Table 6.3 on page 139 shows a breakdown of the types of hate crime and their subcategories. Hate crimes can have more severe psychological consequences and require longer recovery times than other crimes. Younger people aged 12 to 17 were more likely to be accused of hate crimes than older people (Statistics Canada 2009i).

Property Crime

Property crime is the taking of money or property from another without force, the threat of force, or the destruction of property. Breaking and entering, possession of stolen goods, theft, motor vehicle theft, and fraud are examples of property crimes. Table 9.2 shows that over 1 million property crimes were reported in 2007. Overall, property crime has fallen by a quarter since 1998. According to victimization surveys, the most frequent property crime is *breaking and entering*— the unlawful or forcible entry or attempted entry of a residence or business with the intent to commit a serious crime. Breaking and entering usually involves theft—the burglar illegally enters by, for example, breaking a window or slashing a screen (forcible entry) or through an open window or unlocked door (unlawful entry). Although breaking and entering is normally a crime against property, it is more serious than most non-violent crimes because it carries the possibility of violent confrontation and the psychological sense of intrusion that is associated with violent crime. To fully grasp the possibility of violent confrontation, consider the following explanations by two burglars of the pressures—both internal and external—that motivate them to commit breaking and entering:

> Usually what I'll do is a [break and enter], maybe two or three if I have to, and then this will help me get over the rough spot. . . . Once I get it straightened out, I just go with the flow . . . the only time I would go and commit a burglary is if I needed the money at that point in time. That would be strictly to pay the light bill, gas bill, rent. (Dan Whiting, quoted in Wright and Decker 1994:37)

> You ever had an urge before? Maybe a cigarette urge or a food urge, where you eat that and you got to have more and more? That's how that crack is. You smoke it and it hits you [in the back of the throat] and you got to have more. I'll smoke that sixteenth up and get through, it's like I never had none. I got to have more. Therefore, I gots to go do another burglary and gets some more money. (Richard Jackson, quoted in Wright and Decker 1994:39)

According to victimization surveys, the young have a higher risk of being subject to property crime than older people. Risk of victimization is also much higher for families with incomes under $15 000 living in rental property or in inner-city areas. In contrast, people who live in well-maintained residences with security systems on well-lit streets or cul-de-sacs are less likely to be victimized (Logan 2001:1). The UCR likely does not accurately represent the number of burglaries committed because people tend to report them only when very valuable, insured goods are taken.

The most frequently reported crime is called *theft $5000 and under*—unlawfully taking or attempting to take property from another person. This kind of theft includes purse snatching and pickpocketing. Table 9.2 illustrates that in 2007, over 50 percent of the reported property crimes were theft $5000 and under.

Statistics on auto theft are more accurate than those for many other crimes because insurance companies require claimants to report the theft to police. Analysts have identified four basic motives for auto theft:

1. Joyriding—the vehicle is stolen for the fun of riding around in it and perhaps showing off to friends.

2. Transportation—the vehicle is stolen for personal use.

3. Crime—the vehicle is used as an aid in the commission of another crime.

4. Profit—the vehicle is sold or taken to a "chop shop," where it is dismantled for parts, which are then sold separately. (Barlow 1996)

Shoplifting accounts for billions of dollars in losses to retail businesses each year. For some stores, the annual loss can be as high as 2 to 5 percent of the total value of inventory (Vito and Holmes 1994). Early criminologists thought that shoplifters fell into three categories: the *snitch*—someone with no criminal record who systematically pilfers goods for personal use or to sell; the *booster* or *heel*—the professional criminal who steals goods to sell to *fences* (people who receive and dispose of stolen property) or pawnshops; and the *kleptomaniac*—someone who steals for reasons other than monetary gain (e.g., for sexual arousal; Holmes 1983). Most experts think that shoplifting is committed primarily by amateurs across lines of racialization, class, gender, and age (Barlow 1996).

Credit card fraud—using a credit card or account number to obtain property, services, or money under false pretences—has increased sharply with the increase in the availability of cards and the decrease in the use of cheques. Despite the security measures taken by banks and other credit card issuers, credit card fraud is perpetrated in many ways. A lost or stolen wallet or purse can provide a potential offender with all the identification necessary to open up charge accounts in the victim's name and run up large bills before the individual becomes aware of what has happened. Sometimes credit cards are obtained by pickpockets, purse-snatchers, robbers, and burglars, and sometimes by prostitutes who go through their customers' pockets. There are companies using the Internet to sell personal information—such as a person's Social Insurance Number and mother's maiden name—that can be used to apply for and activate some credit cards (Hansell 1996). Credit card information can also be stolen by people who have legitimate access to personal data (e.g., airline or hotel reservationists or department or grocery store personnel) or by computer hackers. Table 9.2 shows that fraud has declined by almost 15 percent since 1998.

One crime that has more than doubled in the past 10 years is kidnapping/forcible confinement. Although the number of victims is very small, the crime deserves scrutiny since it might be related to human trafficking.

Crime Comparisons between Canada and the United States

Canadians absorb much of their crime information from the U.S. media. It is therefore worthwhile to show the differences in Canadian and U.S. crime rates so that we do not automatically assume that their crime problem is our crime problem. Over the past 20 years, Canada has had a much lower violent crime rate than the United States. In 2007, the U.S. homicide rate was three times our rate (almost 6 versus less than 2 per 100 000; Statistics Canada 2008e).

Sociologist Marc Ouimet (1999:403) analyzed these differences and found that they were not uniform throughout the country. For example, homicide rate differences were nine times greater in the United States than Canada for cities with populations of 1 million or more. Ouimet (1999:402) suggested that these differences occur because U.S. cities are much more dangerous than Canadian cities. Unlike U.S. cities, Canadian cities do not contain ghettos, where people are very poor, are disproportionately members of visible minorities, suffer many social problems, and have guns. Whereas two-thirds of U.S. homicides involve firearms, one-quarter of Canadian homicides do (Statistics Canada 2001a). Ouimet refers to Jan van Dijk and his colleagues' international study (1990), which showed that whereas less than 5 percent of Canadian households have a gun, 29 percent of American households own a firearm. Ouimet (1999:401) went on to suggest that this lack of guns might also help explain Canada's higher property crime rate. Canadian burglars might be encouraged to commit more break and enters than their American counterparts since they have less chance of facing an armed householder.

Occupational (White-Collar) Crime

Occupational (white-collar) crime refers to illegal activities committed by people in the course of their employment or normal business activity. When sociologist Edwin H. Sutherland (1949) first introduced the term *white-collar crime,* he was referring to such acts as employee theft, fraud (obtaining money or property under false pretences), embezzlement (theft from an employer), and soliciting bribes or kickbacks. With the advent of personal computers, some white-collar crimes have become easier to commit, and some criminals have developed new types of crime based on computer technology. One type of white-collar crime that has been in the news lately is *insider trading* of securities: an offender buys or sells stocks on the basis of information that isn't publicly known and that he or she obtained only as a corporate insider. A recent high-profile example of this was the case of former Canadian (now British lord) Conrad Black, who was convicted in 2007 in Illinois of diverting for personal use money from Hollinger International when he was CEO. He was sentenced to six-and-a-half years in prison, fined, and forced to return money to his former company, Hollinger. For individual investors without insider knowledge, the losses from the decline in the value of Hollinger stock might have been in the thousands of dollars. For institutional investors, such as in pension funds, losses would have been much higher.

Corporate Crime

Some white-collar offenders engage in **corporate crime**—illegal acts committed by corporate employees on behalf of the corporation and with its support. Examples include acts injurious to the public or employees; pollution; manufacturing of defective products; antitrust violations (seeking an illegal advantage over competitors); deceptive advertising; infringements on patents, copyrights, and trademarks; unlawful labour practices involving the exploitation or surveillance of employees; price fixing; and financial fraud. These crimes arise from deliberate decisions by corporate personnel to profit at the expense of competitors, consumers, employees, and the general public. A striking Canadian example of economic effects of corporate crime was the case of the gold-mining company Bre-X Minerals Ltd. A company geologist, Michael de Guzman, added gold to survey samples, making the results look like those of a great gold mine. When the deception was discovered in 1997, the company and its stock became worthless, wiping out millions of dollars from various portfolios, including pension funds, and de Guzman apparently committed suicide. Other examples are found in the crimes of multinational companies such as Arthur Andersen—convicted in the spring of 2002 of obstructing justice—that have consequences for the companies' branches and accounting practices in Canada.

Recently, much attention has been given to recalls of toys with lead paint imported from China. An example is about 55 000 figures, called the Massive Soldier with Machine Gun, sold in dollar stores between 2007 and 2008 and recalled by Health Canada (CBC News 2008b). The U.S. Consumer Product Safety Commission maintains a list of product recalls by various countries. This includes a rather long list from Canada. Start at their home page (**http://www.cpsc.gov/cpscpub/prerel/prerel.html**).

Corporate crime has huge direct and indirect injurious as well as economic effects. Direct injury and death from corporate crime are immense in comparison to crime rates of murder and manslaughter. Sociologist John L. McMullan reports that before the mid-1980s in Canada, the corporate death rate was more than six times greater than the street crime rate of murder and manslaughter (1992:24). A notable example of lethal corporate crime is Nova Scotia's Westray mine, whose failure to follow good safety procedures resulted in the deaths of 26 workers in 1992. The top executives were not prosecuted for this disaster.

Organized Crime

Organized crime is a business operation that supplies illegal goods and services for profit. These illegal enterprises include drug trafficking, prostitution, gambling, loan sharking, money laundering, and large-scale theft such as truck hijacking (Simon 1996). No single entity controls the entire range of corrupt and illegal enterprises (Chambliss 1988). Instead, there are many groups—syndicated crime networks, including biker gangs—that can thrive because there is great demand for illegal goods and services. Syndicated crime networks operate at all levels of society and even globally (see Box 9.1). Criminologist Margaret Beare (1996) suggests that groups vary according to their dependence on organized crime. Whereas some groups are organized to carry out organized-crime activities (e.g., Russian and Nigerian groups and Colombian cartels), other groups have other goals and use organized-crime activities to support them (e.g., terrorist groups and motorcycle gangs). Sometimes these groups form alliances with businesspeople, law enforcement officials, and politicians. The RCMP website explains how organized crime affects Canadians:

Organized crime can affect your take-home pay (health care and tax losses are recouped by paying for those who are drug addicted, and for people trafficked into Canada); your property tax bill (policing costs and costs of money laundering effects to the local economy); your electricity bill (hydro diversion for drug operations); your car and home insurance bills (organized auto theft rings and property break-ins); your monthly banking fee (as a profit-seeking business, banks need to recover bank fraud costs by billing regular customers); your credit card payment (credit card fraud and identity theft costs to banks are recovered in your interest rate payments), and much more. In terms of economic-related crimes, it is estimated that organized crime costs Canadians $5 billion every year; that's $600 a year for a family of four. This amount, however, does not include costs related to the many other crimes (i.e., drugs, counterfeit goods) that organized crime groups are involved in." (RCMP 2009)

SOCIAL PROBLEMS IN GLOBAL PERSPECTIVE

BOX 9.1 Organized Crime: The Global Empire

According to Havocscope (2008), a website and information centre that focuses on black market activities around the world, the monetary value of global black market products was US$1.02 trillion in 2008. This sum came from the production and sale of marijuana, counterfeit technological products, cocaine, opium/heroin, web video piracy, counterfeit pharmaceutical drugs, cigarettes, counterfeit software, human trafficking, and so on. Canada ranked fifth, after the United States, Japan, China, and Mexico, in a long list of countries involved with the black market, gaining an estimated US$75.6 billion, primarily from the growth, smuggling, and sale of marijuana in British Columbia. According to Misha Glenny, a former BBC reporter who has toured the world investigating global crime and coined the term "McMafia" to describe the global organization of crime and the franchising nature of many criminal organizations, the value of the B.C. operations was over $5 billion in 2006, about 5 percent of British Columbia's GDP. The industry employs around 100 000 workers full- and part-time in the growing, distributing, smuggling (to the United States), and sale of marijuana—thousands more than the 55 000 working in forestry, mining, oil, and gas combined (Glenny 2008:214).

According to Glenny, much of the increase in global crime is due to failed states and the large numbers of unemployed youth and general chaos that result. The collapse of the Soviet Union is "the single most important event promoting the exponential growth of organized crime around the world in the last two decades" (Glenny 2008:52). Glenny found that chaos in other areas led to organized crime, such as the Balkans and India, where the collapse of the textile industry rendered 1.5 million textile workers jobless, causing great hardship to families (Glenny 2008:129). Canada had a similar experience when, contrary to the NAFTA Agreement, the United States imposed a tariff on the export of softwood lumber sales. The Canadian government estimated that 7000 jobs were lost directly in the softwood industry, and another 7000 were lost indirectly in the community. This event produced a ready labour force to produce and sell marijuana. "Most of those who once worked in the traditional industries have moved into marijuana" (Glenny 2008:215).

This is not the only organized crime in Canada. John McFetridge found in researching a novel that over 900 gangs are located in Canada conducting a wide variety of criminal activities, including high-tech crime (software piracy), meth labs, manufacturing and importing of counterfeit goods, and human trafficking (McFetridge 2008:71). While one might expect Canadians to be involved in high-tech crime and meth labs, one might not think that people would resort to human trafficking in Canada. However, human trafficking does not occur only in Europe, the Middle East, and the Far East. "An estimated 600 to 800 people a year are brought into Canada illegally with the promise of better life, and then pushed into prostitution, domestic servitude and forced labour" (Metro 2006:1). Speakers at a sex crimes conference in 2006 said, "Canada is being offered as a land of opportunity." While some people are able to escape from their enslavers, "fear and distrust of police make prosecuting these cases difficult." To help eliminate human trafficking, Canada has a policy of allowing victims of human trafficking to "stay in Canada up to 120 days to help them decide if they wish to assist in the investigation or return home" (Metro 2006:1) (see also Chapter 7).

Globally, seven or eight crime syndicates often operate in collusion. In addition to the Russian syndicate and the Sicilian Mafia, other organized-crime groups allegedly include the Colombian cocaine cartels, which have operations in Spain, and ethnic Chinese from East and Southeast Asia, who have overseas bases in Rotterdam and London. At a lower level, the transport and marketing of drugs and other contraband are managed by syndicates of Nigerians, Moroccans, Pakistanis, Lebanese, Albanians, and others (Viviano 1995).

As consumers of licit (e.g., food cultivated by cheap or forced labour) and illicit (e.g., drugs or pirated products) goods, many of us are involved with the black market. As globalization and deregulation of financial markets (the kind of reduction of control that makes money laundering easy and contributed substantially to the economic meltdown of 2007–2008) is promoted in the world, the more global organized crime we are likely to get. What can Canada do about global organized crime? Can any one nation or organization—such as the United Nations—reduce international human and drug trafficking? What do you think?

Youth Crime

Youth crime involves a violation of law or the commission of a status offence by a young person 12 to 17 years of age. Many behaviours that are identified as youth crime or juvenile delinquency are not criminal acts per se but *status offences*—acts that are illegal because of the age of the offender—such as cutting school, buying and consuming alcoholic beverages, or running away from home. But measuring youth crime is difficult because youth who come into contact with the law can be charged or cleared by a variety of other means, such as a warning or an extrajudicial sanctions program, or the complainant's decision not to lay a charge. The *Youth Criminal Justice Act* (YCJA; 2003) recognizes that effective responses to youth crime may be outside the courts. Figure 9.2 shows that overall youth crime has been stable over the past decade, with declines in property crime and increases in "other" (e.g., drug offenses) and violent crime (Statistics Canada 2008t). Figure 9.3 shows an increase in the cleared otherwise rate since the introduction of the act, resulting in a steady decline in charging youth. The YCJA appears to be effective in diverting youth from courts.

The statistics for youth crime are still high. Whereas people aged 12 to 17 constituted less than 10 percent of the Canadian population, they account for 20 percent of all persons charged in Canada with *Criminal Code* offences, excluding traffic offences (Sauvé 2005:13). Over the past decade, property crime has declined and overall youth crime has declined 25 percent since the peak in 1991. However, the youth violent crime rate increased 12 percent during the past decade, as seen in Figure 9.2. Much of this increase was driven by an increase in assaults. Youth accused of assault represented nearly 80 percent of those apprehended for a violent crime in 2006. Most youth apprehended for assault were accused of common assault, the least serious form of this offence. Overall, 84 young people, 72 boys and 12 girls, were implicated in 54 homicides in 2006. Just over one-half of homicides in which the accused was a youth involved multiple perpetrators, compared with only 15 percent of homicides that involved an adult accused (Statistics Canada 2008j).

SOCIOLOGICAL EXPLANATIONS OF CRIME

As with other social problems, crime and delinquency have been explained in biological, psychological, and sociological terms. Most biological and psychological explanations assume that criminal behaviour is an

FIGURE 9.2   Rates of Youth Crime, 1997 to 2006

Rate per 100 000 youth (aged 12 to 17)

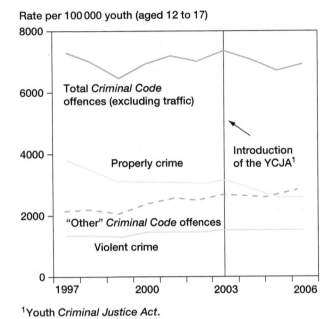

¹Youth *Criminal Justice Act.*

Source: Statistics Canada, 2008, "Youth Crime 2006," The Daily *(May 16).* Retrieved October 29, 2008 (http://www.statcan.ca/Daily/English/080516/ d080516a.htm).

FIGURE 9.3   Rates of Youth Charged, 1997 to 2006

Rate per 100 000 youth (aged 12 to 17)

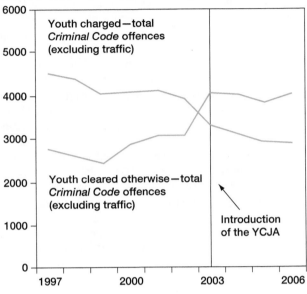

Source: Statistics Canada, 2008, "Youth Crime 2006," The Daily *(May 16).* Retrieved October 29, 2008 (http://www.statcan.ca/Daily/English/ 080516/d080516a.htm).

inherent or acquired individual trait with genetic, biological, or psychological roots. Unlike biological and psychological explanations that focus on individual behaviour, sociological explanations focus on those aspects of society that may contribute to delinquent or criminal behaviour.

The Functionalist Perspective

Although there are numerous functionalist perspectives on crime and delinquency, we will focus on two: strain theory and control theory, as illustrated in social bond theory.

Functionalist explanations for why people commit crimes can be traced to Emile Durkheim, who believed that the macrolevel structure of a society produces social pressures that result in high rates of deviance and crime. Durkheim introduced the concept of *anomie* to describe a social condition that engenders feelings of futility in people because of weak, absent, or conflicting social norms. According to Durkheim (1895/1964), deviance and crime are most likely to occur when anomie is

present in a society. On the basis of Durkheim's theory, sociologist Robert Merton (1938; 1968) developed strain theory to explain why some people conform to group norms while others do not. **Strain theory** states that people feel strain when they are exposed to cultural goals that they cannot reach because they do not have access to a culturally approved means of achieving those goals. When some people are denied legitimate access to cultural goals such as success, money, or other material possessions, they seek to acquire these things through deviant—and sometimes criminal—means. This lack of legitimate access is typical of many of Canada's inmates. According to Robinson and his colleagues (1999: 57), the one-day snapshot of inmates shows that criminals are much more likely to be unemployed than the general population (52 percent versus 7 percent). A more recent study of crime patterns over a 40-year period (from 1962 to 2003) found that economic factors were associated with some kinds of crime. For example, periods of inflation like the 1970s were associated with robbery, breaking and entering, and motor vehicle theft, and unemployment is associated with homicide (Statistics Canada 2005g). The recession of 2008 will also provide an opportunity to test the influence of economic factors.

Merton identified five ways in which people respond to cultural goals: conformity, innovation, ritualism, retreatism, and rebellion (see Table 9.3).

■ *Conformity* occurs when people accept the culturally approved goals and pursue them through the approved means. People who choose conformity work hard and save their money to achieve success. Someone who is blocked from achieving a high level of education or a lucrative career typically conforms by taking a lower-paying job and attending school part-time, joining the military, or trying alternative (but legal) avenues, such as playing the lottery.

■ *Innovation* occurs when people accept society's goals but use illegitimate means to achieve them. Innovations for acquiring material possessions include shoplifting, theft, burglary, cheating on income taxes, embezzling money, and other kinds of occupational crime.

■ *Ritualism* occurs when people give up on societal goals but still adhere to socially approved means for achieving them. People who cannot obtain expensive material possessions or wealth seek to maintain the respect of others by being "hard workers" or "good citizens" to an extreme degree.

■ *Retreatism* occurs when people abandon both the approved goals and the approved means of achieving them. Retreatists include hard-core drug addicts and some middle- or upper-income people who reject conventional trappings of success and the means to acquire them, choosing to "drop out" instead.

■ *Rebellion* occurs when people reject both the approved goals and the approved means for achieving them and advocate an alternative set of goals and means. Rebels may use violence (such as vandalism or rioting) or non-violent tactics (such as civil disobedience) to change society and its cultural beliefs. Or they may withdraw from mainstream society, like the Amish, to live their own life.

Another functionalist perspective—*control theory*—seeks to answer the question, "Why do people *not* engage in deviant behaviour?" According to control theory, people are constantly pulled and pushed toward deviant behaviour. Environmental factors (pulls), such as adverse living conditions, poverty, and lack of educational opportunity, draw people toward criminal behaviour while, at the same time, internal pressures (pushes), such as feelings of hostility or aggressiveness, make people not want to act according to dominant values and norms (Reckless 1967). If this is true, why doesn't everyone who is poor or has a limited education commit crimes? According to control

TABLE 9.3   Merton's Strain Theory

Mode of Adaptation	Method of Adaptation	Agrees with Cultural Goal	Follows Institutional Means
Conformity	Accepts culturally approved goals; pursues them through culturally approved means	Yes	Yes
Innovation	Accepts culturally approved goals; adopts disapproved means of achieving them	Yes	No
Ritualism	Abandons society's goals butto continues to conform approved means	No	Yes
Retreatism	Abandons both approved goals and the approved means to achieve them	No	No
Rebellion	Challenges both the approved goals and the approved means to achieve them	No—seeks to replace	No—seeks to replace

Source: Adapted from Robert King Merton, 1968, Social Theory and Social Structure, *New York: Free Press.*

theorists, people who do not turn to crime or delinquent behaviour have *outer containments*—supportive family and friends, reasonable social expectations, and supervision by others—or *inner containments*—self-control, a sense of responsibility, and resistance to diversions. This lack of outer and inner containments is found among Canada's inmates. According to Robinson and his colleagues, inmates are much more likely to be unmarried than the general adult population (31 percent versus 63 percent; 1999:57) and have high levels of crime-causing needs, such as personal and emotional problems, substance abuse, and problems functioning in the community (1999:66).

The best-known control theory is **social bond theory**—the proposition that criminal behaviour is most likely to occur when a person's ties to society are weakened or broken. According to criminologist Travis Hirschi (1969), who proposed this theory, social bonding consists of (1) *attachment* to other people, (2) *commitment* to conformity, (3) *involvement* in conventional activities, and (4) *belief* in the legitimacy of conventional values and norms. When a person's social bonds are weak and when peers promote antisocial values and violent behaviour, the probability of delinquency and crime increases (Massey and Krohn 1986).

When analyzing violent crime, some functionalists believe that a sense of anomie is the root cause. Others believe that violence increases when social institutions such as the family, schools, and religious organizations weaken and the primary mechanisms of social control in people's everyday lives become external—law enforcement and the criminal justice system. Others accept the **subculture of violence hypothesis**, that violence is part of the normative expectations governing everyday behaviour among young males in the lower classes (Wolfgang and Ferracuti 1967). These violent subcultures are most likely to develop when young people, particularly males, have few legitimate opportunities available in their segment of society and when subcultural values accept and encourage violent behaviour.

Another functionalist perspective on violence, discussed in Chapter 1, is the *lifestyle–routine activity approach* (page 8), which holds that the patterns and timing of people's daily movements and activities as they go about obtaining the necessities of life—such as food, shelter, companionship, and entertainment—are the keys to understanding violent personal crimes and other types of crime in our society (Cohen and Felson 1979). In other words, changes in social institutions, such as more families in which both parents (or the sole parent) work outside the home or the extension of shopping hours into the night, put some people at greater risk than others of being victims of violent crime (Parker 1995).

Functionalist explanations contribute to our understanding of crime by emphasizing that individuals who engage in such behaviour are not biologically or psychologically impaired but are responding to social and economic conditions in society. However, functionalists are not without their critics. Strain theory may point out that people from low-income and poverty-level backgrounds are prevented from achieving success goals through legitimate channels, but it is still criticized for focusing almost exclusively on crimes committed by the lower classes and ignoring crimes committed by people in the middle and upper classes. Critics of social bond theory say that it is limited in its ability to explain more serious forms of delinquency and crime (Krohn 1995).

The Conflict Perspective

Conflict theorists explain criminal behaviour in terms of power differentials and/or economic inequality in society. One approach focuses on how authority and power relations can contribute to some people—but not others—becoming criminals. According to sociologist Austin Turk (1966, 1971), crime is not a *behaviour* but a *status* that is acquired when people with the authority to create and enforce legal rules apply those rules to others.

A second conflict approach focuses on the relationship between economic inequality and crime. Having roots in the work of Karl Marx, the *radical critical-conflict approach* argues that social institutions (such as law, politics, and education) create a superstructure that legitimizes the class structure and maintains capitalists' superior position. In fact, say these theorists, the crimes people commit are based on their class position. Thus, crimes committed by low-income people typically involve taking things by force or physical stealth, while white-collar crime usually involves non-physical means, such as paper transactions or computer fraud. Some critical theorists believe that affluent people commit crimes because they are greedy and continually want more than they have, whereas poor people commit street crimes such as robbery and theft to survive (Bonger 1916/1969).

In sum, the conflict approach is useful for pointing out how inequalities of power, class, and racialization can contribute to criminal or delinquent behaviour. Nevertheless, critics say that conflict theorists have not shown that powerful political and economic elites manipulate law making and enforcement for their own benefit. Rather, say these critics, people of all classes share a consensus that acts such as homicide, sexual assault, and armed robbery are bad (Klockars 1979).

The Interactionist Perspective

Interactionists emphasize that criminal behaviour is learned through everyday interaction with others. We will examine two major interactionist theories: differential association theory and labelling theory. **Differential association theory** states that individuals have a greater tendency to deviate from societal norms when they frequently associate with people who tend toward deviance rather than conformity. According to sociologist Edwin Sutherland (1939), who formulated this theory, people learn not only the techniques of deviant behaviour from people with whom they associate but also the motives, drives, rationalizations, and attitudes. Former gang member Nathan McCall (1994:93–94) describes such a learning process in his own life:

> Sometimes I picked up hustling ideas at the 7-Eleven, which was like a criminal union hall: Crapshooters, shoplifters, stickup men, burglars, everybody stopped off at the store from time to time. While hanging up there one day, I ran into Holt.... He had a pocketful of cash, even though he had quit school and was unemployed. I asked him, "Yo, man, what you been into?" "Me and my partner kick in cribs and make a killin'. You oughta come go with us sometime.... " I hooked school one day, went with them, and pulled my first B&E [breaking and entering].... After I learned the ropes, Shell Shock [another gang member] and I branched out, doing B and Es on our own. We learned to get in and out of houses in no time flat.

As McCall's description indicates, criminal activity often occurs within the context of frequent, intense, and long-lasting interactions with people who violate the law. When more factors favour violating the law than not, the person is likely to become a criminal. Although differential association theory contributes to our knowledge of how deviant behaviour reflects the individual's learned techniques, values, attitudes, motives, and rationalizations, critics note that many individuals who are regularly exposed to people who break the law still conform most of the time. Many critics think that the theory does not adequately take into account possible connections between social inequality and criminal behaviour.

Labelling theory, which was mentioned briefly in Chapter 1, takes quite a different approach from differential association theory. According to **labelling theory,** delinquents and criminals are people who have been successfully labelled as such by others. No behaviour is inherently delinquent or criminal; it is defined as such by a social audience (Erikson 1962). According to sociologist Howard Becker (1963), labelling is often done by *moral entrepreneurs*—people who use their own views of right and wrong to establish rules and label others "deviant." Furthermore, the process of labelling is directly related to the power and status of the people who do the labelling and those who are being labelled. In support of this theory, one study of juvenile offenders has found that youths from lower-income families were more likely to be arrested and indicted than were middle-class juveniles who did the same things (Sampson 1986). Sociologists have also noted that the criminal justice system generally considers such factors as the offender's family life, educational achievement (or lack thereof), and social class in determining how to deal with juvenile offenders. According to one study, the individuals who are most likely to be apprehended, labelled delinquent, and prosecuted are people of colour who are young, male, unemployed, and undereducated and who live in urban high-crime areas (Vito and Holmes 1994).

Sociologist Edwin Lemert (1951) expanded labelling theory by distinguishing between primary and secondary deviance. **Primary deviance** is the initial act of rule-breaking in which the individual does not internalize the delinquent or criminal self-concept. **Secondary deviance** occurs when a person who has been labelled a deviant accepts that new identity and continues the deviant behaviour. The concept of secondary deviance is important to labelling theory because it suggests that when people accept a negative label or stigma that has been applied to them, the label may actually contribute to the behaviour it was meant to control. In other words, secondary deviance occurs if a person is labelled a juvenile delinquent, accepts that label, and then continues to engage in delinquent behaviour. Labelling theory is useful for making us aware of how social control and personal identity are intertwined. Critics, however, do not think that labelling theory explains what causes the original acts that constitute primary deviance, nor do they think that it adequately explains why some people accept deviant labels and others do not (Cavender 1995).

In 1843, Daniel M'Naughton was acquitted of attempting to kill the British prime minister and shooting an official by reason of insanity. This was the beginning of the plea of insanity, but it did not provide any clear definition or measure of irrational behaviour. Since that time, a wide variety of defences involving a loss of self-control by the accused due to medical problems have been advocated by defence attorneys. The process has been called the **medicalization of crime,** the converting of criminal behaviour to a medical condition or disease. It is parallel to the medicalization of deviance—the converting of deviance, such as alcoholism, to a medical condition. Given the current and likely future development of our understanding about the influence of biological factors on serious violent crime, questions about the definition of personal responsibility versus medical conditions for irrational behaviour will be central to many future criminal proceedings.

Feminist Perspectives

Feminist scholarship focuses on why women commit crimes or engage in delinquent behaviour. We have already noted the differences in victimization rates for men and women. Criminologist Elizabeth Cormack (1999) reminds us that studies of offenders in prison often find that the women have experienced physical and/or sexual abuse. Scholars who use a *liberal feminist* framework believe that women's delinquency or crime is a rational response to gender discrimination in society. They attribute crimes such as prostitution and shoplifting to women's lack of educational and job opportunities and to stereotypical expectations about roles women should have in society (Daly and Chesney-Lind 1988). Scholars who espouse *radical feminism* believe that

patriarchy contributes to crimes such as prostitution because, according to society's sexual double standard, it is acceptable for a man to pay for sex but unacceptable for a woman to accept money for such services. A third school of feminist thought, *socialist feminism,* believes that women are exploited by capitalism and patriarchy. Because most females have relatively low-wage jobs and few economic resources, crimes such as prostitution and shoplifting become a means of earning money and acquiring consumer products. Feminist scholars of colour, and other feminist scholars who wish to broaden the perspective of criminology beyond the patriarchy, suggest that consideration be given to "the complex and diverse ways in which patriarchal (along with class and racialization) privilege and power invade people's subjectivities and experiences" (Cormack 1999:166).

Another approach that focuses on differences in males' and females' crime behaviour, specifically on the higher rates of male versus female youth crime, is the power-control theory of sociologist John Hagan and his colleagues (1987). This theory emphasizes the structure of the family and socialization, rating families from "unbalanced," or highly patriarchal, to "balanced," or egalitarian, in the exercise of power by husbands and wives and according to their traditional versus egalitarian socialization of their sons and daughters. In a study in Toronto, Hagan and his colleagues found that gender differences in crime were greater in unbalanced than balanced families. Girls from families where girls were highly controlled and boys were freer committed fewer crimes relative to boys than girls from families with more egalitarian socialization (Hagan et al. 1987).

THE CRIMINAL JUSTICE SYSTEM

The **criminal justice system** is the network of organizations, including the police, courts, criminal prosecutions, and corrections, involved in law enforcement and the administration of justice (CCJS 1999:4). Originally, the criminal justice system was created to help solve the problem of social disorder and crime. Today, however, some social analysts wonder whether the criminal justice system is part of the problem. Most cite two reasons for concern: (1) the criminal justice system fails in its mission to prevent, control, or rehabilitate offenders; and (2) unequal justice occurs because officials discriminate against people on the basis of racialization, class, gender, age, sexual orientation, or other devalued characteristics.

The Police

The police are the most visible link in the criminal justice system because they determine how to apply the law to control crime and maintain order. Four factors seem to influence the occurrence of an arrest:

1. the nature of the alleged offence or problem;
2. the quality of available evidence;
3. the age, racialization, and gender of the alleged offender; and
4. the level of deference shown to police officers. (Mastrofski 1995)

Given these factors, law enforcement officials have fairly wide *discretion*—use of personal judgment regarding whether and how to proceed in a given situation—in deciding who will be stopped and searched and which homes and businesses will be entered and for what purposes (Donziger 1996). Sociologist Jerome Skolnick (1975) argues that because police officers must often make these decisions in a dangerous environment, they develop a sense of suspicion, social isolation, and solidarity.

Some police departments have begun *community policing* as a way of reducing crime. Community policing involves integrating officers into the communities they serve—getting them out of their patrol cars and into a proactive role, recognizing problems and working with neighbourhood citizens to find solutions. In cities where community policing has been implemented, crime rates appear to have dropped; however, it should be noted that there has also been a general trend toward fewer crimes, especially violent crimes, in some cities where community policing is not employed (Sacco and Kennedy 1998:356ff).

The Courts

Criminal courts are responsible for determining the guilt or innocence of people who have been accused of committing a crime. In theory, justice is determined in an adversarial process: a prosecutor (a Crown attorney who represents the state) argues that the accused is guilty and a defence attorney argues that the accused is innocent. In reality, judges have a great deal of discretion. Working with prosecutors, they decide who will be released, who will be held for further hearings, and—in many instances—what sentences will be imposed on people who are convicted.

Because courts have the capacity to try only a small fraction of criminal cases, an attrition process occurs. This process begins with the police, who clear about a third of all offences reported to them. The police clear a fifth of all reports with a charge. About 15 percent of the total reports result in conviction, and 4 percent of reports result in a sentence to custody (CCJS 1999:xiii). This attrition process has been called a "crime funnel" (Silverman et al. 1996, cited in Sacco and Kennedy 1998:205). Many cases are resolved by **plea bargaining**—a process whereby the Crown attorney negotiates with a defence attorney for a guilty plea for a less serious crime. In other words, defendants (especially those who are poor and cannot afford to pay for an attorney) plead guilty to a lesser crime in return for not being tried for the more serious crime for which they were arrested. As cases are sifted and sorted through the legal machinery, steady attrition occurs. At each stage, various officials determine what alternatives will be available for the cases that remain in the system (Hills 1971).

Sometimes plea bargaining occurs to get a conviction in a high-profile case when no other avenue seems available. A notorious example was the case of the sentencing of Karla Homolka to 12 years in prison in return for her testimony and evidence (tapes, missed in the search by police, recording the homicides of two girls) to convict Paul Bernardo of the girls' homicides.

In 2006–2007, just over 372 000 cases were disposed of in adult criminal courts, down 7 percent from five years earlier. Nearly half the cases completed in 2006–2007 involved crimes against the person (25 percent) and crimes against property (24 percent). Almost two-thirds (65 percent) of adult cases received a guilty. In a large majority of these cases (89 percent), the accused had pleaded guilty. The *Criminal Code* traffic offences category had the highest share of cases with a finding of guilt (79 percent), and the lowest (53 percent) occurred in crimes against the person. Probation was the most frequently imposed sanction (43 percent) in cases having a guilty finding. Custody was imposed in 34 percent of cases, and a fine in 30 percent (Statistics Canada 2008a).

Punishment and the Prisons

Punishment is any action designed to deprive a person of things of value (including liberty) because of an offence the person is thought to have committed (Barlow 1996). Punishment is seen as serving four functions:

1. *Retribution* imposes a penalty on the offender. Retribution is based on the premise that the punishment should fit the crime.

2. *Social protection* results from restricting offenders so that they cannot continue to commit crimes.

3. *Rehabilitation* seeks to return offenders to the community as law-abiding citizens. Often, the job skills (such as agricultural work) that are taught in prison do not transfer to the outside world, and offenders are not given help in finding work that fits the skills they might have once they are released.

4. *Deterrence* seeks to reduce criminal activity by instilling a fear of punishment. Criminologists debate, though, whether imprisonment has a deterrent effect, given that 30 to 50 percent of those who are released from prison commit further crimes.

Despite the decline in those sentenced to custody, certain problems remain. For example, there is an over-representation of Indigenous people in prison. Whereas Indigenous people constitute 3 percent of the adult population, they make up 18.73 percent of the federal prison population, according to a report from Statistics Canada (2009f). Incarcerating Indigenous people for crimes such as drunkenness and vagrancy, crimes for which Whites are less likely to be incarcerated, has been a longstanding feature of our justice system. In Box 9.2, this fact and the overrepresentation of Black people is noted in the discussion of whether to use racialization-based statistics.

Restorative Justice

In Canada, Europe, Australia, and New Zealand, the concept of restorative justice comprises diverse practices, including conferencing, sentencing circles, and victim–offender mediation. **Restorative justice** focuses on repairing the harm caused by crime by holding moderated meetings of crime victims, offenders, and others affected by crime, which can be used at different sites in the justice system, for example, as a diversion from court, a pre-sentencing option, and after the release from prison.

Current applications of the idea began to emerge in the 1970s in North America, beginning with a victim–offender reconciliation program in Ontario in 1974. A recent example was the Indigenous sentencing circle created to deal with the bullying situation that resulted in the suicide death of Dawn-Marie Wesley in British Columbia (see also Chapter 12 for more on bullying). According to a report in the *National Post* by Ian Bailey (2002), the mother of Dawn-Marie hugged the girl convicted of criminally harassing her daughter and accepted her apology. The girl also received a sentence of 18 months' probation, a six-month cell-phone ban (the instrument of the harassing), and an assignment of writing a 750-word essay on bullying and doing 20 hours of community work that could include speaking about bullying. Another example is the response of the parents of Reena Virk, killed in 1997, and one convicted killer, Warren Glowatski (see Box 1.2 on page 11 in Chapter 1). In fall 2005 in a church in Mission, B.C., and in the summer of 2006, they hugged each other during an Aboriginal healing circle that was part of his parole hearing (Mason 2006:A3). The Virks hugged him, they said, to release some of the anger that had built up inside them and to help him to not "carry a heavy heart around with him for the rest of his life" (Mason 2006:A3).

SOCIAL PROBLEMS AND SOCIAL POLICY

BOX 9.2   To Collect or Not Collect Racialization and Ethnicity Statistics

Unlike the crime statistics in the United States, those in Canada do not report on ethnic background of victim and accused. We do have information about backgrounds in the Canadian correctional system where, for example, as mentioned above, Indigenous people (3 percent of the population) constitute 18.73 percent of the federal prison population. And the policy question is whether to include racialization/ethnicity information at other levels of the system.

Criminologist Scot Wortley (1999) presents arguments for both sides. Arguments opposed to collecting racialization/ethnicity-based data include

- the risk of publishing inaccurate information due to the problems of official statistics and measuring racialization/ethnicity; and
- the support provided for racist theories.

Arguments in favour of collecting the data include

- the opportunity to learn whether minorities are receiving differential treatment at any level of the system (e.g., To what extent does profiling occur?). In late May 2005, Kingston, Ontario, Chief of Police Bill Closs released data reporting that whereas Blacks were 0.6 percent of the Kingston community, they constituted 2.2 percent of those stopped for questioning and were 9.6 percent of people arrested or charged. But Asians were half as likely to be stopped, and Blacks were seen in higher proportions at the malls, at nightspots, and so on, than other groups. So does this constitute profiling or reflect other kinds of behaviour? The *Toronto Star* and the *Globe and Mail* disagree on the results (*Globe and Mail* 2005:A24). What do you think?
- the identification of crimes that are of particular concern to a minority. While it is well known that homicide is primarily an intraracial problem in the United States, Blacks killing Blacks is also a problem for Canadians. Some Black community leaders, among them, Dudley Laws in Toronto, have spoken out against publishing racialization-based crime statistics. However, in 2001, the Black Action Defence Committee, of which Laws is the executive director, launched a campaign supported by many other associations to stop the killings

of Black youths by other Black youths. From 1996 to 2001, over 100 Black youths were killed by other Black youths, and the agencies were appealing to "society in general to address this very urgent problem" (*Metro Today* August 17, 2001:9). And the killing continues. As shown in this example, members of a minority group may feel comfortable publishing data about their own group but not wish to see it compared to the data for other groups, for fear that the data will be used to label rather than address inequities faced by members of their group.

- a ban on such data does not prevent the spread of racist theories (racialization-based distortions are widely available, for example, on the Internet).
- a report released in November 2008 authored by former Ontario chief justice Roy McMurtry and former Liberal MPP Alvin Curling in response to the shooting of a student, Jordan Manners, in May 2007 in a Toronto high school made a specific recommendation to collect racialization-based data to show the extent of racism in society's treatment of youth. A *Toronto Star* editorial agreed, saying stigmatization did not happen in Britain and is unlikely to happen here. "Rather, the shining of a cold, clear statistical light on the problem could very well help in rolling back discrimination" (2008:AA4).

Do you think racialization/ethnicity-based crime statistics should be published as readily as racialization/ethnicity education data and income data (see Chapters 3 and 12), or should there be no collection of these kinds of data? Or should the collection be limited to certain situations? What situations would they be? Or should the decision be left with the minority group themselves? Would this last approach cause any problems?

Is the solution to our "crime problem" to build more prisons and execute more people? Only about 20 percent of all crimes result in a charge, only half of these lead to a conviction, and fewer than 4 percent of convictions result in a jail term. The "lock 'em up and throw away the key" approach has little chance of succeeding. As for individuals who commit occupational and corporate crime, the percentage that enters the criminal justice system is so minimal that prison is relatively useless as a deterrent to others. Furthermore, the high rate of recidivism strongly suggests that the rehabilitative efforts of our existing correctional facilities are sadly lacking. One thing is clear: the existing criminal justice system cannot solve the crime problem.

Is equal justice under the law possible? As long as social problems exist in our society, equal justice

under the law may not be possible for all people; however, that does not keep it from being a goal that citizens and the criminal justice system should strive to reach.

WHAT CAN YOU DO?

- Seek out a community/police liaison committee in your neighbourhood and learn about local problems and what people are trying to do about them.
- Seek out an advocacy group and participate in one of its activities. For example, in Ontario, an organization called Justice for Children and Youth challenged the Ontario law banning squeegee kids'

solicitations and various kinds of begging (e.g., while intoxicated). This organization seeks participation on its Youth Advisory Committee to help it deal with the problems of young people. It is located in Toronto (tel. 416-920-1633).

- Organize seminars to discuss or debate ideas like the publication of racialization/ethnicity data for crime or the value of restorative justice.
- Work with campus groups to alert female students to the problem of date rape.

SUMMARY

Why Is It Difficult to Study Crime and Youth Crime?

Studying crime, criminals, and youth crime is difficult because it involves complex human behaviour, and many criminals and victims hide their involvement. There also are problems inherent in using official sources of data, such as the *Uniform Crime Report,* because they reflect crimes that are reported rather than crimes that are committed, and they do not provide detailed information about offenders.

How Does Violent Crime Differ from Property Crime?

Violent crime consists of actions involving force or the threat of force against others and includes homicide, sexual assault, robbery, and aggravated assault. Property crime consists of taking money or property from another without force, the threat of force, or the destruction of property.

Why Is Sexual Assault as a Violent Crime Not Well Understood? How Is This Lack of Understanding Reflected in Our Social Response to Sexual Assault?

First, many people think that sexual assault is a sexually motivated crime, but it is actually an act of violence in which sex is used as a weapon against a powerless victim. Moreover, statistics on sexual assault are misleading at best because sexual assault is often not reported. Many reasons keep victims from coming forward. Some victims may be so traumatized that they just want to forget about it. Others fear the attacker will try to get even. Many also fear how they may be treated by the police and, in the event of a trial, by Crown attorneys.

What Is Occupational Crime?

Occupational (white-collar) crime refers to illegal activities committed by people in the course of their employment or normal business activity. Occupational crime includes crimes such as employee theft, fraud (obtaining money or property under false pretences), embezzlement (theft from an employer), soliciting bribes or kickbacks, and insider trading of securities.

How Does Occupational Crime Differ from Corporate Crime?

Occupational crimes are illegal activities committed by people in the course of their employment or normal business activity. Corporate crimes are illegal acts committed by corporate employees on behalf of the corporation and with its support.

What Is Organized Crime and Why Does It Flourish in Canada?

Organized crime is a business operation that supplies illegal goods and services for profit. These illegal enterprises include drug trafficking, prostitution, gambling, loan sharking, money laundering, and large-scale theft. Organized crime thrives because there is great demand for illegal goods and services.

How Does Youth Crime Differ from Adult Crime?

Youth crime refers to a violation of law or the commission of a status offence by people who are younger than a specific age. Many behaviours that are identified as juvenile delinquency are not criminal acts per se but status offences—acts that are illegal because of the age of the offender—such as cutting school or purchasing and consuming alcoholic beverages. Juvenile hearings take place in juvenile courts or before juvenile judges, whereas adult offenders are tried in criminal courts.

Who Is Most Likely to be Arrested for a Crime in Canada?

Men are more likely to be arrested than women. Teenagers and young adults are most likely to be arrested for serious crimes such as homicide, sexual assault, and robbery. Although individuals from all social classes commit crimes, people from lower socio-economic backgrounds are more likely to be arrested for violent and property crimes, whereas people from the upper classes generally commit white-collar or corporate crimes. Indigenous people and Blacks are overrepresented in arrest data.

How Do Functionalists Explain Crime?

Functionalists use several theories to explain crime. According to strain theory, people are socialized to desire cultural goals, but many people do not have institutionalized means to achieve the goals and therefore engage in criminal activity. Control perspectives, such as social bond theory, suggest that delinquency and crime are most likely to occur when a person's ties to society are weakened or broken.

How Do Conflict Theorists Explain Crime?

Conflict theorists explain criminal behaviour in terms of power differentials and/or economic inequality in society. One approach focuses on the relationship between authority and power and crime; another focuses on the relationship between economic inequality and crime.

How Do Interactionists Explain Crime?

Interactionists emphasize that criminal behaviour is learned through everyday interaction with others. According to differential association theory, individuals have a greater tendency to deviate from societal norms when they frequently associate with people who are more likely to deviate than conform. Labelling theory says that delinquents and criminals are those people who have been successfully labelled by others as such.

How Do Feminist Theorists Explain Crime?

Feminist approaches offer several explanations of why women commit crimes: gender discrimination, patriarchy, a combination of capitalism and patriarchy, and a combination of family structure and socialization.

What Are the Components of The Criminal Justice System?

The criminal justice system is a network of organizations involved in law enforcement, including the police, the courts, and the prisons. The police are the most visible link in the criminal justice system because they are responsible for initially arresting and jailing people. Criminal courts are responsible for determining the guilt or innocence of people who have been accused of committing a crime. Imprisonment, conditional sentences, probation, and parole are mechanisms of punishment based on retribution, social protection, rehabilitation, and deterrence.

KEY TERMS

QUESTIONS FOR CRITICAL THINKING

1. Do you think that putting surveillance cameras in public places to monitor people and their possible deviant behaviour is a good idea? Why or why not?

2. How would sociologists argue with the claim that crime is committed by disturbed people?

3. Does the functionalist, conflict, or interactionist perspective best explain why people commit corporate crimes? Organized crimes? Explain your answer.

4. How would you reorganize the criminal justice system so that it would deal more equitably with all people in this country and prevent problems like profiling?

Explore the topics covered in this chapter at **www.mysockit.com** using the access provided with this text. Interactive resources for studying include video clips, practice tests, learning objectives, and Internet resources.

HEALTH, ILLNESS, AND HEALTH CARE AS SOCIAL PROBLEMS

10

The Terry Fox Run

When you get $520 per month and pay $400 for rent, how can you live on $120?

Richard, aged 46, an engineer now on welfare, speaking of the difficulty of purchasing nutritious food on his allowance (author's files)

How many women have that amount of money lying around?

Diana Brynlee, quoted in the **Globe and Mail,** *March 10, 2001:A2, speaking of her ability to pay for a diagnostic test that can detect cancer early*

Since unreasonable wait times for treatment that pose a risk to patients are an infringement of *Charter* rights to "life liberty, and security of person," Quebec patients should be able to pay for insurance to cover treatments already provided by medicare to avoid a long wait.

Supreme Court of Canada ruling June 9, 2005, allowing people to avoid long wait times

Princess Margaret Hospital in Toronto announced same-day diagnosis and treatment plans for those women with breast cancer.

Globe and Mail *May 7, 2009*

Despite the nationwide commitment to build real and lasting change and the infusion of billions of dollars brought about by the 2003 Accord on Health Care Renewal, progress falls short of what could, and should, have been achieved by this time, says the Health Council of Canada's latest report to Canadians, *Rekindling Reform: Health Care Renewal in Canada, 2003 to 2008.*

Health Council of Canada 2009

Richard, quoted above, was speaking to the author at a dinner provided by Street Health, a downtown Toronto agency providing a variety of health and social services to recovering addicts and homeless and poor people. Diana Brynlee made her statement after paying to obtain a PET scan (positron emission tomography takes internal pictures of people to diagnose disease). If she had not had the money to pay for it, she would have had to wait longer for a test and missed the opportunity that early diagnosis afforded. She was wondering about the consequences for people who could not afford the test.

The health situations faced by Richard and Diana Brynlee tend to be viewed as *personal problems,* but lack of access to nutritious food and expensive diagnostic tests is also a *social problem.* For one thing, it affects many people; for another, it is a problem that cannot be reduced or eliminated without a significant social response, such as willingness to devote more money to health and social services. In succeeding years, people have thought that expanding private medicine would solve Diana Brynlee's and others' problems, and even the Supreme Court was appealed to. But in early May 2009, the Princess Margaret Hospital in Toronto announced that it would provide same-day diagnosis and treatment plans for women with breast cancer. It is hoped that this plan will be followed elsewhere to improve accessibility for people suffering from other diseases and conditions. Yet the Health Council of Canada's statement above indicates that even though governments agree to devote more effort and money to health care, problems can still prevent the implementation of individual projects.

This chapter examines health, illness—including both physical and mental illness—and health care problems and current issues in providing health services in this country. The chapter also draws attention to inequalities regarding disease and disability for people of different sex, gender, class, and racialization or ethnicity; recent problems such as HIV/AIDS and obesity; mental illness as a social problem; and the crisis faced by the Canadian health care system and recommendations to improve it. The sociological perspectives are used to explain health problems, and the chapter concludes with suggestions for what you can do to improve your health and the health of others.

HEALTH AND ILLNESS AS SOCIAL PROBLEMS

According to the World Health Organization (WHO; 1946:3), *health* is a state of complete physical, mental, and social well-being. In other words, health is not only a biological issue, but also a social issue. After all, physical and mental health are intertwined: physical illness can cause emotional problems; mental illness can produce physical symptoms. Many people think there is a positive relationship between the amount of money a society spends on health care and the overall physical, mental, and social well-being of its people—that spending a great deal of money on health care should result in physical, mental, and social well-being. But if this were true, people in the United States would be the healthiest and most fit in the world, and they are not.

While physical, mental, and social well-being are difficult to measure, **life expectancy,** an estimate of the average lifetime of people born in a specific year, is relatively easy to measure. If we use this widely accepted measure of the effectiveness of the health care system, we find the relationship between health expenditure and health of the population is not strong. The United States spends the equivalent of more than OECD$6401 (Organisation for Economic Co-operation and Development dollars, adjusted for differences in prices in different countries) per person and Canada spends OECD$3326 per person on health care each year (OECD 2008). The health service industry accounts for more than 15 percent of GDP in the United States and 10 percent in Canada, yet Canadians live longer. Whereas U.S. females born in 2004 can expect to live 80.4 years and males can expect to live 75.2 years (OECD 2008), Canadian females born in 2003 can expect to live 82.4 years and males can expect to live 77.4 (see Table 10.1).

Besides life expectancy, another widely used measure of the effectiveness of the health care system is the **infant mortality rate,** the number of deaths of infants under one year of age per 1000 live births in a given year. During the past century, Canada's infant mortality rate has decreased greatly. Table 10.1 shows that the infant mortality rate (per 1000 live births) for Canada was 5.3 in 2004. The infant mortality rate is an important indication of a society's level of preventive (prenatal) medical care, maternal nutrition, childbirth procedures, and care for infants.

Acute and Chronic Diseases and Disability

Life expectancy in Canada and other developed nations has increased largely because vaccinations and improved nutrition, sanitation, and personal hygiene have virtually eliminated many acute diseases, including measles, polio, cholera, tetanus, typhoid, and malaria. **Acute diseases** are illnesses that strike suddenly and

TABLE 10.1   Canada's Health Indicators

Indicator	Number	Year
Life expectancy in years: Males	77.4	2003
Life expectancy in years: Females	82.4	2003
Infant mortality rate per 1000 live births	5.3	2004
Leading causes of death per 100 000:		
Cancer	215.3 (male)	2003
	148.1 (female)	
Heart diseases	178.9 (male)	
	98.2 (female)	
Cerebrovascular diseases	41.6 (male)	
	34.7 (female)	
Body mass index in % of pop. Females normal (18.5–24.9 BMI)	51.8	2005
% Females obese (30+ BMI)	14.2	2005
% Males normal (18.5–24.9 BMI)	40.5	2005
% Males obese (30+ BMI)	16.8	2005
Fertility rate per 1000 pop.	1.53	2004

Source: Statistics Canada, 2009, Health—Social Indicators. *Retrieved April 2, 2009 (http://www.statcan.gc.ca/pub/11-008-x/2006007/t/ 4097835-eng.htm).*

cause dramatic incapacitation and sometimes death (Weitz 2007). Acute diseases that are still common in Canada are chicken pox and influenza. Recently, too, multi–drug-resistant strains of tuberculosis, Lyme disease, and HIV (the virus that causes AIDS) and various kinds of flu (e.g., swine, bird, and so on) have become pressing health problems, problems exacerbated by global trade—which has increased 1000 percent since World War II—and the worldwide movement of 1.5 billion airplane passengers per year (Donnelly 2003). (See Box 10.1.)

With the overall decline in death from acute illnesses in high-income nations, however, has come a

BOX 10.1   HIV/AIDS Worldwide

Although chronic diseases have replaced infectious diseases as the major cause of death in Canada, infectious diseases are still a problem here and a problem of epidemic proportions in low-income countries. Certainly the most widely publicized of these diseases is HIV/AIDS. In Canada, 49 000 people are living with HIV/AIDS, but in the rest of the world, 33.2 million, including 3.2 million children, are living with the disease. In 2007 alone, 2.7 million people, including 400 000 children, were newly infected with HIV (UNAIDS 2008). Map 10.1 shows the distribution of HIV/AIDS around the world. Note the huge number of 22.5 million people living with the disease in sub-Saharan Africa. While this area contains 10 percent of the world's population, it has 70 percent of its HIV/AIDS cases. Throughout the world, over 20 million people are thought to have died of AIDS, but this figure is difficult to confirm.

MAP 10.1   A Global View of HIV/AIDS

Adults and children estimated to be living with HIV/AIDS, 2007

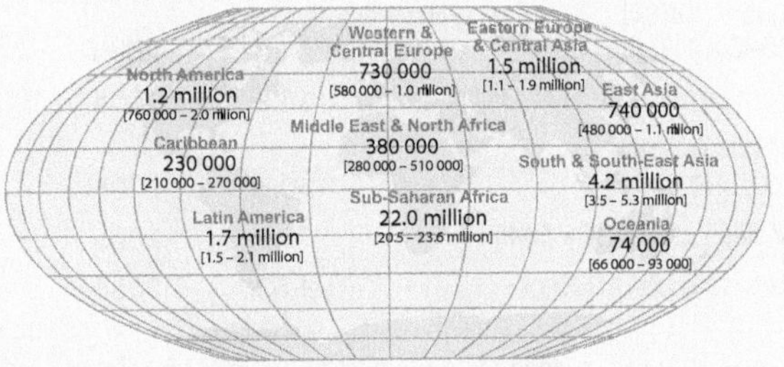

Total: 33 million (30 – 36 million)

Source: UNAIDS 2008. Reproduced with permission of UNAIDS.

In different parts of the world, various approaches have been taken to prevent and treat HIV/AIDS. In Canada and in the Western world generally, since the early 1980s, the approach has been an aggressive educational campaign. A dramatic example of this was the advertising campaign of the AIDS Committee of Toronto urging the use of condoms. These advertisements, called "Condom Country," mimicked Marlborough cigarette advertisements with pictures of rugged cowboys in a Western setting.

Action has also been vigorous in some developing countries. Thailand confronted the problem in 1991 by distributing condoms, shutting down brothels that didn't use them, and requiring radio stations to broadcast HIV/AIDS prevention information hourly. These actions have been effective. In 1990 in Thailand, there were 215 000 new cases of HIV/AIDS; by the early 2000s, the number of new cases was expected to be down to about 90 000 (Shenon 1996).

Fighting HIV/AIDS in India means fighting more than the disease. It means fighting the caste system, because prostitutes and those with HIV/AIDS are discriminated against. It means fighting social taboos against talking about sex. It means fighting poverty, because prostitutes who use condoms lose clients and starve. And it means fighting the denial of the problem by political leaders; only US$35 million of a five-year US$100 million HIV/AIDS prevention program had been spent in four years (Burns 1996).

In many parts of sub-Saharan Africa, the situation is even worse. While this area contains 10 percent of the world's population, it has 70 percent of its HIV/AIDS cases. All governments are undertaking prevention programs, such as the provision of drugs to rape victims and measures to prevent mother-to-child transmission of HIV/AIDS (South Africa reversed its policy of not providing drugs in April 2002).

There is hope, however. In early 2001, after vigorous lobbying by HIV/AIDS activists, the United Nations, and governments of developing countries, five drug companies (Boehringer Ingelheim, Bristol-Myers Squibb, F. Hoffman-LaRoche, GlaxoSmithKline, and Merck) agreed to reduce the price of HIV/AIDS drugs such as antiretrovirals, and generic versions of these drugs are now being produced at costs far below Western prices (UNDP 2001:22). Now over 3 million people are receiving antiretrovirals, costing about US$2.7 billion annually (Picard 2008:A11). In 2008 the federal government will spend $84 million on HIV/AIDS prevention and support programs. How do you think Canada can best contribute to worldwide HIV/AIDS prevention?

corresponding increase in **chronic diseases**—illnesses that are long term or lifelong and that develop gradually or are present from birth (Weitz 2007). Table 10.1 indicates that the three leading causes of death are chronic diseases: cancer, heart, and cerebrovascular diseases. Chronic diseases are caused by various biological, social, and environmental factors. In Chapter 8, we discussed two of the most common sources of chronic disease and premature death: tobacco use, which increases mortality among both smokers and people who breathe the tobacco smoke of others; and alcohol abuse. According to some social analysts, we can attribute many chronic diseases in our society to the *manufacturers of illness*, groups that promote illness-causing behaviour and social conditions, such as smoking (McKinlay 1994). The effect of chronic diseases on life expectancy varies because some chronic diseases are progressive (e.g., emphysema worsens over time), whereas others are constant (e.g., paralysis after a stroke); also, some are fatal (lung cancer), but others are not (arthritis and sinusitis). Because of the combination of longer life expectancies and the disabling consequences of some diseases, new terms have been coined—for example, "active" life or health expectancy and "disability-free" life expectancy. These terms emphasize good health rather than ill health and death. In Canada, from 1995 to 1997, **disability-free life expectancy**—the number of years of life that can be expected to be free of activity limitation—was 70 years for females and 67 years for males, which when subtracted from the life expectancies mentioned above indicate more than 12 years of disability for females and 10 years of disability for males (Statistics Canada 2008o:42).

Sex and Gender, Class, and Indigenous Status

Life expectancy and chronic diseases vary substantially by major demographic variables. Females have had longer life expectancies than males for decades. However, non-fatal diseases or conditions are more common among females. In this chapter, much data comes from early waves of the National Population Health Survey (NPHS). The NPHS was conducted by Health Canada and Statistics Canada to measure the health status of adult, non-Indigenous Canadians and to monitor changes over time. (Children and Indigenous adults [i.e., adults with "Aboriginal status"] were surveyed separately.) The content is multidimensional, including physical, mental, and social components, and the method is in-depth interviewing. The first wave of data collection occurred in 1994–95 and consisted of a sample of 17 626 Canadians, and subsequent waves were undertaken in 1996–97 and 1998–99.

According to the 1998–99 NPHS, larger percentages of females than males aged 12 and over reported having arthritis (19 percent versus 11 percent), high blood pressure (13 percent versus 9 percent), migraine (13 percent versus 4 percent), and bronchitis/emphysema (3 percent versus 2 percent). A higher percentage of males than females reported having heart disease (5 percent versus 4 percent) and diabetes (4 percent versus 3 percent; Statistics Canada 2001b:25). The reasons for these differences could be a combination of factors that contribute to females' longer life expectancies, such as

- consuming lower levels of drugs, tobacco, and alcohol (see Chapter 8);
- not working in hazardous occupations, like mining and construction; and
- having biological protection during the childbearing years, during which females have lower levels of heart disease (but later, women are subject to more disease).

Class, measured by income, is related to longevity. According to the NPHS, people in lower-income groups in 1994–95 had a higher mortality rate than those in upper-income groups (Statistics Canada 1998a). Class, measured by income and education, is also related to chronic conditions. According to the Joint Canada/United States Survey of Health, Canadians (and Americans) who were in the poorest income quintile were much more likely than those in the richest quintile to report fair/poor health status (23 versus 4 percent; see Figure 10.3). As well, higher percentages of people with university degrees than people with elementary or less education reported having excellent or very good health (see Figure 5.5 on page 113 in Chapter 5). The reasons for these differences are likely a combination of people with lower levels of education

- being unable to afford nutritious food (Richard's opening quote is telling, but evidence also comes from a study of welfare incomes and expenses in Toronto: given the cost of housing, welfare did not cover housing and the cost of food for a single-person household, a two-parent two-child family, and a single-parent two-child family [Vozoris et al. 2002]);
- engaging in risky health behaviour such as smoking, drinking, and drug use (see Chapter 8);

- working in dangerous industries; and
- living in some areas, including the North, far from medical care. (In the Yukon and Northwest Territories in 1993, people were an average distance of 23.6 and 155.2 kilometres from the nearest physician, and population per physician was much higher than in the 10 provinces, according to a chart from the Canadian Medical Association [Hewa 2002:66].)

Indigenous status is a very important predictor of life expectancy and illness, both acute and chronic. The high overall life expectancy of almost 80 years for Canadians generally does not hold for Indigenous people. A gap of six years exists between the life expectancy of Indigenous people and that of the general population (Frideres 2002:155). In addition, infant mortality among Indigenous people is still high. It was 12.0 in 1997, or more than twice the rate for Canada as a whole (Frideres 2002:155). According to sociologist James Frideres (2002:156–157), Indigenous people have lower life expectancy, higher infant mortality, and higher rates of infectious diseases, such as tuberculosis and HIV/AIDS, than the general Canadian population; chronic conditions, including diabetes and cancer, are likewise increasing. The reasons for these differences are similar to those for class-related differences in health, including:

- high levels of poverty, with the accompanying poor housing and sanitary conditions;
- higher rates of risky health behaviour; and
- being distant from medical care in Nunavut, Yukon, and the Northwest Territories.

The Canadian Community Health Survey (2000–2001) investigated the health of off-reserve Indigenous people. In comparison with the total population of Canada, a smaller percentage of off-reserve Indigenous people report being in excellent or very good health for both sexes and every age level (see Figure 5.6 on page 115 in Chapter 5). In comparison, the percentage of Indigenous seniors who report this high level of health is just below those with less than high-school education in the general population. This finding might also be predicted from the fact that 79 percent of Indigenous seniors have less than high-school education.

Besides sex and gender, class, and Indigenous status, many other structural variables, including marital status, social support, neighbourhood, and inequality of income in society, affect the health of people. Determining the relative influence of these variables and the health behaviour variables identified in Chapter 8 is not an easy task. With the comprehensive set of questions about health behaviour and social structural variables in the National Population Health Survey, it is possible to begin this analysis. Using the NPHS data, sociologists Margaret Denton and Vivienne Walters (1999) studied the relative influence of health variables—such as smoking, drinking, physical activity, and weight—and structural variables—such as family structure, education, occupation, income, and social support—on subjective health status and functional health status data from the Health Utilities Index (in the NPHS), which inquires into vision, hearing, speech, mobility, cognition, emotion, and so on. They discovered that the social structural variables had a greater effect on health than the health variables. This finding confirms that health and illness are social problems and suggests that changing social conditions would be more helpful than health promotion in improving health. Denton and Walters also found differences between males and females. Females' health was determined more by structural variables (e.g., being in the highest income bracket, working full-time, caring for a family, and having social support) than males' health. Regarding the influence of risky health behaviour, males' health was determined more by smoking and drinking, and females' health was determined more by exercise and weight. For both men and women, a non-heterosexual sexual orientation can also be a factor in health, due to ignorance and discrimination on the part of doctors and other health care professionals.

Disability

Some chronic diseases produce disabilities that significantly increase health care costs for individuals and for society. *Disability* can be defined in several ways. Medical professionals tend to define it in terms of organically based impairments—that is, the problem is entirely within the body (Albrecht 1992). However, disability rights advocates believe that disability is a physical or health condition that stigmatizes or causes discrimination. Perhaps the best way to define disability is, as medical sociologist Rose Weitz (2007) has said, in terms of both physical and social factors: **disability** is a restricted or total lack of ability to perform certain activities as a result of physical or mental limitations or the interplay of these limitations, social responses, and the social environment. In Canada, the Participation and Activity Limitation Survey showed in 2006 that an estimated 4.4 million people, or 14.4 percent of the population, had one or more physical or mental disabilities (Statistics Canada 2007b). Older people have more disabilities than younger; women have more severe disabilities than men; and many kinds of disabilities exist. Mobility and pain-related disabilities are most prevalent among those aged 15 and over. Mobility is the prime disability experienced by 12.2 percent of women and 8.6 of men. While women experience most disabilities more than men, men experience more hearing, learning, and speech problems (Statistics Canada 2004g:16).

Disabilities are an important social problem because people with disabilities have higher unemployment rates and lower incomes than those without disabilities. While some of these differences are likely due to those living with disabilities being unable to work, others point instead to discrimination against those with disabilities. This is called, following the examples of racism and sexism, ableism. **Ableism** is prejudice and discrimination against people because of a physical or mental disability. In the recent past, among those 25 to 64 years of age in 2001, 10.7 percent of the disabled were unemployed versus 5.9 percent of the non-disabled. Among those 25 to 54 years of age in 2001, 47 percent of the disabled had incomes below $15 000 versus 25 percent of the non-disabled (Statistics Canada 2004g:18). In addition, many disabled people need specialized equipment—wheelchairs (some motorized), hearing aids, and so on—and some need help with everyday tasks (Statistics Canada 2004g:17). Since 2001, an improvement in employment has occurred for those with every kind of disability, as shown in Figure 10.1. That

FIGURE 10.1   Employment Rates by Activity Limitation Type

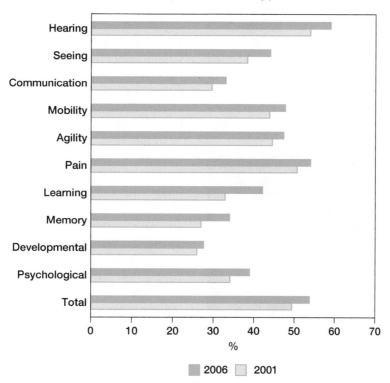

Note: 2001 data are not available for the Yukon, Northwest, Territories, and Nunavut.

Source: Statistics Canada, 2008, "Participation and Activity Limitation Survey," The Daily (July 24).

differences still exist may point to some continuation of ableism.

The number of disabled people continues to increase for several reasons. First, with advances in medical technology, many people who in the past would have died from an accident or illness now survive with impairment. Second, as people live longer, they are more likely to experience chronic diseases (such as arthritis) that may have disabling consequences (Albrecht 1992). Third, people born with serious disabilities are more likely to survive infancy because of medical technology. (However, only a small percentage of people with a disability today were born with it; accidents, disease, and violence account for most disabilities in this country.) Many people with a chronic illness or disability will not live out the full life expectancy for people in their age category.

Obesity

A relatively new health risk—being overweight—is now affecting about half the Canadian population. Excess weight is linked to heart disease, Type II diabetes, back problems, certain forms of cancer, and stroke. A healthy weight range is indicated by the body mass index (BMI), which is calculated by dividing weight in kilograms (kg) by height in metres squared (m^2). A person with a BMI of less than 18.5 is considered underweight; with a BMI of 18.6 to 24.9, of normal

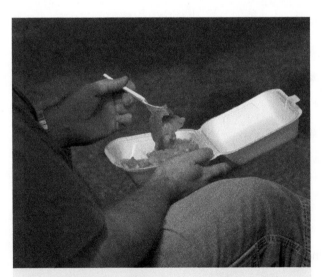

According to a recent Canadian Community Health Survey, 23 percent of adult Canadians are obese. What kinds of problems does this increasing trend present for the health care system in the future?

weight; with a BMI of 25.0 to 29.9, overweight; and with a BMI of 30.0+, obese.

According to a report of the Canadian Community Health Survey (CCHS) in 2004, 2.7 percent of Canadians aged 15 and older were underweight; 46.7 percent were of normal weight; one-third were overweight; and 14.9 percent were obese. Whereas 15.9 percent of men were obese, 13.9 percent of women were obese (Statistics Canada 2004a). These figures were based on self-reports. In 2005 the CCHS released figures obtained with actual measurements and found not only higher rates of obesity (23 percent for Canadian adults), but also big increases for some age groups in comparison with figures obtained in 1978–79. Increases have been seen in obesity for the age groups 12 to 17 (from 3 to 9 percent), 25 to 34 (from 9 to 21 percent), and 75+ (from 11 to 24 percent) over the past 25 years (Statistics Canada 2005b).

A curvilinear pattern was found for age, with middle-aged people being the most likely to be obese. Region of the country is also important. People in Newfoundland and Labrador and New Brunswick were found to have higher rates of obesity than people in the rest of the country. The latest figures from the Canadian Community Health Survey in 2007 show that the dramatic increases in obesity have ended. No change was found in the percentages overweight (32 percent) and obese (16 percent) for those 18 and older (Statistics Canada, 2008c).

Obesity is not just a problem for Canadians; it is a problem worldwide. Although data are difficult to confirm, as of 2000, the WHO estimates the number of obese adults to be over 300 million worldwide. And obesity is not limited to Western societies. The WHO (2003) estimates that over 115 million people in developing countries also suffer from obesity-related problems. If the proportion of overweight to obese people found in Canada were true of the rest of the developed world, nearly 1 billion people would be overweight or obese.

How can we reduce the overweight/obesity problem? Besides the usual suggestions for self-help groups, increased physical activity, and better diets, suggestions now include putting caloric counts on menus; putting health warnings, like those found on cigarette packages, on packages of junk food; and adding a tax to junk food to discourage consumption (see Box 10.2).

SOCIAL PROBLEMS AND SOCIAL POLICY

BOX 10.2   Taxing Food and Restricting Food Additives

In an effort to help reduce obesity, various jurisdictions, including California and New York, have made it mandatory for fast-food restaurants to prominently post caloric counts of their menus. The Ontario Medical Association is recommending something similar (2008). It wants the provincial government to enact legislation requiring caloric labelling on menus and menu boards of school cafeterias and chain restaurants and an educational campaign to inform Ontarians about the relations between the intake of calories and weight gain and obesity.

Few would object to caloric information and educational campaigns to promote weight control and physical activity. But would you go along with increased taxation on sugared drinks? We know that the intake of sugared beverages is associated with increased body weight, and poor nutrition and increasing consumption increases risk for obesity and diabetes (Brownell and Frieden 2009). We know that sugared beverages are marketed extensively to children and adolescents, and in the mid-1990s in the United States, children's intake of sugared beverages surpassed that of milk (Brownell and Frieden 2009). Kelly Brownell, director of Yale's Rudd Center for Food Policy and Obesity, and New York Health Commissioner Thomas Frieden (2009), reporting other studies, state:

> In the past decade, per capita intake of calories from sugar-sweetened beverages has increased by nearly 30 percent; beverages now account for 10 to 15 percent of the calories consumed by children and adolescents. For each extra can or glass of sugared beverage consumed per day, the likelihood of a child's becoming obese increases by 60 percent.

They then argue for a tax on sugared beverages to reduce their consumption and to pay for some of the costs of obesity. Brownell and Frieden report that some have estimated the annual costs at US$79 billion (2009). If this is true, the costs to Canadians could be over $7 billion. Our rates of obesity are slightly lower. To support the effectiveness of a tax, Brownell and Frieden use the analogy that taxing smoking was effective in reducing consumption of tobacco and the huge costs of its health effects.

In the same way, taxing sugared drinks can help reduce consumption and obesity and offset the costs of its effects.

Objections to the tax include that it is regressive in taxing the poor the most; that it singles out one kind of food for a tax (Why soft drinks and not packaged desserts and candy?); and that taxing will not eliminate obesity, as it has not eliminated smoking. However, the poor are at greatest risk from obesity; no other food provides as many extra calories; and taxing smoking did have an influence on reducing, if not eliminating, it (see Chapter 8). Although hefty taxes are recommended by Brownell and Frieden to reduce consumption, too high a tax can have the unintended consequence of encouraging smuggling, as Ontario discovered in 1993–1994 when high tobacco taxes caused cigarette smuggling.

The arguments for restrictions on food additives are similar. Although we know that reducing salt has been related to reducing high blood pressure, considerable controversy exists about whether overall low levels of salt are beneficial in the long run. For example, reducing salt can cause problems with blood flow to the kidneys and insulin resistance, which can increase the risk of strokes and heart attacks. Scientists also have discovered that salt, like chocolate and cocaine, can enhance the mood of rats, and rats deprived of salt experience lack of enjoyment of everyday activities. Thus, salt may prevent feelings of depression (Tierney 2009). Despite these uncertainties, Mayor Bloomberg of New York has proposed a nationwide plan to pressure restaurants and the food industry to cut salt in half over the next decade (Tierney 2009). *New York Times* columnist John Tierney suggests that if these proposals become law, people may have the opportunity to become part of an experiment for which they did not volunteer.

While no figures are available on the support for salt restrictions, Brownell and Frieden report that a small majority of polled New Yorkers support a "soda tax" and that the figure rises to 72 percent when the revenue is to prevent obesity. Would you buy fewer soft drinks if they were taxed an extra 10 percent? Do you think that restricting food additives by large amounts like 50 percent is a good thing?

On the other hand, people of size take exception to the prejudicial attitudes and discrimination they experience from society. They would call this the equivalent of ableism. Several organizations exist to change societies' attitudes and behaviour toward people who are fat, including the International Size Acceptance Association (see **http://www.size-acceptance.org**; a Canadian chapter has a website, but it has not been modified since 2005). The National Association to Advance Fat Acceptance, a U.S. organization, can be found at **http://www.naafa.org**, with up-to-date media releases, education, community, and other links.

MENTAL ILLNESS AS A SOCIAL PROBLEM

Mental illness is a social problem because of the number of people it affects, the difficulty of defining and identifying mental disorders, and the ways in which mental illness is treated. Although most social scientists use the terms *mental illness* and *mental disorder* interchangeably, many medical professionals distinguish between a *mental disorder*—a condition that makes it difficult or impossible for a person to cope with everyday life—and *mental illness*—a condition that requires extensive treatment with medication, psychotherapy, and sometimes hospitalization.

The most widely accepted classification of mental disorders is the American Psychiatric Association's (1994) *Diagnostic and Statistical Manual of Mental Disorders IV* (*DSM-IV*) (see Figure 10.2.) The *DSM* is now in its fourth edition, and with each revision, its list of disorders has changed and grown. Listings change partly because of new scientific findings, which permit more precise descriptions that are more useful than broad terms covering a wide range of behaviours, and partly because of changes in how we view mental

FIGURE 10.2   Mental Disorders Identified by the American Psychiatric Association

1. **Disorders first evident in infancy, childhood, or adolescence**	These disorders include mental retardation, attention-deficit hyperactivity, anorexia nervosa, bulimia nervosa, and stuttering.
2. **Organic mental disorders**	Psychological or behavioural disorders associated with dysfunctions of the brain caused by aging, disease, or brain damage.
3. **Substance-related disorders**	Disorders resulting from abuse of alcohol and/or other drugs, such as barbiturates, cocaine, or amphetamines.
4. **Schizophrenia and other psychotic disorders**	Disorders with symptoms such as delusions or hallucinations.
5. **Mood disorders**	Emotional disorders such as major depression and bipolar (manic-depressive) disorder.
6. **Anxiety disorders**	Disorders characterized by anxiety that is manifest in phobias, panic attacks, or obsessive-compulsive disorder.
7. **Somatoform disorders**	Psychological problems that present themselves as symptoms of physical disease such as hypochondria.
8. **Dissociative disorders**	Problems involving a splitting or dissociation of normal consciousness, such as amnesia and multiple personality.
9. **Eating or sleeping disorders**	Includes such problems as anorexia and bulimia or insomnia and other problems associated with sleep.
10. **Impulse control disorders**	Symptoms include the inability to control undesirable impulses, such as kleptomania, pyromania, and pathological gambling.
11. **Personality disorders**	Maladaptive personality traits that are generally resistant to treatment, such as paranoid and antisocial personality types.

Source: Adapted from American Psychiatric Association, 1994, **Diagnostic and Statistical Manual of Mental Disorders IV,** *Washington, DC: American Psychiatric Association.*

disorders culturally (at one time, for example, homosexuality was considered a mental disorder). Despite these changes, some social analysts still question the extent to which mental health professionals can accurately detect and treat mental disorders.

How many people are affected by mental illness? According to the Canadian Community Health Survey, as shown in Table 10.2, some 4 percent of people interviewed reported having experienced symptoms or feelings associated with major depression, almost 5 percent had experienced anxiety, and when substance dependence was included, 1 in 10 Canadians aged 15 and over had experienced mental problems at some time within 12 months of the interview.

Rates of mental illness are affected by gender, age, class, and Indigenous status. It is often thought that females have higher rates of mental illness, including depression and episodes that cause distress, than males; however, when alcohol and substance dependence are included, the researchers found little difference in prevalence (11 percent for females versus 10 percent for men). The same study found that youth aged 15 to 24 were more likely than other age groups to suffer from mental disorder or substance abuse problems. About 18 percent of them reported experiencing symptoms or feelings consistent with mental disorders or substance dependence. People in lower social classes have higher rates of mental disorders than people in upper classes. But according to sociologist Harley Dickinson (2002), this relationship could be explained by the "downward drift hypothesis"—that people with mental illnesses are unable to function properly, neither getting an education nor keeping a job. Thus, they slip into the lower classes (Dickinson 2002:376). Frideres (2002:157) states that, compared with the rest of the Canadian population, for Indigenous people the suicide rate is three times higher (six times for the 15 to 24 age group), the homicide rate is twice as high, and the rate of violent death is three times higher. Reasons for these differences are attributed to significant differences in living conditions, as mentioned previously, and lack of opportunities.

Treatment of Mental Illness

People who seek professional help for mental illness are treated with medication and psychotherapy to help them understand the underlying reasons for their problem. Because medication is used so routinely today, we tend to forget that institutionalization used to be the most common treatment for severe mental illness. In fact, the development of psychoactive drugs made possible the deinstitutionalization movement of the 1960s.

TABLE 10.2   Measured Mental Disorders or Substance Dependence in the Past 12 Months (as total number and percentage of the Canadian population)

	Total		Males		Females	
	Number	%	Number	%	Number	%
Major depression	1 120 000	4.5	420 000	3.4	700 000	5.5
Mania disorder	190 000	0.8	90 000	0.7	100 000	0.8
Any mood disorder	**1 210 000**	**4.9**	**460 000**	**3.8**	**750 000**	**5.9**
Panic disorder	400 000	1.6	130 000	1.1	270 000	2.1
Agoraphobia	180 000	0.7	40 000	0.4	140 000	1.1
Social anxiety disorder (social phobia)	750 000	3.0	310 000	2.6	430 000	3.4
Any anxiety disorder	**1 180 000**	**4.7**	**440 000**	**3.6**	**740 000**	**5.8**
Alcohol dependence	640 000	2.6	470 000	3.8	170 000	1.3
Illicit drug dependence	170 000	0.7	120 000	1.0	50 000	0.4
Substance dependence	**740 000**	**3.0**	**540 000**	**4.4**	**200 000**	**1.6**
Total—Any measured disorder or substance dependence	**2 600 000**	**10.4**	**1 190 000**	**9.7**	**1 410 000**	**11**

Source: Statistics Canada, 2003, "Canadian Community Health Survey: Mental Health and Well-being," The Daily (September 3), Catalogue no. 11-001.

Deinstitutionalization is the practice of discharging patients from mental hospitals into the community. Although deinstitutionalization was originally devised as a solution for the problem of warehousing mentally ill patients in large, prison-like mental hospitals in the first half of the 20th century, many social scientists now view deinstitutionalization as a problem. To understand how this solution evolved into a problem, one must understand the state of mental health care in Canada during the 1950s and 1960s. The practice of *involuntary commitment* (i.e., without a patient's consent) allowed many patients to be warehoused in mental hospitals for extended periods of time, with only minimal and sometimes abusive custodial care. According to sociologist Erving Goffman (1961), a mental hospital is a classic example of a **total institution**—a place where people are isolated from the rest of society for a period of time and come under the complete control of the officials who run the institution. Patients are stripped of their individual identities—or depersonalized—by being required to wear institutional clothing and follow a strict regimen of activities, meals, and sleeping hours; sometimes they are referred to impersonally as a "CMI" (a person who is chronically mentally ill; see Grobe 1995). The deinstitutionalization movement sought to release patients from mental hospitals so that they could live at home and go about their daily activities. Professionals believed that the patients' mental disorders could be controlled with medication and treatment through community-based mental health services. Other advocates hoped that deinstitutionalization would remove the stigma attached to hospitalization for mental illness.

Deinstitutionalization did occur in a substantial way in Canada. Between 1960 and 1976, the number of beds in mental hospitals declined from 47 633 to 15 011, although the number of beds in psychiatric wards in general hospitals increased from 844 to 5836 (Cochrane et al. 1997:1).

Although deinstitutionalization had worthwhile goals—protection of civil rights, more humane and less costly treatment—in too many cases, it simply moved people out of mental hospitals into the streets and jails. Today, critics of deinstitutionalization argue that it exacerbated long-term problems associated with treating mental illness.

Although there are many causes of homelessness, ranging from lack of affordable housing to drug dependency, some analysts believe that the deinstitutionalization of patients from mental hospitals has significantly increased the number of people living on the streets in Canada. What other alternatives can you suggest for dealing with mental illness?

THE "CRISIS" IN CANADIAN HEALTH CARE

We hear so often that the Canadian health care system is in a state of crisis. In this section, we will outline the development of the system and its current issues.

Development of the National Health Care System

While the idea of universal health care had been circulating for some time, and Saskatchewan had pioneered its major elements, the features of the national health care system emerged with the following pieces of federal legislation and recent changes in funding:

- The *Hospital Insurance and Diagnostic Service Act* 1957 provided insurance for hospital and diagnostic services.

- The *Medical Care Act* 1966 provided insurance for medical services, to which all the provinces agreed by 1972, emphasizing five principles: universality—all Canadians should be covered; accessibility—reasonable access must be unimpeded by financial or other barriers; comprehensiveness—all medically necessary services should be guaranteed; portability—Canadians should be able to have their benefits transferable to other provinces or other countries; and public administration—the system would be operated by a public body on a non-profit basis.

- The *Canada Health Act* 1984 confirmed the five principles and prohibited private charges or extra billing by doctors or hospitals.

- The federal government substantially reduced its contributions to the provinces in the mid-1990s to 26 percent or less of the total cost.

- The federal government increased its contributions to the provinces in 1999, but not to the 50 percent level established at the beginning.

- A federal–provincial agreement in February 2003 saw the federal government state that it would inject almost $35 billion into the health care system over the next five years to deal with catastrophic drug costs, promote electronic health records (EHRs), and so on. This was increased to $41 billion in the 2005 budget. In addition, a Health Care Council was formed to monitor progress toward these goals.

The many health care changes—such as reductions in the size, number, and functions of hospitals; increased use of drugs and home care; increased knowledge of health by patients and consultation of alternative health practitioners; and new technological developments for diagnosis and treatment—have brought about many issues that must be addressed.

Current Issues in the Health Care System

Coverage of Care

Since much of contemporary health care is neither hospital-based nor delivered by physicians, coverage of care is an issue. With the restructuring of hospitals, closing of hospital beds, and increases in out-patient procedures, the need for home care has grown. Home care ranges from visits just after hospital discharge to long-term help in maintaining independence. Not all such care is covered by the public health care system, especially the long-term general support. Although ministers of health have increased support for home care, demand seems to exceed supply. The cost of drugs can also be a problem for those in home care. During the past 25 years, the use and effectiveness of drugs has greatly increased, so that drugs now constitute 17.6 percent of health care costs (CIHI 2008). Drugs taken outside hospitals are not covered by the publicly funded system. Because not everyone, especially those among the poor, has an insurance plan to cover him or her, the need for "pharmacare," or government support of drug purchases, has increased. Several provinces have created plans where citizens pay a yearly fee after which the government pays for the drugs. An example of such a program is the British Columbia plan. In 1995, the B.C. government established its reference-based program where, for each class of drugs, a low-priced (not necessarily the lowest priced), effective drug is selected and the program will pay for it. If a higher-priced drug is desired, but no medical benefit is present, the individual pays the difference (Segall and Chappell 2000:252). Needs for other kinds of care, such as long-term care, palliative care, and dental care, are great and will likely increase as the population ages.

A substantial portion of the money in the governments' agreement of 2003 was supposed to be devoted to solving this set of problems, and the Health Care Council was set up to monitor progress on the plan. In the quote at the beginning of this chapter, the Health Council of Canada indicated that the glass is half full. There is no catastrophic drug care, and home care is covered only for two weeks (much less than people usually need), but progress has occurred in reducing wait times for diagnosis and surgery and providing more access to health information (Health Council of Canada 2008).

Accessibility

A second issue is accessibility. People complain of being unable to find a doctor and waiting lists for treatment. Regarding finding a doctor, data from the 2007 Canadian Community Health Survey show that the vast majority of Canadians have a doctor, but also provide information regarding access to a usual place of care. During 2007, 96 percent of Canadians aged 18 and older had either a regular medical doctor or a usual place of care, such as a walk-in clinic or an emergency room (Statistics Canada, 2008c). Further analysis showed that seniors were the group least likely (3 percent) to be unsuccessful in finding a doctor, and men were less successful than women in finding a doctor (Statistics Canada 2008c). Although many people do not have a regular doctor (some by choice), this is not because of a doctor shortage. Whether this continues to be the case is not possible to determine.

On a more positive note, progress has occurred in wait times, according to the Health Council of Canada (2008). For example, in Ontario, according to a 2008 report, wait times dropped substantially over the previous four years for cataract surgery (from 311 to 118 days), knee replacements (from 440 to 253 days), hip replacements (from 351 to 198 days), and cancer surgeries (from 81 to 57 days) (Ontario Health Quality Council 2008). To improve access, Ontario also has a website program, Ontario Wait Times (**http://ontariowaittimes.ca**), which permits patients to find a hospital for the above procedures with the shortest wait time and by proximity (if desired) by following a simple four-step process.

In early May 2009, the Princess Margaret Hospital in Toronto announced that it would provide a same-day diagnosis and treatment plan for breast cancer patients. The ability to do this so quickly was helped by a $12.5-million gift from private benefactors. But it does show that with organization and support, wait times can be substantially reduced.

In Canada, a major factor affecting access to health care is region. Region can be defined in several ways. Provinces are frequently used as the measure for region in Canada. A better measure for health purposes is the "health region." In Canada, 119 health regions have been designated. The advantage of using this measure is that variation within provinces can be identified. Access to health care both between and within provinces can thus be addressed. In the past, *Maclean's* ranked health regions in Canada according to indicators such as life expectancy,

low birth weight, incidence of pneumonia and flu, preventable hospital admissions, physicians and specialists per capita, and 10 other indicators. The "Fourth Annual Ranking" in 2002 covered 54 of the 119 regions (those with populations over 125 000) and captured 87 percent of the national population (Hawaleshka 2002:23). The ranking showed definite variation in Canada, where comprehensive health services are supposed to be accessible for all citizens. It also seemed to be reliable; a comparison with the "Third Annual Ranking" shows the same geographical differences in access to care (Marshall 2001).

As expected, communities with medical schools (and thus with teaching hospitals) appeared among those with the best scores. Edmonton leads the list (as in the "Second" and "Third" rankings), followed by Hamilton, Saskatoon, Ottawa, and Toronto. Thirteen of 15 "Communities with Medical Schools" appeared in the top half of the ranking. The next group, "Other Major Communities," which included wealthy suburbs like North and West Vancouver, and Mississauga, Brampton, and Burlington (Ontario), demonstrated that communities close to major centres profited from the proximity of medical centres and people's ability to afford the quality services available. These two regions stood first and fourth in the ranking overall. The third group, "Largely Rural Communities," tended to fall in the lower half of the rankings, with the notable exceptions of Kelowna, B.C.; Nanaimo, B.C.; Lethbridge, Alberta; Lévis, Quebec; and Moncton, New Brunswick. The top scorer in this group and the fifth overall, Kelowna, has developed programs to help residents stay healthy; for example, an outreach program teaches coronary-risk patients healthy habits, and a retirement community encourages residents to do as much as possible for themselves to prevent "learned helplessness" (Marshall 2001). While these figures are somewhat old, the Health Council of Canada has noted that regional disparities still exist. It is likely that many of these disparities are similar to those cited from the study of rankings.

Costs and Payment Methods

The overall costs of the health care system and the way they are paid is increasingly an issue. While the overall costs of the system have risen, they have been contained: health care costs were only 10.7 percent of the GDP in 2008 or $5170 per capita (CIHI 2008), a figure a little higher than that in the late 1980s. Although Canada has a single-payer, public method of financing health care, a private segment exists in our system—for cosmetic surgery, dental practice, eyeglasses, drugs outside hospitals, and other out-patient aids and services. It amounts to 30 percent of the total health care expenditures (CIHI 2008). While this private-care figure is high relative to that of some European countries, it is well below the United States' comparable figure of 55 percent.

In some countries with universal health care, people have an opportunity to pay for their own operations and thereby jump the public queue. The two-tier system of health care, with both public and private funding and delivery of health care, results in differential access—poorer access for those who cannot afford to pay. Pressure groups in the private sector are advocating that private clinics and services be made available for people who can afford to pay for them. But many others fear that allowing two tiers in the health system will reduce overall support for the public system.

However, the Supreme Court of Canada made a historic ruling in June 2005 that may significantly alter our health care system. In a battle that originated in Quebec and that pitted against each other two institutions (the public health care system and the *Charter of Rights and Freedoms*) that Canadians hold in high esteem, the Supreme Court of Canada ruled that the Quebec government cannot prevent people from paying for private insurance for procedures covered under the public system. Unreasonable wait times pose a threat to our rights to "life, liberty, and security of the person." While this ruling was for the province of Quebec, it has implications for the rest of the country. The case was brought by an individual who was waiting almost a year for hip surgery and also involved Dr. Chaoulli, who was trying to set up a private hospital in Quebec. The Quebec government has stated that as of October 2009, 56 procedures (e.g., hip and knee replacements, cataracts, mastectomies, and hysterectomies) can be contracted out, and doctors will be able to participate in both the public and private systems. People with private insurance or with cash will not have to wait in a public queue. How this ruling will affect the health care system in Quebec and how many provinces will follow suit are difficult to determine at this time. While people may decide to pay for reasonably inexpensive elective surgery, such as hip replacement and cataract surgery, to get it quickly, they likely would not be able to pay for cancer care that can cost hundreds of thousands of dollars.

What is the recent news about two-tier health care in your province? How do you expect it to change in the future?

Supply and Demand of Health Care Professionals

How can we ensure that we have enough health care professionals? Are health care networks an efficient operating model, and if so, how should practitioners be paid? After laying off nurses in the mid-1990s as a cost-cutting measure and after reducing positions in medical schools because of a fear of a surplus of doctors, Canada's provinces now face the possibility of a severe shortage of nurses and doctors. In May 2009, a nursing report suggested that by 2022, we will need 60 000 nurses, about 27 percent of the current nursing labour force, unless nursing enrolment increases, nurses can be encouraged not to leave the field early, and nurses can become more productive (Picard 2009:L1). In May 2008, the Ontario Medical Association (OMA) placed an advertisement in the *Globe and Mail* to promote its Campaign for Healthier Care, stating that Ontario is short 2000 doctors and that 1 million adults aged 18 and over and 130 000 children do not have access to a doctor. The OMA predicts that with the aging of the population, increased rates of cancer and diabetes, and expected retirement of doctors, a central question will be, "Will I find a doctor?" (OMA 2008). Part of this prediction included the expectation that doctors would retire at age 65. It has been suggested that the recession of 2008–2009 might discourage early retirement of doctors. Perhaps this will happen to nurses also.

Not only is there a need for more professionals, but also their payment and organization of work are concerns. Doctors have seen their salaries fall somewhat in the past 30 years, and nurses have experienced several pay freezes in that time. Doctors are paid on a fee-for-service basis and have been criticized for "churning," or having patients return for multiple visits for a problem. They have also been criticized for trying to see too many in a single day. More imaginative methods of payment, for example, *roster*, or *capitation*—payment per patient in the care of a small network of doctors, nurses, and other health workers, where the incentive is to keep people well and reduce the care they require—should be offered. Local community health centres were formed in Quebec in the 1970s. In Ontario, some health centres exist offering a variety of health and social services. Several years ago, in Ontario, the Ministry of Health asked doctors if they would be interested in setting up family health networks consisting of at least five doctors and some nurses. The doctors would work normal hours, and a nurse triage system (organizing patients according to the severity of their problems) would be available after hours so that patients would have 24/7 coverage. In questionnaires sent to general practitioners, a small percentage of doctors responded positively, but others were not interested in changing their pattern of fee-for-service, perhaps because they were offered only $97 per person per year for the care (Smith 2002:A8). The results suggest that a wider variety of options are likely needed if networks are to gain more support.

Quality of Care

Two measures of quality of care are (a) Canadians' rating of the system and (b) international comparisons. Regarding ratings by Canadians of their health care system, the figures for health indicators from three surveys show that consistently over half of the past decade, 90 percent of Canadians have been "somewhat satisfied" or "very satisfied" with the services provided by physicians (Health Canada 2006).

In terms of international comparisons, in 2008, the Conference Board of Canada rated several OECD countries' health care systems, and Canada's did not rate so well. It ranked 10th out of 16 countries' systems (see Table 10.3). This comparison was based on many measures, including

- life expectancy;
- self-reported health;
- premature mortality;
- mortality due to cancer;
- mortality due to circulatory diseases;
- mortality due to diabetes (due to increased obesity); and
- infant mortality.

TABLE 10.3   Canada's Overall Health Performance

REPORT CARD

Health

#	Country	Grade
1	Japan	A
2	Switzerland	A
3	Italy	A
4	Norway	A
5	Sweden	B
6	France	B
7	Finland	B
8	Germany	B
9	Australia	B
10	Canada	B
11	Netherlands	C
12	Austria	C
13	Ireland	C
14	U.K.	D
15	Denmark	D
16	U.S.	D

Note: Data are not available for Belgium. For the rest, data for the most recent year available were used.

Source: The Conference Board of Canada, 2008, Health Report Card (http://sso.conferenceboard.ca/HCP/deatils/health/aspx).

Canada did well in self-reported health status and low premature mortality (both As), and poorer in infant mortality and mortality due to diabetes (both Cs). Canada has had this middle ranking consistently over the past several years (Conference Board of Canada 2008).

Use of Technology

Large flows of information take place among providers of traditional, alternative, and robotic care (e.g., surgical procedures at a distance). Electronic Health Records (EHRs) have been promoted as a way of dealing with this problem. Because of the cost of implementing this approach, Canada has been slow to move patients to EHRs, and the Health Care Council noted the slow movement in its report. Prince Edward Island and Alberta are the provinces furthest along in this plan. However, in the federal budget of early 2009, new money was made available to promote EHRs, so it is likely that the plan will be implemented more quickly. One other suggestion is that a chip with the EHR be placed on the health card, so that doctors will have a record of the patient's history and thus be able to provide better care. Other pioneering technologies include electronic monitors to permit medical surveillance at a distance and reduce the need for home care.

These are some of the major issues faced by our health care system. Not only do others exist, but more will also emerge with the social and technological developments that are continuously taking place.

PERSPECTIVES ON ILLNESS AND HEALTH CARE PROBLEMS

What are the primary causes of health care problems in Canada? How can health care be improved? The answers that social scientists give to these questions depend on their theoretical framework. Analysts approaching these questions from a functionalist perspective focus on how illness affects the smooth operation of society and how medicine serves as a social institution. Some sociologists, using a conflict perspective, focus on how a capitalist economy affects health and health care delivery. Those who use an interactionist framework look at the social and cultural factors affecting communication between doctors and patients. Finally, feminist theorists look at inequalities of racialization, class, and sex and gender.

The Functionalist Perspective

The functionalist perspective views illness as a threat to a smoothly functioning society, which depends on all people fulfilling their appropriate social roles. According to this view, when people become ill, they cannot fulfill their everyday responsibilities to family, their employer, or the larger society and instead adopt the *sick role*—patterns of behaviour expected from individuals who are ill. Sociologist Talcott

Parsons (1951) identified four role expectations of the sick role:

1. Sick people are not responsible for their incapacity.
2. They are exempted from their usual role and task obligations.
3. They must want to leave the sick role and get well.
4. They are obligated to seek and comply with the advice of a medical professional.

In other words, illness is a form of deviance that must be controlled. According to Parsons, physicians are the logical agents of social control. By certifying that a person is physically or mentally ill and by specifying how the ill person should behave, doctors use their professional authority to monitor people with illnesses, thereby granting them only a temporary reprieve from their usual social roles and responsibilities. Today, however, the dramatic increase in chronic illness and disorganization in the delivery system for medical services mean that many people have less access to doctors, and doctors have less control over those aspects of patients' lives that can increase their chances of becoming ill. Acknowledging these major changes, sociologist Alexander Segall has modified the original conception of the sick role by identifying six expectations. The rights of sick people comprise

- making decisions about health-related matters;
- being exempt from performing usual well roles; and
- making use of social support and depending on others outside the medical profession.

The duties of sick people comprise

- maintaining health and managing illness;
- engaging in routine self-health management; and
- making use of available health care resources. (Segall and Chappell 2000:2)

These changes take into account both the increase in chronic conditions and the need for a more active rather than passive role for the sick person.

Functionalists believe that the problems in Canadian health care are due to macrolevel changes, such as the development of high-tech medicine and drugs; restructuring of the system, including the reduction of the hospital sector; and increased demand for health care by consumers. As a result of these changes, the equilibrium of the system has been greatly affected, and procedures must be implemented to restore the equilibrium. Some observers, writing in a functionalist manner, state that incremental changes will solve the problems. For example, C. David Naylor, then dean of the Faculty of Medicine and now president of the University of Toronto, suggested that incremental changes—such as strengthened home care services, provision of a more equitable coverage of prescription drugs, wider adoption of blended compensation mechanisms (e.g., salary, roster, and fee-for-service) for physicians, primary-care reform, integrated regional services, quality improvement initiatives, and better information gathering—are the best ways for the health care system to "be rendered more accountable, integrated, and sustainable in the next millennium" (Naylor 1999:24).

The Conflict Perspective

The conflict approach is based on the assumption that problems in health care delivery are rooted in the capitalist economy, which views medicine as a commodity available to those who can pay for it and produced and sold by the medical–industrial complex.

The idea that medicine is a commodity is shown in the United States by data on health insurance coverage. Whereas in Canada everyone has health insurance, in the United States in 2006 about 47 million people did not have health insurance (DeNavas-Walt et al. 2007). The health status consequences for Americans in comparison with those for Canadians are significant.

Figure 10.3 shows that while the rich people of both countries are less likely than the poor to report fair/poor health, the poor of the United States are more likely to report fair/poor health than the poor of Canada. Whereas 23 percent of the poorest Canadian group reported fair/poor health, 31 percent of the poorest American group reported fair/poor health (Statistics Canada 2004c).

The **medical–industrial complex** encompasses both local physicians and hospitals as well as global health-related industries such as the pharmaceutical and medical supply companies that deliver health care. Although this expression was coined to typify the U.S.

health care system, it applies in part to the Canadian system also. For example, the pharmaceutical companies have been well known to put profits first, as outlined by physician Joel Lexchin (2002). Lexchin (2002:402) argues that when profit and health considerations come into conflict, profit is likely to be the primary consideration. He gives the examples of Lilly's anti-arthritis drug, benoxaprofen, where the company did not mention to the Canadian Health Protection Branch reviewing the drug that eight deaths had occurred in Britain, and Bristol-Myers Squibb's statin drug, Pravachol (pravastatin), where the Canadian Coordinating Office for Health Technology Assessment reported that all statins were equivalent (Bristol-Myers Squibb sued them).

Radical conflict theorists say that only when inequalities based on sex and gender, class, and racialization/ethnicity—and on occupation, neighbourhood, and region—are reduced and a system based on a different treatment model is developed will inequalities in health outcomes be reduced. For example, observers such as sociologists Pat Armstrong and Hugh Armstrong (2003:160) want to see a

FIGURE 10.3 Fair/Poor Health by Households' Income Quintile, Canada and the United States, 2002 to 2003

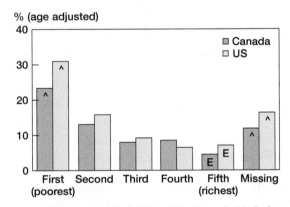

^ Statistically significant difference between Canada and the United States (p<0.05).
E Interpret with caution (high sampling variability).

Source: Statistics Canada, 2004, "Joint Canada/United States Survey of Health," The Daily (June 2), Catalogue no. 11-001.

system that is oriented to a care model and not to a medical model like the present one. They advocate applying the four determinants of health identified in the Lalonde Report (by the then federal minister of health, Marc Lalonde [1974])—human biology, lifestyle, environment, and health care—to the provision of services: emphasizing health maintenance and promotion; improving occupational and income opportunities; and improving the physical and social environment. As long as variable societal conditions—environmental pollution, lack of affordable housing, high levels of stress associated with working conditions or unemployment, inadequate nutrition, lack of early diagnosis for diseases such as breast cancer and heart disease, and type of available health model—affect people, health outcomes will be unequal.

Some conflict theorists also call attention to the unintended negative effects of doctors and suggest that the doctor–patient relationship should be demystified. An early theorist of the negative effects of doctors and the system was Ivan Illich, who coined the term **iatrogenesis** to describe problems caused by doctors and the health care system. These problems are of three types. *Clinical iatrogenesis* occurs when pain, sickness, and death result from medical care. The term used in Canada is "adverse effects." A study of 2000–2001 hospital records in Canada found that adverse effects, such as the wrong medication or dose, infection, adverse transfusion reactions, and in-hospital hip fractures, occurred in 7.5 percent of hospital admissions, and of these, 36.9 percent were preventable and 20.8 percent resulted in death (Baker et al. 2004). Projected to Canada's 2.5 million annual admissions, this study suggests that 185 000 adverse effects occur annually, and 70 000 of these are preventable. *Social iatrogenesis* occurs when the health care system creates dependency and ill health, for example, by discouraging home births. *Cultural iatrogenesis* occurs when the system undermines the ability of people to care for themselves (Illich 1975:165). Conflict theorists argue that if patients were given the information and resources they need for prevention, self-treatment, and home care, the need and demand for expensive medical care would be greatly reduced (Stewart 1995). And some of these theorists are doctors themselves. The Medical Reform Group (http://www.medicalreformgroup.ca) is a Toronto-based voluntary association of physicians and medical students who believe that the medical profession must look to the social, economic, and political forces shaping health and health care in Canada. They believe that health care is a right and that today's health care is too hierarchical, giving too much power to doctors and not enough to patients.

Another group that challenges accepted thinking in the area of health is disability rights organizations. They are especially concerned with the public's support of euthanasia, or "mercy killing," of people with disabilities who cannot speak for themselves. A recent example of this is the Tracy Latimer story (see Box 5.2 on page 119 in Chapter 5). Tracy Latimer was a 12-year-old girl with severe cerebral palsy. Her father asphyxiated her, was tried and convicted of her killing, and was sentenced to prison. Disability rights advocates argue that it would not be a problem to have a disability if persons with disabilities were not discriminated against and oppressed. In the United States, a rights group that campaigns against euthanasia is called Not Dead Yet (from the film *Monty Python and the Holy Grail*, in which someone about to be put on a cart of plague victims says, "I'm not dead yet"). Its website is http://notdeadyetnewscommentary.blogspot.com.

The Interactionist Perspective

Interactionists believe that many problems pertaining to health and illness in our society are linked to social factors that influence how people define our health care system. According to interactionists, we socially construct notions of crisis according to our desire to promote political objectives. The doctors' advertisement mentioned earlier seems to fall into this category.

Interactionists are also interested in using telecommunications to promote health. A relatively new method being tried is Telehealth, a toll-free, confidential telecare service. For example, Telehealth Ontario, a program introduced in Ontario that follows models in other parts of the country, is a free, confidential telephone service anyone can call to get health advice or general health information from a registered nurse. Available 24 hours a day, 7 days a week, it provides information on symptoms, illness, medications, nutrition and health, help for teens, and so on, but does not provide prescriptions or specific doctor referrals, and it is not a substitute for emergency (911) calls.

In the past, most patients relied on doctors for health-related information. Today, many people receive medical information from the media and the Internet. Many thousands of websites are devoted to health and medical information, ranging from potentially life-saving research in top medical journals to alternative therapies such as herbal preparations and colon irrigation (Fisher 1996; Kolata 1996b). Many computer bulletin boards, chat groups, and Usenet newsgroups have emerged to support people with conditions such as HIV/AIDS and multiple sclerosis (Kantrowitz 1993). Some sites (e.g., CarePages and CaringBridge) allow people with a particular disease or condition to write a daily report on their condition so that friends can keep up with how things are progressing. Some U.S. corporations have online ventures that offer not only research on any health care topic but also information on physicians, nurses, hospitals, HMOs, and preferred provider organizations—in the United States, fees come from the providers, not from users viewing the pages (Fisher 1996). Because of the proliferation of medical information on the Internet, Health Canada is working to provide guidance to the consumer. Whether or not this proliferation of information helps to demystify doctor–patient relationships remains to be seen.

Interactionists also examine how individuals can construct their own health, to be producers rather than consumers of health. Writing in the interactionist manner, K. Green (1985) introduced the concept of self-health management, which recommends that people engage in practices to promote their own health—from following good health behaviour guidelines to seeking alternative care to seeking comfort from a friend. **Self-health management** includes self-care practices, mutual aid, and membership in self-help groups (Segall and Chappell 2000:131). While the last two items are self-explanatory, the notion of self-care requires some expansion. This concept originated with Ivan Barofsky (1978) and has been developed by Alexander Segall (Segall and Chappell 2000:135–138). Self-care comprises four components:

- *Regulatory* self-care consists of daily habits that affect health, like eating a balanced diet, getting rest, and exercising.

- *Preventive* self-care consists of deliberate actions taken to reduce the risk of illness, such as brushing and flossing teeth.

- *Reactive* self-care consists of determining what to do when one feels ill and may involve seeking over-the-counter remedies and/or advice from friends or experts.

- *Restorative* self-care consists of compliance with treatments and medications prescribed by professionals, or part compliance, according to self-determination.

Self-care emphasizes lay control over health decision making and health maintenance.

The Feminist Perspective

Feminist theorists examine the extent to which women are treated in a disadvantageous manner in health or health care through processes like medicalization. **Medicalization** is the treating of a person's condition as an illness. This topic is of particular concern to women because many of women's natural conditions have been treated as physical or psychological illnesses. Deborah Findlay and Leslie Miller (2002) have written on the medicalization of women's bodies and women's lives. They begin by describing the rise of the medical profession, showing how healing became "men's work" and women's bodies "offered a lucrative new territory for profit-making" (Findlay and Miller 2002:188). First, mothering, child rearing, and childbirth were defined as medical problems; then, disorders suffered by women—anorexia nervosa, for example—were defined as diseases. Findlay and Miller (2002:202) suggest that, in light of medical talk of "manopause" to typify such youth-seeking behaviour as undergoing cosmetic surgery, buying a sports car, and dating much younger women, men may now be about to experience the same process.

Second, feminists have been critical of the traditional pattern of treating women according to findings from studies of men. Women's College Hospital in Toronto has a brochure with a picture of an orange with "apple?" printed over it. Researchers have found that women and men are not the same when it comes to health problems and thus should be treated differently. For example,

- chest pain is not reported by 43 percent of women during a heart attack;
- women are less likely to be referred for cardiac rehabilitation—despite the fact that they fare much better when they participate;
- women who smoke are about 50 percent more likely to develop lung cancer than men; and
- women are responding differently to some HIV treatments than men.

A third concern of feminists has been the presence and treatment of women in the medical profession itself. It is well known that until a few decades ago, it was not easy for women to enroll in medical faculties and thus not easy to become a doctor. With the increase of women in medical schools came the corresponding increase in women in medicine. In 2007, according to the Canadian Institute of Health Information, women constituted 33 percent of physicians.

WHAT CAN YOU DO?

- Volunteer at an agency, such as Street Health, that deals with people who are on welfare, are homeless, are recovering addicts, or are recently released from prison. Among the sociological insights you will get is an appreciation of how their health is affected by their social status. You may also make a difference in the life of a participant.
- Some students on your own campus may not be able to afford nutritious meals, especially at the end of term when meal cards and money run out. Students at York University organized a program called Food 4 Thought, a food bank for students. The bank gets funds from grants and student fees, gets workers from student volunteers, and gives food to students who can no longer afford it. Unused food is given to community organizations (its website is http://www.yorku.ca/food). Other post-secondary schools have done the same. If your college or university has not created a food bank, you might see if such a need exists and, if so, help to fill it.
- Develop a self-care management program for yourself. Consider how you could make use of mutual aid and the self-help groups that are available on university and college campuses, and how you could follow the four types of self-care to maintain your health.
- Study the way women, and men too, are exploited for profit in cosmetic surgery and other health-related ways. Develop a seminar on body consciousness. You might start with the work of Tovée and associates (1997), who compare the BMIs (see above) of post-secondary female students, glamour and fashion models, and anorexic females. Fashion models (BMI = 17.6) are halfway between the female students (a normal BMI = 21.6) and anorexic females (BMI = 14.7).
- If you plan to do research in this area in the future, apply for a grant from the recently formed Canadian Institute of Health Research. As one of its four directions, it plans to improve the health status of vulnerable populations and create institutes for specific populations, such as Indigenous peoples, and children and youth. Included in this list is the Institute of Gender and Health, which supports research about how sex and gender interact with other health factors, leading to different risk factors and interventions for women and for men. Of particular interest is research on gender inequalities.

SUMMARY

Why Are Illness and Health Care Social Problems?

Health care is a social issue because, according to the World Health Organization, health is a state of complete physical, mental, and social well-being. Although people in Canada pay less for health services than people in the United States, our measures of health show better outcomes than theirs. Thus, high expenditures do not translate into improved life expectancy for everyone.

How Have Health Care Problems Changed Over the Past Century?

Since acute illnesses (e.g., measles, polio) are largely under control with vaccinations and improved public health practices, most health problems today are chronic diseases (e.g., arthritis, diabetes, heart disease) or disabilities (e.g., back injuries, hearing or vision problems, brain injuries), which require long-term treatment. Medical advances mean that many people born with serious disabilities survive, as do many who would have died from acute illnesses or accidents in earlier times. As more people survive and live longer, more are likely to experience chronic illnesses and disabilities.

Why Is Obesity a Social Problem?

Close to half of Canadians over 15 years of age are overweight/obese. Being overweight is related to a number of diseases, such as heart disease and Type II diabetes. People in rural Canada are more likely to be overweight than people in urban Canada. The problem exists worldwide, even in developing countries. Suggestions to reduce this problem are similar to those suggested to reduce smoking, such as warnings on packages and taxes on junk food.

Why Is Mental Illness a Social Problem?

Mental illness is a social problem because of the number of people it affects, the difficulty in defining and identifying mental disorders, and the ways in which it is treated. Deinstitutionalization—discharging mental patients from hospitals into the community—was considered a solution to the problem of warehousing patients, but it has created new problems.

How Do Sex and Gender, Class, and Indigenous Status Affect Physical and Mental Health?

Men, the poor, and Indigenous people have lower life expectancies than women, the rich, and non-Indigenous people. Although women report more chronic conditions and disabilities than men, they do have higher disability-free life expectancies. The poor and elementary-educated report more disability and poorer health than the rich and highly educated. Although women report more mental illness than men, when addictive behaviour is included, men have higher rates of mental illness. Indigenous people have higher rates of suicide than non-Indigenous people.

What Are the Five Characteristics of the Canadian Health Care System?

Our system is universal—covering all Canadians; accessible—unimpeded by financial and other barriers; and comprehensive—providing service on the basis of need. It is portable across provinces. Lastly, it is publicly managed and funded.

Why Is the Health Care System Considered a Problem?

People find a number of issues with the health care system. The coverage of care including home care, drugs, and dental care needs to be expanded. Wait times, though decreasing, could decrease further. Will the supply of health care professionals be adequate with an aging population? What is the future of alternative health care? How can technology help with health care (e.g., EHRs)?

What Are the Sociological Explanations for Health Care Problems?

Functionalists consider the sick role a form of deviance that medicine as an institution controlled until recently. Some functionalists believe that the whole health system must be reorganized; others believe that incremental change is the best answer. Some conflict theorists believe that our health problems are rooted in capitalism and the medical–industrial complex. Some, like Ivan Illich, criticize the control of the system and would like to see people take more responsibility for their own health.

Others, including some doctors, believe that only when inequalities based on sex and gender, class, and Indigenous status are reduced will inequalities in health care be reduced. Interactionists believe that communication problems between politicians and advocates create much of our concern about the health care system, but that these problems can be resolved through negotiation. They believe that people must become more involved in self-health management and health care reform. Feminists believe that women have been treated in a disadvantageous manner regarding their bodies and health, the distribution of money to diseases that affect them, and their participation in medical careers.

KEY TERMS

ableism   p. 229
acute diseases,   p. 225
chronic diseases,   p. 226
deinstitutionalization,   p. 234
disability,   p. 229

disability-free life
   expectancy,   p. 227
iatrogenesis,   p. 241
infant mortality rate,   p. 225
life expectancy,   p. 225

medical–industrial
   complex,   p. 240
medicalization,   p. 242
self-health management,   p. 242
total institution,   p. 234

QUESTIONS FOR CRITICAL THINKING

1.   Because Canadians take pride in their high level of life expectancy, they are usually surprised to learn that the infant mortality rate of Indigenous people is double the rate of Canadians generally. Why is this, and what do you think individuals can do at the community level to save these young lives?

2.   In what ways are sex and gender, class, and Indigenous status intertwined with physical and mental illness? Consider causes and treatments.

3.   Do you know people with mental illness? What do you think would help them function better in our society?

4.   Our health care system is growing in cost and will grow substantially higher with the aging of the population. How much of our gross domestic product would you allocate with your tax dollars to health care in light of our education, research (e.g., on alternate sources of energy), social service, and security needs and our future debt levels because of our current stimulus spending?

PEARSON
mysockit™

Explore the topics covered in this chapter at **www.mysockit.com** using the access provided with this text. Interactive resources for studying include video clips, practice tests, learning objectives, and Internet resources.

11

THE CHANGING FAMILY

I don't need a knight in shining armour to rescue me.

A university student (author's files)

It's difficult to expect people to live together for such a long time.

Another university student (author's files)

Since the divorce what's been hard is worrying about paying the bills—having enough money for food for my son. I don't even get to think about buying him new sneakers.

A 35-year-old secretary, who was married for 16 years and had one child (Kurz 1995:90)

I never had a chance to be young. . . . In high school when they were saying, "Let's move to first base and kiss boys," I was doing things with my father.

Jeannie Hilton (see "Child Abuse" on page 262)

Many people today experience the problems described by these individuals: women wanting equality, worries about long-term commitment, economic hardship after divorce, and sexual abuse. Although most sociologists believe that the family as a social institution will endure in one form or another, they also acknowledge that family-related problems are a challenge not only to individuals but also to our entire society.

THE NATURE OF FAMILIES

What is a family? According to sociologist Robin Wolf (1996), that question generates heated debate: some say that any definition of the family must emphasize tradition and stability; others argue that any useful definition must take into account diversity and social change. Traditionally, *family* has been defined as a group of people who are related to one another by blood, marriage, or adoption and who live together, form an economic unit, and bear and raise children (Benokraitis 1993). Today, however, the traditional definition of family is often modified to incorporate diverse living arrangements and relationships such as single-parent households, cohabiting unmarried couples, domestic partnerships of lesbian or gay couples, and several

generations of family members (grandparent, parent, and child) living under the same roof. To encompass all these arrangements, we will use the following definition as we look at family-related social problems: a **family** is a relationship in which people live together with commitment, form an economic unit and care for any young, and consider the group critical to their identity (Benokraitis 1993; Lamanna and Riedmann 1994).

Changing Family Structure and Patterns

The basis of the traditional family structure is **kinship,** a social network of people based on common ancestry, marriage, or adoption. Kinship is very important in pre-industrial societies because it serves as an efficient means of producing and distributing food and goods (clothing, materials for building shelter) and transferring property and power from one generation to the next. In many pre-industrial societies the primary kinship unit is the **extended family,** a family unit composed of relatives in addition to parents and children, all of whom live in the same household. Extended families typically include grandparents, uncles, aunts, or other relatives in addition to parents and children. When the growing and harvesting of crops is the basis of economic production, extended families mean that large numbers of people participate in food production, which can be essential to survival. Living together also enables family members to share other resources, such as shelter and transportation. Though extended families are not common in Canada, except in some immigrant communities, they are in some countries in Latin America, Africa, Asia, and parts of Eastern and Southern Europe (Busch 1990).

With industrialization, other social institutions begin to fulfill kinship-system functions. The production and distribution of goods and services, for example, largely shifts to the economic sector. The form of kinship that is most typical in industrialized nations is the **nuclear family,** a family unit composed of one or two parents and her/his/their dependent children who live apart from other relatives. The nuclear family in an industrialized society functions primarily to regulate sexual activity, socialize children, and provide family members with affection and companionship. Table 11.1 shows the change in different types of families from 2001 to 2006.

TABLE 11.1   Distribution and Growth of Census Families, Canada, 2001 and 2006

Census families	2001 Number	Percentage	2006 Number	Percentage	Percentage growth 2001 to 2006
Total	8 371 020	100.0	8 896 840	100.0	6.3
Couple families	7 059 830	84.3	7 482 775	84.1	6.0
Married	5 901 420	70.5	6 105 910	68.6	3.5
Common-law	1 158 410	13.8	1 376 865	15.5	18.9
Lone-parent families	1 311 190	15.7	1 414 060	15.9	7.8
Female parent	1 065 360	12.7	1 132 290	12.7	6.3
Male parent	245 825	2.9	281 775	3.2	14.6

Source: Statistics Canada, 2009, 2006 Census: Family Portrait: Continuity and Change in Canadian Families and Households in 2006: Findings. *Retrieved October 22, 2009 (http://www12.statcan.ca/english/census06/analysis/famhouse/cenfam1.cfm).*

In the past many people would have said that an ideal family consisted of a married couple and children. But lone-parent families have existed in the past, often because of a death of one of the parents, and common-law couples have existed in substantial and growing numbers for the last quarter century. What is novel in this table is the slight increase in lone-parent families headed by men.

Are Canadian Families in Decline?

Will the family as a social institution disappear in the future? Social analysts answer this question differently, depending on whether they adopt a traditional definition of the family or a modified definition. But new patterns have emerged over the past 50 years:

- The divorce rate increased sharply from the 1950s to the 1980s but has been stable recently (it is currently 2.3 per 1000 people in Canada; Statistics Canada 2002d), and parents increasingly decide to forgo marriage, so a sizable number of children are being raised in single-parent households apart from other relatives.

- A smaller percentage of people are married (see "Singlehood" on page 254).

- There is a higher percentage of single-parent families.

- Large numbers of married women have left the role of full-time mother and housewife to go into the labour market, and not all the functions of the former role are being fulfilled.

- The focus of many families has shifted away from childbearing to the needs of the adult members. Increasingly, even when parents have young children to raise, they break up if their psychological and self-development needs are unmet in the marriage relationship. Some sociologists have suggested that if marriage and the family weaken enough and no satisfactory substitute for marriage emerges, industrial societies will not survive.

According to some analysts, research has shown that the structure of the family is undergoing profound changes around the world, in both rich and poor nations (see Box 11.1). These analysts say the family isn't declining, it's simply changing. From this social-change perspective, families are becoming more complex and diverse; they are not in a state of irreversible decline (Cherlin 1992; Skolnick 1991). In fact, according to sociologist Andrew Cherlin (1992), the family will last as a social institution precisely because it can adapt to social change and modify its form. However, Cherlin goes on to say that the best way to minimize the costs of change in the family unit is to modify the other social institutions of daily life—such as the economy and workplace.

Changing Views on Marriage and Families

The term *marriage* refers to a legally recognized and/or socially approved arrangement between two individuals that carries certain rights and obligations and usually involves sexual activity. In Canada, the only legal form

BOX 11.1   The Changing Family around the World

Yelena Polyakovskaya lives with her 6-month-old baby, relying on friends and babysitters to watch Aleksandr when she is at work. The father, an unmarried journalist, has never seen his child. Her 6-year-old son, Simeon, is being raised by his grandmother and great-grandmother in Kiev. Polyakovskaya says she hopes to bring him to Moscow, but cannot even afford train fare to visit him.

She loves her job covering music and ballet, but it is ill paid. In her bare one-room apartment, she sleeps on a tiny, fold-out couch next to the baby's crib. An ironing board serves as a desk. But like many women raising children alone, she said she does not want to marry again.

"My life is difficult," she said, "but God, if I had to come home from work and clean, cook and iron for a husband who keeps telling me I am doing it wrong, it would be even worse."

Yelena Polyakovskaya, age 32, a television reporter in Russia (Stanley 1995)

Yelena Polyakovskaya is one of a growing number of women in Russia raising her family without a husband. Approximately 15 to 20 percent of Russian families are single-parent households. This is similar to Canada, but in Russia, single mothers span all social strata; in Canada, single-parent households are much more likely to be poor (Ross et al. 2000:145). In Japan, single-parenthood because of abandonment or divorce is rare, but a practice called *tanshin hunin* has the same effect. When middle managers are transferred, they go without their families so that their children don't have to change schools. When possible, the fathers commute home on weekends, but the mothers are essentially single parents (O'Connell 1994).

Increasing single-parenthood is just one worldwide trend. According to Judith Bruce, author of a report published by the Population Council, a non-profit group in New York, "trends like

unwed motherhood, rising divorce rates, smaller households and the feminization of poverty are not unique to America, but are occurring worldwide" (Lewin 1995:A5). Among the report's findings are the following:

- Divorce rates are rising. In many developed countries, divorce rates doubled between 1970 and 1990; in less developed countries, about one-quarter of first marriages end by the time women are in their 40s.

- Unwed motherhood is increasing virtually everywhere.

- Children in single-parent households are more likely to be poor than are children in two-parent households, especially when the parent is the mother (often termed the feminization of poverty).

- Though the reason varies from country to country, more women are entering the workforce and taking increasing economic responsibility for children. For example, in Bangladesh, older husbands frequently take young wives. When a husband dies, the wife must find work to support her children. In Asia, if a father who migrates for better work opportunities stops sending money, the mother must support the family herself. In sub-Saharan Africa, a woman's husband may go on to another polygamous marriage and support those children instead (Lewin 1995).

The fact that families around the world are changing in similar ways shows that there is nothing inevitable about the form of the family or the roles of women and men even within a single society (O'Connell 1994). The fact of so much change in the most basic unit of society also poses important questions for the 21st century. Is the basic problem really inequality between women and men? Would shared responsibilities in the home and equal opportunities in the workplace create better families? Can some general principles for social policies be developed, given vastly different societal conditions? What do you think?

of marriage is **monogamy,** a marriage between one woman and one man. In some places, such as Bountiful, B.C., polygamy has occurred with no prosecutions until recently (see Box 11.2).

The marriage rate (number of marriages per 1000 population) in Canada is about 4.7, down from 9.2 in 1972 (Milan 2000:6; Statistics Canada 2004h:35). Figure 11.1 shows that over 140 000 marriages were

performed in 2002, down from 200 000 in the early 1970s, and a plateau has occurred since then.

Marriage was once a cultural imperative. There was "something wrong" with a person who didn't marry. But since the 1970s, people's attitudes toward marriage and the family have changed as other aspects of society have changed. Cultural guidelines on marriage and child-bearing have grown weaker as our society has

SOCIAL PROBLEMS AND SOCIAL POLICY

BOX 11.2   Polygamy

In early 2009, the attorney general of British Columbia announced criminal prosecutions against two leaders, Winston Blackmore and Jim Oler, of the Fundamentalist Church of Jesus Christ of Latter Day Saints (FLDS) in Bountiful, B.C., on the charge of polygamy. This will be an important case because it pits the criminal ban on polygamy against freedom of religion in the *Charter of Rights and Freedoms*. This freedom, however, is not supposed to extend to behaviour that harms others, particularly the most vulnerable, such as underage girls.

The FLDS is the Canadian branch of a group now residing in Texas that broke away from the Mormons. The Mormons have rejected this group, whose prophet, Warren Jeffs, is now serving a prison term for being an accomplice to child sexual assault. The Canadian group is divided after a split between Blackmore, who is accused of having 19 wives, and Oler, who is accused of having 3 wives.

In the words of one wife, Elissa Wall, who was forced to marry at 14 a man she hated,

> I was just a child. . . . I was terrified. I was screaming out for help. And nobody would help me.

She was also forced into incest: her husband was her cousin.

> The hardest thing for me was I was marrying my first cousin. . . . I was being forced to marry someone that I had known my whole life—and I had hated my whole life. . . . I didn't even know what sex was. It was horrible because every fibre and grain of my soul screamed out in defiance against this.

She has also accused Canada of being a safe haven for this exploitation because of a lack of prosecutions.

Some say it might be better to charge the FLDS leaders with child and sexual abuse since these men have married many girls under 16 years of age. But B.C. attorney general Wally Oppal said that it is difficult for get people to act as witnesses to sexual exploitation. This has been true in the United States also, but Arizona has been able to convict men on the basis of birth certificates of the brides.

Some say that polygamy is just another marriage form like same-sex marriage. Do you agree with this? Should the *Charter of Rights and Freedoms* be allowed to support bigamy and polygamy?

Source: Terry Milewski, 2009, "Were Polygamy Charges the Best Way to Battle Bountiful?" CBC News (February 24). Retrieved October 22, 2009 (http://www.cbc.ca/canada/story/2009/02/23/f-bountiful.html#socialcomments).

FIGURE 11.1   Number of Marriages and Divorces in Canada, 1921 to 2002

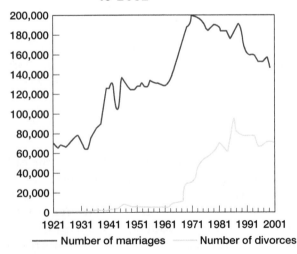

Source: Statistics Canada, 2004, "Divorces 2001 and 2002," The Daily (May 4), Catalogue no. 11-001

experienced a broader cultural shift toward autonomy and personal growth. In the 1970s, according to Cherlin (1992:127), "family life became a matter of personal choice in which individuals made decisions based on a calculus of self-interest and self-fulfillment. Marriage was still desirable, but no one any longer had to be married to be a proper member of society." Marriage also became much less of an economic necessity for women in the 1970s because of new job opportunities and rising incomes. Although women's wages remained low in comparison to men's during this time, their wages rose in absolute terms (Cherlin 1992).

Still, marriage is a persistent preference for most people today. In a national survey conducted by Angus Reid, two-thirds of Canadian adults strongly agreed that their families were the greatest joy in their lives (Angus Reid 1994, cited in Milan 2000:5). According to the 1995 General Social Survey (GSS), 98 percent of those in marriages and 96 percent of those in common-law unions feel that a long-term relationship is important for their happiness (quoted in Milan 2000:5).

On June 28, 2005, the same-sex legislation, Bill C-38, was passed by the House of Commons (and by the Senate in July). Canada was about to become a place where gay and lesbian marriage could take place. Up to that time it was possible for gays and lesbians to marry in some provinces, but it is now possible anywhere in the country. According to the 2006 Census, 45 345 couples were same-sex couples, of which 16.5 percent were married (Statistics Canada 2007c). In the future it will be possible to count same-sex marriages and cohabitations.

Figure 11.1 shows that over 70 000 divorces were finalized in 2002, down from 96 000 in 1987. Though many believe marriage should last "until death do us part," others feel marriage is a commitment "for as long as love allows." Through a pattern of marriage, divorce, and remarriage, many people reaffirm their belief in the institution of marriage, but not to the individual they initially married. This pattern of successive marriages, in which a person has several spouses over a lifetime but is legally married to only one partner at a time, is referred to as *serial monogamy*. Some social analysts consider serial monogamy a natural adaptation to other social changes in society; others think it is detrimental to individuals and to society and serves as further evidence of the decline of the family (see Popenoe 1996). Who is right? As with other social problems we have examined, the view of causes, effects, and possible solutions for family-related problems depends on the theoretical framework the analyst uses.

PERSPECTIVES ON FAMILY-RELATED PROBLEMS

What purposes do families serve in contemporary societies? Do families create problems for society or solve them? The latter, say functionalists, who believe that the family fulfills important functions for individuals at the microlevel and for the entire society at the macrolevel. Conflict and feminist theorists, on the other hand, consider families a primary source of inequality—and sometimes abuse and violence—in society. Taking a microlevel approach, interactionists analyze family-related social problems in terms of socialization and social interactions among family members.

The Functionalist Perspective

Functionalists emphasize the importance of the family in maintaining the stability of society and the well-being of individuals. According to Emile Durkheim, marriage is a microcosmic replica of the larger society; both marriage and society involve a mental and moral fusion of physically distinct individuals (Lehmann 1994). Durkheim also believed that a division of labour contributed to greater efficiency in marriage and families (and in all areas of life). In his study of family life in the United States, sociologist Talcott Parsons (1955) also viewed a division of labour as important. He saw the husband in an ideal nuclear family as fulfilling an *instrumental role*—meeting the family's economic needs, making important decisions, and providing leadership—and the wife as fulfilling an *expressive role*—running the household, caring for children, and meeting family members' emotional needs.

Using Durkheim's and Parsons's work as a basis for their model of the family, contemporary functionalists believe that a division of labour makes it possible for families to fulfill a number of functions that no other social institution in high-income nations can perform as efficiently and effectively:

1. Regulate sexual behaviour and reproduction: Families are expected to regulate the sexual activity of their members and thus control reproduction so that it occurs within specific boundaries. Sexual regulation of family members by the family is supposed to protect the *principle of legitimacy*—the belief that all children should have a socially and legally recognized father (Malinowski 1964).

2. Socialize and educate children: Parents and other relatives are responsible for teaching children the values and norms of their culture.

3. Provide economic and psychological support: Families are responsible for providing for their members' physical (food, shelter) and emotional needs.

4. Provide social status: Families confer social status on their members, including ascribed statuses such as racialization, ethnicity, nationality, class, and religious affiliation, although some of these statuses may change later in life.

Considering their view of the family, functionalists believe that problems in the family are a social crisis. The functional family provides both social order and economic stability by providing for the survival and development of children; the physical and emotional health of adults; and the care of those who are sick, injured, elderly, and have disabilities. The family is also the front line for reinforcing society's norms and values. Functionalists consider the family to be part of the solution to many problems faced by people in contemporary societies. In this view, dysfunctions in families are problems that threaten the well-being of individuals, groups, and nations.

Functionalists believe that changes in other social institutions, such as the economy, religion, education, law, medicine, and the government, contribute to family-related problems. For example, some functionalists think that changing the law to recognize no-fault divorce contributes to higher rates of divorce and dramatically increases single-parent households, which do not provide children with the nurture and guidance they get in a two-parent home (Popenoe 1996).

The Conflict Perspective

Most conflict analysts believe that functionalist views on family problems are idealized and inadequate. Rather than operating harmoniously and for the benefit of all members, families, these analysts say, are sources of social inequality and conflict over values, goals, and access to resources and power.

Conflict theorists who focus on class relations in capitalist economies compare family members to workers in a factory, emphasizing the inequality in each institution. Women are dominated by men in the home just as workers are dominated by managers and capitalists in factories (Engels 1972). As wives and mothers, women contribute to capitalism by producing the next generation of workers and providing the existing labour force with food, clean clothes, and emotional support. Women's work in the family not only benefits the capitalist class but also reinforces women's subordination because the work is unpaid and often devalued. This unpaid work has received much attention in research on the family in Canada (see "Dual-Earner Marriages," on page 255). According to Statistics Canada (2008b), women spent 72 percent more time on unpaid work than men in 2005 (see Figure 4.4 on page 96 in Chapter 4). Meal preparation and cleaning were the most time-consuming activities, but child care and other caregiving, volunteer work, and home maintenance were also time-consuming.

The Feminist Perspective

Many feminist theorists think that male dominance and female subordination began long before capitalism and the private ownership of property arose as an economic system (Mann 1994). They see women's subordination as rooted in patriarchy, particularly in men's control over women's labour power. At the same time that women's labour in the home is directed by men, it is undervalued, which allows men to benefit from their status as the family breadwinner (Firestone 1970; Goode 1982). In a more recent study, sociologist Jane Riblett Wilkie (1993) found that most men are reluctant to relinquish their status as family breadwinner. Although only 15 percent of the families in Canada are supported solely by a male breadwinner, many men continue to construct their ideal of masculinity based on this role. It is acceptable for wives to enter the paid workforce if their role is simply to earn money; they should not, however, challenge the ideal roles of male breadwinner and female homemaker.

Like conflict theorists, feminist theorists argue that family problems derive from inequality—not just within the family, but in the political, social, and economic arenas of the larger society as well (Aulette 1994). In fact, pervasive societal inequality leads to one of the most tragic family problems: spousal violence. According to feminist theorists, wife abuse and other forms of domestic violence may even be conscious strategies that men use to control women and perpetuate gender inequality (Kurz 1989). Fortunately, the rates seem to be declining with the general crime rates, but during the past 30 years, the rate of women being killed in domestic violence has been three to five times greater than the rate of men being killed. According to the 2008 edition of the report *Family Violence in Canada: A Statistical Profile* (Statistics Canada 2008g:39), from 1977 to 2006, the rate of female victims of spousal homicide dropped from 14 per million women in spousal relationships to 6, and the rate of male victims dropped from 5 to 2. (The rates of overall spousal violence are illustrated in Table 11.3.)

According to feminist theorists, family-related problems, including domestic violence and wife abuse, can be solved only if all social institutions work to eliminate the subordination of women in society. Increased educational and occupational opportunities for women over the past quarter-century may be contributing to

TABLE 11.2   Forms of Assisted Reproductive Technology

Name	Description
In vitro fertilization (IVF)	Eggs that were produced as a result of administering fertility drugs are removed from the woman's body and fertilized by sperm in a laboratory dish. The embryos that result from this process are transferred to the woman's uterus.
Micromanipulation	Viewing the process through a microscope, a specialist manipulates egg and sperm in a laboratory dish to improve the chances of a pregnancy.
Cryopreserved embryo transfer (CPE)	Embryos that were frozen after a previous assisted reproductive technology procedure are thawed and then transferred to the uterus.
Egg donation	Eggs are removed from a donor's uterus, fertilized in a laboratory dish, and transferred to an infertile woman's uterus
Surrogacy	An embryo is implanted in the uterus of a woman who is paid to carry the fetus until birth. The egg may come from either the legal or the surrogate mother, and the sperm may come either from the legal father or a donor.

Source: Trip Gabriel, 1996, "High-Tech Pregnancies Test Hope's Limit," New York Times, January 7:1, 10–11.

a reduction in domestic violence. Related to increased opportunities for women, the increase in the age of first marriage (see "Postponing Marriage," on page 254) may be another contributing factor to the decline in violence.

The Interactionist Perspective

Some interactionists view the family communication process as integral to understanding the diverse roles that family members play; therefore, these analysts examine how husbands, wives, and children act out their roles and react to the parts played by others. Although societies differ widely on the rules and norms that should shape family and kin relationships, people are socialized to accept their society's form of the family as the acceptable norm. According to sociologists Peter Berger and Hansfried Kellner (1964), marital partners develop a shared reality through their interactions with each other. Although newlyweds bring separate identities to a marriage, over time they construct a shared reality as a couple. In the process, the partners redefine their past identities to be consistent with their new realities. Interactionists say that the process of developing a shared reality is continuous and occurs not only in the family but in any group in which the couple participates together. In cases of separation and divorce, the process is reversed: couples may start with a shared reality but once again become individuals with separate realities in the process of uncoupling their relationship.

How do interactionists explain problems in a family? Some look at the subjective meanings and interpretations people give to their everyday lives. According to sociologists Charles Jones, Lorna Marsden, and Lorne Tepperman (1990), over the past few decades, women have gained more choice and opportunities in life. Women have become more "individualized." One of the consequences of this dramatic change is that women have few role models to follow; as a result, new expectations about work and child rearing could cause problems for the family. Obviously, men would also be uncertain about how to behave with these changed expectations. According to sociologist Jessie Bernard (1982), women and men experience marriage differently. While the husband may see his marriage very positively, the wife may feel less positive. The reverse may also be true. Evidence for the different realities of marriage comes from research that shows that husbands and wives often give very different accounts of the same event (Safilios-Rothschild 1969).

Still other interactionists view family problems in terms of partners' unrealistic expectations about love and marriage, which can lead to marital dissatisfaction and, sometimes, divorce. These analysts note that our culture emphasizes romantic love—a deep and vital emotion based on significant need satisfaction, caring for and acceptance of another person, and the development of an intimate relationship (Lamanna and Riedmann 1994). Indeed, most couples in Canada get married because they are in love, but being a "nation of lovers" doesn't mean that men and women have the same ideas about what constitutes romantic love. According to sociologist Francesca Cancian (1990), women tend to express their feelings verbally, whereas men tend to express their love through such non-verbal actions as preparing dinner or doing household repairs. Women may not always interpret these actions as signs of love. One man complained (Rubin 1976:146), "What does she want? Proof? She's got it, hasn't she? Would I be knocking myself out to get things for her—like to keep up this house—if I didn't love her? Why does a man do things like that if not because he loves his wife and kids? I swear, I can't figure what she wants." His wife replied, "It's not enough that he supports us and takes care of us. I appreciate that, but I want him to share things with me. I need for him to tell me his feelings."

Whatever their different viewpoints on marriage and family, most social theorists agree on one fact: three decades ago, the nuclear family was the most common family form, and today it is only one of many patterns.

DIVERSITY IN INTIMATE RELATIONSHIPS AND FAMILIES

Greater diversity in intimate relationships and families in Canada has come about because of dramatic increases in (1) singlehood, (2) postponed marriage, (3) living together without marriage (called common-law, cohabitation, or domestic partnerships), (4) dual-earner marriages, and (5) one-parent families.

Singlehood

Although some young singles will eventually marry, 10 percent of the population will remain single for their lives. When this figure is combined with those who have been widowed, separated, or divorced, the proportion of Canadian single-person households is 26.8 percent, according to the 2006 Census (Statistics Canada 2007c). Some people choose singlehood over marriage because it means greater freedom from commitments to another person. Others choose it because of increased career opportunities (especially for women), the availability of sexual partners without marriage, the belief that the single lifestyle is full of excitement, or

the desire for self-sufficiency and freedom to change and experiment (Stein 1976; 1981). Though some analysts think that individuals who prefer to remain single hold more individualistic values and are less family-oriented than are people who choose to marry, sociologist Peter Stein (1981) has found otherwise: many singles still feel a strong need for intimacy, sharing, and continuity and, as a result, develop relationships with other singles, valuing friends and personal growth more highly than marriage and children (Alwin et al. 1985; Cargan and Melko 1982).

Some people are single not by choice but by necessity. Because of structural changes in the economy, many young working-class people cannot afford to marry and set up their own households. Indeed, some college graduates have found that they cannot earn enough money to set up households separate from those of their parents (Boyd and Norris 1999).

Postponing Marriage

Young people today are less eager to get married than they were two decades ago; many are remaining single into their late 20s. In 1997, the average age at which men first married was 29.5 years, and the average age for women was 27.4 years (Milan 2000:6); the pattern continued to 2005, when the average age for men was 29.5 and for women, 26.9 years.

Why are more people postponing first marriages? Although some reasons are the same as those for staying single, sociologist Robin Wolf (1996) suggests four key factors: (1) economic uncertainty due to the changing job structure in Western societies; (2) women's increasing participation in the labour force; (3) the sexual revolution of the 1970s that made sexual relationships outside marriage more socially acceptable; and (4) the rising divorce rate—young people watching their parents divorce may be less anxious to jump into marriage themselves. Other analysts suggest that a significant increase in cohabitation and domestic partnerships also contributes to the percentage of people who are counted as single or postponing marriage.

Common-Law, Cohabitation, and Domestic Partnerships

The popularity of cohabitation has increased in the past two decades. **Common-law,** or **cohabitation,** is two adults living together in a sexual relationship without being legally married. According to the 2006 Census (see Table 11.1), 1.4 million couples—15.5 percent of all couples—were living common-law, up from 5.6 percent in 1981. Now almost 40 percent of men and women aged 30 to 39 are expected to choose common-law as their first union (Statistics Canada 2002d:3). The proportion of cohabiting couples still varies significantly by language spoken. In Quebec, 30 percent of all couples were living common-law in 2001 (Statistics Canada 2002h:5). This seems counterintuitive in a predominantly Roman Catholic province. What do you think?

For some couples, cohabitation is a form of trial marriage and constitutes an intermediate stage between dating and marriage. According to anthropologist Margaret Mead (1966), dating patterns do not adequately prepare people for marriage and parenting responsibilities. Mead proposed a two-stage marriage process, each with its own ceremony and responsibilities. In the first stage, the individual marriage, two people would make a serious commitment to each other but agree not to have children during this stage. In the second stage, the parental marriage, the couple would decide to have children and to share responsibility for their upbringing. Many people today seem to be following this pattern, though without intention, and with different partners. Divorce in the first couple of years of marriage is quite common, and the break-up of a common-law relationship is even more likely. *American Demographics* editor Pamela Paul, having been through an early divorce herself, interviewed 60 other young, divorced couples and wrote a book about what she called a "starter marriage." She claimed that most of her sample had not given marriage much thought before getting married; they had developed "matrimania" due to a marriage-oriented culture (Paul 2002).

For other couples, cohabitation is not necessarily a first step toward marriage. In one study, researchers found that slightly more than 50 percent of cohabitation relationships eventually culminated in marriage, whereas 37 percent broke up and 10 percent were still ongoing at the time of the study (London 1991).

Does cohabitation contribute to marital success? The evidence is mixed. Some studies show that cohabitation has little or no effect on marital adjustment, emotional closeness, satisfaction, and intimacy (Watson and DeMeo 1987). Other studies indicate that couples who cohabit first are more likely to divorce than those who do not (Bennett et al. 1988). Apparently, partners in this study who had cohabited were less satisfied with their marriage and less committed to the institution of marriage than were those who had not lived together before marrying. The researchers theorized that cohabitation may contribute to people's individualistic attitudes and values, while making them more aware that alternatives to marriage exist (Axinn and Thornton 1992; Thomson and Colella 1992).

Dual-Earner Marriages

More than 60 percent of all marriages in Canada are **dual-earner marriages,** marriages in which both spouses are in the labour force. Over half of all employed women hold full-time, year-round jobs, and in a change from the past, there are more married women with young children in the paid labour force today than ever before.

Many married women who are employed outside the household face hours of domestic work and childcare when they get home. Sociologist Arlie Hochschild (1989) refers to the latter half of women's dual workdays as the **second shift**—the domestic work that many employed women perform at home after completing their workday on the job. According to Hochschild, the unpaid housework that women do on the *second shift* (see Chapter 4) amounts to an extra month of work each year. In households with small children or many children, the amount of housework increases (Hartmann 1981). Across racialization and class lines, numerous studies confirm that domestic work remains primarily women's work (Gerstel and Gross 1995).

In recent years, more husbands have been sharing some of the household and child-care responsibilities, especially when the wife's earnings are essential to family finances (Perry-Jenkins and Crouter 1990). But even when husbands assume some of the household responsibilities, they typically spend much less time in these activities than do their wives. Figure 4.4 on page 96 in Chapter 4 shows that though men have been increasing their unpaid work over time (from 2.1 to 2.5 hours per day from 1986 to 2005), their unpaid work is still below that of women. But overall the total paid and unpaid work by men and women is about the same, nine hours per day.

In the age of dual-earner marriages, it has become increasingly important for fathers to assume child-care and household duties. How does this photo show the competing demands faced by many employed parents?

Comparing Two-Parent and One-Parent Households

When the mother and father in a two-parent household truly share parenting, children have the benefit of two primary caregivers. Some researchers have found that when fathers take an active part in raising their children, the effect is beneficial for all family members. Fathers find that increased contact with their children provides more opportunities for personal and emotional gratification (Coltrane 1989).

However, living in a two-parent family does not guarantee children a happy childhood. Children whose parents argue constantly, abuse them, or are alcoholics have a worse family experience than do children in a single-parent family where there is a supportive environment. Women who are employed full-time and are single parents probably have the greatest burden of all. These women must fulfill their paid employment duties and meet the needs of their children and the household, often with little help from ex-husbands or relatives.

How prevalent are one-parent households? The past two decades have seen a significant increase in one-parent households due to divorce, death of a parent, and births outside of marriage. In 2006, lone-parent families made up 16 percent of the total families in Canada (see Table 11.1). Who heads most one-parent households? Table 11.1 shows that today, 81 percent of all one-parent families are headed by single mothers. Men are heads of about 19 percent of one-parent families; a study of one-parent households headed by fathers found that most of the men had very positive relationships with their children (Risman 1987).

What effect does a one-parent household have on children? According to one study based on six nationally representative data sets of more than 25 000 children from various racialized and social-class backgrounds in the United States, children growing up with only one biological parent are at risk of serious problems, including poor academic achievement, dropping out of school, drug and alcohol abuse, teen pregnancy, early marriage, and divorce (McLanahan and Sandefur 1994). Obviously, living in a one-parent family does not necessarily cause these problems. Factors such as poverty, discrimination, unsafe neighbourhoods, and high crime rates must also be considered. (See also the section that follows on parenting styles for another important factor.) In fact, other researchers have found some benefits to growing up in a one-parent family (Lauer and Lauer 1991). For example, children in one-parent families are often less pressured to conform to rigid gender roles. Rather than having chores assigned by gender, as is common in two-parent families, single-parent children typically take on a wider variety of tasks and activities. Many single-parent children also show high levels of maturity and self-sufficiency earlier because they have to help out at a younger age than do children in other families (Lauer and Lauer 1991).

What about the fathers of children in one-parent households headed by women? Although some fathers remain involved in their children's lives, others only occasionally take their children out for recreational activities or buy them presents on birthdays and holidays. Personal choice, workplace demands on time and energy, location of the ex-wife's residence, and limitations placed on visitation by custody arrangements are all factors that affect how often absentee fathers visit their children. Increasingly, parents are receiving joint custody of their children, and it appears that joint custody can minimize the disruption of divorce in a child's life if the ex-spouses cooperate with each other and live in relatively close geographical proximity. Ex-spouses who constantly argue or live far away from each other can create serious problems for "commuter" children, as author David Sheff (1995:64) describes:

> My son began commuting between his two homes at age 4. . . . The commuter flights . . . were the only times a parent wasn't lording over him, so he was able to order Coca-Cola, verboten [forbidden] at home. . . . But such benefits were insignificant when contrasted with his preflight nightmares about plane crashes. . . . Like so many divorcing couples, we divided the china and art and our young son. . . . For the eight years since, he has been one of the thousands of American children with two homes, two beds, two sets of clothes and toys, and two toothbrushes.

The transition from a two-parent family to a one-parent family is only one of many child-related family issues that many people today must deal with, as we discuss in the next section.

CHILD-RELATED FAMILY ISSUES

One of the major issues facing many individuals and families today is reproductive freedom, a term that implies both the desire *to have* and the desire *not to have* a child. As sociologists Leslie King and Madonna Harrington Meyer (1997:8) explain,

> The average woman is fertile, and therefore must attempt to control her reproductivity, for one-half

For a number of decades, there have been intense public confrontations between abortion rights advocates and members of the anti-abortion movement. Demonstrators are a familiar sight outside abortion clinics, hospitals, and government buildings.

of her life. For most women, it is the preoccupation with preventing births that consumes their health care dollars and energies; for a small minority, it is the preoccupation with achieving a birth that dominates. The ability to control fertility is, to a great extent, linked to access to various forms of reproductive health services, including contraceptives and infertility treatments.

Reproductive Freedom, Contraception, and Abortion

Reproductive freedom has been a controversial issue throughout much of Canadian history. In 1869, the Canadian government banned abortion. It was not until 100 years later that a bill was passed making it possible for a woman to get an abortion, with the judgment of three doctors in a hospital that a women's life or health was in danger. That bill, introduced in 1967 by then Justice Minister and future Prime Minister Pierre Elliott Trudeau with the famous expression "The state has no business in the bedrooms of the nation!" also legalized homosexuality and contraception. Earlier in the 1960s the "pill" was introduced, and public opinion about women's reproductive freedom began to change. By 1971, the pill was the most popular form of contraception in Canada (Bélanger 1998:17). Many women spend about 90 percent of their fertile years trying to avoid pregnancy (Gold and Richards 1994).

Over the past 25 years, the methods of contraception have changed greatly. According to the General Social Survey of 1995, the use of contraceptive sterilization doubled in that time. Whereas in 1976, 30.5 percent of couples used sterilization, by 1995, 56.1 percent of couples, mostly older couples with two or more children, were using sterilization (e.g., tubal ligation or vasectomy; Bélanger 1998:17). Since 1976, there has also been a decline in the use of the pill and an increase in the use of condoms. Perhaps this is because of the cost. Perhaps men are willing to take more responsibility for contraception and are more concerned about the spread of sexually transmitted diseases (Bélanger 1998:19).

Although the 1967 law permitted abortion, it was not always easy to obtain one. Some provinces were not sympathetic to abortions, and some hospitals did not set up committees to judge the situations. Because

he felt that women had a basic right to abortions, Dr. Henry Morgentaler started to perform abortions in a clinic in Montreal. Since he was breaking the law, he was tried three times, but no jury would convict him. He took his case to the Supreme Court of Canada and won. The law permitting abortions under strict circumstances was declared unconstitutional in 1988. The next year, the federal government tried once again to pass an abortion bill, but it was defeated in the Senate. No provincial government has tried to pass a bill on abortion since that time, and opportunities for abortion increased in the 1990s. To provide direct and immediate help, Morgentaler set up clinics in several Canadian cities, but not without a struggle: in 1992, his clinic in Toronto was bombed.

Opposition to abortion was strong into the mid-1990s. In 1994, a doctor who performed abortions, Garson Romalis, was shot in Vancouver. Two other anti-abortion shootings took place, one in Ontario in 1995, and one in Manitoba in 1997. While protesting at clinics has continued, no further serious attacks have occurred. This may be due to a decline in the number of abortions being performed. In 2005, 96 615 abortions were performed for Canadian women, a decrease of 3.2 percent from 2004. Now there are fewer than three abortions for every 10 live births in Canada (Statistics Canada 2008k).

At the microlevel, abortion is a solution for some pregnant women and their families but a problem for others, particularly when they face religious or family opposition. At the macrolevel, abortion is both a problem and a solution when activists try to influence the making and enforcement of laws pertaining to women's reproductive rights and the control of new reproductive technologies.

Infertility and New Reproductive Technologies

Infertility is defined as an inability to conceive after a year of unprotected sexual relations. In 40 percent of cases, the woman is infertile, and in another 40 percent, the man is infertile; 20 percent of the time, the cause is impossible to determine (Gabriel 1996).

Sexually transmitted diseases are a leading cause of infertility: each year, many women become infertile as a result of a sexually transmitted disease that develops into pelvic inflammatory disease (Gold and Richards 1994). There are also some women—both married and unmarried—who would like to have a child but cannot because of disabilities. Some analysts point out that a growing number of prospective parents delay childbearing into their 30s and 40s, by which time it may be more difficult for them to conceive.

About 50 percent of infertile couples who seek treatment can be helped by conventional, low-tech treatments such as fertility drugs, artificial insemination, and surgery to unblock fallopian tubes. The other 50 percent require advanced technology, sometimes called assisted reproductive technology (ART). Many middle- and upper-income couples, for example, receive in-vitro fertilization (IVF), which, according to the Infertility Awareness Association of Canada, costs a minimum of $7000 and up to $10 000 (with travel and drugs) per attempt. Despite the popularity of such treatments and the growth of fertility clinics (from 30 slightly over a decade ago to more than 300 today), only one in five couples who receive ART actually become parents (Gabriel 1996). In Canada, the Ontario Hospital Insurance Plan (OHIP) will cover only up to three cycles of treatment and even then, only if the fallopian tubes are completely blocked. Typically, very few private insurance plans will cover this procedure because it is perceived to be too expensive (Infertility Awareness Association of Canada 2003).

Because in-vitro fertilization does not get much financial support and is not always successful, some women have many embryos implanted, and a new situation of more multiple births is occurring. In Canada in 1999, one woman gave birth to six children of whom five survived, and in the United States in 2009, a woman known as "Octomom" gave birth to eight children.

Adoption

Adoption is a legal process through which the rights and duties of parenting are transferred from a child's biological and/or legal parents to new legal parents. The adopted child has all the rights of a biological child. In long past adoptions, a new birth certificate was issued, and the child had no further contact with the biological parents, although more recently agencies have been arranging for people to meet their biological parents or children with mutual consent. Now some provincial acts have made disclosure a right. For example, as of June 2009, in Ontario it is possible to unseal birth records if either a birth parent or adult adoptee requests it, unless a veto has been signed. Five other

provinces in Canada have equivalent legislation, beginning 10 years ago with British Columbia.

Matching children who are available for adoption with prospective adoptive parents can be difficult. The children often have specific needs, and prospective parents often specify the kind of children they want to adopt. Because many prospective parents do not want to adopt children who are non-White (most prospective parents are White), older, or have disabilities or diseases, many children available for adoption are not chosen, and instead move from foster home to foster home (Zelizer 1985).

Prospective parents frequently want infants, but fewer infants are available for adoption than in the past because contraception and abortion are more readily available, and more unmarried teenage parents are deciding to keep their babies. Some teenagers, however, believe that adoption is the best way to solve the problem of early childbearing. Christina, one of many teenagers facing the realities of an early pregnancy and lack of resources to meet the child's needs, explained her decision this way:

I know I can't keep my baby. I can't give it all the things a baby needs and I sure can't dump it on my parents because they can't afford to take care of their own family. I've decided to give it up for adoption. I think it's better for the baby to give it up to parents who can't have a baby themselves. I think that I'm really doing a favour to my baby, although I'm always going to wonder what it looks like and what it's doing. (Luker 1996:163)

Because fewer infants are available for adoption, some Canadians are adopting through a private agency or from a foreign country (e.g., China, Russia, and Haiti have been prominent in the recent past, and, in 2007, Ethiopia moved to second place because of low rates of health disorders and the number of children orphaned because of HIV/AIDS; York 2009:A13).

Parenting Style

Besides the influence of factors such as low income and family structure, other factors, including the way parents treat their children, affect children's development. To study the effect of parenting styles on child development, a massive study was begun in 1994. The National Longitudinal Survey of Children and Youth (NLSCY) is a study of 23 000 families that is investigating a wide variety of variables, including income, family structure, and parenting style, on child development. Parenting style is based on responses to questions about being

- rational (e.g., How often do you think that the kind of punishment you give him/her depends on your mood?);

- responsive (e.g., How often do you praise?);

- reasoning (e.g., When your child breaks the rules … do you: (a) calmly discuss the matter? And (b) describe alternative ways of behaving … ?); and

- firm (e.g., When you give him/her a command to do something, what proportion of the time do you make sure that he/she has done it?).

Based on answers to questions such as these, the parents are divided into four groups ranging from positive (warm and nurturing) to ineffective (very intolerant and erratic). Among the first findings the researchers made was that parenting style had more effect on behavioural problems than family structure or income. Children living with two parents with poor parenting skills were five times more likely to have such developmental problems as aggression, hyperactivity, and depression than children living with a single but effective parent; this is also a wider gap than one due to income differences (Statistics Canada 1998b).

However, if the parenting environment changed from punitive to non-punitive over the ages 2/3 to 8/9 years, then aggressive behaviour will decline (Statistics Canada 2004f). Figure 11.2 shows children's behaviour change to the level of the children in the non-punitive environment if the parent's punitive behaviour changes to non-punitive. Note that the reverse is possible too. Why do you think this occurs?

Teen Pregnancies and Unmarried Motherhood

The birth rate among teenagers has declined substantially over the past few decades. From the early 1970s to the 1990s, the proportion of births to teenagers declined from 11 to 6 percent of all births (Milan 2000:7). Since that time teenage births have dropped from 18.6 to 11.1 per 1000 women under 20 (Statistics Canada 2008k).

Although a popular myth claims that most births to unmarried women occur in the central cities of large

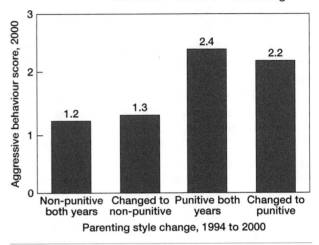

FIGURE 11.2   Children's Aggressive Behaviour Linked with Current Punitive Parenting

Source: Statistics Canada, 2004, "Parenting Style and Children's Aggressive Behaviour, 1994 to 2000," The Daily (October 25), Catalogue no. 11-001.

urban areas, the greatest proportion of unmarried women giving birth occurs in Quebec, Newfoundland and Labrador, and Saskatchewan (Belle and McQuillan 1994:17). Two of the key factors behind this statistic are poverty and lack of employment opportunity.

According to social analysts, the outcome of teen pregnancies is problematic because teenage mothers are typically unskilled at parenting, are likely to drop out of school, and have no social support other than relatives (Chase-Lansdale et al. 1992). Family support is extremely important to unmarried pregnant teens because emotional and financial support from the fathers of their children is often lacking (Nath et al. 1991). Without this support, teen mothers rely on their own mothers and grandmothers to help with child rearing. The picture for the children of teenage mothers without parental support is especially bleak because few of these mothers have adequate parenting skills or knowledge of child development. Children of unwed teenage mothers tend to have severely limited educational and employment opportunities and a high likelihood of living in poverty (Benokraitis 2008). Teenagers are not the only ones having children without getting married. Since 1961 the birth rate for unmarried women between the ages of 25 to 29, and 30 to 34, has doubled. It accounted for 27 and 15 percent, respectively, of births to unmarried women in 1991 (in comparison with 14 and 8 percent in 1961) (Belle and McQuillan 1994:15). Third and fourth births outside marriage are also occurring, most commonly in Quebec, Saskatchewan, and Manitoba (Belle and McQuillan 1994:16). According to demographer Charles Westoff, these rates reflect "the declining significance of marriage as a social obligation or a social necessity for reproduction. Increasing proportions of White women who have not been married are deciding that having a child is more important than any kind of disapproval they might face" (quoted in Connell 1995:A18). With less of a social stigma attached to unmarried pregnancy, fewer women seem to be seeking abortion and are deciding instead to raise the child themselves, whether the pregnancy was planned or not.

DIVORCE AND REMARRIAGE

Divorce is the legal process of dissolving a marriage, which allows former spouses to remarry if they so choose. Have you heard such statements as "Almost one out of every two marriages ends in divorce"? Statistics might initially appear to bear out this statement, but consider the following: most sociologists use a statistic called the *refined divorce rate* to calculate the incidence of divorce. The number of divorces in a year is divided by the total number of marriages in that year. In Canada (see Figure 11.1), there were over 140 000 marriages and over 70 000 divorces in 2002 (Statistics Canada 2004b), and divorces have plateaued since then. However, it is misleading to compare the number of marriages with the number of divorces from year to year and say that the divorce rate is 50 percent, because couples who divorce in any given year are very unlikely to have come from the group that married that year. Also, some people go through several marriages and divorces, which skews the divorce rate because the likelihood of divorce goes up with each subsequent marriage.

Why does divorce occur? A number of factors contribute to a couple's statistical likelihood of becoming divorced, including

- getting married during the teenage years (Balakrishnan et al. 1993);

- getting married after only a short acquaintanceship (Goode 1976);

- having relatives and friends disapprove of the marriage (Goode 1976);

- having limited economic resources and earning low wages (Spanier and Glick 1981);

- both partners having a high-school education or less (Houseknecht et al. 1984);

- having parents who were divorced or who had unhappy marriages (Goode 1976); and

- having children present at the beginning of the marriage (Martin and Bumpass 1989; Morgan et al. 1988; Rankin and Maneker 1985).

Because these factors are interrelated with such other factors as class, racialization, and age, determining the likelihood of divorce is very complicated. For example, age is intertwined with economic resources, and people from low-income families typically marry earlier than do people from more affluent families; but if divorce occurs, which factor—age or economic resources—is more closely associated with it?

Religion may affect the divorce rate of some. People who attend religious services weekly are much more likely to want to keep the family together and place more importance on home life than non-attenders, according to the 1995 GSS (Clark 1998).

Divorce laws in Canada once required the partner seeking the divorce to prove misconduct on the part of the other spouse. Under today's no-fault divorce laws, however, proof of blameworthiness is no longer necessary, and most divorces are granted on the grounds of irreconcilable differences, which means that a breakdown has occurred in the marital relationship and neither partner is to be specifically blamed.

With or without blame, divorce usually has a dramatic economic and emotional impact on family members. An estimated 60 percent of divorcing couples have one or more children. Indeed, some children experience more than one divorce during their childhood because one or both of their parents may remarry and subsequently divorce again. Although we do not know how many Canadians have experienced multiple divorces, we do know about multiple disruptions (including death and/or remarriage of a parent) of the family and their effects on childhood happiness. The 1995 GSS asked about family disruptions and their effects on children's feelings of well-being and closeness to parents. According to Statistics Canada analyst Cara

Williams (2001:3), 8 percent of Canadians (1.9 million people) aged 15 and older experienced one change in parental structure, 800 000 Canadians experienced two, and 200 000 experienced three or more. Disruptions do affect childhood happiness. Whereas 92 percent of those without disruptions reported having a happy childhood, only 50 percent of those with three or more disruptions reported having happiness (Williams 2001:4). Those with one or more disruptions also reported being less close to their mother and father than those without disruptions (Williams 2001:4). The topic of the consequences of divorce quickly brings out strong debate, ranging from those like researcher Anne-Marie Ambert (1998), who say that divorce has negative effects, to those like independent researcher Judith Harris (1998), who dismiss its negative effects. Cherlin (1999) suggests that neither extreme gives a clear portrait of growing up after divorce, because his studies showed that children whose parents would later divorce already showed more emotional problems at age 7 than children from families that would remain intact. Although the effects can be overstated, disruptions do tend to have negative effects on childhood happiness and on relationships with parents.

Divorce changes relationships not only for the couple and children involved but also for other relatives. Some grandparents feel that they are the big losers. Grandparents who wish to see their grandchildren have to keep in touch with the parent who has custody; but if the grandparents are in-laws, they are less likely to be welcomed and may be seen as taking the "other side" simply because they are the parents of the ex-spouse. Recently, some grandparents have sued for custody of minor grandchildren. For the most part, these suits have not been successful except when there has been some question about the emotional stability of the biological parents or the suitability of a foster-care arrangement.

Most people who divorce remarry. In 1997, in more than 34 percent of all marriages, either the bride, the groom, or both had previously been married (Milan 2000:8). Of individuals who divorce before age 35, about half remarry within three years of their first divorce (Bumpass et al. 1990). Most divorced people marry others who have been divorced (London and Wilson 1988), though remarriage rates vary by gender and age. At all ages, a greater proportion of men than women remarry, often relatively soon after the divorce. Among women, the older a woman is at the time of

divorce, the lower her likelihood of remarrying (Wallerstein and Blakeslee 1989). Women who have not graduated from high school and have young children tend to remarry relatively quickly. Women with a college degree and without children are less likely to remarry (Glick and Lin 1986).

Divorce followed by remarriage often creates complex family relationships. A **blended family** consists of a husband and wife or a same-sex couple, children from previous marriages, and children (if any) from the new marriage. At least initially, stress in blended families may be fairly high because of rivalry among the children and hostilities directed toward step-parents or babies born into the family. The NLSCY found that nearly 9 percent of Canadian children under age 12 were living in a blended family. These children were more likely than children from intact families to say they lacked emotional support from their parents and to report difficulties in getting along with siblings and parents (Milan 2000:9). In some cases, when parents divorce and marry other partners, the children become part of a binuclear family, living with one biological parent and a step-parent part of the time and with the other biological parent and another step-parent the rest of the time.

As Cherlin (1992) points out, the norms governing divorce and remarriage are ambiguous, so people must make decisions about family life (such as who should be invited to a birthday celebration or a wedding) on the basis of their own feelings about the people involved. But in spite of the problems, many blended families succeed.

DOMESTIC VIOLENCE

The term *domestic violence* obscures the fact that most victims of domestic violence are women and children. Women are more likely to be assaulted, injured, or raped by their male partners than by any other type of assailant. Children are extremely vulnerable to abuse and violence because of their age and economic and social dependence on their parents or other adult caregivers.

Child Abuse

In 2001, Nico Trocmé and his colleagues published the first Canadian Incidence Study of Reported Child Abuse and Neglect (CIS), a nation-wide study to examine the incidence of reported child maltreatment and the characteristics of children and families investigated by Canadian child welfare services. Most of us, when we hear the words *child abuse*, think in terms of physical injury or sexual abuse, but the most frequent form of child maltreatment, according to the CIS, is child neglect—not meeting a child's basic needs for emotional warmth and security, adequate shelter, food, health care, education, clothing, and protection (Trocmé et al. 2001:xv). In 2005, Trocmé and his associates published the second nation-wide study. (In early 2009 they were analyzing the data from a third study.)

In the past, children in Canada were considered the property of their parents and could be punished or ignored as the parents wished. Now, despite legislation protecting children, through child welfare services in the provinces and territories, many physical injuries to children are intentionally inflicted by parents and other caregivers (see Trocmé et al. 2001:4–5). Parental violence can, in fact, lead to the *battered child syndrome,* a psychological disorder in which a child experiences low self-esteem and sometimes clinical depression associated with former or current abuse by a biological or custodial parent (Kempe et al. 1962).

The first CIS identified four kinds of maltreatment: physical abuse, sexual abuse, neglect, and emotional maltreatment. In 1998, the researchers tracked 7672 cases (excluding Quebec), of which 9 percent were substantiated. In 2003, the researchers tracked 14 200 cases in a representative sample of 63 jurisdictions, of which 47 percent of the cases were substantiated. This is a much higher rate than that substantiated in the first study. This study found 21.71 substantiated cases of abuse per 1000 children. A much higher rate of substantiated exposure to domestic violence and emotional maltreatment accounted for this rise. Regarding the kinds of maltreatment discovered in the 2003 study (excluding Quebec):

- 24 percent were physical abuse;
- 3 percent were sexual abuse;
- 30 percent were neglect;
- 15 percent were emotional maltreatment; and
- 28 percent were exposure to domestic violence. (Trocmé et al. 2005:1–2)

The various kinds of abuse of children in Canada are a serious social problem that remains largely hidden. Some researchers have found that children are most likely to be assaulted in their own homes if their parents were abused, neglected, or deprived as children, and if their parents are socially isolated as adults. Parents who lack a support network and suddenly face a crisis tend to make their children the targets of their frustration and sometimes their aggression (Kempe and Kempe 1978). Other researchers have found that abusive parents characteristically feel unloved and unworthy and totally unprepared to cope with their circumstances (Tower 1996).

In fact, reporting of suspected child abuse has improved significantly in recent years because of increased training, awareness, and legislation, which established that reports of suspected abuse would be investigated promptly and fully. In the past, even when physicians suspected abuse, they often chose to treat the child but not to report the incident, believing that abuse would be too difficult to prove (Tower 1996).

Besides physical harm, instances of emotional harm were noted in 15 percent of investigations. Examples of emotional harm included changes in development (e.g., withdrawal), disruption of sleep patterns, and crying and clinging. Problems in overall functioning were also noted in 44 percent of the investigations. The five most-often indicated problems were behavioural problems, depression or anxiety, negative peer involvement, irregular school attendance, and developmental delay (Trocmé et al. 2001:xxiv).

One of the most disturbing forms of maltreatment of children is sexual abuse. Unfortunately, there is a lack of consensus on how to define *sexual abuse.* In the CIS, *sexual abuse* was defined in seven categories: sexual activity attempted, sexual activity completed, touching/fondling genitals, adult exposing genitals, sexual exploitation (e.g., prostitution), sexual harassment, and voyeurism (Trocmé et al. 2001:33).

According to the CIS, the incidence of sexual abuse investigated declined slightly between studies. Two-thirds of the sexual abuse cases involved female children and one-third involved males (Trocmé et al. 2001:65). Regarding the prevalence of sexual abuse, it appears that between 10 and 15 percent of girls and boys experience some form of sexual contact as children (Finkelhor 1984). While the overall rate of investigations was similar for boys and girls at all ages, females are more likely than males to be victims of sexual abuse as well as incest, or sexual relations between individuals so closely related that they are forbidden to marry by law (Trocmé et al. 2001:66).

In a dramatic example of child sexual abuse, Jeannie Hilton went public with her story about her father, champion boxer Dave Hilton, Jr., and his abuse of her and her sister. In the fall of 2004, Jeannie Hilton published a book detailing the five years of abuse suffered by her and her sister, Anne Marie. Originally written in French, the book was entitled *Le Coeur au buerre noir(The Heart with a Black Eye)*. The father, Dave Hilton, Jr., was convicted in 2001 of sex-related charges and received a seven-year sentence. According to an article in the *Globe and Mail,* he had begun molesting his daughters at age 11, first forcing them to perform oral sex and then taking their virginity through intercourse (Ha 2004:A9). Jeannie Hilton is quoted as saying, "I never had a chance to be young. . . . In high school when they were saying, 'Let's move to first base and kiss boys,' I was doing things with my father." But also affirming, "You have to talk about it. If you don't, it'll eat at you. . . . There is no way out of it" (Ha 2004:A9).

The vast majority (93 percent) of the perpetrators of maltreatment are parents and relatives (Trocmé et al. 2001:49). The alleged perpetrators of physical abuse are almost evenly divided between biological mothers (47 percent) and fathers (42 percent) and of sexual abuse are mostly male—both biological fathers (15 percent) and other relatives (28 percent) (Trocmé et al. 2001:49).

Turning to police reports, according to the 2008 edition of the report *Family Violence in Canada: A Statistical Profile,* reports from 2006 showed that children and youth were more likely than adults to be physically or sexually assaulted. Child and youth victims were likely to know their aggressor. Of the 622 per 100 000 population, 334 were victimized by a friend or acquaintance, 187 experienced violence by a family member, and 101 were victimized by a stranger (Statistics Canada 2009e:6). Rates of family violence were higher for girls than boys (27). Family-related sex assault rates were highest for preteen and teenage girls and for young boys (27).

A usually less severe form of punishment, used by most parents, is spanking. Some people consider this abuse. Box 11.3 presents a discussion of this topic and reference to cases featured in the media. The campaign against spanking is becoming worldwide.

Another kind of abuse that deserves attention is parental abuse. This is not elder abuse (see Chapter 5), but abuse of middle-aged people by their teenaged offspring. Types of parental abuse include physical, psychological, and financial (stealing or damaging the home or possessions). Some children who abuse may have a disorder or condition such as ADHD. Mothers are the most frequent victims of parental abuse, but fathers are susceptible too. Although this abuse can

SOCIAL PROBLEMS AND SOCIAL POLICY

BOX 11.3   Should Spanking Be Permitted?

Every schoolteacher, parent or person standing in the place of a parent is justified in using force by way of correction toward a pupil or child, as the case may be, who is under his care, if the force does not exceed what is reasonable under the circumstances.

Criminal Code, Section 43

In 2000, children's rights advocates appealed to the Ontario Superior Court to have this law declared unconstitutional. Judge David McCombs ruled in July 2000 that spanking does not violate the constitutional rights of children. He agreed with the advocates that corporal punishment should not involve a slap to the head or cause injury, which would be a case of child abuse, and noted that public attitudes to corporal punishment of children are changing. But he also said that parents should have a protected sphere in which to raise children, and reasonable force should be used only with the best interests of the children.

When this decision was appealed to the Ontario Court of Appeal, it ruled in January 2002 that parents and teachers are free to spank children for disciplinary purposes, but only if the force they use is reasonable. The judges acknowledged that many people who were acquitted of abuse before would not be acquitted today. They also suggested such guidelines as not hitting a teenager or a child under 2, not using an object such as a belt or ruler, and not hitting or slapping the head of a child (Makin 2002:A8).

In July 2001, six children, 6 to 14 years of age, were taken from their home in Aylmer, Ontario, because their parents would not promise not to hit them with switches if they disobeyed. The parents belong to a Mennonite church whose members believe in the literal truth of the Bible, which states in the King James version, "He that spareth his rod hateth his son: but he that loveth him chasteneth him betimes" (Proverbs 13:24). The family's pastor, Mr. Hillebrandt, indicated that following the Bible does not mean injuring the child; the children were examined for injuries—none were found. But he does believe that corporal punishment "works in our time to do just like it's written" (quoted in Saunders 2001:A7). Steve Bailey, the executive director of Family and Children's Services of St. Thomas and Elgin, said while they believed that spanking "per se is not child abuse . . . We would look at whether there's any use of inanimate objects such as belts or cords or sticks" (quoted in Saunders 2001:A7). The children were originally taken into foster care and then released. In the summer of 2002, a trial took place in which the authorities sought to allow the children to remain at home, but only under a year-long supervision order, which would see them subject to regular monitoring.

In their chapter "Should Johnny Be Spanked?" Tepperman and Blain (2006:36–37) identify some of the negative consequences of corporal punishment—from immediate depression, anxiety, lower grades, and slower physical development to crime, racism, and violence as adults—while acknowledging

that though a majority of people are spanked, only a minority become abusive or criminal. They conclude that "parents should not spank their children if they want to reduce misbehaviour; it doesn't work. Alternative methods, like reasoning with the child and withholding rewards, are more successful if the parents are consistent." The National Longitudinal Study of Children and Youth also showed that aversive parenting was very often related to behavioural problems.

Many states around the world have enacted laws to eliminate corporal punishment of children. The Global Initiative to End all Corporal Punishment of Children website **(http://www. endcorporalpunishment.org)** identifies ways of tackling the problem and 24 states that have outlawed corporal punishment (2009). These include predictable states, such as the Scandinavian countries; continental European countries, including Spain, Germany, Greece, and the Netherlands; and a variety of others, such as Costa Rica, New Zealand, Ukraine, and Israel.

What do you think about the *Criminal Code* section? Do you think it should be repealed or amended? Do you believe in the parent's right to spank a child? What do you think about the case of the six children? Should the family be monitored for any length of time?

occur in any class or family structure, abused mothers are often single parents (Cottrell 2001).

Spousal Violence

From the days of early Rome to current times, spousal violence has been acknowledged to exist, but until recently, it was largely ignored or tolerated. Fortunately, the rates of abuse seem to be declining in step with the decline of crime generally. According to the 2008 edition of the report *Family Violence in Canada: A Statistical Profile* (Statistics Canada 2009e:6), female and male victim rates dropped for the past years recorded (1998 to 2006), but there are still five times as many female as male victims (see Table 11.3)

The suffering and such other harmful consequences as needing medication are experienced much more strongly by the woman. Unfortunately, some of these abused women end up victims of homicide. As noted above in the section on the feminist perspective, women are more than seven times as likely as men to be killed by their spouses or intimate partners. Fortunately, a substantial decline in spousal homicide is occurring for both sexes (see above).

Social Responses to Domestic Violence

Although every few months we read in the papers about extreme domestic violence, such as a murder (of a woman) and suicide (by a man), many people who are aware of domestic abuse don't do anything about it, feeling that they do not want to become involved in a "private matter."

Historically, in Canada, an ideology of non-intervention—a strong reluctance on the part of outsiders to interfere in family matters—has led people and police officers to ignore or tolerate domestic violence (Lauer 1995). Unfortunately, the pattern of violence that ultimately results in a homicide is eerily similar in many cases of domestic abuse, and in most of those cases, death might have been prevented by earlier intervention. Positive changes in how law enforcement officials handle domestic violence calls are now being made—changes that are long overdue.

One other major change is the growth of shelters for abused women. In Canada, 569 shelters admitted 101 000 women and children between April 1, 2007, and March 31, 2008. A snapshot survey was conducted on

TABLE 11.3   Victims of Spousal Violence by Offence Type and Sex of Victim, Reported to Police, 2006

Offence type	Total number	%	Female number	%	Male number	%
Homicide/attempts	155	0	110	0	45	1
Sexual assault (levels 1, 2, 3)	633	2	622	2	11	0
Major assault (levels 2, 3)	5 555	14	4 047	13	1 508	23
Common assault (level 1)	23 680	61	19 749	62	3 931	60
Criminal harassment	3 053	8	2 705	8	348	5
Uttering threats	4 283	11	3 663	11	620	9
Other violent offences	1 214	3	1 132	4	82	1
Total offences	**38 573**	**100**	**32 028**	**100**	**6 545**	**100**

0   true zero or a value rounded to zero
Note: Percentages may not add up to 100 percent due to rounding, Excludes incidents where the sex and/or the age of the victim was unknown. Includes victims aged 15 to 98.

Source: Statistics Canada, 2008, "Family Violence: Spousal Violence in Canada 2006," The Daily (October 9). Retrieved October 29, 2009 (http://www.statcan.ca/Daily/English/081009/d081009b.htm).

April 16, 2008. On that day, 4273 women and 3361 children were residing in shelters. Nearly 80 percent of these women and children were attempting to flee an abusive situation. Emotional abuse and physical abuse were most cited as reasons for seeking shelter. Three-quarters of the women reported abuse by a spouse or former spouse. Under child abuse (see above), one of the types was witnessing domestic violence; 25 percent of the women sought shelter so their children would not witness violence against their mother. About 90 percent of women who left the shelter did not return to their spouse (Statistics Canada 2009j).

FAMILY-RELATED PROBLEMS IN THE 21ST CENTURY

As we have seen, families and intimate relationships changed dramatically during the 20th century. Because of these changes, some people believe that the family as we know it is doomed; others think that returning to traditional family values can save this important social institution and create a more stable society. Another point of view, however, comes from sociologist Lillian Rubin (1994), who suggests that clinging to a traditional image of families is hypocritical in light of our

society's failure to support the family, whether through family allowances or decent public-sponsored child-care facilities. Some laws even hurt children whose families do not fit the traditional model. Welfare cuts, like those made by the Progressive Conservative government in Ontario in 1995, for example, affect children as well as the adults who are trying to provide for them.

For the family to remain a viable and effective social institution, a macrolevel societal commitment is needed, as sociologist Demie Kurz (1995:232) states:

As a society we should make a commitment to helping all families—traditional nuclear families, two-parent, two-earner families, and single-parent families—and to providing adequately for their members, particularly their children. To help families we must reduce female and male poverty, making special efforts to end institutionalized discrimination against minorities. We must also promote equality between men and women in the family. This includes creating new conceptions of what it means to be a father and what it means to be a partner in a marriage and share family life and household work. It also means taking decisive steps to end violence toward women and children. While the costs of creating humane and just social policies are high, the cost of failing to promote the welfare of family members is far higher.

WHAT CAN YOU DO?

- Investigate if any shelters for women could use help in your community. Volunteer at the shelter; help is always needed.

- Analyze who does what unpaid domestic labour in your household, or suggest that a tutorial be devoted to discussing who should do what unpaid domestic labour in a relationship.

- Find out what family concerns feminist groups on campus have and help them address them.

- Look further into the topic of Canadian parenting styles by studying recommendations of parenting magazines and websites and thinking of new variables or situations for this research topic.

SUMMARY

What Is a Family?

A family is a relationship in which people live together with commitment, form an economic unit, care for any young, and consider the group critical to their identity. This definition modifies the traditional definition to account for today's greater diversity in living arrangements and relationships in families.

Are Canadian Families in Decline?

Not at all, say analysts who take a social change perspective. Families are becoming more complex and diverse, adapting to other changes in society. For one thing, marriage is no longer a cultural imperative; for another, many people reaffirm their belief in the institution through serial monogamy—a succession of marriages over a lifetime.

What Are the Sociological Perspectives on Family-Related Problems?

Functionalists believe that the family provides social order and economic stability; the family is the solution to many societal problems, and dysfunctional families threaten the well-being of individuals and the whole of society.

Conflict theorists see the family as a problem in society, not a solution; they believe that the family is a

major source of inequality in society brought on by capitalism.

Feminist theorists see women's subordination as rooted in the patriarchal system, coming long before capitalism.

Interactionists view the family first in terms of socialization. Some speak of the shared reality of marriage; some view family problems in terms of the subjective meanings that people give to their everyday lives; and some cite partners' unrealistic expectations about love and marriage.

What Characterizes Singlehood in Canada Today?

The proportion of the Canadian households that have a single occupant has risen to a quarter. Some people remain single by choice, others by necessity; many working-class young people cannot afford to marry and set up a household.

Why Do Young People Postpone Marriage Today?

Four factors are important: changing job structures in Canada lead to economic uncertainty; more women are in the labour force; sexual relationships outside of marriage are more socially acceptable than before; and young people observing the rising divorce rate may be cautious about jumping into marriage.

Does Common-Law Living or Cohabitation Usually Lead to a Successful Marriage? What Is a Domestic Partnership?

According to one recent study, only about 50 percent of cohabiting couples marry, and evidence on the success of those marriages is mixed. Some studies show little or no effect; others show that partners who cohabit are more likely to divorce than partners who do not. A domestic partnership is a partnership in which an unmarried couple lives together in a committed relationship and is granted many of the same legal rights and benefits accorded to a married couple.

What Does Research Show about Dual-Earner Marriages?

More than 60 percent of all marriages in Canada are dual-earner marriages; that is, marriages in which both spouses are in the labour force. Many women in these marriages do much of the domestic work at home after completing their workday jobs, though there seems to be a gradual trend toward more egalitarian division of labour.

Is a Two-Parent Family Always Preferable to a One-Parent Family?

If the parents argue constantly, abuse the children, or are alcoholics, a supportive single-parent family would be preferable. However, a child growing up in a single-parent household faces serious risks that are complicated by other factors, such as poverty, discrimination, unsafe neighbourhoods, and high crime rates.

Why Is Reproductive Freedom Such a Controversial Issue?

Reproductive freedom implies the option to have or not to have a child. The roles that religious organizations, physicians, and society (through the legal system) should (and should not) play in controlling a woman's fertility continue to be debated. Contraception, abortion, and new reproductive technologies all raise personal and societal issues.

Which Is More Important, Parenting Style or Income?

A continuing national study has found that parenting styles ranging from positive to ineffective had more influence on behavioural problems than family income or structure.

Are Non-Marital Pregnancies Increasing or Declining?

Births to teenagers, as a percentage of all births, have decreased over the past 30 years, but the birth rate is higher for unmarried teenagers than in the past. In addition, the proportion of births to unmarried women aged 25 to 34 has greatly increased.

Who Gets Divorced? Do Most People Remarry?

Many factors affect who gets divorced (e.g., marrying during the teen years or having limited economic resources), and these factors are interrelated with class, racialization, and age, so it is very difficult to determine any kind of statistical likelihood of divorce. Most people do remarry, and divorce followed by remarriage leads to complex family relationships, such as blended families.

KEY TERMS

blended family, p. 262
common-law, or cohabitation, p. 254
dual-earner marriages, p. 255
extended family, p. 247
family, p. 247
kinship, p. 247
monogamy, p. 249
nuclear family, p. 247
second shift, p. 255

QUESTIONS FOR CRITICAL THINKING

1. Sociologist Andrew Cherlin says that the family is a highly adaptable social institution, but we can minimize the costs of change in the family unit by modifying other social institutions of daily life such as the economy and workplace. What specific suggestions can you give for modifications in work–family arrangements?

2. What do you think of Margaret Mead's proposal of a two-stage marriage? What problems, such as reducing "starter marriages," might it forestall? Would it create any new ones?

3. What suggestions can you offer to help offset the potentially detrimental effects of single-parent households, especially when the parent is a woman who is employed full-time?

4. Why do you think more lesbian couples have children than do gay couples? Do you think this will change in the future?

Explore the topics covered in this chapter at **www.mysockit.com** using the access provided with this text. Interactive resources for studying include video clips, practice tests, learning objectives, and Internet resources.

12 PROBLEMS IN EDUCATION

The current challenge is for the kids to have high standards. I don't want kids to feel victimized. I want to provide them with tools to survive in the dominant culture.

Ainsworth Morgan, a teacher at Nelson Mandela Park School, an inner-city Toronto school, where he was originally a student

But we are concerned in terms of the social polarization that [people choosing a school by factors like math scores, and parental income, education, and immigration status] can cause. We'd be better to look at schools by what sort of programs they have.

Annie Kidder, People for Education, quoted in the Toronto Star *(June 4, 2009:GT5)*

It's as if we're saying to students, technology is not important and working in tech jobs is somehow a second class occupation. For many students these programs keep them interested, keep them in school and provide a pathway to success in secondary school.

Elena Aleinikov, principal of Lord Lansdowne Senior Elementary School, talking about the loss of the Design and Technology program and its effect on students at a press conference to release the eighth annual study by People for Education, June 21, 2005

A study from 10-year-old data but only recently published showed teens in Ontario, Alberta, Saskatchewan, and British Columbia from more advantaged families were more likely to be taking the type of math, science, and English courses that would keep all their post-secondary options open, compared to teens from families in which neither parent had a post-secondary education and in which family incomes tended to be lower (Statistics Canada 2007d). But this did not mean that immigrant children and children whose first language was not English or French were at a disadvantage. They were somewhat more likely to have all post-secondary options open. Devising separate streams, also known as **tracking**—assigning students to specific courses and educational programs on the basis of their test scores, previous grades, or both—can have a positive effect on the achievement of some students, but a negative effect on students not in the post-secondary stream, especially if they are asked to perform at the level of students in the post-secondary stream. The harm isn't intentional. The people who authorized

the test want all students to perform well so that they will be able to thrive in a complex, changing environment. It is possible for inner-city students to do well with the right encouragement, like that from teachers like Ainsworth Morgan (see his story later in the chapter).

Canada and other industrialized nations highly value **education**—the social institution responsible for transmitting knowledge, skills, and cultural values in a formally organized structure. But a wide gap exists between the ideals of Canadian education and the realities of daily life in many schools. As a result, business and political leaders, parents, teachers, and the general public tend to complain about the state of education in this country, even as many parents report feeling relatively positive about the schools their children attend.

In this chapter you will learn about the problems of low-level literacy; opportunities for both high-school completion and post-secondary education available to people from differing family structures, socio-economic backgrounds, racialized/ethnic backgrounds, gender, and regions; school violence and bullying; residential schools for Indigenous children; financing for elementary, secondary, and post-secondary education and the commercialization of post-secondary education; overall learning and the future of education; and what you can do about them.

First, the sociological perspectives—functionalist, conflict, interactionist, and feminist—on education will be outlined to help us understand the problems and to show how educational problems are often intertwined with other issues.

PERSPECTIVES ON EDUCATION

The way a sociologist studies education depends on the theoretical perspective he or she takes. Functionalists, for example, believe that schools should promote good citizenship and upward mobility and that problems in education are related to social disorganization, rapid social change, and the organizational structure of schools. Conflict theorists believe that schools perpetuate inequality and that problems in education are the result of bias based on racialization, class, and gender. Meanwhile, interactionists focus on microlevel problems in schools, such as how communication and teachers' expectations affect students' levels of achievement and dropout rates. Lastly, feminist theorists focus on the differences of male and female performance in, and responses to, the educational system.

Functionalist Perspectives

Functionalists believe that education is one of the most important social institutions because it contributes to the smooth functioning of society and provides individuals with opportunities for personal fulfillment and upward social mobility. According to functionalists, when problems occur, they can usually be traced to the failure of educational institutions—schools, universities, colleges—to fulfill one of their manifest functions. **Manifest functions** are open, stated, and intended goals or consequences of activities within an organization or institution. While the most obvious manifest function of education is the teaching of academic subjects (reading, writing, mathematics, science, and history), education has at least five major manifest functions in society:

1. *Socialization:* From kindergarten through college, schools teach students the student role, specific academic subjects, and political socialization. In kindergarten, children learn the attitudes and behaviour generally considered appropriate for a student (Ballantine and Hammack 2009). In primary and secondary schools, ideally, students are taught specific subject matter that is appropriate to their age, skill level, and previous educational experience. At the college level, students expand their knowledge and seek out new areas of study. Throughout, students learn the democratic process.

2. *Transmission of culture:* Schools transmit cultural norms and values to each new generation and play a major role in *assimilation,* the process whereby recent immigrants learn dominant cultural values, attitudes, and behaviour so that they can be productive members of society.

3. *Social control:* Although controversy exists over whose values should be taught, schools are responsible for teaching values such as discipline, respect, obedience, punctuality, and perseverance. Schools teach conformity by encouraging young people to be good students, conscientious future workers, and law-abiding citizens.

4. *Social placement:* Schools are responsible for identifying the most qualified people to fill available positions in society. Students are often channelled into programs on the basis of their perceived individual ability and academic achievement. Graduates receive credentials generally required for entering the paid labour force.

5. *Change and innovation:* Schools are a source of change and innovation. To meet the needs of student populations at particular times, new programs—such as HIV/AIDS education, computer education, and multicultural studies—are created. In addition, new sustainability teacher education programs are created to promote an inclusive, responsible society that cares about the future. The sixth annual survey (2009) of post-secondary schools found that among teacher education schools, the Ontario Institute for Studies in Education (OISE) had the highest score for these criteria, followed by the education schools of the universities of British Columbia, Saskatchewan, and Alberta (Corporate Knights 2009:48). University faculty members are expected to conduct research and publish new knowledge that benefits the overall society. A major goal of change and innovation in education is to reduce social problems.

In addition to these manifest functions, education fulfills a number of **latent functions**—hidden, unstated, and sometimes unintended consequences of activities in an organization or institution. Consider, for example, these latent functions of education: compulsory school attendance keeps children and teenagers off the streets (and, by implication, out of trouble) and out of the full-time job market for a number of years (controlling the flow of workers). High schools, colleges, and universities serve as matchmaking institutions where people often meet future marriage partners. By bringing people of similar ages, racialized/ethnic groups, and social-class backgrounds together, schools establish social networks.

Functionalists acknowledge many *dysfunctions* in education, but to many, one seems overriding: our public schools were once not adequately preparing students for jobs and global competition. In comparative rankings of students across countries on standardized reading, mathematics, and science tests,

Canadian students were lagging until a decade ago. In the most recent international assessment sponsored by the Organisation for Economic Co-operation and Development (OECD), in 2000, Canadian students made a substantial improvement, placing sixth in mathematics and fifth in science (still behind Singapore and Japan) and second in reading (behind Finland; Statistics Canada 2001c). Canadian students' high ranking continued into 2003 (Statistics Canada 2004d). And between 2003 and 2006, Canadian performance remained unchanged in reading and mathematics; however, more countries outperformed Canada (Statistics Canada 2008m). If these scores are maintained in future tests, this will show that significant change can occur in the educational system.

Other dysfunctions include the fact that our schools are not preparing students for their political responsibilities as citizens of a democracy (to think and question and be well informed). The education departments of different countries understandably have different ways of encouraging their educational goals. Box 12.1 illustrates various ways countries are encouraging their young people's education.

SOCIAL PROBLEMS IN GLOBAL PERSPECTIVE

BOX 12.1   Encouraging Achievement around the World

In Canada, education is a local enterprise. Provinces and local school districts decide on standards, set curricula, and assess—or do not assess—students' achievement. This system may seem to be just fine except that, in international math and science tests, Canada used to rank low in comparison to other modern, industrialized countries and still ranks lower than Japan and Singapore. Critics say that we need higher standards, perhaps national standards backed up by a common nationwide curriculum that culminates in standardized achievement tests. Countries that rank highest in international pupil achievement tests have national standards. Japan, for example, boasts nearly universal literacy and high-school students who can solve complicated math problems.

Today, though, the Japanese Ministry of Education acknowledges that the school system itself may play a role in the problem of truancy. In April 2002, it introduced measures to make education less pressured. Students will be encouraged to be creative and to learn independently, both for themselves and for the needs of the global economy. According to a report by foreign correspondent Geoffrey York (2002:A12), Saturday classes were eliminated, and the mathematics, science, and language programs were cut by 30 percent and replaced by field trips and general studies. Many parents and politicians, thinking, "hardship builds character," are worried that students will do less well on exams. Some wealthy parents will still send their children to *jukus* and other private schools. Assuming that such students will get higher marks, some critics feel that the new approach will result in advantage to the middle class and the wealthy (York 2002:A12).

Japan's neighbour, China, is still conducting the *gao kao*, or high test, that determines the fate of 10 million students for college admission (LaFraniere 2009:L2). Students study 14 to 16 hours a day for a year for a test like the SAT in the United States. But this one is nine hours long and is held only once a year. Various methods are tried to enhance student scores, from sending the student to a military-like boarding school devoted to preparation to placing tiny earpieces in the test-taker's ear to hear answers to the questions—though over 2000 cheaters were caught in 2008 (LaFraniere 2009:L2).

In India an innovative program is helping poor students. Through computer workstations inserted in brick walls for local students to use, Hole-in-the-Wall Education Limited helps them learn math, social sciences, science, and English (the students can also view health videos that show, for example, the value of wearing a helmet when driving a motorcycle and play some computer games). Each computer monitor and keyboard is protected by Plexiglas cover, and an elementary mouse is available for use. A low-hanging cover ensures that only children use it. The project has been described by experts as an opportunity for the poor to act collectively and express themselves—for villagers, the site is a well where children assemble to work collectively and come up with new ideas.

In New Delhi, where a quarter million children do not attend school, Hole-in-the-Wall has set up 56 computer terminals to help these children. The project was expanded to other places and was equally successful. There are now over 300 computers (called Learning Stations) inside and outside India. In urban areas, schools cover the cost of powering the computers. In places separate from schools, computers are powered by solar panels.

The evaluators found an improvement in math, science, and content (on the computer) assimilation and an improvement in scores in school in comparison with a control group. *Slumdog Millionaire*, the runaway winner at the 2009 Academy Awards, was in part inspired by Hole-in-the-Wall.

Conflict Perspectives

Sociologists using a conflict framework for analyzing problems in education believe that schools—which are supposed to reduce social inequalities in society—actually perpetuate inequalities based on class, racialization, and gender (Apple 1982). In fact, conflict theorists such as French sociologist Pierre Bourdieu argue that education *reproduces* existing class relationships (see Bourdieu and Passeron 1990). According to Bourdieu, students have differing amounts of *cultural capital* that they learn at home and bring with them to the classroom (see Chapter 2). Children from middle- and upper-income homes have considerable cultural capital because their parents have taught them about books, art, music, and other forms of culture. According to Bourdieu, children from low-income and poverty-level families have not had the same opportunities to acquire cultural capital. Some social analysts believe it is students' cultural capital—rather than their "natural" intelligence or aptitude—that is measured on the standardized tests used for tracking. Thus, test results may unfairly limit some students' academic choices and career opportunities (Oakes 1985).

Other sociologists using the conflict framework focus on problems associated with the hidden curriculum, a term coined by sociologist John C. Holt (1964) in his study of why children fail. The **hidden curriculum** refers to how certain cultural values and attitudes, such as conformity and obedience to authority, are transmitted through implied demands in the everyday rules and routines of schools (Snyder 1971). These conflict theorists, such as sociologists Samuel Bowles and Herbert Gintis (1976), suggest that elites use a hidden curriculum that teaches students to be obedient and patriotic—values that uphold the status quo in society and turn students into compliant workers—to manipulate the masses and maintain the elite's power in society. An update by Bowles and Gintis (2002) showing that genetic inheritance of cognitive skill explains only a small part of the persistence of status levels among families further supports this finding.

Although students from all social classes experience the hidden curriculum to some degree, working-class and poverty-level students are the most adversely affected (Ballantine and Hammack 2009). When middle-class teachers teach students from lower-class backgrounds, for example, the classrooms are very structured and the teachers have low expectations about the students' academic achievement (Alexander et al. 1987). In one study of five elementary schools with students from different class backgrounds, researchers found significant differences in how knowledge was transmitted despite similar curricula (Anyon 1980). Schools for working-class students emphasize rules and rote memorization without much decision making, choice, or explanation of why something is done a particular way. In contrast, schools for middle-class students stress the processes that are involved in getting the right answer. Elite schools develop students' analytical powers and critical-thinking skills, teaching them how to apply abstract principles to problem solving.

The limitations on what and how these students in lower-track schools are taught mean that many of them do not get any higher education and therefore never receive the credentials to enter high-paying professions (Bowles and Gintis 1976). Our society emphasizes *credentialism*—a process of increasing demands for higher levels of education for a particular position. And credentials are more important than ever. According to a report on post-secondary education by the Canadian Council on Learning, between 1990 and 2007, the number of jobs requiring post-secondary graduates almost doubled. Only half as many jobs were available for those who had not completed high school (2009b:11). Credentialism is closely related to *meritocracy*—a social system in which status is acquired through individual ability and effort (Young 1994). People who acquire the appropriate credentials for a job are assumed to have gained the position through what they know, not who they are or whom they know. According to conflict theorists, however, the hidden curriculum determines in advance that credentials, at least at the higher levels, will stay in the hands of the elites, so Canada is not a meritocracy even if it calls itself one.

Interactionist Perspectives

Whereas functionalists examine the relationship between the functions of education and problems in schools, and conflict theorists focus on how education perpetuates inequality, interactionists study classroom dynamics and how practices such as labelling affect students' self-concept and aspirations.

Interactionists believe that education is an integral part of the socialization process. Through the formal structure of schools and interpersonal relationships with peers and teachers, students develop a concept of self that lasts long beyond their schooling. Overall, social interactions in school can be either positive or negative. When students learn, develop, and function effectively, their experience is positive. For many students, however, the school environment and peer group interactions leave them discouraged and unhappy. When students who might do better with some assistance from teachers and peers are instead labelled "losers," they may come to view themselves as losers and thus set the stage for self-fulfilling prophecies. As noted in Chapter 1, *a self-fulfilling prophecy* occurs when a false definition of a situation evokes a new behaviour that makes the original false conception come true.

According to interactionists, labels such as *learning disabled* stigmatize students and *marginalize* them—put them at the lower or outer limits of a group—in their interactions with parents, teachers, and other students. Such labelling leads to self-fulfilling prophecies (Carrier 1986; Coles 1987). To counteract this possibility, many of these students have been reintegrated into regular classes over the past decade.

At the opposite end of the spectrum, labelling students *gifted* and *talented* may also result in self-fulfilling prophecies. Students who are identified as having above-average intellectual ability, academic aptitude, creative or productive thinking, or leadership skills may achieve at a higher level because of the label. However, this is not always the case. Girls who are identified as gifted may deny their intelligence because of cultural norms about the proper roles of women and men (see Eder 1985; Eder and Parker 1987). Afraid that their academic achievement will make them unpopular, high-achieving girls, and sometimes boys, can become victims of *anti-intellectualism*—hostility toward people who are assumed to have great mental ability or toward subject matter that is thought to require significant intellectual ability or knowledge. White students are overrepresented in gifted-and-talented programs, whereas visible minority students are underrepresented.

The interactionist perspective, emphasizing that society is the sum of interactions of individuals and groups, would also stress the importance of the influence of excellent teachers, the development of special programs to help students overcome barriers to learning, and initiatives of parents to determine which is the best school for their children.

An example of an exceptional teacher is Ainsworth Morgan, a teacher with Nelson Mandela Park School and Pathways to Education. He is actually a graduate of the inner-city school where he now teaches, the first graduate to return to teach there in the school's 150 years. He says that his inspiration comes from his mother, who created, first, an atmosphere of respect at home, believing that "love comes later." With this inspiration, hard work, and considerable athletic ability, he obtained his bachelor's degree in the United States on an athletic scholarship. He returned to Canada to play wide receiver for the Toronto Argonauts and Saskatchewan Roughriders. Realizing his true calling was teaching, he then took teacher training at the University of Toronto and obtained a job teaching science and core grades 7 and 8 at his "alma mater." He added, "I'm a product of the inner city and it's a privilege to give back to the school that supported me." "It's especially important for these communities to have role models. Few who leave the communities return because of the stigma attached to them." Ainsworth creates an atmosphere of respect and emphasizes that "students should have a say in who they are" and "should not be limited by their postal code." He works closely with the students, frequently staying until six o'clock to help them with projects. (When one of the authors visited his class at the end of the school day, he saw a student preparing to storm out of the class. After Ainsworth's quiet request for an explanation for leaving and an expression of interest in her, she returned and was still working when the author left.) He believes, "The current challenge is for the kids to have high standards. . . . I don't want kids to feel victimized. . . . I want to provide them with tools to survive in the dominant culture" (author's files).

An example of a program specially designed to help students with math is the JUMP (Junior Undiscovered Math Prodigies) program. It is a Toronto-based charitable program founded in 1998 by mathematician and writer John Mighton and eight volunteers. JUMP Math is primarily intended to be used by teachers in the classroom. The program offers a complete package of resources intended to cover the curricula for grades 1 to 8. Professional development is also offered to teachers wishing to add to their teaching credentials. While JUMP Math has developed into a mainstream set of curriculum-based resources, it is intended to be flexible and can be used as a support in after-school tutoring by schools and community organizations, as well as by parents at home. The JUMP Math program has been adopted by many classroom teachers in Toronto, Vancouver, Edmonton, Winnipeg, and elsewhere in Canada as well as internationally. Agreeing with the findings of accumulating research in early childhood education, JUMP believes that children, with very few exceptions, are born capable of learning anything, and that when any student fails a test, it should be seen as a failure of the education system. With its innovative teaching program and one-on-one approach, JUMP is adding to the evidence. Summaries of the research showing its effectiveness can be found at **http://jumpmath.org/program/research/researchinitiatives**.

An example of parents' taking initiative in choosing a school for their children is their using a website called School Finder, set up by the Ontario Ministry of Education in 2009. This website allows people to see math and science and background characteristics of students in prospective schools. Whether this

innovation constitutes increasing transparency or creates polarization of classes is uncertain (see Box 12.2).

Feminist Perspectives

Feminist theorists and researchers traditionally emphasized the extent to which girls and women were disadvantaged by receiving less attention in mathematics and science classes, as shown in a study by the American Association of University Women (1992; see also Chapter 4). Recent work has shown that it is no longer easy to show which gender is the more disadvantaged. As noted in the following section on educational opportunity, women have higher rates of educational attainment than men except at the doctoral and some professional (e.g., engineering) degree levels, and women are doing better in mathematics and science at the secondary level. As psychologist Carol Tavris (2002:B7) said in the *Chronicle*,

Who is having more trouble in schools: girls, more likely to be overlooked, or boys, who have more learning disabilities? Who has the greater self-esteem problem: girls, who feel insecure and fall silent, or boys, who feel insecure and brag? Who has the greater bullying problem: girls, who do it verbally, or boys, who do it physically? Who has the eating and body-image disorders: White middle-class girls, with their familiar

SOCIAL PROBLEMS AND SOCIAL POLICY

BOX 12.2   The School Finder

To help parents choose an elementary/secondary school for their children, in April 2009, the Ontario Ministry of Education created a website that presents data about students' academic performance on math and reading tests and demographic characteristics, including family income, parents' education status, and immigration status. These scores can be compared with provincial averages on the variables. Parents at first could compare three schools at a time, but now they can view only one school at a time to prevent invidious comparisons. Some groups, such as People for Education, still object to the presentation of these characteristics. In the quote at the beginning of this chapter, Annie Kidder, spokesperson for People for Education, expressed concern about the social polarization that could occur when parents are seeking for their children to be with other students like them. The Ministry of Education claims that

the website is about transparency and providing information to parents. Parents have indicated that they wish to know more about schools. This information (much from Statistics Canada that is already available) is now at one website. According to Kathleen Wynne, Minister of Education, in June 2009, the website received 600 hits a day for a total of 28 000 hits since April (Brown 2009). Such a response shows that it is considered valuable by thousands of people. The ministry also expects that this kind of information will encourage schools that have low scores to work harder to increase their scores. Visit the website **http://www.edu.gov.on.ca/eng/sift/index.html** and look up your school's characteristics and compare them with neighbouring schools. Do you think this website is a good way to promote transparency and improve math and reading scores, or do you think it will encourage the polarization of children in Ontario?

problems of anorexia and bulimia, or teenage boys, many of whom are taking dangerous amounts of steroids and pumping themselves up to meet a cultural ideal no less damaging than gauntness is for girls?

Some feminists are studying boys and speaking up for their problems, as Carol Gilligan did by giving a keynote address at a recent international conference on educating boys. She said she had "seen some public schools switching over to single-sex classes as a way to boost concentration, reduce distractions and even enhance student performance" (Owens 2002). In October 2009, the Toronto District School Board is considering a boys-only proposal from director Chris Spence. Feminists have traditionally emphasized the disadvantaged situation of women and girls. In the future, we may find them not looking at men as the opposition, but rather conducting programs and research to help anyone at a disadvantage, no matter which gender.

PROBLEMS IN CANADIAN EDUCATION

Although we have already identified a variety of problems in education, other issues must be addressed in planning for the future of this country. These issues include the problem of illiteracy; the impact of high rates of immigration on educational systems; racialized, class, and gender inequalities in educational opportunities; and growing concerns about violence in schools.

What Can Be Done about Illiteracy?

From time to time, reports emerge suggesting that a high percentage of Canadians are **functionally illiterate**—unable to read and/or write at the skill necessary for carrying out everyday tasks. Even more startling, as we learned in November 2005, celebrated people like former Montreal Canadiens Stanley Cup–winning head coach Jacques Demers could neither read nor write. To determine the extent of illiteracy in many industrialized countries, including Canada and the United States, the International Adult Literacy Survey was conducted in 1994–95 and replicated in

2003. Four types of literacy were surveyed in the 2003 version:

- Prose: understanding and responding to instructions
- Document: understanding maps, graphs, or timetables
- Quantitative: calculating costs of various items
- Problem solving

Five levels of each type of literacy were created. For example, Level 1 of prose involved applying instructions on a medicine bottle and Level 5 involved answering a question from a personnel department in terms not used in the question. In Canada, 5660 people aged 16 to 65 were surveyed, and the majority had adequate literacy skills, measured as being at Level 3 or higher for the three types of literacy (Clark 1996:28). Little difference was found between males and females (women scored slightly higher in prose, and men scored slightly higher in quantitative literacy). Younger people scored higher than older people (Clark 1996:30). People who were more highly educated and

FIGURE 12.1   Employment Rate at the Highest and Lowest Levels of Document Proficiency

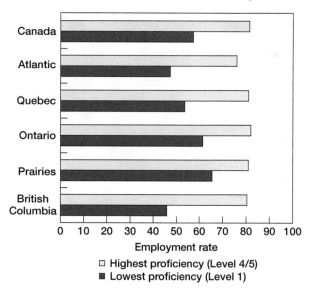

Source: Statistics Canada, 2005, "International Adult Literacy and Skills Survey: Building Our Competencies," The Daily (November 20) Catalogue no. 11-001.

people who read frequently scored predictably higher than those who had not completed high school and did not read newspapers and books (Clark 1996:33). Another analysis of the data showed that whereas anglophones scored higher than francophones, the difference in scores was almost entirely due to education, not language differences. In Canada, until recently, anglophones tended to have higher educational attainment than francophones (Corbeil 1998:6).

Although the majority of Canadians are quite literate, a sizable proportion, one in six people, had literacy skills at Level 1. In 2003, after testing over 23 000 Canadians, the researchers found that this proportion had improved, though not substantially, to one in seven (Statistics Canada 2005a). Perhaps, instead of "functionally illiterate," a new term, such as **low-level literate,** should be used to identify those who can maintain their current occupation but have minimal skills for adapting to a more complex occupation. The problem is that in a complex and rapidly changing world, Canadians need to be functioning at higher levels of literacy to adapt to new challenges. The follow-up survey showed that those with the lowest levels of document literacy have lower levels of employment. Figure 12.1 shows that in every part of Canada, those with lower levels of literacy have lower levels of employment and, as might be predicted, those with higher levels were earning more than those with lower levels (Statistics Canada 2005f).

One ray of hope comes from the general increase in years of schooling, or educational attainment, among younger people. The percentage of people completing secondary school is now almost 90 percent. Thus, the proportion of people who are low-level literate might be expected to decrease in the future. Only 10 percent of secondary-school graduates and no university graduates function at Level 1 (Clark 1996:33).

Volunteers and trained professionals are an important link in reducing adult illiteracy. How can we make it easier for people to learn to read without experiencing embarrassment?

Educational Opportunities and Ascribed Statuses

We have long known that ascribed statuses—such as family structure and socioeconomic status, children's gender or racialized/ethnic status, and geographic region lived in—have a significant effect on educational outcomes. The following sections look at a variety of ascribed statuses and their influence on children's educational outcomes.

Primary Education

Past research showed that girls and boys differed in important ways in their readiness to learn as they entered school at the age of 5. Girls outperformed boys in several areas. However, recent analysis from the National Longitudinal Survey of Children and Youth shows that boys and girls did not differ in mathematics achievement by the time they were aged 9 in either grades 3 or 4. In addition, children from very low-income households scored somewhat lower than those in higher-income households in mathematics achievement in both grades. However, the differences did not reach statistical significance (see Figure 12.2; Statistics Canada 2008n).

What did make a difference in mathematics was school readiness. In the past, the academic achievement of 9-year-olds was strongly linked to the knowledge that children have of numbers, as well as to their ability to copy and use symbols, as they entered school at the age of 5. Longitudinal data from the same children and youth study show that children who had significantly higher scores on these two measures of school readiness at the age of 5 also had high mathematics test scores at the age of 9 (see Figure 12.3).

FIGURE 12.2   Gender and Income Differences in Mathematics Scores

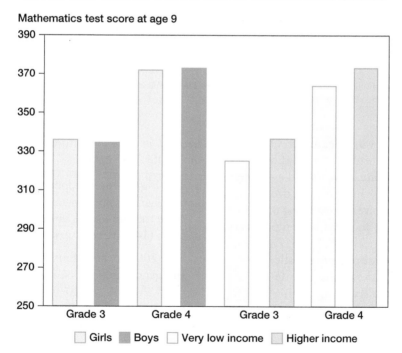

Note: Grade 3 and grade 4 mathematics test scores are not comparable because the tests differed to allow for the different number of years of instruction for students in the two grades.

Source: Statistics Canada, 2008, "National Longitudinal Survey of Children and Youth: School Achievement of Nine-Year-Olds," The Daily *(November 24). Retrieved November 24, 2008 (http://www.statcan.gc.ca/daily-quotidien/081124/cg081124b-eng.htm).*

FIGURE 12.3   Mathematics Scores by School Readiness at Age 5

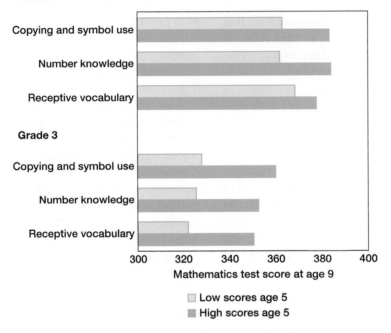

Note: Low scores at age 5 were below the median: high scores at age 5 were above the median. Grade 3 and grade 4 mathematics test scores are not comparable because the tests differed to allow for the different number of years of instruction for students in the two grades.

Source: Statistics Canada, 2008, "National Longitudinal Survey of Children and Youth: School Achievement of Nine-Year-Olds," The Daily (November 24). Retrieved November 24, 2008 (http://www.statcan.gc.ca/daily-quotidien/081124/cg081124b-eng.htm).

In June 2009, a report was released in Ontario advocating full-day kindergarten for 4- and 5-year-olds as a way to solve many problems, from diagnosing disabilities early to reducing high-school dropouts. This would appear to help solve the readiness of those aged 5, though it would cost about $1 billion per year at a time when resources are very scarce. And the report's projected outcomes are open to question since Quebec has had full-day kindergarten since 1997 and its high-school dropout rate is among the highest in the country (see the next section). What do you think might be done to help improve children's readiness for school?

Secondary Education

A wide variety of factors affect whether a student will complete high school. The Canadian Council on Learning's report *Post-Secondary Education in Canada:*

Meeting Our Needs? identified a couple of these factors from 2006–2007 data:

- The high-school dropout rate for 20- to 24-year-olds living in small towns and rural areas was almost twice the rate for the same age group living in large cities (14.9 percent versus 8.3 percent).

- The 2006 Census found that almost half of the Indigenous population in Canada is under the age of 25. Among the 20- to 24-year-old Indigenous population, 40.3 percent had not completed high school, compared to 12.5 percent in the non-Indigenous population. (Canadian Council on Learning 2009b:9)

Other studies show the influence of other factors. The findings of the 1994 General Social Survey show the influence of family structure on the likelihood that children will complete high school.

According to a study by Statistics Canada analyst Judith Frederick and sociologist Monica Boyd (1998:13), children from families living with both biological parents are more likely to complete high school than children from either blended or lone-parent families. Whereas over 80 percent of children living with both biological parents completed high school, slightly less than 70 percent of the children from blended families and slightly more than 70 percent of the children from lone-parent families completed high school. However, if the lone parent had high-school or higher educational attainment, then the chances of the adolescents completing high school increased greatly; about 85 percent of these children completed high school, in comparison with 94 percent of the adolescents from two-parent families (Frederick and Boyd 1998:14). Thus, whereas family structure does affect educational outcomes, parents' education appears be even more influential.

The results of an analysis by Statistics Canada analyst Patrice de Broucker and consultant Laval Lavallée (1998:13) of Canadian data from the previously noted International Adult Literacy Study also show that parents' education continues to count (Statistics Canada 2005f). The probability of earning a diploma or degree is highest for young adults whose parents also have post-secondary education. Whereas over 60 percent of young adults whose parents have post-secondary completion earn a diploma or degree, only about a quarter of young adults whose parents have not completed high school have post-secondary completion. In the replicated study of literacy, young adults whose parents had completed 12 years of schooling scored 24 points higher than young people whose parents completed only eight years (Statistics Canada 2005a).

The social class of the parents is also crucial. De Broucker and Lavallée (1998:13) also discovered that the socioeconomic status (SES—composed of measures of the workers' income and education, and the percentage of women among the workers) of the parents' occupations was related to the educational attainment of the young adults. The higher the SES score of the father, the higher the child's educational level. Even fathers without high-school education but with a higher SES occupation can provide an environment and resources to help their children attain a post-secondary degree. Regarding performance in individual subjects,

in an OECD study of reading, mathematics, and science, students from high SES backgrounds outperformed students from low SES backgrounds (Statistics Canada 2001c).

In regards to high-school completion, women are doing very well. According to Statistics Canada's *Youth in Transition Survey* (Statistics Canada 2002k), only 9 percent of women dropped out of high school in 1999, as measured by the percentage of 20-year-olds who had not completed high school and were no longer in school. This is an important improvement over 1991, when 14 percent dropped out. A higher though decreasing percentage of men drop out: 15 percent of men in 1999 in comparison to 22 percent in 1991. The results of this study also underlined the influence of family structure noted previously. Although the majority of both high-school graduates and dropouts lived in a two-parent family during high school, a greater percentage of dropouts than graduates (32 percent versus 16 percent) lived with a single parent. Dropouts were also three times as likely as graduates to have parents who had not finished high school (27 percent versus 9 percent).

As a result of concern that the dropout rate was trending up in 2005, the Ontario government has decided to make attendance at school compulsory to age 18 (or graduation). New Brunswick has already made attendance to 18 compulsory, but is not enforcing it, so the dropout rate has not changed. Ontario plans to enforce attendance by denying driving licences to those who drop out. Perhaps a better approach would be to support programs like Pathways to Education, a downtown Toronto program that provides tutoring to inner-city secondary school students and a $1000 per year scholarship toward post-secondary education.

For particular subjects, like mathematics and science, a large number of past studies have shown what amounted to gender bias; girls were discouraged from doing well in these subjects or even pursuing them. Now, however, girls are now doing much better in these courses, as shown in recent national test results. According to the OECD study, in which Canadians scored very high, no significant differences between girls and boys were found in science test scores. Scores for reading were significantly higher for girls, and scores for mathematics were significantly higher for boys, but by a slimmer difference than for reading (Statistics Canada 2001c).

Although no clear differences are found among the large regions of Canada for completing high school, Quebec and Prince Edward Island were the provinces with the highest percentages (16 percent) of dropouts, and New Brunswick and Saskatchewan were the provinces with the lowest percentages (8 percent).

Post-Secondary Education

Many educators hoped that with the expansion of post-secondary education, the influence of many ascribed statuses such as gender, ethnicity, region, and class would be eliminated, and to some extent this has happened. Over the past few decades there has been a steady improvement in the percentage of young people, especially women, taking post-secondary education. Figure 12.3 shows that even when young people do not go to post-secondary schools immediately after secondary school, by the time they are 26 years of age, more than 75 percent of them have participated in post-secondary education, ranging from 70 percent of males to over 80 percent of females.

FIGURE 12.4   Participation in Post-Secondary Education by Sex and Age, 2005

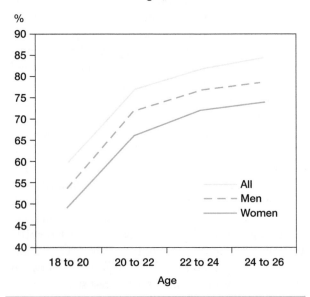

Source: Statistics Canada, 2007, "Youth in Transition Survey: Participation in Postsecondary Education," The Daily (November 20). Retrieved November 20, 2008 (http://www.statcan.gc.ca/daily-quotidien/071120/dq071120b-eng.htm).

Regarding ethnicity, students have differing rates of completion of university depending on their country of origin. Results of a study conducted in 2002 showed children of immigrants tend to achieve higher levels of education than children of Canadian-born parents, but there are wide differences in rates of completing university among young people of different national origins. For example, youth of Asian immigrant parents, except for Filipinos, had higher rates of obtaining a university degree by the time they were aged 25 to 34 in 2002 than most youth of European origin. University completion rates ranged from over 65 percent for youth of immigrant parents from China and India to 24 percent among second-generation German and Central and South American youth. About 28 percent of the children of Canadian-born parents had completed university by the time they were aged 25 to 34 (Statistics Canada 2008q).

Regarding class, students from low-income families are still less likely to pursue a post-secondary education. Only 58.5 percent of 18- to 24-year-olds from families earning less than $25 000 annually participated in post-secondary education in 2006, compared to 80.9 percent of youth of the same age from families with an income over $100 000 (Canadian Council on Learning 2009a:9).

The *Youth in Transition Survey* also showed that Eastern and Central Canadians were slightly more likely to attend post-secondary school than Western Canadians, but the differences were minimal (Statistics Canada 2002k). A more telling measure of the influence of region is commuting distance to university. It has a significant effect on university attendance. High-school students who lived beyond commuting distance of a university (beyond 80 km) were far less likely to attend university than those living within commuting distance (within 40 km). To compound the problem, commuting distance had a much greater negative impact on university access for students with lower family incomes (Statistics Canada 2002c).

Bullying, Cyber Bullying, and School Violence

In the past dozen years, a number of dramatic bullying incidents have been reported. One student—Reena Virk of Victoria, B.C.—was killed and three students—Dawn-Marie Wesley and Hamed Nastoh, also of British

Columbia, and Emmet Fraslick of Halifax—committed suicide because of bullying. Because of incidents like these, bullying has become a very prominent social problem.

As a result of its prominence, questions about bullying—defined as "when one or more people tease, hurt, or upset a weaker person on purpose"—were added by drug use researchers Edward Adlaf and his colleagues (2002:46) to their continuing survey of drug use by older students in Ontario. This study was one of the continuing biennial (since 1977) surveys of Ontario students' drug use by the Centre for Addiction and Mental Health (formerly the Addiction Research Foundation). Previous waves of this study of drug use had asked students in grades 7, 9, 11, and OAC about committing assault and carrying weapons. They found for the year 2001 that 31.8 percent of students in grades 7 through OAC (grade 13, now abolished) reported bullying others at school and 24.6 percent reported being bullied, with 5.7 percent being bullied daily or weekly. The replication of that study in 2007 reported that a reduced percentage of students, 24.7 percent, reported bullying others, but an increased percentage, 29.9 percent, reported being bullied (Adlaf et al. 2007:vi). That a higher percentage of people reported being bullied than bullying and that this percentage has increased over time may be due to the lesser reluctance of people to admit being a victim. Although bullying has become prominent over the past decade, school violence has been a concern for much longer. In his study of officials from 260 school boards and 250 police chiefs across the country, criminologist Thomas Gabor (1995) found that 80 percent of both groups felt that violence and intimidation had grown from the mid-1980s to the mid-1990s. Studying weapons use in Canadian schools, S.G. Walker (1994) found that weapons use increased from the late-1980s to the mid-1990s. Adlaf et al. (2002:43) found that 12.3 percent of the students surveyed had assaulted someone in the past year, and 10.4 percent admitted carrying a weapon at school. In both cases, a higher percentage of males reported the offence, but no significant grade or age differences occurred. In 2007 the percentage carrying a weapon was lower, at 8.7 percent, and the percentage fighting (a slightly different question from assault) at school was 15.8 percent (2007:vi).

It is difficult to know if any trends are present, especially when a new type of bullying, cyber bullying, or bullying online, is occurring. Many extreme examples of cyber bullying have been highlighted by the media, such as that directed at Megan Meier, a 13-year-old Missouri girl who hanged herself after alleged cyber bullying by an adult neighbour masquerading as a teenage boy on MySpace. In an effort to study its extent, Faye Mishna et al., of the University of Toronto, surveyed 2186 students in 33 schools in the Greater Toronto Area. In the past three months, 21 percent reported being bullied, mostly by friends, and 35 percent reported having bullied other kids online, mostly attempting to make them feel bad (2008:5–6).

Most educational analysts acknowledge that technology—for example, metal detectors—alone will not rid schools of violence and crime. In Canada, a wide variety of programs have been developed—from zero tolerance of violence (e.g., Scarborough, a former suburb of Toronto, Board of Education) to Alberta's Safe and Caring School Project to the creation of the Canadian Safe Schools Network (CSSN), a grassroots organization dedicated to reducing youth violence and making schools and communities safer. Years ago, the CSSN launched the Empowered Student Partnerships (EPS) program to empower students to plan, organize, and execute safe-school programs in the Toronto area. Organizations involved include the Toronto Police Service; City Council; ProAction, a concerned business association; and the Toronto School Board. The CSSN has also created a CD-ROM of six bullying incidents and interventions, which can be viewed from the perspective of the victim, perpetrator, and bystander. The Canadian Safe Schools Network's latest work can be found at **http://www.canadiansafeschools.com.**

Ensuring safety at school for students and teachers alike is another challenge facing school districts that are burdened with shrinking budgets, decaying buildings, and heightened demands for services.

Residential Schools

In June 2008, Prime Minister Harper made a formal apology in the House of Commons to former (about 80 000) students of residential schools operated by churches and government. Compensation of $4 billion was offered and an Indian Residential Schools Truth and Reconciliation Commission was established, with $60 million in funding, to hear from the students and their families, communities, and churches, and to educate all Canadians on the residential schools system.

The churches had already begun their Remember the Children campaign in March 2008 (Munnik 2008).

Residential schools were created to assimilate Indigenous children to mainstream culture. The idea of assimilation by force began in the late 18th century, and by 1920 attendance was compulsory for children 7 to 15 years of age. Children were forcibly taken from their families by priests, Indian agents, and police officers. By 1930, 80 residential schools were operating in Canada. The high point of attendance occurred in 1948 with 9368 students in 21 schools. Then schools began to decline in numbers and students decreased, so that in 1979 there were 12 residential schools with 1899 students (Assembly of First Nations 2008).

In the 1980s, students began to disclose forms of abuse at the residential schools. Generally, the Indigenous students experienced more misery than benefit from poor facilities, poor teaching methods, and frequent physical and sexual abuse. In addition, Indigenous languages were forbidden in the school, Indigenous ways were disparaged, and the Euro-Canadian values were considered superior (Miller 2002). Indigenous people began to organize, and the last school was closed in 1996. Various reports, class action lawsuits, apologies by the churches and governments, and offers of compensation occurred before this 2008 offer.

The following quotations from Indigenous people (Stueck and Boesveld 2008:A8–9) illustrate the variety of abuses suffered by many Indigenous children:

One of the first things is they try to institutionalize you by taking away your name. I was given a number and that's [how] I was identified. All my belongings were taken away from me.

—Janice Acoose, associate English professor, First Nations University of Canada

Many children like myself suffered physical, mental, emotional, and sexual abuse. There was nothing ever mentioned at that time in regards to abuse. It was kind of accepted as the norm.... Most of the [sexual abuse] happened at night in the dark in the big crowded room or when you went to the bathroom.

—Darwin Blind, family support worker, Gordon Wellness and Therapy Centre, George Gordon First Nation, Saskatchewan

They instil fear into you. That thing hung around me for a long, long time in my life. Fear of everything—fear of people, of places, institutions, and fear of authority.... [A Parisian priest] saw that I was leaning toward [art] and he said "I will do something about that." ... The art kind of held me in there. It replaced my cultural loss.

—Alex Janvier, artist

[On my first day] I got into a fight with one of the boys. The supervisor locked me in a locker, six feet by two feet....

—Chief Frank Johnson, Wuikinuxv First Nation, B.C.

If we were caught speaking our language, we were punished. It wasn't until I was out of the system ... that I realized that much of the objectives of the residential schools were to disregard our culture.

—Judge Alfred Scow, retired provincial court judge, and first Indigenous person to graduate from law school and be called to the bar in B.C.

Another revelation in October 2008 was that many of the thousands of children who went missing from the schools were buried in unmarked or anonymous graves (Curry 2008). Neither the federal government nor Indigenous leaders know how many students of the residential schools died, let alone where they are buried. The Truth and Reconciliation Commission was asked to undertake to discover how many residential students died and who they were, what they died from (possibly from tuberculosis but also neglect), and where they were buried.

Some have suggested that the schools were not entirely bad. For example, Jim Miller, Canada Research Chair in Native Newcomer Relations at the University of Saskatchewan, said, "From the very early days in the 1990s, the story got framed as a story of abuse. I can understand how that would happen, but it's had an effect of oversimplifying the story." Mr. Wagamsese, a column writer with the *Calgary Herald* and author of several books, said that he did not discount the pain and suffering endured by many who attended residential schools, but "I can't possibly believe that every one of those people functioning as missionaries and clergy were predators" (Stueck and Boesveld 2008:A8).

Another ominous consequence of residential schools is their long-term effect. A survey of off-reserve Indigenous people in 2006 found that, according to the reports of parents who saw report cards and had knowledge of their work, seven of 10 children 6 to 14 years of age were doing well or very well. But off-reserve Indigenous children whose parents had attended residential schools were less likely to do as well or very well than those whose parents had not. About 12 percent of off-reserve Indigenous children had parents (one or both) who indicated that they had been students in the residential school system that operated across Canada between 1830 and the 1990s (Statistics Canada 2009a). Thus, living in residential schools was a problem not only for attenders, but also for future generations.

PROBLEMS IN FINANCING EDUCATION

Declines in Governmental Support

It is well known that governments have been cutting back on school budgets. Although support for elementary and secondary education in Canada is among the highest in the developed world, the contribution by governments per pupil has declined since the mid-1990s. Statistics Canada reported in *Education Indicators* that between 1997/1998 and 2002/2003, combined federal, provincial/territorial, and municipal government expenditure (in constant dollars) in Canada grew by 10 percent at the post-secondary level; expenditure at the elementary–secondary level increased by 5 percent (Statistics Canada 2009d).

Like the other levels of education, the post-secondary level has seen substantial decline in relative governmental support. In *U of T Magazine,* University of Toronto President David Naylor reported comparisons of government support between the United States and Canada. Whereas in 2006–2007, universities in the American Association of Universities similar to the University of Toronto received $60 104 per full-time student, the U of T received $26 738 (Naylor 2009:44) and the absolute value (inflation adjusted) of support per student has not increased since 1991.

In order to make up the shortfall, universities and colleges increased tuition substantially during the past two decades. As a result, a great increase in fees and expenses occurred, on average from $1464 in 1990–1991 to $4172 in 2004–2005. Fees are highest in Nova Scotia (almost $6000) and lowest in Quebec (almost $1700; Statistics Canada 2004j). Since that time the rise has been more gradual. Table 12.1 shows that a 3.6 percent rise in fees occurred between 2007–2008 and 2008–2009.

Moreover, according to the Global Higher Educational Rankings of 2005, Canada ranked 11th out of 16 countries in the affordability of university education (continental European countries having more affordable tuition, and English-speaking countries and Japan having less affordable education; Mascoll 2005:A16).

The provincial governments also deregulated fees for certain courses so that the universities and colleges could charge increased tuition for professional and graduate education. Although student loans were available for paying tuition and expenses, an obvious consequence was that the number of graduating students with large debts increased. Even before the most

TABLE 12.1   Average Undergraduate Tuition Fees for Canadian Full-Time Students, by Province

| | 2007/2008 | 2008/2009 | 2007/2008 to 2008/2009 |
	Current Dollars		% Change
Canada	**4558**	**4724**	**3.6**
Newfoundland and Labrador	2632	2632	0.0
Prince Edward Island	4440	4530	2.0
Nova Scotia	6110	5932	-2.9
New Brunswick	5590	5590	0.0
Quebec	2056	2167	5.4
Ontario	5388	5643	4.7
Manitoba	3271	3276	0.2
Saskatchewan	5015	5015	0.0
Alberta	5122	5361	4.7
British Columbia	4922	5040	2.4

*Source: Statistics Canada, 2008, "University Tuition Fees," **The Daily** (October 9). Retrieved October 9, 2008 (http://www.statcan.gc.ca/daily-quotidien/081009/dq081009a-eng.htm).*

recent big hikes, students were having difficulties. According to the National Graduates Surveys of 2002, just under 50 percent of the 2000 graduates owed money; on average, graduates of universities owed $19 500 and graduates of colleges owed $12 600 (Statistics Canada 2004e). The average debt from all sources in constant 2007 dollars among graduates of the class of 2005 who owed student-related debt did not differ greatly from the class of 2000 (Statistics Canada 2009h). This compares unfavourably with the amounts owed in 1997 by 1995 graduates: $9600 by college students and $13 300 by university students. A more extreme example of tuition increase is that for studying law at the University of Toronto, where the Faculty of Law plans to increase tuition to $22 000 over the next few years. Students entering first year in 2008–2009 paid $20 155 tuition per year. In defence of the increase, former Dean Ronald J. Daniels (2002:A15) wrote in the *Globe and Mail*, "We're pursuing an ideal by offering a challenging intellectual experience steeped in Canadian law and legal institutions that also takes account of broader international experience." He also said the faculty was offering expanded ranks of professors, reduced class sizes, and new courses. Finally, he noted that it was offering increased financial aid and compared the increased tuition to that at top U.S. schools, which charge $27 500 even for in-state students. The Black Law Students Association of Canada was very critical of the tuition hike and asked the Ontario Human Rights Commission to investigate the increase, saying that it would discriminate against minority and low-income students. According to the association, the average annual income for Black families in Toronto is $25 000. Louise James, a member of the association, quoted in the *Varsity,* the student newspaper of the University of Toronto, said that the faculty "don't address the problem that is going to be posed by the tuition hike, in terms of attracting more students of diverse backgrounds and improving their experience at law school" (Holloway 2002:1).

Commercialization of Post-Secondary Education

Another important aspect of school financing is commercialization. The commercialization of universities and colleges takes many forms—for example, the obvious increase in corporate advertisements in washrooms and corridors and the greater numbers of soft-drink machines (see Box 10.2 about taxing soft drinks) and fast-food franchises, such as Tim Hortons. The machines are on almost every floor, and the franchises are in almost every building with classrooms on campus. Another form of commercialization is the opportunity for corporations to name buildings and classrooms. Individual bricks are available for the names of donors. As a speaker at a retirement party for a university president suggested, "Only the doorknobs remain." As a result, the fundraising arm of universities—called by a succession of euphemisms, such as external relations, advancement, and development—has gained in importance and its vice-president is sometimes the highest-paid official at the university. These forms of commercialization are found at both colleges and universities, but a third form of commercialization is more problematic for universities.

Universities are being encouraged to form partnerships with corporations. These relationships are intended to provide research facilities and funding as government funding declines. From the access to university researchers, businesses feel they can be at the cutting-edge of their industry. The university can enhance its image if it can contribute innovative products—from drugs to software. For example, the University of Waterloo is well known for its innovative contributions to computer technology and generating of companies like OpenText and Research In Motion (makers of the BlackBerry). Finally, students can gain because the collaborations can help them find co-op assignments and future employment.

On the other hand, in their book *No Place to Learn: Why Universities Aren't Working,* political scientists Tom Pocklington and Allan Tupper (2002:148) discuss the close links between universities and corporations and conclude that universities

may knowingly or unwittingly link themselves with corporations and thereby operate in ways contrary to other legitimate interests and groups in society. In this way, universities can seriously overextend their mandates as educational institutions. Their priorities can be badly distorted as a result.

EDUCATIONAL GOALS FOR THE 21ST CENTURY

Now that we are in a society of continuous change, we have come to recognize that learning cannot stop with a degree or diploma—we must promote learning outside school, and lifelong learning is crucial. How are Canada and communities within Canada faring regarding overall learning? Although measuring learning is much more difficult than measuring the percentage of people with degrees or even literacy, the Canadian Council on Learning (CCL) has attempted to do so since 2006. It has devised the Composite Learning Index (CLI) based on four learning pillars, developed by the United Nations Educational, Scientific, and Cultural Organization (UNESCO). Each of the pillars has many indicators:

- *Learning to know:* literacy, numeracy, critical thinking, and general knowledge, acquired through participation in post-secondary education
- *Learning to do:* skills like computer training, managerial training, and apprenticeships
- *Learning to live together:* developing values of respect and concern for others, fostering social and interpersonal skills and appreciation of the diversity of Canadians
- *Learning to be, or the development of a person's body, mind, and spirit:* personal discovery through participation in arts and sports. (CCL 2009a)

The four pillars are made up of 17 indicators, such as youth literacy skills, proportion with a diploma or degree, availability of workplace training, access to cultural resources, and participating in clubs and organizations. These indicators have 25 (in total) measures of the indicators. The diagram of the CLI is in the shape of a wheel, with pillars on the inside and measures on the rim. Data are obtained from Statistics Canada and other sources for over 4700 cities and communities in Canada. Top city scores in 2009 went to Calgary (89), Victoria (88), Guelph (85), and Ottawa (84). Toronto (80), Montreal (68), and Vancouver (77) were in the middle of the pack (CCL 2009b). From 2006 to 2008, Canada's overall score rose slightly to 77. In 2009, the overall score declined to 75. The CCL reported that the decline was not related to the recent economic downturn, since many of the measures came from late 2007 and early 2008, but rather to substantial decreases in the "learning to be" pillar, somewhat offset by increases in the "learning to do" pillar. The link **http://www.ccl-cca.ca/CLI2009/2009Scores.html** provides the composite and individual scores for 2009 for the major cities and communities of Canada. Given the difficulties we are facing in this economic downturn, we need to remember the importance of maintaining or increasing all forms of learning to weather this storm and prepare for those in the future. Governmental support is also crucial for support not only of teachers and educational institutions but also of cultural workers, including curators, actors, musicians, and institutions such as museums, art galleries, theatres, and concert halls. We should try to reverse the decline in the CLI and make it possible for Canadians to increase their score in the future.

WHAT CAN YOU DO?

- See if your college or university has a co-operative program with a local elementary or high school to provide mathematics, English, or other kinds of tutoring. If not, you might volunteer your services to a local principal or guidance counsellor.
- Find out if your student government has a program to educate students about the skyrocketing cost of tuition. You might help with the education program or organize a protest.
- Check if your college or university has a peer-mediator program to help settle disputes, or if a local, or your former, elementary or high school needs help with their programs to deal with bullying. If they do not have such programs, you might introduce them to the Canadian Safe School Network (see above) and help them organize a program.
- Familiarize yourself with the wide variety of ways in which girls and boys, and women and men, do poorly or feel at a disadvantage in schools, and do some research to determine what approach can help overcome these problems.
- As a way of following all perspectives, you might consider becoming a teacher, like Ainsworth Morgan and John Mighton, to help students have a say in who they are and not be limited by their backgrounds.

SUMMARY

What Is Education?

Education is the social institution responsible for transmitting knowledge, skills, and cultural values in a formally organized structure.

What Is the Functionalist Perspective on Education?

Functionalists believe that education contributes to the smooth functioning of society when it fulfills its manifest functions. Education has at least five major manifest functions: socialization, transmission of culture, social control, social placement, and change and innovation. Schools also fulfill a number of latent functions—hidden, unstated, and sometimes unintended consequences of its activities—like matchmaking and networking.

What Is the Conflict Perspective on Education?

Conflict theorists believe that schools, which are supposed to reduce inequality in society, actually perpetuate inequalities based on class, racialization, and gender. The sociologist Pierre Bourdieu, for example, says that children from low-income and poverty-level families come to school with less cultural capital (values, beliefs, attitudes, and competencies in language and culture) than middle- and upper-income children. Conflict theorists also think that elites manipulate the masses and maintain their power in society through a hidden curriculum that teaches students to be obedient and patriotic and thus perpetuates the status quo in society.

What Is the Interactionist Perspective on Education?

Interactionists study classroom dynamics and the ways in which practices such as labelling affect students' self-concept and aspirations. If students are labelled "learning disabled," for example, the label may become a self-fulfilling prophecy—that is, an unsubstantiated or erroneous belief that results in behaviour that makes the false belief come true. A student who is erroneously labelled "learning disabled" may stop trying, and teachers may lower their expectations, with the result that the student doesn't succeed in the long run. Interactionists also stress the importance of significant individuals and programs.

What Is the Feminist Perspective on Education?

Feminists were traditionally concerned that girls were not getting equal attention in class with boys, especially for such courses as science and mathematics. Now, girls are performing almost as well as boys on international science and mathematics tests at the secondary level, and women are surpassing men in academic attainment at university, except for engineering and doctoral programs. As a result, some feminists are concerned that boys are at a disadvantage, with higher levels of learning disabilities, lower reading scores on the same international tests, and lower high-school completion rates than girls.

What Is Illiteracy? What Can Be Done About It?

Functional illiteracy is the inability to read and/or write at the skill level necessary for carrying out everyday tasks. Today, one in six adults in Canada has low-level literacy, with higher proportions among lesser-educated and older people. Many of those with test scores at the lowest level of literacy feel that their abilities are good enough for their jobs. To be able to adapt to a modern economy, people need to have a high level of literacy. Perhaps with increasing percentages of people graduating from high school, there will be fewer with low-level literacy. But perhaps extra effort will be required to help people prepare to adapt.

How Do Ascribed Statuses Like Family Structure, Class, Racialization/Ethnicity, Gender, and Region Affect Educational Opportunities in Secondary and Post-Secondary Schools?

Children from lone-parent families, from families with parents having low SES scores, from some racialized/ethnic groups (e.g., Black, Portuguese, and Indigenous), and from some provinces are less likely to graduate from high school than others. Rates of high-school completion are also higher for girls than boys. As they concern post-secondary education and thus graduation, the above factors also apply, as well as how far away from college or university the students live.

How Have Bullying and Violence Affected Our Schools?

Suicides of students who were bullied have highlighted bullying as a significant factor at school. Among grade 7 to OAC students in Ontario, a quarter report being bullied, and almost a third report bullying someone in the past year. Although assault and weapon carrying seem to be declining, the levels are still unacceptably high. In Ontario, in 2007, one in seven students reported fighting with someone in the previous year, and three in ten reported being bullied.

What Is the Crisis in School Financing?

Most educational funds for elementary and secondary education come from provincial and local taxes. Ontario government grants have not kept up with inflation and increasing enrolment. The per-student grant is lower now than in the mid-1990s. Government funds for post-secondary schools have also been reduced, and tuition fees have more than doubled from 1990–1991 to 2004–2005, but since have been rising at inflation-like rates. Since fees for professional and graduate schools have been deregulated, some fees have skyrocketed. An extreme example is the University of Toronto Faculty of Law's plan to increase annual tuition to $22 000. As a result of past increases, some students have high levels of debt. With poor employment prospects, some students have had to default on their loans.

What Educational Goals Should We Set for the 21st Century?

To deal with continuous change, Canada must pursue a policy of providing young people with a high-quality education and opportunities for overall, lifelong learning, including workplace training, volunteer opportunities, and access to cultural programs. The CLI, a measure of this learning, was in a slight decline from 2008 to 2009. We should try to reverse that decline and make it possible for Canadians to increase their score in the future.

KEY TERMS

education, p. 271	latent functions, p. 272	tracking, p. 271
functionally illiterate, p. 277	low-level literate, p. 278	
hidden curriculum, p. 274	manifest functions, p. 272	

QUESTIONS FOR CRITICAL THINKING

1.   How would you convince more parents to spend more time with their children so that they will be ready for school?

2.   What are your learning goals for after graduation? How do you plan to be a lifelong learner?

3.   How would you rate your university or college in comparison with others? Should the provincial governments create a website for post-secondary education like School Finder for primary and secondary education? What characteristics would you like to see compared to help others make the best choice?

Explore the topics covered in this chapter at **www.mysockit.com** using the access provided with this text. Interactive resources for studying include video clips, practice tests, learning objectives, and Internet resources.

PROBLEMS IN THE GLOBALIZED ECONOMY AND POLITICS

13

They did everything they could to make me forget I was human, to make me feel worthless, to make me turn my back on my principles. Though they tried to break us, we all have come out stronger, more militant and more dedicated to changing the world. When will they learn?

Liberty, a woman who was arrested and allegedly brutalized by Canadian police for her participation in the protests against the third Summit of the Americas in Quebec City—the FTAA protest (2001)

There is no activity more intrinsically globalizing than trade, no ideology less interested in nations than capitalism, no challenge to frontiers more audacious than the market. By many measures, corporations today are more central players in global affairs than nations. We call them multinational, but they are more accurately understood as transnational or post-national or anti-national. For they abjure the very idea of nations or any other parochialism that limits them in time or space. Their customers are not citizens of a particular nation or members of a parochial clan: they belong to the universal tribe of consumers defined by needs and wants that are ubiquitous, if not by nature then by cunning or advertising. A consumer is a consumer is a consumer.

Political scientist Benjamin Barber, outlining his understanding of transnational corporations and their role in the world (1995)

The so-called "corporate citizen" is a super-citizen with rights that no flesh-and-blood citizen could ever dream of having. The corporate citizen never sleeps, has virtually unlimited resources, can commit horrendous crimes and never go to jail, and increasingly operates as if the other side of the citizenship coin—responsibilities—simply does not exist.

Murray Dobbin, a member of the Canadian Centre for Policy Alternatives (1998)

The past four years have seen a wave of political organizing and militant protests. Students blockade trade meetings where politicians are bargaining their futures. In First Nations communities, from Vancouver Island to Burnt Church, New Brunswick, there is growing support for seizing back control of the forests and fisheries; people are tired of waiting for Ottawa to grant permission that the courts have already affirmed. In Toronto, the Ontario Coalition Against

Poverty occupies buildings and demands the shelter that is the right of all Canadians.

Naomi Klein, talking about the grassroots protest movements that are growing in Canada (2002)

Nevertheless, if such a movement for radical reform were actually tried and yet failed (we think inevitably) to remove the injustices and irrationalities of the system, there would be no need to go back to square one. Rather the population would be fully justified in such a case in pushing forward and concluding that the entire political-economic structure should be replaced, brick by brick, with another that would meet their genuine needs and be under their democratic control: a system of social use rather than private gain. Already peoples throughout the world have reached the conclusion that the only rational answer is to replace the current rotten system with a more humane order geared to collective needs. For centuries the friends and enemies of social progress have called this alternative of a people-directed economy and society "socialism." We can think of no better name.

Sociologists John Bellamy Foster and Fred Magdoff (2009), speaking about why the current economic crises cannot be dealt with in a similar fashion to the 1930s Great Depression

Healthy national democracies are a necessary foundation for a new global democracy. More and more people in this country feel unrepresented by the existing political system. This democracy deficit is reflected in voter turnout that declines every election: Our voter participation is now close to that in the United States. The democracy deficit is also reflected in the declining number of people who relate to political parties, and in polls that rate politicians and journalists near the bottom of the occupational respect chart. And, finally, it is reflected by the growing number of young people who are taking to the streets because they see no other way to influence government.

Judy Rebick, commenting on the increasing lack of faith Canadians have in the formal political processes (2001a)

Perhaps nothing better signifies our growing awareness of the intertwining of politics and the economy in today's world than the abrupt end of the World Trade Organization (WTO) meeting in Seattle, Washington, in 1999 and subsequent protest actions by broad-based movements worldwide. During the 1999 WTO protest, a series of global trade talks deteriorated into confrontations between diverse protestors, many from Canada, who demanded that large corporations and governments become more accountable for their actions and trade-talk delegates. Many of the delegates to the WTO went home frustrated after a highly unsuccessful meeting, and the world was left with a complicated set of political and economic factors to make sense of. The WTO event served to highlight some important problems that lie at the heart of the global economy and thus affect, and are affected by, Canadian politics. Among these problems are massive job losses, declining wages, welfare state retrenchment, increasing lack of corporate accountability, sweatshop and child labour, and the environmental problems brought about by increased industrialization and decreased regulation (Klein 2000).

Although there have been protests throughout Canadian history, especially during the 1930s and 1960s, the level of radical activism and, maybe most importantly, the broad-based coalition-building that were seen in Seattle had not been visible before. Some analysts believe that a new mood has arisen as more people feel a "loss of control in a world of rapid change and turbocharged global capitalism" (Elliott 1999:37). This overall mood has led to the development of a worldwide anti-globalization movement. Today, the Internet offers protestors and social activists a much wider audience and makes it possible to mobilize a worldwide campaign against political decisions or economic manoeuvres that are viewed as harmful to people and the environment (Elliott 1999).

It will be interesting to chart the actions of the anti-globalization movement through the most recent economic recession. Although Canada entered the global recession later than some other nations, the impact is unparalleled in recent history. This impact is largely due to the fact that Canadians entered the latest recession more vulnerable to an economic downturn than we have been since the 1930s. Overall today, Canadians have little protection against unemployment, little in the way of personal savings, and record-high levels of household debt: in the face of massive job cuts, many of us have nowhere to turn (Yalnizyan 2009). This chapter will examine Canadian and global economic issues and the anti-globalized trade movement.

THREE MAJOR MODERN ECONOMIC SYSTEMS

There are three major modern economic systems: capitalism, socialism, and mixed economies. The Canadian economy is a form of **capitalism,** which is characterized by private ownership of the means of production, from which personal profits can be derived through market competition and without government intervention. **Socialism** is characterized by public ownership of the means of production, the pursuit of collective goals, and centralized decision making. Unlike capitalist economies, in which the primary motivation for economic activity is personal profit, the primary motivation in a socialist economy is the collective good of all citizens. For Karl Marx, socialism was only an intermediate stage to an ideal communist society in which the means of production and all goods would be owned by everyone. Under communism, Marx said, people would contribute according to their abilities and receive according to their needs. Moreover, government would no longer be necessary, since it existed only to serve the interests of the capitalist class.

No economy is purely capitalist or purely socialist; most are mixtures of both. A **mixed economy** combines elements of both capitalism (a market economy) and socialism (a command economy). Some Western European nations, including Sweden, Great Britain, and France, have an economic and political system known as *democratic socialism,* in which private ownership of some of the means of production is combined with governmental distribution of some essential goods and services and free elections. Although most industry in mixed economies is privately owned, there is considerable government involvement in setting rules, policies, and objectives. The government is also heavily involved in providing services such as health care, child care, and transportation. Debates about problems in the Canadian economy often involve comparisons of capitalism with other types of economic systems.

There are four distinctive features of "ideal" capitalism: private ownership of the means of production, pursuit of personal profit, competition, and lack of government intervention. First, capitalism is based on the right of individuals to own various kinds of property, including those that produce income (e.g., factories and businesses). Second, capitalism is based on the belief that people should be able to maximize their individual gain through personal profit, which is supposed to benefit everyone, not just capitalists. Third, capitalism is based on competition, which is supposed to prevent excessive profits. For example, when companies are competing for customers, they must offer innovative goods and services at competitive prices. The need to do this, it is argued, prevents the market pricing of goods from spiralling out of reach of the consumer. Finally, capitalism is based on a lack of government intervention in the marketplace. According to this *laissez-faire* (meaning "leave alone") policy, also called *free enterprise*, competition in a free marketplace—not the government—should be the force that regulates prices and establishes workers' wages.

Problems in the Global Economy

The global financial crisis of 2007–2009 demonstrated how closely connected problems in the Canadian economy are with those of other nations. When Canadian and U.S. financial institutions are in crisis, the economic well-being of many other nations is also in question because it has been widely assumed that high-income nations with advanced economic development will continue to set the pace of global economies. Not all nations are at the same stage of economic development, however, and this creates a widely stratified global economy in which some countries are very wealthy, some are much less wealthy, and still others are very poor. As we discussed in Chapter 2, nations are referred to as high-income, middle-income, and low-income. How these nations are classified is related to their level of economic development and the amount of national and personal income in the country. This development can be traced to the economic organization of societies in the past.

Inequality Based on Uneven Economic Development

Depending on the major type of economic production, a society can be classified as having a preindustrial, industrial, or postindustrial economy. In preindustrial economies, most workers engage in *primary sector production*—the extraction of raw materials and natural resources from the environment. In this type of economy, materials and resources are used without much processing. Today, extracting diamonds in the Canadian Arctic and oil in Alberta are examples of primary sector production.

In comparison with preindustrial economies, most workers in industrial economies are engaged in *secondary sector production*—the processing of raw materials (from the primary sector) into finished products. Work in industrial economies is much more specialized, repetitious, and bureaucratically organized than in preindustrial economies. Assembly-line work, now done on a global basis, is an example.

Although computers and other technology have changed the nature of the production process, factory work is still often specialized, repetitious, heavily supervised, and full of rules for workers to follow, whether these assembly plants are located in Canada, China, or other nations in today's global economy.

Unlike preindustrial and industrial economies, postindustrial economies are characterized by *tertiary sector production*, where workers provide services rather than goods as *their primary source of livelihood*. Tertiary sector production includes work in such areas as fast-food service, transportation, communication, education, real estate, advertising, sports, and entertainment. Inequality typically increases in postindustrial economies where people in high-tech, high-wage jobs often thrive financially and have business connections throughout the world, while workers in low-tech, low-wage jobs in the service sector (such as fast-food servers or hotel cleaning personnel) may have a hard time paying their basic bills and may feel very isolated from the economic mainstream of their own society.

Although Canada still has primary and manufacturing sectors, the service sector has been the one that has grown the most rapidly in recent decades. For this reason, sociologists refer to Canada as an *advanced industrial society*, which is characterized by greater dependence on an international division of labour (Hodson and Sullivan 2008). In Canada, corporations rely on workers throughout the world to produce goods and services for consumers in this country and elsewhere.

Twenty-five years ago, about one-third of the world's workers lived in countries with *centrally planned economies*—economies in which the government decides what goods will be produced and in what quantities—and another third lived in countries only weakly linked to international commerce because of protective barriers to trade and investment. Today, however, it is possible that fewer than 10 percent of the world's workers live in countries that are largely disconnected from world markets (World Bank 1995). While the breakdown in

trade barriers and the turn to economies based on the demands of the marketplace have brought new goods, capital, and ideals to many, they have also brought new fears (see Box 13.1).

BOX 13.1 How "Free" Is Free Trade?

For over a decade, Canada has engaged in negotiating a collection of international trade agreements. In 1989, the Canada–United States Free Trade Agreement (CUFTA) came into effect. Since this time, our government has engaged in several multiyear negotiations that are designed to fully embed the nation in the global economy. Each treaty signed ties Canada's political, social, economic, and environmental well-being more closely to the interests and activities of multilateral trade organizations and transnational corporations.

Many Canadians are deeply troubled by the amount of power these agreements have given corporations and international alliances. These powers are often the same ones that have been taken away from Canadian governments and citizens. This is not a surprising response when 87 percent of our exports go south of the border and 40 percent of Canada's GDP is tied to trade with the United States. No other major country in the world is as dependent upon trade with a single trading partner as Canada is (Barlow 2005). It does nothing to boost confidence when people learn that the world is increasingly dominated by country-size corporations whose "central planning" capacity eclipses that of many countries (M. Barlow 1996) or when Canadians hear Renato Ruggerio, the past director general of the World Trade Organization (WTO), clearly state that the WTO in 1996 was being designed as "the constitution of a single world economy" (Public Citizen 2003).

Governments and businesses justify their support of multilateral trade agreements by invoking the neo-liberal rhetoric of "free market" and free enterprise. While there are clearly economic benefits to corporate involvement in the global economy, the accuracy of the notion of "free market" is questionable. A profile of the global market reveals that it is composed of just 12 industrial sectors, and each of these sectors is controlled by five or fewer firms. The largest of these sectors are consumer durables, automotive, aerospace, electronic components, and steel, with oil, personal computers, and the media not far behind (Dobbin 1998). Based on this information, it could be surmised that, rather than promoting the development of a free market, these multilateral trade agreements primarily promote and protect the interests of shareholders. Canadian policy analyst

Murray Dobbin (1998) warns that this will continue to be the case if corporations are ruling the world.

An analysis of the Canadian economy shows that, for workers, multilateral trade agreements have resulted in the loss of jobs, many in the relatively high-paying, often unionized, manufacturing sector. Today, most new jobs are created in the service sector and are temporary, part-time, and non-unionized. As a result, Canada now has a more "flexible" workforce that earns smaller and smaller wages. For example, by 1999, 52 percent of Canadians were paid less than $15 per hour under the North American Free Trade Agreement (NAFTA). Further, due to NAFTA, hundreds of thousands of jobs have been lost, with re-employed workers earning an average of 77 percent of their previous wages (Steinberg 2001). One of the clearest signals of the decline of workers' rights in Canada under free trade agreements is the decrease in unionization rates. The manufacturing sector felt the sharpest declines, from 45.5 percent in 1988 to 32.6 percent in 2003 (Jackson 2005:170). Although not as sharp, overall unionization rates have declined in Canada—from 39.5 percent to 32.4 percent—reflecting a persistent trend across all sectors of the economy (Scott et al. 2006). These drops reflect the disproportionate closures of unionized facilities and the concentration of new hiring occurring in non-unionized environments. Continental integration, via CUFTA and NAFTA, clearly undercut working families dramatically, with real incomes virtually stagnant, except for those earners at the very top of the scale (Scott et al. 2006).

These job losses and wage cuts are occurring in an era when dramatic cuts to social programs have helped to dismantle Canada's health care system, increased poverty for women and children, and left many sectors of society underserviced (Townson 2003). For example, in the wake of both CUFTA and NAFTA, Canadians were assured that these agreements were an important mechanism for saving the social safety net we are so justly proud of. However, by 2001, government transfers to individuals had dropped from 11.5 percent of the GDP in 1992 to 7.8 percent, and the Canadian government's overall (non-military) spending dropped from 42.9 percent of the GDP in 1992 to 33.6 percent (Scott et al. 2006). Further, the erosion of legislation that protects the environment and

Canada's public natural resources from privatization is currently putting Canada's forests, fish, fresh water, and parks on the international auction block. Under new trade agreements, Canada is being dramatically revamped.

Many Canadians are becoming increasingly concerned that trade deals are not simply about ensuring fair trade between countries; rather, they are about securing power and profit for governments and large corporations. This becomes clear when the socio-economic and political contexts within which multinational agreements are created, negotiated, and signed are analyzed. CUFTA, for example, was signed when over 90 percent of trade between the two countries was already tariff-free and the rest had tariffs of less than 5 percent (Dobbin 1998). It was a decision that was strongly opposed by many Canadians. In 1999, the WTO was negotiated despite the clear protests of over 50 000 people from all walks of life who were opposing the organization's mandate (Klein 2002). In April 2001, the third Summit of the Americas (FTAA) was held in Quebec City—a city that had been barricaded to keep the close to 60 000 citizens expressing their criticism of the summit away from the meeting's headquarters (Editorial Collective 2001). Dobbin (1998) states that the agreements are designed to serve the movement of capital, the removal of restrictions and regulation on that movement, the facilitation of production, and the lowering of production costs. He emphasizes that they are about the rights of capital, not people (Dobbin 1998). Indeed, during the FTAA protest, people's everyday civil rights were violated in Quebec City and the surrounding areas, just as they were in the earlier WTO protests. As one example, local legislators attempted to pass a bylaw that would make it illegal to "wear or have [in your possession] a mask, hood, ski mask, or any other object of the same nature to cover one's face, in whole or in part" (Steinberg 2001). These were all types of clothing protestors could wear as protection against tear gas and pepper spray. In addition, as early as January 2001, people suspected of being protestors were not allowed to cross the border between the United States and Canada (Steinberg 2001).

One of the greatest challenges for Canadians is simply to learn about these agreements and their impacts. This is because many of the treaties are negotiated in secret caucuses; citizens are actively barred or dissuaded from stating dissent at public events; the language used to draft the agreements is often inaccessible; and avenues for direct participation in the official process are blocked. As a clear example, the FTAA protest in Quebec City was not about the actual agreement itself, but rather about the fact that the Canadian government would not allow Canadian citizens access to the trade-deal documents it was discussing and signing with 33 other nations. Because trade deals impact every sphere of our daily life—from the food we eat to the clothes we wear, from the air we breathe to the health care we receive, and so on—if we are not allowed to know what our government is signing on our behalf, what does this say about democracy itself?

A brief overview of the WTO and its role in the protection and perpetuation of multilateral trade agreements, such as the FTAA and the Multinational Agreement on Investment (MAI), demonstrates just how powerful such a governing body is. It also shows how the WTO has the power to directly challenge the ability of Canadian governments and people to protect their own land, resources, and even sovereignty.

The WTO is the international body that codifies the rules upon which global trade systems of production depend. It also administers dozens of trade and commerce agreements and declarations. Initiatives such as the FTAA, the MAI, and the activities of the G-8 (composed of the seven largest economies in the world plus Russia) fall under the auspices of the WTO. The WTO was created in 1995 as a result of the Uruguay Round of negotiations of the General Agreement on Tariffs and Trade (GATT)—the body that for decades has regulated about 90 percent of global trade (Shrybman 1999). Today, the WTO has 153 member countries and is run by its member governments. It covers more than 95 percent of current global trade. The real decision-making authority at the WTO, however, has traditionally been held by the Quad (the European Union, the United States, Japan, and Canada). China's prospective accession as a politically and economically powerful player will add a different dimension to decision making within the WTO. However, at present, "Quad countries basically determine which issues come to the floor, and which issues do not" (Bello, in Shrybman 1999:3). Member nations outside of the Quad, particularly those from poorer nations, complain that the issues of import to 98 percent of the WTO's members are often not meaningfully addressed. In a television interview with delegates to the failed "Millennium Round" of WTO negotiations in Seattle, one delegate from a small nation stated clearly that the people protesting in the streets were saying nothing that delegates from small nations inside the WTO hadn't already been saying for years.

The WTO has authority and influence in part because any country found in contravention of the organization's rulings is vulnerable to economic sanctions "too severe for even the wealthiest nation to ignore" (Shrybman 1999:4). This is alarming when the WTO contains no minimum standards to protect the environment, labour rights, social programs, or cultural diversity and yet is used to strike down a number of key nation-state environmental, food safety, employment, and human rights laws (M. Barlow 1996).

One example is the 1999 WTO ruling that Canada unfairly subsidizes dairy products sold to the United States and New Zealand and must therefore stop its current subsidization activities, which include offering direct export subsidies for tariffs charged by other countries and quota levies that help fund export costs. After going through the court process, Canada grudgingly complied with this ruling. The United States, on the other hand, called it a trade victory. Canada faces $35 million in sanctions from both the United States and New Zealand if it is found in contravention of the ruling one more time (IDFA, NMPF, USDEC 2002). This ruling bolsters the evidence that the WTO is an "international bill of rights for transnational corporations" with a central goal of deregulating international trade for the benefit of these companies (Shrybman 1999:5).

Another initiative that has a great and direct impact on Canada is the North America Free Trade Agreement (NAFTA). This agreement grew out of CUFTA). It was renegotiated as the North America Free Trade Agreement in order to bring Mexico into the cross-border trade agreement. As a result of this agreement, both Canada and Mexico have increased their trade activities both with one another and with the United States. While domestic labour productivity has increased, wages and reliable employment opportunities have not (Campbell et al. 1999). This is not a surprise, however, because the Chapter 11 clause of the agreement grants corporations the authority to override existing laws that govern the behaviour of capital. Corporations are now able to effectively "sue" governments for compensation equal to the loss of profits—including *expected future profits*— if they are a result of policy change or an alteration of the original investment conditions. Typically, under Chapter 11, anything that gets in the way of the free flow of capital is referred to as a "barrier to trade," and Canada can be sued for it.

An increasing number of cases have challenged Canada's ability to protect itself from transnational capital interests. A recent case involving Chapter 11 was the 1997 Ethyl Corporation case, where the corporation filed a $251 million lawsuit against Canada because a new Canadian environmental law stood in the way of potential future profit (Sforza and Vallianatos 1997):

> Canada's decision to ban the import of the neuro-toxin and environmental pollutant MMT was challenged as "expropriation." In the middle of the NAFTA panel's deliberations, Canada threw in the towel, realizing that it was going to lose. Instead of risking a penalty in the hundreds of millions, it settled for US$19 million, apologized to Ethyl, and withdrew the import ban. (Dobbin 1998)

The impact of this case is difficult to calculate. NAFTA allows corporations to bypass democratically adopted laws and, in the case of Canada, may now be contributing to the federal government's reluctance to introduce new environmental or health-protection laws for fear that these legislations would lead to the same allegations (and hence, possible fines) of violating Chapter 11. Moreover, what are the impacts on the health and safety of the citizenry in allowing toxins that would normally be banned by the nation-state to be sold here?

Another example that touches the heart of many Canadians is Canada's universal health plan. As the public system is increasingly underfunded by government, more people call for a two-tier system. However, most Canadians who desire a two-tier system imagine they will have the ability to choose the "kinder, gentler" system of Germany or Sweden and not the American two-tiered model. However, as a signatory of NAFTA, whose rules are clear, it is the American system we are moving toward, and we will not be offered a choice. The exemption for health care under NAFTA, which has, so far, kept large U.S. for-profit health corporations out of Canada, applies only to a fully publicly funded system delivered on a non-commercial basis. Once privatized, the system must give "national treatment" rights to U.S. private hospital chains and Health Maintenance Organizations (HMOs). Not only would U.S. health corporations have the right to set up shop in Canada, they also would have the same right to public funding as Canadian companies. In a short time, the public system could be bankrupt and we could have a corporate health care system based on the American model. If any level of government tried to resist the next *Canadian Health Act*, legal challenges would likely be held in secret at a NAFTA tribunal at World Bank headquarters in Washington.

Even without a Supreme Court ruling on a two-tier system, it is possible that these companies have a right under NAFTA to compete in Canada, because the health system is being privatized so fast. Fully one-third of all health care spending is now private, as services are delisted and doctors opt out of Medicare. There are now at least 240 health care corporations, many of them American, operating in Canada. There are also 140 private health-insurance companies operating here. The Canadian Life and Health Insurance Association states that at least 37 of them are American. Furthermore, 663 private home-care agencies and private companies now control at least 10 percent of the Magnetic Resonance Imaging (MRI) market (Barlow 2005:134–135).

The FTAA was scheduled for completion in 2005. In 2001, Canada hosted the third Summit of the Americas, which was called to further develop the FTAA agreement. The purpose of the FTAA agreement was to extend NAFTA to the entire Western Hemisphere—a total of 34 countries. The final FTAA summit was held in November 2005 at Mar del Plata, Argentina, but no agreement was reached. Despite the fact that 26 of the 34 countries present at the 2005 negotiations agreed to reconvene in 2006 to resume negotiations, no new summit occurred. This fact suggests that there is little likelihood that a comprehensive trade agreement covering the Americas will be signed in the near future.

Regardless of the fate of the FTAA, it is clear that these global trade agreements are already profoundly affecting Canadian democracy, sovereignty, economy, and health. Certainly, finding the balance between economic, social, and environmental health and prosperity is difficult. In part, this is because liberal democracies are inherently challenged by trying to balance an ideology of equality that guides democracy with the imperative of inequality that is integral to "liberal" market economies. The outcry from citizens across the globe and the discontent expressed by ministers involved in these organizations are evidence that the methods and mandates of these global treaties are not fulfilling their commitments to improve trade and *also* to improve the quality of life for the workers who participate in them. What do you think? How has your life been affected by free trade?

Rapid change is never easy. In rich and poor countries alike there are fears of rising insecurity, as technological change, expanding international interactions, and the decline of traditional community structures threaten jobs, wages, and support for the elderly. Nor have economic growth and rising integration solved the problem of world poverty and deprivation. Indeed, the numbers of the poor could rise still further as the world labour force grows to a projected 3.7 billion in 30 years' time. The bulk of the more than a billion individuals living on a dollar or less a day depends on pitifully low returns to hard work. In many countries workers lack representation and work in unhealthy, dangerous, or demeaning conditions. Meanwhile, at the end of 2002, 180 million people were unemployed worldwide, a 20 million increase from 2001 unemployment rates (World Bank 1995:4).

In the wake of latest recession, these numbers have increased dramatically. The rapid changes in economies, and the roles that transnational corporations are playing in those changes, have raised serious concerns about the accountability of corporations.

Transnational Corporations and Canada

Today, the most important corporate structure is the **transnational corporation** (TNC)—a large-scale business organization that is headquartered in one country but operates in many countries, which has the legal power (separate from individual owners or shareholders) to enter into contracts, buy and sell property, and engage in other business activities. These are different from multinational corporations, which have been around since the turn of the last century. The difference is that the **multinational corporation** (MNC)—a complete corporate operation that is taken from its country of origin and integrated into its host country in order to successfully market its products in the local culture—requires a strong host economy to survive. Transnational corporations—by design, truly global entities—prosper by serving global markets in an increasingly economically borderless world. They have advanced global capitalism in unprecedented ways (Dobbin 2001). Some transnational corporations constitute a type of international monopoly capitalism

that transcends the boundaries and legal controls of any one nation. Of the 100 largest economies in the world, 52 percent are private corporations and not national economies (Andersson and Schemberg 2003). The largest transnationals are headquartered in the United States, Japan, Korea, other industrializing Asian nations, and Germany. In 2001, the world's 65 000 transnationals generated over $19 trillion in sales— more than two times the world's exports for that year (Andersson and Schemberg 2002). Examples of true transnational corporations are Asea Brown Boveri, a Swiss–Swedish engineering group, and Philips, a Dutch electronics firm. Both have 85 percent of their sales outside the country in which they are headquartered (Waters 1995). Transnationals dominate in petrochemicals, motor vehicles, consumer electronics, tires, pharmaceuticals, tobacco, soft drinks, fast food, financial consulting, and luxury hotels (Waters 1995). Canadian transnational corporations deal predominantly in gold and other minerals, such as nickel and copper, and oil and gas (Draffan 2003).

Because transnational corporations are large and powerful entities, they play a significant role in the economies and governments of many countries. At the same time, by their very nature, they are not accountable to any government or any regulatory agency. Corporate executives often own a great number of shares in a transnational company. The shareholders in transnational corporations live throughout the world. These people have little control over where plants are located, how much money employees are paid, or how the environment is protected. As transnational corporations gain power, they increasingly determine what will be defined as news, which university departments will receive funding, what technology will be developed, and which political parities will be supported (Dobbin 2001). Because transnationals do not depend on any one country for labour, capital, or technology, they can locate their operations in countries where political and business leaders accept their practices and few other employment opportunities exist for resident workers. For example, when Nike workers went on strike in Indonesia, Nike subcontracted to Korean entrepreneurs operating assembly plants in Vietnam. Although many workers in low-income nations earn less than a living wage from transnational corporations, the products they make are often sold for hundreds of times the cost of raw materials and labour. According to media coverage, managers of these plants are often also physically abusive to the women workers, and union organizing and other human rights organizing are strongly deterred. Designer clothing, athletic shoes, and children's toys are examples of products that are made under exploitative conditions. Young women working in Nike factories in Indonesia and Vietnam, for example, go barefoot and certainly cannot afford to buy the shoes they assemble (Goodman 1996).

Still another concern is that transnational corporations aggressively promote global consumerism. Global consumerism inevitably and dramatically changes local cultures and encourages a "shop till you drop" mentality through advertising and the strategic placement of their business operations around the world. McDonald's golden arches and Coca-Cola signs can be seen from Confederation Square in Ottawa to Red Square in Moscow, and the malls in China could be easily mistaken for the malls in Canada, except that in China they tend to be larger—for example, the US$400 million South China Mall is currently the world's largest shopping mall, covering more than 7.1 million square feet and providing shopping and entertainment for millions of consumers annually (Barboza 2005:C7). Both McDonald's and Coca-Cola are conquering other nations as aggressively as they have Canada. Today, Coca-Cola sells products in more than 195 countries, distributing 37 percent of total gallons sold in the Unites States; 43 percent in Mexico, Brazil, Japan and China; and the remaining 20 percent throughout the rest of the world (Coca-Cola Company 2005). Canada is host to many transnational corporations, like McDonald's, Walmart, and Coca-Cola, primarily from the United States, with some from some Asian countries.

While many Canadian businesses are foreign-owned, the conditions the businesses operate under are a cause of concern for many. The 2001 Canadian Democracy and Corporate Accountability Commission (CDCAC 2002) found that 84 percent of Canadians want the government to promote international agreements to "set minimum enforceable standards for socially responsible corporate behaviour" (CDCAC 2002: Executive Summary). Canadians across the political spectrum are expressing discomfort with transnational activities in many parts of the world, including in this country.

PROBLEMS IN THE CANADIAN ECONOMY

Despite a period of strong economic growth through the late 1990s and early into the 2000s, Canadians entered the global recession in a weaker position than ever before. The impacts of the recession will be felt in many years to come, as we struggle with growing national deficits and debt, growing consumer debt, and rising unemployment. At the same time as individuals and the nation as a whole attempt to ride out the recession with few safety nets left intact, wealth continues to be concentrated in the hands of a few and corporate welfare continues unabated. Since the mid-1990s, inequality in Canada grew faster than in most other OECD countries, including the United States: median incomes in Canada stagnated while the top 5 percent captured the lion's share of income increases (Campbell 2009).

Recession

According to Canadian economist Armine Yalnizyan (2009), Canadians have not been exposed to as much economic risk as we now face since the 1930s. Going into the recession, more than 3 million Canadians were living in poverty. The economic boom in Canada did not impact the distribution of income in any way and certainly did nothing to eliminate poverty or even "child poverty" in Canada. In 2007, for example, one in five Canadians experienced poverty (Yalnizyan and Hennessy 2009). Now, immersed in the worst economic period since the Depression, things look increasingly grim. In 2007, most families needed two income earners to make a living. In the midst of a recession, with mass unemployment, what awaits Canadians in the near future (Yalnizyan and Hennessy 2009)?

Statistics Canada reported in August 2009 that 414 000 jobs were lost in Canada between October 2008 and July 2009, with an additional 436 000 job losses in the private sector. More losses, in the hundreds of thousands, were predicted, while almost 60 percent of the 1.5 million unemployed received no help from the Employment Insurance (EI) program (Statistics Canada 2009g; Yalnizyan and Hennessy 2009). The official unemployment rate climbed to 8.6 percent by July 2009, the highest in 11 years, and is predicted to reach 12 percent before the recession comes to a close (Yalnizyan 2009).

Unemployment affects everyone, but the hardest hit have been young people aged 15 to 24 and men aged 25 to 54 as better-paid and unionized jobs in manufacturing, construction, transportation, and warehousing were eliminated. In June 2009, Yalnizyan predicted the next target would be the service sector, a frightening possibility given that most women's jobs are in the service sector, and in previous recessions, families offset their household income losses through women taking up paid employment. Today, most women are already in the paid labour force, and most families require two incomes to make ends meet. Yalnizyan's predictions were quickly realized, as by July 2009, 75 000 jobs in the private sector and 45 000 public sector jobs were eliminated in that month alone. Those hardest hit in the public sector were young people aged 15 to 24 and women aged 25 to 54, particularly those working in accommodation and food services and construction (Statistics Canada 2009g). In fact, youth experienced particularly difficult conditions as they suffered the highest unemployment rate—20.9 percent—ever recorded since data were first collected in 1977. This represents a 7.1 percent increase from the previous July (2008). Unemployment rates also vary markedly between provinces; for example, by July 2009, Quebec's and Ontario's unemployment rates had reached 9.0 percent and 9.3 percent, respectively, while Newfoundland and Labrador had rates of over 17 percent.

The vulnerability of unemployed Canadians, coupled with high household debt, heavily compromises Canada's ability to emerge quickly from the recession. At approximately one-third of the economy, exports are important to our recovery; however, critical to recovery will be Canadians' own consumer spending, accounting for 57 percent of the economy (Yalnizyan 2009). As unemployment increases, Canadians' purchasing power is severely compromised. Due to program eligibility changes, the majority of unemployed Canadians are unable to access EI benefits, and those who are able receive only 55 percent of their pre-unemployment income. The unemployed, especially those with dependants, are increasingly vulnerable to poverty. Maximum EI benefits today are lower than they were in the 1970s, taking inflation into account. As discussed in Chapter 2, the point of welfare state programs such as EI at their inception was to ensure that consumer spending remained at an adequate level in order to provide stabilization of the economy during its cyclical "bust" era.

The National Deficit and Debt

In July 2009, the Canadian Finance Minister stated the deficit would be $50 billion for the year, in stark contrast to the surplus he had predicted in November 2008. A **deficit** refers to the situation when a government's spending on initiatives and programs, along with the interest charges on its outstanding debts, exceeds its revenues in a given year. When governments run a deficit in any given year, they borrow money, with interest, which becomes a national **debt**—the amount of money borrowed by the government to offset its deficits. So, how did Canada move from a predicted surplus to an enormous $50 billion deficit? In an era of welfare state retrenchment, governments typically lay the blame on social and other normal program spending, urging individuals to do what they can to "tighten their belts" and deal with the "necessary" cuts as best they can. While normal program spending continues to be blamed, an analysis of the deficit by TD Bank's chief economist presents a different picture:

- The 2 percent cut to the GST led to a $12 billion decrease in federal revenue (a $6 billion annual loss for each percentage cut).
- Corporate tax revenues decreased by $10 billion.
- EI payouts increased by $3 billion to $5.5 billion.
- The Canadian auto industry received a $10 billion bailout.
- New infrastructure programs for job creation received $10 billion (Clancy 2009; Department of Finance 2009).

Normal program spending is far from out of control and is clearly not the cause of the deficit. In fact, even in years when government saw a surplus, spending priorities were reducing Canada's substantial debt. For example, in 1997–1998, the federal government of Canada reported its first surplus ($3.5 billion) in approximately 30 years. From 2001 to 2003, the country generated a $39.7 billion surplus, which the federal government used mainly to pay down its considerable debt (Department of Finance 2003). Canada was more than $536 billion in debt, and in the 2001–2002 fiscal year, Canadians paid $37 billion in interest charges alone on this debt. It has consistently been the largest single expenditure item in the federal budget. Moreover, in the 2001–2002 fiscal year, 22 cents out of every

Unemployment is a growing problem in Canada.

revenue dollar went toward maintaining the debt (Manley 2002).

Where have our revenues gone? Whereas in the 1960s, Canadian citizens and business contributed 50–50 to tax revenues collected, today Canadian citizens account for over 92 percent of all tax revenues. Business contributes only 8 percent. Between the federal Liberals and Conservatives, over $200 billion in corporate tax cuts was handed out in recent years (Clancy 2009). As business has withdrawn its tax contribution, the Canadian government has fallen further and further into debt, as have governments all over the world. Like the federal government, many individuals and families in this country are deeply in debt.

Consumer Debt

Canada boasts the ninth-largest economy on the planet. However, only 40 percent of Canadians stated that their standard of living had increased over the past

10 years—26 percent of Canadians stated they were worse off financially, while another 33 percent stated they were in the same financial position (Yalnizyan and Hennessy 2009). Why, following a period of strong economic growth, would this be the case? For many people, a heavy debt load is the culprit; for example, 47 percent of Canadians in a national poll in October 2008 admitted that it was a struggle to keep their personal debt under control—and this was just prior to the recession hitting with full force.

Consumer debt is rising, and household debt was at an all-time high going into the latest recession. What is even more worrisome to analysts is the fact that the ratio of consumer debt to income increased over the past three decades. According to a definitive study of bankruptcy, "the most distinguishing characteristic of bankrupt debtors is their high debts in relation to their incomes" (Sullivan et al. 1989:331). In 2008, Canadians owed $1.40 for every dollar of income compared to the 91 cents owed for every dollar of income in 1990 (Yalnizyan 2009). Personal savings have not been as low as they are today since the late 1930s. Although an increase in consumer debt may benefit the Canadian and global economies in some ways, it is extremely damaging to individuals who cannot pay their bills and to those who must declare bankruptcy (Sullivan et al. 1989). In May 2009, consumer bankruptcies had increased by 34.4 percent over the May previous (BankruptcyCanada.com 2009).

By April 2008, consumer bankruptcy levels were already far ahead of previous years (see Table 13.1). The results of a study released by TD Bank in May 2009 stated that Canadians will declare bankruptcy in record numbers throughout 2009 and 2010. As Craig Alexander, an economist and co-author of the TD Bank report, notes, "unemployment and heightened household debt will drive a substantial increase in consumer insolvencies over the next two years" (CBC News 2009b). The rate of bankruptcies is expected to rise from 1 per 1000 in the 1980s to 6 per 1000 in 2009–2010. The TD report also predicted that the unemployment rate would increase to 10 percent by 2010 and not drop until 2013 (CBC News 2009b). However, as Alexander concluded, "since individuals are carrying a greater amount of debt, they have a greater risk of insolvency regardless of economic conditions" (CBC News 2009b).

Two factors contribute to high rates of consumer debt. The first is the instability of economic life in

TABLE 13.1   Consumer Bankruptcy Statistics, Canada, 1991 to 2008

Year	Total
1991	63 065
1992	61 655
1993	55 399
1994	53 860
1995	65 456
1996	79 664
1997	85 270
1998	75 459
1999	72 994
2000	75 088
2001	79 398
2002	78 210
2003	84 297
2004	84 475
2005	84 675
2006	79 277
2007	79 847
2008	90 610

Source: Statistics Canada. CANSIM Tables 177-0003, 177-0004 (terminated), 177-0007; Office of the Superintendent of Bankruptcy Canada, June 11, 2009.

modern society; unemployment and underemployment are commonplace. The second factor is the availability of credit and the extent to which credit card companies and other lenders extend credit beyond people's ability to repay. It is typical today for many people to use credit (loans, lines of credit, or credit cards) as a means of getting by or even increasing their standard of living (Foster and Magdoff 2009). Many people run up credit card charges that are greatly out of proportion to their income; others cannot pay off the charges they initially believed they could afford when their income is interrupted or drops due to a sudden layoff or decreased work hours. For example, Kenji Peterson (a pseudonym) ran up $20 000 in charges, a sum that was more than half his total yearly income:

It all started when I graduated from college and took a low-paying job. . . . I didn't want to live like a student so I used credit cards to buy myself furniture and eat dinners out. I wasn't extravagant, I just didn't want to deprive myself. . . . When I got a new card with a $5000 credit limit, it felt like someone just handed me $5000. . . . The reality has been that I got in the hole financially. (Tyson 1993:E1, cited in Ritzer 1995:67)

Having a high level of consumer debt is a personal problem for people like Kenji Peterson, but it is also a public issue, particularly when credit card issuers negligently give fifth, sixth, or seventh credit cards to people who are already so far in debt that they cannot pay the interest, much less the principal, on their other cards (Sullivan et al. 1989). One businessman had accumulated a total debt of $183 000 on 41 cards when he received an unsolicited application for still another card, which he accepted and quickly "maxed out" at $5000 (Ritzer 1995).

Statistics Canada reported in 2006 that in the six years between 1999 and 2005, median debt load for

Is this sight a familiar one to you? In stores throughout the world, consumers are increasingly using their credit cards to make purchases of basic necessities such as food and clothing. What are the risks of excessive credit card debt? What are some risks associated with a high national debt and staggering amounts of consumer debt?

families rose 38 percent, with the debt burden being particularly harsh for those families whose major income earner was under the age of 35 (Statistics Canada 2006c). The main increase in debt for Canadians in this time period was in higher mortgage costs and more people having mortgages. The second-largest contributor to the debt load of Canadians, however, was lines of credit, which more than doubled from 1999 to 2005 to $68 billion owing. This meant that for the one-quarter of Canadian families who had a line of credit, it increased from $5800 to $9000 (Statistics Canada 2006c). Canadians also owed, in 2005, $46 billion in automobile loans (a 41.3 percent increase), $25.8 billion in credit card and installment debt (a 58.4 percent increase), and $20 billion in student loans (a 15.8 percent increase) (Statistics Canada 2006c). At the same time as debt loads are increasing, household net worth is decreasing. In the final two quarters of 2008 and through the first quarter of 2009, household net worth in Canada decreased by $438 billion (Statistics Canada 2009g).

According to sociologist George Ritzer (1995), both consumers and credit card companies must become more responsible if consumer debt is to be reduced. Ritzer (1995:71) is particularly critical of banks and credit card companies that entice students in high school or university to become accustomed to buying on credit, saying that this practice lures many people into a "lifetime of imprudence and indebtedness." He believes that the government should restrain credit card companies by limiting the profits they can make and by restricting mail and telephone campaigns offering incentives to accept new credit cards (Ritzer 1995). Many people are adamantly opposed to any kind of government intervention in the marketplace, whether it relates to credit cards or anything else. Interestingly, one kind of government intervention that is institutionalized in the Canadian economy is corporate welfare. As sociologist John Bellamy Foster and plant and soil science professor Fred Magdoff (2009) conclude, "the tragedy of [this economic crisis] is not one of excess consumption but of the ruthless pursuit of wealth by a few at the cost of the population as a whole."

Concentration of Wealth

Through the economic boom of the late 20th and early 21st centuries, corporate wealth became increasingly concentrated in Canada and in many parts of the world.

FIGURE 13.1   Household Net Worth Continues to Decline: Canada and the United States

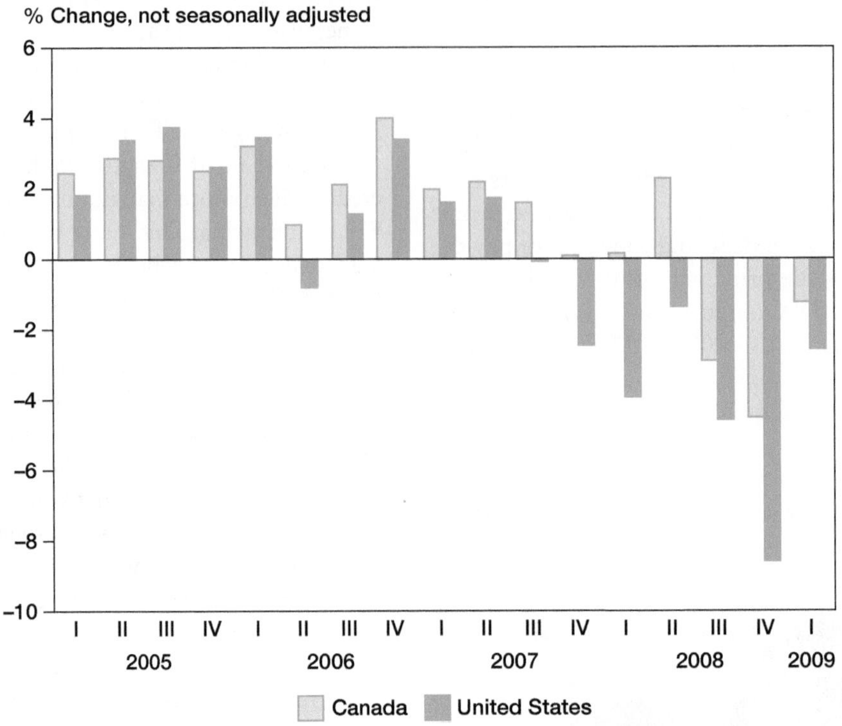

% Change, not seasonally adjusted

Canada   United States

Source: Statistics Canada, 2009, "National Balance Sheet Accounts," The Daily (June 22). Retrieved July 12, 2009 (http://www.statcan.gc.ca/daily-quotidien/090622/dq090622b-eng.htm).

Economic concentration refers to the extent to which a few individuals or corporations control the vast majority of all economic resources in a country. Concentration of wealth is a social problem when it works to society's detriment, particularly when people are unable to use the democratic process to control the actions of the corporations.

The concentration of wealth in Canada has gone through many stages. In the earliest stage, most investment capital was individually owned. Families tended to control all the major trade and financial organizations. Canadian families like the Seagrams or the Irvings controlled whole segments of the Canadian economy.

In early monopoly capitalism, ownership and control of capital shifted from individuals to corporations. As monopoly capitalism grew, a few corporations gained control over major Canadian industries. A **monopoly** exists when a single firm controls an industry and accounts for all sales in a specific market. Monopolies in Canada have ranged from Canadian telephone and power-generating monopolies to the many marketing

boards that cover dairy products, poultry, fruit, and wheat and other grains, as well as Canada Post's monopoly over first-class-mail delivery.

In advanced monopoly capitalism (between 1940 and the present), ownership and control of major industrial and business sectors became increasingly concentrated. After World War II, there was a dramatic increase in **oligopoly**—a situation in which a small number of companies or suppliers control an entire industry or service. These large corporations use their economic resources, through campaign contributions, to lobby and influence the outcome of government decisions that affect their operations (see Table 13.2 for the 19 largest corporations in Canada). Smaller corporations have only limited power and resources to bring about political change or keep the largest corporations from dominating the economy.

Today, mergers often occur *across* industries. In this way, corporations gain near-monopoly control over all aspects of the production and distribution of a product because they acquire both the companies that supply

TABLE 13.2   19 Largest Companies in Canada

1. Agnico-Eagle Mines Ltd.
2. Nortel Networks
3. Magna International
4. Onex Corp.
5. George Weston Ltd.
6. Imperial Oil Ltd.
7. Royal Bank of Canada
8. BCE Inc. (Bell Canada Enterprise)
9. Sun Life Financial Inc.
10. CIBC (Canadian Imperial Bank of Commerce)
11. Loblaw Companies Ltd.
12. TransCanada Corporation
13. TransCanada Pipelines
14. Nucor
15. Alcan Aluminum Ltd.
16. Bombardier Inc.
17. Bank of Nova Scotia
18. Toronto Dominion Bank
19. Manulife Financial Corp.

Source: Reproduced by permission of Transnationale Corporations Observatory, http://www.transnationale.org.

the raw materials and the companies that are the outlets for the product. For example, an oil company may hold leases on the land where the oil is pumped out of the ground, own the refineries that convert the oil into gasoline, and own the individual gasoline stations that sell the product to the public. Corporations that have control both within and across industries and are formed by a series of mergers and acquisitions across industries referred to as *conglomerates*—combinations of businesses in different commercial areas, all of which are owned by one holding company. Media ownership is one case in point (see Chapter 14).

Further complicating corporate structures are **interlocking corporate directorates**—members of the board of directors of one corporation who also sit on the board of one or more other corporations. The problem with such interlocking directorates is that they diminish competition by producing interdependence. People serving on multiple boards are in a position to forge co-operative arrangements that benefit their corporations but not necessarily the general public. When several corporations are controlled by the same financial interests, they are more likely to co-operate with one another than to compete (Mintz and Schwartz 1985).

Wealth is not only concentrated in the hands of corporations or families but increasingly in the hands of a few top CEOs. In 2007, the average CEO took home 259 times the pay of the average worker. Comparing the incomes of the top 50 executives in Canada between 1995 and 2007 shows an exponential increase from 85 times average pay in 1995 to 398 times in 2007 (see Table 13.3). To put these incomes into perspective another way, consider that the top 25 CEOs in Canada take home the equivalent of the total income of Nunavut (see Table 13.4; Mackenzie 2009).

Corporate Welfare

Corporate welfare occurs when the government helps industries and private corporations in their economic pursuits. Corporate welfare, sometimes called "wealthfare,"

TABLE 13.3   Canada's Top 10 CEOs

Rank	Name	Company	Base Salary	Total Compensation
1	Michael Lazaridis	Research In Motion Ltd.	$1 119 952	$51 515 518
2	Gordon Nixon	Royal Bank of Canada	$1 400 000	$44 270 084
3	Robert A. Milton	ACE Aviation Holdings Inc	$1 210 000	$42 928 122
4	James Balsillie	Research In Motion Ltd.	$1 119 952	$32 053 959
5	Paul Desmarais Jr.	Power Corp. of Canada	$961 000	$29 292 829
6	André Desmarais	Power Corp. of Canada	$961 000	$28 675 763
7	Bruce Flatt	Brookfield Asset Management Inc.	$395 864	$27 164 707
8	J.M. Lipton	Nova Chemicals Corp.	$1 289 738	$25 639 972
9	Raymond McFeetors	Great-West Lifeco Inc.	$1 591 666	$24 759 648
10	William Doyle	Potash Corp. of Saskatchewan	$1 117 773	$24 020 161

Source: Hugh Mackenzie, 2009 (January), Banner Year for Canada's CEOs: Record High Pay Increase. Toronto: Canadian Centre for Policy Alternatives. Retrieved July 1, 2009 (http://www.policyalternatives.ca/~ASSETS/DOCUMENT/National_Office_Pubs/2008/Banner_Year_For_CEOs.pdf).

TABLE 13.4   Number of CEOs Needed to Match Total Employment Income of Selected Canadian Urban Areas

	2006 Census Population	Top CEOs to Match Total Earnings
Corner Brook	20 083	17
Summerside	32 174	7
Truro	45 077	41
Edmonton	16 643	12
Shawinigan	56 434	53
Cornwall	45 965	77
Brandon	41 511	89
Prince Albert	40 766	42
Camrose	15 620	12
Penticton	35 944	50
Whitehorse	22 898	35
Yellowknife	18 700	45
Nunavut	29 474	25

Source: Hugh Mackenzie, 2009 (January), Banner Year for Canada's CEOs: Record High Pay Increase. Toronto: Canadian Centre for Policy Alternatives. Retrieved July 1, 2009 (http://www.policyalternatives.ca/~ASSETS/DOCUMENT/National_Office_Pubs/2008/Banner_Year_For_CEOs.pdf).

is not a new phenomenon in Canada. During the industrialization of Canada, corporations received government assistance in the form of public subsidies and protection from competition. To encourage westward expansion, the federal government gave large tracts of land to developers. Tariffs, patents, and trademarks from this era all continue to protect corporations from competition today.

Currently, government intervention includes billions of dollars of subsidies given to corporations in the form of conditionally repayable loans, grants, monies intended for job-creation and job-preservation schemes, and tax breaks to corporations. The majority of financial assistance recipients are among Canada's largest and most profitable companies—those listed in the *Report on Business* 1000 and the *Financial Post* 500. For example, in 1999, the federal government gave a $33 million "gift" to IBM Canada Ltd. under the Technology Partnerships Canada (TPC) program and a $154 million TPC loan to Pratt & Whitney. Approximately 15 percent of the $3.2 billion that Industry Canada has lent large corporations since 1982 has never been repaid and, in the first 10 years, the repayment rate decreased to 2.58 percent

(Canadian Taxpayers Federation 2003)—but such gifts continue to be made. Research is showing that these governmental strategies to retain, expand, and even attract business do not actually influence a corporation's choice of location or its economic growth. This fact does not seem to influence the federal government, however: in 2003, it legislated another cut in corporate income-tax rates to below those in the United States and has continued to make cuts to corporate tax rates in the years since 2003.

Not only have corporations benefitted from increasingly lowered tax rates, but the federal government in 2008–2009 awarded 21 handouts, totalling $1.66 billion, many to the "usual suspects," including CAE ($250 million), Bombardier ($350 million), Ford ($80 million), Husky Oil ($144.6 million), Suncor ($25 million), and Bristol Aerospace ($43.4 million), just to name a few (Gaudet 2009).

The fundamental problem is that, around the world, these corporate welfare programs do not actually promote economic development, and they decrease the revenues available to support governmental spending (Chomsky 1996; Nader 2000). There is growing concern that corporate welfare means that market decisions are being made by politicians and bureaucrats and not by the market; that corporate welfare creates politically driven investments, is inherently unfair, and therefore serves to undermine Canadians' confidence in our democratic institutions; and that it makes business owners and entrepreneurs focus on securing government financing (making them "grantrepreneurs") instead of developing their core competencies. In addition, at least $115 million in repayable contributions is outstanding, and the loss of loan-repayment monies is creating a higher tax burden in Canada for ordinary citizens. This means that indirectly, individuals and small businesses are helping to recoup these losses. It is clear that overall, most large corporations have gained much more than they have lost as a result of government involvement in the economy.

Why do we have corporate welfare programs today? Some can be traced back to the Great Depression in the 1930s, when programs were initiated to bail out companies and stabilize the Canadian economy. This type of system continues today; for example, with the Canadian government bailout of the auto sector. The auto sector in Canada will receive the largest portion of the money intended to soften the consequences of the recession. Supplementing the government's previous announcement of $2.7 billion in loans is a program to encourage Canadians to buy more cars. The newly created Canadian Secured Credit Facility will have $12 billion to help Canadian consumers and businesses finance vehicle and equipment purchases (Gohier 2009).

Some analysts say that the subsidies continue because of lobbying efforts and political contributions by organizations to governments (Tumulty 1996). As a result, many Members of Parliament may find it more within their interests to retrench domestic spending, primarily on health care, education, and other social programs, than to cut corporate handouts (Tumulty 1996). (See Box 2.2 on page 43 of Chapter 2 for a thorough discussion of welfare state retrenchment.)

SOCIAL PROBLEMS IN GLOBAL PERSPECTIVE

BOX 13.2 Heart, Humour, and Hope: The Global Social Justice Movement Gathers Force

"Shame—This is Canada!" These words were scrawled across the Wall of Shame at the Summit of the Americas meeting in Quebec City (April 2001). The Canadian FTAA Summit was one of the earlier international meetings designed to foster the fast proliferation of global trade agreements worldwide. It was also one of the many impressive sites of anti-globalization protest that continue to occur around the world. The result of these protests is that today unfettered global free trade is no longer considered inevitable:

> The last decade has been marked by the explosion of free trade agreements and grassroots opposition to them. . . . It is a battlefield being contested by governments and transnational corporations on one side, and organized labour, environmentalists, human rights advocates and citizens groups on the other. The rules however, are stacked in favour of governments pushing the corporate global agenda. Although, some governments in the global south also find themselves marginalized in the discussions by heavy hitters in the United States, European Union, Canada and Japan. (Corporatewatch 2003)

The effectiveness of these global protests and the threat they pose to the corporate agenda make it unsurprising that mainstream media is most often disparaging and inflammatory in its treatment of protestors, referring to them as anarchists, terrorists, hoodlums, and wayward youth. The people themselves, however, identify as resistors, organizers, citizens, artists, parents, journalists, businesspeople, students, architects, and activists.

Whatever it is called, governments and businesses now acknowledge that this is a global movement of citizens working in solidarity. Increasingly, it is a force to be reckoned with. In 1997, citizens' groups, led in Canada by the Council of Canadians, derailed the powerful and far-reaching Multilateral Agreement on Investment (MAI) negotiations, which were being carried out quietly between 29 industrialized members of the Organisation for Economic Co-operation and Development (OECD). The MAI promoted the interests of international investors

and applied to "all land, territory, internal water and the territorial seas of the contracting [country]" and was designed so that "all corporate behaviour is included and 'protected' from government measures" (OECD 1997). In reference to the derailed MAI meetings, a *Globe and Mail* article in 1998 stated that, while high-powered politicians had reams of statistics and analysis on why a set of international investing rules would make the world a better place, "they were no match . . . for a global band of grassroots organizations, which, with little more than computers and access to the Internet, helped derail a deal" (Drohan 1998). In 1999, the *Globe and Mail* ran an article in a similar vein about the WTO:

> The activists who essentially killed the Multilateral Agreement on Investment launched a campaign yesterday to stop upcoming talks at the World Trade Organization in their tracks—the latest sign of trouble for the next round of WTO negotiations.(*Globe and Mail* 1999:XX)

These were founded concerns, as more than 50 000 people gathered in Seattle to march against the WTO in 1999. It was the meeting place of riot police, the National Guard, and protestors who mainly used the same passive resistance tactics popularized by Gandhi. It marked the beginning of the global movement of citizen protest and the world's recognition of its power. In a post-WTO rally speech in Vancouver, Council of Canadians Chair Maude Barlow eloquently conveyed the point that if these trade talks and their attendant processes were truly democratic and truly what the people wanted, they would not need to be carried out behind the shields of the National Guard. The presence of barricades, riot police, and tens of thousands of protestors diminishes the claim that these trade deals are embraced by the populace (Barlow 1999).

Protestors have been a major force at WTO and other trade-related meetings since 1999 in Seattle—in Quebec City in 2001; in Genoa, Italy, in 2001; in Kananaskis, Alberta, in 2002; in Cancun, Mexico, in 2003; in 2005 in Hong Kong; and so on. These examples of anti-corporate-globalization protests depict a global era of extraordinary hope and optimism within a context of great suffering and desperation. Indian writer Arundati Roy (2003) states, "The corporate revolution will collapse if we refuse to buy what they are selling: their wars, their version of history." The writer urges the world's citizens to tell their own stories, "Another world is not only possible, she's on her way. And if you listen carefully on a quiet day you can hear her breathing" (Roy 2003). This is exactly the kind of message concerned citizens are drawing hope from.

Between January 23 and 28, 2002, 3000 people gathered at the 1st World Social Forum in Puerto Alegre, Brazil. In their call to build this movement, they sent out a statement proclaiming:

> We are meeting in Puerto Alegre in the shadow of a global crisis. . . . We are social movements that are fighting all around the world against neo-liberal globalization, war, racism, capitalism, poverty, patriarchy and all the forms of economical, ethnical, social, political, cultural, sexual and gender discriminations and exclusions. We are all fighting for social justice, citizenship, participatory democracy, universal rights and for the right of peoples to decide their own future.

> We stand for peace and international cooperation, for a sustainable society answering the needs of people for food, housing, health, education, information, water, energy, public transportation and human rights. We are in solidarity with the women engaged against social and patriarchal violence.

> We support the struggle of the peasants, workers, popular urban movements and all those who are urgently threatened by being deprived of homes, jobs, land and their rights. We have demonstrated in millions to say that another world is possible.

> This has never been more true and more urgent. (Institute for Global Communications 2002)

This meeting marked the first global gathering of people in protest to share stories and strategies for addressing global economic and social problems and to create visions for the future. The number of people involved in this movement continues to grow—for example, a reported 133 000 people attended the latest forum in Belem, Brazil, in early 2009—and so too do their skills and commitments to creative, positive, and peaceful alternatives to the current economic world order.

This is a movement with heart, humour, and hope. It is being led by young people primarily and mentored along by those who have lived through wars, embargoes, sanctions, discrimination, and patriarchal rule—those who have long lived with oppression and who understand, first-hand, the importance of working in solidarity to make lasting change. Globalization has not only made commerce everyone's business, it has made informed citizen participation everyone's responsibility. The result is a diverse, intelligent, and highly determined movement of global citizens who know they must stick together in the fight for their lives and for the life of this planet.

PERSPECTIVES ON THE POLITICAL ECONOMY

The economy is so intertwined with politics in Canada that many sociologists speak of the two as a single entity, the *political economy*. At issue for most sociologists is whether political and economic power are concentrated in the hands of the few or distributed among the many in this country. Functionalists adopt a pluralistic model of power, while conflict theorists adopt an elitist model. Symbolic interactionists focus on the microlevel patterns of people's relationships with one another, and feminists adopt a holistic analysis of power inequalities in society.

The Functionalist Perspective

Pluralism is rooted in the functionalist perspective, which assumes that people generally agree on the most important societal concerns—freedom and security—and that government fulfills important functions in these two regards that no other institution can. According to the early functionalists, government serves to socialize people to be good citizens, to regulate the economy so that it operates effectively, and to provide necessary services for citizens (Durkheim 1893/1933). Contemporary functionalists identify four similar functions: a government maintains law and order, plans society and coordinates other institutions, meets social needs, and handles international relations, including warfare.

But what happens when people do not agree on specific issues or concerns? Functionalists say that divergent viewpoints lead to political pluralism; that is, when competing interests or viewpoints arise, government arbitrates. Thus, according to the **pluralist model,** power is widely dispersed throughout many competing interest groups in our political system (Dahl 1961). In the pluralist model, (1) political leaders make decisions on behalf of the people through a process of bargaining, accommodation, and compromise; (2) leadership groups (such as business, labour, law, and consumer organizations) serve as watchdogs to protect ordinary people from the abuses of any one group; (3) ordinary people influence public policy through voting and participating in special interest or lobby groups; (4) power is widely dispersed in society (the same groups aren't equally influential in all arenas); and (5) public policy reflects a balance among competing interest groups, not the majority group's view (Dye 2000).

How might a social analyst who uses a functionalist framework address problems in the globalized economy? Such an analyst might begin by saying that since dysfunctions are inevitable in any social institution, it is important to sort out and remedy the specific elements of the system that create the problems. It should not be necessary to restructure or replace the entire system. Consider, for example, government regulations: some regulations are considered to be good, and some are considered to be bad. The trick, functionalists say, is to keep the good ones and get rid of the bad (Barlett and Steele 1996). Too often, the Canadian government is seen as moving between two extremes: overregulation of business and society, or seeking to end most, if not all, regulation. This perspective is based on the belief that a certain amount of government intervention in the economy is appropriate but that too much—or the wrong kind—is detrimental.

The Conflict Perspective

Most conflict theorists believe democracy is an ideal, not a reality, in our society today. This is because the government primarily benefits the wealthy and the politically powerful, especially business elites. In fact, according to conflict theorists, economic and political elites use the powers of the government to impose their will on the masses. According to the **elite model**, power in political systems is concentrated in the hands of a small group, whereas the masses are relatively powerless. In the elite model, (1) elites possess the greatest wealth, education, status, and other resources and make the most important decisions in society; (2) elites generally agree on the basic values and goals for the society; (3) power is highly concentrated at the top of a pyramid-shaped social hierarchy, and those at the top set public policy for everyone; (4) public policy reflects the values and preferences of the elite, not of ordinary people; and (5) elites use the media to shape the political attitudes of ordinary people (Dye 2000).

According to sociologist C. Wright Mills (1959a), there is a hierarchical structure of power. The rulers are the **power elite,** which at the top is composed of business leaders, the executive branch of the federal government, and the "top brass" of the military. The corporate rich—the highest-paid CEOs of major corporations—are the most powerful because they have the unique ability to parlay their vast economic resources into political power. The next most powerful level is occupied by Members of Parliament, special interest groups, and local opinion leaders. The lowest (and widest) level of the pyramid is occupied by ordinary people, the unorganized masses who are relatively powerless and vulnerable to economic and political exploitation.

Individuals who compose the power elite have similar class backgrounds and interests and interact on a regular basis. Through a revolving door of influence, they tend to shift back and forth between and among the business, government, and military sectors. For example, it is not unusual for people who have served in the prime minister's Cabinet to become directors of major corporations that do business with the government, for powerful businesspeople to serve in Parliament, or for former military leaders to become important businesspeople. Through such political and economic alliances, people in the power elite can influence many important decisions, including how federal tax money will be spent and to whom lucrative subsidies and government contracts are awarded.

In his analysis of the political economy, sociologist G. William Domhoff (1978) speaks of a *ruling class,* which is made up of the **corporate rich**—a relatively fixed group of privileged people who wield power over political processes and serve capitalist interests. The corporate rich influence the political process in three ways: (1) by financing campaigns of candidates who favour their causes; (2) by using loophole contributions to obtain favours, tax breaks, and favourable regulatory rulings; and (3) by gaining appointment to governmental advisory committees, national commissions, and other governmental positions. For example, some members of the ruling class influence international politics through their involvement in banking, business services, and law firms that have a strong interest in overseas sales, investments, or raw materials extraction (Domhoff 1990).

Some analysts who take a conflict perspective say that the only way to overcome problems in politics and the economy is to change the entire system. Our present system exploits poor people, people of colour, women, LGBT individuals, people with disabilities, and all others who are disenfranchised from the political and economic mainstream of society.

Other conflict theorists think that we can solve many problems by curbing the abuses of capitalism and the market economy and thereby reducr the power of political and economic elites. Political scientist Benjamin R. Barber (1996:242) believes that we cannot rely on the capitalist (market) economy to look after common interests:

> It is the job of civil society and democratic government and not of the market to look after common interests and make sure that those who profit from the common planet pay its common proprietors their fair share. When governments abdicate in favour of markets, they are declaring *nolo contendere* [no contest] in an arena in which they are supposed to be primary challengers, bartering away the rights of citizens along the way.

Markets simply are not designed to do the things democratic politics do. They enjoin private rather than public modes of discourse, allowing us as consumers to speak via our currencies of consumption to producers of material goods, but ignoring us as citizens speaking to one another about such things as the social consequences of our private market choices. They advance individualistic rather than social goals. Having created the conditions that make markets possible, democracies must also do all the things that markets undo or cannot do. They must educate citizens so that they can use their markets wisely and contain market abuses well.

The Symbolic Interactionist Perspective

Symbolic interactionism focuses on the micro, or small-scale, interactions that occur between individuals in specific settings. This perspective views society as a dynamic process that is continually being created through human interaction and negotiation. As a result, humans develop subjective interpretations of the physical world at the same time that they are socialized to integrate into society. Symbolic interactionism is particularly interested in how members of society socialize one another and how people utilize shared symbols—objects, words, sounds, and events—to construct social reality and express their experiences of it.

With a focus on the subjective meanings that people attach to their own and other people's behaviour and the processes people engage in to construct and agree upon various definitions of reality, researchers ask very specific questions about human activity. In terms of the political economy, people using this perspective will want to study the interactions that occur between people within democratic processes and business negotiations. How do people experience and interpret laws, fiscal priorities, and budget cuts? How do these societal activities influence people's relationship to and involvement in the democratic process? How do people reach agreements about the role politicians should take in addressing the issues of dissatisfied constituents, and what should citizens do if they are not satisfied with what is happening in their communities? Clearly, it is important to consider the opinions of a diverse range of people in order to build a complete picture of society. People from different racialized/ethnic, gender, and social-class groups, and of different sexual orientations, to name just a few variables, experience the world in dramatically different ways. Their perspectives are essential to the project of understanding the microlevel patterns of human interactions in society.

One question that symbolic interactionists like to ask is, "What happens when a network of people come together to challenge the status quo?" This explains the fascination with the forces that shaped the "Battle in Seattle" (a popular media phrase for the 1999 anti-WTO protests in Seattle). Why did anti-corporate-globalization protestors gather in Seattle; why did people develop and utilize the protest strategies they did during the marches; why did politicians react to the protest in the heavy-handed manner they did; and what shaped the interactions between police and civilians during the protests? While the meaning each individual and small group attributes to the experience is important, so too are the ways in which symbols are used. Symbolic interactionists may focus their attention on ways that mainstream media reporters framed the protestors as dangerous and "anarchistic." They may also do a comparative analysis of the contents of protestors' accounts of police confrontations and the official reports of the same incidents given by police chiefs and elected officials.

Feminist Perspectives

"Black women, be ready. White women, get ready. Red women, stay ready . . ." (Honey, in Brodribb 1999:13). Feminist theoretical perspectives are as diverse as the women who develop them. While feminism as a whole has advanced women's rights and institutional accountability in Canada, there is a wealth of diverse approaches that are responsible for these successes. A close-up look at feminist engagements with the political economy show that liberal, materialist, multicultural, radical, and ecological feminists are among those most concerned with addressing issues of the political economy.

Liberal feminists, for example, work to ensure that women have the rights and abilities to participate fully in political and economic spheres of social life. Securing women's right to vote in Canada; pushing for pay equity, equal opportunity legislation, and universal day care; and supporting women in business are some of the liberal-feminist initiatives. Their work from the 1960s to the mid-1980s dramatically increased the rights of and opportunities available to women in Canada (Elliott and Mandell 2001).

Materialist feminists are concerned with class inequity and the widening gaps between different groups' control over resources, participation in the production of knowledge, and control of power globally. This perspective maintains that social life is inextricably linked to the "materiality of meaning, identity, the body, state, or nation" (Hennessy and Ingraham 1997:1). Central commitments are to analyze, challenge, and work to change business practices, globalization initiatives, and development programs that continue to exploit women's productive and reproductive labour.

Multicultural feminists maintain that global survival depends on meaningful exchanges of knowledge, understanding, and solidarity between peoples across the globe. Multicultural feminists focus on the experiences of African, Asian, Middle Eastern, Latin American, and Caribbean women in Canada and around the world. Institutional, interpersonal, and internalized racism and their impacts on the lives of people such as foreign domestic and sweatshop factory workers and immigrant and refugee women and their communities are a primary concern for these feminists.

Radical feminists see women's personal experiences as political and focus on developing strategies of resistance (Elliott and Mandell 2001:34). This perspective critiques patriarchy and masculinist practices that construct women as passive and submissive. Radical feminists engage in actions such as the fight for the rights and freedoms of women and children who are trafficked in the global sex trade (Kempadoo 1998; see Chapter 7).

Anarcha-feminists analyze the role patriarchy plays in subjugating women and believe that the state is inherently oppressive and should be abolished. Anarcha-feminists view the struggle against patriarchy and the state as the same struggle, with patriarchy being but one of many of the state's tools, as well as being critical in its creation and maintenance (Infoshop 2009).

Ecological feminists draw feminist, ecological, and materialist perspectives together in order to build an understanding of how political and economic activities such as free trade agreements, transnational corporations, and war impact women, the natural environment, and the quality of life of people, animals, and the earth (Sturgeon 1997). The concerns of this perspective are captured in the words of internationally renowned physicist Vandana Shiva, speaking on the consequences of the multinational presence in poorer nations (Shiva 2000):

> Much of the Third World is being re-colonized under the rubric of free trade. You can't miss the KFCs, Pizza Huts and McDonald's. But there is more to it than that. Multinationals like Monsanto and Cargill have penetrated the agricultural sector. They promise green revolutions and greater yields. As chemical inputs increase, monocultures replace bio-diverse crops. In India, farmers are fighting back corporate attempts to patent seeds and herbs. Women are central in the struggle to protect traditional agriculture. They are the seed keepers.

These feminists represent perspectives that, when brought together, can be used to build a holistic understanding of the matrices of oppression that shape our current historical moment. Feminists have impacted theoretical and practical approaches to the political economy in many significant ways in Canada. While women today have many rights and freedoms that women in Confederate Canada did not, feminists point out that some of the advances women have made are still legally tenuous and in times of backlash are slowly revoked. It comes as no surprise, then, that today, Canadian women and children are still the poorest of all the nation's citizens (see Chapter 2).

PROBLEMS IN THE POLITICAL ECONOMY IN THE 21ST CENTURY

What will the Canadian political economy be like as we progress through the 21st century? There is no single vision, of course, but many social analysts think that *digital democracy*—the use of information technologies such as the Internet and the World Wide Web—will dramatically change not only economic relationships but also the way in which politics and government are conducted. For example, digital democracy can inform people about political candidates and issues. Volunteers use e-mail and websites to encourage people to go to the polls and vote for their candidate. These tools can also be used to send messages to voters who indicate an interest in a specific topic, and Canadian voters may soon be exercising their democratic rights via the Internet.

The World Wide Web, cable access channels, and other new information technologies have radically democratized access to political information. However, critics point out that there are some major problems with trying to maintain a pluralist democracy through digital democracy:

> The ultimate threats to [Canadian] democracy in the digital age are not the rise of splinter groups, or new tycoons, or government-imposed limits on speech. The dangers are more subtle and insidious. One is the lack of a common starting point for discussion. . . . The other danger is that leadership as we knew it will disappear as politicians become all too connected to the voters. . . . What if our [leaders] become nothing more than the sum of our whims and misinformation? The "netizens" of the future will have to take their jobs seriously. Are we ready for this much democracy? Let's hope so. (Fineman 1997:52)

Is it possible that the Canadian economy and democratic politics will become obsolete in the face of the global economy and digitized democracy? Despite digital democracy and the transnational nature of politics and the economy, scholars such as Paul Kennedy (1993:134) argue that individual nations will remain the primary locus of identity for most people. Regardless of who their employers are and what they do for a living, individuals pay taxes to a specific government, are subject to its laws, serve in its armed forces, and can travel internationally only by having its passport. Therefore, as new challenges arise, most people in democracies still turn to their own governments and demand solutions.

WHAT CAN YOU DO?

There are many things that individuals can do on their own and in groups to address the important economic and political issues we face as Canadians in a global economy:

- Remember that your consumer habits are a way of registering votes in the global economy—make informed decisions.
- Learn more about globalization and how it affects you.
- Find out what these are—NAFTA, MAI, WTO, FTAA, CUFTA, GATT, NORAD, NATO, OAS—and how their mandates are impacting you in your daily life.
- Find out about anti-sweatshop campaigns and make informed consumer decisions that reflect your knowledge.
- Organize a non-sweatshop fashion show or "anti-fashion" show or another kind of awareness-raising event at your university or in your community.
- If you invest, or know people who do, research companies that invest in things that reflect your politics.
- Explore what kinds of alternative actions you can take if your concerns and priorities are not being addressed.

SUMMARY

What Kind of Economic System Does Canada Have?

Canada has a capitalist economy. Ideally, capitalism is characterized by private ownership of the means of production, pursuit of personal profit, competition, and lack of government intervention.

What Are Multinational Corporations?

Multinational corporations have been around since the turn of the last century. A multinational corporation is a complete corporate operation that is taken from its country of origin and integrated into its host country in order to successfully market its products in the local culture. These operations require a strong host economy to survive.

What Are Transnational Corporations, and Why Do They Pose Social Problems?

Transnational corporations are large-scale business organizations headquartered in one country but operating in many countries. Many transnationals lack accountability to any government or regulatory agency. They are not dependent on any one country for labour, capital, or technology. They can play important roles in the economies and governments of countries that need them as employers and accept their practices.

Why Is the National Debt a Serious Problem? How Is Consumer Debt a Public Issue?

When we increase the national debt, we are borrowing from future generations, leaving them with a social debt of higher taxes, fewer benefits, and a lower rate of economic growth. Consumer debt becomes a public issue when people cannot repay their credit card loans.

What Is Corporate Welfare?

Corporate welfare occurs when the government helps industries and private corporations in their economic pursuits. Many subsidies that were originally put in place to help stabilize the economy continue unnecessarily because of lobbying by special interest groups and business campaign contributions.

What Is the Functionalist–Pluralist Model of the Political Economy?

The functionalists use a pluralist model, believing that power is widely dispersed through many competing interest groups in our political system. Functionalists therefore believe that problems can be solved by identifying dysfunctional elements and correcting them.

What Do Conflict Theorists Say about Power Elites?

Conflict theorists use an elite model, believing that power in political systems is concentrated in the hands of a small group, whereas the masses are relatively powerless. Sociologist C. Wright Mills used the term *power elite* to describe this small group composed of business leaders, the executive branch of the federal government, and the "top brass" of the military.

What Aspect of the Political Economy Do Symbolic Interactionists Focus on?

Symbolic interactionists focus on the micro, or small-scale, interactions that occur between individuals in specific settings. They want to know how humans are socialized, how we develop subjective interpretations of the political economy, and how we find ways to function within it. Specific attention is paid to how people utilize shared symbols—objects, words, sounds, and events—to build, challenge, and change political and economic activities.

What Are Feminist Approaches to the Global Economy?

Feminists are concerned with political, economic, gendered, racialized/ethnic, and sexual power inequalities in the world. Global capitalism is seen as a force that threatens the health and well-being of people and the planet. Feminists are theoretically and socially committed to protecting and improving the rights, freedoms, and opportunities of all people across the globe.

KEY TERMS

capitalism,   p. 293
corporate rich,   p. 309
corporate welfare,   p. 305
debt,   p. 300
deficit,   p. 300
economic
   concentration,   p. 304

elite model,   p. 309
interlocking corporate
   directorates,   p. 305
mixed economy,   p. 293
monopoly,   p. 304
multinational corporation
   (MNC),   p. 298

oligopoly,   p. 304
pluralist model,   p. 308
power elite,   p. 309
socialism,   p. 293
transnational corporation
   (TNC),   p. 298

QUESTIONS FOR CRITICAL THINKING

1.   How would you respond to this Canadian Gallup Poll survey question: "Do you think that the government is run by a few big interests looking out for themselves or that it is run for the benefit of all the people?" Please explain your answer.

2.   Do you favour or oppose sociologist George Ritzer's proposal that the government restrain credit card companies? What do you think about his idea of limiting profit and restricting incentives for accepting new credit cards? What would you propose as other means of reducing consumer debt?

3.   How do you think globalization will affect democratic practices in Canada in the next 10 years?

4.   What roles do you think the Internet has played and will play in future in the political economy?

PEARSON

Explore the topics covered in this chapter at **www.mysockit.com** using the access provided with this text. Interactive resources for studying include video clips, practice tests, learning objectives, and Internet resources.

PROBLEMS RELATED TO MEDIA

14

It is our TV viewing that shapes our understanding of the world and ourselves. However, it is saturated with U.S. influence and media imperialism. How much television has affected [Canadian] culture and sovereignty is yet to be seen. Only time will tell.

Catherine Woods, discussing the role of media in identity construction in Canada (1998)

I've had more than one recent column sliced and diced. I can only assume it was done to remove opinions that did not correspond with those of the new owners. They didn't. And I admit I've also done some self-censoring too, steering clear of certain subjects on which I know the owners have taken a stand for me. . . . Why shouldn't freedom of the press, as legendary press critic A.J. Liebling once put it, be "guaranteed only to those who own one?" Because, quite simply, real democracy depends on the free flow of ideas, on debate and disagreement. And newspapers are the best forum for those debates. Which is why we need to consider the real impact of concentrating so much newspaper ownership in so few hands.

Stephen Kimber, director of the School of Journalism at the University of King's College, describing why he finally quit his job as columnist with the **Daily News** *after 16 years (2002)*

Recently I attended a rally to contest the implementation of "The Gateway" program—a major project which, if implemented, will include the addition of new highways and rail yards to accommodate a four-fold increase in container traffic into and through the container port in Delta, south of Vancouver. At this rally, held locally in a Delta community hall, were opposition MLA's, John Cummins, the local Conservative MP, the provincial Green Party leader, plus other leaders of diverse environmental groups from BC. The hall was packed, estimated attendance for the afternoon event was in the thousands. Unfortunately, there was no mention of this event in the *Vancouver Sun* or *Province,* nor any TV coverage on any of the major outlets that I could find. CBC Radio was the only major media to report on this rally. All of this was hardly surprising. The editorial position of the *Vancouver Sun* has openly stated its support for "Gateway." The local TV coverage, which has been sparse to non-existent, has invariably shown this project in a favourable light. It would be very difficult for any resident of the lower mainland to be aware of the major environmental issues of "Gateway" when coverage

of these issues have been subsumed into the supposed economic spin-offs of this project.

A citizen of Vancouver commenting on the dangers of the concentration of media (Campaign for Democratic Media 2007)

The notion that the Internet would "set us free," and permit anyone to communicate effectively, hence undermining the monopoly power of the corporate media giants, has not transpired. Although the Internet offers extraordinary promise in many regards, it alone cannot slay the power of the media giants. Indeed, no commercially viable media content site has been launched on the Internet, and it would be difficult to find an investor willing to bankroll any additional attempts. To the extent the Internet becomes part of the commercially viable media system, it looks to be under the thumb of the usual corporate suspects.

Robert W. McChesney, professor and acting editor of **Monthly Review,** *in his speech to UNESCO about concerns for the future of global media (2001)*

Media play a vital role in the daily lives of Canadians. Whether we applaud their existence or try to ignore their influence, most of us are constantly inundated with a variety of media. In this chapter we will look at the role media play in contemporary society. In particular, we explore the relationship between media and democracy in Canada. The impact of globalization on media ownership is also reflected upon, as is the importance of critical engagement with media in the 21st century.

What constitutes media? Canadian sociologists Bruce Ravelli and Michelle Webber (2010:443–444) make a helpful distinction between mass communication and mass media: *mass communication* refers to "the transmission of messages by a person or group through a device to a large audience," whereas *mass media* refers to "any medium designed to communicate messages to a mass audience." *Media* is the plural of *medium,*which refers to any device that transmits a message. *Media* therefore includes newspapers, radio, magazines, television, movies, and the Internet, among other things. When sociologists refer to the media (or mass media), however, they are usually speaking of the **media industries**—major businesses that own, or own interests in, radio and television production and broadcasting; cell phones and other Personal Digital Assistants (PDAs); motion pictures, movie theatres, and music companies; newspaper, periodical (maga-zine), and book publishing; and Internet services and content providers, and that influence people and cultures worldwide. To understand how pervasive media indus-tries are in our daily lives, consider one typical day's activities in the life of Scott Schatzkamer, a college student: in the morning he awakened to the sound of an AM/FM adult-contemporary radio station and dur-ing his day and evening, watched ESPN's *SportsCenter* (owned by Disney), read part of Time Warner's *Sports Illustrated*, listened to a radio station owned by Disney, played Electronic Arts' Madden NFL 2000 on his dorm's Sony PlayStation, checked his e-mail several times on AOL, logged on to ESPN.com for sports scores, read assignments in *General Chemistry* (pub-lished by Houghton Mifflin) and *Psychology in Perspective* (published by Pearson), and watched a base-ball game on News Corporation's Fox Network (Heilbrunn 2000). During the course of Scott's day, he

was under the influence of numerous forms of media provided by several media outlets, some of which share corporate ownership at the top.

Recent estimates show that the average person in North America spends more than one-half of her or his waking hours in some media-related activity. Indeed, today, many people spend more time in media-related activities than they do in any other single endeavour, including sleeping, working, eating, or talking with friends and family (Biagi 2009). Consider, for exam-ple, that in 2006, the average Canadian spent 21.4 hours per week watching television (Statistics Canada 2006d; see Table 14.1). Furthermore, approximately one-half the Canadian population uses the Internet at home, almost two-thirds of whom use it every day (Statistics Canada 2006a). Among home Internet users aged 18 to 24, 43 percent of men and 34 percent of women spend more than 10 hours per week online (Statistics Canada 2006a).

TABLE 14.1   Television Viewing by Age and Sex, by Province, 2004

| | Average Hours per Week | | | | |
	Total Population 2 Years and Older	Children 2 to 11 Years	Teens 12 to 17 Years	18 Years and Over Male	Female
Canada	21.4	14.1	12.9	20.9	25.6
Newfoundland and Labrador	22.7	18.9	12.3	21.3	26.8
Prince Edward Island	20.0	14.5	12.3	19.8	23.5
Nova Scotia	22.7	12.9	13.8	22.4	27.2
New Brunswick	23.7	14.7	12.6	23.2	28.4
Quebec[1]	23.3	14.3	13.5	22.4	28.5
Quebec, anglophones[1]	20.6	14.2	13.4	19.8	24.2
Quebec, francophones[1]	23.8	14.3	13.7	22.9	29.2
Ontario	20.6	13.5	13.2	20.1	24.7
Manitoba	22.1	15.5	13.0	22.0	26.4
Saskatchewan	21.2	15.2	12.7	20.5	25.7
Alberta	19.4	14.1	12.4	18.2	23.9
British Columbia	20.7	14.4	11.7	21.5	23.4

Note: Data are collected over the fall period (four weeks of November).

[1]For Quebec, the language classification is based on the language spoken at home. For Quebec as a total, respondents who did not reply to this question or who indicated a language other than English or French are included.

Source: Statistics Canada, (2006), "Television Viewing, by Age and Sex, by Province," Summary Tables (December 22). Retrieved July 17, 2009 (http://www40.statcan.gc.ca/l01/cst01/arts23-eng.htm).

Is this time well spent? Most analysts and media scholars agree that the media industries that emerged in the 20th century are one of the most significant social institutions at work in Canada and in many other nations. The media facilitate human communication and provide news, information, products, and entertainment to their consumers. Therefore, the corporations that own and control media content and distribution have a powerful influence on all the social institutions, including education, health care delivery, religion, families, and politics. Some aspects of this influence are positive, but other aspects may be negative. Some critics who are concerned about possible negative influences note that we are experiencing a media glut and increased commercialization of all aspects of life (Biagi 2009). For example, commercialization of the Internet and the rise of the World Wide Web in the 1990s have magnified the amount of media messages and products that confront people who use computers and online services (McChesney 2004). Other critics question the effects of contemporary media ownership on Canadian democracy (Hackett et al. 2000; McChesney 2004). In our current Canadian cultural context, democracy, consumption, and media have become inextricably linked. Today, radio, television, newspapers, and the Internet are the main sources of news and entertainment for most people. As a result, it is important to know who owns these media, to assess the quality of the information that is disseminated through them, and to understand the roles media play in shaping (and creating) public opinion (Biagi 2009; McChesney 2004).

THE POLITICAL ECONOMY OF MEDIA INDUSTRIES

Over the past three decades, media ownership has become increasingly concentrated. Today, just a handful of companies own a large percentage of television and radio stations, film studios, and publishing houses. In 1983, 50 corporations dominated ownership of most media. In 2007, nine corporations (mainly American) dominated the media world: AOL-Time Warner, Disney, Bertelsmann, Viacom, News Corporation, TCI, General Electric (owner of NBC), Sony (owner of Columbia and TriStar Pictures and major recording interests), and Seagram (owner of Universal film and music interests). (Adnan 2009; Guma 2001).

These few companies and their monopolistic control over media content, production, and distribution are known as Big Media. Many factors have led to the development of Big Media—in the main, the evolution of media-related technology. Technology, in the form of motion pictures, radio, and television, increased competition and broadened media markets throughout the 20th century. Before that, newspapers and books had been the primary means of disseminating information and entertainment to large numbers of people simultaneously. The companies involved in producing these forms of media were usually small and focused on a single output. For example, companies whose only business was newspapers produced newspapers, and books were published by companies that dealt just in books (Biagi 2009). However, at least two factors limited market demands for the information and entertainment provided by the newspaper and publishing industries: the length of time it took to get the product to consumers and the consumers' literacy. Radio, by contrast, offered consumers, from coast to coast, immediate access to information and entertainment. In Canada, the first broadcasting licence was issued in 1919, and by 1922, radio had become a competitor to the newspaper and publishing industries. Simply by turning a knob, consumers could listen to the latest news (sometimes even as it happened!), hear the latest song, laugh with their favourite comedian, or thrill to the adventures of their favourite detective. Consumers and corporate executives alike felt that radio's dominance in the media industries could not be shaken. In 1952, however, a new cable television technology took hold in Canada. By 1958, the Canadian Broadcasting Corporation's (CBC) microwave network extended from Victoria, B.C., to Sydney, Nova Scotia, making it the longest television network in the world (Canadian Museum of Civilization 2003). Television's domination in the media world had begun: it had all the advantages of radio plus one more: *moving images*. Now consumers could not only listen to the world around them, they could watch it unfold.

Media Ownership and Control

Just as technology has played a significant role in the development of media industries, it has played a significant role in the changes that have occurred within these industries.

Consider, for a moment, the effects that fibre-optic cable, broadcast satellites, and computers have had on media industries. The introduction of cable television, for example, brought about a significant shift in media ownership. The development of more sophisticated space satellites in the 1970s made it possible for cable television systems to become interconnected throughout North America and contributed to the success of cable networks such as Shaw Cable, Rogers Communications, StarChoice, Cable News Network (CNN), and COGECO, to which customers pay a monthly subscription fee. Having a variety of cable channels to watch increased the number of cable TV subscribers, resulted in more broadcast stations being built, and inspired the creation of additional cable channels. At the same time, the dramatic increase in cable television viewers drastically reduced the audience share previously held by the original television networks. This evolution of technology and business strategies within the media industry has been characterized by a trend where a few megacorporations own increasing proportions of the media businesses and where companies own more than one form of media business (Biagi 2009).

In Canada, the years between 1983 and 1992 saw the total number of control companies in the media industry shrink from 46 to 20 (Hoynes 2002:1). In the television industry, for example, a few megacorporations gained a great deal of control over all aspects of the television industry. As a result, functions ranging from program production to distribution to the audience fell under Big Media control. As businesses with a goal of generating profit, these corporations also consolidated their holdings in other sectors of the media—ranging from film and music production to books and magazine publishing. They also acquired interests in technologies such as computers and direct broadcasting from satellite (Budd et al. 1999). In 2000, the largest media merger in North America to date occurred when America Online (AOL) merged with Time Warner, garnering access to the Internet for Time Warner and access to cable television systems for AOL—central components in the contemporary music, publishing, and television industries (Hansell 2000). The biggest media merger in Canada also occurred in 2000, when Conrad Black sold 17 percent of his newspapers and Internet properties to Izzy Asper, the now-deceased owner and CEO of CanWest. Asper's empire, run by his three children, is Canada's largest integrated media company. It includes the Global television network, Fox Sports, DejaView, Prime TV, and Fireworks Entertainment, as well as many of the major and minor Canadian dailies and radio stations (Canwest 2009). Analysts describe these types of mergers in the media industries as *convergence,* meaning that a consolidation or amalgamation of the communications, computer, and electronics industries has occurred. Today, Canwest Global Corporation's newspapers control about 30 percent of Canadian daily circulation, with a further 20 percent of circulation controlled under Quebecor, which owns the Sun chain of newspapers (Nesbitt-Larking 2007:44). While these two corporations own and control 50 percent of the daily news circultaion in Canada, an additional three corporations own a further 30 percent, resulting in 80 percent of Canadian newspaper circulation being within the control of just five large chains (Nesbitt-Larking 2007:44). It is important to note, however, that patterns of media ownership change rapidly, and information on media ownership easily becomes outdated.

This type of corporate convergence in the media industry has led to media concentration. **Media concentration** refers to the tendency of the media industries to cluster together in groups with the goal of enhancing profitability (Biagi 2009). Media ownership is more highly concentrated in Canada than almost anywhere else in the industrialized world. Since 2005, almost all private Canadian television stations have been owned by national media conglomerates. And, because of increasing cross-ownership, most of our newspapers are owned by the same corporations that own television and radio stations (Anderson 2009).

As the definition of media concentration suggests, profit is the driving force. According to media scholar Shirley Biagi (2009), media are owned by people whose interest is in making money. Since profits in this sector are high compared with profits in the manufacturing sector, businesspeople view investments in the media industries positively. Thus far, corporate megamergers have led to the following changes in the media industries (Biagi 2009):

1. *Concentration of ownership within one industry:* For example, as this book goes to press, the five largest newspaper chains own 50 percent of all the daily newspapers in Canada. Torstar publishes the *Toronto Star, The Record* in Kitchener-Waterloo, the

Hamilton Spectator, and the *Guelph Mercury.* It also publishes an additional 95 community newspapers in southern Ontario. Osprey Media, a Quebecor media company since 2007, owns 21 dailies in Ontario (including the *Kingston Whig-Standard* and *Peterborough Examiner*) and 36 other newspapers (Lange 2008). In some provinces, media concentration is above the national average. For example, all the daily newspapers in New Brunswick are owned by the Irving family; one company owns all the daily papers in Saskatchewan, Prince Edward Island, and Newfoundland; and in Quebec, only one small independent paper has survived (Press Campaigns 2003). Concentration occurs in part because small presses and independent media sources are not able to access the advertising revenues and large audiences that the larger corporations can. As a result, many small Canadian presses are closing. This is also true of Canadian television, where 60 percent of the market is reached by only five corporations. In 2003, three companies controlled 68 percent of the cable television market and 10 companies controlled 55 percent of the revenue from the radio industry (Biagi 2009; McChesney 2004; Press Campaigns 2003).

2. *Cross-media ownership:* Cross-media ownership occurs when media companies own more than one type of media property. Today, a single giant media corporation may own newspapers, magazines, and radio and television stations. Even among smaller media corporations, cross-media ownership is common. The Canadian company Rogers Communications, for example, has over 2.3 million basic cable subscribers, 1.6 million high-speed Internet subscribers, 8.2 million wireless subscribers (supplying service to 94 percent of Canada's wireless customers), and almost 1 million cable telephone subscriptions (Rogers Communications 2009). As another example, CTVglobemedia owns the CTV network and its 24 affiliates; has full or partial ownership of 40 specialty channels, including MuchMusic and TSN; owns provincial channels such as A Channel, CKX-TV, TQS, and ASN; and owns the *Globe and Mail,* 35 radio stations, and 40 percent of Workopolis.com (Lange 2008; Nesbitt-Larking 2007; Campaign for Democratic Media 2009b). Clearly, cross-media

ownership can have a particularly serious impact in geographical areas where people have access to media owned by only one source. For example, a strike at Irving Oil is likely to receive biased coverage by the media sources that are owned by Irving in the province. Generally, stories that do not support the particular bias of news media owners do not get aired or published or are aired or published in a clearly biased manner, a fact that is problematic when one family (and corporation) owns the two major provincial newspapers, as Canwest does with the *Vancouver Sun* and the *Province* (see **http://thetyee.ca, http://www.democraticmedia.ca,** and numerous publications by Simon Fraser University communications scholar Dr. Donald Gutstein).

3. *Conglomerate ownership:* Conglomerates occur when a single corporation owns companies that operate in different business sectors. For example, Rogers Communications owns 460 retail stores (Video, Plus/mall, and Fido), the Shopping Channel network, 54 radio stations, 70 consumer magazine and trade publications, four Sportsnet regional TV sports networks with national HDTV feed, the five-station Citytv television network, and the five-station OMNI television network, as well as the Toronto Blue Jays and the Rogers Centre event venue (Rogers Communications 2009).

4. *Vertical integration:* Vertical integration occurs when the corporations that make the media content also control the distribution channels. Canwest, for example, owns Canwest Entertainment Inc., one of Canada's largest integrated production, distribution, and financing companies of television programs and motion pictures. The film and television production companies it owns (Canwest Entertainment, Fireworks Television, and Fireworks Pictures) supply programming to its television networks (Global Television Network, Prime TV, and CHECK television). Canwest also partnered with Samuel Goldwyn Films and Stratosphere Releasing, forming IDP Distribution, in order to market and distribute feature films in North America ("Big Media Road Map" 2000; Canwest Entertainment 2003; Rosenwein 2000). As another example, Walt Disney Company owns film and television production companies (Miramax

Films and ABC Entertainment Television Group), which supply programming for its television network (ABC), which helps to promote cable channels that are owned in part by Disney (ESPN, Lifetime TV, and E! Entertainment TV). These, in turn, have ties with Hyperion, the Disney book-publishing unit.

Supporters of convergence believe that much can be gained by these corporate strategies; they speak of synergy. The term *synergy* is often used to describe the process used in capitalizing on a product to make all the profit possible. Media analysts believe that synergy is created, for example, when a corporation acquires ownership of both a production studio and a television network. Theoretically, the products made by one branch of the company may be distributed and sold by the other branch of the company in a more efficient and profitable manner than if separate companies were involved. Shaw Cable, the second-largest cable television operation in Canada, is a good example of synergy. Corus Entertainment, Shaw's media arm, owns 52 radio stations, television services, and Nelvana—the cornerstone of their content and production strategy and one of the world's leading creators, producers, and distributors of animated programming and related consumer products. Nelvana is responsible for popular "brands" such as Babar, Franklin, and Bakugan. Kids Can Press, another branch of Corus, is dedicated solely to children's publishing. Corus also owns the television networks YTV, Treehouse, W Network, CosmoTV, VIVA, CMT, SCREAM, Discovery Kids, Telelatino, TELETOON, and TELETOON Retro; Western Canada's pay TV service Movie Central and HBO Canada in the West; three local over-the-air television stations; and Corus Custom Networks advertising services (Corus Entertainment 2009). This network allows for the programs and products generated by one branch of the company to be promoted through others in an efficient and cost-effective manner.

Most people in the media industries do not see consolidation as a problem. Supporters claim that concentration in media ownership ensures that Canadian voices are able to compete with those promoted by companies from the United States and by the international media market. The former executive vice-president of Canwest Global, Ken Goldstein, claimed Canadian companies could not successfully compete against the more powerful media conglomerates from the United States if they were prevented from consolidating resources. Goldstein stated in a CBC interview, "You would not have a true viable independent media without it" (CBC News 2002). However, some media executives have acknowledged that the close link between their sectors may lead to conflicts of interest or accusations of collusion. Michael Eisner, past chair of Disney, has stated that he believes ABC News (which is owned by Disney) should not cover Disney: "I think it's inappropriate for Disney to be covered by Disney.... By and large, the way you avoid conflict of interest is to, as best you can, not cover yourself" (Rosenwein 2000:94).

Problems Associated with Convergence

Concentration and conglomeration are profitable for investors and media executives. These processes don't only involve the amalgamation of businesses, they also involve initiatives designed to streamline media systems. Strategies to increase profits include asking journalists to report on several separate stories each day as opposed to developing one or two well-researched stories. These stories are then distributed throughout the same conglomerates' different media outlets. Many people watching these trends are concerned about the effects this is having on the quality and integrity of journalism in Canada (Lill 2001). Many analysts indicate that convergence has reduced the amount of *message pluralism*, the "broad and diverse representation of opinion and culture," available to the Canadian public (Biagi 1998:265). This is also a concern when the bias of the small community of media owners influences the nation's media content. As one media scholar has noted:

> Media fare is even more closely linked to the needs and concerns of a handful of enormous and powerful corporations, with annual revenues approaching the [GDP] of a small nation. These firms are run by wealthy managers and billionaires with clear stakes in the outcome of the most fundamental political issues, and their interests are often distinct from those of the vast majority of humanity. By any known theory of democracy, such a concentration of economic, cultural, and political power into so few hands—and mostly unaccountable hands at that—is absurd and

unacceptable. On the other hand, media fare is subjected to an ever-greater commercialization as the dominant firms use their market power to squeeze the greatest possible profit from their products. (McChesney 1999:29–30)

Commercialization and branding have already found their way to the Internet, which, even as it is hailed as a newer source of news and entertainment that is relatively free from corporate constraints, has experienced criticism similar to that levelled at longer-established forms of media.

Among the problems that analysts believe have been brought about by convergence are (1) the decline of journalism as a public service profession; (2) constant pressure for all journalistic endeavors to be immediately profitable; (3) a significant decrease in the quantity and quality of international news available to Canadian audiences; (4) the quashing of public debate about the power of the media industries and how they deal with important social issues; and (5) a dramatic increase in the influence of powerful lobbyists who represent the interests of the media conglomerates (McChesney 2004; Phillips 1999). Because the reach of the media industries is worldwide, these concerns are not limited to Canada.

Global Media Issues

To understand the effect transnational media corporations may have on other nations of the world, consider this: seven major media conglomerates—General Electric (NBC Universal), Walt Disney Company, News Corporation, Time Warner Inc., Viacom Inc., Cox Corporation, and CBS Corporation—control most of the publishing, recording, television, film, and mega–theme park business in the high-income nations of the world (Freepress 2009; McChesney 2004).

Perhaps it should not be surprising that advertising by transnational corporations has fuelled the rise of commercial television—and consequently, the profitability of media conglomerates—around the world. As international agreements over trade, such as NAFTA (the North American Free Trade Agreement) and GATT (the General Agreement on Tariffs and Trade) have come into effect, companies in fields such as oil production, aerospace engineering, and agribusiness have used transnational media corporations to improve

their communication base and extend their international operations (Schiller 1996). All in all, the global economy has proved profitable for media conglomerates (see Chapter 13 for a thorough discussion of trade).

While Canada is not involved in producing, distributing, and controlling media transnationally to the same degree that the major U.S.-based media companies are, Canada still plays a role internationally. For example, Canwest (through a wholly owned subsidiary) is indirectly the controlling shareholder of TEN Television Network and Eye Corp. in Australia. TEN is a national network of commercial television stations in five key Australian markets. Eye Corp. is one of Australia's largest media operators, conducting business in Australia, New Zealand, Asia, Europe, and North America (Canwest 2009).

Among analysts, there is growing concern about the amount of control a few media giants have over the world's information. Some have predicted that a very few major media conglomerates will soon control approximately 90 percent of all global information (Kilbourne 1999). These same few media companies are rapidly gaining the ownership and control of both the hardware and software that will make it possible for them to fully control messages and images appearing in any format (Kilbourne 1999; Schiller 1996). This fact may be particularly alarming to those who are already critical of how the media giants depict other nations.

While global media industries obviously provide news and entertainment to people who otherwise might not know what is going on in the world, according to media critic Robert McChesney (1999), they also contribute to the development of "neoliberal" democracies in those nations in which people have the formal right to vote but where the wealthy actually hold political and economic power:

The global commercial media system is radical, in the sense that it will respect no tradition or custom, on balance, if it stands in the way of significantly increased profits. But it ultimately is politically conservative, because the media giants are significant beneficiaries of the current global social structure, and any upheaval in property or social relations, particularly to the extent it reduced the power of business and lessened inequality, would possibly—no, probably—jeopardize their positions. (McChesney 1999:100)

Many critics also worry that the North American based media giants undermine traditional cultural values and beliefs in other nations, replacing them with North American values—particularly those that support materialism and consumerism. Some call this *media imperialism,* which occurs when one society's media dominates another country's culture (Knight 1998:110). Fewer than 10 global media conglomerates dominate the global media systems, and an additional 50 companies occupy regional and niche markets (Gruber 2009). U.S. media critic Jean Kilbourne (1999:55) states, "Today we export a popular culture that promotes escapism, consumerism, violence and greed." The countries that import media portrayals of Western culture do not have the means to depict values, activities, or perspectives indigenous to their own country in a way that rivals the ability of the United States in particular.

In Canada, a great deal of intra-national legislation is dedicated to protecting the cultural, linguistic, and political differences between English- and French-speaking Canada. The management, editorial priorities, and communications culture of the mass media in French- and English-speaking Canada are characteristically different in some important ways. Internationally, legislation is focused on limiting the percentage of media programming that is imported into Canada, particularly from the United States (Siegel 1996). The historical idea that broadcasting should be a public service created to reflect public, and not private, interests resulted in the creation of the Canadian Broadcasting Corporation (CBC), Le Societé Radio-Canada (SRC), and the Canadian Radio-Television and Telecommunications Commission (CRTC). Within this country, a primary challenge is to maintain control over Canadian ownership of, and content within, the mass media. The CRTC has slowly been changing these protective legislations. Under new rules announced in 2008, the CRTC limited companies to two types of media in a given market—a company may, for example, own television and radio assets in one city, or radio and newspaper, or television and newspaper, but may not own all three simultaneously in one place. Additionally, as ownership of cable specialty channels has become increasingly consolidated under the same few media conglomerates that own most of the country's conventional television stations, the CRTC has imposed a market share cap: no company can own broadcasting assets of more than 45 percent of the country's total television viewership ("CRTC Puts New Restrictions on Media Ownership" 2008).

Increasingly, Canadians are becoming aware of the five basic filters that are used in the media to manage social debate and to "manufacture consent." The first filter is media ownership. Currently, media concentration, which leads to a decrease in the diversity of voices represented through mainstream media, is of grave concern for many Canadians. Media activists and organizations such as MediaWatch, based at Simon Fraser University in British Columbia, as well as SooToday.com, The Tyee, and Rabble.ca, focus their efforts on identifying the blind spots (stories and points of view not covered in the mainstream media) that are the result of media concentration, conglomerate ownership, and other institutional bias. These blind spots contribute to fewer and fewer points of view being meaningfully covered in the media. The second filter is advertising, as it tends not to challenge, criticize, or offer alternative approaches to capitalism or the doctrines of elite social rule in general. Clothing, car, cosmetic, and beer advertisements, for example, consistently reinforce messages that encourage people to consume and to conform to idealized societal norms. The third filter is the sources of news. In North America, the trend is that fewer agencies are generating and monitoring media activity. The Canadian Press, Reuters, and Associated Press are three of the main sources of media in Canada. "Flak" is the fourth filter. Within democratic societies where the ideal of "one voice, one vote" is upheld, media watchdogs serve the role of ensuring that the media production and distribution industries are performing in a democratically appropriate way. In Canada, however, most widely disseminated "flak" is generated by right-wing media watchdogs and industry groups, such as the Fraser Institute and the Canadian Association of Broadcasters. The final filter within North American propaganda production is the "official enemy." Identifying and fighting against an enemy or enemies helps to maintain domestic social discipline and conservative or neo-conservative hegemony. "Enemies" inside Canada include protestors, immigrants, poor people, and people with disabilities, as well as racialized/ethnic, sexual, and religious minorities. International enemies in the post-Soviet world include the Arab world, Afghanistan, Iraqis, "terrorists," and "the Middle East" in general. Understanding the existence and the function of these five filters enables people who are media literate to become informed consumers of media in Canada and critical thinkers about media bias.

Having an awareness of the presence and the function of these filters is one way of making sense of how media are managed. The anti-WTO protests blew the cover off media bias for many Canadians and revealed the dramatic effects media concentration is having on the ability of North Americans to engage in democratic exchanges of mass communication (see Box 14.1).

The social, cultural, and political impacts of the media have also been experienced by Indigenous communities within Canada. John Amagoalik, former president of the Inuit Tapiriit Kanatami, the organization representing the Inuit in Canada, describes the impact of the Canadian government's 1972 decision to bring television into communities in the Far North, in which the population numbered just over 500 people:

> When television first came, the effect of the television on the community was very drastic. People no longer visited their neighbours. Children did not play outside and the interactive activities of the community in general were broken down. The home and the family was the last refuge of the Inuktitut language, and television, by coming into the home, was invading this last refuge. (Raymont 1981)

SOCIAL PROBLEMS IN THE MEDIA

BOX 14.1   Lies, Damned Lies, and Statistics: Critical Thinking about Media Bias

"Most of what has been written is so inaccurate that I can't decide if the reporters in question should be charged with conspiracy or simply incompetence," stated one observer after the 1999 protest against the World Trade Organization (WTO) in Seattle, Washington (Donahue 2000:1). Official media houses reported that violent protestors and "anarchists" had taken to the streets, breaking windows, spraying graffiti on stores such as Starbucks, Nike, and McDonald's, and engaging in confrontational behaviour with police as they progressed through Seattle's downtown. In contrast, most of the 50 000 who attended the protest did so in a spirit of peaceful protest against the WTO and the impacts of globalization. Many of these people have stories to tell about their experiences at the "Battle in Seattle" that differ from those covered by mainstream media.

Critical analysis of media coverage of the Battle in Seattle makes explicit the relationships between media, government, and big business. The close links between these three social institutions call into question the role media play in maintaining the status quo and therefore the degree to which "objectivity" in mainstream reporting is currently being compromised. *Globe and Mail* reporter Barry McKenna (1999:A9) wrote, the morning the WTO summit began, that "nine of the thirteen companies that contributed more than $150 000 to the Seattle organizing committee are high-technology companies." Companies such as these are forecasted to generate trillions of dollars in annual revenue in the next decade. They are the same companies that make up the new global media system and that work in tandem with the five or six super-ad agencies that control the $350 billion global advertising industry. Together they dominate

global trade. In the lead-up to the WTO, these corporations actively lobbied the WTO for tax-free e-commerce regulations to be passed. During the WTO, they dictated to the media houses they own what spin North American reporters should take on reporting the events surrounding the WTO meeting and protests (Gutstein 2000).

Events like the anti-WTO protests demonstrate how media concentration is impacting democratic processes around the globe. Without a voice in the mainstream media, protestors' analyses of and experiences at the WTO were hard for many Canadians to access—unless they were aware of alternative media houses, which carry stories such as those about the Battle in Seattle told by anti-WTO protestors. Alternative media radio and television programs and zines, as well as film and video collectives, have created media pieces such as the Indy Media documentary *This Is What Democracy Looks Like,* which used footage from over 100 independent media activists present at the WTO protest.

These alternative media sources are typically run by volunteers and organized around a commitment to model a democratic media process where a diversity of opinion is expressed and the mainstream is intelligently criticized. For example, the volunteers who run *Adbusters* state on their homepage, "We want folks to get mad about corporate disinformation, injustices in the global economy, and any industry that pollutes our physical or mental commons." This declaration clearly marks this organization's bias about media concentration, which is at odds with the bias of the mainstream media, and invites people to engage with *Adbusters* in a debate about the role of media in the political economy.

As a result of the structure of media in Canada, people who wanted to learn about the common person's experience on the streets of Seattle turned to alternative media sources. Instead of articles discussing the importance of multilateral agreements or the property costs incurred by "anarchistic" protestors, these sites tended to carry critiques of the global political economy and the institutional measures set in place to protect it. During the WTO protests, Web-based sites gave eyewitness reports that challenged official statements made by police, politicians, and other authorities in the mainstream media. For example, many reported on alternative media sites that the police initiated violent attacks against protestors four hours before any vandalism occurred (Donahue 2000). In other stories, people wrote that police violence may have started because the riot squads began to feel intimidated by the unified and committed presence of the non-violent protestors and set about to undermine it. On the Internet, people like Matt Guynn, a non-violence trainer and eyewitness, distributed accounts, such as this one, about police violence:

> In one scene I witnessed this morning, police who had been standing behind a blockade line began marching in lock-step toward the line [of protestors], swinging their batons forward, and when they reached the line they began striking the nonviolent, seated protesters repeatedly in the back. Then they ripped off the protesters' gas masks, and sprayed pepper spray at point-blank range into their eyes repeatedly. After spraying, they rubbed the protesters' eyes and pushed their fingers around on their lips to aggravate the effect of the spray. And after all this, they began striking them again with batons. (in Donahue 2000:1)

Eyewitnesses who had been attacked by police with pepper spray and tear gas returned to their communities to suffer the chemical impacts of these attacks and to share stories about what had really happened on the streets (author's files). It is worth noting that Guynn's account was substantiated by film footage, later used in the documentary *This Is What Democracy Looks Like*. Many families and friends were shocked to learn that the footage shown on television and in national newspapers was almost completely at odds with what the vast majority of protestors reported seeing and experiencing. The discrepancies between the official and unofficial stories were so dramatic that a new era of distrust of the mass media began.

As Kilbourne and other media scholars point out, for the first time in history, people are hearing most stories about life, not from their parents, schools, churches, or friends, but from transnational media conglomerates that have something to sell. If it is true that the media are a crucial influence in shaping and creating global cultural perceptions, then all of us must give careful consideration to the images and information offered to us. Of particular significance is how the news is framed. **Framing** refers to how news content and the accompanying visual images are linked together to create certain audience perceptions and give specific impressions to viewers and readers. When framing occurs in a news story, some analysts use the term "spin," because the process often involves "spinning" information so as to present it from a particular (and different) angle, or point of view. Critics point out that once a frame is established, journalists must adhere to it. The danger is that media coverage falling outside of the frame is not covered by mainstream media. In Canada, media bias is a growing concern for professional journalists.

Media bias, in the form of *structural media bias,* refers to the areas of life and work that are not covered in the media. This distorts how people view the world and can significantly influence the priorities people develop. In the 1990s, the face of national news changed in Canada. Hollinger Press, owned then by Conrad Black, changed its reporting priorities and cut regular columns on the environment, social affairs, education, and health issues and replaced them with entire sections on business affairs. Consequently, today, despite differences in ownership, Canadians continue to be presented with extensive information on stock markets and business concerns while the environment, health, education, and social affairs are treated as "special interest" pieces (M. Barlow 1996). This structural bias results in media coverage that suggests to Canadians that national and international business interests are now the most pressing concerns of the 21st century, while other issues, such as the environment or culture, are only intermittently important.

Potential Media Effects

Today, as we have said, the global media industries are the primary source of news and entertainment for many people. Although these industries may have greater influence over some people than over others, media analysts suggest that all of us are more profoundly influenced by media messages than we realize. The portrayal of violence is one example of a negative media influence.

Violence and the Media

Should we be concerned about how—and the extent to which—media depict violence? A number of media analysts assert that the need of media industries to capture public interest and thus increase the size of their markets has contributed to the use of violence as a means of selling newspapers, television programs, movies, music, and other media-related commodities. A Canadian study reports that television violence affects children of varying age groups differently, and with children between the ages of 10 and 17 spending the majority of their time engaged with media, the overall impacts must be considered (Children Now 1999). A comprehensive economic analysis of television programming led one researcher to conclude that violent fare emerges as a logical extension of commercial broadcasting. While television executives claim their programs reflect audience desires, they do so in a commercially exploitable manner (Hamilton 1998). In other words, when audiences say they want to see justice triumph, television executives make sure justice does triumph in their programs, but only after several violent fights or shootings that hold viewers in their seats even during commercials.

According to Kilbourne, one of the many ways in which the media perpetuate violence against women is through advertising. Kilbourne (1999) analyzed tens of thousands of advertisements to determine what effect they might have on viewers. She found that "the poses and postures of advertising are often borrowed from pornography, as are many of the themes, such as bondage, sadomasochism, and the sexual exploitation of children" (Kilbourne 1999:271). She points out that advertisements showing women as dead or in the process of being killed are particularly popular themes. Advertising in other nations historically has been even more explicit than what is allowed in Canada. For example, an Italian version of *Vogue* showed a man aiming a gun at a nude woman who was wrapped in plastic and had a leather briefcase covering her face (Kilbourne 1999).

That violence against women is an accepted, and seemingly acceptable, part of advertising is highlighted by the use of "crime scene corpse" poses in the popular reality show *America's Next Top Model*. In the show, "wanna-be" models engage in a variety of photo shoots that are designed to expose their suitability as models in the real world of advertising. The one chosen as a winner each season is given a modelling contract. In the 2007 season,

the show featured a photo shoot that pushed the boundaries of popular culture. The contestants were asked to take part in a "crime scene" photo shoot, where each was directed to pose as a corpse. The models posed variously as decapitated, strangled, pushed off a roof, drowned, poisoned, pushed down stairs, stabbed, electrocuted, shot in the head, and even as victims of organ theft.

The following is an excerpt of the judges' comments made about four of the models and their poses:

Responding to the shot model pose:

Miss J: I love the broken-down leg. It's absolute genius.

Tyra: Absolutely beautiful. Jay said that you did well with different shots and that you gave variation, but he had to position you.

Nigel: The reason why this shot works so amazingly well is the positioning of your body. On top of that, the background, the way it's lit—that's one of those shots that if I took all that away from you, then how great would you look?

Twiggy (later): I was rather distressed by what Dionne was wearing today. She doesn't stand out of line for me. She's got no oomph.

Tyra: When you come into this room, no matter how beautiful your pictures are, the judges want to be inspired by what you look like. Almost everybody had a beautiful picture this week, so the judges start thinking about other things—like the way you dress and the way you present yourself outside of the photos.

Media advertising also tends to treat women as sexual objects. As the producers of shows like *America's Next Top Model* clearly are aware, in order to sell products, advertisements frequently show women in compromised positions or as the victims of rape or other violence and thus contribute to the ongoing subordination of women. Such depictions may also normalize the idea that forcing sex on a woman is acceptable, as Kilbourne (1999:273) points out:

Men are also encouraged [by advertisements] to never take no for an answer. Ad after ad implies that girls and women don't really mean "no" when they say it, that women are only teasing when they resist men's advances. "NO" says an ad showing a man leaning over a woman against a wall. Is she screaming or laughing? Oh, it's an ad for deodorant and the second word, in very small print, is "sweat." Sometimes it's "all in good fun," as in the ad for Possession shirts and shorts featuring a man ripping the clothes off a woman who seems to be having a good time. And sometimes it is more sinister. A perfume ad running in several teen magazines features a very young woman, with eyes blackened by makeup or perhaps something else, and the copy, "Apply generously to your neck so he can smell the scent as you shake your head 'no.'" In other words, he'll understand that we don't really mean it and he can respond to the scent like any other animal.

As studies continue on the relationship between violence in the media and in everyday life, we will no doubt learn more about the causes and consequences of extensive media violence in society (see Chapter 4 for more discussion).

PERSPECTIVES ON MEDIA-RELATED PROBLEMS

Just as they do in regard to other social issues, interactionist, functionalist, conflict, and feminist approaches to media-related problems start with differing assumptions about these problems.

The Interactionist Perspective

Perhaps the earliest interactionist theory concerning the media's effect on individuals and groups was the *hypodermic needle theory*, which suggested that audiences were made up of passive individuals who were equally susceptible to the messages of the media. However, a World War II study of military personnel who were shown movies designed to portray the enemy as evil and to increase morale among soldiers concluded that most of the subjects showed little change in their morale level, although the movies did influence their views of the "enemies" as "evil." Based on these findings, researchers suggested an alternative explanation: the theory of limited effects. The **theory of limited effects** states that the media have a minimal effect on the attitudes and perceptions of individuals. According to this theory, people may not always be selective about what

they watch or read, but they gather different messages from the media, and many people carefully evaluate the information they gain. This theory notes that when people are interested and informed about an issue, they are less likely to be influenced by what members of the media report. Those who are poorly informed or have no personal information about a particular topic or issue are more likely to be affected by what other people, including reporters and journalists, say about the social concern.

A similar theory, known as *use and gratification theory*, suggests that people are active audience participants who make conscious decisions about what they will watch, listen to, read, and surf on the Internet. However, this theory assumes that people using different media have specific wishes or desires and will choose media sources that gratify their desires. In other words, people use the media to entertain and inform themselves but are aware of the limitations the media have in their coverage of topics and the forms of entertainment.

Another interactionist theory, mentioned elsewhere in the book, is **social learning theory,** which is based on the assumption that people are likely to act out the behaviour they see in role models and media sources. To support this theory, social psychologist Albert Bandura (1977) conducted a series of experiments on aggression in children. For the experiment, children were divided into four groups. One group watched a film of a man attacking and beating a large, inflatable doll and being rewarded for his behaviour. The second group saw a similar film, except in this version the man was punished for attacking the doll. The third group was shown a version in which the man was neither rewarded nor punished for his behaviour. The final group was not shown any film. Prior to the experiment, researchers believed that the children who saw the man rewarded for hitting the doll would be the most likely to show aggressive behaviour toward the doll. However, this did not prove to be true. Regardless of which version of the film they saw, children who were prone to aggression before the film tended to act aggressively toward the doll but other children did not. As a result, the researchers concluded that many factors other than the media influenced aggressive behaviour in children, including their relationship with their parents, how much formal education their parents possessed, and the personality of the children.

More recent theories have sought to explain the effects of media on individuals by emphasizing the part that viewers, listeners, and readers play in shaping the media. According to the *audience relations approach,* people use their own cultural understandings to interpret what they hear and see in the media. Factors involved in the audience relations approach include how much previous knowledge individuals have about a topic and the availability of other sources of information. This viewpoint is somewhat in keeping with functionalist approaches, which highlight the important contemporary functions of the media.

The Functionalist Perspective

Functionalist approaches to examining the media often focus on the functional—and sometimes dysfunctional—effects the media have on society. Functionalists point out that the media serve several important functions in contemporary societies.

- First, the media provide news and information, including warnings about potential disasters, such as an approaching hurricane.

- Second, the media facilitate public discourse regarding social issues and policies, such as welfare reform.

- Third, the media pass on cultural traditions and historical perspectives, particularly to recent immigrants and children (Lasswell 1969).

- Fourth, the media are a source of entertainment, providing people with leisure-time activities (Biagi 2009).

- Finally, the media confer status on individuals and organizations by frequently reporting on their actions or showing their faces and mentioning their names. According to sociologist Joshua Gamson (1994:186), becoming a media celebrity is a means of gaining power, privilege, and mobility: "Audiences recognize this when they seek brushes with it and when they fantasize about the freedom of fame and its riches and about the distinction of popularity and attention."

As Gamson notes, some people become celebrities *because* the media confers that status on them. In other words, as the popular saying goes, "Some people are famous for being famous." As a fairly recent Canadian example, a Torontonian became possibly the most well-known lawyer in North America for a short while when he sued Starbucks Coffee Company for $1.5 million because of damage to his penis—an injury he received from getting it caught in a toilet seat in the washroom of one of Starbucks' coffee shops. Reporters and producers from across North America deluged the man with requests for interviews. In Toronto, the media focused so heavily on this story that only the WTO talks and protests that year were covered more heavily (Associated Press 1999; Hackett et al. 2000).

Although the media are a source of entertainment for many, functionalist theorists state that the media are dysfunctional when they contribute to a reduction in social stability or weaken other social institutions, such as the family, education, politics, law, and religion. For example, television has brought about significant changes in family interaction patterns, as one media scholar explains:

> The most pervasive effect of television—aside from its content—may be its very existence, its readily available, commanding, and often addictive presence in our homes, its ability to reduce hundreds of millions of citizens to passive spectators for major portions of their waking hours. Television minimizes interactions between persons within families and communities. One writer I know only half-jokingly claims, "I watch television as a way of getting to know my husband and children." Another associate, who spent years in Western agrarian regions, relates how a farmer once told her: "Folks used to get together a lot. Now with television, we see less of each other." (Parenti 1998:188)

When dysfunctions occur, they should be addressed in ways that benefit individuals, families, and the larger society. While the media have changed how people interact with one another, they may have also profoundly influenced the ways in which individuals react to events in their personal and community-based lives. There are other functionalist approaches, however, which suggest that individuals and families are responsible for social change in regard to the media. Analysts who favour this approach believe that rather than changing the nature of television programming, parents should monitor their children's television-watching habits and schools should offer media education for parents and children to make them aware of the classic persuasion and propaganda techniques often used in programming and advertising (Minow and LaMay 1999).

The Conflict Perspective

Conflict theorists typically link the media industries with the capitalist economy. From this approach, members of the capitalist class own and control the media, which, along with other dominant social institutions, instruct people in the values, beliefs, and attitudes that they should have (Curran et al. 1982). All of these efforts to maintain the status quo and the privileged position of the power elites within it are achieved through **hegemony**—the use of the media and other cultural institutions to represent the interests, values, and understandings of the capitalist class and other powerful groups as natural and universal (Knight and Greenberg 2008:108). According to this perspective, the *process of legitimization* takes place as media consumers are continually provided with information that supports the validity of existing class relations. As a result, members of the working class are lulled into a sense of complacency in which they focus more on entertainment and consumption than on questioning existing economic and social relations. This perspective is sometimes referred to as **hegemony theory**—the view that the media are instruments of social control and are used by members of the ruling classes to create "false consciousness" in the working classes. Edward S. Herman and Noam Chomsky, in their book *Manufacturing Consent* (1988) and the 1993 National Film Board film of the same title, discuss this concept at length. One of the major points in this work is that people from the ruling classes need not be involved together in any kind of conspiracy to hoodwink the masses. Rather, the fact that their interests are the same dictates that they act in a manner similar to one another.

Although there are various conflict approaches, most view ownership and economic control of the media as a key factor in determining what kinds of messages are disseminated around the globe. Media analysts such as Michael Parenti (1998:149) believe that media bias is inevitable as transnational media industries become concentrated in the hands of a few megacorporations:

Media bias usually does not occur in random fashion; rather, it moves in the same overall direction again and again, favouring management over labour, corporations over corporate critics, affluent whites over inner-city poor, officialdom over protestors, the two-party monopoly over leftist third parties, privatization and free-market "reforms" over public-sector development . . . domination of the Third World over revolutionary or populist social change, investor globalization over nation-state democracy, national security policy over critics of that policy, and conservative commentators and columnists . . . over progressive or populist ones.

According to Parenti, the built-in biases of the media reflect the dominant ideology that supports the privileged position of members of the capitalist class.

There are a number of ways in which media manipulation can occur: (1) sponsors control broadcasting decisions; (2) information may be suppressed by omitting certain details of a story or the entire story, particularly if the story may have a negative effect on a person or organization to whom members of the media feel beholden; (3) a story may be attacked or the reporting may not present a balanced view of the diverse viewpoints involved; (4) negative labels that stereotype groups of people, for example, "Islamic terrorists," "inner-city gangs," or "welfare cheats," may be used (see Box 14.2); and (5) stories may be framed to convey positive or negative connotations through the use of visual effects, placement, and other means. Like other conflict theorists, Parenti (1998:157) believes that the media tell people what to think before they have had a chance to think about an issue for themselves: "When we understand that news selectivity is likely to favour those who have power, position, and wealth, we move from a liberal complaint about the press's sloppy performance to a radical analysis of how the media serve the ruling circles all too well with much skill and craft." Viewing media activities in Canada from these perspectives inspires one to learn more about the relationship between media, social control, and the economy in the new millennium.

In an era marked by increased concentration of all forms of media, including the Internet, conflict perspectives on media ownership and control raise important questions. Although people engaged in political critique and social activism, such as members of environmental or women's groups, have sometimes been able to marshal the media on their behalf, the media often implicitly support the status quo because of their corporate interests and their need to maintain and enhance advertising revenues.

Feminist Perspectives

Beginning in the late 1960s, Second Wave feminist media scholarship focused on the role of visual representation in women's oppression. Studying media texts that range from television and movies to radio, feminists have critiqued male domination in the media and its role in reinforcing gender stereotypes that sustain socially endorsed and oppressive views of gender:

> Media has consistently misrepresented the goals, activities, and members of the women's movement. Because most editors and media executives are men, they have not experienced the daily frustrations women face in a society where they lack equal rights, opportunities, and status equal to those of men. (Wood 2001:295)

Second Wave feminists radicalized Canadian's understanding of the problem of women's devaluation (be it individualistic, psychological, sociocultural, biologistic, or economic) and the ways traditional relationships between men and women are used to normalize such things as violence against women in the media. Both feminists and conflict theorists are concerned about the role media have in shaping people's values, beliefs, and attitudes. They are also critical of the role the mass media play in supporting and perpetuating hierarchies of oppression.

Feminists maintain that meaning is mediated, and therefore they examine both media texts and the ways in which they are produced (Reinharz 1992:145). As a result, how media present women's roles in both the "public" and "private" spheres of life and the discords that exist between represented and lived experiences are important. Viewing women as agents, feminists also study the ways in which women and girls are receptive to (or rejecting of) the media and the ways these individuals interpret and consume media images. The goal is to challenge male dominance in the media and the devalued status of women in media and society. To this end, women involved in alternative feminist media (i.e., feminist film, documentaries, publishing houses, and art) utilize the media as a political tool by articulating their own perspectives and demands and representing and re-representing themselves. In the 22 years that the women's arm of the Canadian National Film Board, Studio D, was in operation, it actively supported the creation of films by, for, and about women (Shannon 1997).

SOCIAL PROBLEMS IN THE MEDIA

BOX 14.2   How You Can Tell When the Media Poor-Bash

Sometimes poor-bashing is obvious. Calling people on welfare names like "cheats" or "criminally inclined opportunists" is blatant poor-bashing. But subtle poor-bashing can be just as devastating. You must read or listen critically to make sure you're not being taken in by it.

When Newfoundland anti-poverty activist Bev Brown gives workshops on poverty and the media, she asks these questions about media coverage of poverty issues:

What's left out of the story?
Issues usually left out of articles about welfare and EI are the high unemployment rate, the poor quality of jobs that are available (when they are), an explanation of who benefits from poverty, information about the laws that cause poverty (like low welfare rates and minimum wages), and information about who has the funds or could create the jobs or pay the wages to reduce poverty.

Who is speaking?
Do poor people or groups that represent poor people have any voice in the story? Do we hear directly from people in poverty or only from people who work for agencies or charities or from researchers who theorize about them?

Is the story based on false assumptions?
Is it assumed that jobs are available when they aren't? That welfare is generous? That people on welfare are lazy? That welfare is easily available? That people on welfare and EI don't have to look for work? That lone parent moms aren't productive? That people have to be forced to look for work? That training programs will create enough jobs for all who need them?

What are the subtle messages of the story?

Does it suggest—without clearly stating it—that people who have paid work are better than people who have unpaid work (child care, for example)? Does it imply that people on welfare prefer this to a range of other options?

Does the story use facts or gossip and insinuation?

Are the sources named? Are the sources right-wing think-tanks that have a vested interest in policies that cut the taxes and reduce the wages that their member corporations pay? Are the sources "authorities" that promote the typical stereotypes about people on welfare or EI? Would a similar standard of accuracy apply when reporting about a person or a group with a lot of power (e.g., politicians)?

Does the story use the social policy newspeak words?

Does it use words or phrases like "dependent," "incentive," "disincentive," and others . . . that blame the poor and take the pressure off the rich?

Brown recommends these supplementary questions:

1. Does the story ask how to end poverty, or does it merely expose the suffering of poor individuals?

2. Does it ask who benefits from poverty?

3. Does it investigate what laws cause poverty instead of focusing on individual characteristics of poor people?

4. Does it deal with the morality of poverty in the midst of great wealth?

5. If a publication includes stories advising upper-income people how to use RRSPs, does it also print stories advising poor people how to use welfare and EI? If there are stories about welfare fraud, are there any about tax fraud or corporate fraud?

6. Does the story assume charity is the only way to deal with poverty?

A final test: How would it sound if the statements about poor people were made about women or people of colour? Would it be okay to say that women are "criminally inclined opportunists"? That would be sexist. Would it be okay to say that people of colour are "criminally inclined opportunists"? No, that would be racist. Then it's poor-bashing to say that people on welfare are "criminally inclined opportunists."

Source: Jean Swanson, 2001, "Poor-Bashing: The Politics of Exclusion," Toronto: Between the Lines, 191–192. Reprinted by permission of Between the Lines Publishing.

Today, feminist analysis of the media is made more complex by the work of postmodern and post-structural feminists, multicultural feminists, queer feminists, Marxist feminists, anti-racist feminists, "Third World" feminists, and other Third Wave feminists. Feminists today understand that the matrices of oppression are interconnected and, therefore, theory and lived experience cannot be separated (see Chapters 2 and 3 for more discussion). Now, feminists study the impact of gender along with class, racialization/ethnicity, sexual orientation, age, national origin, and physical and mental ability in their analysis of the roles mass media play in shaping the life conditions and life choices of people in media texts and in real life. They also look at the role media play in the construction and deconstruction of identities, nations, and borders, to name but a few, and likewise the role we all play in constructing media.

Theoretically and methodologically, feminists of all persuasions analyze the activities and impacts of the mass media at the institutional, organizational, and individual levels (Valdivia 1995). Institutional analysis is concerned with studying the norms and values that govern the media as an institution and subsequently the smaller institutional entities, such as the press, that compose the

Around the globe, U.S. media conglomerates influence local cultures through continual marketing of films, television programming, and other media. These Harry Potter fans in Tokyo, Japan, wait excitedly in line for tickets to the Japanese premiere of Harry Potter and the Order of the Phoenix. *According to media sources, the film was a gigantic box-office success in Tokyo and other cities worldwide.*

whole. Analysis on an organizational level is concerned with studying the conventions and practices that govern each institution. Finally, individual-level analysis is concerned with the ways in which individuals participate in accepting, challenging, and reproducing societal norms and values. The activities of individuals within the media institution and the ways they function within established practices that are shaped by institutional norms and values are studied. Constructions of "race," class, age, sexual orientation, and ability and the impacts of these constructions on all of us, as well as the constructions of femininity and masculinity and the impacts of the media specifically on men, women, and trans people, are considered important because all groups are negatively affected by gendered discourse in the media.

Regardless of which theoretical perspective on the media industries most closely resembles our own thinking, each of us should take a closer look at the ideas, images, and advertisements that bombard us daily. We can learn a great deal from reflecting upon the ways images are produced and the role media play in maintaining oppressive hierarchies that are all too readily accepted as a satisfactory status quo. While most of us may believe that we are not affected by the constant stream of advertisements we encounter, we should realize, as Kilbourne (1999:27) states, "The fact is that much of advertising's power comes from this belief that advertising does not affect us. The most effective kind of propaganda is that which is not recognized as propaganda." Although individuals alone cannot solve the problems associated with the media industries, they can become more aware of the pervasive impact of television, films, newspapers, the Internet, and other forms of mass communication.

MEDIA IN THE 21ST CENTURY

Problems associated with the media will continue well into this century, and many of the issues will probably become even more complex. For example, it has been suggested that the Internet and e-commerce will affect all aspects of life, particularly in high-income nations such as Canada. Some analysts have suggested that Canadian cities will lose more of their tax base to untaxed Internet commerce, bringing about a need to restructure relations between cities, states, and the federal government (Friedman 2000). Indeed, the ability of a single government to control the activities of transnational media industries may be weakened as globalization continues to occur. Thus, according to journalist Thomas L. Friedman (2000:A31), a world of global communications means that many issues that were once considered the domain of individual nations and governments will have to be viewed from a new perspective:

> Issues such as freedom of speech and libel are going to have to be rethought as the Internet makes everyone a potential publisher in cyberspace—but with no censor or editor in charge. Privacy protection is going to have to be rethought in a world where for $39 Web sites will search out anyone's assets and home address for you. And our safety nets are going to have to be rethought in a world in which access to the Internet is going to be viewed as a human right, essential for basic survival—especially as governments move more services to the Web.

SOCIAL PROBLEMS AND INFORMATION TECHNOLOGY

BOX 14.3   Net Neutrality: Our Newest Endangered Species

Since the Internet became a viable entity, network providers have operated under a principle of **net neutrality**, meaning that they do not *discriminate against,* by degrading, blocking, or slowing access to, or *discriminate for,* by prioritizing and speeding up access to "certain content, services, or applications based on their source, ownership, or destination" (Campaign for Democratic Media 2009a; Save Our Net 2008). However,

because the Canadian Radio-Television and Telecommunications Commission (CRTC) takes a hands-off approach to Internet service provision, many Internet service providers are now claiming they have the right to "'manage' internet content and applications" (Campaign for Democratic Media 2009a).

Using a new technology called Deep Packet Inspection (DPI), Canadian network operators such as Bell, Rogers, and

Shaw Cable are now able to speed up network uses that create more profit for them and slow down any that do not. These companies use "DPI to 'throttle' peer-to-peer (P2P) applications" (Save Our Net 2008), violating the long-held network neutrality that we have come to count on. Today, however, Canada's largest cable and telephone companies want to decide the pace of certain Web activity. This means that content providers who cannot pay the equivalent of a new "toll" will see their sites slowed to a crawl, which ultimately will result in a loss of viewers or customers. This provides an enormous advantage to wealthy corporate sites (Campaign for Democratic Media 2009a).

The Campaign for Democratic Media (2009a) lists three implications of this lack of respect for new neutrality:

■ Entrepreneurs will be muscled out of the marketplace by big corporations that pay Internet providers for dominant placement on the Web. Startup companies left with inferior Internet service will be unable to compete.

■ Political groups could be slowed by a handful of dominant Internet providers who ask them to pay protection money for their websites to work.

■ Independent media creators' costs to post video and audio clips may skyrocket, silencing independent and citizen journalists and limiting the range of debate about important current events.

These implications are certainly not far off when we consider what has already happened in Canada. In 2005, Telus Corporation was able to have access blocked to a website run by striking employees that provided campaign information to the public (from the union's perspective) and provided important strike and picket information to striking workers. Additionally, in 2007, Rogers placed notices carrying the Rogers name and logo over the content of many websites. These messages appeared in the body of the Web page, in place of original website content. Finally, both Bell and Rogers openly admit they have degraded use of certain P2P file-sharing applications, many of which are used by independent filmmakers and citizens. For example, in 2008, Internet users who tried to download CBC's *The Next Greatest Prime Minister* on P2P applications were told it would take three hours to do so (Campaign for Democratic Media 2009a).

Is net neutrality something you take for granted? How might it impact you if it is gone?

In the years to come, new communication technologies will undoubtedly continue to change our lives and bring emergent issues to our attention (see Box 14.3). While new forms of media offer many potential benefits, they also raise serious concerns about social life as many of us know it.

WHAT CAN YOU DO?

■ Become media literate by learning about who owns your local media and identifying their political and economic interests.

■ Critically analyze advertisements and think about how they affect you, your family members, and your friends.

■ Think critically about everything you see, hear, or read (including this textbook) in the media.

■ Find out about current events by accessing both alternative and mainstream media sources in order to see the spin different media give an issue and if the issue is even covered.

■ Contact your local, provincial, and national newspapers and state that you want journalists to dig deeper and to seek out more diverse viewpoints before they write—insist that their employers support this type of journalism.

■ Actively learn about the impacts of "cross-ownership" of broadcast and newspaper holdings (where one company owns both radio or television stations and newspapers) and media concentration in your life.

■ Insist on diversity in the media you consume, so that media owners, journalists, reporters, and stories reflect the diversity of your community and province.

■ E-mail (or call) the customer relations departments of media you engage with and tell them when you feel they are getting something right (or wrong).

■ Check out alternative Canadian media activist associations that might be of interest to you.

SUMMARY

What Are the Media Industries? How Much Time Do Individuals Spend in Media-Related Activities?

According to social scientists, the media industries are media businesses that influence people and cultures worldwide and own interests in radio and television production and broadcasting; motion pictures, movie theatres, and music companies; newspaper, periodical (magazine), and book publishing; and Internet services and content providers. Today, many people spend more time in media-related activities than they do in any other single endeavour, including sleeping, working, eating, or talking with friends and family; therefore, some analysts believe the media have a major influence on how people think, feel, and act.

What Part Does Technology Play in How Various Media Industries Change Over Time?

For many years, newspapers were the primary source of news. However, new technologies brought about radio as the media phenomenon of the 1920s and television as the phenomenon of the 1950s. With the introduction of new communications technologies such as computers, fibre-optic cable, and broadcast satellites, the media industries continue to change rapidly.

How Has Media Ownership Changed?

Although there once were a variety of independent companies that produced books, records, television programs, and films, there are now large corporate conglomerates that own more than one form of the media business.

What Is Convergence? How Does It Relate to Media Concentration?

Convergence refers to a melding of the communications, computer, and electronics industries that gives a few huge corporations control over an increasing proportion of all media sources. Convergence contributes to greater concentration in the media. Media concentration refers to the tendency of the media industries to cluster together in groups.

What Forms May Media Concentration Take?

Media concentration may take place in several forms: (1) within one industry (such as newspaper chains); (2) cross-media ownership, in which media companies own more than one type of media property (such as newspaper chains and television stations); (3) conglomerate ownership, in which corporations own media properties but also own other businesses; and (4) vertical integration, in which the corporations that make the media content also control the distribution channels (such as film and television production companies, television networks, and movie theatres).

Why Do Some People Favour Media Convergence Whereas Others Do Not?

Supporters believe that much can be gained from the synergy created by media convergence because it makes it possible to take a media brand and capitalize on it. This process is clearly profitable for investors and media executives; however, media critics believe convergence limits the news and entertainment that the public receives by reducing message pluralism. Other problems include (1) the decline of journalism as a public service profession; (2) constant pressure for all journalistic endeavours to be immediately profitable; (3) a significant decrease in the quantity and quality of international news available to North American audiences; (4) the quashing of public debate about the power of the media industries and how they deal with important social issues; and (5) a dramatic increase in the influence of powerful lobbyists representing the interests of the media giants.

What Potential Problems Are Associated with Global Media Concentration?

A few large media conglomerates are rapidly gaining control over most of the publishing, recording, television, film, and mega–theme park business worldwide. One major problem is the extent to which a few media giants have almost complete control over the world's information. Some people in other nations have been critical of how the media conglomerates depict nations around the globe and the influence, often negative, that they have on the politics and culture of other nations.

What Is Framing, and How Does It Affect Media Coverage?

Framing refers to how news content and its accompanying visual images are linked together to create certain audience perceptions and give specific impressions to viewers and readers. This process of "spinning" information provides audiences with a particular angle, which usually is favourable to the media and the interests they favour while minimizing or eliminating coverage of other issues and concerns.

Why Are Some Media Critics Concerned about Depictions of Violence in the Media?

Although most scholars do not believe that the media *cause* aggressive behaviour in people, a number of media analysts assert that the media's need to capture public interest has contributed to the gratuitous use of violence as a means of selling newspapers, television programming, movie tickets, music, and other media-related commodities.

What Forms of Media Communication Typically Show Violence Against Women?

According to media scholar Jean Kilbourne, advertising, which often uses sexually violent images and themes such as bondage, sadomasochism, and the sexual exploitation of children to sell products, is one of the ways in which the media perpetuate violence against women. The media also contribute to the view of women as sexual objects who do not need to be taken seriously.

How Do Interactionists Explain the Influence of the Media on Individuals?

According to the theory of limited effects, the media have a minimal effect on individuals' attitudes and perceptions. The use and gratification theory suggests that people are active audience participants who make conscious decisions about what they will watch, listen to, read, and surf on the Internet. However, social learning theory is based on the assumption that people are likely to act out the behaviour they see in role models and media sources. The audience relations approach states that people interpret what they hear and see in the media by using their own cultural understandings as a mental filtering device.

How Do Functionalist and Conflict Perspectives on the Media Differ?

According to some functionalist analysts, the media fulfill several important functions in contemporary societies, including providing news and information, facilitating public discourse on social issues and policies, passing on cultural traditions and historical perspectives, and entertaining people. In contrast, conflict theorists assert that members of the capitalist class (either intentionally or unintentionally) use the media to provide information that supports the validity of existing class relations. Hegemony theory states that the media are an instrument of social control that is used by members of the ruling classes to create false consciousness in the working classes.

What Does the Feminist Perspective Say about the Relationship between Textual or Visual Representations of Women's Lives in Media and the Lived Experiences of Women?

Mass media in Canada have consistently represented women and men in traditional gender roles and relationships of power inequity that undermine efforts to challenge and change oppressive values, beliefs, and attitudes. Contemporary feminists are particularly articulate in their criticism of the discords between reality presented in the media and lived reality. These theorists and activists understand how gender, class, racialization, ethnicity, sexual orientation, age, national origin, and physical ability act together to shape the life conditions and life choices of people in media texts and in real life—realities are seldom depicted with accuracy in the mass media.

KEY TERMS

framing,   p. 325
hegemony,   p. 329
hegemony theory,   p. 329

media concentration,   p. 319
media industries,   p. 316
net neutrality,   p. 332

social learning theory,   p. 327
theory of limited effects,   p. 327

QUESTIONS FOR CRITICAL THINKING

1.   Why might media concentration be a potentially greater social problem than concentration in other industries?

2.   Sociologist Graham Knight (1998:108) has said, "In order to be successful, hegemony must incorporate a range of different viewpoints." Explain why this might be so.

3.   Is continued consolidation in the media a serious threat to democracy? Please explain.

4.   Do media "manufacture consent"?

5.   Should we be concerned about the ability of some companies to "buy" political influence? Why or why not?

6.   Net neutrality means that there is no discrimination, on the part of the Internet network provider, regarding website content, services, or applications based on the source, ownership, or destination. What implications, in addition to the ones discussed in the text, do you foresee if all network operators abandon net neutrality?

PEARSON

Explore the topics covered in this chapter at www.mysockit.com using the access provided with this text. Interactive resources for studying include video clips, practice tests, learning objectives, and Internet resources.

POPULATION, URBANIZATION, AND THE ENVIRONMENTAL CRISIS

15

You see, there are only nine cabins in the steamer launch which comes from Dhaka to Patuakhali. In the nine cabins only 18 people can travel. The ticket is expensive, so only the rich people travel in the cabins. The rest of the common passengers travel in the deck. The latrine facility [restroom] is provided only for the cabin passengers. But sometimes the passengers from the deck want to use the latrines. The cabin passengers allow them to use the latrine because they are afraid that if the poor deck passengers get angry then they might go down and make a hole in the launch. Then the launch will sink; they will die no doubt but the rich cabin passengers will not survive either. So, my dear sisters, do not give birth to more children as they cause a problem for the cabin passengers.

*Writer Farida Ahkter recalling the story she heard one family-planning officer tell a group of poor and illiterate women in a remote village in Bangladesh (*The Ecologist *1993:143)*

Given the already established centrality of cities to the current and future prosperity of the country, then all great social policy questions of the day—education, health, poverty, housing and immigration—become urban policy questions.

Meric S. Gertler, Dean, Faculty of Arts and Science, University of Toronto (2001:128)

A vibrant city depends on communities of mixed incomes and uses.

Pam McConnell, Toronto city councillor (statement to author)

Johannesburg [the World Summit on Sustainable Development, August, 2002] aims to put equal emphasis on the twin aspirations of sustainable development . . . to show that we take this challenge seriously and ultimately to exercise greater responsibility, for one another as well as for the earth on which our progress and well-being depend.

UN Secretary General Kofi Annan writing about challenges for the World Summit and humanity (2002)

We are cooperating [with the United States] to encourage the development of clean energy technologies, to advance our respective environmental and energy objectives, and to reduce greenhouse gases.

The Honourable Jim Prentice, Minister of the Environment, June 30, 2009

Global population control and environment policies are the subject of international controversy. Although some people believe that government policies are essential for curbing overpopulation and protecting the environment, others argue that they are a means by which dominant group members decide "*who* will be born, *how* many will be born, and of *what* race, class, sex and 'quality' they will be" (*The Ecologist* 1993:143) or whether resources will go to protecting the environment.

In this chapter, you will learn about the causes of population growth; fertility, mortality, and migration; the impact of population growth and the consequences for world hunger; suggestions for controlling population growth; immigration and its consequences; problems of Canadian cities; environmental problems including air and water pollution, global warming, soil erosion, deforestation, and solid and toxic wastes; and how sociologists study these problems using the functionalist, conflict, interactionist, and feminist perspectives. We will also discuss what the earth's population and the environment will be like in the future, and what you can do about it.

GLOBAL POPULATION PROBLEMS

During the past 55 years, the world's population has more than doubled, growing from 2.5 billion in the 1950s to over 7 billion today. And it is projected to go above 9 billion by mid-century. Even today, more than 1 billion of the world's people do not have enough food and lack basic health care. Will the earth's resources be able to support such a population? This is an urgent question and one for which we need answers.

Population Growth

Growth rates vary among nations: high-income nations (for example, Canada and the United States) have a lower population growth rate than low-income nations, especially those in Africa, Asia, and Latin America. A *population* is all the people living in a specified geographic area. In some nations, the population growth rate is negative; that is, fewer people are added to the population through birth and immigration than are lost through death and emigration. Current estimates suggest that countries such as Italy, Romania, Russia, and Spain will shrink in population over the next

TABLE 15.1   Population Indicators

Indicator	Number (in thousands)	Year
Population of Canada	33 504	2009
Births	344	2006
Deaths	235	2006
Immigrants	254	2006
Emigrants	39	2006

Source: Statistics Canada, 2009, Population—Social Indicators. Retrieved April 2, 2009 (http://www.statcan.gc.ca/pub/11-008-x/2006007/t/ 4169292-eng.htm and http://www.statcan.gc.ca/start-debut-eng.html).

50 years (Sanger 2000). Table 15.1 shows some of Canada's population figures, including the fact that in early 2009 our population was over 33.5 million people.

Demography is the study of the size, composition, and distribution of populations. Global population changes are important because they have a powerful influence on social, economic, and political structures both within societies and between societies. For example, the population growth imbalance between high-income and middle- and low-income nations is a potential source of global conflict, particularly if world hunger and environmental destruction increase. Three primary factors affect the rate of population growth in any nation or area: fertility (births), mortality (deaths), and migration (movement between geographic areas). We'll look at each in turn.

Fertility

Fertility refers to the number of children born to an individual or a population. The most basic measure of fertility is the number of live births per female. Table 10.1 on page 225 in Chapter 10 showed that in 2004, women in Canada gave birth to about 1.53 children. This low number indicates that the Canadian population is not replacing itself. Women would have to have about 2.1 babies for our population to replace itself. Table 15.1 shows that about 344 000 births occur in Canada per year.

The level of fertility in a society is associated with social as well as biological factors. For example, countries that have high rates of infant and child mortality often have high birth rates. By having many children, parents in these nations are more likely to see a few of them survive to adulthood. In nations without social security systems to provide old-age insurance, parents may view children as an "insurance plan" for their old age. In patriarchal societies, having many children—especially sons—is

proof of manliness. Finally, in cultures in which religion dictates that children are God-given and family planning is forbidden because it "interferes with God's will," many more children are usually born. On the other hand, high-income countries have low fertility, partly because of occupational opportunities for women, effective birth control, and the cost of raising children. Although men are obviously important in the reproductive process, the measure of fertility focuses on women, because pregnancy and childbirth are more easily quantified than biological fatherhood. Biological factors that affect fertility include the general health and nutrition level of women of childbearing age. However, on the basis of biological capability alone, most women could produce 20 or more children during their childbearing years. In industrialized nations, therefore, many people limit their biological capabilities by practising abstinence, refraining from sexual intercourse before a certain age, using contraceptives, being sterilized, or having one or more abortions over the course of their reproductive years. Fertility rates also are affected by the number of partners available for sex and/or marriage, the number of women of childbearing age in the workforce, and government policies regarding families. China, for example, has a one-child policy, so abortion or sterilization can be required by the government when there is an unauthorized pregnancy (Mosher 1994).

Mortality

Births are one factor in population growth; another is a decline in **mortality**—the number of deaths that occur in a specific population. Table 15.1 shows that about 235 000 deaths occur in Canada per year. In many high-income nations, mortality has declined dramatically as diseases such as malaria, polio, cholera, tetanus, typhoid, and measles have been virtually eliminated by vaccinations and improved sanitation and personal hygiene (Weeks 2005).

In addition to measuring deaths, demographers often measure the *infant mortality rate*—the number of deaths of infants under 1 year of age per 1000 live births in a given year. In general, infant mortality has declined worldwide over the past two decades because many major childhood and communicable diseases are now under control. Still, infant mortality rates vary widely between nations. In a high-income nation like Canada, the infant mortality rate is low. As shown in Table 10.1, it was 5.3 per 1000 live births in 2004. In low-income countries like those of sub-Saharan

Africa, the infant mortality rate can be over 100 per 1000 live births.

In any nation, the infant mortality rate is an important reflection of a society's level of preventive (prenatal) medical care, maternal nutrition, childbirth procedures, and neonatal care for infants. In Canada, differential levels of access to these services are reflected in the gap between infant mortality rates for Indigenous and non-Indigenous people. As we saw in Chapter 10, mortality for Indigenous infants was 12 deaths per 1000 live births (Frideres 2002:155).

Demographers also study *life expectancy,* the estimated average lifetime of people born in a specific year. Table 10.1 shows that in 2006, the life expectancy of females in Canada was 82.4, and the life expectancy of males was 77.4. While life expectancy in most areas of the world is rising, in some areas it is falling because of conflict or, in the case of Russia, declining strength of a safety net. Life expectancy also varies by racialization and ethnicity within a country. Indigenous people in Canada have a life expectancy that is six years less than non-Indigenous people (Frideres 2002:155).

Migration

Migration is the movement of people from one geographic area to another for the purpose of changing residency. Migration takes two forms: *immigration*—the movement of people *into* a geographic area to take up residency—and *emigration*—the movement of people *out of* a geographic area to take up residency elsewhere. Today, it is estimated that more than 35 million people live outside their countries of origin.

Table 15.1 shows we received abut 250 000 immigrants in 2006. This is still a large number of people for a country the size of Canada. The number is about twice the size of the natural increase (births minus deaths) in the country. However, it should be noted that official immigration statistics do not reflect the actual number of immigrants who arrive in this country. Canadian immigration authorities record only legal immigration based on entry visas and change-of-immigration-status forms. Some people who enter the country as temporary visitors, coming for pleasure or business, as students, or as temporary workers or trainees, do not leave when their stated purpose has been achieved and their permits expire.

Approximately 20 000 refugees are also admitted to Canada annually as permanent residents. According to the 1951 United Nations Convention on Refugees, the term *refugee* applies solely to those who leave their countries because of persecution for reasons of racialization, religion, nationality, membership in a particular social group, or political opinion (Kane 1995). People who leave home to escape famine or to improve their economic position, for example, do not officially qualify as refugees.

Although some immigrants enter illegally, it is impossible to estimate their number or how many are still in Canada, since many come to Canada to gain access into the United States. Occasionally we learn of large numbers of illegal immigrants because of problems with the boats that were transporting them.

To determine the effects of immigration and emigration, demographers compute the *net migration*—the net number of migrants (total immigrants minus total emigrants) in a given year. Table 15.1 demonstrates that net migration in Canada was about 215 000 in 2006.

The Impact of Population Growth

What is the effect of population growth on a society? Population growth affects **population composition**—the biological and social characteristics of a population, including such attributes as age, sex, racialization, marital status, education, occupation, income, and size of household. In Canada, for example, the age distribution of the population is associated with the demand for community resources such as elementary and secondary schools, libraries, health care, recreational facilities, employment opportunities, and age-appropriate housing.

What are the effects of rapid population growth on individuals? The countries that have the highest rates of growth also have the most human suffering. For example, 20 of the 27 countries listed in the "extreme human suffering" category are in Africa, the fastest-growing region in the world (Population Action International 1992). We also know that while many people in poverty-stricken regions die from hunger and malnutrition each year, people in the high-income nations spend billions of dollars annually on diet products and exercise gear because they think they are overfed and overweight.

What are the consequences of global population growth? Not all social analysts agree on the answer to this question. As you will discover in the sections that follow, some analysts warn that the earth is a finite system that cannot support its rapidly growing population. Others believe that capitalism—if freed from government intervention—could develop innovative solutions to such problems as hunger and pollution. Still others argue that capitalism is part of the problem, not part of the solution.

The Malthusian Perspective

Rapid population growth and overpopulation are not new problems. Causes and solutions have been debated for over two centuries. In 1798, for example, Thomas Malthus, an English clergyman and economist, published *An Essay on Population*. Malthus (1798/1965) argued that the global population, if left unchecked, would exceed the available food supply. The population would increase in a geometric (exponential) progression (2, 4, 8, 16, . . .), but the food supply would increase only by an arithmetic progression (1, 2, 3, 4, . . .). Thus, the population would surpass the food supply, ending population growth and perhaps eliminating the world population (Weeks 2005). Disaster, according to Malthus, could be averted only by positive checks (e.g., famine, disease, and war) or preventive checks (e.g., sexual abstinence before marriage and postponement of marriage for as long as possible) to limit people's fertility.

The Neo-Malthusian Perspective

Today, *neo-Malthusians* (or "new Malthusians") speak of the "population explosion" and "population bomb" to emphasize the urgent need to reduce global population growth. Among the best known neo-Malthusians are biologists Paul Ehrlich and Anne H. Ehrlich, who believe that world population growth is following the exponential growth pattern that Malthus described (Ehrlich and Ehrlich 1991:15):

> Exponential growth occurs in populations because children . . . remain in the population and themselves have children. A key feature of exponential growth is that it often seems to start slow and finish fast. A classic example . . . is the pond weed that doubles each day . . . to cover the entire pond in thirty days. The question is, how much of the pond will be covered in twenty-nine days? The answer, of course, is that just half of the pond will be covered in twenty-nine days. The weed will then double once more and cover the entire pond the next day. As this example indicates, exponential growth contains the potential for big surprises.

To neo-Malthusians, the earth is a dying planet with too many people in relation to the available food supply. Overpopulation and rapid population growth exacerbate global environmental problems ranging from global warming and rainforest destruction to famine and epidemics such as HIV/AIDS.

Demographic Transition Theory

According to **demographic transition theory,** societies move from high birth and death rates to relatively low birth and death rates as a result of technological development. The demographic transition takes place in four stages. The *preindustrial stage* is characterized by little population growth: high birth rates are offset by high death rates. This period is followed by the *transitional* or *early industrial stage,* which is characterized by significant population growth as the birth rate remains high but the death rate declines because of new technologies that improve health, sanitation, and nutrition. Today, large parts of Africa, Asia, and Latin America are in this second stage. The third stage is *advanced industrialization and urbanization*: the birth rate declines as people control their fertility with various forms of contraception, and the death rate declines as medicine and other health care technologies control acute and chronic diseases. Finally, in the *postindustrial stage*, the population grows very slowly, if at all. In this stage, a decreasing birth rate is coupled with a stable death rate.

Proponents of demographic transition theory believe that technology can overcome the dire predictions of Malthus and the neo-Malthusians. Critics point out that not all nations go through all the stages or in the manner outlined. They think that demographic transition theory explains development in Western societies but not necessarily in others. As an example they cite China, which was in the process of significantly reducing its birth rate but only because of the government's mandated one-child-per-family policy, not because of technological advances or urbanization (Weeks 2005).

World Hunger

Food shortages, chronic hunger, and malnutrition are the consequences of rapid population growth, particularly in low-income nations. Approximately one-quarter of all the world's children were undernourished in 2006, though this is a decline from 33 percent in 1990 (United Nations 2008:11). Chronic undernourishment contributes to childhood health problems such as anemia (a blood condition that produces weakness and a lack of energy and can result in child mortality or impaired mental functioning), stunting (impaired physical growth or development), and being underweight (United Nations 1995). In pregnant women, malnutrition increases the risk of anemia, infection, birth complications, and lack of breast milk. In contrast, improvements in nutrition significantly reduce health risks and the spread of some communicable illnesses (Hauchler and Kennedy 1994).

What efforts are being made to reduce global food shortages and world hunger? Organizations such as the United Nations, the World Health Organization, and the International Red Cross have programs in place, but the most far-reaching initiatives are known as the green revolution and the biotechnological revolution.

The Green Revolution

The *green revolution* refers to dramatic increases in agricultural production that have been made possible by high-yield "miracle" crops, pesticides, fertilizers, and good farm management. In the 1940s, researchers at the International Maize and Wheat Improvement Center started the green revolution by developing high-yield varieties of wheat, which increased world grain production. The new dwarf-type wheat, which produces more stalks, has dramatically increased the wheat yield in countries such as India and Pakistan since the 1960s. Researchers have also developed a high-yield dwarf rice with twice as many grains per plant, greatly improving the rice output in India, Pakistan, the Philippines, Indonesia, and Vietnam (Weeks 2005).

How successful has the green revolution been in reducing world hunger? During the 1970s, the green revolution helped to increase the global food supply at a somewhat faster pace than the global population grew; but in the 1980s and 1990s, agricultural production slowed considerably. Also, while the new miracle crops have increased food production in Latin America and Asia, they have not really benefitted Africa (Kennedy 1993).

They have not done so for several reasons. For one thing, the fertilizers, pesticides, and irrigation systems needed to produce these new crops are very costly and beyond the budgets of most middle- and low-income nations. Furthermore, the fertilizers and pesticides often constitute health hazards and become a source of surface water and groundwater pollution (Weeks 2005). Moreover, for the green revolution to eliminate hunger and malnutrition, the social organization of life in many middle- and low-income nations would have to change significantly. People would have to adopt the Western methods of farming on which the green revolution was built, and they would have to be willing to produce a single crop in very high volume. But reliance on a single crop can lead to nutritional deficiencies if other varieties of food are not available. Even with these drawbacks, however, the green revolution continues. Researchers recently developed high-yield sorghum, yams, and other crops that can be grown successfully in the nations of Africa where some of the greatest food shortages exist (Weeks 2005).

The Biotechnological Revolution

A second approach to reducing global food shortages, known as the *biotechnological revolution,* encompasses any technique for improving plants or animals or using micro-organisms in innovative ways. Developing pest-resistant crops, thus reducing the need for pesticides, is one technique. Using growth hormone to increase milk output in cows is another technique. Scientists are also exploring ways to genetically alter the reproductive cells of fish, poultry, sheep, and pigs to speed up conventional breeding times (Kennedy 1993). Scientists have already genetically altered micro-organisms in several ways. Soon, for example, it should be possible to spray frost-sensitive plants, such as strawberries, with a strain of bacteria that will protect the plants against up to 80 percent of frost damage.

Some scientists believe that the biotechnological revolution can close the gap between worldwide food production and rapid population growth, but the new technology is not without problems. First, giving growth hormones to animals can make their meat unfit for human consumption. Hogs that get growth hormones are prone to gastric ulcers, arthritis, dermatitis, and other diseases (Kennedy 1993). Second, the cost of biotechnological innovations is beyond the budgets of most middle- and low-income nations. Third, the new biotechnologies are developed for use with conventional (Western) farming methods (Hauchler and Kennedy 1994). Fourth, genetic erosion (by breeding or gene manipulation) may eventually make the people of the world reliant on only a few varieties of plants and animals for their entire food supply and thus vulnerable to famine as the result of a single pest or disease. Finally, environmental accidents, such as the unintentional release of genetically manipulated microorganisms, pose a potential hazard.

Increasing the food supply is one way of coping with a rapidly growing world population, but hardly the only way. Some people believe that we can forestall the problem by controlling fertility.

CONTROLLING FERTILITY

The global population increase in the 20th century has been unprecedented. As Table 15.2 shows, the global population has increased by a factor of four.

Although demographers know that limiting fertility is the best way to slow down population growth, they also know that the issue is fraught with controversy. Consider the three preconditions that demographer Ansley Coale (1973) believes are necessary before there can be a sustained decline in a society's fertility:

1. People must accept calculated choice as a valid element in marital fertility. If people believe a supernatural power controls human reproduction, it is unlikely that they will risk offending that deity by trying to limit fertility. On the other hand, the more worldly wise people are, the more likely they are to believe they have the right to control reproduction.

2. People must see advantages to reduced fertility. People must have some reason to want to limit fertility. In some places, children become workers for the family and support parents in their old age. Without incentives to reduce fertility, natural attraction could lead to unprotected sexual intercourse and perhaps numerous children.

3. People must know about and master effective techniques of birth control. The means for limiting family size must be available, and people must know how to use them successfully.

Although Coale believes that all three preconditions must be met to limit fertility effectively, most

TABLE 15.2   The Measure of the 20th Century

Item	Increase Factor, 1890s to 1990s
World population	4
Urban proportion of world population	3
Total world urban population	13
World economy	14
Industrial output	40
Energy use	16
Coal production	7
Air pollution	~5
Carbon dioxide emissions	17
Sulfur dioxide emissions	13
Lead emissions to the atmosphere	~8
Water use	9
Marine fish catch	35
Cattle population	4
Pig population	9
Horse population	1.1
Blue whale population (Southern Ocean only)	0.0025 (99.75% decrease)
Fin whale population	0.03 (97% decrease)
Bird and mammal species	0.99 (1% decrease)
Irrigated area	5
Forest area	0.8 (20% decrease)
Cropland	2

Note: Some of the numbers are more trustworthy than others. Comments on their reliability appear in the source from which they are drawn.

Source: From Something New Under the Sun *by J.R. McNeill. Copyright © 2000 by J.R. McNeill. Used by permission of W.W. Norton & Company, Inc.*

government policies in the developing world focus only on the third: family planning measures (Weeks 2005).

Family Planning

Family planning programs in the developing world provide birth control information, contraceptive devices, sometimes sterilization and abortion procedures, and health services. The earliest programs were based on the assumption that women have large families because they do not know how to prevent pregnancy or they lack access to birth control devices. Though we know today that women may have large families for many other reasons, most programs are still based on this assumption. Such programs do little, for example, to reduce a couple's desire to have children, and they ignore the reality that, in some middle- and low-income nations, women are not free to make their own decisions about reproduction. There are a large proportion of married women aged 19 to 45 years with unmet needs for family planning, ranging from 25 percent in sub-Saharan Africa to 10 percent in Northern Africa. In all regions this need is greatest among poor women (United Nations 2008:27).

Zero Population Growth

With **zero population growth,** there is a totally stable population, one that neither grows nor decreases from year to year because births, deaths, and migration are in perfect balance (Weeks 1998). For example, the population growth rate would be zero if a nation had no immigration or emigration and the birth rate and the death rate were the same (Ehrlich and Ehrlich 1991).

Canada is nearing zero population growth because of several factors:

1. A high proportion of women and men in the labour force find satisfaction and rewards outside of family life.

2. Birth control is inexpensive and readily available.

3. The trend is toward later marriage (see Chapter 11).

4. The cost of raising a child from birth to adulthood is rising rapidly.

5. Schools and public service campaigns make teenagers more aware of how to control fertility.

Near-zero population growth is one characteristic of the Canadian population; another is a rapidly changing population.

IMMIGRATION AND ITS CONSEQUENCES

High rates of immigration are changing the composition of the Canadian population. Today, according to the 2006 Census, over 5.4 million people—or more than 20 percent of the total Canadian population—have come here from other nations (see Figure 15.1). This is the highest percentage immigrants in the Canadian population since the early part of the 20th century.

FIGURE 15.1   Number and Share of the Foreign-born Population in Canada, 1901 to 2006

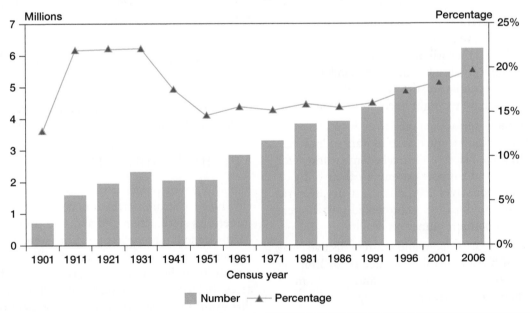

Source: Statistics Canada, 2007, Immigration in Canada: A Portrait of the Foreign-born Population, 2006 Census: Findings. *Catalogue no. 97-557-XWE2006001. Ottawa: Minister of Industry.*

What are the consequences of today's high rate of immigration to Canada as a whole? Not all social analysts agree on the answer to this question. Some believe that immigrants cost taxpayers millions of dollars each year in adjustment and education (e.g., teaching English or French as a second language) costs. But we also know that immigrants contribute as workers and consumers to the economy.

Richard Florida (2002:T8), director of the Martin Prosperity Institute at the University of Toronto, claims the opposite, that Canada's economic future depends on highly educated immigration, which helps to create and nourish a "Creative Class." Some examples of the extraordinary contributions immigrants are making to Canada are found in the Top 25 Canadian Immigrants awards sponsored by *Canadian Immigrant* magazine and the Royal Bank (RBC). They were announced in May 2009 and included people who have helped those abused in their home countries, sisters from Romania who work in neuroscience and cell biology, a founder of an employment service that champions diversity, an internationally acclaimed filmmaker, a president of a radiological diagnostic centre, and many more who made distinguished contributions to Canada (Taylor 2009:GT2). However, although the economic future depends in part on immigrants, recent immigrants do not seem to be sharing in the opportunities as quickly as did their predecessors. Is this due to the immigrants' lack of skills or lack of Canadian work experience, or to discrimination? Statistics Canada (2009c) reported a study to determine some factors (literacy, numeracy, and problem-solving skills) related to this difference. They found first that literacy, numeracy, and problem-solving skills of recent immigrants were less than those of Canadian-born people; that those immigrants who received their education in Canada had higher skills than those who received these skills in the country of origin; and that literacy, numeracy, and problem-solving skills were related to earnings, and once skill levels were controlled, no significant difference was found between earnings of immigrants and Canadian-born people. The authors acknowledge that while lack of skills may be important, lack of Canadian work experience is probably more influential. Those with equal amounts of Canadian work experience tend to have the same earnings (Statistics Canada 2009c). Besides being undesirable, stemming

the flow of immigrants appears to be a virtually impossible task for any one nation. When immigrants come to Canada now they settle in cities, and it is cities and urbanization to which we now turn our attention.

CHANGES IN CANADIAN CITIES

Cities are obviously important to Canada. But over the past couple of decades, the increased services our cities have had to provide—as a result of provincial downloading of hundreds of millions of dollars in new responsibilities with no increase in taxing powers—have put overwhelming strains on their capacity to provide support for Canada's new economy. Can Canadian cities recover from this situation?

Urban problems in Canada are closely associated with the profound socio-economic, political, and spatial changes that have taken place since the Industrial Revolution. Over 100 years ago, many people (about two-thirds of Canadians) lived in rural areas. In the 21st century, about 80 percent of the Canadian population lives in urban areas (see Figure 15.1), and many live in cities that did not exist 200 years ago (Statistics Canada 2002i).

Early Urban Growth and Social Problems

According to sociologists, a *city* is a relatively dense and permanent settlement of people who secure their livelihoods primarily through non-agricultural activities (Weeks 2005). Although cities existed long before the Industrial Revolution, the birth of the factory system brought about rapid *urbanization*, which we defined in Chapter 1 as the process by which an increasing proportion of a population lives in cities rather than in rural areas. Canada industrialized after World War I, and the shift toward urban living is shown in home-ownership rates. About two-thirds of Canadian households own their homes. In 1931, although over three-quarters of rural families owned their own home, less than half of urban families did (Kremarik 2000:18).

Contemporary Urban Growth

The growth of suburbs and outlying areas after World War II forever changed the nature of city life in this country. Suburban areas existed immediately adjacent to many central cities in the 1920s, but after the late 1940s, these communities began to grow in earnest because of the automobile and families wanting homes to raise what is now called the "baby boom" generation. They were referred to as "bedroom communities" because most of the residents were there on nights and weekends but went into the central city for jobs, entertainment, and major shopping. Most suburban dwellers drove to work each day, except where public transit was convenient, establishing a pattern that would result, decades later, in traffic congestion and air pollution, problems that have drastically worsened in the past decade.

To reduce the housing shortage, the federal government subsidized what became a mass exodus from the central city to outlying suburbs. The federal government established the Central (now Canada)

Mortgage and Housing Corporation to grant and insure mortgages. Between 1945 and 1951, the CMHC was responsible for the construction of half a million houses (Kremarik 2000:19). Other factors also contributed to the postwar suburban boom, including the availability of inexpensive land, low-cost mass construction methods for building tract houses, new federally and provincially financed highway systems, inexpensive gasoline, and consumers' pent-up demands, after the Depression and war, for single-family homes on individually owned lots. Although some people lost their homes in the 2008 bursting of the housing bubble, the foreclosures in Canada were not as widespread as in the United States.

Although early suburbanization provided many families with affordable housing, good schools and parks, and other amenities not found in the central city, the shift away from central cities set up an economic division of interests between cities and suburbs that remains in place even today (Flanagan 1995). While many people in the suburbs still rely on the central city for employment,

MAP 15.1   Urban Population as a Percentage of Total National Population

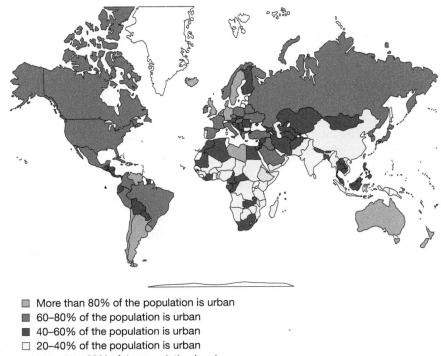

☐ More than 80% of the population is urban
■ 60–80% of the population is urban
■ 40–60% of the population is urban
☐ 20–40% of the population is urban
☐ Less than 20% of the population is urban
☐ Data not available

Source: From Statistical Abstract of the United States, 2001 (118th ed.), U.S. Bureau of the Census, 2001, Washington, DC: U.S. Government Printing Office.

entertainment, or other services, they pay taxes to their local governments and school districts. As a result, suburban police and fire departments, schools, libraries, and recreational facilities are usually well funded and well staffed, with up-to-date equipment. Suburbs also have newer infrastructures (such as roads, sewers, and water treatment plants) and money to maintain them.

Today, edge cities are springing up beyond the central cities and existing suburbs. An **edge city** is a middle- to upper-middle-class area that has complete living, working, shopping, and leisure activities so that it is not dependent on the central city or other suburbs (Garreau 1991). Map 15.2 presents the Canadian population migratory exchanges between the 2001 and 2006 Censuses. It shows the most recent development of edge cities around Toronto, Montreal, and Vancouver, and from Calgary to Edmonton.

Edge cities begin as residential areas; then retail establishments and office parks move into the adjacent area, creating an unincorporated edge city. Automobiles are the primary source of transportation in many edge cities, and pedestrian traffic is discouraged—and even dangerous—because streets are laid out to facilitate high-volume automobile traffic, not walkers or bicyclists. Edge cities may not have a governing body, so they drain taxes from central cities and older suburbs.

MAP 15.2   Migratory Exchanges,¹Canada, 2001 to 2006

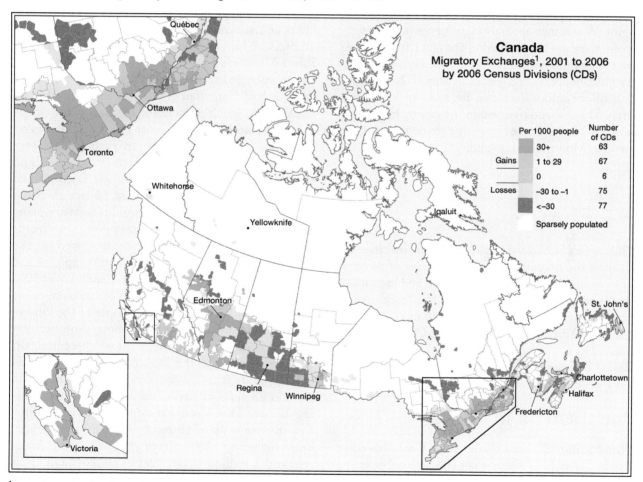

¹Based on net migration rate

Source: Statistics Canada, 2008, Canada Migratory Exchanges 2001–2006. *Retrieved February 16, 2009 (http://geodepot.statcan.ca/Diss2006/Maps/ThematicMaps/National_Maps/NationalMobility_NetMigration_ec.pdf).*

Many businesses and industries move their physical plants—and tax dollars—to these areas because land is cheaper, workers are better educated, and utility rates and property taxes are lower than those in the city. As a result, many jobs move away from poor, visible minority racialized/ethnic workers in central cities, creating structural unemployment.

Over time, large-scale metropolitan growth produces a **megalopolis**—a continuous concentration of two or more cities and their suburbs that have grown until they form an interconnected urban area. The East Coast of the United States, for example, is a megalopolis, with Boston, Providence, Hartford, and their suburbs merging into New York City and its suburbs, which in turn merge southward into Newark, Philadelphia, Baltimore, and Washington, D.C., and their suburbs. It is almost impossible to tell where one metropolitan area ends and another begins. When metropolitan areas merge into a megalopolis, there are big population changes that can bring about or exacerbate social problems and inequalities based on racialization, class, and gender. In Map 15.2, the beginning of megalopolises can be seen in the west, Surrey-Delta-Vancouver; and in the centre, Hamilton-Toronto-Oshawa. In the future, that concentration could extend to Montreal and beyond.

URBAN PROBLEMS IN CANADA

While we traditionally thought that Canadian cities did not have the magnitude of the problems of poverty, crime, racism, homelessness, drug abuse, and inadequate school systems that cities in the United States experience because of years of neglect and deterioration, now "the rebirth of American cities is putting Canada's urban landscapes to shame," according to David Crombie (2001:A15), Toronto's former mayor. Of major concern to mayors of Canadian cities are periodic fiscal crises.

Fiscal Crisis in Cities

It has traditionally been thought that Canadian cities were in better fiscal shape than U.S. cities. No major Canadian city went into financial default like Cleveland in 1978 or to the edge of collapse like New York in 1975. Nor did our cities experience the flight to the suburbs. Major cities have had to deal with major

deindustrialization—the process by which capital is diverted from investment in basic industries (in the form of economic resources, plants, and equipment) to business practices such as mergers and acquisitions and foreign investment—that left so many blighted areas in the centres of U.S. cities. Still, federal and provincial government cutbacks have left Canadian cities, with their limited sources of revenue—primarily property taxes—in desperate financial straits. Out of every $1.00 of taxes collected, $0.07 goes to municipalities, and the federal and provincial governments receive $0.51 and $0.42, respectively (Moloney 2002:A9). Cities have recently received more support, such as revenue from the federal government from a GST rebate and gas taxes. For example, from 2005 to 2008, the Gas Tax Fund contributed $162 million to help in funding public transit, including the purchase of buses and subway cars in Toronto (City of Toronto 2009c:3). Many groups, such as the TD Bank, the Prime Minister's Task Force on Urban Issues, and the Conference Board of Canada, have called for a revitalization of Canadian cities with the help of more stable and ongoing revenue and business partnerships.

One plan to help the cities is to build homes on sites of abandoned factories. In Toronto, Massey-Ferguson, a major maker of farm machinery, and Inglis, a maker of stoves, closed their factories and left land vacant for a decade. Now, houses are being built on the land, and condominium lofts are being built in the 120-year-old Massey-Ferguson headquarters. In 2002, the first residents moved in, and now there are a dozen condominium complexes and hundreds of houses, which will be home to over 5000 people. City planners say that this community, called King West Village, is a good example of the kind of redevelopment they want to promote. Another new large-scale plan is beginning in the south-central part of Toronto, west of the Don River, where factories used to be. It is called the West Don Lands. It will contain 23 acres of parks and public spaces, including 18-acre Don River Park; public transit within a five-minute walk of all residences; 5800 residential units, including 1200 units of affordable rental housing; and 1 million square feet of employment space (for the latest information, go to **http://www.water frontoronto.ca**). With projects like these, planners hope to house up to a million more residents over the next 30 years (Immem 2002:A10).

The Crisis in Urban Health Care

Since about 80 percent of the population lives in cities, most of our social problems are urban problems. This is also true for health care. Although *Maclean's* magazine's (now discontinued) fourth annual ranking of Canadian health centres found that most of the major cities (except Montreal) ranked in the top 10 regions, they were helped by having medical schools in their area (Hawaleshka 2002:24; and see Chapter 10). However, overall scores may mask some problems, particularly with disadvantaged populations. We also know from Chapter 10 that disadvantaged people have greater rates of disease, disability, and death. A study of hospital use in a downtown neighbourhood in Toronto showed that while those from poor neighbourhoods were not discriminated against regarding admission, they had high admission and re-admission rates (Glazier et al. 2000). As a result, the costs of care are about 50 percent greater for poor than for wealthy neighbourhoods. These added costs put greater burdens on hospital emergency, admitting, billing, and discharge departments (Glazier et al. 2000:272). The authors conclude (2000:272) that "Canadian policy makers should take account of the income levels of the neighbourhood when deciding on resource allocation for public health, ambulatory care, community services and hospitals." If hospitals in downtown neighbourhoods do not get additional resources, they will not be able to continue to provide appropriate help to the often disadvantaged people they serve.

Housing Problems

Many regions in Canada lack affordable housing for low-income individuals and families (see Chapter 2). Over the past 15 years, there has been a significant increase in homelessness, especially among families with children. Each year, we are made aware of the plight of homeless people through extensive media coverage during the Christmas holiday season and after winter deaths on the streets. During the rest of the year, many people view the homeless with less compassion.

The Housing Shortage

As mentioned, two-thirds of Canadian households own their homes. And since the rent for a two-bedroom apartment in a major city like Toronto equals the costs of carrying a median-priced townhouse of over $250 000, a good chance exists that the percentage of households that realize their dream of owning their home will increase. But housing is still an income issue, because only 40 percent of people in the lowest income quintile (see Chapter 2) own their homes. In addition, although 86 percent of Canadian households are suitably housed (measured by the homes not needing major repairs and being large enough for their needs), 20 percent of those in the lowest income quintile and 23 percent of female lone parents are not suitably housed (Statistics Canada 2002f).

Although Canadian cities do not have the blighted neighbourhoods and abandoned buildings found in the centre of U.S. cities, they do have pockets of poverty. And for these pockets social housing is needed. According to the Federation of Canadian Municipalities, the completion of social housing units went from a high point of 19 621 in 1992 to 1439 in 1998 (Layton 2000:212). Governments in recent years have again realized the importance or social housing. For example, Toronto plans to compensate for this with its Housing Opportunities Toronto (HOT) project. HOT contains actions to be undertaken by the City of Toronto and the federal and provincial governments, including new investment of $484 million annually for the years 2010 to 2020 to help 257 700 households with high housing costs or inadequate accommodation (City of Toronto 2009b).

Many of the most successful recent initiatives for replacing substandard housing and building lower-cost housing for poor and lower-income families have come from community groups and volunteer organizations. One of the best known of these is Habitat for Humanity, which has received extensive press coverage because of former U.S. president Jimmy Carter's participation. This organization also operates in Canada and, according to its fundraising letter, its volunteers had built, by 2009, 1000 homes across Canada for needy families. Internationally it has built 300 000 homes (Habitat for Humanity Canada 2009).

Perhaps the Pruitt-Igoe project in St. Louis, Missouri, is the all-time worst example of public housing projects. Built as a monolithic high-rise, the building immediately had structural problems, high rates of crime, inadequate maintenance, and poor management. Pruitt-Igoe received media attention and was the subject of sociological research, but finding a solution to the building's many problems was virtually impossible, and it was demolished in the 1970s. Although little high-rise social housing has been built in Canada, St. James Town, in Toronto, is a similar project. It was developed in the 1960s by the private sector and consists of 18 high-rise apartment buildings with 7000 units for 12 000 people. It is one of the most densely populated residential areas in Canada (Hulchanski 1990:16). While it is still standing, this now somewhat shabby development never became the model neighbourhood its proponents claimed it would.

But another large development *has* become a neighbourhood. The St. Lawrence neighbourhood in downtown Toronto is a good example of a large development that is socially mixed. This neighbourhood was conceived in the mid-1970s, with first occupancy in mid-1979. Although it is a large development of 3500 units, it has become a neighbourhood because people who wanted to live there were involved in the planning. St. Lawrence was begun, planned, and implemented by the municipal government (the former City of Toronto) in co-operation with other levels of government, the private sector, and community organizations (such as housing co-operatives and non-profit societies; Hulchanski 1990:4). The neighbourhood is

- socially mixed, including people of different ages, income, and household size (Hulchanski 1990:13);
- tenure mixed, including 39 percent condominium apartments, 30 percent non-profit co-operatives and non-profit rentals, 27 percent municipal non-profit rental, and 4 percent ownership of townhouses (Hulchanski 1990:15); and
- 57 percent non-market, or social, housing (Hulchanski 1990:3). "St. Lawrence demonstrates that public planning of large development projects in an open and democratic fashion can be successful and that desirable high density socially mixed neighbourhoods can be developed by a municipality" (Hulchanski 1990:17).

Toronto's Regent Park, the first subsidized housing project in Canada (built from 1948 to 1957), is now being replaced by a housing complex similar to St. Lawrence with increased housing (and no reduction in subsidized housing), multiple family structures, roads, and commercial development. By August 2009, 85 percent of the first condominium complex was purchased and the first occupants moved in the fall of that year.

Since the 1970s, some middle- and upper-middle-class families and developers have re-entered central city areas and gentrified properties. **Gentrification** is the process by which people renovate or restore properties in central cities. Some people view gentrification as the way to revitalize the central city. Others think that it further depletes the stock of affordable housing for the poor and pushes low-income people out of an area they previously lived in (Flanagan 1995; Palen and London 1984).

Homelessness

The worst outcome of the housing shortage has been a significant increase in the number of homeless people in Canada. Accurate data about the actual number of homeless people are unavailable. It is extremely difficult to count the number of homeless people because most avoid interviews with census-takers and social scientists. The 2001 Census did try to identify one group of homeless people by counting those in shelters for persons lacking a fixed address. On May 14, 2001, 14 145 people were counted in such shelters (Statistics Canada 2002j). This count does not identify all the homeless people, since many others may have been in other accommodations or on the street. A more comprehensive study of the number of homeless people in a major metropolitan area, Toronto, is the survey conducted on the night of April 19, 2006, by more than 1200 people, including 750 volunteers. Key findings include:

- three-quarters of the homeless were male
- average age was 38 years for men and 36 for women; and
- almost three-quarters slept in shelters, 16 percent slept outdoors, 3.4 percent slept in violence-against-women shelters, and 5.4 percent slept in health and treatment facilities.

Of those who slept outdoors:

- one-quarter were Indigenous people;
- they were homeless for longer (six years) than others;
- seventy percent were alone; and
- they were likely to sleep on the sidewalk, grate, doorway or ravine or park (Lewington 2006:A16).

According to social scientists, studies that focus exclusively on personal problems of the homeless, such as mental illness or substance abuse, may result in *specialism*—the

Because of the lack of affordable housing in major Canadian cities, homeless people rely on homeless shelters for food and protection at night, or resort to constructing their own form of shelter in unused city lots or buildings. In 2002, this tent city erected by a number of homeless people in Toronto was ordered destroyed and its residents evicted without notice.

assumption that individual characteristics of poor people cause their homeless condition and that, therefore, the only way to alleviate homelessness is to cure individuals' personal problems (Wagner 1993). This approach downplays the significance of structural factors such as the unavailability of low-income housing and mental-health care, which are the most important determinants of homelessness.

Spatial Separation of the Poor and Visible Minorities

Although it is generally acknowledged that Canada does not have the permanent segregation of poor—especially racialized poor—and non-poor found in the United States, the increasing immigration of racialized/ethnic minorities to our cities leaves open the possibility that the U.S. segregation problems could occur here. Residential segregation in the United States, according to sociologists Douglas S. Massey and Nancy Denton (1992), is associated with many other problems.

Pockets of poverty, measured by the low-income cut-off, do exist in cities. For example, pockets are found in the city of Toronto. While some are in the south-central part, most are in the periphery of the city.

Since the vast majority of recent immigrants have been from East and South Asia, and since they migrate to cities, a big increase in the percentage of visible

minorities has occurred in Canadian cities. Although it is not possible to show the percentage of visible minorities in all the major Canadian cities in these pages, this information is available in a very large table at the 2006 Census website (**http://www12.statcan.gc.ca/ english/census06/data/trends/table_2.cfm?T=CMA& LINE_ID=901&TOPIC_ID=900**). For example, the visible minority population in 2006 in Toronto was 42.9 percent and in Vancouver, 41.7 percent. The table also shows that the percentage of the visible minority population has grown since 1996 in Toronto from 31.6 percent and in Vancouver from 31.1 percent. However, the proportion of visible minorities in a census metropolitan area (CMA) does not indicate the extent of segregation in that area. The 2001 Census release does provide maps of the major CMAs showing the concentration of visible minorities by individual census tracts. It is not possible to include maps for every major city in Canada in this book, but you can see the concentration of visible minorities in the CMAs by going to the Statistics Canada Census Geography website (**http://geodepot.statcan.ca/Diss/Maps/ThematicMaps/ Ethnocultural_e.cfm**). According to these maps, the concentration of visible minorities seems greater in Montreal than in Toronto or Vancouver, where they are more evenly distributed. This segregation may help account for the findings of a report that shows that in Montreal, Blacks had a higher unemployment rate than in the rest of Canada (26.5 versus 19.3 percent) and a much higher rate than non-Blacks (26.5 versus 9.9 percent; Solyom 2001:A14).

To determine the extent of spatial separation of visible minorities in Canada, Hou and Picot (2004) studied the extent to which minority group members are exposed only to one another (isolation index) in their neighbourhoods (census tracts in Toronto, Montreal, and Vancouver) from the 1981 to 2001 Censuses. In tracing the composition of the population over the 20 years, they discovered that the mass immigration of visible minorities has created more visible minority neighbourhoods. The number of visible minority neighbourhoods increased in these cities from 6 in 1981 to 254 in 2001. The majority of these neighbourhoods were Chinese (60 percent), followed by South Asian (about 33 percent; Hou and Picot 2004:11). Few (13) Black neighbourhoods exist, perhaps because Blacks have been in Canada for many generations and come from several places. Toronto and

Vancouver have many more visible minority neighbourhoods (135 and 111, respectively) than Montreal (8) (Hou and Picot 2004:11; see Box 15.1). Far fewer visible minority immigrants go to Montreal than the other two cities. Whether the increase in visible minority neighbourhoods is a good or bad thing is debatable. On the plus side, these neighbourhoods can provide a wide variety of support and services for immigrants and help promote ethnic identity. On the negative side, immigrants may become socially isolated and be slow to learn the host area language and take advantage of available educational and occupational opportunities. These neighbourhoods also have the tendency to have high unemployment and low income rates. This is probably because a third of the population are recent immigrants, and recent immigrants are doing less well than earlier immigrants upon arrival (see Kazemipur and Halli 2001).

SOCIAL PROBLEMS IN GLOBAL PERSPECTIVE

BOX 15.1 Global Cities

Although people have lived in cities for thousands of years, the time is rapidly approaching when more people worldwide will live in or near a city than in rural areas. In 1900, only one person out of 10 lived in a city; now, one person out of two lives in a city. Map 15.1 shows the extent to which certain countries, and not just high-income countries, have become highly urbanized.

Global cities can be classified in several ways. The first and most simplistic is by population. In 1950, New York was the only mega-city with 10 million or more inhabitants. Today, Tokyo is the world's largest city, and by 2015, it will remain among the most populous in the world (see Table 15.3).

Rapid global urbanization is producing a wide variety of problems, including overcrowding, environmental pollution, and the disappearance of farmland. In fact, many cities in middle- and low-income nations are quickly reaching the point at which food, housing, and basic public services are available to only a limited segment of the population. Cities such as Cairo, Beijing, and São Paulo are likely to soon have acute water shortages; Mexico City is already experiencing a chronic water shortage. Natural increases in population (higher birth rates than death rates) account for two-thirds of new urban growth, and rural-to-urban migration accounts for the rest. While many problems of slum development, such as malnutrition and the spreading of disease, occur, industrializing cities grow so big and so fast precisely because they generate vast economic advantages that do not exist in the countryside.

Another way of ranking cities is in terms of the position of their nation in the world economic system. Immanuel Wallerstein (1984) tried to do this by first identifying three kinds of nations:

■ **Core nations** are dominant capitalist centres characterized by high levels of industrialization (e.g., New York, Tokyo, and London).

■ **Peripheral nations** are dependent on core nations and characterized by having exploited resources (e.g., Lagos and Cairo).

■ **Semi-peripheral nations** fit between core and peripheral nations (e.g., São Paulo and Singapore).

But this classification subordinates the city to its nation and cannot account for cities that are major hubs but are not in core nations, such as Beijing, Bangkok, and Mexico City. *Foreign Policy*, an international affairs periodical, has developed an index of global cities based on five criteria: business activity, human capital, information exchange, cultural experience, and political engagement. Their top 10 global cities are New York, London, Paris, Tokyo, Hong Kong, Los Angeles, Singapore, Chicago, Seoul, and Toronto. (Only one Canadian city makes the top 60 list.)

Finally, a less economic, political, and culturally central way of identifying a city as global is the percentage of the population

TABLE 15.3 Population of the World's Largest Cities, 2000 and 2015 (Estimated)

City, Country	Pop. (millions) 2000	Pop. (millions) 2015
Tokyo, Japan	34.5	36.4
Mexico City, Mexico	18.1	21.6
New York, United States	17.8	19.9
São Paulo, Brazil	17.1	20.5
Mumbai, India	16.1	21.9
Shanghai, China	13.2	17.6
Kolkata, India	13.1	17.0
Delhi, India	12.4	18.6

*Source: United Nations, 2009, **World Urbanization Prospects.** Retrieved July 15, 2005 (http://esa.un.org/unup/index.asp?panel=2).*

FIGURE 15.2   Percentage of Foreign Born in the Total Metropolitan Population, 2006

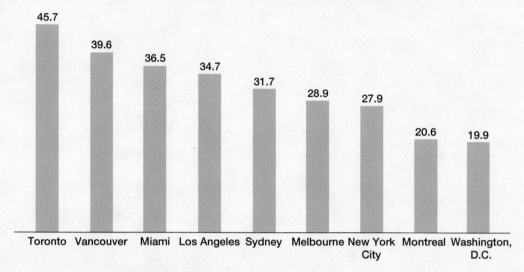

Note: United States data are for 2005.

Source: Statistics Canada, 2008, Census Snapshot—Immigration in Canada: A Portrait of the Foreign-born Population, 2006 Census. *Retrieved November 8, 2008 (http://www.statcan.ca/english/freepub/11-008-XIE/2008001/charts/10556/chart1-en.htm).*

that is foreign born. Figure 15.2 shows that by this measure, Toronto is the most global city (at least of Western cities), with 45.7 percent of its population being foreign born according to the 2006 Census, followed by Vancouver and Miami. Of all the largest cities, only Los Angeles and New York have a high percentage of its citizens who are foreign born.

With increased migration, both internal and international, of people, it is projected that the major cities in Table 15.3 will increase in population in 2015 and that cities like Toronto and Vancouver will have a higher percentage of their population being foreign born. Do you think that Toronto will in the future be rated as a global city by *Foreign Policy*? What problems do you foresee as cities become larger and a higher percentage of the population becomes foreign born? How would you try to prevent these problems?

PERSPECTIVES ON URBAN PROBLEMS

Throughout the 20th century, sociologists analyzed urban problems to determine the causes and consequences of rapid industrialization and urbanization for people's daily lives and the structure of society. The conclusions they reach about the underlying problems and possible solutions depend on the framework they apply.

The Functionalist Perspective

In examining urban problems, most functionalists focus on three processes that have contributed to social disorganization and the disruption of social institutions. First, mass migration from rural areas to urban areas during the industrializing of Canada contributed to social disorganization by weakening personal ties in family, religion, education, and other institutions. Second, large-scale immigration in the late 19th and early 20th centuries was more than most cities could absorb, and many individuals were never fully assimilated into the cultural mainstream. With larger numbers of strangers living close together in central cities, symptoms of social disorganization, such as high rates of crime, mental illness, and suicide, grew more pronounced. So far the high levels of immigration in the late 20th and early 21st century have not caused severe problems, but according to Durkheim (1893/1933), urban life changes people's relationships. Rural areas are characterized by **mechanical solidarity**—social bonds based on shared religious beliefs and a simple division of labour—but

Overcrowded living conditions are a way of life for people residing in this area of Mumbai. How will rapid population growth in the future affect urban areas in global cities?

these bonds are changed with urbanization. Urban areas are characterized by **organic solidarity**—social bonds based on interdependence and an elaborate division of labour (specialization). Although Durkheim was optimistic that urbanization could be positive, he also thought that some things were lost in the process. Third, mass suburbanization created additional social disorganization, and many central cities in the United States, though less so in Canada, have been unable to reach an equilibrium since the mass exodus to the suburbs following World War II. According to urban ecologist Amos Hawley (1950; 1981), new technologies, such as commuter railways and automobiles, have led to the decentralization of city life and the movement of industry from the central city to the suburbs, with disastrous results for some people. Although urbanization, mass immigration, and suburbanization have had functional consequences—including citizenship, job opportunities, and home ownership—for many people, they have also created problems,

particularly for people who are left behind in declining parts of central cities and people who experience discrimination.

Besides emphasizing processes, functionalists also emphasize systems. Sociologist Talcott Parsons (1966:28) identified four systems that interact with one another in urban areas: the cultural system, social system, personality system, and behavioural organism. William Michelson (1976:24) has drawn attention to a fifth system, the environmental system, in particular the human-made physical, or built, environment, most fully illustrated by the urban environment. He suggested that the effects of the phenomena in the built environment on the other systems, and vice versa, should be studied. Michelson also developed the concept of *congruence* to indicate that some states of variables in one system may coexist with some states of variables in another system better than with others. Mismatches of states of variables constitute incongruence. An example of incongruence is the building of economically efficient high-rise subsidized housing for families with small children, like the Pruitt-Igoe project in St. Louis; mothers living in such projects are not able to follow their children to other floors and ground level to supervise or protect them (Michelson 1976:26). High-rise public housing has also had problems with property damage and bullying because of lack of supervision.

The Conflict Perspective

Conflict analysts do not believe that cities grow or decline by chance. Members of the capitalist class and political elites make far-reaching decisions about land use and urban development that benefit some people at the expense of others (Castells 1977; Feagin and Parker 1990). According to conflict theorists, the upper classes have successfully maintained class-based and sometimes racialized segregation (in the United States) through political control and legal strategies such as municipal incorporation, defensive annexation, restrictive covenants, and zoning regulations (Feagin and Parker 1990; Higley 1995). But where do these practices leave everyone else? Marx suggested that cities are the arenas in which the intertwined processes of class conflict and capital accumulation take place; class consciousness and worker revolt are more likely to develop when workers are concentrated in urban areas (Flanagan 1995).

Contemporary conflict theorists Joe R. Feagin and Robert Parker (1990) speak of a *political economy model*, believing that both economic and political factors affect patterns of urban growth and decline. Urban growth, they say, is influenced by capital investment decisions, power and resource inequality, class and class conflict, and government subsidy programs. Members of the capitalist class choose corporate locations, decide on sites for shopping centres and factories, and spread the population that can afford to purchase homes into sprawling suburbs located exactly where the capitalists think they should be located (Feagin and Parker 1990). In this view, a few hundred financial institutions and developers finance and construct most major and many smaller urban development projects, including skyscrapers, shopping malls, and suburban housing projects. These decision makers can make housing more affordable or totally unaffordable for many people. Ultimately, their motivation rests not in benefitting the community, but rather in

making a profit, and the cities they produce reflect this mindset (Feagin and Parker 1990).

The concept of *uneven development*—the tendency of some neighbourhoods, cities, or regions to grow and prosper while others stagnate and decline—is a by-product of the political economy model of urban development (Perry and Watkins 1977). Conflict theorists argue that uneven development reflects inequalities of wealth and power in society. Uneven development not only affects areas in decline but also produces external costs that are paid by the entire community. Among these costs are increased pollution, traffic congestion, and rising rates of crime and violence. According to sociologist Mark Gottdiener (1985:214), these costs are "intrinsic to the very core of capitalism, and those who profit the most from development are not called upon to remedy its side effects." One advantage of the political economy framework is that it can be used to study cities in middle- and low-income nations as well as high-income nations (see Jaffee 1990; Knox and Taylor 1995; Wilson 1997).

Uneven development does not occur in the same way in Canadian cities as it does in U.S. cities. Canadian city governments are more actively involved in land-use management and are committed more strongly than U.S. city governments to public services, including transit, parks, and libraries. Canadian cities are also characterized by more equal distribution of public services than the more politically fragmented U.S. cities (Ley and Bourne 1993). Thus, the land and property values in the Canadian central city remain highly competitive despite a substantial rate of suburban development.

This difference in uneven development does not mean that corporate capitalism does not have an effect on major cities in Canada. For example, Gertler (2001:123) notes that Toronto's share of the top 500 Canadian firms declined from 40 percent to 35 percent from 1989 to 1999 (pre- and post–North American Free Trade Agreement) due primarily to a decline in foreign-based Canadian subsidiaries, from 105 to 85. He suggests that a worldwide concentration of corporate control is likely occurring. However, since then, Toronto's share of headquarters of Canadian firms has increased slightly, from 89 to 91. Other centres, including Calgary, Vancouver, and Ottawa, have seen substantial growth in headquarters placement from both Canadian and foreign firms (Gertler 2001:123).

This movement could have harmful effects for workers and their families and merchants in the older downtowns of Toronto and Montreal unless other projects, such as in-fill housing (for example, King West Village and the West Don Lands mentioned earlier), are developed to fill the void of the former headquarters.

The Interactionist Perspective

Interactionists examine urban problems from the standpoint of people's *experience* of urban life and how they subjectively define the reality of city living. How does city life affect the people who live in a city? According to early German sociologist Georg Simmel (1950), urban life is so highly stimulating that people have no choice but to become somewhat insensitive to events and individuals around them. Urban residents generally avoid emotional involvement with one another and try to ignore the events—including, possibly, violence and crime—that take place nearby. They are wary of other people, looking at others as strangers; some people act reserved to cloak deeper feelings of distrust or dislike toward others. At the same time, Simmel thought that urban living could be liberating because it gives people opportunities for individualism and autonomy (Flanagan 1995).

On the basis of Simmel's observations of social relations in the city, early University of Chicago sociologist Louis Wirth (1938) suggested that urbanism is a "way of life" that increases the incidence of both social and personality disorders in individuals. *Urbanism* refers to the distinctive social and psychological patterns of life that are typically found in the city. According to Wirth, the size, density, and heterogeneity of urban populations result in an elaborate division of labour and in spatial segregation of people by racialization/ethnicity, social class, religion, and/or lifestyle. The division of labour and spatial segregation produce feelings of alienation, powerlessness, and loneliness.

In contrast to Wirth's gloomy analysis of urban life, sociologist Herbert Gans (1962/1982) believed that not everyone experiences the city in the same way. On the basis of research in the West End of Boston in the late 1950s, Gans concluded that many residents develop strong loyalties and a sense of community in central city areas that outsiders often view negatively. According to Gans, in large urban areas, personal behaviour is shaped by the type of neighbourhood a person lives in. For example, *cosmopolites*—students, artists, writers, musicians, entertainers, and professionals—view the city as a place where they can be close to cultural facilities and people with whom they share common interests. *Unmarried people* and *childless couples* live in the city because they want to be close to work and entertainment. *Ethnic villagers* live in ethnically segregated neighbourhoods because they feel most comfortable within their own group. The *deprived* and the *trapped* live in the city because they believe they have no other alternatives. Gans concluded that the city is a pleasure and a challenge for some urban dwellers and an urban nightmare for others.

According to interactionists, the deprived and the trapped contribute to a social construction of reality that stereotypes some city dwellers as poor, down-and-out, and sometimes dangerous, whereas almost all city dwellers are not this way. Because of the U.S. movies and television shows seen by Canadians, and, particularly, because of extensive media coverage of crime or racialized unrest in the largest metropolitan areas of the United States, which presents a very negative image of cities, an anti-urban bias remains strong among many non-urban dwellers. Even urban dwellers can have negative stereotypes of parts of cities. The note about Regent Park shows that social housing for poor people can change over several decades to become an object of media vilification, but when new plans are developed to improve the area, strong sentiments about the area can change, as shown by people's willingness to move into the new buildings.

On the other hand, Richard Florida, like Gans, believes that cities can be pleasurable and tolerant, and thus attract the kind of creative people (what he calls the Creative Class) who will hold the key to Canada's economic future. With Canadian collaborator Meric Gertler, he compiled a Bohemian Index, a measure of talent that looks at Canadian cities' per capita population of artists, poets, novelists, and various entertainers using the 1996 Census. Florida and Gertler concluded that Vancouver had 12.85 bohemians per 1000 population, and, slightly behind it, Toronto had 12 bohemians per 1000 (or about 50 000 people). In comparison with U.S. cities, the two Canadian cities rank below but close to San Francisco, New York, Los Angeles, Seattle, and Washington, D.C. (Florida 2002:T8). Another way of measuring opportunities in a city is with the Composite Learning Index (CLI), mentioned in Chapter 12 (page 287).

The CLI was developed to measure overall learning in Canada and provides scores for our cities. As noted in Chapter 12, the cities with the highest scores for 2009 are Calgary, Victoria, and Guelph. Vancouver and Toronto are close behind on this list. Interactionists believe that the city can be experienced in many ways and the "smarter" cities can help individuals and the country to flourish.

Finally, cities are also known for problems of loneliness and alienation. Some interactionists propose that people who live in large metropolitan areas develop subcultural ties to help them feel a sense of community and identity. A **subculture** is a group of people who share a distinctive set of cultural beliefs and behaviours that set them apart from the larger society. Joining an interest group—from bowling with friends from the office to volunteering in a literacy program—is one way of feeling connected. Ethnic neighbourhoods are an example of subcultures; some are tightly knit, whereas others have little influence on residents' daily lives. Interactionists note that members of subcultures, especially those based on racialization, ethnicity, or religion, sometimes come into conflict with one another. These conflicts can result in verbal exchanges, hate crimes, or other physical violence, or they can cause the individuals to withdraw almost entirely from the larger community and become more intensely involved with the subculture.

Feminist Perspectives

In the same way that great social policy issues are urban policy issues, feminist analyses are germane to virtually every aspect of city life. Many of these analyses have been dealt with in other chapters; here are just a couple of examples of feminism's application to urban problems. Some feminist theorists emphasize the occupational opportunities, freedom, convenience, and stimulation for women present in cities but not available in smaller centres or suburbs—Betty Freidan (1963) and, more recently, Margrit Eichler (1995) have been very critical of the lack of stimulation and the oppressiveness of women's lives in low-density suburbs. In cities, women have the chance to participate in a variety of occupations, and they are very well represented in the (usually low-paid) jobs that constitute the Bohemian Index (e.g., artists and entertainers). Moreover, in cities, women do not have to worry about what the neighbours will think

of their behaviour. They can choose to interact with their neighbours or not. Lastly, women who live in a city instead of a suburb and have the dual roles of worker and mother will usually have a shorter commute to their jobs and more locally available services. Thus, they may feel less stress in fulfilling their responsibilities and have more time for themselves. On the other hand, some feminists have been so concerned about the threats to women at night in cities that they have organized "Take Back the Night" marches in most major centres.

URBAN PROBLEMS IN THE FUTURE

In a best-case scenario, Canada would convert to regional governments to provide water, wastewater (sewage), transportation, schools, parks, hospitals, and other public services. In this scenario, revenues would be shared among central cities, affluent suburbs, and edge cities, since everyone would benefit from the improved quality of life. Cities would get a permanent source of taxation, besides property taxes, and they would create a tolerant and creative climate. Meanwhile, as we wait and hope for solutions to the problems of urbanization at the macrolevel, we can—as citizens, neighbours, tenants, property owners, workers, employers, and users of public and private services throughout the city—exercise some degree of control over the quality of life in our own communities. There is increasing impetus to take control because one thing is certain: as the world population continues to grow in this century, urban problems will intensify, and this will affect us all.

ENVIRONMENTAL PROBLEMS

The environment provides us with the means to survive and thrive.

Although it is popularly believed that most environmental problems arise from rapid growth in middle- and low-income nations, this is not entirely the case. Many scientists believe that high-income nations present a much greater threat to the earth's ecosystems (Ehrlich and Ehrlich 1991). An *ecosystem* is "all the populations of plants and animal species that live and interact in a given area at a particular time, as well as the chemical and physical factors that make up the nonliving environment" (Cable and Cable 1995:124). Thus, an ocean is an ecosystem; a tropical rainforest is an ecosystem; and, on a much smaller scale, a house on a lot is an ecosystem. When all of the earth's ecosystems are put together, they make up the *biosphere.*

Ecosystems do not have an infinite ability to support either population growth or environmental depletion or destruction. In fact, some scientists believe that many of the world's ecosystems have already exceeded their *carrying capacity*—the maximum population that an ecosystem can support without eventually being degraded or destroyed (Cable and Cable 1995). According to Ehrlich and Ehrlich (1991), a baby born in a country like the United States, and to a lesser extent Canada, will have two times the destructive impact on the earth's ecosystems and services as a baby born in Sweden; 140 times the impact of a baby born in Bangladesh or Kenya; and over 280 times the impact of a baby born in Chad, Rwanda, Haiti, or Nepal. Thus the size of the population, its level of affluence, and the harmful technology available in the society are major contributing factors to **environmental degradation**— disruptions to the environment that have negative consequences for ecosystems (Cable and Cable 1995). Environmental degradation involves both removing natural resources from the environment and adding to environmental problems through pollution.

In Canada, environmental degradation increases as people try to maintain the high levels of wealth and material comfort to which they have become accustomed. They consume the earth's resources and pollute its environment with automobiles, airplanes, speedboats, computers, television sets and VCRs, year-round air conditioning and heating, and other amenities that are far beyond the grasp of most of the world's people. Although these products are made possible by high levels of industrial production and economic growth, economic growth often depletes and destroys the environment.

Economic Growth and Environmental Degradation

During most of the 20th century, economic growth in Canada and the world was based on increased output in the manufacturing sector (see Table 15.2 for the increase in industrial output in the 20th century). The environment is affected at all phases of the manufacturing process, from mining and transportation to manufacturing and waste disposal. Industrial production involves extracting raw materials—natural resources—from the environment, usually through mining. Mining depletes mineral resources and fossil fuel reserves—coal, oil, and natural gas. Mining also disturbs ecosystems; this is particularly true of surface mining, which strips bare the land, destroying natural vegetation and wildlife habitats. Other problems typically follow, including erosion of the land by wind and water and runoff of acids, silt, and toxic substances into nearby surface water and groundwater; this leads to the pollution of rivers and streams with toxic compounds that kill fish and other aquatic life (Cable and Cable, 1995).

Table 15.2 provides some indication of the enormous effects humanity's activity has had on our planet during the past 100 years. This chart ignores huge expansions that took place after 1900, like automobiles—in Canada, from zero to 14 million by the end of the century—and huge declines of natural resources of special interest to Canadians, such as the 99 percent decrease in the cod fishery, which has not returned and may never return to 1980s levels despite a continuing moratorium on fishing.

The environmental impact of mining doesn't stop when the raw materials have been mined. Now the raw materials must be transported to a plant or factory, where workers will transform them into manufactured products. Transporting requires the use of energy— particularly the burning of fossil fuels—which contributes to air pollution because motor vehicles produce carbon monoxide, nitrogen oxides, and photochemical pollutants. Each of these pollutants is associated with various illnesses, including heart and respiratory disease and cancer. The manufacturing process further depletes the supply of fossil fuels and contributes to air pollution. (See Table 15.2 for the amount of various kinds of pollution produced in the 20th century.) People who work in or live near facilities that pollute the environment are often harmed by the solid or toxic wastes resulting from the manufacturing process.

Many analysts believe that we cannot continue this pattern of environmental degradation. They believe future economic development—in Canada and globally—will require drastic changes in the structure of industry, especially in the energy, transportation, chemical, and agricultural sectors of the economy. If we don't make changes, environmental degradation—of our air, water, soil, and forests—constitutes a major threat to the well-being of all human beings and ecosystems on the earth. On the other hand, not all types of industries are harmful. Green industries, like wind turbines, solar power, and industrial water purification projects, could provide future sources of economic development and jobs.

Air Pollution and Smog

Nature performs many *ecosystem services*—valuable, practical functions that help to preserve ecosystems. For example, if the atmosphere is not overburdened, it can maintain a proper balance between carbon dioxide and oxygen, as well as provide ozone for protection against ultraviolet radiation. However, air pollution interferes with many ecosystem services. The carbon dioxide that pollutes the air we breathe keeps the sun's heat from radiating back into space, thereby causing the earth to heat up (the greenhouse effect, discussed in the next section).

The drastic increase in air pollution during the 20th century has placed an undue burden on the atmosphere's ecosystem services (Stevens 1997). Beginning with the Industrial Revolution in the late 19th and early 20th centuries, more and more pollutants have been emitted into the atmosphere by households, industries, and automobile traffic. Though these three sources have become more fuel-efficient, constantly increasing amounts of carbon dioxide, carbon monoxide, nitrogen oxide, and sulphur oxide, as well as such heavy metals as lead, zinc, and copper, still pollute our air (Hauchler and Kennedy 1994).

Air pollution affects all life and ecosystems on the planet. Air pollution in the form of acid rain destroys forests, streams and lakes, and other ecosystems. **Acid rain** is rainfall containing large concentrations of sulphuric and nitric acids (primarily from the burning of fuel and car and truck exhausts). Canadian efforts to reduce acid rain from the United States have been blocked by the automobile industry; companies that mine, haul, and sell high-sulphur coal; and coal miners. Fortunately, new industries are less dependent on burning coal than are older factories in the industrial northeast and midwest states (Petersen 1994).

The word *smog* is a combination of the words "smoke" and "fog." Smog is the most visible form of air pollution. According to the North American Commission for Environmental Cooperation (CEC 2009), gases and particulate matter have declined from the mid-1990s to 2005. In Canada, the releasing of particulate matter was stable from 2001 to 2005, but at least 30 percent of Canadians live in communities with particulate matter above the Canada-wide standard. The communities affected were in southern Ontario, Quebec, and British Columbia (CEC 2009:17).

To monitor air pollution in Ontario, the Air Quality Index (AQI) was devised to measure ground-level ozone, nitrogen dioxide, carbon monoxide, sulphur dioxide, sulphur compounds, and fine suspended particles. An AQI of 50+ may cause eye irritation, breathing difficulties, and even lung damage to those physically active. Since the inception of the AQI in 1993, the number of smog alerts has been growing, though few smog alerts occurred in 2009 because of cool and wet weather. To discover the pollution level by contaminant in Ontario cities for today go to **http://www.airqualityontario.com/history/ summary.cfm**.

Showing relationships between long-term exposure to air pollution and mortality has been difficult because of a wide variety of confounding variables and the problems of measuring air pollution consistently. A Toronto Public Health publication by research consultant Ronald Macfarlane and his colleagues (2000:5) states that air pollution in Toronto is linked to about 1000 early deaths, and 5500 hospital visits are linked to heart and lung diseases every year, based on 1995 data. But this is only one centre. A study that followed 1.2 million adults in more than 150 cities in the United States since 1982 confirmed the health hazards of air pollutants. The results of this study, by economist C. Arden Pope III and colleagues (2002), among whom were Canadian colleagues, showed fine particulate and sulphur oxide were associated with all-cause lung cancer and cardiopulmonary mortality. Furthermore, they showed that elevations in the amount of pollutants were associated with definite percentage increases in mortality. The Toronto Public Health Department conducted a retrospective study for the period 1954–2000 to determine the relative influence of hot and cold weather and air pollution on mortality. The analysis showed an annual excess of 822 deaths due to air pollution for that period. If current global warming trends continue, it is projected that the annual mortality will rise to 1070 per year in 2080 (McKeown 2005:iii).

In the past, air pollution in middle- and low-income nations was attributed primarily to the fight for survival and economic development, whereas most air pollution in high-income nations was attributed to relatively luxurious lifestyles. However, distinctions between air pollution in high-income and middle- and low-income nations are growing weaker; in 2009 China surpassed the United States in carbon dioxide emissions. Still, Western industrial nations account for about

68 percent of the carbon monoxide in the atmosphere (World Resources Institute 1992). Automobile ownership, once considered a luxury, is rising rapidly in urban centres in middle-income nations such as Mexico, Brazil, Taiwan, Indonesia, and China (Bradsher 1997). Cities such as Mumbai, Shanghai, and Jakarta have also seen a significant increase in the number of automobiles, bringing a corresponding rise in air pollution and traffic problems (Bradsher 1997). In the summer of 2002, southern and lower eastern Asia was suffering from a "brown cloud," a three-kilometre-thick haze, from combustion of wood and fossil fuels.

But there are some hopeful signs that we are curbing fossil fuel pollution. In Canada, antipollution laws have brought about changes in how automobiles are made and the fuels they consume. Cars are now equipped with catalytic converters and other antipollution devices, and leaded gasoline (a major offender) has been phased out. However, while some middle-income nations are requiring antipollution devices on new vehicles, many leaded-gas-burning cars—often used cars from Canada and the United States—are still a significant source of air pollution. In October 2006, the federal government introduced its *Clean Air Act* to fight air pollution. Given that its mandatory standards come in the future, it is difficult to know how much of an impact the act will have.

The Greenhouse Effect

Emissions from traffic and industry not only add to general air pollution but also contribute to the enhanced **greenhouse effect**—an environmental condition caused by excessive quantities of carbon dioxide, methane, and nitrous oxide in the atmosphere. When carbon dioxide CO_2) molecules build up in the earth's atmosphere, they act like the glass roof of a greenhouse, allowing sunlight to reach the earth's surface but preventing the escape of infrared radiation back into space. The radiation that cannot escape is reradiated as heat, causing the earth's surface temperature to rise (Weiner 1990). Over the past century, average temperatures in the northern hemisphere have been trending up .5 degrees Celsius, as shown on the National Climate Data Center website (**http://www.ncdc.noaa.gov/oa/ncdc.html**). Scientists believe that the earth will have a temperature increase of from 1.5 to as much as 5 degrees over the next hundred years. In fact, if current rates of emission

Air pollution is a pressing problem in many nations, but nowhere more so than in Mexico City, where daylight hours often look like they do in this photo. How is air pollution related to people's health and life expectancy?

into the atmosphere remain unchanged, temperature increases might eventually bring about catastrophic consequences.

One consequence could be significant changes in weather patterns and climate. Changes in weather patterns could bring increased evaporation, creating new deserts and decreasing regional water reserves. Changes in air circulation and climatic conditions could also result in more frequent and intense storms, hurricanes, flooding, and droughts. Vegetation zones could shift, and forests in the northern hemisphere might be infested with new insects or die off (see Map 15.3 for the possible consequences of climate change in different parts of Canada). On the other hand, Greenland is now benefiting from warming by growing vegetables and exploring for minerals in areas once covered by ice.

Not all scientists believe that the greenhouse effect exists or that its effects will be this disastrous. However, studies show a marked retreat of glaciers and the beginning of a shift in vegetation, and one likely cause is the greenhouse effect (Lomborg 2008). Canada's greenhouse gas emissions have increased substantially over the past two decades. One of the major contributors is the oil sands (Statistics Canada 2008f). Not only does it take a lot of energy to separate the oil from the sand, but large amounts of water are used and large areas of forests are cut down. But the oil sands do not deserve to be called a "big war crime," as Greenpeace has called it, since oil production currently accounts for less than one-tenth of 1 percent of global greenhouse gas (GHG) emissions (Levi 2009). To reduce GHGs, new plans have been suggested since the failure of the Kyoto Protocol (see Box 15.2).

MAP 15.3   Climate Change across the Country

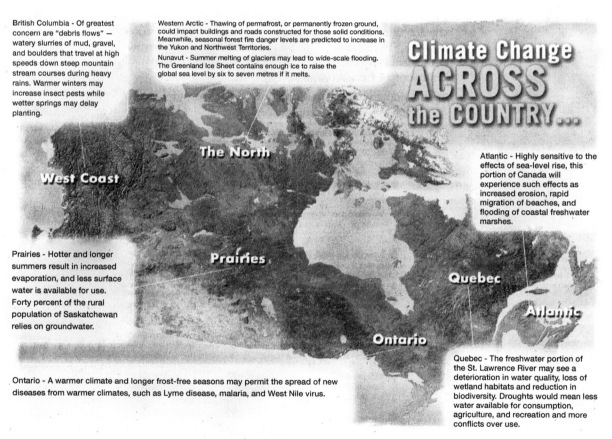

British Columbia - Of greatest concern are "debris flows" — watery slurries of mud, gravel, and boulders that travel at high speeds down steep mountain stream courses during heavy rains. Warmer winters may increase insect pests while wetter springs may delay planting.

Western Arctic - Thawing of permafrost, or permanently frozen ground, could impact buildings and roads constructed for those solid conditions. Meanwhile, seasonal forest fire danger levels are predicted to increase in the Yukon and Northwest Territories.

Nunavut - Summer melting of glaciers may lead to wide-scale flooding. The Greenland Ice Sheet contains enough ice to raise the global sea level by six to seven metres if it melts.

Atlantic - Highly sensitive to the effects of sea-level rise, this portion of Canada will experience such effects as increased erosion, rapid migration of beaches, and flooding of coastal freshwater marshes.

Prairies - Hotter and longer summers result in increased evaporation, and less surface water is available for use. Forty percent of the rural population of Saskatchewan relies on groundwater.

Ontario - A warmer climate and longer frost-free seasons may permit the spread of new diseases from warmer climates, such as Lyme disease, malaria, and West Nile virus.

Quebec - The freshwater portion of the St. Lawrence River may see a deterioration in water quality, loss of wetland habitats and reduction in biodiversity. Droughts would mean less water available for consumption, agriculture, and recreation and more conflicts over use.

Visit www.climatechange.gc.ca for more info.

Source: Environment Canada, 2006. Reproduced with the permission of the Minister of Public Works and Government Services.

Depletion of the Ozone Layer

There is some indication that the ozone layer of the atmosphere has been endangered by air pollution. In 1992, a hole the size of North America was reported in the ozone layer over Antarctica, and scientists have concluded that the ozone layer was thinning out at a rate of 6 percent a year in the 1990s (Hauchler and Kennedy 1994). Ozone is vital to life on earth because it is the only gas in the atmosphere that can absorb the sun's dangerous ultraviolet radiation. A thinning ozone layer increases risk of skin cancer, damages marine life, and lowers crop yields. It is important to note that the ozone shrinkage that scientists are currently measuring is the result of emissions in the early 1980s. Thus, the emissions we produce today will exert their destructive effects in the future (Hauchler and Kennedy 1994). Many countries, hoping to control damage to this delicate ecosystem in the future, are now phasing out products that contain CFCs, which damage the ozone layer and do not break down quickly. In 1987, 49 countries signed the Montreal Protocol to cut CFC production and consumption by 50 percent by the year 2000 (Harper 2001:131). By 2006, the cut amounted to 96 percent of original ozone-depleting substances (United Nations 2008:37). This decline has also reduced GHGs and helped reduce climate change.

SOCIAL PROBLEMS AND SOCIAL POLICY

BOX 15.2   What to Do about Global Warming?

The problem of global warming has the highest profile of any of the environmental problems we face. According to most scientists, a major contributor to global warming is greenhouse gases (GHG), primarily CO_2 and primarily released by consuming fossil fuels. In an attempt to reduce GHG emissions, 150 nations met in Kyoto, Japan, in 1997 and agreed to a plan, called the Kyoto Protocol, to reduce the amount of emissions expected in the year 2012 by 20 to 30 percent. The Canadian Liberal government ratified the Kyoto Protocol in 2002. In 2006, after Prime Minister Harper acknowledged that Canada would not meet its GHG emissions target on time, the Conservative government took a different approach. In October 2006, they introduced the *Clean Air Act,* which calls for a reduction in intensity of emissions, not an absolute reduction in emissions, and makes no mention of the Kyoto Protocol. The act's proposals include

- in 2007 limiting emissions from vehicles and products including motorcycles and personal watercraft and tighter standards for appliances;

- in 2011 making mandatory fuel-efficiency standards for new cars and trucks sold in Canada and fixed caps on emissions by industrial polluters;

- in 2025 putting a cap on greenhouse gas emissions through national targets for smog and ozone levels; and

- in 2050, the target year to reduce greenhouse gas emissions, reducing 2003 levels by 45 to 65 percent. (Curry 2006:A4)

The approach of the Harper government is called the "cap-and-trade" method where an overall level of emissions is mandated and according to whether a particular polluter is above or below their standard they can buy or sell, respectively, emissions credits. This approach is also used in Europe, and in early 2009 President Obama indicated the United States will follow this approach. In opposition to this approach is the "carbon tax," where people pay a tax on the fossil fuels they consume. The latter approach was supported by former Liberal leader Stéphane Dion, Premier Gordon Campbell of British Columbia, former President Bill Clinton, and James Henson, a pioneer in the campaign against GHG. The former approach is criticized by its opponents as a licence to pollute and the latter approach is branded as an additional tax by its opponents. Since no one wants to pay extra taxes, cap-and-trade may have an advantage. This may not be a great problem since it is possible to increase one kind of tax (on pollution) and lower another kind of tax, such as the GST. The cap-and-trade approach is also easier for international agreements, since it would be impossible for countries to verify that taxes were being extracted in other countries. Since it is possible to monitor overall emissions of a country, it would be easier to determine whether countries were keeping emissions below a set level. So which approach would you support?

Although Canada has not met its Kyoto targets (it's about 35 percent above its target in 2009), it has reduced its GHG intensity level. GHG intensity is a ratio of GHG in megatonnes emitted to the growth in GDP in billions of dollars. This GHG intensity has declined by 21 percent since 1990, meaning it's now taking less GHG emissions to produce more GDP.

The second issue for this policy box is how money should be allocated to reduce GHG and their effects. It's been estimated that it would take $180 billion per year to meet Kyoto targets (Lomborg 2008:107). Instead of allocating such a large sum of money over a very long period to reduce GHG with uncertain results, Bjorn Lomborg, a former Greenpeace advocate and now a skeptical environmentalist, after acknowledging that global warming is real and manmade, stresses that bringing hundreds of millions of people out of poverty is also desirable. He suggests that tackling individual problems such as those identified in the GHG section separately could be cheaper, at $52 billion per year, and this total includes tackling more problems, including HIV/AIDS; the need for micronutrients, like vitamin A, to prevent blindness in children; increased drinking water projects and sanitation; and increased research for energy without fossil fuels. For example, he suggests

- prohibiting the hunting of polar bears;
- acknowledging that though heat kills people, so does cold, and a slightly warmer climate in the temperate areas could provide a net benefit with the help of air conditioning;
- increasing use of levees to reduce flooding;

- acknowledging that increasing desert in some areas is offset by increasing agricultural fertility in other areas;
- increasing support for anti-malaria policies directly (providing more nets and better drugs); and
- improving building controls, preventing draining of wetlands, and avoiding building on the coasts to reduce the costs of hurricanes. (Lomborg 2008:162)

Tackling problems specifically is an interesting approach, especially when targets such as reducing HIV/AIDS and starvation coincide with the United Nations' Millennium Goals for 2015 (http://www.un.org/millenniumgoals). This is not to suggest that nothing need be done to reduce GHG. Many countries, like Canada, are now doing much to prevent GHG increases. For example, the oil and gas extraction industry led the way with expenditures of $495.4 million on alternative energy and energy reduction technologies in 2006. Most of this amount, $472.9 million, was directed at capital projects (Statistics Canada 2008f). But we could allocate resources with the goal not just to reduce GHG, but to improve the overall quality of life for everyone on the planet. How do you think money should be allocated to world problems?

Toxic Air Pollutants

Toxic air pollutants refer to a wide variety of chemicals found in the air in low but sufficient concentrations to be associated with a lifetime cancer risk greater than one in a million. *Corporate Knights* magazine, in a 2005 report on the top 50 polluters in Canada, noted that 82 companies from the Toronto stock market index released 2.06 billion kilograms of toxic chemicals into Canada's air. The primary polluting companies were mining, forestry, and energy companies ("The Toxic 50" 2005:39). The National Pollutant Release Inventory (NPRI) keeps track of the quantities of pollutants released at **http://www.ec.gc.ca/inrp-npri/default.asp?lang=En&n=4A577BB9-1.** A study commissioned by Toronto Public Health assessed the potential for exposure to 10 key carcinogens, including asbestos, benzene, and polycyclic aromatic hydrocarbons (PAHs), in Toronto workplaces and environments. The results showed that Toronto residents are routinely exposed to a variety of carcinogenic chemicals in the environment, and "many of these people are exposed to additional and even higher levels of carcinogens at work" (Basrur 2002:iii). The report recommends finding ways to determine people's actual exposure to these chemicals and reduce the release of them. The higher concentration of pollutants in areas of high levels of poverty (described as *environmental classism*, below) is also a concern.

Problems with Water, Soil, and Forests

Water, soil, and forests (vegetation) are interdependent, crucial resources that face increasing degradation or destruction because of pollution. As a result of climate changes, waste, pollution, and rapid depletion, the earth's drinking water is endangered and its fertile land is being lost.

Water Shortages and Pollution

Water depletion and pollution are serious problems. A shocking example occurred in 2000 in the small town of Walkerton in southern Ontario. Seven people died and about 2300 became ill as a result of *E. coli* contamination in the water. The primary source of the contamination was manure that had been spread on a farm near a major well. This well had not been monitored appropriately by the water utility operators. In the end, Ontario Premier Mike Harris was forced to admit that he and his government were, in part, responsible for the tragedy: despite ongoing strong public support for environmental protection, they had slashed funding for environmental programs (along with funding for welfare, education, and health); at the same time, they had devolved responsibility in many areas—including water testing and manure management—to the municipalities, which had neither the money nor the knowledge needed to handle these responsibilities.

Obviously, such problems are not limited to Canada. Although approximately 70 percent of the earth's surface is covered by water, most water is not drinkable: 97 percent is saltwater, 2 percent is in ice caps and glaciers, and most of the remaining 1 percent is so far underground that it is beyond human reach (Petersen 1994). The primary sources of water for use and consumption are rainfall, streams, lakes, rivers, and aquifers (accessible underground water supplies). Canada is often thought to be a source of limitless fresh water, but according to the Water Quickfacts website of Environment Canada (2002), we have only 7 percent of the world's renewable, or flowing, fresh water, as opposed to the stationary fresh water in lakes; moreover, 60 percent of our fresh water runs north.

Because of the current rate of world population growth and existing climatic conditions, water scarcity is increasing throughout the world. According to the *United Nations World Water Development Report 3*, a global assessment of the world's freshwater supply, about 7 billion people, two-thirds of the world's population in the middle of this century, will likely face water scarcity. Areas that already experience water shortages, like India, Pakistan, the Middle East, and sub-Saharan Africa, will experience the most severe problems (UN-Water 2009).

Where does the water go? The largest amount (about 70 percent) is used for crop irrigation; in some African and Asian countries, as much as 85 percent of the available water is used in agriculture. The second largest use of water is in industry (23 to 25 percent). Industrial use of water depends on the level of development in a country and the structure of its economy. For example, high-income nations use as much as 60 percent of their water for industry, whereas a middle- or low-income nation may use less than 10 percent. (In Canada, industry uses about 70 percent of the water and agriculture 12 percent.) A mere 8 percent of all available water is used for domestic or private household use. Over the past 100 years, global use of water has gone from 1000 to 2000 litres per day (Lomborg 2001:151), with affluent people in high-income nations using far more water than do families living in African villages, where water must often be carried several kilometres (about 2 to 5 litres is the physical minimum needed per person per day). According to the *United Nations World Water Development Report 3* (UN-Water 2009), about 3 million people per year die because of inadequate water, sanitation, and hygiene (primarily as a result of diarrhea, malnutrition, and malaria). On the plus side, since 1990, 1.6 billion people have gained access to safe water, but 1 billion people still lack safe drinking water (United Nations 2008:42).

Water pollution seriously diminishes the available supply of water. Water may be polluted in a variety of ways. Most often, though, the cause is unpurified or insufficiently treated sewage from households and industry discharged into groundwater, or surface water, or pesticides and mineral fertilizers leached from farmland. The pollutants range from nitrates and phosphates to metals, salts, and disease-causing micro-organisms.

Environment Canada studied 345 southern Canadian freshwater sites from 2001 to 2003 and found that less than half were rated good or excellent for meeting guidelines that set limits for pollutant levels, a third were rated as fair, and a quarter as marginal or poor. It is estimated that 100 000 tonnes of toxic pollutants were discharged into surface waters in 2003 (Statistics Canada 2005c).

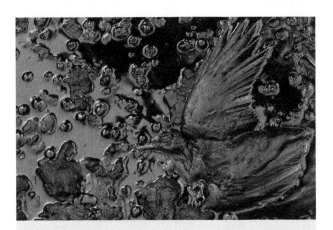

In our delicate ecosystem, water pollution has a disastrous effect on all forms of life—not just on human life. What measures might we implement to reduce water pollution like this?

The future will see increased pressure on water resources, and this pressure will be aggravated by climate change and population growth.

Soil Depletion and Desertification

About 11 percent of the earth's surface is used for growing crops, 32 percent is forest, and 24 percent is used to graze animals. Each year, however, many acres of usable land are lost through erosion and contamination. *Deforestation*—excessive removal of trees—usually results in serious erosion. Since the 1992 Earth Summit in Rio de Janeiro, high-income nations have made an effort to protect forests. Unfortunately, prior industrialization in Canada and other high-income nations has already taken a serious toll on forests, and the pattern is continuing in some middle- and low-income nations as they become more industrialized. In Canada, especially in the Pacific Northwest, logging is an issue. Environmentalists say that logging, besides destroying old-growth forests, increases landslides, floods, and changes in rivers and streams, which devastate fish stocks (Goldberg 1997).

Today, many regions are losing an increasing amount of usable land as a result of **desertification**—the process by which usable land is turned into desert because of overgrazing, harmful agricultural practices, or deforestation. It is estimated that desertification destroys as many as 6 million hectares (15 million acres) of land a year. An additional 20 million hectares (50 million acres) of crop and pasture land become inefficient each year because of excessive application of herbicides and pesticides, insufficient crop rotation, and intensified agricultural production (United Nations Environment Programme 2002).

In Canada's Prairies, according to the North American Commission for Environmental Cooperation (2002), in the mid-1990s, soil loss through erosion is thought to have amounted to about 177 million tonnes annually, despite successful efforts to reduce loss by the planting of winter cover crops and windbreaks. Although soil erosion has declined, more soil is being lost than is being regenerated naturally, because heavy use of chemical fertilizers has harmed soil structure.

Although desertification takes place in both high-income and middle- and low-income nations, its effects are particularly devastating in middle- and low-income nations. When a country is already hard hit by rapid population growth, virtually any loss of land or crops is potentially devastating to large numbers of people. The United Nations and other international organizations have therefore tried to make protection of the environment an integral part of all economic development policy. However, environmental protection specialists say that to translate policy into action, conservation programs must be supported by the people, and the major sources of the problem—population and poverty—must also be addressed. As part of their conservation program, the United Nations has developed a campaign to plant 7 billion trees by the end of 2009. As of early August 2009, they had planted over 4 billion trees. To find out more about the campaign, including how you can participate, visit the United Nations Environment Programme at **http://www.unep.org/billiontreecampaign**.

Solid, Toxic, and Nuclear Wastes

Even with a rapidly growing world population and ongoing economic development in industrialized nations, the planet might be able to sustain life for a long time if it weren't for all the solid and toxic chemical waste that is dumped into the environment.

Solid Waste

In Canada and some other high-income nations, people consume a vast array of products and—in these *disposable societies*—throw away huge quantities of paper, plastic, metal, and other materials. *Solid waste* is any and all unwanted and discarded materials that are not liquids or gases. For example, in 2000, each person in Canada disposed of about 0.75 tonnes of waste (Statistics Canada 2002g), of which only 30 percent was recycled—reused resources that would otherwise be discarded. While Canadians may not be recycling as much as possible, they report participating in recycling as well as other environmentally favourable behaviours. Table 15.4 shows the extent to which Canadians are participating in recycling and other resource saving behaviours like conserving water, composting, and reducing GHGs.

Toxic Waste

At the same time that technology has brought about improvements in the quality and length of life, it has

TABLE 15.4   National Household Participation Rates for Six Environmental Behaviours, 2006

	Participation rate[1] (%)
Recycling	97
Compact fluorescent light bulbs	59
Low-flow showerheads	56
Lowering temperatures	54
Reduced volume toilets	37
Composting	30

[1] **As a percentage of all households that had a thermostat and that had access to at least one recycling program.**

Source: Statistics Canada, 2008, "Study: Participation in Environmentally Active Lifestyles," The Daily *(December 9).*

created the potential for new disasters. One source of a potential disaster is *toxic waste,* the hazardous chemical by-products of industrial processes. Perhaps the most widely known U.S. case of toxic waste is Love Canal. In the late 1970s, residents of Niagara Falls, New York, learned that their children were attending a school that had been built on top of a toxic landfill (Gibbs 1982). After large numbers of children became ill and the smell and appearance of the chemicals permeated the entire area, many people mobilized against Hooker Chemical Company, which had dumped tons of chemicals there (Gibbs 1982). Eventually, the federal government bought many of the houses, moved the residents out, and removed as much of the toxic waste as possible. A lesser-known Canadian example of chemical discharge, by Uniroyal Chemical, permanently contaminated the water supply in Elmira, Ontario, with a "toxic soup of cancer-causing chemicals." In 1989, the Ontario Ministry of the Environment ordered Uniroyal to cease the discharge and clean up the local environment (Cameron 1995:298).

Government regulates the disposal of toxic wastes, but some hazardous wastes are not covered by regulations, and some corporations avoid the regulations by locating their factories in other countries (see also Chapter 2).

The Canadian government estimates that about 6 million tonnes of hazardous waste are generated each year (Commission for Economic Cooperation 2009:2).

Some good news is that total releases of carcinogens and developmental/reproductive toxicants were reduced by 26 percent between 1998 and 2004 (Commission for Economic Cooperation 2009:1).

Nuclear Waste

Nuclear, or radioactive, wastes are the most dangerous of all toxic wastes. Radioactive waste in Canada comes primarily from 22 nuclear power plants, which provide enough electricity in Canada to power 6 million homes (Canadian Nuclear Association 2002). In addition, small amounts of waste are by-products of certain medical procedures. According to the *Harper's* Index, citing an Organisation for Economic Co-operation and Development report, Canada generates more grams of nuclear waste per capita than either Britain or the United States (50 versus 15 and 7, respectively; "*Harper's* Index" 2002). Nuclear waste remains deadly for prolonged periods of time. For example, uranium waste from nuclear power plants (an estimated 40 000 tonnes by early 2009) will remain dangerously radioactive for the next 10 000 years, and plutonium waste for the next 240 000 years (Petersen 1994). Although there are many problems with nuclear power, some environmentalists are reconsidering its value, because it does have the advantage of not producing CO_2 emissions.

Technological Disasters

Technological disasters, such as the 1986 meltdown and radiation leak at the Chernobyl nuclear power plant in Ukraine, which caused over 50 immediate deaths, exposed hundreds of thousands to radiation, and likely precipitated thousands of cancer deaths, have increased global awareness of the problems associated with radioactive waste. However, despite the disaster, the former Soviet Union was still using 19 similar reactors in 1994 (Petersen 1994). Sociologist Kai T. Erikson (1991:15) sees the world facing a new species of trouble today:

> [Environmental problems] contaminate rather than merely damage . . . they pollute, befoul, taint, rather than just create wreckage . . . they penetrate human tissue indirectly rather than just wound the surfaces by assaults of a more straightforward kind. . . . And the evidence is growing that they scare human beings in new and special ways, that they elicit an uncanny fear in us.

The chaos that Erikson (1991:141) describes is the result of *technological disasters*—"meaning everything that can go wrong when systems fail, humans err, designs prove faulty, engines misfire, and so on." Chernobyl, Love Canal, and Elmira were technological disasters, as were radiation leakage at the Three Mile Island nuclear power plant in Pennsylvania in 1979 and the leakage of lethal gases at the pesticide plant in Bhopal, India, which killed over 3000 people in 1984. In the worst-case scenario, technological disasters kill tens of thousands of people; in the best-case scenario, they place tremendous stress on the world's ecosystems and greatly diminish the quality of life for everyone.

PERSPECTIVES ON POPULATION AND THE ENVIRONMENT

As sociologists have examined how human behaviour affects population and environmental problems, the subdiscipline of environmental sociology has emerged. According to Cable and Cable (1995:5), "*environmental sociology* examines people's beliefs about their environment, their behaviour toward it, and the ways in which the structure of society influences them and contributes to the persistent abuse of the environment." Like all sociologists, environmental sociologists—as well as demographers—approach their study from one or another perspective.

The Functionalist Perspective

Some functionalists focus on the relationship between social structure, technological change, and environmental problems. On the one hand, they say, technological innovation serves important functions in society. For example, automation and mass production have made a wide array of goods—from automobiles and computers to McDonald's burgers—available to many people. On the other hand, technological innovation has latent dysfunctions; automation and mass production, for example, create air pollution, overuse and depletion of natural resources, and excessive solid waste. From this point of view, some environmental problems are the price a society pays for technological progress. If this is true, the best way to alleviate the problem is to develop new technologies. This is what happened, some functionalists note, when the catalytic converter and other antipollution devices were developed for automobiles.

Other functionalists take a neo-Malthusian perspective and believe that to reduce food shortages and environmental problems, population must be controlled. In other words, the more people there are alive, the greater are the overuse of finite resources and degradation of soil, water, and land.

No matter which view functionalist environmental sociologists take, they believe that solutions to overpopulation and environmental degradation lie in social institutions such as education, the government, and business. Educators can encourage population control by teaching people about the limits to agriculture and the difficulty of feeding rapidly increasing populations. Government leaders and international organizations such as the United Nations can co-operate to find far-reaching and innovative solutions and develop understandings about more equitable use of the world's resources (Ehrlich and Ehrlich 1991). Business can be helpful by becoming "greener"—applying environmentally friendly principles to its buildings and operations, putting gardens on plant roofs, using alternative energy sources to coal and oil, sequestering greenhouse gases in underground storage, and cutting waste. Business can also develop environmentally friendly products such as cars powered by a hybrid of gasoline-powered engines and electric motors (e.g., the Toyota Prius, Honda Insight, Ford Escape) and solar- and wind-powered devices.

To show the extent to which countries are protecting their environment, the Yale Center for Environmental Law and Policy, the Center for International Earth Science Information Network at Columbia University, and the World Economic Forum have devised an index to rank countries' efforts to meet two objectives: to reduce environmental stress on human health and to promote ecosystem vitality and sound resource management.

In total, 25 indicators of these two objectives were selected, ranging from reducing air pollution and increasing water safety to protecting critical habitats, reducing climate change, and improving management of fisheries, agriculture, and forestry (CIESIN 2009). Map 15.4 shows the different levels of effort of countries. Switzerland, Norway, Sweden, Finland, and Costa Rica have scores over 90. On this scale Canada ranks 12th with a score of

86; and the United States ranks 39th with a score of 81. While our score can provide some comfort, we are still very deficient in reducing greenhouse gases.

Within Canada some variation exists among provinces for their climate change plans, according to the David Suzuki Foundation. Whereas British Columbia and Quebec rank high in their plans to reduce emissions, Alberta and Saskatchewan expect to have an increase in their emissions by 2020. Some variation also exists among cities regarding sustainability. Among large cities, Edmonton and Toronto rank high; among medium cities, Halifax and Quebec rank high; and among small cities, Yellowknife and Saskatoon rank high (Shin 2009:27).

The Conflict Perspective

Analysts using a conflict framework believe that population and environmental problems have less to do with overpopulation and shortages of resources than with power differentials in societies and in the larger global economy. For example, early conflict theorists,

such as Karl Marx and Friedrich Engels (1848/1976), did not think that the food supply was threatened by overpopulation because agricultural technology (even in their era) could meet the food needs of the growing world population, if it were not for poverty. According to Marx and Engels (1848/1976), poverty exists because workers are exploited by capitalists. They argued, for example, that poverty existed in England because the capitalists skimmed off some of the workers' wages as profits. Thus, the labour of the working classes was used by capitalists to earn profits, which, in turn, were used to purchase machinery that could replace the workers rather than supply food. From this classical Marxist point of view, population growth is encouraged by capitalists who use unemployed workers (the industrial reserve army) to keep other workers from demanding higher wages or better working conditions.

According to contemporary conflict theorists, corporations and the government are the two main power institutions in society. As a result, when economic decisions made by members of the capitalist class and elite

MAP 15.4   Environmental Performance Index

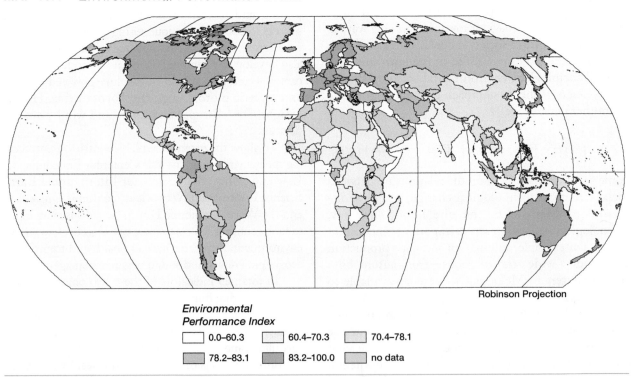

Robinson Projection

Environmental
Performance Index

☐ 0.0–60.3	☐ 60.4–70.3	☐ 70.4–78.1
☐ 78.2–83.1	☐ 83.2–100.0	☐ no data

Source: The Trustees of Columbia University in the City of New York. Daniel C. Esty, M.A. Levy, C.H. Kim, A. de Sherbinin, T. Srebotnjak, and V. Mara, 2008, Environmental Performance Index. New Haven: Yale Center for Environmental Law and Policy (http://sedac.ciesin.columbia.edu/es/epi).

political leaders lead to environmental problems, the costs are externalized, or passed along to the people (Cable and Cable 1995:13):

> [The externalization of environmental costs of production] . . . means that the costs of production's negative impact on the environment (for example, the expense of cleaning polluted water to make it suitable for drinking) are not included in the price of the product. The company neither pays for the privilege of polluting the water nor cleans it; it saves the cost of proper waste disposal and makes environmentally conscious competition impossible. Not even the consumer of the product pays the environmental costs of production directly. Rather, the public at large essentially subsidizes the company, by either paying for the cleanup of the environment or enduring degraded environmental quality.

Another conflict approach uses an *environmental justice framework*, examining how class affects the struggle for scarce environmental resources. Of particular interest to these theorists is **environmental classism**, which occurs when a disproportionate number of hazardous facilities are present in areas with large proportions of poor people (measured by low-income cut-offs). Hazardous facilities include waste disposal and treatment plants and chemical plants (Schneider 1993). PollutionWatch (2008) combined maps of poverty areas and combined air pollutants in Toronto from 2005 data. Areas with poverty rates above the national average of 11.8 show a disproportionate number of sources of air pollution from the National Pollutant Release Inventory (NPRI). To map the pollution in your area, go to **http://pollutionwatch.org/mapsearch.do**.

The Interactionist Perspective

Since interactionists take a microlevel approach, viewing society as the sum of all people's interactions, they look at environmental problems in terms of individuals' social construction of reality.

According to sociologist John A. Hannigan (1995), environmental claims-makers assemble, present, and contest the claims they make about various environmental problems. To gain public attention and support, the claims must be newsworthy, have scientific credibility, and get past various interests. It is helpful to have

- supporters who span science and media, such as David Suzuki, the award-winning scientist (the UN Environmental Medal and many honorary degrees), host of the CBC program *The Nature of Things*, and author of many books concerned with the environment;

- incentives for change, such as better health; and

- sustaining support by major international organizations, such as the United Nations. (Hannigan 1995)

Having institutional support can lead to the creation of international protocols, like the Kyoto Protocol for global warming, though it cannot guarantee full international co-operation.

The social construction approach also helps us understand people's accounts of the estimation of environmental risk and their response to different kinds of communication. McMaster University researchers John Eyles and his colleagues (1993) studied the effects of the tire fire in 1990 in Hagersville, Ontario—a fire broke out on a site on which 13 to 14 million tires were located and burned for 17 days before being extinguished. When the fire broke out, 300 households were evacuated. Eyles and his colleagues conducted in-depth interviews among a small sample of those who experienced the evacuation and were helped by local groups. The researchers found (1993:287) that although the effects of the fire were short-lived, many residents had anxieties about future problems, such as their children's health, toxic water runoff, and the value of their property. Eyles and colleagues (1993:287) also found that the authorities did not do a good job of communicating with people about the evacuation, the de-evacuation, the cleanup, and compensation for loss. Since perceived risk is increased when the threat is uncontrollable, involuntary, and problematic for future generations, the researchers "conclude that the nature of the message is as important as information itself" (Eyles et al. 1993:288). For the authorities to communicate better with people, they must "recognize and cater to ways in which lay publics act, think and talk" (Eyles et al. 1993:288).

Feminist Perspectives

Two strands of feminist theorizing in population and the environment are *women's agency* and *ecofeminism*. Regarding overpopulation, the relationship between women's literacy and fertility is well established. Higher-educated women have fewer children, not only in developed countries, but also in developing countries. While the fertility rate in India is over 3.0, the rate in Kerala, a state in which women are well educated and participate in the labour force, is below replacement level at 1.7 (Sen 1999:199). Thus, encouraging women's education and participation in the labour force would contribute to both women's well-being and the reduction of fertility rates.

The term *ecofeminism* was coined by French writer Françoise d'Eaubonne, who thought that men's oppression of women and of the environment were two components of the same phenomenon (Eckersley 2001). Ecofeminists believe that women are more nurturing, co-operative, and conservation-minded than men and point to the term "Mother Nature" to support the general acceptance of women as being closer to nature. The viewpoint that women have a unique capacity to construct a new approach to the environment is combined with activism (Mies and Shiva 1993).

An example of ecofeminism was the 1993 protest against clear-cutting a temperate rainforest at Clayoquot Sound on Vancouver Island, British Columbia. It was organized by women and still ranks as the largest example of civil disobedience in Canada. News of the protest spread worldwide, and cutting was stopped. Since that time, members of environmental groups and Indigenous groups have worked with logging companies, including the Indigenous-run Iisaak Forest Resources. In 2006, Clayoquot Sound was opened to carefully managed logging.

POPULATION AND THE ENVIRONMENT IN THE FUTURE

The problems we have considered in this section include some of the greatest challenges that humans face in the 21st century. Global overpopulation and environmental depletion and devastation have irreversible consequences, and actions taken—or not taken—today will be with us far into the future. Futurists believe that we must use a wide-angle lens to examine population and environmental concerns (Petersen 1994). We must see the world and our role in it in a much different way than we did in the

past. We must understand that environmental issues are *security* issues—as much as a terrorist threat or a missile or bomb (Petersen 1994). Once we understand that, we will think of environmental problems in a completely different light. For example, to eliminate the global threats posed by overpopulation and environmental degradation, all societies can make the following changes (based on Petersen 1994:109):

- Reduce the use of energy.
- Shift from fossil fuels to solar-based energy systems or other energy-efficient systems such as water power, wind power, or geothermal energy.
- Develop new transportation networks and city designs that reduce automobile use.
- Push for equality between women and men in all nations, emphasizing literacy training, educational opportunities, and health care (including reproduction and contraception information) for women.
- Effect a rapid transition to smaller families.
- Co-operate internationally to reduce the consumption of resources by the wealthy nations and bring higher living standards to poorer nations.

Are these changes likely to occur? Not if people in high- and middle-income nations adhere to their current belief systems. Some social analysts think that it will take a threatening event—a drastic change in the earth's weather patterns or a sudden increase in natural disasters—to capture the attention of enough of the earth's people and convince political leaders that a serious change in direction is required if the planet is to continue to support human life (Petersen 1994). We can only hope that people will not wait until it's too late.

WHAT CAN YOU DO?

For this cause, there is no shortage of opportunities to do something. Here are a few places to start for the environment:

- Visit the Environment Canada website, which describes just about every opportunity imaginable, at http://**www.ec.gc.ca/education**. At this site, one is invited to take action on a wide variety of topics and learn your environmental impact. Reduce energy consumption (e.g., by driving less, having a fuel-efficient car, not idling the car engine, and, at home, reducing heating fuel use through proper insulation, lowering water and air heating, etc.); reduce waste (e.g., by recycling and composting); and reduce consumption—you know what we mean.

■ Lobby Members of Parliament, by yourself or with others, to encourage them to take action to protect the environment.

■ Join with others to change energy use (e.g., urge people idling their cars to stop, as students in Mississauga, Ontario, are doing as part of an environmental internship program with City Council and their Environmental Studies Program at the University of Toronto).

Here are some things you can do for cities:

■ If you live in a city, you might join your local residents' association. These associations are always looking for volunteer help for committees: to undertake liaison with the police, to have representatives for every street in the area, to keep track of problems like drug dealing and prostitution, and to undertake social projects. Be aware that some of the members of some of these groups are more concerned with enhancing the value of their properties than with solving social problems in the area and may seek to reduce local shelters and social agencies.

■ If you are searching for a place to live and like the idea of working with your neighbours, try co-operative housing. You will gain a great experience working with others.

■ Join a group lobbying for the homeless. Public interest research groups are found on many university and college campuses, and sometimes, like the Ontario Public Interest Research Group in Toronto, they support action to help the homeless.

■ Participate in irregular programs to plant trees or clean up your neighbourhood.

■ Sit in on a city council meeting so you can learn more about the activities and governance of a city and meet other interested citizens and lobby your councilor or mayor.

SUMMARY

What Is the Global Population? Why Is Population Growth a Problem?

The world's population was more than 6.7 billion in 2009; it doubled in the past 50 years and, if this trend continues, could increase by 50 percent in the next 50 years. Can the earth's resources support this rapid population growth?

What Are the Primary Factors that Affect Population Growth?

Three factors affect population growth: fertility, the actual number of children born to an individual or population; mortality, the number of deaths that occur in a specific population; and migration, the movement of people from one geographic area to another for the purpose of changing residency.

How Does Population Growth Affect a Society?

Population growth affects population composition—the biological and social characteristics of a population, including such attributes as age, sex, racialization, marital status, education, occupation, income, and size of household. In Canada, for example, the age distribution of the population affects the need for schools, employment opportunities, health care, and age-appropriate housing.

What Are the Major Theoretical Perspectives on Overpopulation?

According to the Malthusian perspective, population expands geometrically while the food supply increases arithmetically; disaster can be averted through positive checks (e.g., famine, disease, war) or preventive checks (e.g., sexual abstinence, delayed marriage). The neo-Malthusians believe that the earth is a ticking bomb because population problems exacerbate environmental problems. The third perspective is more hopeful. According to demographic transition theory, societies move from high birth and death rates to low birth and death rates as a result of technological development. However, critics say that demographic transition theory applies chiefly to Western societies.

What Solutions Do We Have to World Hunger?

Two of the most far-reaching initiatives are the green revolution (the growing of high-yield "miracle" crops) and the biotechnological revolution, which involves "improving" plants or animals or using micro-organisms in innovative ways. However, some social analysts believe that the solution is not to produce more food but to control fertility.

How Is Immigration Changing the Population Composition of Canada?

Today, the proportion of Canadian immigrants in the population is about 20 percent. If immigration continues at the present rate, it will account for half of the expected population growth in the next 50 years. (Canada is otherwise below zero population growth—a stable population.) Immigration could lead to higher taxes, but it also brings substantial economic and cultural benefits.

How Did Urbanization Come About?

Urbanization—the process by which an increasing proportion of a population lives in cities rather than rural areas—began with industrialization. Before the Industrial Revolution, most people lived in sparsely populated rural areas, where they farmed. Industrialization led to the growth of cities, and urbanization brought about profound changes in societies and spawned new social problems, such as housing shortages, overcrowding, unsanitary conditions, environmental pollution, and crime.

How Did Mass Suburbanization Occur? What Were the Results?

Mass suburbanization began with government efforts to correct the housing shortage that followed World War II. The Central (now Canada) Mortgage and Housing Corporation contributed to the building of half a million homes between 1946 and 1951 by granting mortgages. Other factors included the availability of inexpensive land, low-cost mass construction methods, new federally financed highway systems, inexpensive gasoline, and consumer demand for single-family homes on individually owned lots. Mass suburbanization brought about a dramatic shift in the distribution of the Canadian population and set up an ongoing economic division of interests between cities and suburbs.

Why Are Many Cities in Fiscal Crisis?

Cities do not have regular sources of income such as income or sales taxes. They have taxes on property values, which can vary widely over time; levies such as service fees; and a portion of gas taxes. They have a wide variety of services to provide, from social services to transportation. Many middle- and upper-income people have moved back into the central cities, but this does not compensate for increased needs. Moreover, suburbanites who regularly use city services do not pay taxes to the city to keep up these services.

Why Is There a Housing Shortage in Canada? What Is Being Done about It?

A major reason for the housing shortage is that Canada has yet to find a way to provide safe, livable, low-income housing. In addition, as part of governmental cutbacks in the mid-1990s, the federal and provincial governments stopped building social housing. Some non-governmental groups have been doing good work. Among the most successful initiatives for creating affordable housing are developments like St. Lawrence in Toronto and the volunteer organization Habitat for Humanity.

How Great a Problem Is Homelessness? Are There Any Solutions?

Accurate data on the actual number of the homeless are extremely difficult to get because homeless people avoid interviews with census-takers and social researchers. Most experts agree that any long-term, successful solution to homelessness must take structural factors into account, especially low-income housing and mental-health care.

Does Residential Racialized or Ethnic Segregation Exist?

Spatial separation of the poor and non-poor is greater than separation of racialized/ethnic groups. While, in contrast to in U.S. cities, there are no extensive areas of blight, decay, or abandoned housing in Canadian cities, pockets of poor racialized/ethnic groups coexist beside upscale neighbourhoods.

What Are the Major Problems in Global Cities?

In 2010, one out of every two people in the world lives in a city. Increasing population accounts for two-thirds of the new urban growth, and rural-to-urban migration accounts for the rest. Rapid urban growth brings a wide variety of problems, including overcrowding, environmental pollution, and the disappearance of farmland.

What Is the Functionalist Perspective on Urban Problems?

Functionalists believe that today's urban problems are the result of mass migration from rural areas during the Industrial Revolution, large-scale immigration in the early and late 20th and early 21st centuries, and mass suburbanization. One solution is to create regional governments.

What Is the Conflict Perspective on Urban Problems?

Conflict theorists believe that cities grow or decline according to decisions made by capitalists and the political elite. In other words, these theorists use a political economy model. Urban problems can be reduced through political activism and organized resistance to oppressive conditions.

What Is the Interactionist Perspective on Urban Problems?

Interactionists look at how people subjectively experience urban life. According to German sociologist Georg Simmel, urban life is so stimulating that people have no choice but to become somewhat insensitive to people and events around them. On the other hand, urban living gives people opportunities for individualism and autonomy. Sociologist Louis Wirth expanded on Simmel's ideas, saying that urbanism produces feelings of alienation and powerlessness. Herbert Gans concluded from his research that city life is a pleasure for some and a nightmare for others. Commenting on Toronto and Vancouver, Richard Florida states these cities have a high rate of Creative Class people because of the stimulation and tolerance in these cities and, according to the CLI, they are "smarter" cities, which is a key to a bright economic future. A way to avoid the nightmare of alienation is to develop subcultural ties.

What Is the Feminist Perspective on Urban Problems?

Feminist theorists emphasize the occupational opportunities, freedom from scrutiny, and convenience of short distances between work and home that allow fulfillment of multiple roles for women.

What Is Environmental Degradation? What Are Its Causes?

Environmental degradation is caused by disruptions to the environment that have negative consequences for ecosystems. Human beings, particularly as they pursue economic development and growth, cause environmental degradation.

What Are the Major Sources of Air Pollution? What Are Its Effects?

The major sources of fossil fuel pollution are transportation and industry. One of the most serious consequences of air pollution is the greenhouse effect, an environmental condition caused by excessive quantities of carbon dioxide, methane, and nitrous oxide in the atmosphere, leading to global warming. Another is depletion of the ozone layer, the part of the earth's atmosphere that absorbs dangerous ultraviolet radiation from the sun. Although the great reductions in the use of CFCs may prevent serious depletion, the already present CFCs will continue to adversely affect the ozone layer.

What Water, Soil, and Forest Problems Do We Face?

Water is increasingly scarce throughout the world, and water pollution further diminishes the available water supply. However, desertification is greatest in middle- and low-income nations.

Why Are Solid, Toxic, and Nuclear Wastes a Problem?

High-income nations are running out of space for the amount of solid waste produced by their "disposable societies." Toxic waste (hazardous chemical by-products of industry) causes death and disease if it is not disposed of properly. Canada has become a significant importer of toxic waste. Nuclear, or radioactive, waste is a problem because of the length of time it remains deadly.

What Is the Functionalist Perspective on Population and the Environment?

Functionalists say that the latent dysfunctions of technology cause environmental problems but that new technologies can solve these problems. Most functionalists take a neo-Malthusian perspective on population but believe that social institutions, especially education and the government, can co-operate to solve population and environmental problems.

What Is the Conflict Perspective on Population and the Environment?

In the classical Marxist view, there would be enough food for all people if poverty were alleviated; poverty exists because capitalists skim workers' wages for profits. Contemporary conflict theorists believe that the two main power institutions in society—corporations and the government—make economic decisions that result in environmental problems.

What Is the Interactionist Perspective on Population and Environment?

Interactionists see population and environmental problems in microlevel—individual—terms. Social constructionists show how environmental claims-makers assemble, present, and contest the claims they make about various environmental problems. Sometimes scary scenarios are created, and those who challenge this definition of reality are dismissed as wishful thinkers. Social contructionists can also help us understand people's estimation of environmental risk.

What Is the Feminist Perspective on Population and the Environment?

Feminists emphasize the importance of promoting women's literacy and participation in the labour force to help control fertility. Ecofeminism emphasizes that patriarchy is the root cause of the oppression of women and of nature. Living off the backs of others and living beyond ecological means are both unsupportable.

KEY TERMS

acid rain,   p. 359
deindustrialization,   p. 348
demographic transition
    theory,   p. 341
demography,   p. 339
desertification,   p. 365
edge city,   p. 347

environmental classism,   p. 369
environmental
    degradation,   p. 358
fertility,   p. 339
gentrification,   p. 350
greenhouse effect,   p. 360
mechanical solidarity,   p. 353

megalopolis,   p. 348
migration,   p. 340
mortality,   p. 339
organic solidarity,   p. 354
population composition,   p. 340
subculture,   p. 357
zero population growth,   p. 344

QUESTIONS FOR CRITICAL THINKING

1. Which perspective on population growth do you favour—neo-Malthusian or demographic transition theory—and why?

2. Where do you live—in a core central city, an edge city, a suburb, or a megalopolis? What examples from your everyday life can you give that relate to the problems described in this chapter? Which sociological perspective do you think best explains the urban problems you observe?

3. The government has so far failed to eliminate homelessness. What new initiatives can you suggest?

4. The 2006 Census releases have included tables on various characteristics of cities, including age and sex distribution, family structures, income, and visible minority percentages. One table about visible minorities from the 2006 Census can be found at **http://www12.stat-can.gc.ca/english/census06/data/trends/table_2.cfm? T=CMA&LINE_ID=901&TOPIC_ID=900.** Using various demographic variables, write a social study of your area.

5. If you had to focus on a single aspect of environmental degradation—air pollution; water, soil, or forest problems; or solid, toxic, or nuclear waste disposal—which would it be, and why? What would you do to make people aware of the seriousness of the problem? What new solutions could you propose?

6. Is it possible to have development without environmental degradation?

PEARSON

Explore the topics covered in this chapter at **www.mysockit.com** using the access provided with this text. Interactive resources for studying include video clips, practice tests, learning objectives, and Internet resources.

16 GLOBAL SOCIAL PROBLEMS

Beware the leader who bangs the drums of war in order to whip the citizenry into a patriotic fervor, for patriotism is indeed a double-edged sword. It both emboldens the blood, just as it narrows the mind. And when the drums of war have reached a fever pitch and the blood boils with hate and the mind has closed, the leader will have no need in seizing the rights of the citizenry. Rather, the citizenry, infused with fear and blinded by patriotism, will offer up all of their rights unto the leader and gladly so. . . .

A famous quote about the drawbacks of patriotism that is credited by many to Gaius Julius Caesar (100 BCE–44 BCE)

The worldwide enthusiasm for the election of Barack Obama signaled a global desire for change, people around the world are sick of the lies and wars, of the guns and bombs. A return to the rule of law and an end to the Iraq war is what Obama promised, not only to the American electorate, but to the entire world. The election of the first Black President was an ecstatic moment for people of colour around the world, as it was for those White populations sickened by the racism and violence of American empire-building. People around the world took Obama up on his promise of hope, daring to believe that political change was coming. Whether President-Elect Obama will, or can deliver what he promised is a question people of colour passionately debate with eyes wide open.

Dr. Sunera Thobani, UBC women's studies professor and expert on nationalism and immigration (2009)

Naturally the common people don't want war. . . . That is understood. But, after all, it is the leaders of the country who determine the policy and it is always a simple matter to drag the people along, whether it is a democracy, or a fascist dictatorship, or a parliament, or a communist dictatorship. Voice or no voice, the people can always be brought to the bidding of the leaders. That is easy. All you have to do is tell them they are being attacked, and denounce the peacemakers for lack of patriotism and exposing the country to danger. It works the same in any country.

Hermann Goering, president of the Reichstag, Nazi Party, and Luftwaffe commander in chief, testifying at the Nuremberg Trials in 1946 (in Gilbert 1995)

Nations must understand that a casualty spent in Rwanda trying to resolve conflict has as much significance as one in the defence of our nation, because, as Kofi Annan wrote . . . "we are in the millennium of humanity. All humans are human. Not one human is more human than the other."

Canadian Lt. General Romeo Dallaire on the need for Canada's military to assist those in need, stabilize situations, and provide an atmosphere for rebuilding in war-torn nations (in Barris n.d.)

Deep down we must have a real affection for each other, a clear realization or recognition of our shared human status. At the same time, we must openly accept all ideologies and systems as means of solving humanity's problems. One country, one nation, one ideology, one system is not sufficient. It is helpful to have a variety of different approaches on the basis of a deep feeling of the basic sameness of humanity. We can then make a joint effort to solve the problems of the whole of humankind. The problems human society is facing in terms of economic development, the crisis of energy, the tension between the poor and the rich nations, and many geopolitical problems can be solved if we understand each other's fundamental humanity, respect each other's rights, share each other's problems and sufferings, and then make a joint effort to address them.

His Holiness the Dalai Lama, speaking about pathways to peace (1990:13)

With the collapse of the former Soviet Union and the end of the Cold War between the United States and the former Soviet bloc in the 1980s, prospects for world peace were bright. This hope was challenged in 2001 by the United States' declaration of sustained war against nations that harbour terrorism. The war was mandated to expand anywhere in the world and has been fought with the participation of several other allied nations, including Canada. In 2003, Iraq was invaded by the United States, which maintained that the Iraqi government, with its nuclear capacities and potential for terrorist activity, posed a threat to the world. Citizens across the globe feared this would mark the beginning of World War III. In spite of extensive searches for the so-called weapons of mass destruction, the U.S. government was forced to concede that these weapons did not exist and that Saddam Hussein did not in fact have links to al Qaeda (McQuaig 2006). Today, combat troops are still in Iraq, and though they are scheduled to leave by August 2010, up to 50 000 troops will remain as part of "advisory and assistance brigades."

The U.S. "war on terror" is still very active in the Middle East, though it is continually taking on new form and direction, and despite the change in U.S. presidents, the new president, Barack Obama, shows no signs of pulling troops out of Afghanistan either—in fact, he may be intent on just the opposite (Porter 2009).

In addition to the threat of a third world war, there is a civil war in Sri Lanka that has been raging for more than 25 years, along with wars in Africa. Africa, to a greater extent than any other continent, is afflicted by war. Africa has been besieged by over 20 major civil wars since 1960. Among those countries that have experienced recent armed conflict are Rwanda, Somalia, Angola, Sudan, Liberia, and Burundi (Pike 2009).

Military conflicts that result in 1000 battlefield deaths per year have been defined by the United Nations as "major wars" (Pike 2009). In 1965, there were 10 major wars occurring; in 2003, 15; and by mid-2005, this number had been reduced to 8, with approximately two dozen additional "lesser" conflicts going on worldwide. Most of these lesser conflicts are civil or "intrastate" wars, fuelled variously by ethnic, religious, and ideological rationales as well as by economic ones. The factor that sets contemporary major and lesser wars apart from historical ones is that today, most victims are civilians. During World War I, civilians made up fewer than 5 percent of all those killed. Today, 75 percent or more of people killed or wounded in wars are civilians (Pike 2009). Most conflicts are fought primarily with small arms and light weapons, which account for 60 to 90 percent of direct conflict deaths, some 250 000 each year (Gillis 2009:2).

Many countries possess nuclear and chemical weaponry that is capable of destroying all life on the planet (Daley 1997). The importance of peaceful resolutions to armed conflict has never been greater.

The 20th century saw the development of advanced technologies that provided new potential for wars that could be far more deadly than those in the past. These technologies are now defining what war looks like. Long-range, hypersonic munitions that strike from the air have made it unnecessary to send aircraft and soldiers into the theatre of war (Friedman and Friedman 1996). Moreover, the stockpile of nuclear weapons from the arms race between the former Soviet Union and the West has vastly increased the potential for waging war on a massive scale.

In olden times when there was a war, it was a human-to-human confrontation. The victor in battle would directly see the blood and suffering of the defeated enemy. Nowadays, it is much more terrifying because a man in an office can push a button and kill millions of people and never see the human tragedy he has created. The mechanization of human conflict poses an increasing threat to peace. (Dalai Lama 1991:6).

This scenario was recently poised to play out exactly as the Dalai Lama suggests. In a 2005 press conference on the Nuclear Non-Proliferation Treaty Review Conference that was occurring at the time, former United States Secretary of Defense Robert McNamara stated that

the United States had deployed about 6000 strategic nuclear warheads. . . . Each one on average had a destructive power of roughly 20 times that of the Hiroshima bomb, which killed something on the order of 100 000 civilians. Of those 6000 weapons, 2000 were on hair trigger alert, ready to launch on a 15-minute warning by the decision of one man—the President of the United States. The so-called "football" was at his side 24 hours a day, 365 days a year. (United Nations 2005)

However, as the capability of waging mechanized war is increasing, so too is global resistance to it. As social analyst and critic Barbara Ehrenreich (1997:239) has said:

If the twentieth century brought the steady advance of war and war-related enterprises, it also brought the beginnings of organized resistance to war . . . in the situation where everyone is expected to participate in one way or another, and where anyone can become a victim whether they participate or not, opposition to the institution of war itself could at last develop.

This chapter will examine some of the characteristics of war and terrorism and look at Canada's role in past and upcoming conflicts. We will examine some of the consequences of war—even before it happens, in Canada's case—and look at possible explanations for seeing war as a solution to global conflicts. Finally, we will look at resistance and prospects for peace and discuss the roles and effectiveness of citizens' groups in opposing war.

WAR AS A SOCIAL PROBLEM

What is war? Most people think of war as armed conflict between two countries or two factions within a country, such as the historical 1775 U.S. invasion of the St. Lawrence region of Quebec or the Korean War of 1950. But social scientists define *war* more broadly, including not only *declared* wars between nations or parties but also *undeclared* wars, civil and guerrilla wars, covert operations, and some forms of terrorism (Wright 1964). To social scientists, *general warfare* refers to violent armed conflict between nations, whereas *regional warfare* refers to conflict between rival factions located within a specific geographic area. Social scientists also say that societies that are prepared at all times for war possess a **war system**—components of social institutions (e.g., the economy, government, and education) and cultural beliefs and practices that promote the development of warriors, weapons, and war as a normal part of the society and its foreign policy (Cancian and Gibson 1990).

How, then, do social scientists define *peace*? Sociologists Francesca M. Cancian and James William Gibson (1990) believe that peace is a less clearly defined concept than war. Cancian and Gibson note that people generally agree that peace is highly desirable, but they often have different ideas of what constitutes peace. Some equate peace with harmonious relations in a world where there is no bloodshed between groups; but sometimes nations equate peace with prevailing in battle (Gibson and Cancian 1990). Despite the problems associated with distinguishing between war and peace, we can conclude that both consist of actions and beliefs held by people like ourselves and that these actions and beliefs have serious consequences for individuals, groups, and nations.

THE CHARACTERISTICS OF WAR

First and foremost, war is an institution that involves *violence*—behaviour intended to bring pain, physical injury, psychological stress, and/or death to people or to harm or destroy property (Sullivan 1997). Violence occurs on both micro and macro levels. As we have

seen, violence is a component of many social problems, including violent crime and sexual assault. Both of these are forms of *interpersonal violence* and typically involve a relatively small number of people who are responding to a particular situation or who are pursuing their own personal goals. In contrast, war is a form of **collective violence** that involves organized violence by people seeking to promote their cause or resist social policies or practices that they consider harmful, oppressive, and unjust (Sullivan 1997).

War is an abstract concept for many Canadians. It is less abstract for those who have experienced combat, or who are friends and family members of people who have experienced it, or who are survivors of war. Early in Canada's history, during the fighting of civil wars and rebellions, war was much less abstract: it took place at home or close to home. But in the 20th century, military action was transformed: wars were now fought on foreign soil and vastly more Canadian military personnel were sent into combat. In World War I, for example, Canada, with a population of 8 million people, sent 418 000 of them overseas to fight. In World War II, Canada entered the war with an entirely Canadian command and forces. At that time, Canada had a population of 12 million people, and 1.1 million of them got into uniform (Ehrenreich 1997; Veteran Affairs Canada 2002).

The two world wars were different from each other in a very significant way. In World War I, killing civilians was considered unduly violent, but in World War II civilians were killed intentionally. The targeting of civilians during World War II added a new dimension (Hynes 1997). This is how Ehrenreich (1997:206–207) describes the shift to civilians as the targets of war-related violence:

> By World War II, the destruction (and exploitation) of civilians was deliberate policy on all sides. The British used air power to "de-house" the German population; the U.S. bombed the civilian populations of Hiroshima, Nagasaki, and Dresden; the Germans and Japanese destroyed cities and exploited defeated populations as slave labour. . . . Air power made the mass bombings of civilians possible, but it was the huge involvement of civilians in the industrial side of war that made it seem strategically necessary. . . . In this situation, there were no "innocent" civilians, except

possibly children, and the war took on a genocidal character unknown to the more gentlemanly conflict of [World War I].

One of the most significant characteristics of war is its persistence. Following World War II, Canada emerged as a leading "middle power"—assuming the role of peacekeeper and negotiator in international disputes. This was a natural extension for Canada, as the protocol from 1909 to 1946 was that the prime minister was to serve as the Canadian Secretary of State for External Affairs. Canadian prime ministers have maintained that tradition and have endeavoured to remain prominent in international affairs, taking part in visits from foreign heads of state, world tours, treaty negotiations, and other activities (National Library of Canada 2003). Today, some view Canada as a "moral superpower"—one that exercises a "soft power" when it comes to world affairs. Since 1956, Canada has sent peacekeeping forces into operations around the world. Soldiers, police, and civilians have all played prominent roles in separating armies and in the resolution of conflicts in places such as Cypress, the Middle East, Haiti, Bosnia, Cambodia, El Salvador, and Angola. In 2002, Canadian peacekeepers were serving in 14 operations in Europe, Asia, Africa, South America, and the Middle East. However, more than 160 Canadians were killed while on peacekeeping duties around the world in 2007, and operations in Somalia and Rwanda have led to a crisis of confidence in the Canadian military's peacekeeping efforts (McCluskey 2002). In Somalia in 1993, as part of a United Nations humanitarian effort, members of Canada's elite Airborne Regiment brutally and fatally tortured and beat a Somali teen they took captive. They documented the hours-long torture with photos, marring the international reputation of Canadian soldiers as peacekeepers. Two other unarmed Somali teens were shot in the back by the regiment just days before the murder of 16-year-old Shidane Arone. The whistle blower was physician and major Barry Armstrong. The Airborne Regiment was disbanded after an official inquiry in 1995 (CBC Digital Archives 2009; O'Reilly 1998).

At approximately the same time, UN peacekeeping forces were also stationed in Rwanda, under the leadership of Canadian Brigadier General Romeo Dallaire. The 1993–1994 mission to Rwanda has been nearly unanimously described as "doomed" and as a "failure" of humanity to support the United Nations (Barris n.d.). UN peacekeepers managed to save tens of thousands of

lives but could only stand by as 1 million more people were massacred in the violent civil war. Dallaire had requested 5000 additional soldiers from the UN, but instead had forces cut to 450: "The explosion of genocide could have been prevented. If the political will had been there and if we had been better skilled . . . it could have been prevented" (Veterans Affairs Canada 2009; Barris n.d.:26).

Canada's role in armed conflicts seems to have been shifting over the past two decades. For example, in 1991, we had approximately 1150 soldiers involved in UN peacekeeping missions, but by the fall of 2006, only 55 of the 100 000 UN peacekeepers were Canadian (LaBerge 2008). The legacy of peacekeeping lives on in the Canadian imagination, regardless of the reality, however; in a 2007 public opinion poll, two-thirds of those polled mistakenly agreed that "Canada is an essential

Brigadier General Romeo Dallaire

contributor to peacekeeping" (LaBerge 2008). Recently, Canada seems to have diplomatic trouble maintaining its role as peacekeeper in the world as well as keeping the peace with the United States, our closest neighbour and primary trading partner.

According to Ehrenreich (1997), the end of World War II was marked by the U.S. government's declaration of itself as the "leader of the free world." The ideology supporting this pronouncement gave the nation's political and economic leaders the impetus to perpetuate the United States' position as a world military superpower. Since that time, the American Congress has established defence spending as a national priority, and the U.S. **military–industrial complex**—a term referring to the interdependence of the military establishment and private military contractors—that had emerged during World War II became a massive industrial infrastructure that today produces an array of war-related goods, such as uniforms, tanks, airplanes, and warships. This military–industrial complex flourished during the 1950s, when the international arms race brought about what became known as the *Cold War*—a conflict between nations based on military preparedness and the threat of war but not actual warfare. Between 1950 and the mid-1990s, the U.S. government responded to the perceived "Soviet threat" by spending approximately US$10.2 trillion for its arms buildup. In 1991 alone, the defence industry received more than US$121 billion in government contracts, giving some corporations a virtual monopoly over an entire market in which there was only one buyer (the U.S. government) and very few (if any) competitors.

THE CONSEQUENCES OF WAR

The direct effects of war are loss of human life and serious physical and psychological harm to survivors. It is impossible to determine how many human lives have been lost in wars throughout human history. Were we to attempt to do so, we would need a more precise definition of what constitutes war, and we would have to assume that there would always be survivors available to count the dead (Hynes 1997).

Despite these difficulties, social analyst Ruth Sivard (1991; 1993) has tackled the problem in a limited way. She

determined that 589 wars have been fought by 142 countries since 1500 and that approximately 142 million lives have been lost. But according to Sivard, more lives were lost in wars during the 20th century than in all of the other centuries combined. Since early 2002, when the Canadian military was deployed to Afghanistan, 121 Canadian soldiers, one diplomat and two aid workers have been killed (Canwest News Service 2009). These numbers, while unacceptably high, stand in sharp contrast to the over 100 000 Iraqis, mainly civilians, killed since the beginning of 2003 (Iraq Body Count 2009).

The consequences of all these wars pale when compared to the consequences of an all-out nuclear war. The devastation would be beyond description. Today, some nuclear warheads held by governments throughout the world are more than 4000 times as powerful as the bombs that were dropped on Japan. In fact, scientists estimate that a nuclear war would kill more than 160 million people outright and that more than 1 billion people would die in the first few hours as a result of radiation poisoning, environmental contamination and destruction, and massive social unrest (Friedman and Friedman 1996). At the beginning of 2008, those nations with nuclear weapons (the United States, Britain, France, Russia, China, Pakistan, Israel, and India) possessed more than 23 000 nuclear warheads, more than 8000 of which are operational and several thousand of which are kept on high alert, ready to be launched within minutes (Gillis 2009:3).

Even though an international treaty bans underground nuclear tests, it is believed that a number of nations are developing and stockpiling nuclear weapons. The idea that "others" may be secretly building and stockpiling weapons and the inability to substantiate such claims reliably provided the rationale for the 2003 U.S.–led invasion of Iraq. For example, the Bush Administration claimed that the regime of Iraqi President Saddam Hussein was in possession of **weapons of mass destruction (WMD)**—nuclear, biological, chemical, or radiological weapons that can kill thousands of people and destroy vast amounts of property at one time—and had to be overthrown as a preemptive measure to protect the United States and other nations. When no weapons of mass destruction were found in Iraq, extensive public debate and much criticism of the Bush Administration followed for having inaccurately represented the scope and immediacy of the threat posed (Moeller 2004) (see Box 16.1).

What justifications are sufficient to support a war in which the final death toll is almost certain to include millions of children?

The use of supercomputers and advanced technology has created a new era of military activity. Military technology is rapidly evolving, and often the danger of handling new weapons as well as deploying them is largely unknown. Technology has also impacted military strategy. Today, military strategy calls for deploying bombs and long-range missiles to eliminate the enemy's weapon-production plants and supply centres. Because these plants are located in major cities, civilians are more likely to be killed than they were in the past. The trend toward more civilian casualties that began in World War II has continued in subsequent wars (Colhoun 1992; Ehrenreich 1997). Using Iraq as a contemporary example, of the millions of people in Iraq, nearly 40 percent of the population are children under the age of 14, and the average age in Iraq is 20.4 years (Bellamy 2003; CIA 2009). Moreover, hospitals are typically damaged or destroyed. In some cases, when nearby power plants are hit, hospitals can no longer operate basic equipment or provide emergency medical care to people injured by bombs (Burleigh 1991). With each successive war, more civilians are killed. What justifications are sufficient to support a war in which the final death toll is almost certain to include millions of children (Hicks et al. 2009)?

SOCIAL PROBLEMS IN GLOBAL PERSPECTIVE

BOX 16.1   "Weapons of Mass Destruction": Political Spin and Media Framing of a War

June 25, 2008: **What I do know is that war should only be waged when necessary, and the Iraq war was not necessary.**

—Scott McClellan (2008), former White House press secretary, wrote in his memoir, *What Happened: Inside the Bush White House and Washington's Culture of Deception,* that he had been mislead by Administration officials about the necessity for war with Iraq and that he, in turn, unintentionally misinformed the media and the general public about the alleged importance of the war to spread democracy in the Middle East.

March 17, 2003: **Intelligence gathered by this and other governments leaves no doubt that the Iraq regime continues to possess and conceal some of the most lethal weapons ever devised. . . . [We] cannot live under the threat of blackmail. The terrorist threat to America and the world will be diminished the moment that Saddam Hussein is disarmed.**

—President George W. Bush (2003b) in an address to the nation

March 19, 2003: **The people of the United States and our friends and allies will not live at the mercy of an outlaw regime that threatens the peace with weapons of mass murder.**

—President George W. Bush (2003a) in an address to the nation

These statements by a former government official and by then President George W. Bush show the contentious nature of what has happened in the United States in regards to the war in Iraq. During the weeks before the U.S. invasion of Iraq on March 20, 2003, former President George W. Bush conveyed the message to journalists and the general public that he believed an invasion of Iraq, with the subsequent removal of President Saddam Hussein from office and the establishment of a new government, were necessary to protect vital security interests of the United States and other nations. Through extensive media coverage of the president's comments on weapons of mass destruction and the imminent threat posed by Saddam Hussein, the "war on terror" was launched, making Iraq the "big" international news story and overshadowing coverage of the U.S. military's unsuccessful search in Afghanistan for Osama bin

Laden, the alleged mastermind behind a number of terrorist attacks.

Many news reporters and television anchors quickly embraced the language of war, including terms such as "weapons of mass destruction" (WMD) and "war on terror." Stations that carry "all news, all the time," such as the FOX cable news network, had a dramatic increase in the number of viewers because of their patriotic spin on the "situation" in Iraq and what the United States should do about it (BBC News 2003). And, although he now apparently regrets his decision, Scott McClellan helped to publicize this perspective to the world as the president's press secretary.

Does it matter how the media cover topics such as war and terrorism? According to one media scholar, "The public relies on the media to separate facts and tangible realities from assumptions and spin" (Moeller 2004). How well did the media perform in this case? Not very well, according to journalism scholar Susan D. Moeller (2004), whose study provides insights on how political spin may be incorporated into media

What should we do when we think that political leaders and journalists are not providing us with the information we need to make informed judgments about what we think Canada should do with regard to domestic and international problems?

framing of news stories about war and terror. "Spin" is the act of selectively describing or deliberately shading an event in a way that favours one partisan response over another or that attempts to control a negative political reaction before it fully emerges and becomes detrimental to the spinners' interests (based on Safire 1993; see Chapter 14).

As you will recall, journalists use a variety of frames to shape the news stories they present to their audiences. Frames are cognitive shortcuts that help readers and viewers make sense of social life. Facts have no intrinsic meaning and instead take on meaning when they are embedded in a frame or story line that organizes them and gives them coherence.

Anticipating opposition to launching a war against Saddam Hussein, particularly when U.S. military personnel were already deployed in Afghanistan and the country had numerous other pressing problems, political leaders used "spin" in their speeches and conversations with the media to aggressively market the war before their critics could attempt to refute claims that Hussein possessed WMDs or disagree about linkages between Iraq and international terrorist activity. Many journalists and news commentators absorbed the political language of the WMD debate when they framed their news reports, adding credibility to the administration's claims (Moeller 2004). The following are findings in Moeller's (2004:11) study of media coverage of the weapons of mass destruction issue:

- Virtually all news coverage of WMDs did not question the political formulation of "weapons of mass destruction" as a single category of threat.

- Based on political spin, the media associated mass destruction agents with the phenomenon of terrorism despite the fact that no terrorist organization had demonstrated the capability of performing an act of mass destruction under a strict definition of that term.

- Media framing of stories on WMDs and war results less from political bias on the part of journalists, editors, and producers than from the use of standard journalistic procedures such as the "inverted pyramid" style of news writing that gives the "lead" in stories to the "most important" information and/or the "most important" players. In the case of reporting on WMDs and problems in Iraq, the president of the United States and other top officials in his administration would be considered the most important players (Moeller 2004:iii).

From a sociological perspective, Moeller's findings should encourage us to take a new look at how political spin and media framing might influence our beliefs on war, as well as other social problems. What should we do when we think that political leaders and journalists are not providing us with the information we need to make informed judgments about what we think Canada should do with regard to domestic and international problems?

Civilians are not the only ones adversely affected by war. Veteran Affairs Canada provides benefits to veterans who served in wars that Canada has been involved in (Veteran Affairs Canada 2002). Many of these veterans are totally disabled, and not all injuries sustained in wars are physical. We have no accurate count of the soldiers and civilians—of all nations involved—who experience psychological trauma that affects them the remainder of their lives. One psychological disorder that has been getting a great deal of attention in recent years is known as *post-traumatic stress disorder* (PTSD). Symptoms include difficulty sleeping and concentrating, anxiety, and recurring flashbacks or nightmares, many of which are triggered by loud, sudden noises such as thunder, automobiles backfiring, or other things that sound like gunshots or explosions. When some stimulus triggers a flashback, the individual re-experiences the horror of some deeply traumatic wartime event. High rates of drug abuse and suicide among war veterans are attributed to PTSD.

Civilians in Canada have shown evidence of high levels of PTSD from participating in military operations; for example, medical staff and war correspondents suffer from the effects of witnessing death and destruction. Many of the artists commissioned to paint the World War I and II canvasses also suffered deep depression and other emotional side-effects upon returning from the wars (Abbott 2000). PTSD, however, is most documented among war vets and peacekeepers. In Canada, 20 percent of peacekeeping troops are believed to have the symptoms. Consider, for example, the psychological effects experienced by General Romeo Dallaire, the UN commander in Rwanda who left that country, shaken and suicidal, to go on indefinite sick leave:

It took nearly two years ... of ... not being able to cope; not being able to hide it; not being able to forget it or to put it in, keep it in a drawer.... I became suicidal because there was no other solution. You couldn't live with the pain and the sounds and the smell and the sights. I couldn't sleep. I couldn't stand the loudness of silence.... And sometimes I wish I had lost a leg instead of having all those brain cells screwed up. You lose a leg, it's obvious; you've got therapy, all kinds of stuff. You lose your marbles; very very difficult to explain, very difficult to gain that support that you need. But those who don't recognize it and don't go to get the help are going to be at risk to themselves and to us. (CBC TV 1999)

Today many war veterans are suspicious that military doctors are reluctant to diagnose PTSD because this diagnosis can oblige the government to make lifetime disability payments to those affected. According to the organization Veterans Against the Iraq War, doctors may be encouraged to either not diagnose PTSD or to misdiagnose it as a minor anxiety disorder. Money that goes to the treatment of injured soldiers and to those with psychological disorders like PTSD may be seen as being diverted from financing weapons and the army generally (Yoanna and Benjamin 2009).

While we cannot put a price tag on loss of life, physical disability, or psychological trauma associated with war, we know that the direct economic costs of war are astronomical. Consider, for example, that since the 1990s, military budgets have risen 45 percent (Gillis 2009:1) and around the world in 2008, governments spent approximately US$1464 billion to arm themselves (Hill and Acheson 2008). This number represents US$216 for every person in the world. The figure for the United States alone was US$607 billion or nearly 42 percent of the total (Gillis 2009:2). In 2008, Canada's military spending budget was $18.2 billion, 27 percent higher than prior to 9/11, and the 2008 budget pledged a 2 percent per year increase in Canada's military for 20 years, beginning in 2011, adding an additional $20 billion over the 20 years (CBC News 2008a; Gillis, 2009:2; Staples and Robinson 2007).

To put defence and war-related expenditures in perspective, 30 years ago, one analyst calculated that a single aircraft carrier would build 12 000 high schools, and the cost of developing one new bomber would pay the annual salaries of 250 000 teachers to staff the schools (de Silva 1980). Within the 26-member NATO alliance, Canada now occupies sixth place (from seventh) in terms of military spending (CBC News 2008a; Staples and Robinson 2007).

War on Ecology

Ecological and human health is an important aspect of military activity. Landscapes and human bodies reveal a great deal about the long-term effects of violence, toxicity, and invasions. As images of ecological devastation and human suffering around the world are depicted in mainstream media, such as on CNN, it is becoming more and more difficult to ignore these issues. People are also recognizing that, in this global era, citizens and their economies, health, and environments are interconnected. In a recent brief to the International Peace Bureau (IPB) in Geneva, Disarmament Coordinator for the Bureau David Hay-Edie (2002:2) advised:

> Some of the major threats to human security come from the deterioration of the physical environment. Air and water pollution, the depletion of underground water tables, deforestation, desertification, loss of biodiversity, and above all climate change, are having profound effects on many societies today. . . . Military activities place a number of stresses on the physical environment, but their contribution to overall environmental deterioration has not received its share of attention.

To illustrate Hay-Edie's concerns: the world's military forces are responsible for more than two-thirds of the chlorofluorocarbon-113 released into the ozone layer. For example, if the current war was ranked as a nation in terms of emissions, it would emit more CO_2 annually than 139 nations—the equivalent of 25 million more cars on the road in the United States in one year (Reisch and Kretzmann 2008). Greenpeace and the European Renewable Energy Council have estimated that global investment needs to reach $2.89 billion by 2030 in order to achieve a 50 percent reduction in CO_2 emissions by 2050 and to help avoid average warming over two degrees centigrade (Greenpeace and European Renewable Energy Council 2007; Reisch and Kretzmann 2008).

In the early 2000s, the estimated cost to clean up military-related sites was thought to be more than $500 billion (Hay-Edie 2002:2). However, in a recent book by Stiglitz and Bilmes (2008), the total budgetary cost of the current war (operations plus veteran's benefits and other military expenses) is realistically

War can have disastrous ecological effects.

estimated to be US$2.655 trillion. What is the cost to Canada? Each additional war, terrorist attack, military training manoeuvre, and peacetime nuclear test adds to this social and ecological debt.

The impact of specific conflicts and wars must be considered. The use of chemical and biological warfare—such as scorched-earth tactics, "Agent Orange," and other toxic materials felt to be linked to the Gulf War "syndrome"—are all examples of the long-term impacts these weapons have. In Vietnam, for example, about one-third of the country was rendered a wasteland by military activity. It will take many generations to repair these agricultural areas. In the Gulf War, 4 to 8 million barrels of oil spilled into the sea, damaging 740 kilometres of coastline—creating an inestimable loss for generations to come. Air attacks in Kuwait and during the NATO military action in Kosovo and the Federal Republic of Yugoslavia have destroyed oil refineries and caused the leakage of oil products and chemicals into lands, rivers, lakes, and oceans (Hay-Edie 2002). The U.S.–led attack on Iraq damaged their water and sewage systems as well as the nation's fragile desert ecosystem. Additionally, oil well fires spew smoke across the countryside (Institute for Policy Studies and Foreign Policy In Focus 2004). These actions devastate the integrity of drinking water, arable land, yards, school grounds, and public parks, as well as natural habitats and ecological reserves.

As humans and the earth are connected, toxic attacks on the earth are equally damaging to humans. One particularly potent hazard to human and ecological health is depleted uranium—a waste product that arises during the production of enriched uranium for nuclear weapons and reactors. It is a very dense material that has the capability of slicing through heavily armoured vehicles. Seventy percent of the uranium burns on impact, turning into a fine ceramic dust of depleted uranium oxide particles that get distributed across great distances by wind and water activity. One of the most devastating aspects about this compound is that it has a radioactive half-life of 4.5 billion years. Environmental educator Guy Dauncey (2003:1) states:

> This means that the cities, battlefields, and locations where depleted uranium is used will be radioactive and remain radioactive for the next 4.5 billion years. . . . That's as long as the Earth has existed. That's twice as long as the entire evolution of life on Earth. Seventy times longer than the time since the dinosaurs became extinct.

Depleted uranium was used by the U.S. army in Iraq, in Kosovo, and in Afghanistan. Even though the United Nations wants a worldwide ban on it, reports indicate that the United States is currently using it in its war against Iraq: "U.S.-fired depleted uranium weapons have contributed to pollution of Iraq's land and water, with inevitable spillover effects in other countries. The heavily polluted Tigris River, for example, flows through Iraq, Iran and Kuwait" (Dauncey 2003:1; Institute for Policy Studies and Foreign Policy in Focus 2004).

There are several reasons why the military continues to contribute to the devastation of human and ecological health. One is an antiquated notion of maintaining national security through traditional military methods. In a global age characterized by interdependence as well as by the ability to end life on earth with the "flick of a switch," old techniques of arms build-up and confrontation are no longer appropriate. There is also an underlying ideological view of the earth as an infinite resource that allows for incredible assaults against ecological integrity to occur without significant thought about the qualitative and quantitative results of these actions. Finally, there is a refusal to see the military as a money-making "industry" and an unwillingness to submit armed forces to levels of transparency and accountability that are required of other governmental or civil-society actors. But the increasingly widespread evidence of the profound impacts of landmines, nuclear testing, and other invasive military techniques on the environment is beginning to change this (Hay-Edie 2002). Rosalie Bertlee, winner of the International Peace Bureau's Sean MacBride Peace Prize in 2001, insists that we must set up a co-operative, not a dominant, relationship with the earth—this is in part because ultimately the gift of life is the legacy we pass on to our children and the generations to follow (International Peace Bureau 2001).

GLOBAL TERRORISM

Terrorism is the use of calculated, unlawful physical force or threats of violence against a government, organization, or individual to gain some political, religious, economic, or social objective. Terrorists, however, are often difficult to conclusively identify, because those who are perceived as terrorists in one country may be perceived as freedom fighters by another. There are some things that are relatively easy to agree upon however, such as identification and assessment of terrorist tactics. Typically, these include bombing, kidnapping, hostage taking, hijacking, assassination, and extortion (Vetter and Perlstein 1991). Although terrorists sometimes attack government officials and members of the military, they more often target civilians as a way of pressuring the government.

Collective violence and terrorism share certain commonalities with war. Both terrorism and war pose major threats to world stability and domestic safety. Terrorism and war also extract a massive toll on individuals and societies by producing rampant fear, widespread loss of human life, and extensive destruction of property and the environment.

One form of terrorism—political terrorism—is actually considered a form of unconventional warfare. *Political terrorism* uses intimidation, coercion, threats of harm, and other violent attempts to bring about a significant change in or overthrow of an existing government. There are three types of political terrorism: revolutionary terrorism, repressive terrorism, and state-sponsored terrorism.

Revolutionary terrorism refers to acts of violence against civilians that are carried out by internal enemies of the government who want to bring about political change. Some groups believe that if they perpetrate enough random terrorist acts, they will achieve a political goal. Modern terrorism is not always based in a single country, as we have learned from efforts to apprehend Osama bin Laden and the al Qaeda network, who have been accused of planning the September 11, 2001, attacks on the United States and attacks at other times and sites associated with U.S. interests and citizens. Money usually is a crucial ingredient in terrorism, and following the so-called money trail has been a key way in which law enforcement agencies have sought to apprehend those accused of violent terrorist attacks and of financing terrorism. In some circumstances, revolutionary terrorists receive economic help from other governments that support their objectives (Vetter and Perlstein 1991).

Unlike revolutionary terrorism, **repressive terrorism** is conducted by a government against its own citizens for the purpose of protecting an existing

Protestors marching against the "War on Terror".

political order. Repressive terrorism has taken place in many countries around the world, including Haiti, the People's Republic of China, and Cambodia, where the Pol Pot regime killed more than 1 million people in the four years between 1975 and 1979 (Mydans, in Pran 1997).

In the third type of political terrorism, **state-sponsored terrorism,** a government provides financial resources, weapons, and training for terrorists who conduct their activities in other nations. In Libya, for example, Colonel Muammar Qaddafi provided money and training for terrorist groups such as the Arab National Youth Organization, which was responsible for skyjacking a Lufthansa airplane over Turkey and forcing the Bonn government to free the surviving members of the terrorist group responsible for killing Israeli Olympic athletes in the 1970s (Parry 1976). Other countries that have been charged with using terrorism as a form of surrogate warfare include Iran, Syria, Yugoslavia, Bulgaria, Israel, and the United States (Vetter and Perlstein 1991). The United States conducted surrogate warfare when it supported the Contras, who waged war against the Sandinista government of Nicaragua until the Sandinistas were defeated in a 1990 election (Vetter and Perlstein 1991).

Terrorism also occurs intra-nationally. Domestic terrorism is sometimes referred to as "home-grown terrorism" by the media because the perpetrator is usually a resident of the country in which the incident occurs or has other strong ties to the country, such as relatives or acquaintances who live there. Like international terrorism, domestic terrorism typically is used to reach some political goal. The most famous example of Canadian domestic terrorism involves the Front de Liberation du Quebec (FLQ), which sought to turn Quebec into an independent state. In the late 1960s, the group set off several bombs, and in the 1970s, they kidnapped British Trade Commissioner James Cross and Quebec's Liberal Labour and Immigration minister, Pierre Laporte. Prime Minister Pierre Trudeau invoked the *War Measures Act* in response to the kidnappings. The night after the *War Measures Act* was proclaimed, Laporte's body was found in the trunk of an abandoned car. Eventually, Cross was freed by his captors, who were given free passage to Cuba in exchange for his life (NFB 1973; Zolf 2003). There were no similar incidents of domestic terrorism in Canada since that time until fall 2008.

Since October 2008, the EnCana natural gas pipeline in northeastern British Columbia has been the target of several explosions. The first occurred just shortly after EnCana received a letter demanding it cease operations in the area. Then, in July 2009, a local newspaper received a second letter addressed to EnCana, alerting the company and the RCMP Anti-Terrorism Unit—the Integrated National Security Enforcement Team—that the company would be given a three-month reprieve to formulate plans to withdraw from the area. The letters' authors also recommended that EnCana shift its focus to green alternative fuels (Stolte 2009). To date, no one has been injured in the blasts, and apparently there is no danger to the public or to the environment from the leaks caused by them. At the point this book went to press, no one had been arrested in connection with the explosions. However, the reward for information leading to conviction, in what the RCMP is calling "domestic

terrorism," has been increased to $1 million by EnCana (Mercer 2009; Stolte 2009).

How widespread is terrorism? Despite popular conviction that global terrorism is on the increase, researchers at Simon Fraser University suggest that it is actually declining (SFU 2008). It is difficult to measure terrorism-related deaths due to differences in data recording and inconsistent records. Definitions of "terrorism" and "attack" appear to vary greatly globally. New statistics would appear to show, in some cases, that terrorism-related deaths have increased dramatically. SFU researchers report, however, that this seeming increase comes from the new practice by some groups of counting the large percentage of deadly assaults against civilians by non-state armed groups in civil wars (SFU 2008). This counting approach is unusual because the intentional killing of civilians in wartime is not normally described as "terrorism," but as a "war crime" or "crime against humanity" (SFU 2008).

CANADIAN POLITICS AND TERRORISM

Canada was quick to show its support to the United States in the form of infrastructural, citizen, and military support; freezing the assets of suspected terrorists; and working with the United States to improve security along the 8850-kilometre Canada–U.S. border (Council on Foreign Relations 2003). Canada also supported the NATO decision to invoke Article V of the NATO charter, which declares an armed attack against any member of the council is considered "an attack against them all." In October 2001, former Canadian Prime Minister Jean Chrétien committed Canadian forces to the U.S.–led war in Afghanistan (Ljunngren 2003). And since the fall of the Taliban regime in late 2001, Canadian involvement in Afghanistan has increased steadily. In fact, the military mission in Afghanistan could cost Canadians up to $1.8 billion, or $1500 per household, by 2011. These costs are likely to be an underestimation of the total costs of the mission, however, noted a report created by the parliamentary budget officer (CBC 2009). U.S. President Barack Obama has asked NATO allies to continue the fight against the resurgent Taliban (CBC 2009). At this point, Canada has made no new promises.

Sociologists critically analyze the motives and actions of people and their governments in times of war or anticipated war. They ask questions such as, "Why is Canada participating in the 'war on terror' in the ways it is, and how are these actions affecting people in Canada?"

Historically, wars and periods of national crisis have resulted in serious and unjustified losses of civil rights for many, and especially for immigrants, refugees, and people of colour. This is because war is not simply a fight for justice; rather, war is an institution that shapes the economic, environmental, civic, ideological, and political activities and practices of civilians and governments. For example, almost immediately after the September 11 attack in New York, the Canadian federal government passed Bill C-36, an *Anti-Terrorism Act*. Bill C-36 is a key component of the government of Canada's anti-terrorism plan and gives wide-ranging powers to the government, presumably to deal with the threat of terrorism. The controversial December 2001 omnibus bill has four objectives:

1. Stop terrorists from getting into Canada and protect Canadians from terrorist acts.
2. Bring forward tools to identify, prosecute, convict, and punish terrorists.
3. Prevent the Canada–U.S. border from being held hostage by terrorists and impacting on the Canadian economy.
4. Work with the international community to bring terrorists to justice and address the root causes of such hatred (Department of Justice 2001).

The bill was passed in haste and within a panicked civic environment. It comes under the *Criminal Code* and is linked to at least 12 UN Anti-Terrorism Conventions. Unlike the *War Measures Act*, Bill C-36 is not emergency legislation. It changed, forever, laws and conduct under the *Criminal Code*, the *Official Secrets Act*, the *Privacy Act*, and the *Canada Evidence Act*.

The government maintained that this act ensured that Canadian values of respect and fairness are preserved and "rigorous safeguards ensure that the fundamental rights and freedoms of Canadians are upheld" (Department of Justice 2001). The Canadian Centre for Policy Alternatives (CCPA), in a brief to the House of Commons Justice Committee, challenged this proclamation. The following are the aspects of the

bill that the CCPA (2003) identified as posing the greatest potential for civil liberties violations or for rendering our justice system and government more secretive and less accountable:

- the definition of "terrorist activity," which could encompass legitimate protest and dissent;
- the process whereby organizations are put on a public "terrorist" list without procedural protections;
- the vague definitions of the new terrorist offences of "participating, facilitating, instructing and harbouring," offences that carry substantial penalties;
- intrusive new investigative procedures, including a new investigatory hearing that removes the right to silence;
- important changes to the *Privacy Act* and the *Access to Information Act* that would prohibit the disclosure of information to Canadians; and
- the creation of new layers of scrutiny for charities that will significantly hamper their legitimate operations.

Generally speaking, Bill C-36 was criticized because many Canadians believed that many of its features were incompatible with our existing *Charter of Rights and Freedoms*. Some provisions of the bill regarding preventative arrest and investigative hearings expired in March 2007, despite the urgings of the Conservative government to renew them.

Bill C-36, similar to the U.S. *Patriot Act*, passed at the same time, is not the only controversial bill. Other bills that were ratified around the same time included the new *Citizenship of Canada Act* (Bill C-18—replacing the 1977 *Citizenship Act*), the *Immigration and Refugee Protection Act* (Bill C-11), and the *Public Safety Act* (Bill C-42).

Bill C-42 raises anxieties about the need to balance fundamental rights with security interests. Of particular concern is a provision that allows the Minister of Defence to declare certain areas—even in major cities—security zones, thereby curtailing the right of peaceful assembly and protest (Canadian Human Rights Commission 2003). Given the extent of legitimate and peaceful protest against the G-20 and various trade acts, many people see this bill as being more about unfettered access to trade than about citizen "security" per se. The Ontario Council of Agencies Serving Immigrants (OCASI) is concerned that Bill C-18 will create a two-tiered approach to citizenship in Canada—the implications of which are immensely disturbing. For example, a child born outside of Canada to a first-generation Canadian (even if the mother has lived all but the first couple of months of her life in Canada) does not have the right to citizenship and may even become stateless. There are no citizenship restrictions faced by a Canadian-born mother who lives outside of the country but gives birth in Canada (Casipullai 2003). The bill also gives broad powers to Cabinet to refuse citizenship to a person who has "demonstrated a flagrant and serious disregard for the principles and values underlying a free and democratic society" (in Casipullai 2003). The act does not clearly outline the aforementioned "principles" and "values" but rather leaves it up to the interpretation of cabinet ministers and other individuals in a given historical moment. The possibility of an abuse of power and a decision to refuse citizenship within this framework is real. The revocation of citizenship is yet another potential for the violation of human rights, as is the policy that evidence used against an individual in an immigration process may not be disclosed to the person in question, giving a person no way of addressing, or even knowing about, allegations against them (in Casipullai 2003).

The impact of these bills is already being felt by many people—most significantly, those involved in immigration processes, those who belong to "visible minorities," and those citizens who are the victims of racialized or ethnic profiling. Some critics say that these are all cases of *scapegoating*—a process where people blame visible and generally marginalized "others" for a perceived threat. The implementation of tighter immigration laws, legislation such as that discussed above, and cases of civilian hostility against people most easily identified as immigrants and refugees are all aspects of this larger movement of "nationalist protectionism." Many point out, however, that these attitudes are not new. Rather, feelings of vulnerability to attack lead people to create a hostile climate where underlying attitudes of suspicion, discrimination, and intolerance gain strength and even become institutionalized as new legislation and policies (Choudry 2001). Recalling the internment of Japanese Canadians and German Canadians during World War II provides easy examples.

Ethnic or racialized profiling is a controversial policing technique that involves identifying and pursuing suspects on the basis of their ethnicity or racialization. It is becoming increasingly common practice among Canada–U.S. immigration officers in a post-9/11 world. While proponents of ethnic/racialized profiling say that it can provide a government with a tool for risk analysis, they acknowledge that it inevitably involves injustices (Gillis 2001). The result is that a person fitting the profile for a "high-risk" group—these days, a person from any of Afghanistan, Algeria, Bahrain, Djibouti, Egypt, Eritrea, Indonesia, Iran, Iraq, Jordan, Kuwait, Lebanon, Libya, Malaysia, Morocco, Oman, Pakistan, Qatar, Saudi Arabia, Somalia, Sudan, Syria, Tunisia, Turkey, the United Arab Emirates, and Yemen—may be searched, fingerprinted, photographed, registered, detained, and even deported without real evidence of wrongdoing. As the criterion for this invasive treatment is a person's ethnicity or racialization, authorities assume that all people from certain ethnic/racialized groups have the potential to be affiliated with terrorists from their country (or region) of origin—or of ancestral origin—and could therefore pose a threat to national security. An example of this is the case of one of Canada's most celebrated writers, Indian-born Canadian Rohinton Mistry. Mistry was given such humiliating and traumatic treatment by U.S. border officials while on a U.S. book release tour that he cancelled the second half of tour (Gillis 2001).

The most notorious example is found in the case of Maher Arar. In September 2002, Arar, a Syrian-born Canadian engineer, on his way home to Montreal from Zurich after a family vacation, landed at Kennedy Airport in New York. U.S. authorities suspected ties to al Qaeda and deported him to Syria without consulting Canadian officials. When Canada's Foreign Affairs Department learned of the deportation, they protested it, saying there was no information that the man posed a security threat, but to no avail (Arar 2009; *Migration News* 2002). While he was imprisoned, Arar was beaten, tortured, refused contact with family or a lawyer, and forced to make a false confession (Arar 2009). He was finally released in October 2003 and returned home to Canada. In September 2006, Arar was finally cleared of all terrorism allegations, based on the fact that there was "no evidence to indicate that Mr. Arar has committed any offence or that his activities constitute a threat to the security of Canada" (Arar 2009).

Ethnic/racialized profiling is a procedural practice that affects Canadians of all walks of life. Andrew

Telegdi (2002), Minster of Parliament for Kitchener–Waterloo, addressed Parliament in November 2002:

> We are a nation of immigrants who come from all over the world. . . . Fifty-two members of the House were not born in Canada. . . . There are members of Parliament who originally came from some of those [targeted] countries. . . . Under these procedures they too are subjected to being registered and having their fingerprints taken. . . . I understand that in the context of 9/11 we do look at the world in a different fashion but practices such as ethnic profiling do not work. They require a great deal of resources and they are not effective.

Ethnic/racialized profiling in fact exacerbates the racism found throughout Canada by giving people formal, or state-sanctioned, justifications for their dislikes. Today, the subjective character of immigration practices and the vulnerability of immigrants is a great concern for Canada. Clearly, the numerous changes that have been made to the immigration and citizenship acts in Canada contain potential threats to present and future citizens' civil liberties. While this is true, mechanisms of appeal, such as the Refugee Appeal Division (RAD) of Bill C-18, have not yet been implemented even though all other aspects of the bill have been. The result is that those people denied refugee status by the Immigration and Refugee Board of Canada still do not have a means of recourse (Neve 2003). This is particularly important for those individuals seeking asylum in Canada who face harsh penalties in their countries of origin.

The Canada Race Relations Foundation (CRRF) has tried to put current legislative activities into a historical context. It has drawn the country's attention to the injustices suffered by the Japanese Canadian community during World War II and attempted to draw parallels to the current "backlash" being visited today upon Muslim and Arab Canadians in a post-9/11 world. "We have witnessed grave injustices that befell a community and, from this, have a clearer understanding of what can arise in response to increased security concerns in a society that has not yet stripped itself of racism" (CRRF 2001). Indeed, Indigenous people and other non-White Canadian citizens have always faced, and continue to face, "racial" profiling, not only in war times, but also in everyday life. "Racial" profiling accompanies racist attitudes and structures. This is not a new phenomenon, although a broader awareness does seem new. In this current historical moment, Canadians are actively engaged in shaping the face of Canadian politics. In this global age, people understand that all things are connected—including the causes and effects of war and terrorism on national and international levels.

SOCIAL PROBLEMS IN THE MEDIA

BOX 16.2   The First Casualty of War Is Truth

On October 1, 2001, Sunera Thobani, sociologist, professor of women's studies at the University of British Columbia, and former president of the National Action Committee on the Status of Women, addressed the Women's Resistance—From Victimization to Criminalization conference in Ottawa. In her address, Thobani, who is an expert in globalization, citizenship, immigration, and nationalism, spoke out in opposition to colonialism and imperialism. She criticized the U.S. government's foreign policy and its declaration of a unilateral war against terrorism. In her speech, Thobani (2001a) spoke about military violence and focused her comments on the current U.S.–led build-up to an attack on Iraq, referring to it as another form of patriarchal and racist violence:

> The women's movement, we have to stand up to this. There is no option. There's no option for us, we have to fight back against this militarization, we have to break the support that is being built in our countries for this kind of attack. We have to recognize that the fight is for control of the vast oil and gas resources in central Asia, for which Afghanistan is a key, strategic point! . . . There's nothing new about this, this is more of the same, this is more of the same that we have been now fighting for, for so many decades.

While the 500 people attending Thobani's impassioned and well-researched speech gave her a standing ovation, much of the mainstream media published statements of outrage against her. Newspaper, television, and radio reports asked how this "Tanzanian-born immigrant" dared to speak out against the U.S. government's response to the September 11, 2001, attacks. British Columbia Premier Gordon Campbell called

Thobani's speech "hateful," and an editorial in the right-leaning *National Post* said Thobani "condensed her febrile misandry and vicious anti-war hatred into a spit ball aimed squarely at the memory of those who died on Sept. 11" (in Mick 2001). Others maintained that she was wrong to criticize the Canadian government's position, particularly at a women's conference that had received funding of $80 000 from the federal government (McElroy 2001; O'Neill 2001). Terry O'Neill (2001) of the right-wing magazine *Report* wrote that it is "ironic" that at "one of those all-too-frequent feminist conferences about the alleged evils of the patriarchy," one of Canada's leading multiculturalists had revealed herself to be "ungrateful" and a "first-class hater of the very country that so warmly welcomed her." O'Neill continued, "Ultimately, Ms. Thobani has made it clear that the hotbed from which multiculturalism grows is a noxious mixture of bitterness and envy. . . . At a time when, as President Bush said, you're either with freedom or with the terrorists, it is clear Sunera Thobani has made her choice."

Citizens also wrote editorials to mainstream newspapers in Canada to express their contempt for Sunera Thobani's position. On Saturday, October 13, 2001, the *Vancouver Sun* ran a story with the headline "Thobani's views bring call to halt support for UBC." The article profiled a letter Charles Huntzinger, president and CEO of Imperial Parking, had written to the *Vancouver Sun*. In the letter, Huntzinger accused Thobani of being "anti-American" and called on alumni of the University of British Columbia to withhold contributions to the university for as long as Sunera Thobani is employed there. Huntzinger wrote (2001:XX):

> Obviously in free societies like Canada and the United States, people like Thobani have the right to free speech, even if they are apologists for terrorist murderers. However, Canadians have the right to show their

Sunera Thobani

displeasure towards her attitudes. . . . The idea that such a terrorist sympathizer is teaching your children is a scary picture of the future.

One unnamed B.C. resident even filed a hate crimes complaint with the RCMP against Thobani, accusing her of inciting hatred against Americans.

The same type of coverage was given in the United States. On October 16, 2001, journalist Wendy McElroy gave this report on the FOX News Channel:

> On October 1st, the Tanzanian-born Thobani grabbed headlines by denouncing the "bloodthirsty" U.S. government as "the most dangerous global force" with a "foreign policy . . . soaked in blood." Thobani labeled the War as "patriarchal racist violence" conducted to colonize coloured people. In response to these remarks, Canadian authorities are now investigating Thobani for hate speech. Under Section 319(1) of Canada's Criminal Code, she faces a jail sentence if convicted of inciting public hatred of an "identifiable group"—in this case, Americans—that is likely to lead to a breach of the peace.

McElroy (2001) mused that prosecuting Thobani under hate speech laws has a morbid justice about it: "feminists and the Left have championed these sorts of laws to stifle 'offensive' words and attitudes toward minorities and women. But stifling anyone's speech cannot be tolerated by a free society." McElroy concluded her report with the statement that Thobani had been spreading "intolerance at tax-payer expense since at least as early as 1993" and that as president of Canada's National Action Committee on the Status of Women, "she became notorious for driving the white leadership out of power and for shifting the focus of Canadian feminism away from women and on to race."

Thobani's comments challenged many aspects of the status quo, including the assumption of White hegemony. In a fashion typical of backlash, those people who felt that their privilege was being challenged were quick to fight back. While most called upon the media or the criminal justice system to punish Thobani for her statements, members of government criticized each other for letting her speak. Opposition MPs chastised Canadian Secretary of State Hedy Fry and indicated that the government should fire her for failing to renounce Thobani's statements at the conference itself (McElroy 2001; O'Neill 2001). Chuck Strahl, then deputy leader of the Tory–Democratic Representative coalition, said, "[Fry] should apologize to Canadians and our American cousins for not condemning these comments and [immediately] walking out on this insulting inflammatory speech." Fry responded to these allegations by saying that, while she defended the freedom of speech within Canada, she did not applaud Thobani's speech, and immediately left the event after Thobani spoke (O'Neil 2001). The political environment was becoming hostile of dissident voices and those who did not move to quickly quell them.

The heat was also felt at the University of British Columbia, which, as an institution of higher education, is a place mandated to foster critical engagements with society. Barry McBride, academic vice-president of UBC, drew upon the notion of academic freedom in his interviews with reporters. "I'm not here to judge on the content . . . but to defend [Thobani] as an academic and her . . . academic freedom" (in McElroy 2001). Tineke Hellwig, chair of UBC's women studies program, told the media, "It's essential that people see different sides to an issue," and Thobani (2001b) herself told FOX's McElroy, "They are trying to silence dissent in this country."

Thobani was not alone in her statements about silencing dissent in Canada. New Zealand academic Aziz Choudry observed in his November 21, 2001, article titled "Canada's Dirty War Over Words" that backlash to Thobani's words was extraordinary in the sense that many others have made similar points. He pointed out, however, that it demonstrates the strength of racist ideology that lies just under Canada's liberal façade:

> Sunera Thobani is a woman of colour living in a society founded on the attempted extermination of Indigenous Peoples and maintained by denial of that genocide. For speaking the truth about U.S. foreign policy she has been variously attacked as a nutty professor, an ungrateful immigrant, a brown bitch and a terrorist sympathizer or a combination thereof. (2001:XX)

Forms of social difference, freedom of expression, and the right of association of oppressed groups are all constituent aspects of an unshakable democratic nation. Choudry (2001) warns that approaches to national security that include attacking the democratic rights of such groups threaten the foundations of democracy. In the month following Thobani's speech, journalists and public figures critical of the United States were "censored, reprimanded and, in some cases, fired for offering anything other than wholehearted support of the United States government and whatever course of action George W. Bush deems fit to follow" (Coady 2001). Canadian journalist Judy Rebick (2001b), a White woman and leader of the National Action Committee before Sunera Thobani took over the post, stated in her CBC.ca column that the ferocity of the attack on Thobani smacks of a new kind of McCarthyism. The reality is that an overwhelming number of Canadians—and many Americans—share Thobani's critiques of the foreign policy of the U.S. government.

Many Canadians are neither "with" the United States nor "with" the terrorists; rather, they are working to create tolerant, intelligent, and long-term solutions to global conflicts—as are many Americans. Sunera Thobani is one woman who "refused to play the submissive role expected from immigrant women of colour" and who "defied the agreed-upon rules of debate set by the ruling elite" (Rebick 2001b). Thobani's insights, the outcry produced by mainstream media, and the myriad critical analyses generated by academics, activists, and everyday citizens alike have raised important questions about the way wars are created and support for them generated in Canada and around the world. When the first casualties of war are truth telling and support for diversity in Canada, this gives us, as citizens, a great deal to think about.

EXPLANATIONS OF WAR AND TERRORISM

What causes collective violence such as war and terrorism? Can war and acts of terrorism be reduced? Despite centuries of war and terrorism, we still know little about the origins of violence or how to reduce such acts (Turpin and Kurtz 1997). We will now examine four sociological approaches to violence as they relate to war and terrorism.

The Functionalist Perspective

Some functionalist explanations focus on the relationship between social disorganization and warfare or terrorism. According to these explanations, disorganization in social institutions, such as the government, contributes to overall political instability. Militia members believe that governments no longer serve the purposes for which they were intended—namely, to protect the individual's rights and freedom. In their eyes, governments have become dysfunctional. Some militia groups engage in acts of terrorism to undermine a particular government in the hope that it will change radically or be abolished.

Other functionalists focus on the functions that war serves. Looked at from this perspective, war can settle disputes between nations. However, in the age of nuclear weaponry, many nations seek other means to deal with their disagreements. Among these means are *economic sanctions*, or cutting off all trade. Thus, in the past Canada has imposed economic sanctions rather than engaging in war or military action against countries engaging in terrorism, environmental violations, abuse of workers' rights, regional strife, drug trafficking, human and political rights abuses, and nuclear proliferation (Myers 1997). However, some political analysts

FIGURE 16.1   State of Peace in the World Today

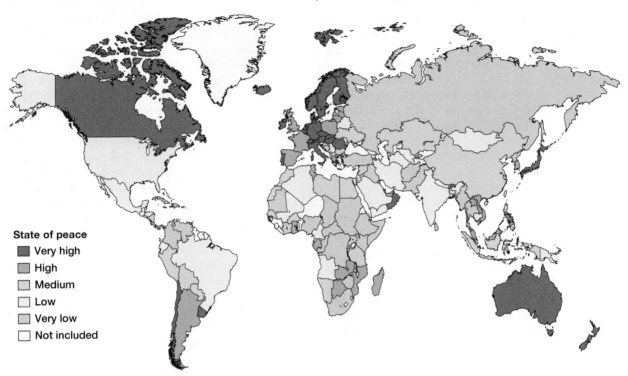

State of peace
- Very high
- High
- Medium
- Low
- Very low
- Not included

Source: Vision of Humanity, 2008, "Global Peace Index—World Map" (http://www.visionofhumanity.org/gfx/m ap-GPI-RYB.gif).

argue that Canada is cutting off its nose to spite its face when it imposes economic sanctions against other governments. This is because economic sanctions are dysfunctional for another social institution—the economy. Also, even though Canada has used sanctions against other nations from its earliest days, corporations are concerned that the sanctions deny them access to the world's markets and the profits in those markets (Myers 1997).

Some functionalists believe we will always have wars because of other important functions that they serve in societies. First, war demonstrates that one nation or group has power over another. Historically, conquering forces acquire the "spoils of war," including more territory and material possessions. Second, war functions as a means of punishment in much the same manner that the Canadian government uses sanctions to force other nations to comply with our viewpoint on certain issues. Third, war is a way to disseminate ideologies, usually political or religious. For example, under the slogan "making the world safe for democracy," the United States has fought its largest

wars in defence of a democratic form of government (Crossette 1997). Canada explains its involvement in contemporary conflicts using the same ideological commitment to the protection and strengthening of democracy in the world. But there is more to democracy than one may think. Larry Diamond, a scholar who has examined new democracies in nations outside North America, explains (cited in Crossette 1997:E3):

> Political freedom has deteriorated in several of the longest-surviving democracies of the developing world, including India, Sri Lanka, Colombia, and Venezuela. . . . It isn't enough to have elections. . . . Democracy is not something that is simply present or absent. It's not like a light switch that you flip on or off. It emerges in different fragments in different sequences in different countries and in different historical periods.

Finally, many functionalists point out the economic function of war: war benefits society because it stimulates the economy through increased war-related production and provides jobs for civilians who otherwise might not be able to find employment. Conflict analysts also see an economic side to war, but they are not so optimistic.

Conflict and Interactionist Perspectives

Conflict theorists view war from the standpoint of how militarism and aggressive preparedness for war contribute to the economic well-being of some, but not all, people in a society. According to sociologist Cynthia Enloe (1987:527), people who consider capitalism the moving force behind the military's influence "believe that government officials enhance the status, resources, and authority of the military in order to protect the interests of private enterprises at home and overseas." In other words, the origins of war can be traced to corporate boardrooms, not to governmental war rooms. Those who view war from this standpoint note that workers and business owners alike come to rely on military spending for jobs.

A second conflict explanation focuses on the role of the nation and its inclination toward coercion in response to perceived threats. From this perspective, nations inevitably use force to ensure compliance within their societies and to protect themselves from outside attacks.

A third conflict explanation is based on patriarchy and the relationship between militarism and masculinity. Across cultures and over time, the military has been a male institution, and the "meanings attached to masculinity appear to be so firmly linked to compliance with military roles that it is often impossible to disentangle the two" (Enloe 1987:531).

Interactionists would call this last perspective the *social construction of masculinity*. That is, certain assumptions, teachings, and expectations that serve as the standard for appropriate male behaviour—in this case, values of dominance, power, aggression, and violence—are created and re-created, presumably through gender socialization, and particularly in military training. Historically, the development of manhood and male superiority has been linked to militarism and combat—the ultimate test of a man's masculinity (Cock 1994; Enloe 1987). This is also a perspective held by some feminists who have focused a great deal of attention on the relationships between patriarchy and military violence.

Feminist Perspectives

Feminist scholarship on war has proliferated since the late 1980s. Women are the targets of massacres in wars, the victims of systematic rape during warfare, and the largest percentage of the population that is forced to flee war-torn areas. Women are also increasingly participating as soldiers in the military and are continuing to work together internationally for peace (Goldstein 2001:1). While war and gender are connected, feminists take many theoretical and political approaches to understanding issues of women and war. As a result, a cohesive "feminist theory" of war does not exist; rather, a "polyphonic chorus of female voices" constitutes current scholarship and political debate about women and war (J. Elshtain, in Goldstein 2001:2).

Most feminists share a concern with changing "masculinism" in both scholarship and political–military practice, where *masculinism* is defined as an ideology justifying male domination. Within this framework, women are seen as a disadvantaged class, unjustly dominated and exploited by men. In addition to their substantive objections to arguments of biological determinism, some feminists challenge the methods of knowledge generation that they see as based on masculine qualities—such as objectivity, control, and theoretical parsimony (especially binary dualisms)—at the expense of detailed knowledge about complex social relationships (Goldstein 2001).

Liberal feminists, with their emphasis of classical individual rights to full participation in all social and political roles, maintain that women should also be able to assume war roles without facing discrimination. They argue that women equal men in ability and that the gendering of war reflects male discrimination against women (i.e., sexism). Furthermore, the exclusion of women from positions of power in international relations is unfair and prevents women from contributing fully to society (Goldstein 2001). Liberal feminist scholars often include women as subjects of study—female state leaders, female soldiers, and other women operating outside the traditional gender roles in international relations. This brand of feminism pays homage to women who succeed in nontraditional positions despite the obstacles they face in a sexist society (Goldstein 2001).

Materialist feminists draw upon a Marxist approach to class differences and their role in the perpetuation of power inequalities in and between societies. To this end, materialist feminists have studied the construction of productive and reproductive roles of women and men beginning in horticultural societies and progressing through to post-capitalist economies (Mies 1986). Through paying particular attention to the links between economies and warfare, these feminists have come to challenge the construction of gender roles in general, and those concerning violence and aggression in particular. Research by materialist feminists shows that the claims that gender roles are genetically determined, natural, difficult to change, and adaptive in an evolutionary sense are easily proven false (Goldstein 2001; Mies 1986). While war has existed perhaps as long as humans have, an explanation for the roots of war is often sought. Anthropologists, for example, have turned to an evolutionary model to explain the origins of war. Such scholars have tended to argue, for example, that in early societies, man-the-hunter used his tools to protect woman-the-gatherer. With the advent of agricultural economies, men began to engage in larger-scale conflicts in order to protect accumulated wealth, land, and community and, finally, in capitalist societies, men engaged in large, often international modes of warfare (Mies 1986). The underlying argument is that males have an evolutionary predisposition to wage war. Materialist feminists show that man-the-hunter actually used violence to control his own communities and that warfare across the ages is more often linked to battles for control over resources and power than it is about adaptive protection and preservation tactics (Meis 1986).

Multicultural feminism theorizes about war and peace from the perspective of "Third World" and Indigenous women. It is a perspective that shows how globalization and colonization remain rooted together. It also demonstrates that there will be no true and sustainable social justice, no anti-racism, feminist emancipation, or liberation of any kind for anybody until Indigenous people have self-determination and the fundamental divide between the North and the South, between "Third World" people and those in the West, is ended (Thobani 2001a).

Ecofeminism brings together theories of feminism, environmentalism, and movements for social justice and equality under one theoretical perspective. Ecofeminists begin with critiques of the 17th-century philosopher of science, Francis Bacon, who cast nature as female and used explicit sexual metaphors to demonstrate the requisite relations of domination and

seduction that were to replace an earlier attitude of wonder and contemplation (Merchant 1983; Sturgeon 1997). Ecofeminists argue that all forms of oppression are deeply connected, although they pay particular attention to the types of violence that are created by patriarchal systems of rule and anthropocentrism, which permit people to exploit the natural world based on an ideology of human supremacy.

War is seen as an extension of the aggressive and exploitative relationships embodied in sexism, racism, and the "rape" of the environment. Ecofeminism influenced the character of women's peace movements in the 1980s and 1990s, and of the Greens political parties in Europe (Goldstein 2001; Mies 1986; Sturgeon 1997). These feminists trace war to an "ideology of control" that gives rise to various forms of oppression; ecofeminism sees the problem of war in very broad terms, connecting peace to a deep restructuring of society (Goldstein 2001).

OVERCOMING WAR AND TERRORISM IN THE 21ST CENTURY

What will happen during this new century? How will nations deal with the proliferation of arms and nuclear weapons? What should be done with the masses of nuclear waste being produced? How can we best deal with the inevitable consequences of war to humans, animals and our planet? No easy answers are forthcoming, as Ehrenreich explains (1997:239):

> War . . . is a more formidable adversary than it has ever been . . . war has dug itself into economic systems, where it offers a livelihood to millions. . . . It has lodged in our souls as a kind of religion, a quick tonic for political malaise and a bracing antidote to the moral torpor of consumerist, market-driven cultures. In addition, our incestuous fixation on combat with our own kind has left us ill-prepared to face many of the larger perils of the situation in which we find ourselves: the possibility of drastic climatic changes, the depletion of natural resources, the relentless predations of the microbial world. The wealth that flows ceaselessly to the project of war is wealth lost, for the most part, to the battle against these threats.

Ehrenreich, like most other social analysts, is not totally pessimistic about the future. She believes that human resistance to war can provide a means to spare this nation and the world from future calamities.

The anti-war movements of the late 20th and early 21st centuries show that "the passions we bring to war can be brought just as well to the struggle *against* war" (Ehrenreich 1997). But, she notes, people must be willing to educate, inspire, and rally others to the cause. As with other forms of warfare, the people struggling for peace must be willing to continue that struggle even when the odds seem hopeless. Ehrenreich's point is supported by Gibson and Cancian (1990:9), who believe that making peace can be more difficult than making war:

Making peace requires democratic relationships: soldiers who refuse to fight in a war they do not support; citizens who claim the right to participate in making decisions instead of accepting rule by elites who make decisions in secret; newspaper reporters, magazine editors, movie makers, and others in the mass media who question the necessity of casting another nation as an "enemy" and instead look for ways to communicate with other human beings who are potentially our friends.

Why do we end our discussion of social problems with war and terrorism? They are the ultimate category of social problems. When class, racialization, ethnicity, or any of the other dominant/subordinate categories discussed in this book escalate to a level of "doing something about it" regardless of the consequences, terrorism or war may be the result. Redressing inequality is an admirable goal, but perhaps the goal should be the one stated by Tim O'Brien, who wrote about his tour of duty in Vietnam (quoted in Hynes 1997:283–284):

I would wish this book could take the form of a plea for everlasting peace, a plea from one who knows, from one who's been there and come back, an old soldier looking back at a dying war. . . . That would be good. It would be fine to integrate it all to persuade my younger brother and perhaps some others to say "No" to wars and other battles.

The international society—the community of all the nations of the world—must work to alleviate inequalities and create a better—more peaceful—world for future generations. What role will you play during the 21st century? Will you work toward a better world

for all? Will you be part of the solution? The answers to these questions are up to all of us: each of us individually and all of us collectively.

WHAT CAN YOU DO?

- Check in with your local pro-peace or anti-war action groups to see what rallies and actions are happening in your area. Participate in them!

- Call, fax, or e-mail your MLAs, MPs, and senators DAILY—several time a day if possible—to express your opposition to current military activities, including sanctions, questionable peacekeeping missions, anti-terrorist initiatives, and invasions.

- Write a letter to the editor of your local newspaper saying why you oppose a particular military initiative. Your letter should be from one to three paragraphs long. You can find out where to send it by looking on the Letters to the Editor page of your local newspaper.

- E-mail a friend and ask her or him to join you in supporting peace. Send this list of things you can do to stop war to a friend along with a copy of information about current conflicts you wish to oppose.

- Distribute flyers about why people should stop war before it starts. Good, heavily trafficked locations include bus stops, subway stations, grocery stores, college and university campuses, libraries, and churches, among other sites. Look for sample flyers on the Internet.

- Organize a weekly vigil against current wars and conflicts at your parliament buildings, the office of an MLA or MP who supports the war, city hall, or another public place.

- Call a press conference where local community leaders, religious leaders, veterans, politicians, and others can speak out against war. Once you have some community leaders who are willing to speak out, determine the time and location of the press conference, send a news release to local media outlets, and then follow up with a phone call to tell editors and reporters what you are doing.

- Connect with the local peace group in your community and/or with an international peace organization. They will have many other ideas for how you can work to stop war.

- Speak out against racist and anti-immigrant attacks. Ensure that the needs of victims (and those at risk for attack) are front and centre.
- Circulate the criticisms of Bill C-42, Bill C-36, Bill C-18, and Bill C-11 that have been raised by many community groups. Find out about these bills from government, social justice organizations, and alternative media sources, and conduct your own critical analysis.

- Work with Canadian and U.S. immigrant and refugee-rights groups, such as the Canadian Council for Refugees (**http://www.web.net/~ccr**) or the Lesbian and Gay Immigration Task Force (**http://www. legit.ca**) to ensure that no new draconian legislation or regulations are introduced.
- Subscribe to local, regional, or national organizations that are addressing the effects of military activity on the health of humans and their environments.

SUMMARY

How Do Social Scientists Define War and Peace?

Social scientists define war broadly. The term *war* includes armed conflict between two countries, undeclared wars, civil and guerrilla wars, covert operations, and some forms of terrorism. War is a form of collective violence that involves organized violence by people seeking to promote their cause or resist social policies or practices that they consider oppressive. Peace seems less easy to define as, while people generally agree that peace is desirable, they have different ideas about what it looks like. Some people equate peace with global harmony while others define it as prevailing in battle.

What Are the Consequences of War?

The most direct effect of war is loss of human life. In World War I and before, it was mostly military personnel who lost their lives, but in World War II and thereafter, war was waged against civilians. If a nuclear war took place, the devastation would be beyond description. Other consequences for both military personnel and civilians are physical and psychological damage, including post-traumatic stress syndrome. Finally, the economic costs of war and war preparedness are astronomical.

How Does War Affect Human and Ecological Health?

The impacts of military activity in times of war and peace are often left out of mainstream debates about war. The effects, however, include both visible and invisible reminders of the impact military activity has on people and environments. Some examples of this are high CO_2 emission levels, the effects of depleted uranium on human and ecological life, the loss of millions of lives through contaminated water and air, and post-traumatic stress disorder (PTSD).

What Is Terrorism?

Terrorism is the use of calculated unlawful physical force or threats of violence against a government, organization, or individual to gain some political, religious, economic, or social objective. Tactics include bombing, kidnapping, hostage taking, hijacking, assassination, and extortion.

What Are the Three Types of Political Terrorism?

Revolutionary terrorism involves acts of violence against civilians that are carried out by internal enemies of the government who want to bring about political change. Repressive terrorism is terrorism conducted by a government against its own citizens for the purpose of protecting an existing political order. In state-sponsored terrorism, a government provides financial resources, weapons, and training for terrorists who conduct their activities in other nations.

What Is the Functionalist Perspective on War and Terrorism?

Some functionalists focus on the relationship between social disorganization and warfare or terrorism.

Examining the growth of militias, they note that disorganization in social institutions contributes to overall political instability. Other functionalists say that war serves certain functions: war settles disputes, demonstrates that one nation or group has power over another, punishes, is one way to disseminate religious and political ideologies, and stimulates the economy.

What Are the Conflict and Interactionist Perspectives on War and Terrorism?

Some conflict theorists say that militarism and preparedness for war contribute to the economic well-being of some—not all—people. Another conflict perspective says that nations inevitably use force to ensure compliance within their society and to protect themselves from outside attacks. A third conflict perspective is based in patriarchy: across cultures and over time, the military has been a male institution; it is almost impossible to untangle masculinity from militarism. Interactionists call this last perspective the *social construction of masculinity*—the connection between manhood and militarism is historically created and re-created through gender socialization.

What Are Feminist Perspectives on War?

Feminist scholarship focuses on the links between war and gender. There is no such thing as a cohesive "feminist theory" of war. There are many thoughts that feminist scholars do agree upon, including constructions of masculinism, which is an ideology that justifies male domination. Liberal feminists focus on issues of women's equality with men and therefore work for women's rights to participate fully in all aspects of war. Materialist feminists analyze the relationship between economics, patriarchy, and power on a world scale and how this affects the life conditions of women in times of peace and conflict. Multicultural feminism theorizes from the perspective of "Third World" and Indigenous women and demonstrates how globalization and colonization remain rooted together. Ecofeminists take a holistic approach to war and maintain that ideologies of control over nature mirror patriarchal ideologies of men's control over women and anthropocentric attitudes of human's dominion over the earth.

KEY TERMS

collective violence,   p. 379
environmental racism,   p. 387
military–industrial
    complex,   p. 381

repressive terrorism,   p. 387
revolutionary terrorism,   p. 387
state-sponsored terrorism,   p. 387
terrorism,   p. 386

war system,   p. 379
weapons of mass
    destruction (WMD),   p. 381

QUESTIONS FOR CRITICAL THINKING

1.   In World War II and every war since, more civilians than military personnel have died. Is killing civilians possible in armed conflicts today?

2.   What impacts does the U.S.–led war on terrorism have on Canada and on the rest of the world today?

3.   Considering the massive resistance against the war in Iraq, why did it go ahead anyway?

4.   Consider the question posed in the last paragraph of this chapter: What can you yourself do to make the world a better—more peaceful—place in the 21st century?

PEARSON
mysockit™

Explore the topics covered in this chapter at **www.mysockit.com** using the access provided with this text. Interactive resources for studying include video clips, practice tests, learning objectives, and Internet resources.

HOW CAN SOCIAL PROBLEMS BE SOLVED?

The _____ Hotel here is a favorite watering hole of the well-heeled and is known for its fantastic views of the city. . . . Just across the street in _____ Park, homeless people, more concentrated here than in most parts of the city, spend the day sipping from half-empty juice boxes and picking through the garbage discarded by children using the playground. . . . The gap between rich and poor . . . is widening, spurred by economic and social change.

Stephanie Strom (2000:A1)

Does this scenario describe Vancouver? Regina? Montreal? Another large urban centre in Canada? No, this is a reporter's description of what was going on in Tokyo, Japan, as the 21st century began. Although the similarity of patterns associated with such social problems as poverty and homelessness in Canada and Japan leaves us concerned about their persistence, we are also hopeful that we may be able to find ways to reduce or alleviate some of these problems—across cities, provinces, and nations—in the 21st century. However, as social analysts have said, solving social problems is a far more complex undertaking than simply identifying them and pinpointing their social locations:

> Identifying social problems and calling for action are quite different matters from actually designing and implementing programs to solve them. Calling attention to the problem, for example, can often be accomplished relatively quickly and easily. Trying to actually carry out a solution, by contrast, involves innumerable obstacles, delays, and frustrations, and demands immense dedication and perseverance. (Weinberg et al. 1981:6)

Perhaps the first obstacle that we face in trying to solve social problems is the difference between ideal solutions and "do-able" solutions. As sociologists Martin S. Weinberg, Earl Rubington, and Sue Kiefer Hammersmith (1981:6) have stated, "There is usually considerable conflict between what the _ideal_ solution would be and what a _workable_ solution might be." Sometimes, for example, the ideal solution to a problem entails high costs that governments may be unwilling to pay. Sometimes there is little or no agreement about what the problem _is_ and what efforts should be made to reduce or eliminate it. After all, the people and organizations involved in the problem-defining stage of a social problem generally are not the same people and organizations involved in the problem-solving stage. Social problems are often identified and defined by political or social activists, journalists, social scientists, and religious leaders. In contrast, the problem-solving stage usually involves elected officials and/or people working in agencies and governmental bureaucracies. Moreover, sometimes a proposed solution to a problem only gives rise to a whole new set of unforeseen problems (Weinberg et al. 1981). In this short epilogue, we will review several approaches for dealing with social problems and reiterate a pressing question: What are you willing to do to reduce or eliminate the social problems that you are concerned about?

The underlying theoretical assumptions that we hold regarding social problems have a profound influence on what we feel may be the best solution for a specific problem. Do we believe society is based on stability, or conflict? Is conflict good or bad for society? Each of the four sociological perspectives summarized below suggests ways in which social problems may be reduced. In doing so, they produce divergent views on social changes that might reduce or eliminate social problems.

According to the functionalist perspective, a society is a stable, orderly system that is composed of a number of interrelated parts, each of which performs a function that contributes to the overall stability of the society. From the functionalist perspective, social problems arise when social institutions do not fulfill the functions they are supposed to or when dysfunctions (undesirable consequences of an activity or social process that inhibit a society's ability to adapt or adjust) occur. Dysfunctions create social disorganization, which in turn causes a breakdown in the traditional values and norms that serve as social control mechanisms. As shown in Table E.1, the social disorganization approach of functionalists traces the causes of social problems to any social change that leaves existing rules inadequate for current conditions. In societies undergoing social change—for example, retrenchment of social programs, high rates of immigration or emigration, rapid changes in technology, and increasingly complex patterns of social life—social disorganization can produce stress at the individual level and inefficiency and confusion at the institutional and societal levels (Weinberg et al. 1981). Thus, the functionalist approach to reducing social problems has as central factors the prevention of rapid social changes, the maintenance of the status quo, and the restoration of order.

TABLE E.1   Perceived Problems and Possible Solutions

Perspective	Causes	Possible Solutions
Functionalist:		
Social disorganization	Social change; inadequacy of existing social rules	Development and implementation of social rules that are explicit, workable, and consistent
Conflict:		
Value conflict	Conflict between different groups' values; economic, social, and cultural diversity	Group action involving confrontation of opponents for lasting changes in policy or legislation
Critical conflict (Marxist)	Relations of domination and subordination are reinforced by the global capitalist economy and political leaders who put other priorities ahead of the good of the people	Changing the nature of society, particularly inequalities that grow more pronounced as the wealthy grow richer and the poor worldwide become increasingly impoverished
Interactionist:		
Deviant behaviour	Inappropriate socialization within primary groups	Resocialize or rehabilitate individuals so that they will conform
Labelling	How people label behaviour, how they respond to it, and the consequences of their responses	Changing the definitions through decriminalization; limit labelling
Feminist:		
Interlocking oppressions	Patriarchy, capitalism, and other hierarchical systems that cause competition between groups and place value on one group over another	Consider the ways that oppressions are interconnected; educate oneself and others about inequities; change one's own behaviours; join with others to create models of change and visions of co-operative society; help to alleviate the suffering of individuals and groups who experience discrimination while simultaneously working to make broad-based and foundational social and political change

Source: Based on Martin S. Weinberg, Earl Rubington, and Sue Kiefer Hammersmith, 1981, **The Solution of Social Problems: Five Perspectives** *(2nd ed.), New York: Oxford University Press; and Joe R. Feagin and Claireece Booher Feagin, 1997,* **Social Problems: A Critical-Conflict Perspective** *(5th ed.), Upper Saddle River, NJ: Prentice Hall.*

In contrast, the conflict perspective assumes that conflict is natural and inevitable in society. Value conflict approaches focus on conflict between the values held by members of divergent groups. These approaches also highlight the ways in which cultural, economic, and social diversity may contribute to misunderstandings and problems. According to Marxist, or critical-conflict, theorists, groups are engaged in a continuous struggle for control of scarce resources. As a result of the unjust use of political, economic, or social power, certain groups of people are privileged while others are disadvantaged. Thus, for critical-conflict theorists, social problems arise out of major contradictions that are inherent in the ways in which societies are organized. When this approach is used, the root causes of social problems—capitalism and spending priorities that place corporate tax breaks and military spending ahead of social services, for example—must be radically altered or eliminated altogether. Focusing on the political economy, one critical-conflict approach states that the capitalist economy, which is now global, maintains and reinforces domination and subordination in social relations. This approach also examines how political leaders and the economic elite may put their own interests ahead of any common good that might exist (Feagin and Feagin 1999). Clearly, any solutions to social problems proposed by this approach would require radical changes in society and thus are not always viewed positively in societies in which economic prosperity based on individual attributes rather than collective activities is considered a mark of personal and social achievement. This is particularly problematic, conflict theorists point out, when elites maintain power through hegemony. Change can only be achieved, then, through counter-hegemonic means.

Operating at the microlevel, the interactionist perspective focuses on how people act toward one another and make sense of their daily lives. From this perspective, society is the sum of the interactions of individuals and groups. Thus, interactionists often study social problems by analyzing the process whereby a behaviour is defined as a social problem and how individuals and groups then come to engage in activities that a significant number of people view as major social concerns. Interactionist theories of deviance note that inadequate socialization or interacting with the "wrong" people may contribute to deviant behaviour and crime and, hence, to some social problems. Similarly, interactionists who use the labelling framework for their analysis of social problems study how people label behaviour, how they respond to people engaged in such behaviour, and the consequences of their responses (Weinberg et al. 1981).

Feminist theorists concentrate analyses at both macro and microlevels of interaction. Social problems are therefore examined on the basis of power in individual relations and in ideologies and structures, in particular looking at gender as a key component. Society is seen as a matrix of interlocking oppressions, organized according to specific relations of domination–subordination. Sexism, along with other forms of oppression, such as classism, homophobia, biphobia or transphobia, racism, and ableism, are examined in terms of the ways they privilege and disadvantage whole groups of people as well as the ways that these forms of oppression work in tandem to reinforce a paradigm of oppression, competition, and hierarchy. Feminist theorists who look at social problems look at the roles people play in resisting and/or perpetuating oppressions and at the locations or standpoints people come from. The inequalities and harm stemming from interlocking systems of oppression and domination are viewed as central to social problems. The solutions for reducing or eliminating social problems are therefore multifaceted: pivotal is the push for a paradigm shift that holds the values of co-operation, diversity, and power sharing in highest regard; also key is changing the unequal dynamics embedded in current racialized/ethnic, class, and gender relations and in relationships between individuals that get played out within these and other contexts. Paradigm shifts require dramatic changes in the ways we view society and the ways we interact with one another individually and collectively. Further, paradigm shifts require us to retrain ourselves so that our behaviours fall into line with our new ways of thinking. This takes a great deal of commitment and hard work and is one of our challenges in the new millennium.

The Internet has dramatically opened up new possibilities for activists to get information to those they would like to mobilize. Many sites serve as national and international mobilizing vehicles for groups seeking avenues to foster social change. Through news groups, bulletin boards, social networking sites, YouTube and other similar vehicles, people are able to learn from one another and share information about social problems. They are also able to join in collective action or encourage others to take some specific action.

Do you follow the news about any social issues? If so, do you get your information primarily from television, radio, the Internet, or other sources? Based on the information you receive from various media sources, are you motivated to participate in organizations or actions that endeavour to bring about social change?

According to some analysts, we need to develop a human agenda that focuses on the needs of people and offsets the corporate agenda that is currently taking precedence over other issues and concerns. Social activists Jeremy Brecher and Tim Costello (1998) suggest that any proposed human agenda should,

- improve the lives of the great majority of the world's people;
- correspond to widely held common interests as well as integrate the interests of people worldwide;
- provide opportunities for action at a variety of levels;
- include elements that can be implemented independently, at least in part, but that are compatible or mutually reinforcing;
- make it easier to solve social problems such as environmental protection; and
- grow out of social movements and coalitions that have developed in response to the needs of diverse peoples.

But perhaps you would like us to take a step backward and ask a more fundamental question: Can social problems be solved? We believe wholeheartedly that they can; after all, what has been created can be re-created. So what do we need to re-create a more just world? Foundationally, we need social analysis, for as Swift, Davies, Clarke, and Czerny (2003:202) state in their book *Getting*

Started on Social Analysis in Canada, "the very activity of social analysis . . . helps to 'lift the fog' and overcome ideological confusion. . . . It can also lead directly into effective action." Take the quiz in Figure E.1 and evaluate your tendency toward social analysis.

We need some kind of shared vision and some shared values, without compromising the rich diversity that makes the world such a dynamic and joyful place. In their book on globalization and social problems, Peterson, Wunder, and Mueller (1999:414)

provide an example of shared visioning and collective values using a statement derived from the 1993 Parliament of the World's Religions called *Toward a Global Ethic*. Some of the values stated in this document include equality between men and women; the dignity and worth of all humans, regardless of ethnicity, gender, language, religion, ability, and so on; generosity, compassion, and caring for one another; economic and social justice; respect for the environment and human rights; truthfulness and honesty;

FIGURE E.1   Social Paralysis Quiz

5	4	3	2	1
strongly agree	agree	don't know	disagree	strongly disagree

☐ Canadian society is too complicated for me to understand.

☐ In Canada there's a premium on authority and obedience: the prudent thing, whenever there's social tension, is to stay out of it.

☐ Things are always getting worse and I feel the news is too awful to take in.

☐ If the experts cannot agree among themselves on any social problem, much less the solution, I haven't a chance.

☐ Faced with issues too big and complicated for me, I feel overwhelmed–it's better not to start.

☐ Because decisions about social issues are very personal, I feel alone and isolated in facing the social world.

☐ There are too many facts to absorb, and it's like I'm drowning in a deluge of information.

☐ I have no control over the important decisions that shape life in Canada.

☐ Economics is a science so mysterious that even economists can't understand how the Canadian economy works.

☐ We will never reach a perfectly just society, because human greed and the lust for power will always reassert themselves, so why bother?

☐ I want to live a well-ordered life–I keep my world quite small.

☐ Social analysis might work in a Third World country, where the inequities are obvious, but it's nearly impossible to analyze a free society like Canada, with its complex issues.

☐ People used to understand the world from the viewpoint of the community they lived in all their lives, but now things are moving too fast for us to understand.

☐ There are tendencies towards evil built into human nature, and until individual hearts are changed there's no point in tampering with social structures.

☐ Political decisions are too weighty for most citizens to grasp.

☐ Total score

This quiz tests people's disposition towards social analysis. The higher you score, the more you have to struggle against social complacency or paralysis–the tendency to leave social concerns to experts, professionals, or activists. A lower score suggests that people believe they can understand their society and hope to have some impact on it.

In a group, everyone's scores could be averaged to see if they tend towards a belief that they have the power to change society for the better, or towards paralysis and disbelief. There could be a discussion of the items that group members tended to score on the pessimistic side.

Source: Jamie Swift, Jacqueline M. Davies, Robert G Clarke, and Michael Czerny S.J., 2003, Getting Started on Social Analysis in Canada, *4th ed., Toronto: Between the Lines, p. 8.*

moderation and modesty; loyalty; freedom as long as it does not impose on others; safety; security; and so on. The ability to participate freely and fully in social life is at the core of these values, so, lastly, we need participation. Many of us feel paralyzed by the idea that social problems are big and we are small. Even small changes, however, can create critical mass, turning "seemingly impossible change into an inevitable one" (Swift et al. 2003:203). For a homegrown example of the difference small changes can make, look at what 12-year-old Craig Kielburger accomplished when he gathered together a small group of his grade seven classmates to try to put an end to child labour in Pakistan and other countries. Today, Free the Children, the organization he founded in 1995 as a child, includes more than 1 million children and young people networking to help other children and operates programs in 45 countries.

Two less well-known but equally influential young Canadians are Jennifer Corriero and Michael Furdyk, who founded the youth website TakingITGlobal (TIG), which marries volunteers to good causes online. With 250 000 young people in 261 countries as TIG members, it's the biggest online community for youth for social change. As well as linking people around the world, this site offers background information on such issues as global warming and human rights. Four million people used the site in 2008. Someone in Iraq

Craig Kielburger

found the site and translated it into Arabic. Jennifer has won a World Economic Forum Young Global Leader award.

What kind of world you hope for? What kind of world are you willing to participate to (re)create? What values do you hold that may propel you toward that participation? What answers has your social analysis brought you? What questions? As we conclude this book and our time together, won't you join sociologists, social activists, and others who seek to use these tools to face up to one of the greatest challenges of the 21st century: bringing peace, justice, and equality to all?

QUESTIONS FOR CRITICAL THINKING

1. What is most useful about applying a sociological perspective to the study of social problems? Is there anything not useful in such an approach? How can you contribute to a better understanding of the causes, effects, and possible solutions to social problems?

2. Do you believe that corporations can be trusted to "do the right thing" when it comes to reducing or eliminating existing social problems? Is good corporate citizenship a possibility in the global economy today? Why or why not?

3. Suppose you were given the economic resources and political clout to reduce or eliminate a major social problem. Which problem would you choose? What steps would you take to alleviate this problem? How would you measure your success or failure in reducing or eliminating the problem?

4. Do governments at all levels in Canada listen to their constituents about social issues? What evidence can you find to support that they do or do not? Why is the situation the way it is? What can we do to make the situation better?

GLOSSARY

ableism prejudice and discrimination against people because of a physical or mental disability.

absolute poverty a condition that exists when people do not have the means to secure the most basic necessities of life (food, clothing, and shelter).

acid rain rainfall containing large concentrations of sulphuric and nitric acids (primarily from the burning of fuel and car and truck exhausts).

acute diseases illnesses that strike suddenly and cause dramatic incapacitation and sometimes death.

ageism prejudice and discrimination against people on the basis of age.

amalgamation a process in which the cultural attributes of diverse racialized or ethnic groups are blended together to form a new society incorporating the unique contributions of each group.

androcentricity putting males at the centre.

Anglo-conformity model a pattern of assimilation whereby members of subordinate racialized/ethnic groups are expected to conform to the culture of the dominant (White) Anglo-Saxon population.

anti-Semitism prejudice and discriminatory behaviour directed at Jews.

assimilation the process by which members of subordinate racialized and ethnic groups become absorbed into the dominant culture.

biphobia fear and intolerance of bisexuality.

blaming the victim a practice suggesting that the cause of a social problem emanates from within the individual or group who exhibits the problem, by virtue of some inherent lack or flaw on the part of the individual or group.

blended family a family that consists of a husband and wife or a same-sex couple, children from previous marriages, and children (if any) from the new marriage.

capitalism an economic system characterized by private ownership of the means of production, from which personal profits can be derived through market competition and without government intervention.

chronic diseases illnesses that are long term or lifelong and that develop gradually or are present from birth.

civil disobedience non-violent action that seeks to change a policy or law by refusing to comply with it.

codependency a reciprocal relationship between the alcoholic and one or more non-alcoholics who unwittingly aid and abet the alcoholic's excessive drinking and resulting behaviour.

collective behaviour voluntary, often spontaneous activity that is engaged in by a large number of people and typically violates dominant group norms and values.

collective violence organized violence by people seeking to promote their cause or resist social policies or practices that they consider harmful, oppressive, and unjust.

common law, or cohabitation two adults living together in a sexual relationship without being legally married.

compulsory heterosexism a belief system that offers no options other than heterosexual behaviour and feelings and denies, denigrates, and stigmatizes gay, lesbian, or bisexual behaviour, identity, relationships, and community.

conflict perspective a framework for viewing society that is based on the assumption that groups in society are engaged in a continuous power struggle for control of scarce resources.

core nations dominant capitalist centres characterized by high levels of industrialization and urbanization.

corporate crime illegal acts committed by corporate employees on behalf of the corporation and with its support.

corporate rich a relatively fixed group of privileged people who wield power over political processes and serve capitalist interests.

corporate welfare a situation in which the government helps industries and private corporations in their economic pursuits.

crime a behaviour that violates criminal law and is punishable by fine, jail term, or other negative sanctions.

criminal justice system the network of organizations, including the police, courts, criminal prosecutions, and corrections, involved in law enforcement and the administration of justice.

cultural capital social assets, such as values, beliefs, attitudes, and competencies in language and culture, that are learned at home and required for success and social advancement.

date rape forcible sexual activity that meets the legal definition of sexual assault and involves people who first meet in a social setting.

debt the amount of money borrowed by the government to offset its deficits.

deficit the situation when a government's spending on initiatives and programs, along with the interest charges on its outstanding debts, exceeds its revenues in a given year.

deindustrialization the process by which capital is diverted from investment in basic industries (in the form of economic resources, plants, and equipment) to business practices such as mergers and acquisitions and foreign investment.

deinstitutionalization the practice of discharging patients from mental hospitals into the community.

demographic transition theory the theory that societies move from high birth and death rates to relatively low birth and death rates as a result of technological development.

demography the study of the size, composition, and distribution of populations.

desertification the process by which usable land is turned into desert because of overgrazing, harmful agricultural practices, or deforestation.

differential association theory the belief that individuals have a greater tendency to deviate from societal norms when they frequently associate with people who tend toward deviance rather than conformity.

disability a restricted or total lack of ability to perform certain activities as a result of physical or mental limitations or the interplay of these limitations, social responses, and the social environment.

disability-free life expectancy the number of years of life that can be expected to be free of activity limitation.

discrimination actions or practices of dominant group members (or their representatives) that have a harmful impact on members of subordinate groups.

dominant group the group whose members are disproportionately at the top of the hierarchy, "with maximal access to society's power resources, particularly political authority and control of the means of economic production" (Marger 1999:273). See also majority (or dominant) group.

drug any substance—other than food or water—that, when taken into the body, alters its functioning in some way.

drug addiction (or drug dependency) a psychological and/or physiological need for a drug to maintain a sense of well-being and avoid withdrawal symptoms.

drug subculture a group of people whose attitudes, beliefs, and behaviours pertaining to drug use differ significantly from those of most people in the larger society.

dual-earner marriages marriages in which both spouses are in the labour force.

economic concentration the extent to which a few individuals or corporations control the vast majority of all economic resources in a country.

edge city a middle- to upper-middle-class area that has complete living, working, shopping, and leisure activities so that it is not dependent on the central city or other suburbs.

education the social institution responsible for transmitting knowledge, skills, and cultural values in a formally organized structure.

elderly dependency ratio the number of workers necessary to support those over age 64 or the ratio of seniors to 100 workers aged 20 to 64.

elite model a view of society in which power in political systems is concentrated in the hands of a small group, whereas the masses are relatively powerless.

environmental classism the belief that a disproportionate number of hazardous facilities are placed in areas with large proportions of poor people.

environmental degradation disruptions to the environment that have negative consequences for ecosystems.

environmental tobacco smoke the smoke in the air as a result of other people's tobacco smoking.

ethnic group a category of people who are distinguished, by others or by themselves, on the basis of cultural or nationality characteristics. These can include language, country of origin, and adherence to culture.

ethnic pluralism the coexistence of diverse racialized/ethnic groups with separate identities and cultures within a society.

ethnocentrism the assumption that one's own group and way of life are superior to all others.

extended family a family unit composed of relatives in addition to parents and children, all of whom live in the same household.

family a relationship in which people live together with commitment, form an economic unit and care for any young, and consider the group critical to their identity.

feminization of poverty the trend whereby women are disproportionately represented among individuals living in poverty.

fertility the number of children born to an individual or a population.

fetal alcohol spectrum disorder (FASD) an umbrella term used to describe the range of disabilities and diagnoses that result from drinking alcohol during pregnancy.

functionalist perspective a framework for viewing society as a stable, orderly system composed of a number of interrelated parts, each of which performs a function that contributes to the overall stability of society.

functionally illiterate being unable to read and/or write at the skill level necessary for carrying out everyday tasks.

gender socially constructed sets of attitudes that dictate what behaviours, thoughts, and emotions are appropriate for each sex—these are culturally specific, change over time, and are associated with notions of femininity or masculinity.

gender ideology ideas of masculinity and femininity that are held to be valid in a given society at a specific historical time.

gendered division of labour the process whereby productive tasks are separated on the basis on gender.

gendered racism the interactive effect of racism and sexism in exploiting Indigenous women and women "of colour."

generalizations ideas held about a group of people that are open to revision or change and that can be rejected entirely at any time.

genocide the deliberate, systematic killing of an entire people or nation.

gentrification the process by which people renovate or restore properties in central cities.

glass ceiling the invisible institutional barrier constructed by male management that prevents women from reaching top positions in major corporations and other large-scale organizations.

grassroots groups organizations started by ordinary people who work in concert to change a perceived problem in their neighbourhood, city, province or territory, or nation.

greenhouse effect an environmental condition caused by excessive quantities of carbon dioxide, methane, and nitrous oxide in the atmosphere.

hate crime an act of violence motivated by prejudice against people on the basis of racialized identity, ethnicity, religion, gender, or sexual orientation. This can include the dissemination of materials intended to incite hatred.

heterosexism the belief that heterosexuality is the only normal, natural, and moral mode of relating, and hence is superior to homosexuality or bisexuality.

hidden curriculum how certain cultural values and attitudes, such as conformity and obedience to authority, are transmitted through implied demands in the everyday rules and routines of schools.

homicide the unlawful, intentional killing of one person by another.

homophobia the irrational and excessive fear or intolerance of homosexuals and homosexuality.

hospice an organization that provides a homelike facility or home-based care (or both) for people who are terminally ill.

iatrogenesis problems caused by doctors and the health care system.

income the economic gain derived from wages, salaries, and income transfers (governmental aid, such as income assistance [welfare], or ownership of property).

indictable offence more serious crimes, such as murder or aggravated assault, that are punishable by more than a year's imprisonment.

individual discrimination one-on-one acts by members of the dominant group that harm members of the subordinate group or their property.

industrialization the process by which societies are transformed from a dependence on agriculture and handmade products to an emphasis on manufacturing and related industries.

infant mortality rate the number of deaths of infants under one year of age per 1000 live births in a given year.

institutional discrimination the day-to-day practices of organizations and institutions that have a harmful impact on members of subordinate groups.

interactionist perspective a framework that views society as the sum of the interactions of individuals and groups.

interlocking corporate directorates members of the board of directors of one corporation who also sit on the board of one or more other corporations.

internal colonialism a process that occurs when members of a racialized/ethnic group are conquered or colonized and forcibly placed under the economic and political control of the dominant group.

internalized dominance all the ways that White people learn they are normal, feel included, and do not think of themselves as "other" or "different."

intersectionality when people experience oppression in more than one aspect of their lives (e.g., sexism plus racism plus homophobia), the resulting oppression is greater than the sum of these oppressions.

intersexed having either unrecognizably male or female genitalia, or having both male and female genitalia.

kinship a social network of people based on common ancestry, marriage, or adoption.

labelling theory the proposition that delinquents and criminals are those people who have been successfully labelled as such by others.

latent functions hidden, unstated, and sometimes unintended consequences of activities in an organization or institution.

life chances the extent to which individuals have access to important societal resources such as food, clothing, shelter, education, and health care.

life expectancy an estimate of the average lifetime of people born in a specific year.

lifestyle–routine activity approach the belief that the patterns and timing of people's daily movements and activities as they go about obtaining the necessities of life—such as food, shelter, companionship, and entertainment—are the keys to understanding violent personal crimes and other types of crime in our society.

low-level literate those who can maintain their current occupation but have minimal skills for adapting to a more complex occupation.

macrolevel analysis focuses on social processes occurring at the societal level, especially in large-scale organizations and major social institutions such as politics, government, and the economy.

majority (or dominant) group a group that is advantaged and has superior access to resources and rights in a society.

manifest functions open, stated, and intended goals or consequences of activities within an organization or institution.

mass murder the killing of four or more people at one time and in one place by the same person.

master status the most significant status a person possesses, the one that most determines how the individual views him- or herself and how he or she is treated by others.

mechanical solidarity social bonds based on shared religious beliefs and a simple division of labour.

media concentration the tendency of the media industries to cluster together in groups with the goal of enhancing profitability.

media industries major businesses that own, or own interests in, radio and television production and broadcasting; cell phones and other Personal Digital Assistants (PDAs); motion pictures, movie theatres, and music companies; newspaper, periodical (magazine), and book publishing; and Internet services and content providers, and that influence people and cultures worldwide.

medical–industrial complex encompasses both local physicians and hospitals as well as global health-related industries such as the pharmaceutical and medical supply companies that deliver health care.

medicalization the treating of a person's condition as an illness.

medicalization of crime the converting of criminal behaviour to a medical condition or disease.

megalopolis a continuous concentration of two or more cities and their suburbs that have grown until they form an interconnected urban area.

meritocracy a nation where the best person can rise to the top in any situation, despite his or her antecedents.

microlevel analysis focuses on small-group relations and social interaction among individuals.

migration the movement of people from one geographic area to another for the purpose of changing residency.

military–industrial complex a term referring to the inter-dependence of the military establishment and private military contractors.

minority (or subordinate) group a group whose members, because of supposed physical or cultural characteristics, are disadvantaged and subjected to negative discriminatory treatment by the majority group and regard themselves as objects of collective discrimination.

mixed economy an economic system that combines elements of both capitalism (a market economy) and socialism (a command economy).

monogamy a marriage between one woman and one man.

monopoly a situation that exists when a single firm controls an industry and accounts for all sales in a specific market.

mortality the number of deaths that occur in a specific population.

multinational corporation (MNC) a complete corporate operation that is taken from its country of origin and integrated into its host country in order to successfully market its products in the local culture.

net neutrality the situation where net providers do not discriminate against or for website content, services, or applications based on the source, ownership, or destination.

norms established rules of behaviour or standards of conduct.

nuclear family a family unit composed of one or two parents and her/his/their dependent children who live apart from other relatives.

occupational (white-collar) crime illegal activities committed by people in the course of their employment or normal business activity.

oligopoly a situation in which a small number of companies or suppliers control an entire industry or service.

organic solidarity social bonds based on interdependence and an elaborate division of labour (specialization).

organized crime a business operation that supplies illegal goods and services for profit.

patriarchy a hierarchical system of social organization in which cultural, political, and economic structures are controlled by men.

peripheral nations nations that depend on core nations for capital, have little or no industrialization (other than what may be brought in by core nations), and have uneven patterns of urbanization.

perspective an overall approach or viewpoint toward some subject.

plea bargaining a process whereby the Crown attorney negotiates with a defence attorney a reduced sentence in exchange for a guilty plea.

population composition the biological and social characteristics of a population, including such attributes as age, sex, racialization, marital status, education, occupation, income, and size of household.

poverty rate the proportion of the population whose income falls below the government's official poverty line—the level of income below which a family of a given size is considered to be poor.

power the ability of people to achieve their goals despite opposition from others.

power elite rulers of Canada, at the top is composed of business leaders, the executive branch of the federal government, and the "top brass" of the military.

prejudice a negative attitude about people based on such characteristics as racialization, gender, age, religion, or sexual orientation.

prestige the respect, esteem, or regard accorded to an individual or group by others.

primary deviance the initial act of rule breaking.

primary groups small, less-specialized groups (see secondary groups) in which members engage in face-to-face, emotion-based interactions over an extended period of time.

property crime the taking of money or property from another without force, the threat of force, or the destruction of property.

prostitution the sale of sexual services (of oneself or another) for money or goods and without emotional attachment.

punishment any action designed to deprive a person of things of value (including liberty) because of an offence the person is thought to have committed.

racialized group a category of people who have been singled out, by others or themselves, as inferior or superior, on the basis of subjectively selected physical characteristics such as skin colour, hair texture, and eye shape.

racism a set of attitudes, beliefs, and practices used to justify the superior treatment of one racialized or ethnic group and the inferior treatment of another racialized or ethnic group.

rape culture the pervasive system of cultural values, attitudes, and practices that support and perpetuate sexualized violence against women.

relative poverty a condition that exists when people may be able to afford basic necessities, such as food, clothing, and shelter, but cannot maintain an average standard of living in comparison to that of other members of their society or group.

restorative justice the focus on repairing the harm caused by crime by holding moderated meetings of crime victims, offenders, and others affected by crime; restorative justice practices can be used at different sites in the justice system.

repressive terrorism acts of violence conducted by a government against its own citizens for the purpose of protecting an existing political order.

revolutionary terrorism acts of violence against civilians that are carried out by internal enemies of the government who want to bring about political change.

routine activities crime crime that occurs when a motivated offender finds a suitable target in the absence of suitable guardianship.

secondary deviance the process that occurs when a person who has been labelled a deviant accepts that new identity and continues the deviant behaviour.

second shift the domestic work that many employed women perform at home after completing their workday on the job.

segregation the spatial and social separation of categories of people by racialization, ethnicity, class, gender, religion, or other social characteristics.

self-fulfilling prophecy the process by which a false definition of a situation results in new behaviour that makes the original false conception become true.

self-health management includes self-care practices, mutual aid, and membership in self-help groups.

semiperipheral nations nations that are more developed than peripheral nations but less developed than core nations.

serial murder the killing of three or more people over more than a month by the same person.

sex the biological, physiological, hormonal, and chromosomal attributes of females, males, and intersex people.

sexism the subordination of one sex, female, based on the assumed superiority of the other sex, male.

sexual assault an act of violence in which sex is used as a weapon against a powerless victim.

sexual harassment a form of intentional, institutionalized gender discrimination that includes all unwelcome sexual attention affecting an employee's job conditions or creating a hostile work environment.

sexuality attitudes, beliefs, and practices related to sexual attraction and intimate relationships with others.

sexual orientation a preference for emotional–sexual relationships with individuals of the "same" sex (homosexuality), the "opposite" sex (heterosexuality), or both (bisexuality).

situational approach the belief that violence results from a specific interaction process, termed a "situational transaction."

social bond theory the proposition that criminal behaviour is most likely to occur when a person's ties to society are weakened or broken.

social change the alteration, modification, or transformation of public policy, culture, or social institutions over time.

social construct the classification of people based on social and political values—rather than a biological given.

social control the systematic practices developed by social groups to encourage conformity and discourage deviance.

social disorganization the conditions in society that undermine the ability of traditional social institutions to govern human behaviour.

social gerontology the study of the social (nonphysical) aspects of aging.

socialism an economic system characterized by public ownership of the means of production, the pursuit of collective goals, and centralized decision making.

social movement an organized group that acts collectively to promote or resist change through collective action.

social problem a social condition (such as poverty) or a pattern of behaviour (such as violence against women) that people believe warrants public concern and collective action to bring about change.

social stratification the hierarchical arrangement of large social groups on the basis of their control over basic resources.

society a large number of individuals who share the same geographical territory and are subject to the same political authority and dominant cultural expectations.

sociological imagination the ability to see the relationship between individual experiences and the larger society in which they are contextualized.

sociology the academic and scholarly discipline that engages in systematic study of human society and social interactions.

state-sponsored terrorism political terrorism resulting from a government providing financial resources, weapons, and training for terrorists who conduct their activities in other nations.

stereotypes fixed and distorted generalizations about the appearance, behaviour, or other characteristics of all members of a particular group.

strain theory the proposition that people feel strain when they are exposed to cultural goals that they cannot reach because they do not have access to culturally approved means of achieving those goals.

subculture a group of people who share a distinctive set of cultural beliefs and behaviours that set them apart from the larger society.

subculture of violence hypothesis the hypothesis that violence is part of the normative expectations governing everyday behaviour among young males in the lower classes.

subordinate group a group whose members, in relation to the dominant group (or groups), do not occupy positions of power. See also minority group.

summary offence a relatively minor crime that is punishable by a fine or less than a year in jail.

sustainable development meeting the needs of the present generations without compromising the ability of future generations to meet their needs.

terrorism the use of calculated, unlawful physical force or threats of violence against a government, organization, or individual to gain some political, religious, economic, or social objective.

theory a set of logically related statements that attempt to describe, explain, or predict social events.

theory of racial formation a theory that states that the government substantially defines racialized and ethnic relations.

tolerance a condition that occurs when larger doses of a drug are required over time to produce the same physical or psychological effect that was originally achieved by a smaller dose.

total institution a place where people are isolated from the rest of society for a period of time and come under the complete control of the officials who run the institution.

tracking assigning students to specific courses and educational programs on the basis of their test scores, previous grades, or both.

transnational corporation (TNC) a large-scale business organization that is headquartered in one country but operates in many countries, which has the legal power (separate from individual owners or shareholders) to enter into contracts, buy and sell property, and engage in other business activities.

urbanization the process by which an increasing proportion of a population lives in cities rather than in rural areas.

values collective ideas about what is right or wrong, good or bad, and desirable or undesirable in a specific society.

victimless crime a crime that many people believe has no real victim because it involves willing participants in an economic exchange.

violence the use of physical force to cause pain, injury, or death or damage to property.

wage gap the disparity between women's and men's earnings.

war system components of social institutions (e.g., the economy, government, and education) and cultural beliefs and practices that promote the development of warriors, weapons, and war as a normal part of the society and its foreign policy.

wealth the value of all economic assets, including income and savings, personal property, and income-producing property, minus one's liabilities or debts.

weapons of mass destruction (WMD) nuclear, biological, chemical, or radiological weapons that can kill thousands of people and destroy vast amounts of property at one time.

welfare state a nation in which the government intervenes in the welfare of its citizens through various social policies, programs, standards, and regulations.

withdrawal a variety of physical and/or psychological symptoms that habitual drug users experience when they discontinue drug use.

youth crime a violation of law or the commission of a status offence by a young person 12 to 17 years of age.

zero population growth a situation in which a population is totally stable, neither growing nor decreasing from year to year because births, deaths, and migration are in perfect balance.

REFERENCES

Aalbers, Manuel B. 2005. "Big Sister Is Watching You: Gender Interaction and the Unwritten Rules of the Amsterdam Red-Light District." *The Journal of Sex Research*, 42:54–62.

Abbate, Gay. 1998. "Gangs Small But Growing Roots: Police Hope to Arrest Development." *Globe and Mail* (November 20):A10.

Abbott, Roberta. 2000. "From Shell Shock to Post-Traumatic Stress Disorder: What Are We Asking of Our Armed Forces Personnel?" Presented at the Third Annual Graduate Student Symposium Conference of Defence Associations Institute (November 3–4).

Abella, Irving. 1989. *A Coat of Many Colours: Two Centuries of Jewish Life in Canada.* Toronto: Lester and Orpen Dennys.

Abella, Irving, and Harold Troper. 1991. *None Is Too Many: Canada and the Jews in Europe 1933–1948* (3rd ed.). Toronto: Lester and Orpen Dennys.

A Commitment to Training and Employment for Women (ACTEW). 1998. "ACTEW's Top 8 Reasons Why Workfare Won't Work." In Luciana Ricciutelli, June Larkin, and Eimear O'Neill (Eds.), *Confronting the Cuts: A Sourcebook for Women in Ontario.* Toronto: Inanna, pp. 96–97.

Adams, Karen L., and Norma C. Ware. 1995. "Sexism and the English Language: The Linguistic Implications of Being a Woman." In Jo Freeman (Ed.), *Women: A Feminist Perspective* (5th ed.). Mountain View, CA: Mayfield, pp. 331–346.

Adams, Tom. 1991. *Grass Roots: How Ordinary People Are Changing America.* New York: Citadel Press.

Aday, David P., Jr. 1990. *Social Control at the Margins: Toward a General Understanding of Deviance.* Belmont, CA: Wadsworth.

Adlaf, Edward, and Angela Paglia-Boak. 2007. *Drug Use among Ontario High School Students.* Toronto: Centre for Addiction and Mental Health.

Adlaf, Edward, Angela Paglia-Boak, Joseph Beitchman, and David Wolfe. 2007. *Mental Health and Well-Being of Ontario Students 1991–2007.* Toronto: Centre for Addiction and Mental Health.

Adler, Patricia A., Steven J. Kless, and Peter Adler. 1995. "Socialization to Gender Roles: Popularity Amongst Elementary School Boys and Girls." In E.D. Nelson and B.W. Robinson (Eds.), *Gender in the 1990s: Images, Realities and Issues.* Toronto: Nelson, pp. 119–141.

Adnan. 2009. "Understanding the Global Media." *Global Issues* (March 3). Retrieved July 19, 2009 **(http://adnanglobalissues.blogspot.com/ 2009/03/understanding-global-media.html)**.

Akers, Ronald L. 1992. *Drugs, Alcohol, and Society: Social Structure, Process, and Policy.* Belmont, CA: Wadsworth.

Albrecht, Gary L. 1992. *The Disability Business: Rehabilitation in America.* Newbury Park, CA: Sage.

Alcoholics Anonymous. 1998. "A.A. Fact File." Retrieved July 18, 2005 **(http://www.alcoholics-anonymous.org)**.

Alexander, Karl L., Doris Entwisle, and Maxine Thompson. 1987. "School Performance, Status Relations, and the Structure of Sentiment: Bringing the Teacher Back In." *American Sociological Review,* 52:665–682.

Alexander, Priscilla. 1987. "Prostitution: A Difficult Issue for Feminists?" In Frederique Delacoste and Priscilla Alexander (Eds.), *Sex Work: Writings by Women in the Sex Industry.* San Francisco: Cleis Press, pp. 184–214.

Allen, Paula Gunn. 1986. *The Sacred Hoop: Recovering the Feminine in American Indian Traditions.* Boston: Beacon Press.

Allman, Dan. 1999. *M Is for Mutual, A Is for Acts: Male Sex Work and AIDS in Canada.* Co-published with Health Canada; AIDS Vancouver; The HIV, Social, Behavioural, and Epidemiological Studies Unit, Faculty of Medicine, University of Toronto; and the Sex Workers Alliance of Vancouver. **(http://www.walnet.org/ members/dan_allman/mutualacts/index.html)**.

Allport, Gordon. 1958. *The Nature of Prejudice* (abridged ed.). New York: Doubleday/Anchor.

Almaguer, Tomás. 1995. "Chicano Men: A Cartography of Homosexual Identity and Behavior." In Michael S. Kimmel and Michael A. Messner (Eds.), *Men's Lives* (3rd ed.). Boston: Allyn and Bacon, pp. 418–431.

Alvi, Shahid, Walter DeKeseredy, and Desmond Ellis. 2000. *Contemporary Social Problems in North American Society.* Don Mills, ON: Addison-Wesley.

Alwin, Duane, Philip Converse, and Steven Martin. 1985. "Living Arrangements and Social Integration." *Journal of Marriage and the Family,* 47:319–334.

Ambert, Anne-Marie. 1998. *Divorce: Facts, Figures, and Consequences.* Ottawa: Vanier Institute of the Family.

American Association of University Women (AAUW). 1992. *The AAUW Report: How Schools Short-Change Girls.* Washington, DC: The AAUW Educational Foundation and National Educational Association.

American Psychiatric Association. 1994. *Diagnostic and Statistical Manual of Mental Disorders IV.* Washington, DC: American Psychiatric Association.

Amott, Teresa, and Julie Matthaei. 1991. *Race, Gender, and Work: A Multicultural Economic History of Women in the United States.* Boston: South End Press.

Anders, George. 1996. *Health against Wealth: HMOs and the Breakdown of Medical Trust.* Boston: Houghton Mifflin.

Andersen, Margaret L., and Patricia Hill Collins (Eds.). 1997. *Race, Class, and Gender: An Anthology* (3rd ed.). Belmont, CA: Wadsworth.

Anderson, S. 2009. "Why Big Media Is Failing." *The Tyee* (March 11). Retrieved July 19, 2009 **(http://thetyee.ca/Mediacheck/2009/03/11/ MediaFailing)**.

Anderssen, Erin. 2002. "Same-Sex Census Numbers Due Today." *Globe and Mail* (October 22):A9.

Andersson, Thomas, and Georgina Schemberg. 2003. *Transnational Corporations and Export Competitiveness: A Summary and Comment.* Retrieved February 8, 2009 (**http://www.iked.org/pdf/UNCTAD.pdf**).

Angus Reid. 2006a. "Canadians Examine What Is Immoral." *Angus Reid Global Monitor: Polls & Research* (June 15). Retrieved October 4, 2006 (**http://www.angus-reid.com/polls/index.cfm/fuseaction/viewItem/itemID/12241**).

Angus Reid. 2006b. "Same-Sex Marriage Issue Settled, Say Canadians." *Angus Reid Global Monitor: Polls & Research* (June 21). Retrieved October 4, 2006 (**http://www.angus-reid.com/polls/index.cfm/fuseaction/viewItem/itemID/12288**).

Angus Reid. 2008. "Health Care Is a Key Concern for Canadian voters." *Angus Reid Global Monitor: Polls & Research* (September 2). Retrieved June 23, 2009 (**http://www.angusreid.com/polls/view/health_care_is_key_issue_for_canadian_voters**).

Angus Reid. 2009. "American Majority Opposes Same-Sex Marriage." *Angus Reid Global Monitor: Polls & Research* (January 5). Retrieved June 23, 2009 (**http://www.angus-reid.com/polls/view/american_majority_opposes_same_sex_marriage**).

Annan, Kofi. 2002. "Beyond the Horizon." *Time* (August 26):46–47.

Anyon, Jean. 1980. "Social Class and the Hidden Curriculum of Work." *Journal of Education*, 162:67–92.

Appelbe, Alison. 2001. "Culture War: Trans-Sexual Fights for Right to Counsel Rape Victims." *CNS News* (April 17). (**http://www.cnsnews.com/culture/archive/200104/CUL20010417c.html**).

Apple, Michael W. 1982. *Education and Power: Reproduction and Contradiction in Education.* London: Routledge & Kegan Paul.

Applied Research and Evaluation Services. 2009. *Estimating the Presence of Alcohol and Drug Impairment in Traffic Crashes and Their Costs to Canadians: 1999 to 2006.* Vancouver: University of British Columbia. Retrieved March 9, 2009 (**http://madd.ca/english/research/estimating_presence.pdf**).

Arar, Maher. 2009. "Maher's Story in Brief." Maherarar.ca. Retrieved August 24, 2009 (**http://www.maherarar.ca**).

Ash, Roberta. 1972. *Social Movements in America.* Chicago: Markham.

Assembly of First Nations. 2008. "Residential Schools." Retrieved November 29, 2008 (**http://www.afn.ca/residentialschools/index.html**).

Associated Press. 1999. "Crushed Cock Earns Cash." (December 2). (**http://www.geocities.com/athens/thebes/9940/taboo/sexnews.html**).

Atchley, Robert C. 2000. *Social Forces and Aging: An Introduction to Social Gerontology* (9th ed.). Belmont, CA: Wadsworth.

Aulette, Judy Root. 1994. *Changing Families.* Belmont, CA: Wadsworth.

Axinn, William G., and Arland Thornton. 1992. "The Relationship between Cohabitation and Divorce: Selectivity or Casual Influence?" *Demography*, 29(3):357–374.

Bailey, Ian. 2002. "Dead Girl's Mother Hugs Bullying B.C. Teenager." *National Post* [online] (May 15).

Bailey, Ian. 2008. "The Inside Story of Vancouver's Safe Injection Site." *Globe and Mail* (October 6):A3.

Baird, Vanessa. 2007. *The No-Nonsense Guide to Sexual Diversity* (updated ed.). Toronto: Between the Lines.

Bakanic, Von. 2009. *Prejudice: Attitudes about Race, Class and Gender.* Upper Saddle River, NJ: Pearson Prentice Hall.

Baker, G. Ross, Peter C. Norton, Virginia Flintoft et al. 2004. "The Canadian Adverse Effects Study: The Incidence of Adverse Effects in Canadian Hospitals." *Canadian Medical Association Journal*, 170 (11):1678–1686.

Baker, Jean M. 2001. *How Homophobia Hurts Children: Nurturing Diversity at Home, at School, and in the Community.* London: Harrington Park Press.

Balakrishnan, T.R., Evelyn Lapiere-Adamoyk, and Karol J. Krotk. 1993. *Family and Childbearing in Canada: A Demographic Analysis.* Toronto: University of Toronto Press.

Ballentine, Jeanne H., and Floyd M. Hammack. 2009. *The Sociology of Education: A Systematic Analysis* (6th ed.). Upper Saddle River, NJ: Pearson/Prentice Hall.

Bandura, Albert. 1973. *Aggression: A Social Learning Analysis.* Englewood Cliffs, NJ: Prentice-Hall.

Bandura, Albert, and R.H. Walters. 1977. *Social Learning Theory.* Englewood Cliffs, NJ: Prentice Hall.

Bannerji, Himani. 1995. *Thinking Through: Essays on Feminism, Marxism and Anti-Racism.* Toronto: Women's Press.

Barber, Benjamin. 1995. *Jihad vs. McWorld.* Toronto: Random House.

Barber, Benjamin R. 1996. *Jihad vs. McWorld: How Globalism and Tribalism Are Reshaping the World.* New York: Ballantine Books.

Barboza, David. 2005. "China, New Land of Shoppers, Builds Mall on Gigantic Scale." *New York Times* (May 25):A1, C7.

Barlett, Donald L., and James B. Steele. 1996. *America: Who Stole the Dream?* Kansas City: Andrews and McMeel.

Barlow, Hugh D. 1996. *Introduction to Criminology* (7th ed.). New York: HarperCollins.

Barlow, M. 2005. *Too Close for Comfort: Canada's Future Within the Fortress of North America.* Toronto: The Canadian Publishers.

Barlow, Maude. 1996. "Globalization and the Dismantling of Canadian Democracy, Values and Society." *PCD Forum*, Article 17 (March 10). (**http://iisd1.iisd.ca/pcdf**).

Barofsky, I. 1978. "Compliance, Adherence and the Therapeutic Alliance: Steps in the Development of Self-Care." *Social Science and Medicine*, 12:369–376.

Barrett, Stanley R. 1991. "White Supremists and Neo-Fascists: Laboratories for the Analysis of Racism in Wider Society." In Ormond McKague (Ed.), *Racism in Canada.* Saskatoon: Fifth House, pp. 85–99.

Barris, Ted. 2009. "Romeo Dallaire: Peacekeeping in the New Millennium." *The Memory Project: Stories of the Second World War.* Retrieved August 24, 2009 (**http://www.thememory project.com/Vol3Dallaire.pdf**).

Barry, Kathleen. 1995. *The Prostitution of Sexuality.* New York: New York University Press.

Basow, Susan A. 1992. *Gender Stereotypes and Roles* (3rd ed.). Pacific Grove, CA: Brooks/Cole.

Basrur, Sheila V. 2002. *Ten Key Carcinogens in Toronto Workplaces and Environment: Assessing the Potential for Exposure.* Toronto: Toronto Public Health.

Bauerlein, Monika. 1995. "The Borderless Bordello." *Utne Reader* (November–December):30–32.

Bawer, Bruce. 1994. *A Place at the Table: The Gay Individual in American Society.* New York: Touchstone.

BBC News. 2003. "Who Won the US Media War?" *BBC News.* Retrieved August 26, 2005 (**http://news.bbc.co.uk/go/pr/fr/-/2/hi/americas/2959833.stm**).

"B.C. Man Guilty in Beating Death of Gay Man." 2004. *CTV News* (December 11). Retrieved October 23, 2006 (**http://www.ctv.ca/servlet/ArticleNews/story/CTVNews/1102715020316_56/?hub=**).

Beare, Margaret E. 1996. *Criminal Conspiracies.* Scarborough, ON: Nelson.

Becker, Howard S. 1963. *Outsiders: Studies in the Sociology of Deviance.* New York: Free Press.

Bedard, Gabriel. 2000. "Deconstructing Whiteness: Pedagogical Implications for Anti-Racism Education." In George J. Sefa-Dei and Agnes Calliste (Eds.), *Power, Knowledge and Anti-Racism Education: A Critical Reader.* Halifax: Fernwood, pp. 41–56.

Beeghley, Leonard. 1989. *The Structure of Social Stratification in the United States.* Boston: Allyn and Bacon.

Bélanger, Alain. 1998. "Trends in Contraceptive Sterilization." *Canadian Social Trends* (Autumn):16–19.

Bellamy, Carol. 2003. UNICEF Briefing on Iraq at the Palais, Geneva (January 28). (**www.unicef.org/ newsline/2003/03bn01iraq.htm**).

Belle, Marilyn, and Kevin McQuillan. 1994. "Births Outside Marriage: A Growing Alternative." *Canadian Social Trends* (Summer): 14–17.

Belsky, Janet. 1990. *The Psychology of Aging: Theory, Research, and Interventions* (2nd ed.). Pacific Grove, CA: Brooks/Cole.

Bem, S.L. 1974. "The Measurement of Psychological Androgyny." *Journal of Consulting and Clinical Psychology,* 42:155–162.

Bennett, Niel G., Ann Klimas Blanc, and David E. Bloom. 1988. "Commitment and the Modern Union: Assessing the Link between Premarital Cohabitation and Subsequent Marital Stability." *American Sociological Review,* 53:127–138.

Benokraitis, Nijole V. 1993. *Marriage and Families: Changes, Choices, and Constraints.* Englewood Cliffs, NJ: Prentice-Hall.

Benokraitis, Nijole V. 2008. *Marriages and Families: Changes, Choices and Constraints* (6th ed.). Upper Saddle River, NJ: Prentice Hall.

Benokraitis, Nijole V., and Joe R. Feagin. 1995. *Modern Sexism: Blatant, Subtle, and Covert Discrimination.* Englewood Cliffs, NJ: Prentice-Hall.

Berger, Peter. 1963. *Invitation to Sociology: A Humanistic Perspective.* New York: Anchor.

Berger, Peter, and Hansfried Kellner. 1964. "Marriage and the Construction of Reality." *Diogenes,* 46:1–32.

Berger, Peter, and Thomas Luckmann. 1967. *The Social Construction of Reality: A Treatise in the Sociology of Knowledge.* Garden City, NY: Anchor Books.

Bernard, Jessie. 1982. *The Future of Marriage.* New Haven, CT: Yale University Press.

Bess, Irwin. 1999. "Widows Living Alone." *Canadian Social Trends* (Summer):2–5.

Besserer, Sandra, and Catherine Trainor. 2000. "Criminal Victimization in Canada, 1999." *Juristat,* 20(10).

Biagi, Shirley. 1998. *Media Impact: An Introduction to Mass Media* (3rd ed.). Belmont, CA: Wadsworth.

Biagi, Shirley. 2009. *Media/Impact: An Introduction to Mass Media* (8th ed.). Belmont, CA: Wadsworth/Cengage.

Bibby, Reginald. 1995. *The Bibby Report: Social Trends Canadian Style.* Toronto: Stoddart.

"Big Media Road Map." 2000. *Brill's Content* (January):99–102.

Bishop, Anne. 2002. *Becoming an Ally: Breaking the Cycle of Oppression in People* (2nd ed.). Halifax: Fernwood.

Blackwood, E. 1986. "Breaking the Mirror: The Social Construction of Lesbianism and the Anthropological Discourse on Homosexuality." In *The Many Faces of Homosexuality: Anthropological Approaches to Homosexual Behavior.* New York: Harrington Park Press, pp. 1–17.

Blasius, Mark. 2001a. "An Ethos of Lesbian and Gay Existence." In Mark Blasius (Ed.), *Sexual Identities—Queer Politics.* Princeton, NJ: Princeton University Press, pp. 143–177.

Blasius, Mark. 2001b. "Sexual Identities, Queer Politics, and the Status of Knowledge." In Mark Blasius (Ed.), *Sexual Identities—Queer Politics.* Princeton, NJ: Princeton University Press, pp. 3–19.

Blauner, Robert. 1972. *Racial Oppression in America.* New York: Harper & Row.

Bonacich, Edna. 1972. "A Theory of Ethnic Antagonism: The Split Labor Market." *American Sociological Review,* 37:547–549.

Bonacich, Edna. 1976. "Advanced Capitalism and Black–White Relations in the United States: A Split Labor Market Interpretation." *American Sociological Review,* 41:34–51.

Bonger, Willem. 1969. *Criminality and Economic Conditions* (abridged ed.). Bloomington: Indiana University Press (orig. published in 1916).

Bonnin, Julie. 1997. "Knockout Drugs." *Austin American-Statesman* (February 2):E1, E12.

Bourdieu, Pierre, and Jean-Claude Passeron. 1990. *Reproduction in Education, Society, and Culture.* Newbury Park, CA: Sage.

Bourgeois, Philippe. 1995. *In Search of Respect: Selling Crack in el Barrio.* New York: Cambridge University Press.

Bowles, Samuel, and Herbert Gintis. 1976. *Schooling in Capitalist America: Education and the Contradictions of Economic Life.* New York: Basic Books.

Bowles, Samuel, and Herbert Gintis. 2002. "Schooling in Capitalist America Revisited." *Sociology of Education,* 75(1):1–18.

Boyd, Monica, and Doug Norris. 1999. "The Crowded Nest: Young Adults at Home." *Canadian Social Trends* (Spring):2–5.

Bradsher, Keith. 1997. "In the Biggest, Booming Cities, a Car Population Problem." *New York Times* (May 11):E4.

Brannigan, Augustine, Louis Knafla, and Christopher Levy. 1989. *Street Prostitution: Assessing the Impact of the Law—Calgary, Regina, Winnipeg.* Ottawa: Department of Justice Canada.

Brecher, Jeremy, and Tim Costello. 1998. *Global Village or Global Pillage: Economic Reconstruction from the Bottom Up* (2nd ed.). Cambridge, MA: South End Press.

Brenna, Shannon, and Andrea Taylor-Butts. 2008. *Sexual Assault in Canada, 2004 and 2007.* Canadian Centre for Justice Statistics Profile Series. Catalogue no. 85F0033M–No. 19. Ottawa: Minister of Industry. (**http://www.statcan.gc.ca/pub/85f0033m/ 85f0033m2008019-eng.pdf**).

British Columbia (B.C.) Ministry of Attorney General. 1996. *Community Consultation on Prostitution in British Columbia: Overview of Results.* Victoria, BC: Ministry of Attorney General, Government of British Columbia.

British Columbia Ministry of Community Services, Women's Services. 2006. *A Minute of Silence: Statistics on Violence Against Women.* Retrieved July 31, 2006 (**http://www.mcaws.gov.bc.ca/ womens_services/a-minute-of-silence/weq_print.htm**).

Brodribb, Somer. 1999. "Introduction." In Somer Brodribb (Ed.), *Reclaiming the Future: Women's Strategies for the 21st Century.* Charlottetown, PEI: Gynergy Books, pp. 13–22.

Brody, Jane E. 1996. "Good Habits Outweigh Genes as Key to a Healthy Old Age." *New York Times* (February 28):B9.

Brown, J. Larry. 2002. *Child Hunger and Food Insecurity: The Scientific Evidence and Possible Solutions.* Retrieved August 11, 2002 (**http://www.jeffbridges.com/Larry.html**).

Brown, Louise. 2009. "Call to Remove School-Finder Website Ignored." *Toronto Star* (June 4):GT5.

Browne, Jan, and Victor Minichiello. 1995. "The Social Meanings Behind Male Sex Work: Implications for Sexual Interactions." *British Journal of Sociology,* 46(4):598–623.

Brownell, Kelly D., and Thomas R. Frieden. 2009. "Ounces of Prevention: The Public Policy Case for Taxes on Sugared Beverages." *New England Journal of Medicine.* Retrieved April 15, 2009 (http://content.nejm.org/cgi/content/full/NEJMp0902392?resourcetype=HWCIT).

Budd, Mike, Steve Craig, and Clay Steinman. 1999. *Consuming Environments: Television and Commercial Culture.* New Brunswick, NJ: Rutgers University Press.

Bullough, Vern, and Bonnie Bullough. 1987. *Women and Prostitution: A Social History.* Buffalo, NY: Prometheus.

Bumpass, Larry, James E. Sweet, and Teresa Castro Martin. 1990. "Changing Patterns of Remarriage." *Journal of Marriage and the Family,* 52:747–756.

Burke, Mary Anne, Joan Lindsay, Ian McDonald, and Gerry Hill. 1997. "Dementia among Seniors." *Canadian Social Trends* (Summer): 24–27.

Burleigh, Nina. 1991. "Watching Children Starve to Death." *Time* (June 10):56–58.

Burns, John F. 1996. "Denial and Taboo Blinding India to the Horror of Its AIDS Scourge." *New York Times* (September 22):A1.

Busch, Ruth C. 1990. *Family Systems: Comparative Study of the Family.* New York: P. Lang.

Bush, George W. 2003a. "President Bush Addresses the Nation." Retrieved September 3, 2005 (http://www.whitehouse.gov/news/releases/2003/03/20030319-17.html).

Bush, George W. 2003b. "President Says Saddam Hussein Must Leave Iraq Within 48 Hours. Remarks by the President in Address to the Nation, March 17, 2003." Retrieved September 3, 2005 (http://www.whitehouse.gov/news/releases/2003/03/20030317-17.html).

Butler, Robert N. 1969. "Ageism: Another Form of Bigotry." *The Gerontologist,* 9:243–246.

Byrne, Caroline. 2005. "CCTV Helps Police Close in on Suspects." *Globe and Mail* (July 28): A9.

Cable, Sherry, and Charles Cable. 1995. *Environmental Problems, Grassroots Solutions: The Politics of Grassroots Environmental Conflict.* New York: St. Martin's Press.

Callender, Claire. 2003. *Attitudes to Debt: School Leavers' and Further Education Students' Attitudes to Debt and Their Impact on Participation in Higher Education.* London: Universities UK.

Callender, Claire, and Jon Jackson. 2004. "Fear of Debt and Higher Education Participation." Families and Social Capital ESRC Research Group Working Paper No. 9 (November). London: London South Bank University.

Cameron, David. 1995. "The Making of a Polluter: A Social History of Uniroyal Chemical in Elmira." In Michael D. Mehta and Eric Ouellet (Eds.), *Environmental Sociology Theory and Practice.* North York, ON: Captus Press, pp. 297–320.

Campaign for Democratic Media. 2007. "Excerpts from Comments Made in the Summer of 2007 through the Campaign for Democratic Media's 'Stop the Big Media Takeover' Campaign" (Summer). Retrieved July 19, 2009 (http://democraticmedia.ca/sites/democraticmedia.ca/files/crtcdiversity_commentsCC_0.pdf).

Campaign for Democratic Media. 2009a. "Net Neutrality." Retrieved July 11, 2009 (http://www.SaveOurNet.ca).

Campaign for Democratic Media, 2009b. "Private Media Ownership in 2008." Retrieved August 17, 2009 (http://democraticmedia.ca/sites/democraticmedia.ca/files/ownership%20chart.pdf).

Campbell, B. 2009. "Canadian Vulnerability in the Face of the Global Economic Crisis." *Canadian Centre for Policy Alternatives* (March 31). Retrieved July 11, 2009 (http://www.policyalternatives.ca/editorials/2009/03/editorial2176).

Campbell, Bruce, Maria Teresa Gutierrez Haces, Andrew Jackson, and Mehrene Larudee. 1999. *Pulling Apart: The Deterioration of Employment and Income in North America Under Free Trade.* Ottawa: Canadian Centre for Policy Alternatives.

Canadian Advisory Council on the Status of Women. 1984. *Prostitution in Canada.* Ottawa: Canadian Advisory Council on the Status of Women.

Canadian Association of Food Banks. 2002. *Hunger Count 2002—Eating Their Words: Government Failure on Food Security.* Prepared by Beth Wilson and Emily Tsoa. Toronto: Canadian Association of Food Banks.

Canadian Association of Food Banks. 2005. *Time for Action: Hungercount 2005.* Toronto: Canadian Association of Food Banks.

Canadian Centre for Justice Statistics (CCJS) (Ed.). 1999. *The Juristat Reader: A Statistical Overview of the Canadian Justice System.* Toronto: Thompson.

Canadian Centre for Policy Alternatives (CCPA). 2003. *CCPA Analysis of Bill C-36: An Act to Combat Terrorism* (February 12). Retrieved June 30, 2009 (www.policyalternatives.ca/publications/c-36.html).

Canadian Centre for Policy Alternatives (CCPA). 2008. "Majority Want Leadership on Poverty: Poll" (October 27). Retrieved June 30, 2009 (www.policyalternatives.ca/news/2008/10/pressrelease1988).

Canadian Centre for Policy Alternatives (CCPA). 2009. "Canada's EI Benefits Well Below OECD Average: Study." Retrieved June 30, 2009 (www.policyalternatives.ca/news/2009/06/pressrelease2259/?pa=BB736455).

Canadian Centre for Policy Alternatives, BC Office. 2008. *The Time Is Now: A Poverty Reduction Plan for BC* (December). Vancouver: CCPA BC.

Canadian Council on Learning. 2009a. *Canadian Composite Learning Index.* Retrieved June 13, 2009 (http://www.ccl-cca.ca/CCL/Reports/CLI/index.htm?Language=EN).

Canadian Council on Learning. 2009b. *Post-secondary Education in Canada: Meeting Our Needs?* Retrieved March 11, 2009 (http://www.ccl-cca.ca/CCL/Reports/PostSecondaryEducation/?Language=EN).

Canadian Council on Social Development (CCSD). 2009a. *Consumer Price Index Info.* Retrieved June 30, 2009 (http://www.ccsd.ca/factsheets/labour_market/employment/index.htm).

Canadian Council on Social Development (CCSD). 2009b. *Economic Security: Poverty Fact Sheet.* Retrieved June 30, 2009 (http://www.ccsd.ca/factsheets/economic_security/poverty/ccsd_es_poverty.pdf).

Canadian Council on Social Development (CCSD). 2009c. *Economic Security: Spending Patterns, 2001–2005.* (http://www.ccsd.ca/factsheets/economic_security/spending/index.htm).

Canadian Democracy and Corporate Accountability Commission (CDCAC). 2002. "Executive Summary." In *The New Balance Sheet: Corporate Profits and Responsibility in the 21st Century* (http://www.corporate-accountability.ca).

Canadian Federation of Students. 2009a. "Canada Student Loan Program." *Campaigns and Lobbying.* Retrieved July 1, 2009 (http://www.cfs-fcee.ca/html/english/campaigns/canstudent-loan.php).

Canadian Federation of Students. 2009b. "Student Debt in Canada: Education Shouldn't Be a Debt Sentence." *Media: Canadian Federation of Students Newswire* (Winter). Retrieved July 1, 2009 (www.cfs-fcee.ca).

Canadian Federation of Students. 2009c. "Students Continue to Struggle with Debt: Statistics Canada." *Media: Canadian Federation of Students Newswire* (April 22). Retrieved July 1, 2009 (http://www.cfs-fcee.ca/html/english/media/mediapage.php?release_id=983).

Canadian Human Rights Commission. 2003. *Annual Report 2001: The Health of Human Rights in Canada.* (http://www.chrc-ccdp.ca/ar-ra/RapportAnnuel2001/AR01RA/annualReport_1_rapportAnnuel.asp?l=e).

Canadian Institute of Health Information (CIHI). 2007. "Percentage of Women Doctors." Retrieved February 27, 2009 (http://secure.cihi.ca/cihiweb/dispPage.jsp?cw_page=statistics_results_topic_physicians_e&cw_topic=Health%20Human%20Resources&cw_subtopic=Physicians).

Canadian Institute of Health Information (CIHI). 2008. "Spending on Health Care to Reach $5,170 per Canadian in 2008." Retrieved November 14, 2008 (http://secure.cihi.ca/cihiweb/dispPage.jsp?cw_page=media_13nov2008_e).

Canadian Labour Congress. 2006. *Report Card 2005: Is Your Work Working for You?* Ottawa: Canadian Labour Congress. (http://www.canadianlabour.ca).

Canadian Labour Congress. 2009a. "Georgetti Says EI Must Be Improved" (June 5). Retrieved June 30, 2009 (http//canadian-labour.ca/en/georgette-says-ei-must-be-improved).

Canadian Labour Congress. 2009b. "Women's Economic Equality." Retrieved June 30, 2009 (http://www.canadianlabour.ca/action-center/womens-economic-equality).

Canadian Museum of Civilization, 2003. (http://www.civilization.ca).

Canadian Nuclear Association. 2002. Retrieved July 30, 2002 (http://www.cna.ca).

Canadian Race Relations Foundation (CRRF). 2001. "Canadian Race Relations Foundation Urges Balance in Anti-Terrorism Act; Provisions on Hate Crime Lauded, But Revisions to Bill Still Needed." *Media Centre* (November 19) (www.crr.ca/en/MediaCentre/NewsReleases/eMedCen_NewsRel20011119.htm).

Canadian Taxpayers Federation. 2003. (http://www.taxpayer.com).

Cancian, Francesca M. 1990. "The Feminization of Love." In C. Carlson (Ed.), *Perspectives on the Family: History, Class, and Feminism.* Belmont, CA: Wadsworth, pp. 171–185.

Cancian, Francesca M., and James William Gibson. 1990. *Making War, Making Peace: The Social Foundations of Violent Conflict.* Belmont, CA: Wadsworth.

Canwest. 2009. "About Us." Retrieved July 20, 2009 (http://www.canwestglobal.com/about/default.asp).

Canwest Entertainment. 2003. "Our Brands" (January 14). (http://www.canwestglobal.com).

Cargan, Leonard, and Matthew Melko. 1982. *Singles: Myths and Realities.* Newbury Park, CA: Sage.

Carmichael, Stokely, and Charles V. Hamilton. 1967. *Black Power: The Politics of Liberation in America.* New York: Vintage.

CARP. 1998. *CARP's National Forum on Scams and Frauds.* Toronto: CARP.

CARP. 2005a. "CARP Announces Canada's Best Employers for the 50+." Retrieved October 3, 2006 (http://www.carp.ca/display.cfm?DocumentID=1490&cabinetID=304&libraryID=70).

CARP. 2005b. *CARP's Fight Against Scams and Frauds.* Toronto: CARP.

Carrier, James G. 1986. *Social Class and the Construction of Inequality in American Education.* New York: Greenwood Press.

Carroll, William K. 1997. "Social Movements and Counterhegemony: Canadian Contexts and Social Theories." In William K. Carroll (Ed.), *Organizing Dissent: Contemporary Social Movements in Theory and Practice.* Toronto: Garamond Press, pp. 3–38.

Casipullai, Amy. 2003. "Bill C-18 (Citizenship Bill)." Ontario Council of Agencies Serving Immigrants (OCASI). (www.ocasi.org/sys/anno_detail.asp?AnnoID=70).

Cass, Vivien C. 1984. "Homosexual Identity Formation: Testing a Theoretical Model." *Journal of Sex Research,* 20:143–167.

Castells, Manuel. 1977. *The Urban Question.* London: Edward Arnold.

Catalyst. 2009. "Women Still Largely Shut Out from Senior Ranks of FP500 Companies: 2008 Catalyst Census of Women Corporate Officers and Top Earners of the FP500 Reveals 'a Glass Half-Empty'" [Press Release] (March 6). Retrieved July 31, 2009 (http://www.catalyst.org/press-release/145/women-still-largely-shut-out-from-senior-ranks-of-fp500-companies).

Cavender, Gray. 1995. "Alternative Approaches: Labeling and Critical Perspectives." In Joseph F. Sheley (Ed.), *Criminology: A Contemporary Handbook* (2nd ed.). Belmont, CA: Wadsworth, pp. 349–367.

CBC Digital Archives. 2009. "The Somalia Affair, 1992–1997." Retrieved August 24, 2009 (http://archives.cbc.ca/war_conflict/peacekeeping/topics/723).

CBC News. 2002. "Media Ownership." CBCNews.ca (November 27). Retrieved (http://www.cbc.ca/stories/2002/11/27/media_ownership021127).

CBC News. 2008a. "Canadian Forces in the 21st Century." CBCNews.ca (April 21). Retrieved August 13, 2009 (http://www.cbc.ca/news/background/cdnmilitary).

CBC News. 2008b. "Recalls and Advisories: Soldier Toy Has Lead Paint." CBCNews.ca (August 8). Retrieved March 5, 2009 (http://www.cbc.ca/consumer/recalls/2008/08/soldier_toy_has_lead_paint.html).

CBC News. 2008c. "Retiring Mandatory Retirement." CBCNews.ca (August 20). Retrieved October 25, 2008 (http://www.cbc.ca/news/background/retirement/mandatory_retirement.html).

CBC News. 2009a. "B.C. Voters Turn Thumbs Down on STV." CBCNews.ca (May 12). Retrieved July 6, 2009 (http://www.cbc.ca/canada/bcvotes2009/story/2009/05/12/bc-election-stv.html).

CBC News. 2009b. "Canada's Individual Bankruptcies to Hit Record in 2009: TD Bank." CBCNews.ca (May 1). Retrieved August 7, 2009 (http://www.cbc.ca/money/story/2009/05/01/canada-2009-bankruptcy.html).

CBC TV. 1999. *Peacekeeping: The Invisible Wounds.*

Chambliss, William J. 1988. *Exploring Criminology.* New York: Macmillan.

Chandler, Michael, and Christopher Lalonde. 2004. "Transferring Whose Knowledge? Exchanging Whose Best Practices? On Knowing about Indigenous Knowledge and Aboriginal Suicide." In J. White, P. Maxim, and D. Beavon (Eds.), *Aboriginal Policy Research: Setting the Agenda for Change,* Vol. 2. Toronto: Althouse Press, pp. 111–123.

Channel 4. 2009. "Ghosts and Human Trafficking." Retrieved January 29, 2009 (http://www.channel4.com/more4/drama/g/ghosts_traffik_campaign.html).

Chapkis, Wendy. 1997. *Live Sex Acts: Women Performing Erotic Labour.* New York: Routledge.

Chase-Lansdale, P. Lindsay, Jeanne Brooks-Gunn, and Roberta L. Palkoff. 1992. "Research and Programs for Adolescent Mothers: Missing Links and Future Promises." *Family Relations,* 40(4):396–403.

Cherlin, Andrew J. 1992. *Marriage, Divorce, and Remarriage* (rev. and enlarged ed.). Cambridge, MA: Harvard University Press.

Cherlin, Andrew J. 1999. "Going to Extremes: Family Structure, Children's Well-Being, and Social Science." *Demography,* 36(4):421–428.

Chermak, Steven M. 1995. *Victims in the News: Crime and the American News Media.* Boulder, CO: Westview.

Children Now. 1999. "Children Now Annual Report 1999 Highlights." (http://www.childrennow.org/annual-reports/annual-report-1999.htm).

The Chilly Collective (Eds.). 1995. *Breaking Anonymity: The Chilly Climate for Women Faculty.* Ontario: Wilfred Laurier University Press.

Chomsky, Noam. 1996. *Class Warfare: Interview with David Barsamian.* Monroe, ME: Common Courage Press.

Choudry, Aziz. 2001. "Canada's Dirty War Over Words." *ZMag* (November 21). (www.zmag.org/sustainers/content/2001-11/21choudry.cfm).

Chudacoff, Howard P. 1989. *How Old Are You? Age Consciousness in American Culture.* Princeton, NJ: Princeton University Press.

CIA. 2009. "The World Factbook: Iraq." Retrieved July 29, 2009 (https://www.cia.gov/library/publications/the-world-factbook/geos/iz.html#People).

CIESIN. 2009. *2008 Environmental Performance Index.* Retrieved June 30, 2009 (http://epi.yale.edu).

City of Toronto. 2009a. "Fact Sheet: Impact of Firearms in Canada." Retrieved June 23, 2009 (http://www.toronto.ca/handgunban/pdf/factsheet.pdf).

City of Toronto. 2009b. "Housing Charter Highlights HOT." Retrieved October 8, 2009 (http://www.toronto.ca/affordablehousing/hot.htm).

City of Toronto. 2009c. *Submission for the Federal Budget.* Retrieved July 6, 2009 (http://www.toronto.ca/city_hall/pdf/2009FedBudget Submission.pdf).

Clancy, J. 2009. "Lies about the Deficit." *National Union of Public and General Employees* (June 2). Retrieved July 12, 2009 (http://www.nupge.ca/node/2334).

Clark, Warren. 1996. "Adult Literacy in Canada, the United States, and Germany." *Canadian Social Trends* (Winter):27–33.

Clark, Warren. 1998. "Religious Observance, Marriage and the Family." *Canadian Social Trends* (Autumn):2–7.

Clinard, Marshall B., and R.F. Meier. 1989. *Sociology of Deviant Behavior* (7th ed.). Fort Worth, TX: Holt, Rinehart and Winston.

Coady, Lynn. 2001. "Mediating Thobani." *Rabble News* (October 10). (www.rabble.ca/everyones_a_critic.shtml?x=2898).

Coale, Ansley. 1973. "The Demographic Transition." Proceedings of the International Population Conference, Liege. Vol. 1, pp. 53–72.

The Coca-Cola Company. (2005). United States Securities and Exchange Commission: Form 10-K (December 31). Retrieved July 11, 2009 (http://www.sec.gov/Archives/Edgar/data/21344/0001047469060 02588/a2167326z10-k.htm).

Cochrane, J., J. Durbin, and P. Goering. 1997. *Best Practices in Mental Health Reform.* Discussion paper prepared for the Federal/Provincial/Territorial Advisory Network on Mental Health. Ottawa: Health Canada.

Cock, Jacklyn. 1994. "Women and the Military: Implications for Demilitarization in the 1990s in South Africa." *Gender and Society,* 8(2):152–169.

Cohen, Lawrence E., and Marcus Felson. 1979. "Social Change and Crime Rate Trends: A Routine Activity Approach." *American Sociological Review,* 44:588–608.

Coleman, Eli. 1981/2. "Developmental Stages of the Coming Out Process." *Journal of Homosexuality,* 7:31–43.

Coles, Gerald. 1987. *The Learning Mystique: A Critical Look at "Learning Disabilities."* New York: Pantheon.

Collins, Patricia Hill. 1991. *Black Feminist Thought: Knowledge, Consciousness, and the Politics of Empowerment.* New York: Routledge.

Coltrane, Scott. 1989. "Household Labor and the Routine Production of Gender." *Social Problems,* 36:473–490.

Commission for Economic Cooperation. 2009. *Industrial Pollution and Waste.* Retrieved July 29, 2009 (http://www.cec.org/soe/files/en/SOE_IndustrialPollution_en.pdf).

Community Childhood Hunger Identification Project. 1995. *A Survey of Childhood Hunger in the United States.* Washington, DC: Food Research and Action Committee (July).

Conference Board of Canada. 2008. *Health Report Card.* Retrieved February 6, 2009 (http://sso.conferenceboard.ca/HCP/Details/Health.aspx#_ftn5).

Connell, Christopher. 1995. "Birth Rate for Unmarried Women Surges." *Austin American-Statesman* (June 7):A18.

Conseil du statut de la femme. 2002. *Is Prostitution Work or Exploitation: Further Consideration Is Needed.* Quebec: Gouvernement du Québec, Conseil du statut de la femme.

Cooke, Richard, Michael Barkham, Kerry Audin, Margaret Bradley, and John Davy. 2004. "Student Debt and Its Relation to Student Mental Health." *Journal of Further and Higher Education, 1469–9486,* 28(1):53–66.

Corbeil, Jean-Pierre. 1998. "Literacy: Does Language Make a Difference?" *Canadian Social Trends* (Winter):2–6.

Cormack, Elizabeth. 1999. "New Possibilities for a Feminism 'in' Criminology." *Canadian Journal of Criminology,* 41(2):161–170.

Corporate Knights. 2009. *6th Annual Knight Schools Ranking,* 8(1):48.

Corporate Watch. 2003. (http://www.corporatewatch. org.uk).

Corr, Charles A., Clyde M. Nabe, and Donna M. Corr. 1994. *Death and Dying, Life and Living.* Pacific Grove, CA: Brooks/Cole.

Corus Entertainment. 2009. "About Corus." Retrieved July 20, 2009 (http://www.corusent.com/home/Corporate/AboutCorus/tabid/1668/Default.aspx).

Cottrell, Barbara. 2001. *Parent Abuse: The Abuse of Parents by Their Teenage Children.* Family Violence Prevention Unit, Ottawa: Health Canada. Cat. no. H72-21/180-2000E. Retrieved October 25, 2006 (http://www.phac-aspc.gc.ca/ncfv-cnivf/familyviolence/html/fvparentsabu_e.html).

Council of Canadians. 1999. "Trade and Investment Must Serve ... "Retrieved March 7, 2003 (http://www.canadians.org/display_document.htm?COC_token=1@@465cb4da239ed216035817807630876d&id=332&isdoc=1&catid=133).

Council on Foreign Relations. 2003. "How Did Canada, Australia, and New Zealand Respond to September 11?" (February 22). (http://www.terrorismanswers.com/coalition/canada.html).

Cowley, Geoffrey. 1997. "Can Marijuana Be Medicine?" *Newsweek* (February 3):22–27.

Cox, Brian J., Nancy Yu, Tracie O Afifi, and Robert Ladouceur. 2005. "A National Survey of Gambling Problems in Canada." *Canadian Journal of Psychiatry,* 50(4):213–218.

Cox, Oliver C. 1948. *Caste, Class, and Race.* Garden City, NY: Doubleday.

Crombie, David. 2001. "Grow Smart or Grow Worse." *Globe and Mail* (April 4):A15.

Crossette, Barbara. 1997. "Democracies Love Peace, Don't They?" *New York Times* (June 1):E3.

Crowe, Cathy. 2007. *Dying for a Home: Homeless Activists Speak Out.* Toronto: Between the Lines.

"CRTC Puts New Restrictions on Media Ownership." 2008. *Globe and Mail.* Retrieved July 20, 2009 (**http://www.reportonbusiness.com/servlet/story/RTGAM.20080115.wCRTC0115/BNStory/robNews/home**).

CTV. 1995. *Hearts of Hate: The Battle for Young Minds.* Toronto: Investigative Productions.

Curatolo, Peter W., and David Robertson. 1983. "The Health Consequences of Caffeine." *Annals of Internal Medicine,* 98:641–653.

Currah, Paisley. 2001. "Queer Theory, Lesbian and Gay Rights, and Transsexual Marriages." In Mark Blasius (Ed.), *Sexual Identities—Queer Politics.* Princeton, NJ: Princeton University Press, pp. 178–199.

Curran, James, Michael Gurevitch, and Janet Woollacott. 1982. "The Study of the Media: Theoretical Approaches." In Michael Gurevitch, Tony Bennett, James Curran, and Janet Woollacott (Eds.), *Culture, Society and the Media.* London: Methuen, pp. 5–35.

Curry, Bill. 2006. "Critics Blast Ottawa's 'Shameful' Green Plan." *Globe and Mail* (October 20):A1, A4.

Curry, Bill. 2008. "Hunt Begins for Long Missing Students." *Globe and Mail* (October 27):A1.

Curtis, Polly. 2008. "Women Take Longer To Repay Student Loans." *The Guardian* (**http://www.guardian.co.uk/politics/2008/jan/02/uk.studentfinance/print**).

Dahl, Robert A. 1961. *Who Governs?* New Haven, CT: Yale University Press.

Dalai Lama. 1990. *Ocean of Wisdom: Guidelines for Living.* New York: Harper & Row.

Daley, Suzanne. 1997. "Zaïre's Fall Jolts Neighboring Angola's Frail Peace." *New York Times* (June 8):3.

Daly, Kathleen, and Meda Chesney-Lind. 1988. "Feminism and Criminology." *Justice Quarterly,* 5:497–533.

Daniels, Ronald J. 2002. "Let's Reach for the Gold in Higher Education." *Globe and Mail* (March 1).

Danziger, Sheldon, and Peter Gottschalk. 1995. *America Unequal.* Cambridge, MA: Harvard University Press.

Dauncey, Guy. 2003. "101 Ways to Stop the War on Iraq." (**http://www.earthfuture.com**).

Dauvergne, Mia, and Holly Johnson. 2001. "Children Witnessing Family Violence." *Juristat,* 21(6).

Davidson, Julia O'Connell. 1996. "Sex Tourism in Cuba." *Race and Class,* 38(1):39–49.

Davis, Kingsley. 1937. "The Sociology of Prostitution." *American Sociological Review,* 2:744–755.

Davis, Kingsley, and Wilbert E. Moore. 1945. "Some Principles of Stratification." *American Sociological Review,* 10:242–249.

Daw, James. 2008. "What Retirement?" *Toronto Star* (December 6):B1, B2.

de Broucker, Patrice, and Laval Lavallée. 1998. "Getting Ahead in Life: Does Education Count?" *Canadian Social Trends* (Summer):11–15.

DeKeseredy, Walter S., and Ronald Hinch. 1991. *Woman Abuse: Sociological Perspectives.* Toronto: Thompson.

Demczuk, Irene, Michele Caron, Ruth Rose, and Lyne Bouchard. 2002. *Recognition of Lesbian Couples: An Inalienable Right.* Ottawa: Status of Women Canada.

DeNavas-Walt, Carmen, Bernadette D. Proctor, and Jessica Smith. 2007. *Current Population Reports, P60-233, Income, Poverty, and Health Insurance Coverage in the United States: 2006.* Washington, DC: U.S. Government Printing Office.

Denton, M., and V. Walters, 1999. "Gender Differences in Structural and Behavioural Determinants of Health: An Analysis of Social Production of Health." *Social Science and Medicine,* 48:1221–1235.

Department of Finance Canada. 2003. "Chapter One: The Budget Plan." (February 18). (**http://www.fin.gc.ca/ scripts/register_e.asp**).

Department of Finance Canada. 2009. *Canada's Economic Outlook and Policy Framework.* Retrieved July 7, 2009 (**http://www.fin.gc.ca/activty/pubs/EPFrmwrk08_eng.asp**).

Department of Justice, Canada. 2001. "The Royal Assent of Bill C-36, The Anti-Terrorism Act." *NewsRoom* (December 18).

Department of Justice, Canada. 2006. "*Criminal Code*: Part XXII, Sentencing." Retrieved July 21, 2006 (**http://laws.justice.gc.ca/en/c-46/268353.html**).

DePasquale, Katherine M. 1999. "The Effects of Prostitution." Retrieved December 3, 1999 (**http://www.feminista.com/v1n5/depasquale.html**).

de Silva, Rex. 1980. "Developing the Third World." *World Press Review* (May):48.

Devereaux, Anna. 1987. "Diary of a Prostitute." *Cosmopolitan* (October 1987):164, 166.

Devor, Aaron. 2003. Interview with Aaron Devor, Dean of Graduate Studies, University of Victoria, by Vicki Nygaard, February 20, 2003. See also Devor's website for more information and additional publications (**http://web.uvic.ca/~ahdevor**).

Devor, Holly. 1989. *Gender Blending: Confronting the Limits of Duality.* Bloomington: Indiana University Press.

Devor, Holly. 1997. *FTM: Female to Male Transsexuals in Society.* Bloomington: Indiana University Press.

Dews, Peter B. 1984. "Behavioral Effects of Caffeine." In Peter B. Dews (Ed.), *Caffeine: Perspectives from Recent Research.* Berlin: Springer-Verlag, pp. 86–103.

Diamond, Jared. 2000. "The Greening of Corporate America." *New York Times* (January 8):A31.

Dickinson, Harley D. 2000. "Work and Unemployment as Social Issues." In B. Singh Bolaria (Ed.), *Social Issues and Contradictions in Canadian Society* (3rd ed.). Toronto: Harcourt Brace, pp. 26–50.

Dickinson, Harley D. 2002. "Mental Health Policy in Canada: What's the Problem?" In B. Singh Bolaria and Harley D. Dickinson. (Eds.), *Health, Illness, and Health Care in Canada* (3rd ed.). Scarborough, ON: Nelson.

Dietz, P. 1986. "Mass, Serial and Sensational Homicide." *Bulletin of the New England Medical Society,* 62:477–491.

DiFranza, Joseph R., and Robert A. Lew. 1995. "Effect of Maternal Cigarette Smoking on Pregnancy Complications and Sudden Infant Death Syndrome." *The Journal of Family Practice,* 40:385–394.

Dobbin, Murray. 1998. *Myth of the Good Corporate Citizen: Democracy Under the Rule of Big Business.* North York, ON: Stoddart.

Dobbin, Murray. 2001. "Globalization: A World Ruled by Corporations." *CCPA Monitor* (April). (**http://www.policyalternatives.ca**).

Dobinson, Cheryl, 2004. "Everyday Acts of Survival and Unorganized Resistance: Gay, Lesbian and Bisexual Youth Respond to

Oppression." In James McNinch and Mary Cronin (Eds.), *I Could Not Speak My Heart: Education and Social Justice for Gay and Lesbian Youth*. Regina, SK: Canadian Plains Research Centre, University of Regina, pp. 49–80.

"Do Canadians Feel Secure?" 2005. Editorial. *Globe and Mail* (August 11):A5.

Doezema, Jo. 1998. "Forced to Choose: Beyond the Voluntary v. Forced Prostitution Dichotomy." In Kamala Kempadoo and Jo Doezema (Eds.), *Global Sex Workers: Rights, Resistance and Redefinition*. New York: Routledge, pp. 34–50.

Domhoff, G. William. 1978. *The Powers That Be: Processes of Ruling Class Domination in America*. New York: Random House.

Domhoff, G. William. 1990. *The Power Elite and the State: How Policy Is Made in America*. New York: Aldine de Gruyter.

Donahue, Paul. 2000. "The WTO Protests in Seattle: This Is What Democracy Looks Like." *The Maine Woods: A Publication of the Forest Ecology Network* (Winter):4–1.

Donavon, Tina. 2001. "Being Transgender and Older: A First Person Account." *Journal of Gay and Lesbian Social Services: Issues in Practice, Policy and Research*, 13(4):19–22.

Donnelly, John. 2003. "CIA Had Idea of Contagion, and of Governments' Reactions." *Boston Globe*. Retrieved April 26, 2003 **(http://www. boston.com/dailyglobe2/117/ nation)**.

Donziger, Steven R. (Ed.). 1996. *The Real War on Crime: The Report of the National Criminal Justice Commission*. New York: HarperPerennial.

Doob, Anthony N., and Jane B. Sprott. 2006. "Punishing Youth Crime in Canada: The Blind Men and the Elephant." *Punishment and Society*, 8(2):223–233.

Doyle, James A. 1995. *The Male Experience* (3rd ed.). Madison, WI: Brown and Benchmark.

Drohan, Madelaine. 1998. "How the Net Killed the MAI: Grassroots Groups Used Their Own Globalization to Derail Deal." *Globe and Mail* (April 29).

Dua, Enakshi. 1999. "Canadian Anti-Racist Feminist Thought: Scratching the Surface of Racism." In Enakshi Dua and Angela Robertson (Eds.), *Scratching the Surface: Canadian Anti-Racist Feminist Thought*. Toronto: Women's Press, pp. 7–31.

Dubois, Julie. 2006. *Trends in Student Borrowing and Pathways: Evidences from the 1990, 1995 and 2000 Classes*. Human Resources and Skills Development Canada, Cat. No.: HS28-39/2006E-PDF. Retrieved September 25, 2006 **(http://www11.hrsdc.gc.ca/ en/cs/sp/hrsdc/lp/publications/2006-002850/page01.shtml)**.

Duffy, Ann, and Nancy Mandell. 2001. "The Growth in Poverty and Social Inequality: Losing Faith in Social Justice." In Dan Glenday and Ann Duffy (Eds.), *Canadian Society: Meeting the Challenges of the 21st Century*. Don Mills, ON: Oxford University Press, pp. 77–116.

Dunlap, David W. 1996. "Role of Openly Gay Episcopalians Causes a Rift in the Church." *New York Times* (March 21):A8.

Durkheim, Emile. 1933. *Division of Labor in Society*. George Simpson (Trans.). New York: Free Press (orig. published in 1893).

Durkheim, Emile. 1964. *The Rules of Sociological Method*. Sarah A. Solovay and John H. Mueller. (Trans.). New York: Free Press (orig. published in 1895).

Dye, Thomas R. 2000. *The Irony of Democracy: An Uncommon Introduction to American Politics* (millennium ed.). Fort Worth, TX: Harcourt College.

Dynes, Wayne R. (Ed.). 1990. *Encyclopedia of Homosexuality*. New York: Garland.

Eckersley, Robyn. 2001. "Ecofeminism and Environmental Democracy: Exploring the Connections." *Women & Environments International Magazine*, 52/53 (Fall):23–26.

The Ecologist. 1993. *Whose Common Future? Reclaiming the Commons*. Philadelphia: New Society Publishers.

Eder, Donna. 1985. "The Cycle of Popularity: Interpersonal Relations among Female Adolescents." *Sociology of Education*, 58(July): 154–165.

Eder, Donna, and Stephen Parker. 1987. "The Cultural Production and Reproduction of Gender: The Effect of Extracurricular Activities on Peer Group Culture." *Sociology of Education*, 60:200–213.

Editorial Collective. 2001. *Resist: A Grassroots Collection of Stories, Poetry, Photos and Analyses from the Quebec City FTAA Protests and Beyond*. Halifax: Fernwood.

Ehrbar, Ned. 2009. "Golden Girl Says 'Yes' to Role." *MetroNews* (June 17):49.

Ehrenreich, Barbara. 1997. *Blood Rites: Origins and History of the Passions of War*. New York: Metropolitan Books.

Ehrlich, Paul R., and Anne H. Ehrlich. 1991. *The Population Explosion*. New York: Touchstone/Simon & Schuster.

Eichler, Margrit (Ed.). 1995. *Change of Plans: Towards a Non-Sexist City*. Toronto: Garamond Press.

Elliott, Michael. 1999. "The New Radicals." *Newsweek* (December 13): 36–39.

Elliott, Patricia, and Nancy Mandell. 2001. "Feminist Theories." In Nancy Mandell (Ed.), *Feminist Issues: Race, Class, and Sexuality* (3rd ed.). Toronto: Prentice Hall, pp. 23–48.

Engels, Friedrich. 1972. *The Origin of the Family, Private Property and the State*. New York: Pathfinder (orig. published in 1884).

Enloe, Cynthia H. 1987. "Feminists Thinking about War, Militarism, and Peace." In Beth Hess and Myra Marx Feree (Eds.), *Analyzing Gender: A Handbook of Social Science Research*. Newbury Park, CA: Sage, pp. 526–547.

Enloe, Cynthia. 1990. *Bananas, Beaches, and Bases: Making Feminist Sense of International Politics*. Berkeley: University of California Press.

Epstein, Cynthia Fuchs. 1988. *Deceptive Distinctions: Sex, Gender, and the Social Order*. New Haven, CT: Yale University Press.

Erickson, Patricia G., Jennifer Butters, Patti McGillicuddy, and Ase Hallgren. 2000. "Crack and Prostitution: Gender, Myths and Experiences." *Journal of Drug Issues*, 30(4):767–788.

Erikson, Kai T. 1962. "Notes on the Sociology of Deviance." *Social Problems*, 9:307–314.

Erikson, Kai T. 1991. "A New Species of Trouble." In Stephen Robert Crouch and J. Stephen Kroll-Smith (Eds.), *Communities at Risk: Collective Responses to Technological Hazards*. New York: Peter Land, pp. 11–29.

Essed, Philomena. 1990. *Everyday Racism: Reports from Women of Two Cultures*. Claremont, CA: Hunter House.

Essed, Philomena. 1991. *Understanding Everyday Racism*. Newbury Park, CA: Sage.

Evans, Robert G., Kimberlyn M. McGrail, Steven G. Morgan, Morris L. Barer, and Clyde Hertzeman. 2001. "Apocalpyse Now: Population and the Future of Health Care Systems." *Canadian Journal on Aging*, 20(suppl. 1):160–191.

Eyles, John, S. Martin Taylor, Jamie Baxter, Doug Sider, and Dennis Willms. 1993. "The Social Construction of Risk in a Rural Community: Responses of Local Residents to the 1990 Hagersville (Ontario) Tire Fire." *Risk Analysis*, 13(3):281–290.

Farley, Melissa, and Jacqueline Lynne. 2004. "Prostitution in Vancouver: Pimping Women and the Colonization of First Nations." In Rebecca Whisnant and Christine Stark (Eds.), *Not for Sale: Feminists*

Resisting Prostitution and Pornography. Melbourne, AU: Spinifex Press, pp. 106–130.

Farr, Kathryn. 2005. *Sex Trafficking: The Global Market in Women and Children.* New York: Worth.

Feagin, Joe R. 1975. *Subordinating the Poor: Welfare and American Beliefs.* Englewood Cliffs, NJ: Prentice-Hall.

Feagin, Joe R., and Clairece Booher Feagin. 1999. *Social Problems: A Critical-Conflict Perspective* (5th ed.). Upper Saddle River, NJ: Prentice Hall.

Feagin, Joe R., and Robert Parker. 1990. *Building American Cities: The Urban Real Estate Game* (2nd ed.). Englewood Cliffs, NJ: Prentice-Hall.

Feagin, Joe R., and Melvin P. Sikes. 1994. *Living with Racism: The Black Middle-Class Experience.* Boston: Beacon Press.

Feagin, Joe R., and Hernán Vera. 1995. *White Racism: The Basics.* New York: Routledge.

Feodorowycz, Orest. 2001. "Homicide in Canada." *Juristat,* 21(9).

Fields, B.J. 1990. "Slavery, Race, and Ideology in the United States of America." *New Left Review,* 181(May/June):95–118.

Filax, Gloria. 2006. *Queer Youth in the Province of the "Severely Normal."* Vancouver: University of British Columbia Press.

Findlay, Deborah A., and Leslie J. Miller. 2002. "Through Medical Eyes: The Medicalization of Women's Bodies." In B. Singh Bolaria and Harley D. Dickinson (Eds.), *Health, Illness, and Health Care in Canada* (3rd ed.). Scarborough, ON: Nelson.

Fineman, Howard. 1997. "Who Needs Washington?" *Newsweek* (January 27):50–52.

Finkelhor, David. 1984. Child Abuse: New Theory and Research. New York: Free Press.

Firestone, Shulamith. 1970. *The Dialectic of Sex.* New York: Morrow.

Fisher, John. 1999. *A report on lesbian, gay, and bi-sexual youth issues in Canada.* Ottawa: EGALE.

Fisher, Lawrence M. 1996. "Health on Line: Doctor Is In, and His Disk Is Full." *New York Times* (June 14):C1, C8.

Fitzgerald, Robin. 1999. *Family Violence in Canada: A Statistical Profile, 1999.* Ottawa: Statistics Canada.

Flanagan, William G. 1995. *Urban Sociology: Images and Structure* (2nd ed.). Boston: Allyn and Bacon.

Fleras, Augie. 2001. *Social Problems in Canada: Conditions, Constructions, and Challenges* (3rd ed.). Toronto: Prentice Hall.

Fleras, Augie. 2010. *Unequal Relations: An Introduction to Race, Ethnic, and Aboriginal Dynamics* (6th ed.). Toronto: Pearson Canada.

Fleras, Augie, and Jean Leonard Elliott. 1996. *Unequal Relations: An Introduction to Race, Ethnic and Aboriginal Dynamics in Canada.* Scarborough, ON: Prentice Hall.

Fleras, Augie, and Jean Leonard Elliott. 1999. *Unequal Relations: An Introduction to Race, Ethnic, and Aboriginal Dynamics in Canada* (3rd ed.). Scarborough, ON: Prentice Hall/Allyn and Bacon.

Florida, Richard. 2002. "Toronto 2020." *Globe and Mail* (June 24):T8.

Food Banks Canada. 2009a. "Difficult Economic Climate Increases Stress on Canadian Food Banks" [News Release] (June 1). Retrieved July 3, 2009 (**http://foodbankscanada.ca/main2.cfm?id=107185FA-B6A7-8AA0-672CE43DAF6DE6E3**).

Food Banks Canada, 2009b. "Facts and Statistics." Retrieved June 25, 2009 (**http://www.foodbankscanada.ca**).

Food Banks Canada, 2009c. *HungerCount 2008: A Comprehensive Report on Hunger and Food Bank Use in Canada.* Retrieved June 30, 2009 (**http://foodbankscanada.ca/documents/hungercount_en_fin.pdf**).

Forbes.com. 2009. *The World's Billionaires 2009 (Special Report)* (March 11). Retrieved June 25, 2009 (**http://www.forbes.com/2009/03/11/worlds-richest-people-billionaires-2009-billionaires_land.html**).

Forcese, D. 1997. *The Canadian Class Structure* (4th ed.). Toronto: McGraw-Hill Ryerson.

Foster, J.B., & Magdoff, F. 2009. *The Great Financial Crisis.* New York: Monthly Review Press.

Frederick, Judith A., and Monica Boyd. 1998. "The Impact of Family Structure on High School Completion." *Canadian Social Trends* (Spring):12–18.

Freepress. 2009. "Ownership Chart: The Big Six." Retrieved July 21, 2009 (**http://www.freepress.net/ownership/chart/main**).

Freiler, Christa, and Judy Cerny. 1998. *Benefiting Canada's Children: Perspectives on Gender and Social Responsibility* (March). Ottawa: Research Directorate, Status of Women Canada.

French, Dolores, with Linda Lee. 1988. *Working: My Life as a Prostitute.* New York: E.P. Dutton.

Freund, Matthew, Nancy Lee, and Terri Leonard. 1991. "Sexual Behavior of Clients with Street Prostitutes in Camden, New Jersey." *Journal of Sex Research,* 28(4) (November): 579–591.

Frideres, James S. 1999. "Altered States: Federal Policy and Aboriginal Peoples." In Peter S. Li (Ed.), *Race and Ethnic Relations in Canada.* Toronto: Oxford University Press, pp. 115–146.

Frideres, Jim S. 2002. "Overcoming Hurdles: Health Care and Aboriginal People." In B. Singh Bolaria and Harley D. Dickinson (Eds.), *Health, Illness, and Health Care in Canada* (3rd ed.). Scarborough, ON: Nelson.

Friedan, Betty. 1963. *The Feminine Mystique.* New York: Norton.

Friedan, Betty. 1993. *The Fountain of Age.* New York: Simon & Schuster.

Friedman, Thomas L. 2000. "Boston E-Party." *New York Times* (January 1):A31.

Friedman, George, and Meredith Friedman. 1996. *The Future of War: Power, Technology, and American World Dominance in the 21st Century.* New York: Crown.

Friend, Tim. 1996. "Teens and Drugs: Today's Youth Just Don't See the Dangers." *USA Today* (August 21):1A, 2A.

Fullilove, Mindy Thompson, E. Anne Lown, and Robert E. Fullilove. 1992. "Crack 'Hos and Skeezers: Traumatic Experiences of Women Crack Users." *Journal of Sex Research,* 29(2):275–288.

Gabor, Thomas. 1995. *Responding to School Violence: An Assessment of Zero Tolerance and Related Policies.* Ottawa: Solicitor General of Canada.

Gabriel, Trip. 1995. "Some On-Line Discoveries Give Gay Youths a Path to Themselves." *New York Times* (July 2):1, 9.

Gabriel, Trip. 1996. "High-Tech Pregnancies Test Hope's Limit." *New York Times* (January 7):1, 10–11.

Gailey, Christine Ward. 1987. "Evolutionary Perspectives on Gender Hierarchy." In Beth B. Hess and Myra Marx Ferree (Eds.), *Analyzing Gender: A Handbook of Social Science Research.* Newbury Park, CA: Sage, pp. 32–67.

Galabuzi, Grace-Edward. 2006. *Canada's Economic Apartheid: The Social Exclusion of Racialized Groups in the New Century.* Toronto: Canadian Scholars' Press.

Galabuzi, Grace-Edward. 2008. "Social Exclusion: Socio-economic and Political Implications of the Racialized Gap." In Maria A. Wallis and Siu-ming Kwok (Eds.), *Daily Struggles: The Deepening Racialization and Feminization of Poverty in Canada.* Toronto: Canadian Scholars' Press, 81-93.

Galt, Virginia. 2008. "Older Workers a Drain? Not a Chance, Study Finds." *Globe and Mail* (May 23):B5.

Gamson, Joshua. 1994. *Claims to Fame: Celebrity in Contemporary America.* Berkeley: University of California Press.

Gamson, Joshua. 1996. "Must Identity Movements Self-Destruct? A Queer Dilemma." In Steven Seidman (Ed.), *Queer Theory/Sociology.* Cambridge, MA: Blackwell, pp. 395–420.

Gamson, William. 1990. *The Strategy of Social Protest* (2nd ed.). Belmont, CA: Wadsworth.

Gans, Herbert. 1982. *The Urban Villagers: Group and Class in the Life of Italian Americans* (updated and expanded ed.). New York: Free Press (orig. published in 1962).

Gardner, Carol Brooks. 1995. *Passing By: Gender and Public Harassment.* Berkeley: University of California Press.

Garreau, Joel. 1991. *Edge City: Life on the New Frontier.* New York: Doubleday.

Gawin, F.H., and E.H. Ellinwood, Jr. 1988. "Cocaine and Other Stimulants: Actions, Abuse, and Treatment." *New England Journal of Medicine,* 318:1173–1182.

Gaudet, K. 2009. "Top 100 Federal Handouts for 2008–09: $5.8 Billion." Taxpayer.com (June 23). Retrieved July 12, 2009 (http://www.taxpayer.com/taxpayer/news-archive?news _id=3543).

Gay and Lesbian Alliance Against Defamation. 2009. *Where We Are on TV: GLAAD's 13th Annual Diversity Study Examines 2008–2009 Primetime Television Season.* Retrieved April 5, 2009 (http://www.glaad.org/eye/ontv/2008/where_we_are.pdf).

Geddes, John. 2009. "What Canadians Think of Sikhs, Jews, Christians, Muslims . . ." *Maclean's* (May 4):20–24.

Gee, Ellen, and M. Kimball. 1987. *Women and Aging.* Toronto: Butterworths.

Gerstel, Naomi, and Harriet Engel Gross. 1995. "Gender and Families in the United States: The Reality of Economic Dependence." In Jo Freeman (Ed.), *Women: A Feminist Perspective* (5th ed.). Mountain View, CA: Mayfield, pp. 92–127.

Gertler, Meric S. 2001. "Urban Economy and Society in Canada: Flows of People, Capital and Ideas." *Isuma,* 2(3):119–130.

Gfellner, Barbara M., and John D. Hundleby. 1995. "Patterns of Drug Use among Native and White Adolescents: 1990–1993." *Canadian Journal of Public Health,* 86:95–97.

Gibbs, Lois Marie, as told to Murray Levine. 1982. *Love Canal: My Story.* Albany: State University of New York Press.

Gibson, James William, and Francesca M. Cancian. 1990. "Is War Inevitable?" In Francesca M. Cancian and James William Gibson (Eds.), *Making War, Making Peace: The Social Foundations of Violent Conflict.* Belmont, CA: Wadsworth, pp. 1–10.

Gil, Vincent E., Marco S. Wang, Allen F. Anderson, Guo Matthew Lin, and Zongjian Oliver Wu. 1996. "Prostitutes, Prostitution and STD/HIV Transmission in Mainland China." *Social Science and Medicine,* 42(1):141–153.

Gilbert, Gustave. 1995. *Nuremberg Diary.* Cambridge, MA: DaCapo Press.

Gilbert, Richard J. 1986. *Caffeine: The Most Popular Stimulant.* New York: Chelsea House.

Gilder, George. 1981. *Wealth and Poverty.* New York: Basic Books.

Gillis, Charlie. 2001. "Racial Profiling Inevitable: Courts Expected to Permit Practice at Points of Entry." *National Post* [online] (October 10). (http://www.geocities.com/CapitolHill/2381/CanadaCustomsand Revenue Agency/cdnracialprofileinevitable.html).

Gillis, Melissa. 2009. *Disarmament: A Basic Guide.* New York: United Nations. Retrieved July 20, 2009 (http:// www.un.org/disarmament/HomePage/ODAPublications/AdhocPublications/PDF/guide.pdf).

Giobbe, Evelina. 1993. "Surviving Commercial Sexual Exploitation." In Diana E.H. Russell (Ed.), *Making Violence Sexy: Feminist Views on Pornography.* New York: Teachers College Press, pp. 37–41.

Giobbe, Evelina. 1994. "Confronting the Liberal Lies about Prostitution." In Alison M. Jaggar (Ed.), *Living with Contradictions: Controversies in Feminist Social Ethics.* Boulder, CO: Westview, pp. 120–136.

Glaser, Barney, and Anselm Strauss. 1968. *Time for Dying.* Chicago: Aldine.

Glazier, Richard H., Elizabeth M. Badley, Julie E. Gilbert, and Lorne Rothman. 2000. "The Nature of Increased Hospital Use in Poor Neighbourhoods: Findings from a Canadian Inner City." *Canadian Journal of Public Health,* 91(4): 268–273.

Gleick, Elizabeth. 1996. "The Children's Crusade." *Time* (June 3):30–35.

Glenny, Misha. 2008. *McMafia: A Journey Through the Global Criminal Underworld.* Toronto: House of Anansi Press.

Glick, Paul C., and Sung-Ling Lin. 1986. "More Young Adults Are Living with Their Parents: Who Are They?" *Journal of Marriage and the Family,* 48:107–112.

Global Initiative to End all Corporal Punishment of Children. 2009. "End All Corporal Punishment of Children." Retrieved March 16, 2009 (http://www.endcorporalpunishment.org/).

Globe and Mail. 2005. "Those Racial Statistics." Editorial (May 28):A24.

Goffman, Erving. 1961. *Asylums: Essays on the Social Situation of Mental Patients and Other Inmates.* Chicago: Aldine.

Gohier, P. (2009). "Budget '09: Bailout." *Maclean's* (January). Retrieved July 20, 2009 (http://www2.macleans.ca/2009/01/27/budget-09-bailout).

Gold, Rachel Benson, and Cory L. Richards. 1994. "Securing American Women's Reproductive Health." In Cynthia Costello and Anne J. Stone (Eds.), *The American Woman, 1994–1995.* New York: Norton, pp. 197–222.

Goldberg, Carey. 1997. "Quiet Roads Bringing Thundering Protests." *New York Times* (May 23):A8.

Goldberg, Joshua. 1998. Personal correspondence to a friend. Author's Files. Victoria, BC.

Goldberg, Robert A. 1991. Grassroots Resistance: Social Movements in Twentieth Century America. Belmont, CA: Wadsworth.

Goldie, Terry (Ed.). 2001. *In a Queer Country: Gay and Lesbian Studies in the Canadian Context.* Vancouver: Arsenal Pulp Press.

Goldstein, Joshua. 2001. *War and Gender: How Gender Shapes the War System and Vice Versa.* Cambridge, MA: Cambridge University Press.

Goode, Erich. 1989. *Drugs in American Society* (3rd ed.). New York: McGraw-Hill.

Goode, William J. 1976. "Family Disorganization." In Robert K. Merton and Robert Nisbet (Eds.), *Contemporary Social Problems* (4th ed.). New York: Harcourt Brace Jovanovich, pp. 511–554.

Goode, William J. 1982. "Why Men Resist." In Barrie Thorne with Marilyn Yalom (Eds.), *Rethinking the Family: Some Feminist Questions.* New York: Longman, pp. 131–150.

Goodman, Peter S. 1996. "The High Cost of Sneakers." *Austin American-Statesman* (July 7):F1, F6.

Gordon, David M. 1996. *Fat and Mean: The Corporate Squeeze of Working Americans and the Myth of Managerial "Downsizing."* New York: Martin Kessler Books/ The Free Press.

Gordon, Frances Linzee. 2000. *Lonely Planet Guide to Ethiopia, Eritrea, and Djibouti* (1st ed.). Victoria, Australia: Lonely Planet.

Gordon, Milton M. 1964. *Assimilation in American Life: The Role of Race, Religion, and National Origins.* New York: Oxford University Press.

Gordon, Robert M. 2000. "Criminal Business Organizations, Street Gangs and 'Wanna-be' Groups: A Vancouver Perspective." *Canadian Journal of Criminology,* 42(1):39–60.

Gottdiener, Mark. 1985. *The Social Production of Urban Space.* Austin: University of Texas Press.

Graham, Ian D., and Paul M. Baker. 1989. "Status, Age, and Gender: Perceptions of Old and Young People." *Canadian Journal on Aging,* 8(3):255–267.

Graham, John R., Karen J. Swift, and Roger Delaney. 2000. *Canadian Social Policy: An Introduction.* Scarborough, ON: Prentice Hall/Allyn and Bacon.

Grant, Tavia. 2008. "When the Nest Egg Shatters, Keep at It." *Globe and Mail* (December 1):B1.

Green, K. 1985. "Identification of the Facets of Self-Health Management." *Evaluation and the Health Professions,* 8:323–338.

Greenberg, Edward S., and Benjamin I. Page. 1993. *The Struggle for Democracy.* New York: HarperCollins.

Greene, Mark. 2003. Press Release for The Lysistrata Project. Retrieved March 2, 2003 **(http://www.pecosdesign. com/ lys/press1)**.

Greenpeace and European Renewable Energy Council. 2007. *Futu[r]e Investment: A Sustainable Investment Plan for the Power Sector to Save the Climate* (July). **(http://www.greenpeace.org/international/ press/reports/future-investment)**.

Grillo, Trina, and Stephanie M. Wildman. 1996. "Obscuring the Importance of Race: the Implication of Making Comparisons Between Racism and Sexism (or Other isms)." In Stephanie M. Wildman (Ed.), *Privilege Revealed: How Invisible Preference Undermines America.* New York: New York University Press, pp. 85–102.

Grobe, Jeanine (Ed.). 1995. *Beyond Bedlam: Contemporary Women Psychiatric Survivors Speak Out.* Chicago: Third Side Press.

Gross, Leonard. 1983. *How Much Is Too Much: The Effects of Social Drinking.* New York: Random House.

Gruber, M. 2009. "Globalisation." *International Federation of Journalists* (July 21). Retrieved July 21, 2009 **(http://www.ifj.org/en/pages/ globalisation)**.

Guma, Greg. 2001. "Corporate Media and the Indy Challenge— A Talk for FTAA Convergence Conference." *The MediaChannel* (April 14). **(http://www.mediachannel. org)**.

Gutstein, Donald. 2000. "Blindspots: Big Business Escapes the Critical Media Spotlight." *Media Magazine* (Winter). **(http://www.caj.ca/ mediamag)**.

Ha, Tu Thanh. 2004. "Former Boxer's Daughter Breaks Silence on Incest." *Globe and Mail* (October 14):A9.

Habitat for Humanity Canada. 2009. "What Is Habitat for Humanity Canada?" Retrieved October 8, 2009 **(http://habitat.ca/faqp1.php)**.

Hackett, Robert A, Richard Gruneau, Donald Gutstein, Timothy A. Gibson, and NewsWatch Canada. 2000. *The Missing News: Filters and Blind Spots in Canada's Press.* Aurora, ON: Canadian Centre for Policy Alternatives/Garamond Press.

Hagan, John, John H. Simpson, and A.R. Gillis. 1987. "Class in the Household: A Power-Control Theory of Gender and Delinquency." *American Journal of Sociology,* 92:788–816.

Hall, Neal. 2005. "The Highway of Tears." *Vancouver Sun* (December 10).

Hallgrimsdottir, Helga K., Rachel Phillips, and Cecilia Benoit. 2006. "Fallen Women and Rescued Girls: Social Stigma and Media Narratives of the Sex Industry in Victoria, B.C., from 1980–2005." *The Canadian Review of Sociology and Anthropology,* 43(3):266–280.

Hamilton, James T. 1998. *Channeling Violence: The Economic Market for Violent Television Programming.* Princeton, NJ: Princeton University Press.

Hannigan, John A. 1995. *Environmental Sociology: A Social Constructionist Perspective.* New York: Routledge.

Hanon, Andrew. 2005. "A Story That No One Wanted Told." *Edmonton Sun* (September 30).

Hansell, Saul. 1996. "Identity Crisis: When a Criminal's Got Your Number." *New York Times* (June 16):E1, E5.

Hansell, Saul. 2000. "America Online Agrees to Buy Time Warner for $165 Billion; Media Deal Is Richest Merger." *New York Times* (January 11):A1, C11.

Hardina, Donna. 1997. "Workfare in the U.S.: Empirically Tested Programs or Ideological Quagmire?" In Eric Shragge (Ed.), *Workfare: Ideology for a New Under-Class.* Toronto: Garamond Press, pp. 131–148.

Harper, Charles L. 2001. *Environment and Society: Human Perspectives on Environmental Issues* (2nd ed.). Upper Saddle River, NJ: Prentice Hall.

"*Harper's* Index." 2002. *Harper's* (March 13).

Harris, Judith R. 1998. *The Nurture Assumption: Why Children Turn Out the Way They Do.* New York: Free Press.

Harrison, Susan. 1997. "Working with Women." In Susan Harrison and Virginia Carver (Eds.), *Alcohol and Drug Problems: A Practical Guide for Counsellors.* Toronto: Addiction Research Foundation, pp. 219–244.

Hartmann, Heidi. 1976. "Capitalism, Patriarchy, and Job Segregation by Sex." *Signs: Journal of Women in Culture and Society,* 1 (Spring):137–169.

Hartmann, Heidi. 1981. "The Family as the Locus of Gender, Class, and Political Struggle: The Example of Housework." *Signs,* 6:366–394.

Hartnagel, Timothy F. 2004. "The Rhetoric of Youth Justice in Canada." *Criminal Justice,* 4(4):355–374.

Hauchler, Ingomar, and Paul M. Kennedy (Eds.). 1994. *Global Trends: The World Almanac of Development and Peace.* New York: Continuum.

Havighurst, Robert J., Bernice L. Neugarten, and Sheldon S. Tobin. 1968. "Disengagement and Patterns of Aging." In Bernice L. Neugarten (Ed.), *Middle Age and Aging.* Chicago: University of Chicago Press, pp. 161–172.

Havocscope. 2008. "Havocscope Black Markets." Retrieved October 21, 2009 **(http://www.havocscope.com/country.htm)**.

Hawaleshka, Danylo. 2002. "Measuring Health Care." *Maclean's* (June 17):23–31.

Hawley, Amos. 1950. *Human Ecology.* New York: Ronald Press.

Hawley, Amos. 1981. *Urban Society* (2nd ed.). New York: Wiley.

Hay, David I. 2009. *Poverty Reduction Policies and Programs.* Social Development Report Series. Ottawa: CCSD. Retrieved July 1, 2009 **(http://www.ccsd.ca/SDR2009/Reports/Canada_Report_ FINAL.pdf)**.

Hay-Edie, David. 2002. "The Military's Impact on the Environment: A Neglected Aspect of the Sustainable Development Debate." In *A Briefing Paper for States and Non-Governmental Organisations* (August). Geneva: International Peace Bureau.

Hays, Constance L. 1995. "If the Hair Is Gray, Con Artists See Green: The Elderly Are Prime Targets." *New York Times* (May 21):F1, F5.

Health Canada. 1993. *Family Violence and Substance Abuse.* Ottawa: National Clearinghouse on Family Violence.

Health Canada. 1998. *Canada's Drug Strategy.* Ottawa: Minister of Public Works and Government Services Canada.

Health Canada. 2006. *Healthy Canadians: A Federal Report on Comparable Health Indicators 2006.* Retrieved May 1, 2008 (**http://www. hc-sc.gc.ca/hcs-sss/pubs/systemregime/2006-fed-comp-indicat/ 2006-fed-comp-indicat-3_e.html**).

Health Canada. 2009a. "Costs of Substance Abuse in Canada." Retrieved January 19, 2009 (**http://www.hc-sc.gc.ca/hl-vs/pubs/adp-apd/ straight_facts-faits_mefaits/appendix-annexe-eng.php#costs**).

Health Canada. 2009b. "Factsheets." Retrieved January 19, 2009 (**http://www.hc-sc.gc.ca/hl-vs/tobac-tabac/res/newsnouvelles/ risks-risques-eng.php**).

Health Canada. 2009c. "Fetal Alcohol Spectrum Disorder." Retrieved January 19, 2009 (**http://www.hc-sc.gc.ca/hl-vs/iyh-vsv/diseases- maladies/fasd-etcaf-eng.php**).

Health Canada. 2009d. "Smoking Prevalence, Canada, 1999–2008." Retrieved January 10, 2009 (**http://www.hc-sc.gc.ca/hl-vs/tobac- tabac/research-recherche/stat/ctums-esutc_2008-eng.php**).

Health Canada. 2009e. "What Is Canada's Drug Strategy?" Retrieved January 19, 2009 (**http://www.hc-sc.gc.ca/hl-vs/pubs/ adp-apd/straight_facts-faits_mefaits/drug_strategy-antidrogue_ Strategie-eng.php**).

Health Council of Canada. 2009. *Rekindling Reform: Health Care Renewal in Canada, 2003 to 2008.* Retrieved October 21, 2009 (**http://health- councilcanada.ca/en/index.php?option=com_content&task=view &id=216&Itemid=99999999**).

Heilbrunn, Leslie. 2000. "Mind Control?" *Brill's Content* (January): 105–109.

Hendriks, Aart, Rob Tielman, and Evert van der Veen. 1993. *The Third Pink Book: A Global View of Lesbian and Gay Liberation and Oppression.* Buffalo, NY: Prometheus.

Hennessy, Rosemary, and Chrys Ingraham. 1997. "Introduction: Reclaiming Anticapitalist Feminism." In Rosemary Hennessy and Chrys Ingraham (Eds.), *Materialist Feminism: A Reader in Class, Difference, and Women's Lives.* New York: Routledge, pp. 1–16.

Hennessy, Trish, and Armine Yalnizyan. 2008. *Ready for Leadership: Canadians' Perceptions of Poverty* (October). Toronto: Canadian Centre for Policy Alternatives. Retrieved July 30, 2009 (**http://www. growinggap.ca/files/Ready%20for%20Leadership.pdf**).

Henry, Frances, and Carol Tator. 1999. "State Policy and Practices as Racialized Discourse: Multiculturalism, the *Charter,* and Employment Equity." In Peter S. Li (Ed.), *Race and Ethnic Relations in Canada* (2nd ed.). Don Mills, ON: Oxford University Press, pp. 88–115.

Henry, Frances, Carol Tator, Winston Mattis, and Tim Rees. 2000. *The Colour of Democracy: Racism in Canadian Society.* (2nd ed.). Toronto: Harcourt Brace.

Herek, Gregory M. 1995. "Psychological Heterosexism and Anti-Gay Violence: The Social Psychology of Bigotry and Bashing." In Michael S. Kimmel and Michael A. Messner (Eds.), *Men's Lives* (3rd ed.). Boston: Allyn and Bacon, pp. 341–353.

Herman, Edward S., and Noam Chomsky. 1988. *Manufacturing Consent: The Political Economy of the Mass Media.* New York: Pantheon Books.

Hewa, Soma. 2002. "Physicians, the Medical Profession, and Medical Practice." In B. Singh Bolaria and Harley D. Dickinson (Eds.), *Health, Illness, and Health Care in Canada* (3rd ed.). Scarborough, ON: Nelson.

Hicks, Madelyn Hsiao-Rei, et al. 2009. "The Weapons That Kill Civilians—Deaths of Children and Noncombatants in Iraq,

2003–2008." *The New England Journal of Medicine,* 360(1585–1588, April 16). Retrieved August 13, 2009 (**http://content.nejm.org/ cgi/content/full/360/16/1585**).

Higley, Stephen Richard. 1995. *Privilege, Power and Place: The Geography of the American Upper Class.* Lanham, MD: Rowman & Littlefield.

Hill, Felicity, and Ray Acheson. 2008. "Paying the Price: Looking Back, Learning, Looking Forward." *International Peace Update: Paying the Price,* 3(September).

Hill, Lawrence. 2001. *Black Berry Sweet Juice: On Being Black and White in Canada.* Toronto: HarperCollins.

Hills, Stuart L. 1971. *Crime, Power, and Morality.* Scranton, PA: Chandler.

Hirschi, Travis. 1969. *Causes of Delinquency.* Berkeley: University of California Press.

Hochschild, Arlie Russell, with Ann Machung. 1989. *The Second Shift: Working Parents and the Revolution at Home.* New York: Viking/Penguin.

Hodson, Randy, and Teresa A. Sullivan. 2008. *The Social Organization of Work.* Belmont, CA: Wadsworth.

Holloway, Kelly. 2002. "Black Students Slam U of T for Law Tuition Hike." *Varsity* (February 25).

Holmes, Ronald M. 1983. *The Sex Offender and the Criminal Justice System.* Springfield, IL: Charles C. Thomas.

Holmes, Robert M. 1988. *Serial Murder.* Beverly Hills, CA: Sage.

Holt, John C. 1964. *How Children Fail.* New York: Dell.

hooks, bell. 1984. *Feminist Theory: From Margin to Centre.* Boston: South End Press.

Hooyman, Nancy, and H. Asuman Kiyak. 2008. *Social Gerontology: A Multidisciplinary Perspective* (8th ed.). Boston: Allyn and Bacon.

Houseknecht, Sharon, Suzanne Vaughn, and Anne Macke. 1984. "Marital Disruption among Professional Women: The Timing of Career and Family Events." *Social Problems,* 31(1):273–284.

Hoynes, William. 2002. "Why Media Mergers Matter." (January 16). (**http://www.opendemocracy.net/debates/article-8-24-47.jsp**).

Huber, Manfred. 2005. *Long-Term Care for Older People.* Paris: Organisation for Economic Co-operation and Development.

Hulchanski, J. David. 1990. "Planning New Urban Neighbourhoods: Lessons from Toronto's St. Lawrence Neighbourhood." In *UBC Planning Papers.* Vancouver: School of Community and Regional Planning, University of British Columbia.

Hunter, Justine. 2008. "Freed Latimer to Take Campaign to Ottawa." *Canadian Press* (February 28).

Hynes, Samuel. 1997. *The Soldiers' Tale: Bearing Witness to Modern War.* New York: Allen Lane/Penguin.

IDFA, NMPF, and USDEC. 2002. "News Release: U.S. Dairy Industry Applauds WTO Ruling Against Canada on Compliance with Dairy Export Subsidies." (June 25). Retrieved (**http://www.idfa.org/ news/releases/2002/usdairy.cfm**).

Illich, Ivan. 1975. *Medical Nemesis.* London: Calder and Brown.

Immem, Wallace. 2002. "Village Scores High Marks for Quality of Urban Life." *Globe and Mail* (August 5):A10.

Inciardi, James, Dorothy Lockwood, and Anne E. Pottieger. 1993. *Women and Crack-Cocaine.* New York: Macmillan.

Infertility Awareness Association of Canada. 2003. Retrieved April 20, 2003 (**http://www.iaac.ca/english/articles/insurance.asp**).

Infoshop. 2009. *Anarcha-feminism.* Retrieved July 7, 2009 (**http:// infoshop.org/page/Anarcha-feminism**).

Institute for Policy Studies and Foreign Policy In Focus. 2004. "Foreign Policy in Focus." *International Relations Center.* Retrieved July 30, 2009 (**http://www.fpif.org/papers/0406costsofwar.html**).

International Lesbian and Gay Association. 2009. Retrieved April 5, 2009 (http://www.ilga.org/index.asp).

International Peace Bureau. 2001. (www.ipb.org).

Iraq Body Count. 2009. "Documented Civilian Deaths from Violence" (June 14). *Iraq Body Count.* Retrieved July 28, 2009 (http://www.iraqbodycount.org/database/).

Jackson, A. 2005. *Work and Labour in Canada: Critical Issues.* Toronto: Canadian Scholars' Press.

Jaffee, David. 1990. *Levels of Socio-economic Development Theory.* Westport, CT: Praeger.

Jankowski, Martín Sánchez. 1991. *Islands in the Street: Gangs and American Urban Society.* Berkeley: University of California Press.

Janoff, Douglas Victor. 2005. *Pink Blood: Homophobic Violence in Canada.* Toronto: University of Toronto Press.

Javed, Noor. 2008. "Safe Haven for Abused Seniors Vital to Aiding Their Escape." *Globe and Mail* (June 17):A17.

Jeffrey, Leslie Ann, and Gayle MacDonald. 2006a. "'It's the Money, Honey': The Economy of Sex Work in the Maritimes." *Canadian Review of Sociology and Anthropology,* 43(3):313–327.

Jeffrey, Leslie Ann, and Gayle MacDonald. 2006b. *Sex Workers in the Maritimes Talk Back.* Vancouver: UBC Press.

Jensen, Michael. 2007. "*Ugly Betty* Is Freaking Fabulous (and Gay)." Afterelton.com. Retrieved May 26, 2008 (http://www.afterelton.com/TV/2007/3/uglybetty).

Jiwani, Yasmin. 1997. "Reena Virk: The Erasure of Race." The FREDA Centre for Research on Violence against Women and Children, Simon Fraser University, BC. (December). Retrieved (http://www.harbour.sfu.ca/freda/articles/virk.htm).

Johnson, Allan G. 2006. *Privilege, Power and Difference* (2nd ed.). New York: McGraw-Hill.

Johnson, Bruce D., Paul J. Goldstein, Edward Preble, James Schmeidler, Douglas S. Lipton, Barry Spunt, and Thomas Miller. 1985. *Taking Care of Business: The Economics of Crime by Heroin Abusers.* Lexington, MA: Lexington Books.

Johnson, Holly. 1996. *Dangerous Domains: Violence against Women in Canada.* Toronto: Nelson.

Jolin, Annette. 1994. "On the Backs of Working Prostitutes: Feminist Theory and Prostitution Policy." *Crime and Delinquency,* 40(1):69–83.

Jones, Charles, Lorna Marsden, and Lorne Tepperman. 1990. *Lives of Their Own: The Individualization of Women's Lives.* Don Mills, ON: Oxford University Press.

Joyce, Greg. 2008. "Prostitutes to Open Brothel in Time for Vancouver 2010." TheStar.com (December 17). Retrieved January 31, 2009 (http://www.thestar.com/news/canada/article/555509).

Jung, John. 1994. *Under the Influence: Alcohol and Human Behavior.* Pacific Grove, CA: Brooks/Cole.

Kalish, Richard A. 1985. *Death, Grief, and Caring Relationships* (2nd ed.). Monterey, CA: Brooks/Cole.

Kane, Hal. 1995. "Leaving Home." *Transaction: Social Science and Modern Society* (May–June):16–25.

Kantrowitz, Barbara. 1993. "Live Wires." *Newsweek* (September 6):42–48.

Katz, Stephen. 2000. "Busy Bodies: Activity, Aging, and the Management of Everyday Life." *Journal of Aging Studies,* 14(2):135–152.

Kazemipur, Abdolmohammad, and Shiva S. Halli. 2000. *The New Poverty in Canada: Ethnic Groups and Ghetto Neighbourhoods.* Toronto: Thompson.

Kazempur, Abdolmohammed, and Shiva S. Halli. 2001. "The Changing Colour of Poverty in Canada." *Canadian Review of Sociology and Anthropology,* 38(2):217–238.

Kemp, Alice Abel. 1994. *Women's Work: Degraded and Devalued.* Englewood Cliffs, NJ: Prentice Hall.

Kempadoo, Kamala. 1998. "Introduction: Globalizing Sex Workers' Rights." In Kamala Kempadoo and Jo Doezema (Eds.), *Global Sex Workers: Rights, Resistance and Redefinition.* New York: Routledge, pp. 1–28.

Kempadoo, Kamala. 2005. "Victims and Agents of Crime: The New Crusade against Trafficking." In Julia Sudbury (Ed.), *Global Lockdown: Race, Gender, and the Prison-Industrial Complex.* New York: Routledge, pp. 35–55.

Kempe, C. Henry, F. Silverman, B. Steele, W. Droegemueller, and H. Silver. 1962. "The Battered-Child Syndrome." *Journal of the American Medical Association,* 181:17–24.

Kempe, Ruth S., and C. Henry Kempe. 1978. *Child Abuse.* Cambridge, MA: Harvard University Press.

Kendall, Diana. 2000. *Sociology in Our Times: The Essentials* (2nd ed.). Belmont, CA: Wadsworth.

Kendall, Diana, Vicki L. Nygaard, and Edward G. Thompson. 2008. *Social Problems in a Diverse Society* (2nd Canadian ed.). Toronto: Pearson Education Canada.

Kennedy, Paul. 1993. *Preparing for the Twenty-First Century.* New York: Random House.

Kidron, Michael, and Ronald Segal. 1995. *The State of the World Atlas.* New York: Penguin.

Kiel, Douglas P., David T. Felson, Marian T. Hanna, Jennifer J. Anderson, and Peter W.F. Wilson. 1990. "Caffeine and the Risk of Hip Fracture: The Framington Study." *American Journal of Epidemiology,* 132:675–684.

Kilbourne, Jean. 1999. *Deadly Persuasion: Why Women and Girls Must Fight the Addictive Power of Advertising.* New York: Free Press.

Kimber, Stephen. 2002. "Last Word: The Last Spike." *Media Magazine,* 8(4, Winter). (http://www.caj.ca/mediamag/winter2002/lastword.html).

King, Leslie, and Madonna Harrington Meyer. 1997. "The Politics of Reproductive Benefits: U.S. Insurance Coverage of Contraceptive and Infertility Treatments." *Gender and Society,* 11(1):8–30.

Kingsley, Cherry, and Melanie Mark. 2000. *Sacred Lives: Canadian Aboriginal Children and Youth Speak Out about Sexual Exploitation.* Vancouver: Save the Children Canada.

Kirsch, Max H. 2000. *Queer Theory and Social Change.* London: Routledge.

Kitzinger, Celia. 1987. *The Social Construction of Lesbianism.* London: Sage.

Kivel, Paul. 1996. *Uprooting Racism: How White People Can Work for Racial Justice.* Philadelphia: New Society Publishers.

Kivel, Paul. 2002. *Uprooting Racism: How White People Can Work for Racial Justice* (rev. ed.). Gabriola, BC: New Society Publishers.

Klein, Naomi. 2000. *No Logo: Taking Aim at the Brand Bullies.* Toronto: Vintage.

Klein, Naomi. 2002. *Fences and Windows: Dispatches from the Front Lines of the Globalization Debate.* Ed. Debra Ann Levy. Toronto: Vintage.

Klockars, Carl B. 1979. "The Contemporary Crises of Marxist Criminology." *Criminology,* 16:477–515.

Knapp, Caroline. 1996. *Drinking: A Love Story.* New York: Dial.

Knight, Graham. 1998. "The Mass Media." In Robert Brym (Ed.), *New Society: Sociology for the 21st Century.* Toronto: Harcourt Brace, pp.103–127.

Knight, Graham, and Josh Greenberg. 2008. "The Mass Media." In Robert J. Brym (Ed.), *New Society* (5th ed.). Toronto: Thomson Nelson, pp. 104–133.

Knox, Paul L., and Peter J. Taylor (Eds.). 1995. *World Cities in a World-System*. Cambridge, UK: Cambridge University Press.

Kolata, Gina. 1996a. "Experts Are at Odds on How Best to Tackle Rise in Teen-Agers' Drug Use." *New York Times* (September 18):A17.

Kolata, Gina. 1996b. "On Fringes of Health Care, Untested Therapies Thrive." *New York Times* (June 17):A1, C11.

Kremarik, Frances. 2000. "One Hundred Years of Urban Development." *Canadian Social Trend*s (Winter):18–22.

Krohn, Marvin. 1995. "Control and Deterrence Theories of Criminality." In Joseph F. Sheley (Ed.), *Criminology: A Contemporary Handbook* (2nd ed.). Belmont, CA: Wadsworth, pp. 329–347.

Kübler-Ross, Elisabeth. 1969. *On Death and Dying*. New York: Macmillan.

Kunisawa, Byron. 1996. "Designs of Omission." Workshop handout. Cultural Solutions. Author's Files, Victoria, BC. (http://www.byronkunisawa.com).

Kurz, Demie. 1989. "Social Science Perspectives on Wife Abuse: Current Debates and Future Directions." *Gender and Society*, 3(4):489–505.

Kurz, Demie. 1995. *For Richer, for Poorer: Mothers Confront Divorce*. New York: Routledge.

LaBerge, Roy. 2008. "May 2008: The Truth about Canada: Some Truly Appalling Things We Should Know about Our Country." Canadian Centre for Policy Alternatives. Retrieved July 26, 2009 (http://www.policyalternatives.ca/monitorissues/2008/05/monitorissue1934/?pa=BB736455).

LaFreniere, Sharon. 2009. "Forget All-Nighters—You'll Have to Cram All Year for This Test." *Globe and Mail* (June 15):L2.

Laird, Gordon. 2007. *Shelter: Homelessness in a Growth Economy. Canada's 21st Century Paradox*. Calgary: Sheldon Chumir Foundation for Ethics in Leadership. Retrieved June 30, 2009 (http://www.ccsd.ca/pubs/2007/upp/SHELTER.pdf).

Lamanna, Marianne, and Agnes Riedmann. 1994. *Marriages and Families: Making Choices and Facing Change* (5th ed.). Belmont, CA: Wadsworth.

Lange, A. 2008. "The Star." *Media Ownership in Canada* (January 16). Retrieved July 19, 2009 (http://www.thestar.com/article/ 294381).

Langelan, Martha J. 1993. *Back Off! How to Confront and Stop Sexual Harassment and Harassers*. New York: Fireside/Simon & Schuster.

Lappé, Frances Moore, and Paul Martin Du Bois. 1994. *The Quickening of America: Rebuilding Our Nation, Remaking Our Lives*. San Francisco: Jossey-Bass.

Laqueur, Thomas. 1992. *Making Sex: Body and Gender from the Greeks to Freud*. Cambridge, UK: Harvard University Press.

Lasswell, Harold D. 1969. "The Structure and Function of Communication in Society." In Wilbur Schramm (Ed.), *Mass Communications*. Urbana: University of Illinois Press, pp. 103–130.

Lauderback, David, and Dan Waldorf. 1993. "Whatever Happened to ICE: The Latest Drug Scare." *Journal of Drug Issues*, 23:597–613.

Lauer, Robert H. 1995. *Social Problems and the Quality of Life* (6th ed.). Madison, WI: Brown.

Lauer, Robert H., and Jeannette C. Lauer. 1991. "The Long-Term Relational Consequences of Problematic Family Backgrounds." *Family Relations*, 40:286–290.

Lauer, Robert H., Jeanette C. Lauer, Zelda Abramson, and Jeanette A. Auger. 2006. *Social Problems and the Quality of Life* (Cdn. ed.). Toronto: McGraw-Hill Ryerson.

Layton, Jack. 2000. *Homelessne*ss: *The Making and Unmaking of a Crisis*. Toronto: Penguin/McGill Institute.

Lee, Jeff. 2007. "Coalition Pushes for Legal Brothel." *Vancouver Sun* (November 12). Retrieved January 31, 2009 (http://www2.canada.com/compnents/print.aspx?id=0057e9b8-1508-499c-9268-7610a233).

Lefrançois, Guy R. 1999. *The Lifespan* (6th ed.). Belmont, CA: Wadsworth.

Lehmann, Jennifer M. 1994. *Durkheim and Women*. Lincoln: University of Nebraska Press.

Lehne, Gregory K. 1995. "Homophobia among Men: Supporting and Defining the Male Role." In Michael S. Kimmel and Michael A. Messner (Eds.), *Men's Lives* (3rd ed.). Boston: Allyn and Bacon, pp. 325–336.

Lehrer, Jonah. 2009. "Gambling Blows Your Mind." *Times Online* (February 20). Retrieved March 1, 2009 (http://entertainment.timesonline.co.uk/tol/arts_and_entertainment/books/non-fiction/article5772806.ece).

Lemert, Edwin. 1951. *Social Pathology*. New York: McGraw-Hill.

Lengermann, Patricia Madoo, and Jill Niebrugge-Brantley. 1992. "Contemporary Feminist Theory." In George Ritzer (Ed.), *Contemporary Sociological Theory* (3rd ed.). New York: McGraw-Hill, pp. 308–357.

Leuchtag, A. 2003. "Human Rights, Sex Trafficking, and Prostitution." *Humanist*, 63(1):10–15.

Levi, Michael A. 2009. "Living on Canada's Oil." *Slate*. Retrieved June 19, 2009 (http://www.slate.com/id/2220878/pagenum/all/#p2).

Levin, Jack, and Jack McDevitt. 1993. *Hate Crimes: The Rising Tide of Bigotry and Bloodshed*. New York: Plenum.

Levin, William C. 1988. "Age Stereotyping: College Student Evaluations." *Research on Aging*, 10(1):134–148.

Levine, Peter. 1992. *Ellis Island to Ebbets Field: Sport and the American Jewish Experience*. New York: Oxford University Press.

Levinthal, Charles F. 1996. *Drugs, Behavior, and Modern Society*. Boston: Allyn and Bacon.

Levinthal, Charles F. 2007. *Drugs, Behaviour and Modern Society* (5th ed.). Boston: Allyn and Bacon.

Lewin, Tamar. 1995. "The Decay of Families Is Global, Study Says." *New York Times* (May 30):A5.

Lewington, Jennifer. 2006. "At Least 5,000 Homeless in City." *Globe and Mail* (June 24):A16.

Lewis, Oscar. 1966. *La Vida: A Puerto Rican Family in the Culture of Poverty—San Juan and New York*. New York: Random House.

Lexchin, Joel. 2002. "Profits First: The Pharmaceutical Industry in Canada." In B. Singh Bolaria and Harley D. Dickinson (Eds.), *Health, Illness, and Health Care in Canada* (3rd ed.). Scarborough, ON: Nelson.

Ley, D.F., and L.S. Bourne. 1993. "Introduction: The Social Context and Diversity of Urban Canada." In L.S. Bourne and D.F. Ley (Eds.), *The Changing Social Geography of Canadian Cities*. Montreal: McGill-Queen's University Press, pp. 3–30.

Liebow, Elliot. 1993. *Tell Them Who I Am: The Lives of Homeless Women*. New York: Free Press.

Lill, Wendy. 2001. "Media Chaos Reigns in Canada." Media Channel. Retrieved December 20, 2001 (http://www.mediachannel.org/ownership).

Lindsey, Linda L. 1994. *Gender Roles: A Sociological Perspective* (2nd ed.). Englewood Cliffs, NJ: Prentice Hall.

Lindsey, Linda L. 2005. *Gender Roles: A Sociological Perspective* (4th ed.). Upper Saddle River, NJ: Pearson Prentice Hall.

Lips, Hilary M. 1993. *Sex and Gender: An Introduction* (2nd ed.). Mountain View, CA: Mayfield.

Ljunggren, David. 2003. "Canada Sending Up to 2,000 Troops to Afghanistan." Reuters (February 13). (http://www.reuters.com).

Logan, Ron. 2001. "Crime Statistics in Canada, 2000." *Juristat*, 21(8).

Lombardi, Emilia L., Riki Anne Wilchins, Dana Priesling, and Diana Malouf. 2001. "Gender Violence: Transgender Experiences with

Violence and Discrimination." *Journal of Homosexuality*, 42(1):89–101.

Lomborg, Bjorn. 2001. *The Skeptical Environmentalist: Measuring the Real State of the World.* Cambridge, UK: Cambridge University Press.

Lomborg, Bjorn. 2008. *Cool It: The Sceptical Environmentalist's Guide to Global Warming.* New York: Vintage Books.

London, Kathryn A. 1991. "Advance Data Number 194: Cohabitation, Marriage, Marital Dissolution, and Remarriage: United States 1988." U.S. Department of Health and Human Services. Vital and Health Statistics of the National Center, January 4.

London, Kathryn A., and Barbara Foley Wilson. 1988. "Divorce." *American Demographics,* 10(10):23–26.

Lorber, Judith. 1986. "Dismantling Noah's Ark." *Sex Roles,* 14(11–12):567–579.

Lorber, Judith. 1994. *Paradoxes of Gender.* New Haven, CT: Yale University Press.

Lowman, John. 1997. "Submission to the Subcommittee on Solicitation Laws of the Standing Committee on Justice, Human Rights, Public Safety and Emergency Preparedness." Retrieved October 20, 2006 **(http://users.uniserve.com/~lowman/).**

Lowman, John. 2000. "Violence and the Outlaw Status of (Street) Prostitution in Canada." *Violence Against Women,* 6(9):987–1011.

Lowman, John, and Chris Atchison. 2006. "Men Who Buy Sex: A Survey in the Greater Vancouver Regional District." *Canadian Review of Sociology and Anthropology,* 43(3): 282–296.

Lowman, John, Chris Atchison, and Laura Fraser. 1997. *Sexuality in the 1990s: Survey Results—Men Who Buy Sex, Phase Two.* Retrieved October 20, 2006 **(http://users.uniserve.com/~lowman/ICSS/icss.htm).**

Lowman, John, and Laura Fraser. 1995. *Technical Report: Violence against Persons Who Prostitute: The Experience in British Columbia.* Department of Justice Canada TR1996-14e, Research, Statistics and Evaluation Directorate Policy Sector. Retrieved October 20, 2006 **(http://users.uniserve.com/~lowman/).**

Lowman, John, and Laura Fraser. 1996. *Violence Against Persons Who Prostitute: The Experience in British Columbia.* Technical Report No. TR1996-14e. Ottawa: Department of Justice Canada.

Luckenbill, David F. 1977. "Criminal Homicide as a Situated Transaction." *Social Problems,* 25:176–186.

Luker, Kristin. 1996. *Dubious Conceptions: The Politics of Teenage Pregnancy.* Cambridge, MA: Harvard University Press.

Lundy, Katherine Coleman. 1995. *Sidewalk Talk: A Naturalistic Study of Street Kids.* New York: Garland.

Lunman, Kim. 2002. "Privacy Watchdog Sues RCMP Over Cameras." *Globe and Mail* (June 22):A1.

MacDonald, Eleanor. 2000. "Critical Identities: Rethinking Feminism Through Transgender Politics" (1998). In Barbara Crow and Lise Gotell (Eds.), *Open Boundaries: A Canadian Women's Studies Reader.* Toronto: Prentice Hall, pp. 282–290.

Macdonald, Gayle. 2004. "Bring Back Geezer TV." *Globe and Mail* (January 19):R3.

Macdonald, Scott. 1995. "The Role of Drugs in Workplace Injuries: Is Drug Testing Appropriate?" *Journal of Drug Issues,* 25(4):703–723.

Macfarlane, Ronald, Monica Campbell, and Sheela V. Basrur. 2000. *Toronto's Air: Let's Make It Healthy.* Toronto: Toronto Public Health.

Macionis, John J., and Linda M. Gerber. 2002. *Sociology* (4th Cdn. ed.). Toronto: Pearson.

Mackenzie, Hugh. 2009. "Banner Year for Canada's CEO's: Record High Pay Increase" (January). The Canadian Centre for Policy Alternatives.

Retrieved July 1, 2009 **(http://www.policyalternatives.ca/~ASSETS/DOCUMENT/National_Office_Pubs/2008/Banner_Year_For_CEOs.pdf).**

Mackie, Marlene. 1987. *Constructing Women and Men: Gender Socialization.* Toronto: Holt, Rinehart.

Maclean's. 1999. "Annual Poll." (December 20).

MacLeod, Jay. 1995. *Ain't No Makin' It: Aspirations and Attainment in a Low-Income Neighbourhood.* Boulder, CO: Westview Press.

MacMillan, Craig S., and Myron G. Claridge. 1998. "Criminal Proceedings as a Response to Hate." Paper presented at the "Hatred in Canada" conference, University of Victoria, Victoria, BC (September).

Macy, Marianne. 1996. *Working Sex: An Odyssey into Our Cultural Underworld.* New York: Carroll & Graf.

Mahoney, Jill. 2002. "Proposals Back Private Care." *Globe and Mail* (January 9):A3.

Makin, Kirk. 2002. "Ontario Court Upholds Parents' Right to Spank." *Globe and Mail* (January 16):A1, A8.

Malarek, Victor. 2003. *The Natashas: The New Global Sex Trade.* Toronto: Viking Canada.

Malatest, R.A., and Associates Ltd. 2007. *The Class of 2003: High School Follow-Up Survey.* Montreal: Millennium Scholarship Foundation.

Malette, Louise, and Marie Chalouh (Eds.). 1991. *The Montreal Massacre.* Marlene Wildman (Trans.). Charlottetown, PEI: Gynergy Books.

Malinowski, Bronislaw. 1964. "The Principle of Legitimacy: Parenthood, the Basis of Social Structure." In Rose Laub Coser (Ed.), *The Family: Its Structure and Functions.* New York: St Martin's Press.

Malthus, Thomas R. 1965. *An Essay on Population.* New York: Augustus Kelley, Bookseller (orig. published in 1798).

Manley, John. 2002. "The Economic and the Fiscal Update to the House of Commons Standing Committee on Finance." Presented by the Honourable John Manley, P.C., M.P. Halifax, Nova Scotia (October 30).

Mann, Patricia S. 1994. *Micro-Politics: Agency in a Post-Feminist Era.* Minneapolis: University of Minnesota Press.

Marable, Manning. 1995. *Beyond Black and White: Transforming African-American Politics.* New York: Verso.

Marger, Martin. 1999. *Social Inequality: Patterns and Processes.* Toronto: Mayfield.

Marger, Martin N. 1994. *Race and Ethnic Relations: American and Global Perspectives.* Belmont, CA: Wadsworth.

Marlowe, Julian. 1997. "It's Different for Boys." In Jill Nagle (Ed.), *Whores and Other Feminists.* New York: Routledge.

Marshall, Barbara L. 2000. *Configuring Gender: Explorations in Theory and Politics.* Peterborough, ON: Broadview Press.

Marshall, Katherine. 2006. "Converging Gender Roles." *Perspectives:* 5–17. Statistics Canada Catalogue no. 75-001-XIE.

Marshall, Robert. 2001. "Where Can We Get the Best Care? *Maclean's* (June 11):31–43.

Marshall, Victor W. 1980. *Last Chapters: A Sociology of Aging and Dying.* Monterey, CA: Brooks/Cole.

Marshall, Victor W., and Judith Levy. 1990. "Aging and Dying." In Robert H. Binstock and Linda George (Eds.), *Handbook of Aging and the Social Sciences* (3rd ed.). New York: Academic Press.

Martin, Dianne. 2002. "Demonizing Youth, Marketing Fear: The New Politics of Crime." In Joe Hermer and Janet Mosher (Eds.), *Disorderly People: Law and the Politics of Exclusion in Ontario.* Halifax: Fernwood, pp. 91–104.

Martin, Patricia Yancy. 1992. "Gender, Interaction and Inequality in Organizations." In Cecilia Ridgeway (Ed.), *Gender, Interaction and Inequality.* New York: Springer-Verlag, pp. 208–231.

Martin, Teresa Castro, and Larry L. Bumpass. 1989. "Recent Trends in Marital Disruption." *Demography,* 26:37–51.

Marx, Karl, and Friedrich Engels. 1971. "The Communist Manifesto." In Dirk Struik (Ed.), *The Birth of the Communist Manifesto.* New York: International (orig. published in 1847).

Marx, Karl, and Friedrich Engels. 1976. *The Communist Manifesto.* New York: Pantheon (orig. published in 1848).

Mascoll, Philip. 2005. "Canada Lags on Affordable Universities." *Toronto Star* (April 19):A16.

Mason, Gary. 2006. "Why Grieving Parents Forgave Reena's Killer." *Globe and Mail* (July 27):A3.

Massey, Douglas S., and Nancy A. Denton. 1992. *American Apartheid: Segregation and the Making of the Underclass.* Cambridge, MA: Harvard University Press.

Massey, James L., and Marvin D. Krohn. 1986. "A Longitudinal Examination of an Integrated Social Process Model of Deviant Behavior." *Social Forces,* 65:106–134.

Mastrofski, Stephen D. 1995. "The Police." In Joseph F. Sheley (Ed.), *Criminology: A Contemporary Handbook* (2nd ed.). Belmont, CA: Wadsworth, pp. 373–405.

Maticka-Tyndale, Eleanor, Jacqueline Lewis, and Megan Street. 2005. "Making a Place for Escort Work: A Case Study." *Journal of Sex Research,* 42(1):46–53.

Maxwell, Milton A. 1981. "Alcoholics Anonymous." In Martin S. Weinberg, Earl Rubington, and Sue Kiefer Hammersmith (Eds.), *The Solution of Social Problems: Five Perspectives* (2nd ed.). New York: Oxford University Press, pp. 152–156.

Maynard, Joyce. 1994. "To Tell the Truth." In Jay David (Ed.), *The Family Secret: An Anthology.* New York: William Morrow, pp. 79–85.

McCall, Nathan. 1994. *Makes Me Wanna Holler: A Young Black Man in America.* New York: Random House.

McChesney, Robert W. 1999. *Rich Media, Poor Democracy: Communication Politics in Dubious Times.* Urbana: University of Illinois Press.

McChesney, Robert W. 2004. *The Problems of the Media: US Communications Politics in the 21st Century.* New York: Monthly Review Press.

McCluskey, Peter. 2002. "Keeping the Peace." CBC News [online]. **(http://www.cbc.ca/news/indepth/peacekeepers/index.html).**

McDonald, Lynn, Brooke Moore, and Natalya Timoshkina. 2000. *Migrant Sex Workers from Eastern Europe and the Former Soviet Union: The Canadian Case.* Ottawa: Research Directorate, Status of Women Canada.

McElroy, Lori. 2005. *Student Aid and University Persistence: Does Debt Matter?* Montreal: Millennium Scholarship Foundation.

McElroy, Wendy. 2001. "Free Speech Protects All Speech." FOX News Channel (October 16). **(http://www.foxnews.com/story/ 0,2933,36565,00.html).**

McFetridge, John. 2006. "Modern Day Slavery." *Metro* (Torstar News Service) (November 21).

McFetridge, John. 2008. "Pot of Gold." *Driven* (October):70–71.

McIntosh, Peggy. 1995. "White Privilege and Male Privilege: A Personal Account of Coming to See Correspondences through Work in Women's Studies." In Margaret A. Andersen and Patricia Hill Collins (Eds.), *Race, Class, and Gender: An Anthology.* Belmont, CA: Wadsworth, pp. 76–87.

McKenna, Barry. 1999. "U.S. Election Strategy Helps Shape WTO Agenda." *Globe and Mail* (November 29):A9.

McKeown, David. 2005. *Summary Report: Influence of Weather and Air Pollution on Mortality in Toronto.* Toronto: Toronto Public Health.

McKinlay, John B. 1994. "A Case for Refocusing Upstream: The Political Economy of Illness." In Peter Conrad and Rochelle Kern (Eds.), *The Sociology of Health and Illness.* New York: St. Martin's Press, pp. 509–530.

McLanahan, Sara, and Gary D. Sandefur. 1994. *Growing Up with a Single Parent: What Hurts, What Helps.* Cambridge, MA: Harvard University Press.

McClellan, Scott. 2008. *What Happened: Inside the Bush White House and Washington's Culture of Deception.* New York: PublicAffairs Books.

McMullan, John L. 1992. *Beyond the Limits of the Law: Corporate Crime and Law and Order.* Halifax: Fernwood.

McMullin, J.A., and Victor W. Marshall. 1996. "Family, Friends, Stress, and Well-Being: Does Childlessness Make a Difference?" *Canadian Journal on Aging,* 15(3):355–373.

McNamara, Robert P. 1994. *The Times Square Hustler: Male Prostitution in New York City.* Westport, CT: Praeger.

McPherson, Barry D. 1990. *Aging as a Social Process: An Introduction to Individual and Population Aging* (2nd ed.). Toronto: Butterworths.

McQuaig, Linda. 2006. *War, Big Oil, and the Fight for the Planet.* Toronto: Doubleday Canada.

McWilliams, Peter. 1996. *Ain't Nobody's Business If You Do: The Absurdity of Consensual Crimes in Our Free Country.* Los Angeles: Prelude Press.

Mead, Margaret. 1966. "Marriage in Two Steps." *Redbook,* 127:48–49, 85–86.

Meadahl, Marianne. 2007. "Lack of Violence Among Off-Street Sex Workers." *Simon Fraser News* (June 28). Retrieved January 31, 2009 **(http://www.sfu.ca/sfunews/print/Stories/sfunews06280710.html).**

Mehta, Bina, and Kevin Spooner. 2000. "Glimpses of a Canadian Interracial Relationship." In Carl E. James (Ed.), *Experiencing Difference.* Halifax: Fernwood, pp. 150–162.

Merchant, Carolyn. 1983. *The Death of Nature: Women, Ecology and the Scientific Revolution.* San Francisco: Harper and Row.

Merton, Robert. 1938. "Social Structure and Anomie." *American Sociological Review,* 3(6):672–682.

Merton, Robert King. 1968. *Social Theory and Social Structure*(enlarged ed.). New York: Free Press.

Messner, Michael. 2003. "Becoming 100 Percent Straight." In Michael J. Kimmel and Abby L. Ferber (Eds.), *Privilege: A Reader.*Cambridge, MA: Westview Press, pp. 181–194.

Michael, Robert T., John H. Gagnon, Edward O. Laumann, and Gina Kolata. 1994. *Sex in America: A Definitive Survey.* New York: Warner Books.

Michelson, William H. 1976. *Man and His Urban Environment: A Sociological Approach.* Don Mills, ON: Addison-Wesley.

Mick, Hayley. 2001. "Thobani." *UBC Journalism Review* [Thunderbird Online], 4(2). (December). **(http://www.journalism.ubc.ca/ thunderbird.html).**

Mies, Maria. 1986. *Patriarchy and Accumulation on a World Scale: Women in the International Division of Labour.* UK: Zed Books.

Mies, Maria, and Vandana Shiva. 1993. *Ecofeminism.* Atlantic Highlands, NJ: Zed Books.

Migration News. 2002. "Canada: Immigration, Border." *Migration News,* 9(12,December). **(http://www.migration.ucdavis.edu: 80/mn/archive_mn/dec_2002-06mn.html).**

Milan, Anne. 2000. "One Hundred Years of Families." *Canadian Social Trends* (Spring):2–12.

Milkman, Harvey, and Stanley Sunderwirth. 1987. *Craving for Ecstasy: The Consciousness and Chemistry of Escape.* Lexington, MA: Heath.

Millar, Alison E. 2002. "Leaving the Trade: Exiting Experiences of Former Sex Trade Workers in the CRD." Unpublished master's thesis, University of Victoria, Department of Sociology, Victoria, BC.

Miller, Casey, and Kate Swift. 1991. *Words and Women: New Language in New Times* (updated). New York: HarperCollins.

Miller, Eleanor M. 1986. *Street Woman*. Philadelphia: Temple University Press.

Miller, J.R. 2002. "Residential Schools." *The Canadian Encyclopedia.* Retrieved October 20, 2002 **(http://www. thecanadianencyclopedia.com/index.cfm?PgNm=TCE&TCE_Version=A&ArticleId=A0011547&MenuClosed=0).**

Miller, Michael W. 1994. "Quality Stuff: Firm Is Peddling Cocaine, and Deals Are Legit." *Wall Street Journal* (October 17):A1, A14.

Mills, C. Wright. 1959a. *The Power Elite*. Fair Lawn, NJ: Oxford University Press.

Mills, C. Wright. 1959b. *The Sociological Imagination.* London: Oxford University Press.

Minaker, Joanne C., and Bryan Hogeveen. 2009. *Youth, Crime, and Society: Issues of Power and Justice.* Toronto: Pearson Prentice Hall.

Minnich, Elizabeth Kamarck. 1995. "Transforming Knowledge." In Sheila Ruth (Ed.), *Issues in Feminism* (3rd ed.). Mountain View, CA: Mayfield, pp. 413–429.

Minow, Newton N., and Craig L. LaMay. 1999. "Changing the Way We Think." In Robert M. Baird, William E. Loges, and Stuart E. Rosenbaum (Eds.), *The Media and Morality.* Amherst, NY: Promethus Books, pp. 309–330.

Mintz, Beth, and Michael Schwartz. 1985. *The Power Structure of American Business.* Chicago: University of Chicago Press.

Mirchandani, Kiran, and Wendy Chan. 2007. *Criminalizing Race, Criminalizing Poverty: Welfare Fraud Enforcement in Canada.* Halifax: Fernwood.

Mirchandani, Kiran, and Wendy Chan. 2008. "The Racialized Impact of Welfare Fraud Control in British Columbia and Ontario." In Maria A. Wallis and Siu-ming Kwok (Eds.), *Daily Struggles: The Deepening Racialization and Feminization of Poverty in Canada.* Toronto: Canadian Scholars' Press, pp. 167–182.

Mishna, Faye, Charlene Cook, Tahany Gadalla, Joanne Daciuk, Steven Solomon, and Robert McFadden. 2008. *Cyber Bullying Survey.* Toronto: University of Toronto.

Mitchell, Barbara A. 2009. *Family Matters: An Introduction to Family Sociology in Canada.* Toronto: Canadian Scholars' Press.

Moeller, Susan D. 2004. "Media Coverage of Weapons of Mass Destruction." Centre for International Security Studies at Maryland, University of Maryland, College Park **(http://www.cissm.umd.edu/documents/WMDstudy_full.pdf).**

Moloney, Paul. 2002. "Canadian Cities to Urge Ottawa for Tax Powers." *Toronto Star* (May 23):A9.

Mooney, Linda A., David Knox, Caroline Schacht, and Adie Nelson. 2001. *Understanding Social Problems* (1st Cdn. ed.). Scarborough, ON: Nelson Thomson Learning.

Mooney, Linda A., David Knox, Caroline Schacht, and Adie Nelson. 2003. *Understanding Social Problems* (2nd Cdn. ed.). Scarborough, ON: Nelson Thomson Learning.

Morel, Sylvie. 2002. *The Insertion Model or the Workfare Model? The Transformation of Social Assistance within Quebec and Canada.* Ottawa: Research Directorate, Status of Women Canada.

Morgan, Robin. 1993. *The Word of a Woman: Selected Prose 1968–1992.* London: Virago Press.

Morgan, S. Philip, Diane N. Lye, and Gretchen A. Condran. 1988. "Sons, Daughters, and the Risk of Marital Disruption." *American Journal of Sociology,* 94(1):110–129.

Mosher, Steven W. 1994. *A Mother's Ordeal: One Woman's Fight against China's One-Child Policy.* New York: HarperPerennial.

Mothers Against Drunk Driving (MADD) Canada. 2005. " 'If You're High You Can't Drive'—Awareness Campaign Against Drug Impaired Driving." Retrieved July 18, 2005 **(http://www.madd.ca/english/news/high_drive_2005.html).**

Muggeridge, Peter. 2001. "Report on Ageism." *CARPNews* (December 5).

Munnik, Katie. 2008. "First, Confess Then, Celebrate." *Presbyterian Record* (May):22–23.

Muszynski, Alicja. 2000. "The Social Construction/Deconstruction of Sex, Gender, Race and Class." In B. Singh Bolaria (Ed.), *Social Issues and Contradictions in Canadian Society* (3rd ed.). Toronto: Harcourt Brace, pp. 95–131.

Myers, Steven Lee. 1997. "Converting the Dollar into a Bludgeon." *New York Times* (April 20):E5.

Myles, John. 2000. "The Maturation of Canada's Retirement Income System: Income Levels, Income Inequality and Low Income among Older Persons." *Canadian Journal on Aging,* 19(3):287–316.

Nader, Ralph. 2000. *Cutting Corporate Welfare.* New York: Seven Stories Press.

Nangeroni, Nancy R. 2001. "Transgenderism: Transgressing Gender Norms." *GenderTalk.* **(http://www.gendertalk.com/tgism/tgism.shtml).**

Nath, Pamela S., John G. Borkowski, Thomas L. Whitman, and Cynthia J. Schellenbach. 1991. "Understanding Adolescent Parenting: The Dimensions and Functions of Social Support." *Family Relations,* 40:411–420.

National Council of Welfare. 1999. *A New Poverty Line: Yes, No, or Maybe?* **(http://www.ncwcnbes.net/htmdocument/ reportnewpovline/newpovline_e.htm).**

National Council of Welfare. 2001. *The Cost of Poverty,* 115 (Winter 2001–2). Ottawa: Minister of Public Works and Government Services Canada.

National Council of Welfare. 2004. *Poverty Profile, 2001.* Ottawa: National Council of Welfare.

National Film Board of Canada (NFB). 1973. *The October Crisis.* Director Pierre Perrault.

National Library of Canada. 2003. "First Among Equals: The Prime Minister in Canadian Life and Politics" (February 21). **(http://www.nlc-bnc.ca/history/4/h4-2231-e.html).**

National Victims Resource Center. 1991. *Juvenile Prostitution: Fact Sheet.* Rockville, MD: Victims Resource Center.

Nava, Michael, and Robert Dawidoff. 1994. *Created Equal: Why Gay Rights Matter to America.* New York: St. Martin's Press.

Navarro, Mireya. 1996. "Marijuana Farms Are Flourishing Indoors, Producing a More Potent Drug." *New York Times* (November 24):13.

Naylor, C. David. 1999. "Health Care in Canada: Incrementalism under Fiscal Duress." *Health Affairs,* 18(3):9–26.

Naylor, David. 2009. "A Special Message from the President." *U of T Magazine,* 36(3):39–45.

Nelson, Adie. 2006. *Gender in Canada* (3rd ed.). Toronto: Pearson Prentice Hall.

Nelson, Adie. 2010. *Gender in Canada* (4th ed.). Toronto: Pearson Education.

Nesbitt-Larking, P. (2007). *Politics, Society and Media* (2nd ed.). Peterborough, ON: Broadview Press.

Neve, Alex. 2003. "The Refugee Appeal Division (RAD) Must Be Implemented—Take Action Now." Amnesty International. **(http://www.amnesty.ca/Refugee/actRAD.htm)**.

Newman, Zoe. 2001. "The Bisexuality Wars: The Perils of Identity as Marginality." In Terry Goldie (Ed.), *In a Queer Country: Gay and Lesbian Studies in the Canadian Context.* Vancouver: Arsenal Pulp Press, pp. 122–137.

North American Commission for Environmental Cooperation (CEC). 2002. "Highlights from *The North American Mosaic: A State of the Environment Report.*" Retrieved July 16, 2002 **(http://www. cec.org/files.PDFPUBLICATIONS/soehigh_en.PDF)**.

Novak, Mark, and Lori Campbell. 2006. *Aging and Society: A Canadian* Perspective (5th ed.). Toronto: Nelson.

Oakes, Jeannie. 1985. *Keeping Track: How Schools Structure Inequality.* New Haven, CT: Yale University Press.

O'Connell, Helen. 1994. *Women and the Family.* Prepared for the UN-NGO Group on Women and Development. Atlantic Highlands, NJ: Zed Books.

O'Grady, William. 2007. *Crime in Canadian Context: Debates and Controversies.* Don Mills, ON: Oxford University Press.

Oliver, Melvin L., and Thomas M. Shapiro. 1995. *Black Wealth/White Wealth: A New Perspective on Racial Inequality.* New York: Routledge.

Olsen, Gregg M. 2002. *The Politics of the Welfare State: Canada, Sweden, and the United States.* Don Mills, ON: Oxford University Press.

Olzak, Susan, Suzanne Shanahan, and Elizabeth H. McEneaney. 1996. "Poverty, Segregation, and Race Riots: 1960 to 1993." *American Sociological Review,* 61(August):590–613.

Omi, Michael, and Howard Winant. 1994. *Racial Formation in the United States: From the 1960s to the 1990s* (2nd ed.). New York: Routledge.

O'Neil, Peter. 2001. "Feminist's Anti-U.S. Speech Causes Uproar—Hedy Fry Jeered by Opposition for Sitting Silent." *Vancouver Sun* (October 2).

O'Neill, Terry. 2001. "As Chrétien Moves Closer, Multiculturalism Is Shown to Have Given Birth to Ingrates Who Hate." *Report: Canada's Independent News Magazine* (October 22).

Ontario Health Quality Council. 2008. *Report on Ontario's Health System: Highlights.* Retrieved May 23, 2008 **(http://www.ohqc.ca/ en/index.php)**.

Ontario Medical Association. 2008. "Physician Human Resources: The Facts." Retrieved May 12, 2008 **(http:// www.healthiercare.ca)**.

Ontario Medical Association. 2009. "Ontario's Doctors Call for Calorie Labelling on Fast Food and Cafeteria Menus" [media release]. Retrieved April 15, 2009 **(http://www.oma.org/media/news/ pr090407-a.asp)**.

O'Reilly, Michael. 1998. "MD at Centre of Somalia Controversy Finds Peace in Northern Ontario." *CMAJ,* 158:244–245. Retrieved August 24, 2009 **(http://epe.lac-bac.gc.ca/100/201/300/ cdn_medical_association/cmaj/vol-158/issue-2/0244.htm)**.

Organisation for Economic Co-operation and Development (OECD). 1997. *Draft of the Multilateral Agreement on Investment, Consolidated Text and Commentary* (May 13):II. Paris: OECD.

Organisation for Economic Co-operation and Development (OECD). 2008. *OECD Health Data 2008.* Retrieved February 2, 2009 **(http://www.oecd.org/document/44/0,3343,en_2649_34631_2085 228_1_1_1_1,00.html)**.

Osberg, Lars. 2009. *Canada's Declining Social Safety Net: The Case for EI Reform.* Ottawa: Canadian Centre for PolicyAlternatives. Retrieved June 30, 2009 **(http://www.policyalternatives.ca)**.

Otis, Leah. 1985. *Prostitution in Medieval Society.* Chicago: University of Chicago Press.

Ouimet, Marc. 1999. "Crime in Canada and in the United States: A Comparative Analysis." *Canadian Review of Sociology and Anthropology,* 36(3):389–408.

Overall, Christine. 2000. "Heterosexuality and Feminist Theory." In Barbara A. Crow and Lise Gotell (Eds.), *Open Boundaries: A Canadian Women's Studies Reader.* Toronto: Prentice Hall/Allyn and Bacon, pp. 262–269.

Owens, Anne Marie. 2002. "Feminist Shifts Focus to Boys." *National Post.* Retrieved June 27, 2002 **(http://www.nationlpost.com)**.

Palen, J. John, and Bruce London. 1984. *Gentrification, Displacement, and Neighborhood Revitalization.* Albany: State University of New York Press.

Palmer, Hazelle. 2004. Foreword to *Hear Me Out: True Stories of Teens Educating and Confronting Homophobia.* Toronto: Second Story Press, pp. 1–7.

Parenti, Michael. 1998. *America Besieged.* San Francisco: City Lights Books.

Parents and Friends of Lesbians and Gays. 2009. Home Page. Retrieved April 5, 2009 **(http://www.pflagcanada.ca/ en/index-e.asp)**.

Parker, Robert Nash. 1995. "Violent Crime." In Joseph F. Sheley (Ed.), *Criminology: A Contemporary Handbook* (2nd ed.). Belmont, CA: Wadsworth, pp. 169–185.

Parrot, Andrea, and Nina Cummings. 2008. *Sexual Enslavement of Girls and Women Worldwide.* Westport, CT: Praeger.

Parry, A. 1976. *Terrorism: From Robespierre to Arafat.* New York: Vanguard Press.

Parsons, Talcott. 1951. *The Social System.* New York: Free Press.

Parsons, Talcott. 1955. "The American Family: Its Relations to Personality and to the Social Structure." In Talcott Parsons and Robert F. Bales (Eds.), *Family, Socialization, and Interaction Process.* Glencoe, IL: Free Press, pp. 3–33.

Parsons, Talcott. 1966. *Societies: Evolutionary and Comparative Perspectives.* Englewood Cliffs, NJ: Prentice Hall.

Pateman, Carole. 1994. "What's Wrong with Prostitution?" In Alison M. Jaggar (Ed.), *Living with Contradictions: Controversies in Feminist Social Ethics.* Boulder, CO: Westview, pp. 127–132.

Paul, Pamela. 2002. *The Starter Marriage and the Future of Matrimony.* New York: Random House.

Pedicelli, Gabriella. 1998. *When Police Kill: Police Use of Force in Montreal and Toronto.* Montreal: Vehicule Press.

Perreaux, Les. 2009. "Quebec Medical College Cautiously Endorses Limited Euthanasia." *Globe and Mail* (November 4):A8.

Perry, David C., and Alfred J. Watkins (Eds.). 1977. *The Rise of the Sunbelt Cities.* Beverly Hills, CA: Sage.

Perry-Jenkins, Maureen, and Ann C. Crouter. 1990. "Men's Provider Role Attitudes: Implications for Household Work and Marital Satisfaction." *Journal of Family Issues,* 11:136–156.

Peterborough Social Planning Council. 1998. "A Report on Hunger in Peterborough." In Luciana Ricciutelli, June Larkin, and Eimear O'Neill (Eds.), *Confronting the Cuts: A Sourcebook for Women in Ontario.* Toronto: Inanna, pp. 124–132.

Petersen, John L. 1994. *The Road to 2015: Profiles of the Future.* Corte Madera, CA: Waite Group Press.

Peterson, R. Dean, Delores F. Wunder, and Harlan L. Mueller. 1999. *Social Problems: Globalization in the Twenty-First Century.* Upper Saddle River, NJ: Prentice Hall.

Peterson, V. Spike, and Anne Sisson Runyan. 1993. *Global Gender Issues.* Boulder, CO: Westview Press.

Pheasant, Valerie Bedassigae. 2001. "My Mother Used to Dance." In Carl E. James and Adrienne Shadd (Eds.), *Talking About Identity: Encounters in Race, Ethnicity and Language.* Toronto: Between the Lines, pp. 38–43.

Picard, André. 2008. "World Makes Gains in Battle Against AIDS." *Globe and Mail* (July 30):A1, A11.

Picard, André. 2009. "Six Steps Urged to Reverse RN Shortfall." *Globe and Mail* (May 12):L1.

Pike, John. 2009. "The World at War: Current Conflicts." GlobalSecurity.org (July 12). Retrieved July 26, 2009 **(http://www.globalsecurity.org/military/world/war/ index.html)**.

Pocklington, Tom, and Allan Tupper. 2002. *No Place to Learn: Why Universities Aren't Working.* Vancouver: UBC Press.

PollutionWatch. 2008. "PollutionWatch Fact Sheet." Retrieved July 7, 2009 **(http://pollutionwatch.org/pressroom/factSheetData/PW_Toronto_Fact_Sheet.pdf)**.

Ponse, Barbara. 1978. *Identities in the Lesbian World: The Social Construction of Self.* Westport, CT: Greenwood Press.

Pope, C. Arden III, Richard T. Burnett, Michael J. Thun, Eugenia E. Calle, Daniel Krewski, Kazuhiko Ito, and George D. Thurston. 2002. "Lung Cancer, Cardiopulmonary Mortality, and Long-Term Exposure to Fine Particulate Air Pollution." *Journal of the American Medical Association,* 287(9):1132–1141.

Popenoe, David. 1996. *Life without Father: Compelling New Evidence That Fatherhood and Marriage Are Indispensable for the Good of Children and Society.* New York: Martin Kessler/Free Press.

Population Action International [formerly Population Crisis Committee]. 1992. *Human Suffering Index.* Washington, DC: Population Crisis Committee.

Porter, Gareth. 2009. "Report: Despite Obama's Vow, Combat Brigades Will Stay in Iraq." *Democracy Now!* (March 26). **(http://www.democracynow.org/2009/3/26/report_despite_obamas_vow_combat_brigades)**.

Potterat, John J., Donald E. Woodhouse, John B. Muth, and Stephen Q. Muth. 1990. "Estimating the Prevalence and Career Longevity of Prostitute Women." *Journal of Sex Research,* 27(May):233–243.

Pran, Dith. 1997. *Children of Cambodia's Killing Fields.* New Haven, CT: Yale University Press.

Press Campaigns. 2003. Home Page. (January 14). **(http://www.presscampaigns.org)**.

Public Citizen. 2003. *Global Trade Watch.* **(http://www.citizen.org/trade/issues/mai/articles.cfm?ID=1500)**.

Purvis, Andrew. 1996. "The Global Epidemic: AIDS Is Tightening Its Grip on the Developing World." *Time* (December 30):76–78.

Queen, Carol. 1997. *Real Live Nude Girl: Chronicles of Sex-Positive Culture.* Pittsburgh, PA: Cleis Press.

Rabinovich, Jannit, and Megan Lewis. 2001. *The Story of PEERS: Prostitutes Empowerment, Education and Resource Society.* Vancouver: Save the Children.

Rankin, Robert P., and Jerry S. Maneker. 1985. "The Duration of Marriage in a Divorcing Population: The Impact of Children." *Journal of Marriage and the Family,* 47(February):43–52.

Raphael, Ray. 1988. *The Men from the Boys: Rites of Passage in Male America.* Lincoln: University of Nebraska Press.

Ratner, Robert S. 1997. "Many Davids, One Goliath." In William K. Carroll (Ed.), *Organizing Dissent: Contemporary Social Movements in Theory and Practice.* Toronto: Garamond Press, pp. 271–286.

Ravelli, Bruce, and Michelle Webber. 2010. *Exploring Sociology: A Canadian Perspective.* Toronto: Pearson Education Canada.

Raymont, Peter (Director). 1981. *Magic in the Sky* [Motion picture]. Canada: National Film Board of Canada.

RCMP. 2009. "Organized Crime" (September 9). Retrieved March 1, 2009 **(http://www.rcmp-grc.gc.ca/oc-co/index-eng.htm)**.

Rebick, Judy. 2001a. "PR Can Help Solve Canada's Democracy Deficit." *Policy Options,* 22(6/July–August):15.

Rebick, Judy. 2001b. "Soaked in Censorship." *Rabble* (October 5). **(http://www.rabble.ca/columnists/soaked-censorship)**.

Reckless, Walter C. 1967. *The Crime Problem.* New York: Meredith.

Reinharz, S. 1992. *Feminist Methods in Social Research.* New York: Oxford University Press.

Reisch, Nikki, and Steve Kretzmann. 2008. "A Climate of War: The War in Iraq and Global Warming." *Oil Change International* (March). Retrieved July 30, 2009 **(http://priceofoil.org/wpcontent/uploads/2008/03/A%20Climate%20of%20War%20FINAL%20(March%2017%202008).pdf)**.

Renzetti, Claire M., and Daniel J. Curran. 1995. *Women, Men, and Society* (3rd ed.). Boston: Allyn and Bacon.

Reskin, Barbara F., and Irene Padavic. 1994. *Women and Men at Work.* Thousand Oaks, CA: Pine Forge.

Reynolds, Helen. 1986. *The Economics of Prostitution.* Springfield, IL: Charles C. Thomas.

Ricciutelli, Luciana, June Larkin, and Eimear O'Neill. 1998. Preface to Luciana Ricciutelli, June Larkin, and Eimear O'Neill (Eds.), *Confronting the Cuts: A Sourcebook for Women in Ontario.* Toronto: Inanna, pp. I-iii.

Rich, Adrienne. 1984. "Compulsory Heterosexuality and Lesbian Existence." In Ann Snitnow, Christine Stansell, and Sharon Thompson (Eds.), *Desire: The Politics of Sexuality.* London: Virago Press, pp. 212–241.

Richardson, Laurel. 1993. "Inequalities of Power, Property, and Prestige." In Virginia Cyrus (Ed.), *Experiencing Race, Class, and Gender in the United States.* Mountain View, CA: Mayfield, pp. 229–236.

Risman, Barbara J. 1987. "Intimate Relationships from a Microstructural Perspective: Men Who Mother." *Gender and Society,* 1:6–32.

Ritzer, George. 1995. *Expressing America: A Critique of the Global Credit Card Society.* Thousand Oaks, CA: Pine Forge.

Roberts, Nickie. 1992. *Whores in History: Prostitution in Western Society.* London: HarperCollins.

Robertson, Angela. 1999. "Continuing on the Ground: Feminists of Colour Discuss Organizing." In Enakshi Dua and Angela Robertson (Eds.), *Scratching the Surface: Canadian Anti-Racist Feminist Thought.* Toronto: Women's Press, pp. 309–329.

Robinson, David, Frank J. Porporino, William A. Millson, Shelley Trevethan, and Barry McKillop. 1999. "The One-Day Snapshot of Inmates in Canada's Adult Correctional Facilities." In Canadian Centre for Justice Statistics (Eds.), *The Juristat Reader: A Statistical Overview of the Canadian Justice System.* Toronto: Thompson, pp. 54–66.

Rochlin, M. 1982. "The Heterosexual Questionnaire." *Changing Men* (Spring).

Rogers Communications. 2009. "Second Quarter 2009 Corporate Fact Sheet." Retrieved August 17, 2009 **(http://www.rogers.com/cms/investor_relations/pdfs/factsheet.pdf)**.

Roos, Patricia A., and Barbara F. Reskin. 1992. "Occupational Desegregation in the 1970s: Integration and Economic Equity?" *Sociological Perspectives,* 35:69.

Ropers, Richard H. 1991. *Persistent Poverty: The American Dream Turned Nightmare.* New York: Plenum.

Rose, Arnold. 1951. *The Roots of Prejudice.* Paris: UNESCO.

Rosenberg, Janet, Harry Perlstadt, and William Phillips. 1993. "Now That We Are Here: Discrimination, Disparagement and Harassment at Work and the Experience of Women Lawyers." *Gender and Society,* 7(3):415–433.

Rosenthal, Carolyn J. 1987. "Aging and Intergenerational Relations in Canada." In Victor W. Marshall (Ed.), *Aging in Canada Social Perspectives* (2nd ed.). Markham, ON: Fitzhenry and Whiteside, pp. 311–342.

Rosenwein, Rifka. 2000. "Why Media Mergers Matter." *Brill's Content* (January):93–95.

Ross, David P., Katherine J. Scott, and Peter J. Smith. 2000. *The Canadian Fact Book on Poverty.* Ottawa: Canadian Council on Social Development.

Rossi, Peter H. 1989. *Down and Out in America: The Origins of Homelessness.* Chicago: University of Chicago Press.

Rothenberg, Paula S. (Ed.). 2008. *White Privilege: Essential Readings on the Other Side of Racism* (3rd ed.). New York: Worth.

Rowan, Ruby. 2001. "Sleeping with the Enemy and Liking It: Confessions of a Bi-Sexual Feminist." In Allyson Mitchell, Lisa Bryn Rundle, and Lara Karaian (Eds.), *Turbo Chicks: Talking Young Feminisms.* Toronto: Sumach Press, pp. 238–244.

Rowland, Robyn, and Renate Klein. 1996. "Radical Feminism: History, Politics, Action." In Diane Bell and Renate Klein (Eds.), *Radically Speaking: Feminism Reclaimed.* London: Zed Books, pp. 9–36.

Roy, Arundati. 2003. "Confronting Empire." Paper presented to People's Summit, Port Alegre, Brazil, January 27. **(http://www.dawn.com/ 2003/02/10/op.htm).**

Rubin, Lillian B. 1976. *Worlds of Pain: Life in the Working-Class Family.* New York: Basic Books.

Rubin, Lillian B. 1994. *Families on the Fault Line.* New York: HarperCollins.

Sacco, Vincent F., and Leslie W. Kennedy. 1998. *The Criminal Event* (2nd ed.). Scarborough, ON: Nelson.

Sachs, Aaron. 1994. "The Last Commodity: Child Prostitution in the Developing World." *World Watch,* 7(4) (July–August):24–31.

Safire, William. 1993. *Safire's New Political Dictionary.* New York: Random House.

Safilios-Rothschild, Constantina. 1969. "Family Sociology or Wives' Family Sociology? A Cross-Cultural Examination of Decision-Making." *Journal of Marriage and the Family,* 31(2):290–301.

Sallot, Jeff. 1999. "Latimer Sentence Too Harsh, Poll Told." *Globe and Mail* (January 11):A5.

Sampson, Robert J. 1986. "Effects of Socioeconomic Context on Official Reactions to Juvenile Delinquency." *American Sociological Review,* 51(December):876–885.

Sanday, Peggy Reeves. 1996. *A Woman Scorned: Acquaintance Rape on Trial.* New York: Doubleday.

Sanger, David E. 2000. "In Leading Nations, a Population Bust?" *New York Times* (January 1):YNE8.

Sangera, Jyoti. 1997. "In the Belly of the Beast: Sex Trade, Prostitution and Globalization." Paper presented to the South Asia Regional Consultation on Prostitution, Bangkok, Thailand.

Satzewich, Victor. 1989. "Racism and Canadian Immigration Policy: The Government's View of Caribbean Migration, 1962–66." *Canadian Ethnic Studies,* 30(1):77–97.

Satzewich, Vic, and Nikolaos Liodakis. 2007. *"Race" and Ethnicity in Canada: A Critical Introduction.* Don Mills, ON: Oxford University Press.

Saunders, John. 2001. "Furor Erupts as Police Seize Spanked Children." *Globe and Mail* (July 6):A1, A7.

Sauvé, Julie. 2005. "Crime Statistics in Canada, 2004." *Juristat,* 25(5).

Sauve, Julie, and Mike Burns, 2009. "Residents of Canada's Shelters for Abused Women, 2008." *Juristat,* 29(2, May). Component of Statistics Canada catalogue no. 85-002-x. Ottawa: Minister of Industry. Retrieved July 16, 2009 **(http://www.phac-aspc. gc.ca/ncfv-cnivf/pdfs/fem-residents-eng.pdf).**

Save Our Net. 2008. *Fact vs. Fiction: Five Myths about Network Neutrality* (September 9). Retrieved July 12, 2009 **(http://www.SaveOurNet.ca).**

Sawyer, Janet. 1989. "Internalized Dominance." *Quarterly Change,* 1(4):16–23.

Sayej, Nadja. 2008. "Battle of the Ages." *Globe and Mail* (November 18).

Schiller, Herbert I. 1996. *Information Inequality: The Deepening Social Crisis in America.* New York: Routledge.

Schlaadt, R.G. 1992. *Alcohol Use and Abuse.* Guilford, CT: Duskin.

Schmalleger, Frank, and Rebecca Volk. 2008. *Canadian Criminology Today: Theories and Applications* (3rd ed.). Toronto: Pearson Education Canada.

Schneider, Keith. 1993. "The Regulatory Thickets of Environmental Racism." *New York Times* (December 19):E5.

Schur, Edwin M. 1965. *Crimes without Victims: Deviant Behavior and Public Policy.* Englewood Cliffs, NJ: Prentice-Hall.

Schwartz, Saul. 1999. "The Dark Side of Student Loans: Debt Burden, Default, and Bankruptcy." *Osgoode Hall Law Journal,* 37(1&2).

Scott, Denise Benoit. 1996. "Shattering the Instrumental-Expressive Myth: The Power of Women's Networks in Corporate-Government Affairs." *Gender and Society,* 10(3):232–247.

Scott, James C. 1990. *Domination and the Arts of Resistance: Hidden Transcripts.* New Haven, CT: Yale University Press.

Scott, R.E., Salas, C., & Campbell, B. (2006, September 28). "Revisiting NAFTA: Still Not Working for North American Workers." Economic Policy Institute. Retrieved July 12, 2009 **(http://www. policyalternatives.ca/documents/National_Office_Pubs/2006/ Revisiting_NAFTA.pdf).**

Scully, Diana, and Joseph Marolla. 2005. "Riding the Bull at Gilley's': Convicted Rapists Describe the Rewards of Rape." In Raquel Kennedy Bergen, Jeffrey L. Edleson, and Claire M. Renzetti (Eds.), *Violence Against Women: Classic Papers.* Boston, MA: Pearson Allyn and Bacon, pp. 317–333.

Seabrook, Jeremy. 2002. *The No-Nonsense Guide to Class, Caste, and Hierarchies.* Carlisle, UK: Carel Press.

Seager, Joni. 1997. *The State of Women in the World Atlas* (2nd ed.). London: Penguin.

Seager, Joni. 2003. *The Penguin Atlas of Women of the World* (rev. ed.). Brighton, UK: Penguin Books.

Seccombe, Karen. 2007. *Families in Poverty.* Families in the 21st Century Series, Vol. 1. Susan J. Ferguson, General Ed. Boston: Pearson Education.

Segall, Alexander, and Neena L. Chappell. 2000. *Health and Health Care in Canada.* Toronto: Prentice Hall.

Seidman, Steven. 1992. "An Investigation of Sex-Role Stereotyping in Music Videos." *Journal of Broadcasting & Electronic Media* (Spring):212.

Sen, Amartya. 1999. *Development as Freedom.* New York: Knopf.

Serbeh-Dunn, Gifty, and Wayne Dunn. 2001. "We Are All the Same—Just Because You Are Black Doesn't Matter." In Carl E. James and Adrienne Shadd (Eds.), *Talking About Identity: Encounters in Race, Ethnicity and Language.* Toronto: Between the Lines, pp. 267–276.

Sexually Exploited Youth Committee of the Capital Regional District. 1997. *Report of the Sexually Exploited Youth Committee of the Capital Regional District, Victoria, British Columbia.* Victoria, BC: City of Victoria.

Sforza, Michelle, and Mark Vallianatos. 1997. "NAFTA & Environmental Laws: Ethyl Corp. v. Government of Canada: Chemical Firm Uses Trade Pact to Contest Environmental Law." **(http://www.globalpolicy.org/socecon/envronment/ethyl.htm)**.

Shelton, Beth Ann. 1992. *Women, Men and Time: Gender Differences in Paid Work, Housework and Leisure.* Westport, CT: Greenwood.

Shenon, Philip. 1996. "AIDS Epidemic, Late to Arrive, Now Explodes in Populous Asia." *New York Times* (January 21):A1.

Shepard, Dennis. 1999. "Dennis Shepard's Statement to the Court" (November 4). Retrieved November 15, 1999 **(http://www.matthewsplace.com/dennis2.htm)**.

Sher, Kenneth J. 1991. *Children of Alcoholics: A Critical Appraisal of Theory and Research.* Chicago: University of Chicago Press.

Sherman, Lawrence, Patrick R. Gratin, and M.E. Buerger. 1989. "Routine Activities and the Criminology of Place." *Criminology,* 27(1):27–55.

Shin, Melissa. 2009. "Green Space." *Corporate Knights* (Winter):23–29.

Shiva, Vandana. 2000. *Tomorrow's Biodiversity.* London: Thames and Hudson.

Short, G. 1991. "Combating Anti-Semitism: A Dilemma for Antiracist Education." *British Journal of Educational Studies,* 39(1).

Shragge, Eric. 1997. "Workfare: An Overview." In Eric Shragge (Ed.), *Workfare: Ideology for a New Under-Class.* Toronto: Garamond Press, pp. 17–34.

Shrybman, Steven. 1999. *A Citizens Guide to the World Trade Organization.* Ottawa: Canadian Centre for Policy Alternatives/Lorimer.

Sidel, Ruth. 1996. *Keeping Women and Children Last: America's War on the Poor.* New York: Penguin.

Siegel, Arthur. 1996. *Politics and the Media in Canada* (2nd ed.). Toronto: McGraw-Hill Ryerson.

Simmel, Georg. 1950. *The Sociology of Georg Simmel.* Kurt Wolff (Trans.). Glencoe, IL: Free Press (orig. written in 1902–1917).

Simon, David R. 1996. *Elite Deviance* (5th ed.). Boston: Allyn and Bacon.

Single, Eric, Linda Robson, Jurgen Rehm, and Xiadi Xie. 1999. "Morbidity and Mortality Attributable to Alcohol, Tobacco and Illicit Drug Use in Canada." *American Journal of Public Health,* 89:385–390.

Single, Eric, Linda Robson, Xiadi Xie, and Jurgen Rehm. 1996. *The Cost of Substance Abuse in Canada.* Ottawa: Canadian Centre on Substance Abuse.

Single, Eric, Minh Van Truong, Edward Adlaf, and Anca Ialomiteanu (Eds.). 1999. Canadian Profile Alcohol, Tobacco and Other Drugs/Profil Canadien L'alcool, le tabac et les autres drogues. Toronto: Centre for Addiction and Mental Health, and Ottawa: Canadian Centre on Substance Abuse.

Sivard, Ruth L. 1991. *World Military and Social Expenditures—1991.* Washington, DC: World Priorities.

Sivard, Ruth L. 1993. *World Military and Social Expenditures—1993.* Washington, DC: World Priorities.

Skolnick, Arlene. 1991. *Embattled Paradise: The American Family in an Age of Uncertainty.* New York: HarperCollins.

Skolnick, Jerome H. 1975. *Justice without Trial* (2nd ed.). New York: Wiley.

Sleeter, Christine E. 1996. "White Silence, White Solidarity." In Noel Ignatiev and John Garvey (Eds.), *Race Traitor.* New York: Routledge, pp. 257–265.

Small, Shirley. 1978. "Canadian Narcotics Legislation, 1908–1923: A Conflict Model Interpretation." In William K. Greenaway and Stephen L. Brickey (Eds.), *Law and Social Control in Canada.* Scarborough, ON: Prentice Hall.

Smith, Charlie. 2006. "Exposing the Boss's Pay." *Georgia Straight.* Retrieved February 23, 2006 **(http://www.matthewsplace.com/dennis2.htmwww.straight.com/content.cfm?id=16227)**.

Smith, Graeme. 2002. "Doctors Reluctant to Form Networks." *Globe and Mail* (March 1):A8.

Smith, Michael D. 1993. "Women's Fear of Male Violence." *Canada Watch,* 1:68–70.

Snell, Cudore L. 1995. *Young Men in the Street: Help-Seeking Behavior of Young Male Prostitutes.* Westport, CT: Praeger.

Snyder, Benson R. 1971. *The Hidden Curriculum.* New York: Knopf.

Solyom, Catherine. 2001. "Pigment Matters in Montreal: Survey." *Gazette* (October 26).

Spanier, Graham, and Paul Glick. 1981. "Marital Instability in the U.S.: Some Correlates and Recent Changes." *Family Relations,* 30(July):329–338.

Speier, Suzu G. 1991. "Stereotypes Exercise." *Anti-Racism and Community Development Train the Trainer Workshop Manual.* Quesnel, BC: College of New Caledonia and 42nd Street Consulting.

Squires, Gregory D. 1994. *Capital and Communities in Black and White: The Intersections of Race, Class, and Uneven Development.* Albany: State University of New York Press.

Stanley, Alessandra. 1995. "Russian Mothers, from All Walks, Walk Alone." *New York Times* (October 21):A1.

Stanley, Julia P. 1972. "Paradigmatic Woman: The Prostitute." Paper presented at South Atlantic Modern Language Association, Jacksonville, FL, cited in Jessie Bernard, *The Female World.* New York: Free Press, 1981.

Staples, Steven, and Bill Robinson. 2007. "More Than the Cold War: Canada's Military Spending 2007–08." *Foreign Policy Series,* 2(3). Retrieved August 13, 2009 **(http://www.poli-cyalternatives.ca/documents/National_Office_Pubs/2007/More_Than_the_Cold_War.pdf)**.

Stasiulis, Daiva K. 1999. "Feminist Intersectional Theorizing." In Peter S. Li (Ed.), *Race and Ethnic Relations in Canada* (2nd ed.). Don Mills, ON: Oxford University Press, pp. 347–397.

Statistics Canada. 1999a. "Assets and Debts Held by Family Units, Canada and Provinces, 1999." Retrieved April 23, 2003 **(http://www.statcan.ca/english/pgdb/famil99d .htm)**.

Statistics Canada. 1999b. *A Portrait of Seniors in Canada* (3rd ed.). Ottawa: Ministry of Industry.

Statistics Canada. 2001a. "Crime Comparisons Between Canada and the United States." *The Daily* (December 18).

Statistics Canada. 2001b. "How Healthy Are Canadians?" *Health Reports,* 12(3).

Statistics Canada. 2001c. "Measuring Student Knowledge and Skills: The Performance of Canada's Youth in Reading, Mathematics and Science." *The Daily* (December 4).

Statistics Canada. 2002a. "Average Earnings by Sex and Work Pattern." CANSIM II, Table 202-0102. **(http://www.statcan.ca/english/Pgdb/labor01a.htm)**.

Statistics Canada. 2002b. "Control and Sale of Alcoholic Beverages." *The Daily* (July 12).

Statistics Canada. 2002c. "Distance to School and University Participation." *The Daily* (June 24).

Statistics Canada. 2002d. "Divorces." *The Daily* (December 2).

Statistics Canada. 2002e. "Family Income, 2000." *The Daily* (October 30).

Statistics Canada. 2002f. "Housing: An Income Issue." *The Daily* (June 21).

Statistics Canada. 2002g. "Human Activity and the Environment: Annual Statistics." *The Daily* (November 6).

Statistics Canada. 2002h. "Profile of Canadian Families and Households: Diversification Continues." Retrieved October 22, 2002 (http://www12.statcan.ca/english/census01/ release/index.cfm).

Statistics Canada. 2002i. "A Profile of the Canadian Population: Where We Live." 2001 Census Analysis Series. Retrieved March 30, 2002 (http://www.statcan.ca/english/dai-quo/ note.htm).

Statistics Canada. 2002j. "2001 Census: Collective Dwellings." Retrieved November 6, 2002 (http://www12.statcan.ca/english/census01/ products/analytic/companion/coll/contents.cfm).

Statistics Canada. 2002k. "Youth in Transition Survey." *The Daily* (January 23).

Statistics Canada. 2004a. "Canadian Community Health Survey." *The Daily* (June 15).

Statistics Canada. 2004b. "Divorces." *The Daily* (May 4).

Statistics Canada. 2004c. "Joint Canada/United States Survey of Health." *The Daily* (June 2).

Statistics Canada. 2004d. "Measuring Up: Canadian Results of the OECD PISA Study." Retrieved September 16, 2005 (http://www.statcan.ca:8096/bsolc/english/bsolc? catno=81-590-X).

Statistics Canada. 2004e. "National Graduates Survey: Student Debt." *The Daily* (April 26).

Statistics Canada. 2004f. "Parenting Style and Children's Aggressive Behaviour." *The Daily* (October 25).

Statistics Canada. 2004g. "Profile of Disability in 2001." *Canadian Social Trends* (Spring):14–18.

Statistics Canada. 2004h. "Social Indicators." *Canadian Social Trends* (Winter):35.

Statistics Canada. 2004i. "Study: The Sandwich Generation." *The Daily* (September 28).

Statistics Canada. 2004j. "University Tuition Fees." *The Daily* (September 2).

Statistics Canada. 2005a. "Adult Literacy and Life Skills Survey." *The Daily* (May 11).

Statistics Canada. 2005b. "Canadian Community Health Survey: Obesity among Children and Adults." *The Daily* (July 6).

Statistics Canada. 2005c. "Canadian Environmental Sustainability Indicators." *The Daily* (December 14).

Statistics Canada. 2005d. "General Social Survey: Criminal Victimization." *The Daily* (November 24).

Statistics Canada. 2005e. "Health Reports: Use of Alternative Health Care." *The Daily* (March 15). Retrieved May 13, 2008 (http://www.statcan.ca/Daily/English/050315/ d050315b.htm).

Statistics Canada. 2005f. "International Adult Literacy and Skills Survey: Building Our Competencies." *The Daily* (November 30).

Statistics Canada. 2005g. "Study: Exploring Crime Patterns in Canada." *The Daily* (June 29).

Statistics Canada. 2005h. "Study: Trends in Income Inequality in Canada from an International Perspective." *The Daily* (February 10).

Statistics Canada. 2006a. "Canadian Internet Use Survey." *The Daily* (August 15). Retrieved July 17, 2009 (http://www.statcan.gc.ca/daily-quotidien/ 060815/dq060815b-eng.htm).

Statistics Canada. 2006b. "General Social Survey: Paid and Unpaid Work, 2005." *The Daily* (July 19).

Statistics Canada. 2006c. "Survey of Financial Security." *The Daily* (December 7). Retrieved July 12, 2009 (http://www.statcan.gc.ca/daily-quotidien/061207/dq061207b-eng.htm).

Statistics Canada. 2006d. "Television Viewing, by Age and Sex, by Province" *Summary Tables* (December 22). Retrieved July 17, 2009 (http://www40.statcan.gc.ca/l01/cst01/arts23-eng.htm).

Statistics Canada. 2006e. "Violence Against Women: Statistical Trends." *The Daily* (October 2).

Statistics Canada. 2006f. "Violence Against Women in Canada, by the Numbers." *The Daily* (December 8).

Statistics Canada. 2006g. "Women in Canada." *The Daily* (March 7).

Statistics Canada. 2006h. *Women in Canada: A Gender-based Statistical Report* (5th ed.). Ottawa: Minister of Industry.

Statistics Canada. 2007a. *Food Statistics 2006*. Ottawa: Minister of Industry. (http://www.statcan.ca/english/freepub/21-020-XIE/ 2006001/part1.htm).

Statistics Canada. 2007b. "Participation and Activity Limitation Survey." *The Daily* (December 3). Retrieved May 5, 2008 (http://www.statcan.ca/Daily/English/071203/d071203a.htm).

Statistics Canada. 2007c. "2006 Census: Families, Marital Status, Households and Dwelling Characteristics." *The Daily* (September 12). Retrieved February 24, 2009 (http://www.statcan.gc.ca/daily-quotidien/070912/dq070912a-eng.htm).

Statistics Canada. 2007d. "Study: Streaming in Grade 10 in Four Provinces." *The Daily* (June 19). Retrieved June 5, 2009 (http://www.statcan.ca/daily-quotidien/070619/dq070619c-eng.htm).

Statistics Canada. 2008a. "Adult Criminal Court Statistics." *The Daily* (May 20).

Statistics Canada 2008b. "Are Women Spending More Time on Unpaid Domestic Work Than Men in Canada?" *Matter of Fact*. Retrieved November 7, 2008 (http://www.statcan.ca/english/freepub/ 89-630-XIE/2008001/article/ 10705-en.htm).

Statistics Canada, 2008c. "Canadian Community Health Survey." *The Daily* (June 18).

Statistics Canada. 2008d. "Canadian Tobacco Use Monitoring Survey." *The Daily* (August 25).

Statistics Canada. 2008e. "Crime Rates." *The Daily* (July 17).

Statistics Canada. 2008f. "Environmental Protection Measures by Businesses." *The Daily* (November 17).

Statistics Canada. 2008g. *Family Violence: A Statistical Profile 2008*. Catalogue no. 85-224-X. Retrieved October 22, 2008 (http://www.statcan.gc.ca/bsolc/olc-cel/olc-cel?catno=85-224-XIE& lang=eng).

Statistics Canada. 2008h. *Gambling: Perspectives on Labour and Income*. Retrieved February 24, 2009 (http://www.statcan.gc.ca/pub/ 75-001-x/2008109/topics-sujets/gambling/5203656- eng.htm).

Statistics Canada. 2008i. "Gay Pride . . . By the Numbers." (June 24). Retrieved February 24, 2009 (http://www42.statcan.ca/smr08/ smr08_118-eng.htm).

Statistics Canada 2008j. "Homicide in Canada." *Juristat* (October). Retrieved March 6, 2009 (http://www.statcan.gc.ca/pub/ 85-002-x/2008009/article/10671-eng.htm).

Statistics Canada. 2008k. "Induced Abortions." The Daily (May 21). Retrieved May 7, 2009 (http://www.statcan.gc.ca/daily-quotidien/ 080521/dq080521c-eng.htm).

Statistics Canada. 2008l. "Leading Causes of Death 2001 to 2004." *The Daily* (December 4).

Statistics Canada. 2008m. *Measuring Up: Canadian Results of the OECD 2006 PISA Study*. Retrieved June 9, 2009 (http://www.statcan.gc.ca/pub/81-590-x/81-590-x2007001-eng.htm).

Statistics Canada. 2008n. "National Longitudinal Survey of Children and Youth: School Achievement of Nine-Year-Olds 2006." *The Daily*

(November 24). Retrieved November 24, 2008 **(http://www. statcan.gc.ca/daily-quotidien/081124/ cg081124a-eng.htm)**.

Statistics Canada. 2008o. "Participation and Activity Limitation Survey: Employment." *The Daily* (July 24). Retrieved February 6, 2009 **(http://www.statcan.gc.ca/ daily-quotidien/080724/dq080724 a-eng.htm)**.

Statistics Canada. 2008p. "Study: Hate-Motivated Crime." *The Daily* (June 9). Retrieved April 5, 2009 **(http://www.statcan.gc.ca/ daily-quotidien/080609/dq080609a-eng.htm)**.

Statistics Canada. 2008q. "Study: University Completion Rates among Children of Immigrants." *The Daily* (September 22).

Statistics Canada. 2008r. "2006 Census: Earnings, Income and Shelter Costs." *The Daily* (May 1). Retrieved June 25, 2009 **(http:// www.statcan.gc.ca/daily-quotidien/080501/ dq080501a-eng.htm)**.

Statistics Canada. 2008s. "2006 Census Information on Same-Sex Common-Law and Married Couples." *2006 Census: Reference Material* (October 15). Retrieved February 24, 2009 **(http://www12. statcan.ca/census-recensement/2006/ref/info/same_sex-meme_ sexe-eng.cfm)**.

Statistics Canada. 2008t. "Youth Crime Statistics." *The Daily* (May 16).

Statistics Canada. 2009a. "Aboriginal Peoples Survey: School Experiences of Children Aged 6 to 14 Living Off Reserve." *The Daily* (January 16).

Statistics Canada. 2009b. "Census 2006 Summary Tables." *2006 Census: Analysis Series*. Retrieved March 12, 2009 **(http://www 12. statcan.ca/english/census06/analysis/famhouse/cenfam1.cfm)**.

Statistics Canada. 2009c. "Earning Differences Between Immigrants and Canadian-Born: The Role of Literacy Skills." *Education Matters: Insights on Education, Learning and Training in Canada* (March). Retrieved July 7, 2009 **(http://www.statcan.gc.ca/pub/81-004-x/ 81-004-x2008005-eng.htm)**.

Statistics Canada. 2009d. *Education Indicators*. Retrieved June 8, 2009 **(http://www.statcan.gc.ca/pub/81-582-x/2007001/ 4148950- eng.htm#B)**.

Statistics Canada. 2009e. *Family Violence in Canada: A Statistical Profile 2008*. Retrieved March 15, 2009. **(http://www.statcan.gc.ca/pub/ 85-224-x/85-224-x2008000-eng.pdf)**.

Statistics Canada. 2000f. "Incarceration of Aboriginal People in Adult Correctional Services." *The Daily* (July 21). Retrieved October 21, 2009 **(http://www.statcan.gc.ca/daily-quotidien/090721/ dq090721b-eng.htm)**.

Statistics Canada. 2009g. "National Balance Sheets Accounts." *The Daily* (June 22). Retrieved July 12, 2009 **(http://www.statcan.gc.ca/ daily-quotidien/090622/dq090622b-eng.htm)**.

Statistics Canada. 2009h. "National Graduates Survey." *The Daily* (March 22). Retrieved June 22, 2009 **(http://www.statcan.gc.ca/ daily-quotidien/090422/dq090422a-eng.htm)**.

Statistics Canada. 2009i. "Police-Reported Hate Crimes." *The Daily* (May 13). Retrieved May 13, 2009 **(http://www.statcan.gc.ca/ daily-quotidien/090513/dq090513c-eng.htm)**.

Statistics Canada. 2009j. "Residents of Canada's Shelters for Abused Women." *Juristat* (May). Retrieved May 13, 2009 **(http://www. statcan.gc.ca/pub/85-002-x/85-002-x2009002-eng.htm)**.

Steed, Judy. 2008. "Ontario Braces for an Age Wave." *The Star* (November 8). Retrieved November 28, 2008 **(http://www. thestar.com/Atkinson2008/article/532921)**.

Stein, Peter J. 1976. *Single*. Englewood Cliffs, NJ: Prentice-Hall.

Stein, Peter J. (Ed.). 1981. *Single Life: Unmarried Adults in Social Context*. New York: St. Martin's Press.

Steinberg, Michelle. 2001. "If You Thought NAFTA Spelled Trouble." *Media Reader Quarterly*. Retrieved February 17, 2003 **(http:// www.mediareader.org)**.

Stevens, William K. 1997. "How Much Is Nature Worth? For You, \$33 Trillion." *New York Times* (May 20):B7, B9.

Stewart, Charles T., Jr. 1995. *Healthy, Wealthy, or Wise? Issues in American Health Care Policy*. Armonk, NY: M.E. Sharpe.

Stiglitz, Joseph, and Linda Bilmes. 2008. *The Three Trillion Dollar War: The True Cost of the Iraq Conflict*. New York: W.W. Norton.

Stolte, Elise. 2009. "EnCana Ups Reward for Info on B.C. Pipeline Bomber." *Edmonton Journal* (July 30). Retrieved August 24, 2009 **(http://www.globaltvedmonton.com/EnCana+bomber+reward/ 1845057/story.html)**.

Stormfront. 2009. "White Pride Marchers Fight Running Battles with Communists and Anti-Racists in Calgary." Retrieved March 21, 2009 **(http://www.stormfront.org/forum/showthread.php? t=583276)**.

Strom, Stephanie. 2000. "Tradition of Equality Fading in New Japan." *New York Times* (January 4):A1, A6.

Stueck, Wendy, and Sarah Boesveld. 2008. "Schools Not Entirely Bad, Native Writer Contends." *Globe and Mail* (June 12):A8.

Sturgeon, Noel. 1997. *Ecofeminist Natures: Race, Gender, Feminist Theory and Political Action*. New York: Routledge.

Sulaimanova, Saltanat. 2006. "Trafficking in Women from the Former Soviet Union for the Purposes of Sexual Exploitation." In Karen Beeks and Delila Amir (Eds.), *Trafficking and the Global Sex Industry*. Oxford, UK: Lexington Books, pp. 61–76.

Sullivan, A. 1997. "The Conservative Case." In A. Sullivan (Ed.), *Same Sex Marriage: Pro and Con*. New York: Vintage, pp. 146–154.

Sullivan, Harmony B., and Maureen C. McHugh. 2009. "The Critical Eye: Whose Fantasy Is This? Media Review of Dreamworlds 3: Desire, Sex and Power in Music Video." *Sex Roles*, 60(9–10):745–747.

Sullivan, Teresa A., Elizabeth Warren, and Jay Lawrence Westbrook. 1989. *As We Forgive Our Debtors: Bankruptcy and Consumer Credit in America*. New York: Oxford University Press.

Sullivan, Thomas J. 1997. *Introduction to Social Problems* (4th ed.). Boston: Allyn and Bacon.

Sutdhibhasilp, Noulmook. 2002. "Migrant Sex-Workers in Canada." In Susanne Thorbek and Bandana Pattanaik (Eds.), *Transnational Prostitution: Changing Global Patterns*. London: Zed Books, pp. 173–192.

Sutherland, Edwin H. 1939. *Principles of Criminology*. Philadelphia: Lippincott.

Sutherland, Edwin H. 1949. *White Collar Crime*. New York: Dryden.

Swanson, Jean. 1997. "Resisting Workfare." In Eric Shragge (Ed.), *Workfare: Ideology for a New Under-Class*. Toronto: Garamond Press, pp. 149–170.

Swanson, Jean. 2001. *Poor-Bashing: The Politics of Exclusion*. Toronto: Between the Lines.

Swift, Jamie, Jacqueline M. Davies, Robert G. Clarke, and Michael Czerny S.J. 2003. *Getting Started on Social Analysis in Canada* (4th ed.). Toronto: Between the Lines.

Swingewood, Alan. 2000. *A Short History of Sociological Thought* (3rd ed.). London: Macmillan Press.

Sydie, Rosalind A. 1983. "Sociology and Gender." In M. Michael Rosenberg et al. (Eds.), *An Introduction to Sociology*. Toronto: Methuen, pp. 185–223.

Tallarico, Claire M., and Susan Black. 2005. "Latest Count of Top Women in Canadian Business Shows Little Progress Since Last

Catalyst Census." *Catalyst News Release* (April 27). **(http://www. catalystwomen.org)**.

Tannen, Deborah. 1990. *You Just Don't Understand: Women and Men in Conversation*. New York: William Morrow.

Tavris, Carol. 2002. "Are Girls Really as Mean as Books Say They Are?" *Chronicle of Higher Education*, 48(43):B7–B9.

Taylor, Leanne. 2008. "Looking North: Exploring Multiracial Experiences in a Canadian Context." *New Directions for Student Services*, 123(Fall). Published online by Wiley InterScience **(http://www.interscience.wiley.com)**.

Taylor, Lesley Ciarula. 2009. "Activist Keeps Paying Forward." *Toronto Star* (May 26):GT2.

Taylor, Verta, and Nicole C. Raeburn. 1995. "Identity Politics as High-Risk Activism: Career Consequences for Lesbian, Gay, and Bisexual Sociologists." *Social Problems*, 42(2):252–273.

Teeple, Gary. 2000. "The Decline of the Canadian Welfare State: Policies and Implications of Retrenchment." In B. Singh Bolaria (Ed.), *Social Issues and Contradictions in Canadian Society* (3rd ed.). Toronto: Harcourt Brace, pp. 434–468.

Telegdi, Andrew. 2002. Statement made at the 37th Parliament, 2nd Session. *Hansard* (November 7):No. 024.

Tepperman, Lorne. 2009. *Betting Their Lives: The Close Relations of Problem Gamblers*. Don Mills, ON: Oxford University Press.

Tepperman, Lorne, and Jenny Blain. 2006. *Think Twice! Sociology Looks at Current Social Issues* (2nd ed.). Upper Saddle River, NJ: Prentice Hall.

Terkel, Studs. 1996. *Coming of Age: The Story of Our Century by Those Who've Lived It*. New York: St. Martin's Griffin.

Thobani, Sunera. 2001a. Speech at the "Women's Resistance: From Victimization to Criminalization" conference, October 1. Transcript provided by the Cable Public Affairs Channel **(http://www.casac.ca/ conference01/ conf01_thobani.htm)**.

Thobani, Sunera. 2001b. "War Frenzy" (October 15). **(http://www.casac.ca/ conference01/thobani_response.htm)**.

Thobani, S. 2009. "Desparately Seeking Obama." *Rabble* (January 2). Retrieved August 23, 2009 **(http://www.rabble.ca/news/ desperately-seeking-obama)**.

Thomas, Cal. 1996. "Overrule Same-Sex Marriage." *Austin American-Statesman* (December 6):A15.

Thomas, Gale E. 1995. "Conclusion: Healthy Communities as a Basis for Healthy Race and Ethnic Relations." In Gail E. Thomas (Ed.), *Race and Ethnicity in America: Meeting the Challenge in the 21st Century*. Bristol, PA: Taylor & Francis, pp. 335–342.

Thompson, Kenneth. 1998. *Moral Panics*. London: Routledge.

Thomson, Elizabeth, and Ugo Colella. 1992. "Cohabitation and Marital Stability: Quality or Commitment?" *Journal of Marriage and the Family*, 54:259–267.

Thornton, Michael C., Linda M. Chatters, Robert Joseph Taylor, and Walter R. Allen. 1990. "Sociodemographic and Environmental Correlates of Racial Socialization by Black Parents." *Child Development*, 61:401–409.

Tierney, John. 2009. "Public Policy That Makes Test Subjects of Us All." *New York Times* (April 6). Retrieved April 15, 2009 **(http://www.nytimes.com/2009/04/07/science/07tier.html)**.

Toner, Robin, and Robert Pear. 1995. "Medicare, Turning 30, Won't Be What It Was." *New York Times* (July 23):1, 12.

Totten, Marilyn. 2004. "A Mother's Story: Critical Consciousness, Conscience and Homophobia." In James McNinch and Mary Cronin (Eds.), *I Could Not Speak My Heart: Education and Social Justice for Gay and Lesbian Youth*. Regina, SK: Canadian Plains Research Centre, University of Regina, pp. 43–48.

Totten, Mark D. 2001. *Guys, Gangs and Girlfriend Abuse*. Peterborough, ON: Broadview Press.

Tovée, M.J., S.M. Mason, J.L. Emery, S.E. McCloskey, and E.M. Cohen-Tovee. 1997. "Supermodels: Stick Insects or Hourglasses." *Lancet*, 350(9089):1474–1475.

Tower, Cynthia Crosson. 1996. *Child Abuse and Neglect* (3rd ed.). Boston: Allyn and Bacon.

"The Toxic 50." 2005. *Corporate Knights*, 4(3):38–42.

Towle, Evan B., and Lynn M. Morgan. 2002. "Romancing the Transgender Native: Rethinking the Use of the 'Third Gender' Concept." *GLQ: A Journal of Lesbian and Gay Studies*, 8(4):469–497.

Townson, Monica. 2003. "Women's Poverty Rates Reach 20-Year High." *Straight Goods* (February 19). **(http://www.straightgoods.com)**.

Transcend Transgender Support and Education Society. 2001. *Transforming Community: Resources for Trans People, Intersexed People and their Families*. Victoria, BC: Transcend Transgender Support and Education Society.

Trice, Harrison M., and Paul Michael Roman. 1970. "Delabeling, Relabeling, and Alcoholics Anonymous." *Social Problems*, 17(4):538–546.

Trinity Western University v. British Columbia College of Teachers. May 17, 2001. Retrieved April 5, 2009 **(http://csc.lexum. umontreal.ca/en/2001/2001scc31/2001scc31.html)**.

Trocmé, Nico, Bruce MacLaurin, Barbara Fallon, Tara Black, and Jules Lajoie. 2005. "Child Abuse and Neglect Investigations in Canada: Comparing 1998 and 2003 Data." *CECW Information*, 26E. Retrieved May 12, 2009 **(http://www.cecw-cepb.ca/sites/ default/files/publications/ en/CISComparisons26E.pdf)**.

Trocmé, Nico, Bruce MacLaurin, Barbara Fallon, Joanne Daciuk, Dianne Billingsley, Marc Tourigny, Micheline Mayer, John Wright, Ken Barter, Gale Burford, Joe Hornick, Richard Sullivan, and Brad McKenzie. 2001. *The Canadian Incidence Study of Reported Child Abuse and Neglect: Final Report*. Ottawa: Minister of Public Works and Government Services.

Tumulty, Karen. 1996. "Why Subsidies Survive." *Time* (March 25):46–47.

Turcotte, Martin, and Grant Schellenberg, 2007. *A Portrait of Seniors in Canada*. Ottawa: Statistics Canada, Social and Aboriginal Statistics Division.

Turk, Austin T. 1966. "Conflict and Criminality." *American Sociological Review*, 31:338–352.

Turk, Austin T. 1971. *Criminality and Legal Order*. Chicago: Rand McNally.

Turner, Francis J. 1995. "Social Welfare in Canada." In Joanne C. Turner and Francis J. Turner (Eds.), *Canadian Social Welfare* (3rd ed.). Scarborough, ON: Allyn and Bacon, pp. 2–11.

Turpin, Jennifer, and Lester R. Kurtz. 1997. "Introduction: Violence: The Micro/Macro Link." In Jennifer Turpin and Lester R. Kurtz (Eds.), *The Web of Violence: From Interpersonal to Global*. Urbana and Chicago: University of Illinois, pp. 1–27.

UNAIDS. 2008. *2007 Aids Epidemic Update*, 39.

UNICEF. 2009. *Child Protection from Violence, Exploitation and Abuse*. Retrieved January 29, 2009 **(http://www.unicef.org/protection/ index_exploitation.html)**.

"Unionize Prostitutes, Nfld. Labour Leader Urges." 2004. *CBC News* (September 8). Retrieved October 16, 2006 **(http://www.cbc.ca/ canada/story/2004/09/06/prostitute040906.html)**.

Unitarian Universalist Association of Congregations. 2009. "Unitarian Universalists Support Freedom to Marry!" (March 2). Retrieved

April 5, 2009 (http://www.uua.org/ visitors/justicediversity/ 128897.shtml?cid=fm15&gclid=CLTvr5Kv25kCFRk_awodkx 79XA).

United Nations. 1995. *The World's Women 1995: Trends and Statistics.* New York: United Nations.

United Nations. 2000. *Protocol to Prevent, Suppress and Punish Trafficking in Persons, Especially Women and Children, Supplementing the United Nations Convention Against Transnational Organized Crime.* Retrieved January 29, 2009 (http://www.uncjin.org/Documents/Conventions/ dcatoc/final_documents_2/convention_%20traff_eng.pdf)

United Nations. 2005. "Press Conference on Nuclear Non-Proliferation Treaty." (May 24). (http://www.un.org/News/briefings/docs/2005/ NPTpc050524.doc.htm).

United Nations. 2008. *The Millennium Development Goals Report 2008.* Retrieved July 2, 2009 (http://www.undp.org/publications/ MDG_Report_2008_En.pdf).

United Nations Development Programme (UNDP). 2001. *Human Development Report 2001.* New York: Oxford University Press.

United Nations Environment Programme (UNEP). 2002. *Global Environmental Outlook 3.* Retrieved December 14, 2002 (http://www.unep.org/geo/geo3/english/overview/020.htm).

UN-Water. 2009. *The United Nations World Water Development Report 3: Water in a Changing World.* Retrieved August 3, 2009 (http:// www.unesco.org/water/wwap/wwdr/wwdr3/pdf/WWDR3_Facts_ and_Figures.pdf).

Uribe, Esteban. 2008. *Not Ready for Prime Time: Canadians in the Sub-Prime, High-Interest Lending.* Ottawa: Public Interest Advocacy Centre.

Urschel, Joe. 1996. "How Girls Get Scared Away from Computers." *USA Today* (June 26):1D–2D.

Valdivia, Angharad N. 1995. *Feminist Media Studies in a Global Setting: Beyond Binary Contradictions and Into Multicultural Spectrums in Feminism, Multiculturalisms, and the Media.* Thousand Oaks, CA: Sage.

Valverde, Mariana. 1998. "Sexuality." In Robert J. Brym (Ed.), *New Society: Sociology for the 21st Century* (2nd ed.). Toronto: Harcourt Brace, pp. 74–102.

Valverde, Mariana. 2000. "Lesbianism: A Country That Has No Language" (1987). In Barbara A. Crow and Lise Gotell (Eds.), *Open Boundaries: A Canadian Women's Studies Reader.* Toronto: Prentice Hall/Allyn and Bacon, pp. 255–261.

Van Brunschot, Erin Gibbs. 2003. "Community Policing and 'John Schools.'" *Canadian Review of Sociology and Anthropology,* 40(2):215–232.

van Dijk, Jan J.M., Pat Matthews, and M. Killans. 1990. *Experiences of Crime around the World: Key Findings from the 1989 International Crime Survey.* Deventer, Netherlands: Klower.

Vanneman, Reeve, and Lynn Weber Cannon. 1987. *The American Perception of Class.* Philadelphia: Temple University Press.

Veteran Affairs Canada. 2002. "Veteran's Week 2002: Remembering Our Past, Preserving Our Future." (http://www.vac-acc.gc.ca).

Vetter, Harold J., and Gary R. Perlstein. 1991. *Perspectives on Terrorism.* Pacific Grove, CA: Brooks/Cole.

Vissing, Yvonne M. 1996. *Out of Sight, Out of Mind: Homeless Children and Families in Small-Town America.* Lexington: University of Kentucky Press,

Vito, Gennaro F., and Ronald M. Holmes. 1994. *Criminology: Theory, Research and Policy.* Belmont, CA: Wadsworth.

Viviano, Frank. 1995. "The New Mafia Order." *Mother Jones* (May–June):45–55.

Vozoris, Nicholas, Barbara Davis, and Valerie Tarasuk. 2002. "The Affordability of a Nutritional Diet for Households on Welfare in Toronto." *Canadian Journal of Public Health,* 93:36–40.

Wagner, David. 1993. *Checkerboard Square: Culture and Resistance in a Homeless Community.* Boulder, CO: Westview.

Waldron, I. 1997. "Changing Gender Roles in Health Behavior." In D. Gochman (Ed.), *Handbook of Health Behavior Research I: Personal and Social Determinants.* New York: Plenum, pp. 303–328.

Walker, S.G. 1994. *Weapons Use in Canadian Schools.* Ottawa: Solicitor General of Canada.

Wallerstein, Judith, and Sandra Blakeslee. 1989. *Second Chances: Men, Women and Children a Decade after Divorce.* New York: Ticknor & Field.

Ward, Martha, and Monica Edelstein, 2009. *A World Full of Women* (5th ed.). Boston: Pearson Education.

Warshaw, Robin. 1994. *I Never Called It Rape.* New York: HarperPerennial.

Waters, Malcolm. 1995. *Globalization.* New York: Routledge.

Watson, Roy E.L., and Peter W. DeMeo. 1987. "Premarital Cohabitation Versus Traditional Courtship and Subsequent Marital Adjustment: A Replication and a Follow-Up." *Family Relations,* 36:193–197.

Weedon, Chris. 1999. *Feminism, Theory and the Politics of Difference.* Oxford, UK: Blackwell.

Weeks, Carly. 2008. "Safe Injection May Save System $14 Million." *Globe and Mail* (November 18):L1.

Weeks, John R. 2005. *Population: An Introduction to Concepts and Issues* (9th ed.). Belmont, CA: Wadsworth.

Weinberg, Martin S., and Colin Williams. 1975. *Male Homosexuals.* New York: Penguin.

Weinberg, Martin S., Earl Rubington, and Sue Kiefer Hammersmith. 1981. *The Solution of Social Problems: Five Perspectives* (2nd ed.). New York: Oxford University Press.

Weinberg, Martin S., Colin J. Williams, and Douglas W. Pryor. 1994. *Dual Attraction: Understanding Bisexuality.* New York: Oxford University Press.

Weiner, Jonathan. 1990. *The Next One Hundred Years: Shaping the Fate of Our Living Earth.* New York: Bantam.

Weitz, Rose. 1996. *The Sociology of Health, Illness, and Health Care: A Critical Approach.* Belmont, CA: Wadsworth.

Weitzer, Ronald. 2005. "New Directions in Research on Prostitution." *Crime, Law and Social Change,* 43:211–235.

Wellman, David T. 1993. *Portraits of White Racism* (2nd ed.). New York: Cambridge University Press.

Wente, Margaret. 2008. "The War over Drug Policy." *Globe and Mail* (May 6):A17.

Wildman, Stephanie M., and Adrienne D. Davis. 2002. "Making Systems of Privilege Visible." In Paula S. Rothenberg (Ed.), *White Privilege: Essential Readings on the Other Side of Racism.* New York: Worth, pp. 89–96.

Wilkie, Jane Riblett. 1993. "Changes in U.S. Men's Attitudes toward the Family Provider Role, 1972–1989." *Gender and Society,* 7(2):261–279.

Wilkinson, Sue, and Celia Kitzinger. 1996. "The Queer Backlash." In Diane Bell and Renate Klein (Eds.), *Radically Speaking: Feminism Reclaimed.* London: Zed Books, pp. 375–382.

Williams, Cara. 2001. "Family Disruptions and Childhood Happiness." *Canadian Social Trends* (Autumn):2–4.

Williams, Christine L. 1995. *Still a Man's World: Men Who Do Women's Work.* Berkeley, CA: University of California Press.

Williams, Robin M., Jr. 1970. *American Society: A Sociological Interpretation* (3rd ed.). New York: Knopf.

Williamson, Robert C., Alice Duffy Rinehart, and Thomas O. Blank. 1992. *Early Retirement: Promises and Pitfalls*. New York: Plenum.

Wilson, David (Ed.). 1997. "Globalization and the Changing U.S. City." *The Annals of the American Academy of Political and Social Science*, 551(May). Special Issue. Thousand Oaks, CA: Sage.

Wilson, Susannah J. 2001. "Paid Work, Jobs and the Illusion of Economic Security." In Nancy Mandell (Ed.), *Feminist Issues: Race, Class, and Sexuality* (3rd ed.). Toronto: Pearson, pp. 219–241.

Wilson, William Julius. 1996. *When Work Disappears: The World of the New Urban Poor*. New York: Knopf.

Wilton, Tamsin. 2000. *Sexualities in Health and Social Care: A Textbook*. Buckingham, UK: Open University Press.

Wirth, Louis. 1938. "Urbanism as a Way of Life." *American Journal of Sociology*, 40:1–24.

Wirth, Louis. 1945. "The Problem of Minority Groups." In Ralph Linton (Ed.), *The Science of Man in the World Crisis*. New York: Columbia University Press, p. 38.

Wolf, Robin. 1996. *Marriages and Families in a Diverse Society*. New York: HarperCollins.

Wolff, Lee, and Dorota Geissel. 2000. "Street Prostitution in Canada." In *Canadian Social Trends*, 3. Ottawa: Minister of Supply and Services Canada, and Toronto: Thompson, pp. 253–257.

Wolfgang, Marvin E., and Franco Ferracuti. 1967. *The Subculture of Violence: Towards an Integrated Theory in Criminology*. Beverly Hills, CA: Sage.

Women's International Network. 1995. "Sex Trade Flourishing in Japan." *WIN News* 21(Winter):42.

Wood, Julia T. 2001. *Gendered Lives: Communication, Gender and Culture* (4th ed.). Belmont, CA: Wadsworth/Thomson Learning.

Woods, Catherine. 1998. "TV and Media Imperialism." *MTheory*, 2 (Fall). **(http://www.mala.bc.ca/soules/mtheory/vol2/index.htm).**

Woolley, Pieta. 2008. "Vancouver Women's Groups at Odds over East Side Brothels." *The Georgia Straight* (March 13). Retrieved January 31, 2009 **(http://www.straight.com/article-134799/vancouver-womens-groups-at-odds-over-east-side-brothels).**

World Bank. 1995. *World Development Report: 1995*. New York: Oxford University Press.

World Health Organization (WHO). 1946. *Constitution of the World Health Organization*. New York: World Health Organization Interim Commission.

World Health Organization (WHO). 2003. Retrieved February 16, 2003 **(http://www.who.int/nut/obs.htm).**

World Resources Institute. 1992. *World Resources 1992–93*. New York: Oxford University Press.

Wortley, Scot. 1999. "A Northern Taboo: Research on Race, Crime, and Criminal Justice in Canada." *Canadian Journal of Criminology*, 41(2):261–274.

Wren, Christopher. 1996. "Teen-Agers Find Drugs Easy to Obtain and Warnings Easy to Ignore." *New York Times* (October 10):A12.

Wright, Erik Olin. 1979. *Class Structure and Income Determination*. New York: Academic Press.

Wright, Erik Olin. 1985. *Class*. London: Verso.

Wright, Erik Olin. 1997. *Class Counts: Comparative Studies in Class Analysis.* Cambridge, UK: Cambridge University Press.

Wright, Quincy. 1964. *A Study of War*. Chicago: University of Chicago Press.

Wright, Richard T., and Scott Decker. 1994. *Burglars on the Job: Streetlife and Residential Break-ins*. Boston: Northeastern University Press.

Yalnizyan, A. 2009. "Exposed: Revealing Truths about Canada's Recession." Growing Gap.ca (April). Retrieved July 8, 2009 **(http://growinggap.ca/files/Exposed_Revealing_Truths_About_Canadas_Recession.pdf).**

Yalnizyan, A., & Hennessy, T. 2009. "Canada's Income Gap: Why a Good News Story Isn't Great." GrowingGap.ca (June 4). Retrieved July 1, 2009 **(http://www.growinggap.ca/node/183).**

Yea, Sallie. 2005. "When Push Comes to Shove: Sites of Vulnerability, Personal Transformation, and Trafficked Women's Migration Decisions." *Sojourn*, 20(1):67–95.

Yinger, J. Milton. 1994. *Ethnicity: Source of Strength, Source of Conflict?* Albany, NY: SUNY Press.

Yoanna, Michael De, and Mark Benjamin. 2009. "Coming Home: The Army's Fatal Neglect." *Salon* (April 8). Retrieved August 12 2009 **(http://www.salon.com/news/special/coming_home/2009/04/08/tape).**

York, Geoffrey. 2002. "Japan's Students Can't Spell Relax." *Globe and Mail* (June 10):A1, A12.

York, Geoffrey. 2009. "International Adoptions to Canada 2004–2007." *Globe and Mail* (June 22):A13.

Young, J.H. 1961. *The Toadstool Millionnaires: A Social History of Patent Medicine in America before Federal Regulation*. Princeton, NJ: Princeton University Press.

Young, Malcolm C., and Jenni Gainsborough. 2000. "Prosecuting Juveniles in Adult Court: An Assessment of Trends and Consequences." *The Sentencing Project* **(http://www.sentencingproject.org).**

Young, Michael Dunlap. 1994. *The Rise of the Meritocracy*. New Brunswick, NJ: Transaction.

Zelizer, Viviana. 1985. *Pricing the Priceless Child: The Changing Social Value of Children*. New Haven, CT: Yale University Press.

Zolf, Larry. 2003. "1970—The October Crisis." CBC News Online. Retrieved February 2003 **(http://www.cbc.ca/millenium/timelines/feature_octobercrisis.html).**

NAME INDEX

Note: Entries for notes are followed by "*n*."

SUBJECT INDEX

Note: Entries for figures and tables are followed by "*f*" and "*t*," respectively.

social problems
  alcohol-related social problems, 177–180
  crime, 201–203
  defined, 3
  early urban growth, 345
  ethnic inequality, 57–60
  gambling-related social problems, 192
  gender inequality, 82–84
  grassroots groups, 17–19, 19t
  health and illness, 224, 230–231
  individual solutions to personal problems, 16
  macrolevel analysis, 6, 19–25
  mental illness, 232–234
  microlevel analysis, 6, 16
  mid-range solutions, 16–19
  national social movements, 21–25
  objective view of, 6
  racism, 57–60
  reducing social problems, 15–25
  self-help groups, 17
  social movement, 18–19
  sociological examination, 3
  and the sociological imagination, 6
  sociological perspectives, 7–15
  special-interest groups, 20–21
  study of, 3, 5–6
  tobacco (nicotine) use, 180–182
  war, 379
social programs, 32, 36
social protection, 218
social stratification, 32
social tasks, 118
social welfare
  in Canada, 42–47
  deserving poor, 45
  undeserving poor, 46
  welfare dependency, 45
  welfare state, 42–47
  workfare, 43–46
socialism, 293
socialist feminism, 50, 99, 216
socialization
  agents of socialization, 88–89
  and education, 272, 275
  and gender inequality, 88–91
  gender-role socialization, 100
  racialized socialization, 69–70
societal racism, 67
society
  defined, 3
  tensions in, 141
socioeconomic status, 281
sociological imagination, 6
sociological perspectives, 7–15
  conflict perspective, 9–12
  feminist perspectives, 14–15
  functionalist perspective, 7–9
  interactionist perspective, 12–14

sociology, 3
soil depletion, 365
solid waste, 365
spanking, 264–265
special-interest groups, 20–21
specialism, 350
spiritual tasks, 118
split-labour market theory, 70
spousal violence, 265, 253t
spouse, definition of, 134
St. James Town, 350
stage-based approach, 118
state-sponsored terrorism, 387
status, 328
status offences, 211
stereotypes
  age-based stereotypes, 108
  "Bubba" stereotype, 64
  defined, 61
sterilization, 258
stimulants, 186–187
stomach remedies, 183
straight, 127
strain theory, 212–213, 213t
street gangs, 206
streetwalkers, 159, 161–162
strippers, 159
structural approach, 88
structural functionalist perspective. See functionalist perspective
structural media bias, 325
student debt, 37–38, 38t
subculture, 357
subculture of violence hypothesis, 214
subordinate group, 5, 59
subsidies, 306
suburbs, 346
success, 47–48
suicide
  assisted suicide, 119
  community factors, 72f
  Indigenous youth suicide, 71
summary conviction offences, 203
Summit of the Americas, 296–297, 307
supercomputers, 382
supply of health care professionals, 237–238
symbolic interactionist perspective. See interactionist perspective
syndicated crime networks, 210
synergy, 321
systemic racism, 66–67
systems of prostitution, 151–152

T

table dancers, 159
talented, 275
tardiness, 179
task-based approach, 118

tax rates, 306
taxing food, 231
technological disasters, 366–367
technological innovations, 121, 238–239, 298, 367, 378
teen pregnancies, 260–261
Telehealth, 241
television viewing statistics, 317t
terminal phase, 118
terrorism, 386–391
  Anti-Terrorism Act, 389–390
  and Canadian politics, 388–391
  and collective violence, 387
  conflict perspective, 395
  defined, 386
  domestic terrorism, 388
  ethnic or racialized profiling, 390
  explanations of, 393–396
  feminist perspectives, 395–396
  functionalist perspective, 393–395
  home-grown terrorism, 388
  intra-national terrorism, 388
  media coverage, 382–383
  media response to Thobani's speech, 391–393
  overcoming terrorism, 396–397
  political terrorism, 387
  repressive terrorism, 387
  revolutionary terrorism, 387
  state-sponsored terrorism, 387
tertiary prevention, 195, 196
tertiary sector production, 294
theft, 207
theft $5000 and under, 208
theory, 7
theory of limited effects, 327
theory of racial formation, 71
therapeutic community approach, 196–197
"third gender" examples, 85
Third Wave feminists, 331
Third World feminist perspective, 155, 171
This Is What Democracy Looks Like, 324–325
Thobani, Sunera, 391–393
Tobacco Act, 182
tobacco use, 180–182
tolerance, 176
total institution, 234
toxic air pollutants, 363
toxic waste, 365–366
tracking, 271
trade agreements, 295–297
trafficking in persons, 155–156, 211
Trafficking in Persons Report, 153
tranquilizers, 187
trans people, 84–87
transitional space, 156
transitional stage, 341

PHOTO CREDITS

Page 1: The Canadian Press/Ryan Remiorz; p. 5: Cesar Lucas Abreu /Getty Images; p. 22: Edmonton Sun/The Canadian Press/Jason Franson; p. 23: Courtesy Council of Canadians; p. 30 The Canadian Press; p. 62: The Ottawa Press/Nick Corrigall; p. 66: George Burdi; p. 78: Richard Lautens/ The Toronto Star; p. 81: Family Violence Prevention Fund, www.endabuse.org; p. 86: Vicki L. Nygaard; p. 88: Vicki L. Nygaard; p. 93: Souce: Gable, Regina Leader Post 84. Reprinted by permission of Biran Glable and the Regina Leader Post; p. 105: David Young-Wolff/PhotoEdit; p. 116: Christina Beamish; p. 125: Shutterstock; p. 134: Newscom; p. 141: Shutterstock; p. 150: Shutterstock; p. 165: Pearson; p. 174: Shutterstock; p. 200: The Canadian Press/Jacob Henefin; p. 223: Toronto Star/The Canadian Press/Rene Johnston;

p. 230: Shutterstock; p. 234: Shutterstock; p. 246: Christopher Thomas/Photographer's Choice/Getty Images; p. 257: The Canadian Press/Fred Chartrand; p. 270: AL Harvey/Slide Farm; p. 278: © Bill Bachman/Alamy; p. 291: The Canadian Press/Kevin Frayer; p. 301: Artizans Entertainment Inc.; p. 303: David Young-Wolff/PhotoEdit; p. 316: The Canadian Press/Andrew Vaughan; p. 331: The Canadian Press; p. 337: ©Dick Hemingway; p. 351: Shutterstock; p. 354: Shutterstock; p. 360: Shutterstock; p. 364: Shutterstock; p. 376: Dev Carr/Getty Images; p. 380: Courtesy Romeo Dallaire; p. 382: Photo: © Allan Lissner; p. 383: Photo: © Allan Lissner; p. 385: Shawn Baldwin; 9. 387: Photo: © Allan Lissner; p. 392: Courtesy Sunera Thobani; p. 405: Free The Children www.freethechildren.com;